The Boys of Winter

THE *Boys* OF WINTER

LIFE AND DEATH IN THE U.S. SKI TROOPS DURING THE SECOND WORLD WAR

Charles J. Sanders

UNIVERSITY PRESS OF COLORADO

© 2005 by Charles J. Sanders

Published by the University Press of Colorado
5589 Arapahoe Avenue, Suite 206C
Boulder, Colorado 80303

All rights reserved
First paperback edition 2005
Printed in the United States of America

FAUP The University Press of Colorado is a proud member of
the Association of American University Presses.

The University Press of Colorado is a cooperative publishing enterprise supported, in part, by
Adams State College, Colorado State University, Fort Lewis College, Mesa State College,
Metropolitan State College of Denver, University of Colorado, University of Northern Colorado,
and Western State College of Colorado.

∞ The paper used in this publication meets the minimum requirements of the American National
Standard for Information Sciences—Permanence of Paper for Printed Library Materials. ANSI
Z39.48-1992

Library of Congress Cataloging-in-Publication Data

Sanders, Charles J. (Charles Jeffrey), 1958–
   The boys of winter : life and death in the U.S. ski troops during the Second World War /
Charles J. Sanders.
      p. cm.
   Includes bibliographical references and index.
   ISBN 0-87081-783-3 (alk. paper) — ISBN 0-87081-823-6 (pbk. : alk. paper)
   1. Konieczny, Rudy, d. 1945. 2. Nunnemacher, Jacob, d. 1945. 3. Bromaghin, Ralph, d. 1945.
4. United States. Army. Mountain Division, 10th—History. 5. United States. Army—Ski troops.
6. World War, 1939–1945—Campaigns—Italy. 7. World War, 1939–1945—Regimental
histories—United States. 8. Soldiers—United States—Biography. I. Title.
   D769.310th.S26 2004
   940.54'451'092273—dc22

                                                                                              2004017421

Design by Daniel Pratt
Typesetting by Laura Furney

14   13   12   10   9   8   7   6   5

Every reasonable effort has been made to obtain permission for all copyrighted material included in this
work. Any errors that may have occurred are inadvertent and will be corrected in subsequent editions,
provided notification is sent to the publisher.

For my father,
my son,
and those boys of winter
to whom the gift of long life was denied

I hope they will remember—not with sackcloth, not with tears—but just by contemplating a little, what these men gave, willingly or not, has contributed toward an opportunity still to travel the trails.

—DAVID BROWER (10th Mt. Div.), The Sierra Club Bulletin, 1945, in *For Earth's Sake: The Life and Times of David Brower*

See again in your mind's eye the handsome suntanned face . . . a quiet smile on his lips, a twinkle in those dark eyes squinting into the sun. Recall with me in happy memory those mountain days . . . of sunshine and snow, of ski races won—and lost; of pitches on steep rock faces, summits gained—of retreats from storms and danger; of less happy yet wonderful days of army service, of combat in Italy, of comrades lost but victory gained; of fireside songs, of the Winter Song itself, which always ends in the pledge "of fellowship, of fellowship."

—ERLING OMAR OMLAND (10th Mt. Div.), Eulogy for Sergeant Walter Prager, 1984, in "Leaves from a Skier's Journal," *New England Ski Museum Newsletter*

Montani Semper Liberi—Mountaineers Are Always Free.

—LOWELL THOMAS, *Book of the High Mountains*

Contents

Contents

Illustrations

MAPS

PHOTOGRAPHS

Foreword

IT WAS IN THE YEAR 2000, ON A TENTH MOUNTAIN DIVISION REUNION TRIP TO Italy, that I experienced a startling moment of grief that bears directly on my feelings for *The Boys of Winter* and its poignant subject matter.

Beta Fotas was a young skier from my hometown of Seattle. As one of the senior officers of the Eighty-seventh Mountain Regiment, the Mountain Training Center, and later the Tenth Recon/Mountain Training Group, I had the opportunity during the early 1940s to oversee his training at Mount Rainier and later at Camp Hale, Colorado. He was a fine young man, always ready to do whatever task might be assigned to him. Everyone liked Beta and admired his mountaineering skills. I thought of him as one of the truly good kids I had the privilege to mentor during my years of army service.

Though I have kept in contact over the years with a good many veterans of the division, especially those like myself who continued to be avid skiers after the war, I assumed that Beta was among the men who preferred to put their combat experiences behind them by limiting their ties to former comrades in arms. I was certain that he had made it all the way through to the end of our campaign, moved from Seattle, married, raised a family, and gone on with his life. Perhaps he still skied and climbed with his grandchildren, I hoped, whenever thoughts of him crossed my mind.

One of the highlights of our reunion trip to Italy was a visit to the Florence Military Cemetery, where many of our friends are buried. Though the families of the majority of the boys killed in action opted to bring their loved ones home for reinterment, others believed it was better to let their sons rest in the land where they died (we hope not in vain), with the buddies with whom they served.

When our tour group arrived at the cemetery, we found a touching tribute in the form of a single rose placed at the foot of each Tenth Mountaineer grave marker, allowing us to find our friends among the thousands of American servicemen and -women from other divisions buried there. We passed among the rows of markers, paying our respects, here and there recognizing a name that set off a rush of memories and emotions.

And then I passed one cross with a rose resting beneath it, and glanced up to read the inscription. I can only describe my feeling upon seeing that name as a brutal shock. I was standing before the grave of Beta Fotas, killed in action on April 14, 1945. There had been, it turns out, no joyful homecoming for Beta, no family life after the war, no rewarding career, and no leisure time spent in the mountains. Those were legends I had optimistically created and taken comfort in for more than fifty years. Having them evaporate in a single instant drove home again the very painful reality that every combat veteran knows but tries hard not to dwell on: Beta Fotas had given *everything*. Unexpectedly finding his resting place stayed in my mind for the rest of the trip, and has remained with me ever since.

There was a time when a book delving into the innermost, personal feelings of the men of our division during our months of combat—especially of those who did not come home—might have been viewed by the division's survivors as needlessly intrusive. With the passage of time, however, priorities often shift. At some point, the desire to honor fallen friends in order to ensure that their very personal sacrifice is remembered surpasses the desire to protect the unique privacy of the battlefield.

It was my honor to know all the young men whose lives are painstakingly recounted in *The Boys of Winter.* As with Beta Fotas, I can say without exaggeration that they were among the most exceptional individuals I have ever known, and I am extremely gratified that their stories are now memorialized in print.

Veterans of the Tenth Mountain Division are fortunate to have authors such as Charles Sanders, and archivists such as Debbie Gemar of the Denver Public Library, who are willing to scour the records and interview the survivors in order to provide the public with a more intimate view of the unique young men—like Ralph Bromaghin, Jake Nunnemacher, and Rudy Konieczny—who made our division the very special group it was. The dozens of letters these men sent home, preserved in the Tenth Mountain Division archives at the DPL, have made it possible for the author to let the protagonists speak *in their own voices* about what they did and how they felt during those times of utmost worry and concern. The final product is a powerful and moving testament to the sacrifice of those most deserving of remembrance.

More than once I have stood with the author at memorial services near the monument erected to honor the members of the Tenth Mountain Division who fell in combat. During the most recent of those services, which take place once or twice a year at the base of our old ski training center on Cooper Hill at Tennessee Pass, Colorado, my mind had drifted back to that moment in Italy when I came upon the grave of Beta Fotas. It has caused me to focus with renewed clarity on what an awesome sacrifice all those boys whose names are engraved on that memorial made, and how wonderful it would be if those who did not have the privilege of serving with them knew what good men they were and what great things they might have accomplished had they returned home.

The publication of *The Boys of Winter* goes far toward making that hope a reality. They were among the very best the Tenth—and indeed our country—had to offer, and I am so glad that the reader will now get a chance to know it, too.

—Major John B. Woodward (Ret.)
(10th Mt. Div., 87-HQ-1)

Preface

LEGEND SAYS IT WAS THE GREAT AUSTRIAN *SKIMEISTER* HANNES SCHNEIDER, AFTER participating in the deadly artillery and avalanche duels of World War I in the Italian Alps that killed tens of thousands, who first proclaimed that "if everyone skied, there would be no more war." The premise of that hopeful sentiment is that skiing, like all winter mountain sports, exposes the participant to much of the freedom and natural beauty the world has to offer. No person familiar with the wonders of the high alpine, Schneider reasoned, would willingly choose to defile man and earth and risk losing those gifts through war.

Dartmouth's philosophical ski coach Otto Schniebs, Schneider's German-born contemporary, put it another way. "Skiing is not a sport," he insisted. "It is a way of life." That way of life is by its essence destined to bring the follower closer to nature, and thereby closer to "God." The closer to the deity, the more the adherent appreciates life, and the less likely he or she is to take the consequences of armed conflict lightly. Once again, skiing as a metaphor for enlightenment: *if everyone skied, there would be no more war.*

Though captivating in its simplicity, the theory is, of course, a Utopian pipe dream. Everyone does not ski. There are those who will never understand the things that would prevent them from seeking to attain their goals through brutality, and so at times there must also be those who put aside their own plans and dreams in order to oppose the aggressors. That is perhaps the greatest curse of the complex, global society in which we live, as threatening today as it was in the 1930s and 1940s, when the world in its entirety went to war.

This is the story of three boys of that extraordinary era, who by their affinity for the mountains were imbued with a special quality of wonder and appreciation of the natural world. They adored the snow, the mountains, and life itself, each clearly recognizing how much he had to lose by placing himself in harm's way. Each volunteered to do exactly that, however, as a member of the Tenth Mountain Division, America's World War II ski troops, in order to put a stop to what he saw as an evil of such dimension that it simply had to be defeated.

The men of the Tenth Mountain accomplished great things, in both war and peace. Those lucky enough to return home from the Division's victorious but bloody struggles in the mountains of northern Italy literally founded the U.S. ski industry, and contributed mightily to the growth of the American ecological movement. They led the nation's drive toward greater physical fitness, and pioneered sports and nature programs for the handicapped. They founded great companies and charities, and became some of America's most admired political and social leaders. And they accomplished all of this in large part, each one would readily admit, on the shoulders of their fallen comrades.

For that and so many other reasons, Rudy Konieczny, Jake Nunnemacher, and Ralph Bromaghin deserve to be remembered as more than just names and numbers on a casualty list. This book is in appreciation of their sacrifice, and of the sacrifice of each of the 999 members of the Tenth Mountain Division who gave their lives during the Second World War.

Ultimately, it is also in recognition of how much these three heroes of American skiing still have to teach us: about our world, our values, ourselves, and most of all, about the precious things we place at risk whenever we go to war.

Acknowledgments

THANK YOU TO ALL WHO MADE THE RETELLING OF THIS STORY POSSIBLE:

Veterans of the United States Tenth Mountain Division whom I was privileged to interview: Luterio Aguilar, Nelson Bennett, Bruce Berends, Jeddie Brooks, Tom Brooks, David Burt, Ross Coppock, Marty Daneman, Donald Dwyer, George Earle, Victor Eklund, Newc Eldredge, John Engle, Hugh Evans, Sid Foil, William Gall, Norman Gavrin, Nick Hock, Lewis Hoelscher, Paul Kitchen, Ralph Lafferty, Don Linscott, John Litchfield, Gordie Lowe, Bruce Macdonald, Charles McLane, Albert Meinke, Bob Meservey, Robert Meyerhof, John Montagne, Lyle Munson, Charles Murphy, Bob Parker, Jacques Parker, Ruso Perkins, Dan Pinolini, Frank Prejsnar, Phil Puchner, Percy Rideout, Herbert Schneider, Albert Soria, John Tripp, Duke Watson, Dick Wilson, John Woodward, and especially Professor John Imbrie, whose dedication to keeping alive the accurate history of the division with which he so proudly served is above and beyond the call of duty.

Their friends and families: Adelbert Ames, Charles Bradley Jr., Nina Bradley, Fred Brendemihl, Ralph Clough, Ray Clough, Robert Craig, Michael Fagan, Theresa Frees, Norma Johnson, Madi Kraus, my good friends Adolph Konieczny and Jean Nunnemacher Lindemann, Denny Pace, Audrey Pertl, Marvin Sanders, Heidi Nunnemacher Schulz, Rene Tripp, Fritz Trubshaw, Harriet Clough Waldron, and Edward Wilkes.

And other appreciated contributors: E. John B. Allen, Norman Cohen, Lou Dawson, Gerd Falkner, Nicole Fortier, Michael Hamilton, Staciellen Heasley, Bob and Iris Hermann, Alvin Kane, Jeff Leich and the New England Ski Museum, Robert Levine, Morten Lund, Blair Mahar, Maryanne Moore,

John Nilsson, Al Ossoff, Pat Pfeiffer and the Colorado Ski Museum, Seth Pietras, Kim Schefler Rodriguez, Lowell Skoog, Licia Smith, Patrick Sullivan, Peter Thall, Katherine Trager, Sabina Wolf, Debbie Gemar of the Denver Public Library, whose tireless assistance was indispensable, and Sandy Crooms of the University Press of Colorado for believing so strongly in the importance of this project.

And most of all, thank you to my wife, Nina, and to our extended family who comprise the civilian 3947th Mountain Regiment for your endless love, patience, and good humor. We do what others just talk about.

RIVA RIDGE–MT. BELVEDERE BATTLE DIAGRAM
February 18 – 25

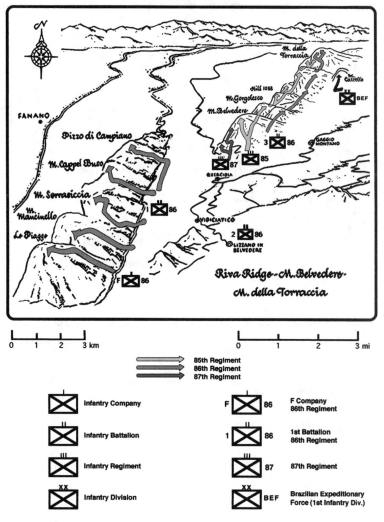

0 1 2 3 km

0 1 2 3 mi

85th Regiment
86th Regiment
87th Regiment

⊠ Infantry Company	F ⊠ 86 — F Company 86th Regiment
⊠ Infantry Battalion	1 ⊠ 86 — 1st Battalion 86th Regiment
⊠ Infantry Regiment	⊠ 87 — 87th Regiment
⊠ Infantry Division	⊠ BEF — Brazilian Expeditionary Force (1st Infantry Div.)

Courtesy of Tenth Mountain Division Association.

MARCH OFFENSIVE BATTLE DIAGRAM
March 3 – 6

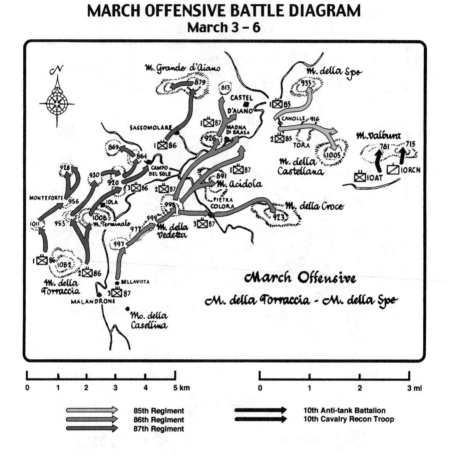

Courtesy of Tenth Mountain Division Association.

SPRING OFFENSIVE BATTLE DIAGRAM
April 14 – 16

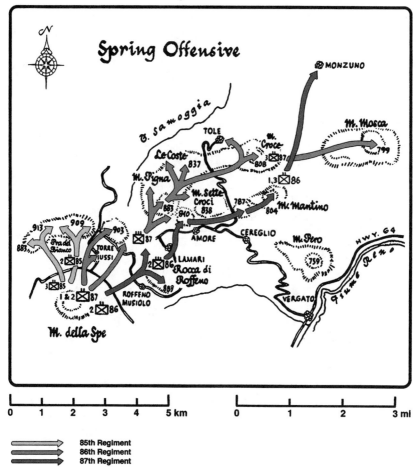

The small town of Torre is located slightly to the north of Tole. Mount Serra is a short distance northeast of Torre. The small village of Madna di Rodiano is located midway between Mount Croce and Mount Mosca. The hamlets of Casa Costa and Casa Bacucchi are located slightly north of Mount Croce. Courtesy of Tenth Mountain Division Association.

The Hero of the Thunderbolt (Rudy Konieczny)

THE STORMS ROLLED ACROSS WESTERN MASSACHUSETTS IN FEBRUARY 1936 AS they always had, leaving a blanket of white on the hills around Adams that turned luminous under the full moon. Down the road in the southern Berkshires, Norman Rockwell was capturing on canvas the idealized images of small-town life in Depression-era America. On this night, he would have done well to travel a few miles north for his inspiration.

On the wooded slopes behind the old Konieczny farm in Adams, several young men shivered in the moonlight, shouldering their seven-foot hickory skis toward the modest summit. In front of the pack, as always, was a slightly built teen of medium height, with short blond hair and baby-faced, angular features. Over and over, he would lead his gang up, and then beat them to the bottom. His name was Rudolph Konieczny (Kon-EZ-nee), but to everyone in town he was just plain "Rudy." And Rudy liked to win.

In the near distance of this idyllic scene loomed the behemoth, "the highest wave of the great landstorm of all this billowing region," as native son Oliver Wendell Holmes described it.[1] Dark and foreboding even in bright moonlight, Mount Greylock rose far above them, teasing the boys into dreams of racing glory. Herman Melville had drawn his inspiration for the hulking Moby Dick from the snowcapped peak. It was the "great white hump" the author could see through the window above his writing desk.[2] Now the mountain was pulling on Rudy in a way reminiscent of the beast's inexorable tug at Ahab.

When the church bells tolled nine, Rudy led his tired, happy group back to the farm. Skiing was their passion, and little satisfied more than a rare and exhausting moonlight practice. As they skated toward the house and the main road, their conversation yielded a consensus that this night had been particularly exhilarating. The snow had been good for a change, not the usual mixture of New England slush and ice. The weather was clear and cold. They had done well. All was right with the world.[3]

Moving along at Rudy's demanding pace, his younger brother Adolph—Rudy's shadow—struggled to keep up. Though the gangly Adolph was several years Rudy's junior, he was already taller, which irked the smaller Konieczny. His little brother's sudden growth spurt toward an eventual 6'4" was particularly difficult for Rudy to accept, since for years he himself had been tagging after his older brother Charlie, a local star athlete who towered over both his younger brothers and their five sisters.[4]

The growing frustration over the "averageness" of his height, according to Adolph, led the seventeen-year-old Rudy increasingly to place his highest priority on excelling at activities that proved his physical prowess and daring. Prior to finding his true love of skiing, Rudy had even talked his older brother into managing his fledgling boxing career.[5]

Rudy, in fact, won his first amateur bout at sixteen. His initial pugilistic success came as a surprise to everyone, including Charlie, who was quite amused when the young boxer announced that getting into the ring seemed about the easiest way in the world to earn three dollars. Rudy's second match against a more seasoned Holyoke boxer with the ominous pseudonym "Kid Shamrock," however, was his last. It was a reluctant career choice with which everyone in attendance at the bout—*especially* Charlie—concurred. Rudy returned to the slopes after his brief fling with the sweet science having demonstrated that, if nothing else, he wasn't the type to back down from a scrap.

"As a kid, I think that Rudy might actually have liked fighting," remembered Adolph. Rudy, however, was no bully. "Quite to the contrary, he never picked on anyone. He just wouldn't brook nonsense from anybody. He could not back down. It was not in his nature."[6]

Gliding along between the two brothers that night was Rudy's gang of neighborhood ski cronies. First behind the leader was Maurice "Greeny" Guertin, a fine skier possessed of an even wilder streak of teenage insanity than Rudy. Guertin once scaled the outside of the huge Adams church steeple for the simple, extraordinarily dangerous pleasure of waving to his friends below.[7] Behind Greeny came Roy Deyle, a good athlete, but definitely the more cautious "follower" of the group. And finally, there was Gerard "Stumpy" Gardner, who at five feet tall had something even greater to prove than Rudy did. Gerard understood what drove Rudy, and vice versa. He was the only one permitted to call Rudy by his rhyming nickname "Tooty," a reference to Rudy's occasional tooting of his own horn, without risking reprisal. They were both in the process of molding themselves into first-class downhill racers, and each respected that in the other.[8]

More than anything else this night, the five boys exuded pride. Every one wore the badge "Adams Man" with the same sense of self that the young fishermen from across the state in Gloucester wore theirs, the name of the town itself a synonym for the utter tenacity of its sons. Fearlessness in the mountains was identical to courage on the sea, as far as the Berkshire boys were concerned, and that belief caused them to move with a purpose, their heads high. To a man, they were out to conquer Greylock, where they agreed to meet again to practice at first light.

೮೨೦೮೨

By 1936, Adams, Massachusetts, had already earned a reputation as one of the skiing capitals of the eastern United States. The first American ski boom of the early 1930s coincided with, and was in part fueled by, the activities of the New Deal's Civilian Conservation Corps. Looking for projects to keep its workers busy in the midst of a seemingly endless Depression, President Roosevelt's CCC had decided in 1934 to cut a "Class A" ski trail in the hill country of western Mass in the hopes of stimulating local business and tourism.[9] The site chosen was the highest peak in the Berkshires, Mount Greylock, smack in Adams's backyard. They called the trail the Thunderbolt, and even without the installation of one of the popular, new rope tows recently invented to pull skiers uphill, it instantly became one of America's legendary ski runs.[10]

The Thunderbolt was tough to climb, and even tougher to ski. In the words of 1934 U.S. National Downhill Ski Champion Joseph Duncan Jr. of Colorado (a future Tenth Mountain Division officer), those who made the nearly two-mile, forty-five-minute hike to the summit were faced with "undoubtedly the most thrilling wooded run yet built in the country—it beats anything in the Rocky Mountains."[11] Dartmouth Ski Team member and another future Tenth Mountaineer, Bob Meservey, had a less exuberant view. "It just scared the hell out of you. Steep, icy, and full of nasty surprises. It was the toughest run we had to ski."[12]

From all over New England, the best skiers in the eastern United States flocked to the Berkshires to take their crack at the mighty 'Bolt. These pilgrimages of the elite exposed the local Berkshire youth to championship-caliber racing, and Rudy Konieczny and his friends were among the many who contracted skiing fever as a result. The first Massachusetts Downhill Championship was held on the Thunderbolt in 1935 and won by the superb Dartmouth racer Dick Durrance. Fellow Olympian Jarvis Schauffler of Amherst College followed Durrance by setting a new speed record on the run several months later.[13]

Before long, Rudy and the others were flocking to the hills of Adams on primitive, homemade equipment that often included bicycle inner tubes fashioned into bindings and nailed to their skis. Inspired by the thrills they had witnessed and willing to take enormous risks in pursuit of the speeds they had seen Durrance and Schauffler achieve on *their* mountain, the young Berkshire skiers painfully learned their sport by imitation, and then quickly organized themselves into ski racing clubs. These included the Mount Greylock and Pittsfield organizations and Rudy's first affiliation, the Thunderbolt team.[14]

As their skill and confidence progressed, Rudy's gang soon set out to procure skis with real metal edges and leather bindings. The working-class kids of Adams received a tremendous stroke of fortune in that pursuit when local furniture store owner Art Simmons himself caught the ski bug and took on the role of Santa Claus for the fledgling racers. At the height of the Depression, Art's store, A. C. Simmons, sold twenty-dollar pairs of Groswold skis to Rudy and his cohorts—some of whom were lucky enough to be making $10.40 a week at the Berkshire Mills—for one dollar down and interest-free terms. For those Saroyan-esque acts of kindness, Simmons is recalled with fondness nearly seventy years later by the surviving club members, who continue to patronize the family-owned A. C. Simmons Department Store on Main Street in Adams in the twenty-first century.[15]

Now more properly outfitted, Rudy, Greeny, and their friends began training in earnest on the Thunderbolt. They would frequently scale Greylock three times in a single afternoon to practice racing down. "We'd strip down to our undershirts on the way up," Adolph remembered, "to keep the perspiration to a minimum. The wetter your clothes got on the way up, the colder you were going to be once you stopped moving. We were cold most of the time, I guess, but we just ignored it."[16]

On those rare occasions when the light and conditions were just right, they'd ski all day on the mountain and come back to the Konieczny farm to continue their workouts at twilight. From the start, however, it was apparent that Rudy—frequently adorned in his trademark, floppy-brimmed ski hat (a knitted gift from an older sister that he believed created a look that was unique if not outright jaunty)—was head and shoulders above the rest.

"Rudy skied like water flowing over a waterfall," was friend Lester Horton's assessment.[17] According to Bill Linscott, the Thunderbolt champion of 1942, "[a]nyone who saw Rudy ski would try to imitate him because he had such great style. He was such a natural. When you saw Rudy coming down, you watched, because you knew it was going to be beautiful."[18]

Rudy was not only better than the rest, he was also more committed. During the winter, he refused to work at the mill (where he had started at age fifteen after quitting school), saving his factory earnings the rest of the year to get him through the months in which he did nothing but train and race. Rudy would pay room and board to his parents, but he spent most of his time on Greylock. According to his younger brother, he'd hike up alone, stay at the Bascomb Lodge on top with caretaker Charlie Parker if the weather came in, and ski down himself. Skiing alone has always been a dangerous pursuit. "Some good skiers got killed in those mountains," recalled Adolph, "but one thing Rudy wasn't short on was confidence."[19]

Rudy and Greeny Guertin, who gradually became best friends based upon their obsession with achieving speed on skis, also became familiar figures on the slopes around Hancock, Massachusetts, that today comprise the Berkshires' largest ski area, Jiminy Peak. Actually, the two pushed each other both on *and* off the slopes. "A lot of people thought they were nuts," said Adolph. "But they were just challenging themselves. Not showing off, just marching to their own drums."

It wasn't only ski racing that gave the boys their requisite charge of adrenaline. While Greeny amused himself scaling church steeples and doing front flips and other acrobatics on skis, Rudy reveled in riding a bicycle without brakes around the hills of Adams, figuring out ways to stop only as the absolute necessity arose. He also liked to dive off a high ledge at the local reservoir into four feet of water, just for the excitement of it. "When the other kids told him he'd break his neck, he'd just tell them he knew what he was doing," continued Adolph. "Pretty soon, they were all doing it, too."

Rudy, Adolph concluded, was from a very early age what might today be called a "thrill junkie." "A lot of people, when they think of Rudy, automatically recall first and foremost that he could be very funny, a real smart aleck. That's not what I think of, and that really, to me, wasn't the core of his personality. It was that perpetual search for the next big thrill that really defined my brother. School and pretty much everything else was secondary to adventure. That's really what made him tick. As a kid, he hadn't figured out yet how skiing could be his ticket to bigger things, but he wasn't going to make that mill his life. If there was anything in this world that scared him, it was that. That he'd have to live a life limited by that mill."[20]

ℰℭℬℛ

Rudy came into the world on April 7, 1918, the fourth of eight children born to Sophie and Charles Konieczny. His parents had emigrated to Massachusetts in the early part of the century from the central European cities of Warsaw and Prague, respectively, and retained certain "Old World" notions of proper behavior for good Catholic youth. As a result, they were frequently driven to distraction by Rudy's antics. "My father had a very low tolerance for nonsense, and he was pretty strict with all of us," recalled Adolph. "Rudy would never rebel against my folks in obvious ways, but he'd do little sly, humorous things that gave him a feeling he was getting away with something."[21]

As youngsters, Rudy and Adolph were frequently enlisted by their father to assist him in doing chores on the farm. "Rudy really made a game out of that," his brother remembered. "My father would ask us to help him move hay across the farm on a large wagon, for instance, and he'd be red in the face pushing from the rear. I'd push as hard as I could from one front side, and Rudy would pretend to be pushing with every ounce of strength from the other. Of course, I knew he was really coasting, and every once in a while he would shoot me a wink. Lucky for him, my old man never caught on, and I was no snitch. But that was Rudy."

Rudy didn't get away with everything, though, such as the time he lent his bicycle to his father, conveniently failing to mention its lack of brakes. That incident did not end happily for Rudy, who didn't feel like sitting on his bike again, or on anything else, for a week. "Sure, my father would whack him every once in a while when a point really needed to be made," Adolph continued. "That's the way it was done back then. Rudy could take that. What he really hated was when my mother would try to drag him to church. He was good natured about it because he knew better than to challenge her, but he'd generally end up sneaking out the side door when the priest wasn't looking, and would head straight for Greylock with Greeny, Roy, and Gardner. He wasn't much for religion, or for sitting still, and I think eventually my parents understood through their exasperation that it just wasn't in him to change."

Understanding that his growing and relentless search for adventure required the constant indulgence of others, Rudy soon cultivated a notoriously charming and effective power of persuasion. It was a skill, his brother recalled, that Rudy did not always use to unselfish ends. "When I first learned to drive, he talked me into splitting the cost of an old jalopy with him," remembered Adolph. "I knew it would be me who kept it gassed up all the time. . . . One night Rudy had a big date, and didn't bother to check the fuel gauge. He ran out of gas in the middle of a downpour, and his evening went downhill from there. The girl was really upset, and he ended up doing a lot of walking in the rain. [Apparently, even Rudy's superior abilities to persuade had a limit.] When he finally got home, he just heaved his sopping wet jacket on the bed to wake me up, and that started quite a riot. But damned if he didn't almost convince me that his running out of gas was somehow my fault."[22]

Adolph pointed out, however, that whatever tension might have developed over the course of a year between the brothers was swept away each winter on Greylock. Rudy would mentor his younger brother precisely and enthusiastically on the finer points of ski racing, refusing to allow Adolph to make a single concession to the fact he had the use of only one arm since birth. "He helped turn me into a pretty good racer," Adolph admitted, and the race results published at the time prove it.[23] Though he never won an official race, the younger Konieczny made creditable showings in several Thunderbolt downhills with the benefit of Rudy's encouragement. "I didn't take all of his advice, though," Adolph asserted. "He once told me that it made sense to go into a deep tuck and *schuss* [ski straight without making turns] the entire last, steep section of the Thunderbolt. 'Don't worry about how much speed you build up,' he told me, 'the run-out is short, but it's uphill. You'll stop. I always do.'" Adolph's retrospective comment on that advice was a long pause, followed by the words, "yeah, right."

"Rudy had that racer's mentality of total invincibility," his brother concluded, "and it showed in everything he did, down to his personal motto: Never worry about falling down a mountain; you'll always stop at the bottom."[24]

Before long, the hard work began to produce results for Rudy. He quickly developed, without formal instruction (other than a pointer here and there from Dartmouth's legendary skiing coach Otto Schniebs, who would sometimes talk with the local kids after a competition), into one of the strongest and most fearless racers in New England.[25] He missed the 1937 Eastern Championships when they were relocated to the Nosedive at Stowe, Vermont, because of a lack of snow on the Thunderbolt, but he began the next season by winning the 1938 New Year's Day race on the Pittsfield Forest Shadow Trail.[26]

Rudy had by that time developed such powers of concentration that he would almost go into a trance before a race. Adolph recalled waiting in the warming hut above the Thunderbolt for the start of a competition, and noticing that his brother was staring off into space. He asked Rudy if he was okay. Rudy just smiled, put his index finger to his lips, and went back to his thoughts. "He was visualizing, long before that became standard preparation for most racers," said Adolph. "Racing was his life, and he took it seriously . . . It's hard to explain, but Rudy was both incredibly intense and incredibly happy at the same time. I guess it's as simple as the fact that he was flat out doing what he loved. He was going for it."[27]

ℰℭ

On Sunday, January 16, 1938, it all came together for Rudy Konieczny. Under perfect conditions in the qualifying heats for the 1938 Eastern Downhill Championships, Rudy set the course record on the Thunderbolt. The years of practice and risk up and down the face of Greylock had paid off. His time of 2:57.4 bested the records previously set by Durrance and Schauffler, and it changed his life forever.[28]

Suddenly, young Rudy Konieczny was famous in eastern U.S. skiing circles. Even the *New York Times* reported on his feat, and the local newspapers went wild for the new record holder.[29] In gushing prose, the *Berkshire Eagle*'s Norman H. Ransford wrote: "A modest and popular 19-year-old boy, Rudolph Konieczny of Adams, and his sensational officially recorded time on the new Thunderbolt ski run are providing . . . many colorful anticipations for the Eastern Downhill Championship race on the trail. . . . Chances are widely

8

conceded this new and slim young figure in Berkshire skiing may win or place close to the top in the season's biggest race, notwithstanding the fact that it will bring into competition some of the leading ski runners in the world. . . . All Adams and its environs are quietly pulling for 'Rudy' to make a good run in the big test."[30]

Almost overnight, Rudy became a symbol, a crucible for the hopes of people throughout the Berkshires who—after enduring nearly a decade of Depression—wanted something to cheer about. "There were things going on here that went well beyond skiing," said Adolph. "You have to understand that the emotional depth of the hopes placed on Rudy also stemmed from who Rudy was racing against."[31]

It was the Ivy League college kids with a little more money and opportunity who always seemed to win the races. "Now here comes a local mill kid who sets the record on the Thunderbolt," continued Adolph. "That gets a lot of area people thinking about their own place in the world, and it's possible that Rudy started to feel a bit like it was up to him to win not only for himself but for everyone else, too."

Many of the most fervent hopes for Rudy's success were harbored by members of the army of Berkshires "ski townies," of whom Rudy was now the undisputed leader. They, too, had learned their skills without coaches and raced on equipment not nearly as good as the gear used by their collegiate rivals. They had also seen firsthand how the college stars would often congratulate each other on the medal stand after a race but ignore Rudy, which the locals regarded as an intentional snub of their hero. "He'd laugh it off," recalled Adolph, "but I think it hurt him a little. Everybody wants the recognition of his peers."[32]

Many years later, the competitive but usually affable Dartmouth star Dick Durrance told an interviewer that "collegiate skiing [in the 1930s] *was* skiing in this country."[33] That statement appears to reveal a conceit—whether conscious or not—that the Berkshire townies believed permeated the ranks of both college skiers and the large-circulation newspaper reporters who lionized them, when it came to their regard for locals like Rudy. On the other hand, Rudy's brash reputation and recklessness on the slopes did nothing to win him friends among the college racers. "I liked Rudy. He was a sharp kid, very amusing, but it wasn't hard to get rubbed the wrong way by him when we competed," said Bob Meservey of Dartmouth. "He knew the Thunderbolt like nobody else, and it made him a little cocky when we raced there. Did he have a chip on his shoulder? Who knows? Maybe we put it there."[34]

Another former Dartmouth Ski Team star from the prewar era, Charles McLane (who also holds the distinction of being the first enlisted member of the Tenth Mountain Division) suggested a different explanation. "This wasn't a class thing. The colleges were filled with skiers from middle- and working-class backgrounds, in addition to those from well-to-do families. There was just a wonderful camaraderie among the college competitors because we all knew each other from the various university winter carnivals, parties, sing-alongs and the like. The locals like Rudy—and every ski area in New England had them—mistook the familiarity the college racers had with one another for an exclusionary attitude or aloofness that simply did not exist."[35] Meservey concluded the debate by staking out the middle ground, stating that in general, "over-awareness of each other's feelings was never one of [most] competitive skiers' failings (or mine)."[36]

One racer who both appreciated Rudy's skills and understood his personality was the great Austrian skier and two-time U.S. National Downhill Champion, Toni Matt. So friendly did they become that after a race on the Thunderbolt, Matt stayed at the Konieczny farm, which reminded him of his own family's home in the Alps. "Toni Matt's friendliness kind of reinforced our perception that the college guys looked down on the townies, no matter how nice Rudy tried to be," said Adolph. "I mean, if a truly great European skier like Matt could accept Rudy as an equal, how could the college guys not? That's one of the reasons we all wanted so badly for Rudy to do well against them."[37] After the Thunderbolt time trials, hard as it was for some of them to believe, the country's best university skiers sensed that the local kid formerly of Adams High might just be the favorite going into the big race on his home mountain.

Rudy spent the next two weeks before the 1938 Eastern Championship training intensively, but the pressure and distractions steadily began to build. That was especially the case after he received his "Class A" racing certification from the U.S. Eastern Amateur Ski Association, placing him in the same category as Durrance, Schauffler, Matt, and the other greats of the sport. "Just because I happened to win New Year's and last Sunday, they expect me to win every time," he lamented to the newspapers, referring to local ski racing fans who were disappointed over his nasty fall in a preliminary heat. "An ordinary skier [like me] can't do that."[38]

His self-effacing words were counterbalanced by the multitude of local spokesmen lauding his record. "We think he's a great little skier who's going places," Thunderbolt Club president Henry Neff told reporters. "Best of all, it can't spoil him. He's a grand little guy, who refuses to get a swelled head."[39] Even Durrance jumped on the bandwagon, perhaps employing a little psychology of his own. He was quoted in the *Berkshire Eagle* as having told friends "he doubts Konieczny's time will be beaten," referring to Rudy with somewhat faint praise as a "particularly competent skier."[40]

As Rudy struggled to stay focused, he could not possibly have known that his life was strangely on a collision course with international politics. Over the next seven years, the ill winds from Europe that would soon blow across New England and into Rudy's life would affect nearly every living soul on earth. That February, however, Rudy Konieczny and the skiers of Adams got an early look at the coming storm.

߷

The fascist Nazi regime, which had taken power in Berlin in 1933 on a platform that stressed the doctrine of Aryan racial superiority, placed enormous emphasis on developing and demonstrating the physical pre-eminence of German athletes. These supposed gods of sport were invariably portrayed as tall, muscular, and blond, with carved, Nordic features.[41] The two leading proponents of this Nazi doctrine of eugenics, the wild-eyed, dark-haired, and mustached Chancellor Adolf Hitler and his diminutive and polio-scarred propaganda minister, Joseph Goebbels, themselves seemed to provide stark proof that persons of Teutonic ancestry vary widely in their physical traits and abilities. Nevertheless, Goebbels utilized the theory of Aryan superiority as the cornerstone of his ubiquitous propaganda program, and was in constant search of athletic champions from the Reich to tout as the proof behind Hitler's racist rants.[42]

In the early years of Hitler's rule, Goebbels was presented with several such opportunities. In 1930, German boxer Max Schmeling won the vacant heavyweight championship of the world. Six years later, having lost his title and considered past his prime, Schmeling traveled to New York to face an undefeated and heavily favored, up-and-coming African American fighter named Joe Louis. In a shocking upset, he pummeled Louis, providing a propaganda bonanza for the Nazis. Despite the nontitle nature of the 1936 fight, Goebbels was again enabled to proclaim Schmeling the model of the Aryan superman, against whom members of "inferior" races stood no chance in honest competition.[43]

Unfortunately for Goebbels, Schmeling remained unwilling to play the role of Nazi idol, and refused the constant urging of both the propaganda minister and Hitler himself to join the *Nationalsozialistische Deutsche Arbeiterpartei* (National Socialist German Worker's Party). Schmeling further infuriated the rabidly anti-Semitic Nazi leadership by refusing to fire his Jewish American manager.[44] Eager to find more malleable sports stars to exploit, Goebbels turned his attention to the Olympics. The Nazi regime had been given the opportunity by the International Olympic Committee to host both the 1936 Winter and Summer Games, and in February of that year the world's greatest winter athletes traveled to Garmisch-Partenkirchen in the Bavarian Alps to compete.

The reporting of the Winter Games by the American press was less than flattering toward the Nazis. Correspondent Westbrook Pegler compared the atmosphere in Garmisch to activities behind the front lines in a war, so pervasive was the presence of Nazi symbols and men in military uniforms. The burliest members of Hitler's feared "Black Guard" handled security for the events, primarily through overt physical intimidation meted out with self-important enthusiasm.[45]

Still, Goebbels got in large part what he wanted out of the international forum. Whereas the United States led the field in the 1932 Winter Games held in Lake Placid, New York, with six gold medals and twelve medals overall, the German games four years later were dominated by athletes from the "Aryan" nations of northern Europe, with Norway, Germany, Sweden, Finland, Switzerland, and Austria finishing in that order in the medal count. These were also the first games to feature an alpine skiing event, the downhill and slalom combined. Goebbels had to have been thrilled that Germans Franz Pfnur (coached by the great Austrian ski stylist Toni Seelos) and Christl Cranz took the gold for the men's and women's divisions, respectively.[46] The American alpine ski team, led by Dick Durrance, made a respectable showing without collecting a medal.

The Berlin Summer Games in August were an equally sycophantic show of reverence for Hitler and Nazism, with the German team doing its part by winning an astonishing eighty-nine medals. The United States was a distant second with fifty-six, followed by Hungary with just sixteen.[47] Amid this utter domination, however, was the realization even among the Nazi elite that the games had been commandeered by African American sprinter Jesse Owens, who captured four gold medals and earned appreciative ovations from the German sports fans.[48]

Following the embarrassment suffered by the Reich as the result of Owens's performance at the 1936 Summer Games and Schmeling's refusal to endorse the Nazi regime, the propaganda minister apparently concluded that winter sports (in which mainly Caucasian athletes from cold weather nations compete against one another) were simply the safest and most promising vehicles for his crusade to identify proof in athletics of the Aryan super race. Thus, although there are no surviving records in Germany revealing exactly who in the Nazi hierarchy chose to permit their tour of the United States to proceed only a few weeks prior to the Reich's highly anticipated annexation of Austria known as the *Anschluss,* a team of world-class skiers from Bavaria arrived in the United States to compete against North America's best in late January 1938.[49]

≈⊃✕⊂≈

They were known as the German Universities Skiing Team of Munich. The elite group—which had already won the Intercollegiate Championship of Europe—featured German intercollegiate downhill champion Kurt Riehle, intercollegiate jumping champion and downhiller Franz Machler, intercollegiate cross-country and combined champion Walter Ringer, British downhill and slalom champion Xavier "Haver" Kraisy, and intercollegiate Langlauf jump champion Richard May. Captain Karl Ringer, Gerri Lantschner, Siegfried List, the late-arriving star Ulrich "Ulli" Beuter, and a promising young downhiller, University of Munich Ph.D. candidate Fritz Dehmel, rounded out the squad.[50] They arrived in America five days prior to the 1938 U.S. Eastern Alpine Championships, the race Rudy Konieczny was favored to win.

At a Manhattan dinner given in the team's honor by the German Ski Club of New York on February 1, 1938, it was announced that the Bavarian skiers intended to compete by invitation in several upcoming North American ski tournaments, including the Bates and Dartmouth Winter Carnivals. No mention, however, was made of the Eastern Championships on the Thunderbolt, which coincided with the Bates College event over the coming weekend.[51]

Nevertheless, eight members of the German team arrived in Pittsfield and began practicing on Mount Greylock early that week.[52] The day they first appeared on the hill, resplendent in their sweaters featuring the German Eagle and Nazi Swastika across their chests, was the last day for young Rudy as race favorite. Noting that the "German Aces" had arrived in Massachusetts seeking the Eastern U.S. downhill title, the *New York Times* reported on February 5, 1938, that "the course record . . . set recently by 19-year-old Rudolph Konieczny, is likely to be shattered by one of the big stars in the field."[53] The first thing broken by the German skiers, though, was American confidence.

According to those locals on the hill, the German team arrived sporting an arrogance that made even the haughtiest collegiate racer appear downright friendly in comparison. During practices, the German stars used assistants to caddy their skis up the Thunderbolt, permitting them to arrive at the top of the mountain fresher than their American rivals. And when they skied, it was nearly flawlessly, faster than anyone had ever skied on Greylock.[54]

Those U.S. racers who watched the Germans' displays of skill in practice seemed psychologically beaten before the event began on February 6. Greeny Guertin recalled that Rudy's self-assurance was shaken for the first and only time in his memory. "He said to me, 'Jeez, Greeny, I don't even feel like racing. We can't beat these guys.' I said, hey, they could have some bad days, too, you know," but neither really believed he had a chance to win.[55]

For Rudy, things went from bad to worse. First, he suffered a serious ankle sprain in a fall during a weekday practice run.[56] Then, of the fifteen names of the top-seeded racers placed into a hat to determine starting order, Rudy's name was pulled first. With the unenviable task of leading off among fifty of the world's best downhillers, Rudy fell hard on the icy, uneven course and lost precious time favoring his injured ankle. He finished sixteenth, not bad in the larger scheme, but disastrous considering the circumstances. The huge crowd of local fans who lined the bottom of the course was crestfallen.[57]

"I can't say that the pressure got to him," said Adolph. "But again, he carried a lot of folks' hopes with him into that race, as well as his own big dreams. That's a lot of weight to put on the back of an inexperienced, nineteen-year-old kid with a bum ankle. But Rudy made no excuses. He'd have none of that."[58]

The day belonged to Germany's Fritz Dehmel, who—as predicted—broke the three-week-old course record. No one expected, however, that Rudy's mark would be eclipsed by a remarkable thirty-one seconds. Ted Hunter and Edward Meservey (Bob's older brother) of Dartmouth finished a distant second and third.[59] Rudy's time was still good enough to best such skiing luminaries as Williams College captain and future Tenth Mountaineer Tommy Clement and Australian slalom champ Tom Mitchell, but according to his younger brother, Rudy remembered only the dashed expectations and all of those racers who finished ahead of him. Unfortunately, that is also what many of those who rooted for him would remember, and Rudy knew it.

Dehmel accepted his medal as Eastern U.S. Alpine champion, and together with his teammates departed in a private touring car waiting near the victory platform. With that, the Germans disappeared into the fading

Berkshire mountain light. It was unclear at the time whether there would ever be a rematch, but one can imagine Joseph Goebbels laughing back in Berlin when he got the news. The headline in the *New York Times* the next day read, "Dehmel Annexes Eastern Ski Race."[60]

The last that New Englanders saw of the official German Team was their appearance at the National Ski Jumping Championships in Brattleboro, Vermont. During that event, there were several attempts to pull down the Nazi flag as it flew alongside the banners of the other competing nations at the bottom of the jumping hill.[61] "The people of New England knew who these guys were, and what that flag stood for," said another of Rudy's skiing buddies and a future Tenth Mountaineer from Adams, Frank Prejsnar. "Who could blame them?"[62] Joe Dodge, the legendary manager of the Appalachian Mountain Club's camp at Pinkham Notch, New Hampshire, reportedly refused the Germans permission to stay at the Tuckerman Ravine Shelter.[63]

Interestingly, the perceptions of the western American skiers regarding the German Team were decidedly different from the initial impressions of most New Englanders. Ralph Lafferty, a member of the University of Oregon Ski Team and another future Tenth Mountain Division officer, remembered meeting the Bavarians on their swing through the northwestern United States and Canada, and was taken by their gregarious nature. "They were drinking beer and singing all the time when they stayed with us out here, jabbering away in German that we somehow understood," he recalled. "They even staged some performances as a singing group. It's possible that they relaxed once they acclimated themselves, won some races, and got away from the political stuff that was so prevalent in the first days of their trip. As far as we could tell, they were just a bunch of skiers having a good time, and we liked them."[64] Fritz Dehmel similarly made friends on his return back east, racing in the National Championship that March at Stowe, which was won by his teammate and an equally enthusiastic partier, Ulli Beuter.[65]

Ralph Lafferty remembered that he maintained correspondences with Machler and Kraisy for a while, until the Second World War intervened. "After that," he said, "I never heard from those guys again."[66]

⁊⁊⁊⁊

Following the disappointment of the 1938 Eastern Championships, Rudy and Greeny dedicated themselves to reclaiming the Thunderbolt as *their* mountain. They also began to take their leadership roles more seriously.

15

After much debate, the two broke from their respective clubs and formed a new one, the now legendary Ski Runners of Adams. Among other goals, Rudy and Greeny wanted to establish a team that young, local skiers could afford to join. The other area racing clubs charged up to twenty-five dollars a year for membership, a small fortune in the midst of the Depression. Joining the new Adams team cost nothing but dedication.[67]

They also wanted a fresh start. Now that they were the undisputed cocaptains of their own squad, it was woe to those teammates or competitors who attempted to beat them on the Thunderbolt, whether climbing up or racing down. "The Ski Runners of Adams were definitely fun loving," recalled Adolph Konieczny, "but their attitude was that they wanted to win every time down the hill. This was their lives. They worked to earn money to train. They trained to become better racers. And they raced because they loved it. No steady girlfriends. No cultural pursuits beyond a favorite radio program. Just ski racing. My brother became more intensely focused than ever."[68]

In his handmade Peter Limmer ski boots and top-notch Groswold skis, which he had for months saved his mill salary to purchase, Rudy finished second in the 1938 Massachusetts Championships to Peter Garrett of Yale. A year later, he placed second to his friend Toni Matt in the 1939 Greylock Trophy Race, with Greeny Guertin coming in third.[69] No one dared suggest, however, that even a maturing Rudy might still be half a step behind the upper echelon of the world's best skiers. "He was too proud for anyone to risk his reaction to something like that," said Adolph. "He'd give you the shirt off his back, but for that, he might have popped you one."[70]

Store owner Art Simmons also lent a hand in trying to help Rudy develop into a more poised and experienced racer. Late in the 1938 season, he drove Konieczny three hours north to Stowe, Vermont, to compete in the Nationals against Dehmel, Beuter, and the American college stars, so that the young racer could experience a world-class competition on the Nosedive run at Mount Mansfield.[71] (Rudy, who raced with low expectations owing to his lack of familiarity with the course, was indeed disqualified for unintentionally cutting through a control flag.)[72] In a letter written some sixty years later, David Burt of Stowe, who would later become one of Rudy's closest army buddies, gave his recollections of that event at which Rudy played a very unassuming role: "As a high school boy, seeing so many 'A' racers was a vision; there were the Durrances, there was Ted Hunter, Al Beck, and [the Townsend brothers from the University of New Hampshire]. Who won I don't recall but I do remember seeing a table full of racers at a supper, post race, put on by our local ski club in the basement of the Congregational Church, and the . . . lean, almost frail looking (at first sight) Rudy was there. . . . There was nothing in those days to hint that before long Rudy would be one of the people I most admired."[73]

At long last, at the Massachusetts Downhill Championships held in January 1939 on the Thunderbolt, Rudy and the Ski Runners of Adams enjoyed a day in the sun. Facing a strong field that included a Dartmouth team led by Olympian Ted Hunter and coached by Walter Prager—the Swiss racer and technical innovator who had succeeded Otto Schniebs—Rudy, Greeny, Gardiner, Roy Deyle, and the rest of the Ski Runners took home the team trophy.[74] That satisfying hometown victory was celebrated before six thousand ski racing fans and hundreds of jubilant local supporters. For Rudy, however, even this memorable achievement proved bittersweet. The tuck and schuss approach on the last section of the Thunderbolt, which he had urged his brother Adolph to adopt, may have done him in. Describing the race, the *Berkshire Eagle* reported:"Hardest luck of all hit Rudy Konieczny, 20-year-old Adams 'A' skier, who ran in extremely fast time to a point 10 yards from the finish line. Then misfortune smacked him squarely in the face, as his ski caught in a rut of the steep embankment and he pitched forward, convoluting in a whirl of arms, legs and skis. Fighting to collect himself, he regained his feet and stumbled across the rope to place eighth. It was a heartbreaking finish, that cost him at least 20 seconds and a place much nearer the top of the list. But Rudy became justly elated when it became apparent that the Ski Runners of Adams . . . had won the team competition."[75]

It is unclear whether Rudy's disappointing spill cost him the individual title, won by Ted Hunter, but his breakneck performance as captain of the team champions was impressive enough to refocus the attention of the American Federation of International Skiing (the sport's national governing body) on him. The Federation informed Rudy that a top-five finish in the 1940 FIS qualifying race, or a win in the Massachusetts or Eastern Championships, would likely secure him a spot on the U.S. National Team and perhaps a shot at competing in the next Olympic Games.[76] It was electrifying news, but it surely put the pressure back on.

The 1940 Massachusetts Championship was run on the Thunderbolt on February 18, one week prior to the Eastern Championships. It proved a bitter disappointment for both Rudy and his teammates, all of whom had practiced for a full year in anticipation of defending their title and sending one of their own to the national team. In conditions termed "excellent" by most, Rudy had been expected to contend for top honors. Instead, he inexplicably crossed the finish line in twenty-fourth place. Though Greeny Guertin placed well, the Ski Runners of Adams lost the Massachusetts state title to their Dartmouth archrivals by a wide margin.[77] The local boys and their rooters were devastated.

With just six days in which to help himself and his team to put the disastrous loss behind them, Rudy plumbed the depths of his resolve. "He poured all the determination he had into rallying the guys and motivating himself," Adolph remembered, "for what he figured was probably the make or break race of his career."[78]

Conditions on the Thunderbolt the Sunday of the 1940 Eastern Championships were even better than they had been the week before. Eager to regain the pride that their humbling defeat in the state championships had stolen, the home team decided to throw all caution to Greylock's icy wind. This time, they did not disappoint. Former U.S. Olympian and future Tenth Mountain Division officer Robert Livermore took home the individual trophy, but Rudy finished eighth among one of the most talented fields ever to race for the eastern skiing crown. It was enough to lead the Ski Runners to the Championship over a tough Dartmouth squad, which that day featured stars Bob Meservey and Jack Tobin, and Dartmouth's future team captain, a handsome and dedicated racer from Wisconsin named Jake Nunnemacher.[79]

Once again, Rudy had failed to win an individual title. For the second time in the course of a year, however, he had led the Ski Runners to a major championship. His shot at securing a spot on the U.S. National Team was tenuous, but he was most definitely still in the running as he stepped up his preparations dramatically for the FIS National Championship to be held that March in Sun Valley, Idaho, a three-day train ride away. "He believed he could race his way onto the team," sighed Adolph. "With Rudy, though, fate kind of always seemed to intervene in a very disappointing way."[80]

On March 3, 1940, the star-crossed Rudy took off at full speed on a Thunderbolt training run. Well down the hill and running flat out in a deep crouch, he was shocked to come upon another skier who should not have been on the course. Rudy attempted to negotiate one of the most dangerous sections of the trail while trying to avoid the interloper, but in the end opted for a slide into the trees rather than a collision. He lay in the woods for some time before anyone heard his calls for help. The resulting leg fracture ended his season, and his shot at the U.S. National Ski Team.[81]

Deep gloom set in, at least for a few days. That is, until Greeny Guertin went out a week later and broke *his* leg while simply walking on skis at the bottom of the Thunderbolt. "It was pretty comical, seeing the two of them on crutches together," said Adolph, "and it got Rudy laughing at the irony of it all. But I think that we all kind of secretly worried that we were coming to the end of a very special time." Factors beyond the control of its members were conspiring to bring down the curtain on the Ski Runners of Adams.

The Nazis were now waging full-scale war and well on their way toward conquering nearly all of Europe. Czechoslovakia, Poland, and France—the ancestral homes of many Berkshire skiers—had already been brutally over-run, and bombs were falling on London. The Olympic Games were canceled in 1940, and there was little hope for the resumption of international sports competition anytime soon. For the first time in their young lives, many of the local Berkshire racers began to recognize the triviality of sport in comparison with the threat of world war.

"By that time, with Germany on a rampage and the Japanese doing the same, most folks in the Berkshires thought our involvement in the war was inevitable," recalled Adolph. Recruitment drives by the U.S. Armed Forces were stepped up appreciably in the summer of 1940, and a lot of young men in the Berkshires, including Rudy and Roy Deyle, decided the time had come to join up. "They figured," said Adolph, "that it was better to choose the branch of service in which they wanted to serve now, rather than being drafted into one they didn't want to serve in later."[82]

On September 25, 1940, a headline in the *Berkshire Eagle* declared, "Skiing Star . . . to Join Army." The article detailed the decision of Rudy Konieczny to enlist in, of all things, the army's Coast Artillery unit.[83] Both he and Roy Deyle had made the difficult decision to trade the mountains for the windy beaches of New England.

Perhaps the frustrations and personal disappointments of the past few ski seasons had convinced Rudy that he needed a break from the racing circuit. Maybe he wanted time away from Adams, where some remained disenchanted over his perceived racing failures. It was even possible that Rudy had tired of constantly being ignored by the large-circulation sportswriters who had already begun the subtle process of writing him out of the history of New England skiing in favor of collegiate racing heroes. If these or other motivations were at work, though, he wasn't saying. Whatever Rudy's reasons, the article concluded with a simple, declarative sentence that landed heavily on the hearts of many Berkshire readers: "Konieczny's signing up for soldiering means the breaking up of an unusual group of young skiers known as the Ski Runners of Adams."[84]

The Pied Piper of Pine Lake (Jake Nunnemacher)

IT WAS A SWELTERING SUMMER NIGHT IN THE APTLY NAMED TOWN OF HARTLAND, Wisconsin, and the tiny theater wasn't air-conditioned. Still, the movie playing was the new sensation of 1939, *Gone with the Wind,* and the raves had prompted young couples from all over the Lake Country west of Milwaukee to brave the heat for the chance to see it first. When intermission finally came, the movie house crowd spilled out onto the sidewalk and headed straight for the drugstore counter across the street. Everyone wanted ice cream sodas to fortify themselves for the burning of Atlanta, which would probably make the theater feel even hotter.[1]

Among the many couples populating this real-life, Thornton Wilder tableau, only one appeared unfazed by the weather. He was tall, blond, poised, and engagingly handsome, home for the summer after his freshman year at Dartmouth. She was petite and striking, still a junior in high school. "I had known Jacob most of my life," remembered the former Jean Schmidt. "We had sailed together, and skied together, and basically grew up together, but this was our very first date. It was very exciting." The two had been in love for some time, but hadn't yet grasped it until that evening with Rhett and Scarlet. "Who cared about heat on a night like that?" asked Jean. "This was the boy I was going to marry."[2]

Even to the most casual observers, Jake Nunnemacher appeared to be Jack Armstrong come to life. Twenty years old that summer, with the world spread out gloriously before him as the result of being born into a family of means, Jake's opportunities to pursue his talents and dreams were nearly unlimited. "All that," sighed Jean, "and someone everybody knew as just a really good guy. I'm not exaggerating about that. I cannot remember, even growing up, anyone ever having a bad word to say about Jacob."[3]

Jake Nunnemacher was a member of the fifth generation of Nunnemachers in Milwaukee. His great-grandfather and namesake, a German-speaking Swiss immigrant who had arrived in the 1840s, made enough money as a meat and liquor distributor not only to stake Jake's grandfather Robert to a career in banking and global travel, but also to finance Milwaukee's first opera house. Great-Grandfather Nunnemacher and his wife Catherine also bought property thirty miles west of the city at a secluded spot known as Pine Lake. There, many of the most well-to-do local families of German extraction followed the popular couple in building their country homes.[4]

The various clans of German Milwaukee socialized at Pine Lake, encouraging their children to pursue together all manner of outdoor sporting activities. Sailing, however, was emphatically the favored form of recreation. The woodland lake itself, over two miles long and a mile wide, was bordered at the end of the nineteenth century by the homes and extravagant boathouses of about thirty families. Nearly all of them participated in the racing of sailboats organized by their own Pine Lake Yachting Club, a pastime that for many bordered on obsession.

In 1889, Grandfather Robert took time out from banking and art collecting (his fine collections of coins, art, and guns were later donated to the Milwaukee Public Museum) to found the Galland Henning Malting Drum Manufacturing Company. The family-owned business, still active more than a century later, began by servicing the famous Milwaukee breweries. It proved immensely profitable. Robert began grooming his son, Jake's father Henry James "H. J." Nunnemacher, at an early age to assume the running of the concern. In the traditions of Pine Lake, he also taught H. J. to race sailboats.[5]

The stern and serious H. J. developed under Grandfather Robert's tute-lage into an excellent and aggressive lake sailor, and took over the running of Galland Henning soon after marrying in 1910. His bride and Jacob's mother, the former Gertrude Fink, was a member of another of Milwaukee's leading families and the niece of the famous German painter Carl von Marr. Together, H. J. and Gertrude had three boys in the years prior to 1919—Robert, Rudolph, and Hermann—and for many years, life was very good indeed.

In 1919, however, everything changed. First the family's eldest son, Rob-ert, contracted polio. He deteriorated quickly, and died in his mother's arms at the age of nine.[6] Then the business began to falter badly, as the ratification of Prohibition sent the American breweries and the firms that serviced them into a tailspin. Meanwhile, the worldwide influenza pandemic of 1918–19 (which eventually killed more people than did the First World War) contin-ued to rage in the United States. Still in shock over their beloved Bobbie's death, H. J. and Gertrude were extremely apprehensive over the vulnerability of their remaining children, a fear heightened by the birth of Jacob Robert on July 30, 1919. Luckily, though many in Milwaukee and its surrounding areas succumbed to the Spanish Flu, the remaining Nunnemachers all survived. The family, however, was left reeling.[7]

Over the next four years, H. J. and Gertrude had two more children, daughters Audrey and Barbara. Unfortunately, their joy for life had been sub-stantially diminished by Robert's death. That is not to say that young Jacob and the other children failed to receive the love and attention they needed at home. Gertrude, a firm but loving woman, referred to baby Jacob in German as her "replacement gift," and showered him with attention and affection.[8] Inevitably, however, the children lived in an atmosphere of residual grief that hung over the family for a good part of their early lives.

Finally, in 1927, H. J. decided it was time to shake himself and his wife out of their lingering sadness. Mother Nunnemacher had recently become captivated by the book *Ports and Happy Places* by Cornelia Stratton Parker, in which the author described the pleasure of traveling abroad as a family. Con-vinced that this was the right time to follow their hearts, H. J. and Gertrude simply packed up the family, closed down their beautifully appointed man-sion in Milwaukee, and moved the entire household to Europe—principally to the Bavarian Alps—for two years.[9]

By the time of their arrival in Germany, local political unrest was already being fomented by thugs in nearby Munich, led by former army corporal Adolf Hitler. In the dramatic setting of the mountains, however, most people paid scant attention to such doings, and life went on much as it always had.

H. J. and Gertrude committed to reviving for themselves and their children a bygone era of tranquil simplicity in the Alps. Pictures of Jacob and his younger sisters hiking with their parents beneath the Zugspitze glacier near Garmisch, the father and his son in lederhosen and the mother and her girls in traditional mountain dresses with braided hair, fill the family photo albums. The family's two oldest sons, Rudolph and Hermann, meanwhile, had the opportunity to attend the famous Glarisegg school in Switzerland, where each participated in alpine winter sports. After extensive sojourns in eight other European countries, the entire family met up for Christmas 1928 at Waldhaus Flims in the Swiss Alps to ski.[10]

The trip did for the entire family what H. J. had hoped it would. It gave them all a fresh start, at the same time exposing them to their ancestral heritage. Jacob returned speaking German fluently, a skill he would retain for his entire life.[11] That, unfortunately, would turn out to be a decidedly mixed blessing.

Newly invigorated and back at Pine Lake, the demanding Father Nunnemacher decided it was time for his teenage sons to start taking their sailing more seriously. H. J. therefore embarked on his next great crusade, the struggle to turn them into great yachtsmen. Though Jacob went along with the plan and grew to love life in the lowland lakes, a good part of his heart remained in the mountains. "The trip to the Alps made a profound impression on Jacob, even at such a young age," said Jean. "He spent his whole life trying to figure out how he would be able to balance his passion for both the water and the mountains. But Father Nunnemacher was a sailor first and always, and he impressed that as much as he could on his children."[12]

"H. J. really took his boating seriously," recalled Jacob's friend and racing partner Fritz Trubshaw.[13] The Nunnemachers had named their lake home *Tranquility*, but it was anything but that after a sailboat race, Fritz remembered. "H. J. would gather all of us around the kitchen table and deliver these incredibly serious lectures on racing technique. He'd go over everything that had gone on during that day's race, dissecting every move Jakey and the other boys had made, good and bad. The brothers tolerated it out of respect for their father, and because they learned a great deal from him." At times, though, the advice was neither happily delivered nor gladly received, especially by Hermann. Jake also chafed, though more quietly.[14]

By all accounts, his brothers and sisters became fine sailors. Jacob, however, became a champion. Before long, he emerged as one of the very best of the Pine Lake yachtsmen, who as a group captured nearly every inland American sailing trophy one could win in the 1920s and 1930s. "Pine Lake was one of the inland sailing capitals of the United States during that period," according to Jean, whose family also owned property at the lake, "and Jacob was winning just about every one of the popular C Class [single sail] cat boat races he entered, even on Lake Michigan."[15] "He was such a great skipper," remembered Fritz, "because there was never any fear or hesitation in what he did."[16]

"I think H. J. was very proud of Jacob," Jean continued, "but not being a demonstrative man, he rarely showed it. Jacob, of course, was always striving to please him, but was never sure he was succeeding, even by winning all those trophies. After a while, Jacob got used to the situation, but he never really got from Father Nunnemacher the kind of acknowledgement that he probably longed for." As hard as H. J. might have been on Jake, according to his sister Audrey, he was even tougher on the older Hermann. "My father was not an easy man to please," she recalled, "especially in his younger days. Giving praise did not come easily to him, and the sons [toward] whom he was so demanding had to deal with that."[17]

Nevertheless, in a few short years, Jake had grown from a quiet youngster into one of the most popular and self-confident young men on Pine Lake. More than simply being admired by his peers for his sailing ability and his good graces, Jacob had the additional honor of being adored by the local children, who followed him around as if he were the lake's own pied piper. "Jakey was just a great teacher, always patient and encouraging," recalled Fritz. "He had a glow about him that way. The kids just adored him."[18]

William F. Stark, author of the authoritative volume on life at Pine Lake and one of Jake's young students, seconded Fritz Trubshaw's recollections: "Jake Nunnemacher was more than just an excellent skipper. For a number of summers, while he was in his late teens, he taught sailing to young Pine Lake sailors, and looked after the welfare of the Cub Fleet. His own sportsmanlike conduct set an example for the youngsters and he was hero worshipped by more than one neophyte sailor at the time."[19]

It was sailing that first brought Jake and Jean together, too, when Jean was just learning the sport. "Jacob and Fritz were just tremendous together in the *Wildcat*," she recalled. "Naturally, I gravitated toward them because I wanted to learn from the best, but also because I loved Jacob's charm."

Jean was only thirteen at the time, and acutely aware that she likely wouldn't be taken seriously by Jake and Fritz as a potential crewmember, especially being a girl. "I stayed after them, though," she remembered. "Mainly due to my enthusiasm and my small size—all ninety pounds of me—I finally started getting the calls when they needed an additional, light-weight crewmember for stability on particularly stormy days. So years later I became Jacob's wife, but I really started out as ballast on his boat."[20]

⅏

Though sailing remained the principal sporting preoccupation at Pine Lake throughout Jake's early life, in the mid-1930s the alpine skiing craze suddenly took hold, and gave boating a run for its money as the most intensely pursued activity for the lake's younger inhabitants. Predictably, the Nunnemachers were in the forefront of the new winter sports boom.

In the mid-1930s, the family sent Hermann back to Europe on a grand tour. There he reunited with Glarisegg classmate René Roch, the younger brother of renowned avalanche expert and ski mountaineer Andre Roch. The younger Roch taught Hermann the Arlberg controlled turning technique currently being perfected in Austria by ski pioneer Hannes Schneider. Andre Roch (at the time developing a Swiss variation to the "snowplow/stem Christiania"–based Arlberg method) would soon come to America to design the first ski run at Aspen, Colorado, for investor and American Olympic bobsled champion Billy Fiske. Fiske viewed Aspen as potentially the best ski mountain in North America, and planned to turn the Colorado backwater into a world-class center of interconnected Colorado ski towns.[21]

Hermann, in the meantime, returned to Wisconsin full of enthusiasm for the new sport of downhill skiing. He taught Jacob the Arlberg method, and together they joined a number of other local devotees in preaching to the rest of the kids at Pine Lake that alpine skiing could be more fun than their occasional pursuit of Nordic cross-country and ski jumping.

Nevertheless, Jacob and Hermann were also acutely aware that there were regional stigmas to overcome. In the 1930s, the Scandinavian immigrants of the Upper Midwest who dominated the sport of ski jumping still regarded alpine skiing with disdain. There was something vaguely unmanly about making turns to slow down on the snow. The idea was to build up as much speed as possible in order to fly. Those who meandered down a slope were generally those who had chickened out at the top of the jumping ramp.[22]

What Schneider and his Arlberg followers were teaching to a new generation of ski enthusiasts was that sustained and *controlled* speed on the snow, not a short burst of speed followed by a long jump, was the most exhilarating aspect of skiing. And what more apt group to embrace the new technique than the kids of Swiss, Austrian, and German heritage growing up on Pine Lake?

"We all just went nuts for the sport," remembered Jean. "Before long, as good a sailor and ice boater as Jacob was, he became an equally superb skier. His love for snow and mountains suddenly had a focus, even though he hadn't left Wisconsin."[23] Soon after Hermann's return, he, Jake, and other adventurous Pine Lakers, such as pioneering environmentalist Fritz Meyer and Fred Pabst of the local brewing family (who would later found Big Bromley ski area in Vermont), went scouting for a location that could serve as a ski hill for the local gang.[24] After an extensive search of the low terrain that curses the state, the boys finally settled on a four-hundred-foot-high slope outside Milwaukee known as "Holy Hill," situated above the red brick Carmelite Cathedral, which is a famous local landmark.[25]

Dissatisfied with such an angelic designation for the peak that would serve as their mighty winter proving ground, one of the local boys suggested that a German translation of the name might give it greater cachet. Thus, the "Heiliger Huegel" Ski Club was born, becoming the first downhill and slalom ski club in the Midwest. Since girls were always included in Pine Lake activities, Heiliger Huegel was from its inception a coeducational club open to everyone.[26]

Two years after leasing a portion of the hill from the farmer who owned it and clearing it of trees, Hermann and Jacob also arranged to rent his tractor during the winter months. They used the machine's engine to power a rope tow, one of the first in the midwestern United States. Thanks principally to the Nunnemachers and their friends, the youth of Pine Lake and its surrounding areas now had their own winter sports playground, and the kids came running from as far away as Chicago. "Like everyone who learned to downhill ski in the Midwest," concluded Hermann, "what we lacked in vertical we made up for in enthusiasm. We loved the sport, and it didn't matter that it wasn't the Alps or the Rockies or the Sierras or even New England. We were skiing, and that's all that mattered."[27]

Over a very short period of time, Jacob became Pine Lake's best skier, too. "He had tremendous natural ability," Jean maintained, "and he was just wild for the feeling of flying on the snow. Before long, he was finishing near the top in ski races across the state and teaching the local kids how it was done." To keep pace with her heart's desire, Jean also became a good skier, visiting Sun Valley with her family during its inaugural season in early 1937. "Everything about the sport was romantic back then," she said. "It was the perfect counter-point to our summers of sailing."[28]

❧❦❧

During the summer of 1937, Jake traveled to Cape Cod, Massachusetts, where his oldest brother Rudolph was a research fellow at Woods Hole Oceanographic Center. There, he experienced ocean racing for the first time, and fell in love with it.

Jake's trip coincided with the annual pilgrimage to the Cape organized by Nunnemacher family friend Professor Harold Bradley. Bradley, an immensely popular science professor at the University of Wisconsin at Madison, had grown up in the High Sierras of California, and had raised his seven boys to be mountain men as well as sailors. The professor and his wife were quite affluent (she being an heiress to the Chicago Crane fortune), and frequently took local students and friends of the family, along with their own sons, on trips to the mountains to ski and to the ocean to sail.[29]

In the members of the Bradley family with whom he sailed at Woods Hole, Jake Nunnemacher found kindred spirits.[30] His path would cross those of the Bradleys many times in the future. Three of the Bradley boys, Dave, Steve, and Richard, would go on to star with the Dartmouth Ski Team, while a fourth, Charles, would serve with Jake in the Tenth Mountain Division.[31]

"The time that Jacob spent with the Bradleys confirmed his conviction that there was a way to divide time between the water and the mountains while still leading a full and productive working life," remembered Jean. "He came back from Woods Hole inspired about the path his life would take. It was a very happy time for him."[32]

In 1938, Jacob received his high school diploma from the Milwaukee University School, where he had been class treasurer and a member of the school's basketball and swimming teams. Now faced with choosing a college, Jake had only two principal criteria in mind. It had to have snowcapped mountains nearby, and it had to have lake and ocean sailing within a short distance. He also suspected that H. J. might insist the school be of a certain academic standing, a condition to which he was not averse in principle.[33]

Sitting down with his father and family friends such as the Bradleys, Fritz Meyer, and Fred Pabst, all of whom had strong ties to Dartmouth College in Hanover, New Hampshire, the choice seemed obvious. "Jake took one look at the Dartmouth Ski Team roster and knew that it was the place for him," Jean remembered. "It was the 'who's who' of college ski racing, probably of all time."[34] Though Olympians Ted Hunter, Linc Washburn, and Warren Chivers were among the stars who had graduated after leading the team to near sweeps of U.S. collegiate races over the previous four seasons,[35] Howard Chivers, Charles McLane, Percy Rideout, and Olympians Dick Durrance and John Litchfield all remained.[36] "These would be his teammates his first year at school if he made the team, plus two of the Bradley boys," said Jean. Walter Prager, the famous Arlberg-Kandahar champion from Davos, Switzerland, would be his coach. "How could Jacob turn all that down?" Jean asked rhetorically.[37] So off Jake went that fall to join the legendary Dartmouth ski circus.

ɛɔɼ

Like the Berkshires, the mountains of even northernmost New England cannot approach the majesty of those that dominate the American West and the Alps. The White Mountains of New Hampshire and Maine and the Green Mountains of Vermont, however, have their own seasonal magnificence. According to Jean, "Jacob was taken right away with the rustic charms of New England mountain life, arriving by train just in time to see the gorgeous fall foliage."[38]

He also got an immediate taste of the brutality of New England weather. On September 21, 1938, the worst hurricane to hit the northeastern United States in the twentieth century roared out of the Atlantic across Long Island Sound and up through New England, leaving devastation in its wake. Hundreds lost their lives from Long Island to Maine, as rivers crested fifteen feet over flood level and ten feet of ocean water filled the streets of Providence, Rhode Island.[39] In the words of Dartmouth's hometown newspaper, the *Hanover Gazette,* parts of its own little city were "hammered into shambles of destruction" by the storm. Sustained winds in the nearby White Mountains were clocked at 168 miles per hour, killing nearly half of the millions of white pines in the state.[40]

"Jacob was one of the many Dartmouth students who immediately volunteered to help with emergency assistance, and then with the cleanup," Jean remembered. "By doing that, I believe he instantly felt a part of the community."[41] Still, with centuries of tradition seeping from its ivy walls, the Dartmouth campus was a daunting place for a young man from the Midwest on his own essentially for the first time.

Jake's transition, however, was further eased by his acquaintance with yet another Bradley-esque spirit named Jack Tobin. They became fast friends af-

28

ter discovering a common passion for skiing and sailing, and remained inseparable buddies for their four years at college.[42]

According to Tobin, one of his first encounters with Jake was an odd gathering of ski team hopefuls, who were summoned to a "practice" on the wet grass near a steep embankment at the Hanover golf course around Thanksgiving 1938. There, in full skiing regalia, team captain and legendary international ski racer Dick Durrance gave a clinic that required the attendees to ski the brown golf course. The assumption was, apparently, that if an aspirant could ski the grass with form, he could probably ski the snow. Both Jake and Jack impressed their young mentor, and were on their way to making the Dartmouth Ski Team.[43]

Jake wrote excitedly to Jean about his encounters not only with Durrance, but also with many others among the best skiers in the world who had fortuitously gathered in the White Mountains of New Hampshire in the late 1930s. Among the ski pioneers to whom the underclassmen at Dartmouth suddenly had access was the great *skimeister* himself, Hannes Schneider, the father of modern skiing. Schneider arrived at Mount Cranmore, New Hampshire, in early 1939, having been repatriated from imprisonment in his hometown of St. Anton am Arlberg, Austria, through the machinations of New England financier Harvey Gibson.[44]

The reasons for the antifascist Schneider's incarceration immediately following the 1938 Anschluss of Austria by Germany remain murky to this day. It is generally thought that his friendship with a Jewish officer of the Austrian Ski Federation, and his firing of a Nazi ski instructor only days before the German takeover, brought about the reprisals against him.[45] Some, however, also claimed to see the fingerprints of the infamous propaganda filmmaker and friend to Hitler and Goebbels, former actress Leni Riefenstahl. The controversial diva of German cinema best known for her paean to Nazism, *Triumph of the Will*, had forged a deep hatred for the devoutly Catholic Schneider during the filming of Arnold Fanck's pioneering ski films in which she and Hannes had starred. Schneider undoubtedly looked askance at Riefenstahl's unbridled lifestyle, and she likely bristled over his disapproving rigidity. It was speculated by some, including Schneider himself, that she influenced local Nazi authorities in Austria to seize his ski school and jail him in revenge for his perceived slights against her.[46]

By the time Hannes Schneider stepped off the train in New Hampshire's beautiful Mount Washington valley, to a congratulatory chorus of the antifascist rallying cry *Ski Heil*, his former ski school in St. Anton had already produced a legion of great instructors whose own arrivals in the United States preceded their mentor's by periods ranging from several months to several years. This coterie of famous disciples—who defended the Arlberg dogma "with a devotion bordering on religious fanaticism"[47]—included Otto Lang, who had set up his Arlberg school at Mount Rainier; European downhill champion Friedl Pfeifer, who was now teaching at Sun Valley; Luggi Foeger, who had opened a school in Yosemite Valley; and, most importantly to New England skiers, Sepp Ruschp and Benno Rybizka, the former of whom was teaching at Stowe, and the latter, Schneider's head instructor, who had recently established the Schneider Ski School at Mount Cranmore in North Conway.[48]

It was indeed ironic that as a result of the pervasive spread of Nazism throughout Alpine Europe and especially Austria, Jacob Nunnemacher, Jack Tobin, and the rest of the Dartmouth team now had only to take a short automobile ride rather than an ocean voyage to observe the world's greatest downhill skiers. The knowledge imparted by these European émigrés (several of whom would later serve in the Tenth Mountain Division) contributed considerably to the success of the Dartmouth skiing program in the 1930s and early 1940s, and to the growing popularity of the sport of alpine skiing in general throughout the mountainous regions of the United States.[49] Moreover, whether by imitation as in the case of Rudy Konieczny, or by direct instruction as with Jake Nunnemacher, Hannes Schneider's Arlberg technique had quickly developed into the predominant style of skiing not only in prewar America but throughout the world.

&)Q&

The Dartmouth Ski Team of 1938–39 had a tremendously successful season. As a freshman, however, Jake Nunnemacher spent most of his time observing and practicing, not racing.

One of the more memorable highlights of Jake and Tobin's initial season on the team was a good-natured brawl at Pinkham Notch fought between them over an orphaned Peruvian knit ski cap. It was a mock fight to be sure, but it was also indicative of the competition that permeated every aspect of the ski team members' lives. Even roughhousing became a sport with winners and losers. Tobin recalled that the two walked out of the warming hut high on Mount Washington, and simultaneously spotted the hat hanging high above the Appalachian Mountain Club sign. A lengthy row ensued over who would be first to shimmy up the pole and grab the cap, during which a substantial crowd of rooters gathered. The struggle at last came to an end when Jake momentarily knocked the wind out of Tobin. He was up and down the frozen pole in an instant, much to the delight of the crowd, which awarded him an ovation and a curtain call when he put the hat on.

"It looked so well on him," Tobin recalled without a hint of sarcasm, "brown and white with a high peak and earflaps, [that Jake adopted it as his] trademark."[50] "Jake was always a great guy," concluded teammate Bob Meservey, "but he could be as competitive as the rest of us when he wanted to be."[51] Charles McLane chuckled in agreement.[52]

The most eye-opening skiing event for Jake that first year at Dartmouth was the landmark 1939 Inferno downhill race at Tuckerman Ravine on Mount Washington, which closed the eastern ski season. Jean recalled that "Jacob and a few of the other Dartmouth freshmen went to watch the daredevils like Durrance try to survive" what was then the steepest run in the United States.[53] Just getting down the nine-hundred-foot head wall of ice and crud in one piece remains an accomplishment. On the day of the 1939 race, there were the additional complications of eighty-mile-per-hour wind gusts and single-digit temperatures. Tobin, whose Class A certification allowed him to race that day, recalled that the race officials gave up and went indoors, sending each skier down the course by ringing a bell rigged from the inside of the warming hut.[54]

"Lo and behold, Jacob told me," said Jean, "here came Toni Matt [yet another of Schneider's young St. Anton acolytes] over the lip of the head wall, and he schussed the entire run straight down, at full speed without a turn. He won the race by more than a couple of minutes, I think. Jacob said it was the most amazing athletic feat he'd ever seen, and didn't see how he could ever compete with men possessed of that level of skill." Tobin recalled that the Austrian's skis clattering over the ripples of ice on his way down sounded like gunshots reverberating across the valley.[55] Matt's schuss of the head wall at Tuckerman remains the most legendary feat in New England skiing history.

∞)(∞

A somewhat humbled Jake returned to Milwaukee after his first year to date Jean, to sail, and to work at Galland Henning, where he was expected by H. J. to begin concentrating more intensively on learning the family business. Enjoying the summer social season at Pine Lake with Jean, though, was the principal reason for Jake to look forward to his time back home.

"The summer parties were so extravagant, and so much fun," Jean recalled. "We'd have cotillions and debutante parties, and the host—usually one of the brewery tycoons—would bring in Benny Goodman's band from Chicago, or Glenn Miller's group as they came through Milwaukee, and they'd play for us at the lake as if it were a high school dance. That was pretty heady stuff for teenagers." After a party and on most other nights, Jake and Jean would stroll the perimeter of the lake arm in arm, staring at the stars and discussing their future together.[56]

Jake and Jean had other fairy-tale aspects to their young social lives at Pine Lake. "Jacob was a very good dancer, and we'd go to local dances during the summers for fun," said Jean. "One of our favorite spots was a local club at Genesse Depot, the community where Alfred Lunt and Lynn Fontanne had their estate, *Ten Chimneys*." At the time, the husband-and-wife acting team were the most celebrated stage personalities in the country. "One night, the two of them came in to dance and socialize while we were there," Jean continued. "We ended up switching partners, and there I was with Alfred Lunt, and Jacob had Lynn Fontanne in his arms, and it was quite a thrilling moment for us. Jacob looked so handsome. We were very lucky growing up."[57]

Among the charms of life at the highly insular refuge of Pine Lake has always been the celebration of eccentricity among its inhabitants. In considering some of the antics that took place in the wealthy and conservative community during an economic depression that many members hardly seemed to notice (the repeal of Prohibition in 1933 may have had something to do with that), a real-life version of the screwball comedies of period moviemakers Preston Sturges and Frank Capra comes to mind.

As one example among many, several generations of Nunnemachers have served as caretakers for one of Pine Lake's most beloved relics, the *Nunnemacher Cannon*. The Civil War–era gun was "rescued" by Jake's grandfather Robert from an army depot after the war, and relocated to the lawn of the Nunnemacher property. There, it and its twin (which the family somehow procured to replace the original after government officials demanded its return) have served since the nineteenth century as the centerpiece of the lake's ardent Fourth of July celebrations. Few communities outside of Pine Lake can boast of a family with its own artillery piece, able to fire out onto the water everything from croquet balls to confetti—to the occasional round of live ammo—to dress up the usual humdrum of Independence Day skyrockets and Roman candles. "I'm not joking about the live ammo, either," asserted Jean.[58]

"I want to emphasize," she continued, "that with all the privilege and nuttiness, it would have been very easy for someone in Jacob's position to become—for lack of a better description—'spoiled.' Aside from the fact that his personality did not lend itself to that, however, there was simply no way that his parents would have allowed it. Despite all of the advantages he had been given in life, Jacob was taught and retained a humility and compassion that drew people toward him—especially young people—whether we're talking about kids around the lake, local teens in New Hampshire he was coaching on ski racing, or later on, displaced children in Italy during the war."[59]

Jake returned to Dartmouth as a sophomore for the 1939–40 ski season under the captaincy of future Tenth Mountain Division officer Percy Rideout. For the sixth consecutive year, the team won the Intercollegiate Ski Union Championship. The squad also captured first place in the Dartmouth Winter Carnival Meet (generally regarded at the time as the biggest annual winter event in New England) and several other major races.[60] The Dartmouth boys, however, had a tough day on February 25, 1940, when they raced for the Eastern Championships on Greylock against Rudy Konieczny's Ski Runners of Adams.

The Eastern Championships that year represented the third time within a four-week period that Jake, Jack Tobin, and freshman Bob Meservey had driven down to Massachusetts to race on the Thunderbolt with the Dartmouth team. Reflecting on the experience, Meservey recalled: "The first race in January for the [individual] Greylock Trophy was my initial time on the Thunderbolt. I was an eighteen-year-old freshman, and my only memory is one of fear. Waiting to be called to the starting gate I had to sit down because my legs were shaking so badly. I still see the terrifying view approaching the first schuss: a view of the brick buildings of Adams two miles below with apparently nothing in between. All I know is, I didn't win."[61]

The modest Meservey did not come in first, but rather finished third to two of the world's top downhillers, Toni Matt and German Olympian Heinz Krebs. He also managed to beat every one of the Dartmouth upperclassmen in the contest.[62]

The second race of the three was for the Massachusetts state title, which featured the largest field of skiers—ninety-three—ever to race on Greylock. Rudy Konieczny's Ski Runners were the defending team champions, and their legion of local supporters hoped to see them repeat. This time, however, the Dartmouth squad led by Charles McLane and Tobin won handily. Jake Nunnemacher placed an impressive eighteenth in the large, excellent field, several spots better than both a devastated Konieczny and the young Bob Meservey.[63]

The stage was set for the biggest race of the season, the Eastern Championships, held a week later. This time, ninety-five of the country's best skiers entered the race, and a huge contingent of spectators from New York and Boston arrived on the ski trains to watch dozens of "A" skiers compete on the nation's toughest downhill course.

"We knew how badly those Adams guys wanted to win, after we'd taken away their State title the week before," Meservey recalled. "Jacob and I watched Rudy Konieczny warming up, and he was just flying. . . . I remember during practice Rudy sweeping smoothly through a fast and bumpy section of the trail looking a little like Durrance. We had a feeling it might be their day."[64] It was. The Ski Runners of Adams took the team trophy by six full seconds.[65] "In retrospect, I'm glad that Rudy was able to enjoy that moment," Meservey concluded, "but, boy, we hated to lose."[66]

Jake and Tobin finished out their sophomore season in style at the famed little Vermont ski area known as Suicide Six. There, along with good friend Karl Acker—who was coaching future American Olympic champion Andrea Mead Lawrence at Pico Peak in Vermont and would later serve in Jake's company with the Tenth Mountain Division—the three raced and finished in a dead heat for the mountain's coveted top-to-bottom, all-time speed title. Each chose the same dangerous route through a narrow gap between the on-mountain spruce trees, and each skied the line perfectly. Tobin, eager to avenge his loss to Jake in the Pinkham Notch hat brawl, went back to "the Six" a few days later and knocked three-tenths of a second off the record, a time not surpassed for another seven ski seasons. But for three glorious days, Jake Nunnemacher shared the Suicide Six all-time speed record, not bad for a kid from the flatlands of Wisconsin.[67]

In Jake's junior year, 1940–41, future Tenth Mountain Division officer Charles McLane took over as Dartmouth Ski Team captain, and again led the team to a stellar year. For the seventh consecutive season, Dartmouth captured the Intercollegiate Ski Union Championship.[68] For Jake, however, the year was highlighted by his ascendancy to the head of Dartmouth's prestigious honor society known as Casque and Gauntlet, the membership of which consisted of fourteen selected campus leaders. He also played a role in the stupendous success of the Dartmouth College Yachting Club, which had a fine season (and would go on to win every major competition of the New England Section of the Intercollegiate Yacht Racing Association the following year).[69]

Carrying a full academic load, however, Jake was spreading himself very thin. Before long his grades were sinking badly, and though H. J. was displeased, it was not enough to prompt Jake to change his focus.[70] A dispassionate observer might even conclude that rebellion against his father was playing a less-than-subtle role in Jake's relaxed attitude toward academics. But there were also other, more tangible reasons for his diminishing grades.

"We'd be traveling with the ski team from Friday to Tuesday every week of the season," Meservey explained, "and that really made it tough to keep our grades up. Sometimes we'd have a bus or van, although most of the time it was just a bunch of private cars. The Dartmouth Outing Club paid for gas, and that was it. We got no money from the school. So I would sit in the back of the bus, or the car, and have my physics books out and be studying, and Jake would be up front giving pointers on sailing, or talking about ski racing or politics, pursuing what interested him. I don't think he felt the pressure to get A's the way I did. We all knew that Jake was one of the guys heading into a family business, and we were just happy with the fact that he took on the role of being an engaged leader."[71]

The question was, did Jake really want to go into the family business? According to Jean, he simply hadn't made up his mind.

Upon his return to Pine Lake that summer, Jacob's mother opted to try a little psychological motivation on Jake regarding his grades. According to Jean, Mother Nunnemacher raised the possibility to him that in a depressed economy he might not be able to depend on a secure position at Galland Henning. She suggested that perhaps he should buckle down and take academics a bit more seriously, just in case he needed to pursue an alternative course to earn a living.

Jake had returned home practiced and ready for such a conversation. "Well, if things don't work out," Jean remembered him telling his mother matter-of-factly, "I've been thinking that I can always just teach skiing at Sun Valley. That might suit me better, anyway." Jean chuckled over the horrified expression that came over Mother Nunnemacher's face. "That was the last Jacob heard about there not being a job at Galland Henning for him after college."[72]

As time went on, Jake's sunny disposition made him one of the most popular students on the Dartmouth campus, despite the fact that he refused to change his unbending ways when it came to personal discipline. That steadfastness slowly became a subject of great amusement among many of his friends. Jean came to visit for Dartmouth Winter Carnival as a senior in high school during 1941, a trip she remains amazed her parents permitted her to make. "Everyone just trusted Jacob to be a gentleman, including my parents," she explained.[73] During the visit, she recalled, Jake was the subject of constant, affectionate ribbing among his teammates and his Casque and Gauntlet housemates.

"They thought he was too straight-laced," she continued. "They'd call him a prude, and tease him for not drinking enough, but that was the way he was raised. Jacob took it all in his stride, even laughed about it. He was just an old-fashioned romantic."[74]

"Jake got kidded a lot because everybody liked him so much," remembered Meservey. "That, and he was good-natured, which made him a pretty safe target for pranks." On a ski team trip to McGill College in Canada that year, Meservey was in the lead car with several racers, and Jake in the car behind with the rest of the team. As they reached the Canadian border, the boys in Meservey's car got an idea. "Remember, this was 1941, and the British-Canadian Commonwealth was already at war with the Nazis," he recalled. "So, we told the Canadian border guards that we had overheard that there was a German national in the car behind us who spoke great English, and that we were all pretty suspicious about why he wanted to get into Canada so badly. Of course, we gave them Jake's description, and he looked about as German as anyone I've ever seen. They held Jake's car up for hours before they let them cross over. Jake took some time to see the humor in that one, but eventually he did."[75]

Jacob's good humor and leadership qualities led in his senior year to the indisputable highlight of his college athletic career. He was given the honor of serving as captain of the Dartmouth Ski Team for 1941–42, making him (along with Meservey, who would captain the 1942–43 squad) one of the final links in a dynasty of the greatest American collegiate ski teams of all time. Though clearly Jake was neither the best nor the most accomplished racer on the team, Tobin summed up the rationale for his selection with a simple expression of the opinion shared by every member of the squad. "In every way Jake lived and acted the part of the ideal Dartmouth skier," he wrote.[76] The same integrity, intensity, and sportsmanship that were so appreciated by his young sailing students at Pine Lake had similarly moved his Dartmouth teammates, enough to make them want him to lead them.

Jake's sister Audrey, a ski racer who started at Middlebury College in Vermont that year and would soon join the U.S. National Women's Ski Team, would frequently travel with the Dartmouth squad to practices and meets. She became, in her words, their "mascot." "Above everything else," she recalled, "I had the chance to observe how much my brother's teammates respected him as a person. That made me very proud, that they could see the same things in him that his family did. He was so fair-minded and earnest, and at the same time so poised, you couldn't help but trust his judgment and his decisions." Audrey believed it was their mother who had instilled that sense of fair play so deeply in Jake. "Rather than having a formal religion, she had been raised as a 'free-thinker,' and raised her children that way, too. Fairness, goodness, and honor were her religious convictions, and Jake took that teaching very much to heart."[77]

In addition to assuming the captaincy of the ski team in his senior year, Jake was honored by his election to head the Winter Sports Council of the famed Dartmouth Outing Club. The DOC had been established at the turn of the century with the financial assistance of a conservation-minded alumnus. By the 1920s, it had become the leading group in the eastern United States in the organization of winter sports competitions, as well as an important link in the maintenance of the Appalachian Trail system.[78] "Jacob was very proud to hold those two positions at the same time," Jean recalled. "He understood the historical significance, and spent enormous energy helping to keep the traditions of those organizations alive under very difficult circumstances."[79]

₭)꜒

Those "difficult circumstances" included the December 7, 1941, attack by the Japanese on Pearl Harbor, thrusting the United States into the Second World War. Jake, according to Jean, was torn over his desires both to enlist in the armed forces immediately and to finish his last semester and complete his commitments to Dartmouth. "He made the choice to stay on and fulfill his duties in Hanover," Jean said, "but he was embarrassed a little by not joining up right away." Jean was by that time attending Pine Manor Junior College in Wellesley, Massachusetts, enabling Jake to visit on weekends. They discussed their future in the weeks leading up to Christmas that year, and over the holidays, Jacob proposed marriage. Jean accepted. He was twenty-two, she eighteen.

"Father Nunnemacher thought we were too young, and acting impulsively due to the war," Jean recalled. "Jacob and I thought that was nonsense on both scores. We were wholly committed to one another, and the engagement was announced with the blessings of our families." The couple returned to their respective schools right after the holidays, full of a combination of joy and dread. "We were happy for ourselves," said Jean, "but apprehensive for what the future might hold for everyone we knew."[80]

Dartmouth ski coach Walter Prager had already been called to serve in the armed forces in early 1941, and so the recently graduated Percy Rideout returned on a temporary basis to replace him.[81] With only his new captain Jake Nunnemacher, Tobin, and Meservey (and a precious few others, like sophomore Phil Puchner) to lean on after years of depth and experience throughout the team, Rideout's squad quickly ran into trouble. Despite winning at Williams in January, the team was crushed on consecutive weekends at the Dartmouth and New Hampshire Winter Carnivals by a University of New Hampshire team led by future Olympian and Tenth Mountaineer Steve Knowlton.[82] That left Rideout and Jake one week to prepare their dazed squad for the defense of its cherished seven-year winning streak in the Intercollegiate Ski Union Championships, the record that most personified the dominance of the Dartmouth ski program for the entire era of the first American ski boom.

Just as Rudy Konieczny had done at the 1940 Eastern Championships on the Thunderbolt, Jake Nunnemacher rallied his team against equally long odds. He took them to Middlebury College for their most important race of the year, and exercising the leadership that was expected of him when he was selected as captain, he willed them to win. Jake, Tobin, and Meservey paced the squad to its unprecedented eighth consecutive ISU championship, beating the University of New Hampshire by a whisker and capping four spectacular years of team accomplishments during Jake's tenure as a Dartmouth skier.[83] For good measure, the captain took his squad up to McGill the next weekend, and won there, too.

"Looking back, it's true that Jake Nunnemacher didn't win a lot of ski races and that I did win a few," Meservey said, referring in part to the individual Eastern Downhill Championship he won in 1942. "A good part of the reason for that was I think he got a greater thrill out of teaching than he did out of the pursuit of personal glory."[84] Jake, in fact, never won an individual race during his entire four-year college skiing career.

"He may have figured he was dealt a pretty good hand in life," Meservey continued, "and that he just liked helping others better than competing. He was a strong and graceful skier, but I think he lacked a certain 'killer instinct' essential to competitive racing. When I raced, emotionally, I *had* to win. It just wasn't that kind of priority for him."[85]

Teammate Phil Puchner, who also went on to serve with Jake in the Tenth Mountain Division, summed up the feelings of the Dartmouth team members after their last victory at McGill, which in many ways also marked the end of an era in New England skiing history. "We won our share of races over the years," he reflected, "but on the whole, what I think most of us remember best is just how much fun it was to be a part of a great team in a sport with so much enthusiasm built up around it. The camaraderie, the songs, the gags, all made for a very close group. We got a kick out of the ski trains coming up, and the parties and the big crowds. . . . But once the war came, that was over. Nobody really cared how someone fared in a ski race. Everybody's mind was correctly refocused on other matters. We still loved to ski, but we had another job to do, and it was time to go do it."[86]

Jake's final academic ranking at Dartmouth was dismal. Still, in all, he had done what he wanted to do for four years, and brought honor to himself and to his school in the process by holding the Outing Club and the ski team together in the months after Pearl Harbor. Thus, the Dartmouth trustees voted to award him a diploma, though the issue remained in doubt until the last few weeks prior to graduation.[87] His family remains baffled by his academic underachievement in college, especially in light of the pride he took in the liberal arts education he received. "Jake was so bright and well read," his sister Audrey insisted. "I'm at a loss to explain why he didn't get better grades, but he could hardly have been a better representative of the school."[88]

ଛଠଓଷ

In June 1942, Jake returned to Wisconsin and informed Jean and his family that he would be following Prager, Rideout, McLane, Litchfield, and many of his other Dartmouth teammates into military service with the ski troops. The news, naturally, was greeted with anxiety by his parents and Jean. H. J. probably could have pulled enough strings to ensure a safe, stateside assignment for Jacob, but the young skier would have nothing to do with preferential treatment. He wanted to be a ski trooper, and would accept no interference from anyone regarding that decision.[89]

It was a strange time of change at Pine Lake. Its residents had to come to grips with the fact that the outside world had finally encroached on theirs. "As much as the Depression hadn't affected life very much at the lake, there might have been a delusion at the very beginning of the war that life still might go on as usual," remembered Jean. "That hope dissolved quickly."[90]

One might also suspect that in a wealthy, politically conservative area populated by German Americans such as Pine Lake, some residents may have harbored a certain myopic admiration for the Nazi regime of the type that afflicted Henry Ford, Charles Lindbergh, and other sympathizers and members of the German American Bund.[91] According to Jean, however, with very few exceptions that was not the case. The isolationism being preached by many at both political extremes found few supporters in Pine Lake, the proof being that more than fifty boys from the area joined the military to fight fascism, many signing up before the attack on Pearl Harbor.[92]

That is not to say that the decision to join up was ever an easy one. Jake himself expressed reservations to his Casque and Gauntlet housemate and future comrade in arms, John de la Montagne, over facing his German cousins in combat.[93] In the end, however, as with the vast majority of the boys at Pine Lake, loyalty to America, combined with deep disdain for the Nazi regime, overwhelmed ancient familial ties.

"Every lake family had at least one, and often more than one boy, serving overseas," said Jean. "For all of us, life changed drastically from lightheartedness to fear, in what seemed like an instant. The one blessing, I guess, was that we were all in it together."[94]

The Sun Valley Serenader (Ralph Bromaghin)

IT WAS MIDNIGHT ON JULY 4, 1937, AND THE TEENAGE MEMBERS OF BOY SCOUT Troops 150 and 158 of Seattle, Washington, had something to celebrate. They had been given an ultimatum by the national Boy Scouts of America: either stop climbing such dangerous mountains peaks under the Boy Scout banner or find yourselves another organizational sponsor.[1]

The boys chose the latter course, and did so in style. To cap off Independence Day that year, and to announce their formation of the now legendary northwestern climbing club known as the Ptarmigans, they split into groups and independently scaled three of the most storied mountains in the country: Mount St. Helens, Mount Adams, and Mount Hood. There on the summits as the clock struck twelve, the teams simultaneously fired flares equal to one million candlepower. It was quite a fireworks display. They were quite a collection of young mountaineers.[2]

The Ptarmigans' principal members, all of whom had already accomplished the most difficult climbs in the Pacific Northwest (several of which were first ascents), included Ralph and Ray Clough, Tup Bressler, Mitzi Metzger, Wimpy Myers, Chuck Kirschner, and a tall, lanky kid from Seattle with a perpetually hangdog expression on his long face, Ralph Bromaghin.[3] It was Bromaghin who served as the ski and snow expert of the group. "Brom could climb, no doubt about it," recalled Ray Clough, "but he was first and foremost a skier, and he was adamantly proud of that."[4]

Like their counterparts to the east, Ralph Bromaghin and his friends had taught themselves to ski, climbing up and hurtling down the local mountains to the point of exhaustion. "This was the Depression," remembered Ralph Clough, "and so we *had* to get the most out of our investments. We'd bought the skis and the Arlberg method instruction books. We'd scrounged the fifty cents in gas money it took to drive to Municipal Hill on Snoqualmie Pass in a borrowed Model A. Damned if we weren't going to ski all day and get good at it."[5] "For the rest of us," added Ray, "skiing was a nice break from climbing. For Ralph Bromaghin, it was his calling."[6]

Bob Craig, another Seattle contemporary who went on to become one of America's most celebrated international ski mountaineers, referred unabashedly to Bromaghin as his mentor. "He had a gift on skis that he could impart to others," Craig recalled. "Whether you were a Ptarmigan or not, and I wasn't, Ralph was willing to teach you. All of those guys had an infectious enthusiasm for the mountains, but it was Ralph's amazing passion for skiing that instilled in me an excitement and devotion to the sport that has literally lasted a lifetime."[7]

஫௸

The city of Seattle, and in fact the entire northwestern region of the United States, are dominated both spiritually and physically by the gigantic volcanoes that form the chain known as the "Ring of Fire." The largest and most famous of those spectacular peaks, the glaciated Mount Rainier, presides over Seattle like a snowcapped fortress. On clear days its white mass glows against the blue sky, appearing so close that though it sits some sixty miles away, one might be able to reach out and touch it from downtown. On those frequent days of northern Pacific overcast, Rainier still often floats visibly above the clouds. It is a siren, luring the adventurous to test its dangerous slopes. Bromaghin and the rest of the Ptarmigans found its draw irresistible.

"Ralph grew up loving that mountain, just like the rest of us," remembered Harriet Clough Waldron, the sister of Ptarmigans Ralph and Ray Clough. "It became a part of us, really, reminding us every day of where our hearts lay."[8]

Ralph Bromaghin was born on January 27, 1918, to a middle-class Seattle couple of Norwegian and Scots-Irish descent who raised him along with his two older sisters, Leone and Florence, in a strict although not an exceptionally close or religious environment.[9] As exacting as Fred and Norma Bromaghin tried to be in raising their son, however, they soon realized that his convictions in the pursuit of outdoor adventure ran deeper than any punishments could reach. After a while, they gave up trying to stop him from sneaking off to the mountains, even though the time he spent climbing and skiing might have taken away from the overall quality of his formal education.[10]

Thus, throughout his primary and secondary schooling, Ralph went to class, did his work, and left for the mountains. His extracurricular activities, according to his classmate Harriet, were limited to following his dreams, along with the rest of the Ptarmigans, into the high country. "If you could climb on it, Brom and my brothers and their friends would be out trying to conquer it," recalled Harriet.

As the years went by, the Ptarmigans developed into superior, dedicated athletes. "It was a joy to go into the mountains with them," Harriet continued. "But I'll tell you something else. They were way ahead of their time. One of the reasons those boys found leaving the Boy Scouts such an easy decision was that they didn't like excluding girl climbers like me. They were all extreme individualists, and they would not abide being told where and with whom they could climb. We really appreciated that." Like Jake Nunnemacher's Heiliger Huegel Ski Club in Wisconsin, the Ptarmigans soon included female members like Harriet, and Chuck Kirschner's sister, Erlene.

Of the three climbing and skiing Cloughs, however, it was Harriet who spent the most time with Ralph. "We were the same age, and went all through school together," she remembered. "He was just a wonderful guy to be around. He was very introspective, you might even say a bit of a loner. But he was also lots of fun, with a real offbeat, ironic sense of humor. That took some getting used to, and some people never got it. But he also wasn't nearly as argumentative as most of the others. The Ptarmigans, my brothers included, could just drive you nuts with their endless debates."[11]

The Ptarmigans earned legendary status for their willingness to battle with one another passionately on any subject, almost as much as for their athletic skills. "One thing that kept our membership down was the stern, strong individuality of the hard core," admitted Tup Bressler, one of those hard-core members. "We had many visitors who were amazed . . . by our knockdown, drag-out arguments, administering fearful beatings to Robert's Rules."[12] A story related by Ptarmigan Wimpy Myers summed up that aspect of Ptarmigan life concisely: "The Ptarmigans . . . were as varied a collection of rugged individualists as you would be likely to find anywhere, bound together closely by a common love of the high country and a burning desire to climb mountains. On one winter trip with the objective of traversing [Mount] Baker, a severe storm blew up at about 9,000 feet on the Coleman Glacier. Opinion as to the best course of action was equally divided [among]: (1) continuing on, (2) going back, or (3) bivouacking on the spot. From the foregoing it should be obvious that the party consisted of three members."[13]

Ralph Bromaghin's more malleable disposition was almost certainly a byproduct of his split allegiance between two separate passions. As much as his skills as a ski mountaineer, Ralph took tremendous pride and pleasure in his musicianship.

"Ralph was just as intense as the rest of them," according to Harriet, but his tremendous love of music gave him a bit more perspective than the others had in gauging the relative importance of the choices he faced. "The inner satisfaction he got from playing and listening to jazz allowed him to compromise on such momentous issues as choosing the optimal climbing or skiing route on a particular trip," she asserted with a laugh, "without feeling that he had somehow compromised himself. The only thing that mattered to Ralph as much as the mountains was music, and that sort of balanced him."

Harriet recalled the many car trips with Ralph to ski near Paradise Lodge at Mount Rainier National Park, during which he'd sing jazz standards all the way. "It was such great fun," she remembered. "He'd come over to our house with his guitar, too, or he'd play our piano—Ralph was one of those people who could play any instrument you handed him—and he would get everyone to sing along. That became a regular thing for our family. Jazz . . . was the thing that brought him out of his shell a little bit. He really came alive when he was playing music."[14]

Though one might not imagine it, Seattle was a Pacific Coast jazz outpost in the 1930s, presided over by recording artist, drummer, and nightclub owner–turned–populist politician Vic Meyers. Meyers was a musical *and* comic inspiration to young local jazz enthusiasts like Ralph, who particularly appreciated the drummer's willingness to engage in campaign activities more suited to

Spike Jones and the Marx Brothers than to the serious New Deal Democrat that he was. He launched his first candidacy in 1932 for lieutenant governor of Washington State (a post he won and held for some thirty years) by dressing up as Mahatma Gandhi and leading a goat up Seattle's Fourth Avenue.[15] Another time, he purportedly hired a Shakespearean actor to impersonate his opponent, paying him to attend a women's auxiliary club to speak out in favor of legalized gambling and prostitution. "The humor of those stunts was not lost on Ralph, or anyone else with an appreciation for the absurd," remembered Harriet. "Brom thought it was just hilarious."[16]

Bromaghin was also especially fond of the great singer-songwriter Fats Waller, the three-hundred-pound New York piano impresario as famous for his innovative sense of humor as for his hit recordings such as "I Can't Give You Anything but Love" and "Gonna Sit Right Down and Write Myself a Letter." (One Waller coast-to-coast radio broadcast began with his classic pronouncement, "What a party! Everybody's here but the po-lice. And they'll be here soon!") "Bromaghin loved that stuff," recalled his army buddy, the omnipresent former Dartmouth Ski Team captain Charles McLane. "He talked about Harlem jazz all the time, and he made fans out of the rest of us. Nobody loved it the way Ralph did, though. He breathed it."[17] There may not have been an overabundance of "hep cats" living near Seattle in the 1930s, but Ralph Bromaghin was one of them.

By the time he graduated from Roosevelt High in 1936, Ralph had added watercolor painting to his artistic pursuits. He had also become one of the best young skiers in the northwestern United States. Faced with a decision over whether to enter college immediately or to pursue at least temporarily a career as a ski instructor, he chose the latter. Ralph secured employment first as an instructor at Municipal Hill at Snoqualmie Pass east of Seattle, and later at both Rainier and rugged Mount Baker, the northern Washington volcano known for its prodigious snowfalls, bulletproof ice, and poor weather.[18] His choice of work over college also enabled him to stay current with the activities of the Ptarmigans, and he continued to climb each summer with the Cloughs, including a two-day trip with Ray up and down Ruth Mountain that is noted in local lore as a first ski descent.[19]

⊱⊰

The big story in 1936 for American skiers was the opening of Sun Valley Ski Resort that December. The Union Pacific Railroad, in an effort to increase ridership in the midst of the Depression, had set out in 1935 under the leadership of skiing enthusiast Averell Harriman to find a suitable place for an American alpine center that could compete with the best of the European resorts.

To conduct the search for a promising site along the routes controlled by the Union Pacific, Harriman hired an Austrian count, Felix Von Schaffgotsch. The count's sole job qualification, apparently, was his brother's affiliation with Hannes Schneider's ski school in St. Anton. According to famed Arlberg instructor and two-time European Kandahar Downhill Champion Friedl Pfeifer, it is even possible that Harriman thought he *was* hiring the count's brother.[20] Whatever the case, it was Felix Von Schaffgotsch who showed up in America, and who traveled throughout the western United States on behalf of Union Pacific during the winter of 1935–36 searching for Harriman's ski Shangri-la.

The arrogant count, who advisedly kept his Salzburg-based Nazi affiliations mainly to himself, rejected such potential sites as Mount Rainier, Mount Hood, Alta, Aspen, Badger Pass near Yosemite, and Grand Targhee in the Tetons, before wiring Harriman that he had found the perfect spot near Ketchum, Idaho. What he had found was a sunny valley having one of its most significant snow years of the century, a meteorological fact that the locals kept well hidden.[21]

Harriman rushed out to Ketchum, and determined that good weather, easy track access, and cheap local real estate made this the ideal place for his resort. He immediately imported former Olympic skier Charley Proctor from New Hampshire to help design the slopes and to install the world's first chairlift (inspired by a conveyor belt used to load bananas onto ships) on tiny Dollar Mountain.[22] Magnificent Bald Mountain, the peak up the road that has served for decades as the area's signature ski hill, was not recognized by either Schaffgotsch or Harriman for its potential and was for the time being ignored.

While Harriman set about building a grand lodge and putting into effect an even grander public relations plan touting the newly dubbed "Sun Valley" as the ne plus ultra of ski resorts, Schaffgotsch was dispatched back to Europe to round up a crew of suitably accented ski instructors. Predictably, the count headed straight for Obersalzburg on the German-Austrian border near Hitler's beloved Berchtesgaden, an area much more highly influenced in the mid-1930s by the growth of Nazism than Hannes Schneider's Tyrolean and Arlberg sections of western Austria.[23] In short order, Schaffgotsch hired the overbearing Hans Hauser of Salzburg as the leader of his new group of instructors ("all Nazis," Schaffgotsch proudly confided) and imported the whole pack of them to Sun Valley well in advance of the resort's celebrated opening on December 21, 1936.[24] That day, there was no snow on Dollar Mountain, but plenty of movie stars mingling with Hauser's instructors at the bar in what would soon become famously known as the "Duchin Room." Snow or no snow—and it did eventually arrive—Sun Valley became *the* place for winter leisure among the members of the American aristocracy during the later years of the Depression.[25]

Back in Seattle, the year 1936 also marked the arrival from St. Anton, Austria, of Hannes Schneider protégé Otto Lang. Not only did Lang's mission involve setting up the Arlberg method ski school at Mount Rainier, but as a burgeoning moviemaker he was also charged with shooting a film at Mounts Baker and Rainier advertising the beauty and poetry of skiing in the Pacific Northwest. Lang quickly became one of the focal points of the region's ski community, and though it is impossible to pinpoint just exactly how and where their paths first crossed, it is clear that Ralph Bromaghin got to know Lang during the filming of *Ski Flight* at Baker. The film proved an amazing success, running as a second feature at Radio City Music Hall in New York for six weeks during the winter of 1937.[26]

Lang's next project was the publication of the most comprehensive guidebook on the Arlberg ski method to date, *Downhill Skiing*. In it, the alpine romantic proselytized passionately about both the Arlberg style and the spiritual benefits of winter days spent in the mountains. "We should all look on skiing as an art akin to ballet, dancing to imaginary music," he wrote. "It's not only exercise, or merely sport, but revelation for body and soul."[27]

The book instantly became the blueprint for anyone learning to ski in North America.[28] As a result of his growing popularity as a ski instructor, Lang was next tapped in December 1937 by the University of Washington to coach its ski team on an emergency basis. The Huskies had accepted an invitation to compete head to head with the Dartmouth Ski Team at Sun Valley, and Lang's job was to minimize the embarrassment that seemed sure to result.[29]

The 1937–38 Dartmouth squad that visited Sun Valley featured Dave and Steve Bradley, Warren and Howard Chivers, and John Litchfield, and predictably ran roughshod over the Huskies team. The U.W. racers, however, conducted themselves in a serious and sportsmanlike manner, and everyone back in Seattle was satisfied that true disaster had been averted thanks to Lang. More important, the coach utilized his first Sun Valley visit (and subsequent ones) to reacquaint himself with fellow Schneider alumnus and new Sun Valley ski instructor Friedl Pfeifer, solidifying a firm link for the future between the skiers of the Pacific Northwest and the Sun Valley establishment.[30] That relationship would shortly bear fruit for one Ralph Bromaghin, currently sitting in the snowy fog of Mount Baker.

By the beginning of the 1938–39 ski season, Averell Harriman had decided to replace Hauser as Sun Valley Ski School director. His primary motivation was to avoid any embarrassment to Union Pacific that might have resulted from either Hauser's suspected Nazi sympathies or his personal dating habits (which included regular public rendezvous with Virginia Hill, former moll of the late gangster Bugsy Siegel). Shortly before the opening of the season, Harriman asked Friedl Pfeifer to take over the school. Though Pfeifer kept Hauser on, he made it clear that the "non-stop party" for Hauser's marauding band of Salzburgers was over.[31]

The demotion of Hauser was greeted by several in the Sun Valley community with unrestrained glee, including members of the Duchin Room waitstaff. According to then-waiter and lifelong Sun Valley employee Denny Pace, "I don't know if Hauser was a real Nazi, but I'm quite sure that he was a real [jerk]. More than once, I saw him linger at a table until the rest of his fellow diners had started for the door, and then pocket the waiter's tip for himself. That's the type of guy he was."[32]

Friedl Pfeifer, on the other hand, was most Sun Valley residents' idea of a gentleman. Though some of his comrades in arms would later think of him as being aloof, to most in Sun Valley he appeared soft-spoken and good-humored. Harriman also likely viewed Friedl, who was happily devoted to a Salt Lake City debutante, as a safer alternative to Hauser in that regard, too.[33]

Pfeifer quickly set out to restructure the ski school in a way that would make Hannes Schneider proud. One of his first acts, therefore, was to recruit his hometown friend Otto Lang to serve as his assistant director, and to solicit opinions as to which good, young American skiers might make appropriate additions to the school's expanding roster of instructors.[34] Among those skiers that Lang recommended for the job was the impressive young man he'd seen ski and teach at Mount Baker, Ralph Bromaghin.[35]

According to Harriet Clough Waldron, Ralph was extremely excited over the prospect of teaching at the glamorous, state-of-the-art facility at Sun Valley. In the interim, he continued to serve during the winter of 1938–39 as an instructor in the Seattle area, honing his skills under Lang's occasional tutelage. "I remember Ralph and I being in such a giddy mood one day that spring, when the snow was up to the second floor of the Paradise Inn at Mount Rainier," said Harriet, "that we herringboned [ski-walked] up the side of the roof on one side and skied down the other. As they used to say, we had the world on a string."[36]

∽)(∝

Sometimes in a young life, a defining moment arises unexpectedly, presaging the future of the individual by testing his or her character under pressure, or even in crisis. Rudy Konieczny's test came on the Thunderbolt in the 1940 Eastern Championships. Jake Nunnemacher's arose in the Intercollegiate Championships of 1942 at Middlebury. Ralph Bromaghin's moment arrived on March 18, 1939, and involved circumstances far more serious and emotional than a ski race. It was during Harriet Clough's spring break, and Ralph, as usual, accompanied his friend to Rainier to enjoy a day of outdoor winter sports.

The nearby Boeing Aircraft Company had chosen that day to test its revolutionary new "Stratoliner," the world's first pressurized commercial aircraft. It was designed as a variation of the soon-to-be-famous American B-17 bomber (nicknamed the "Flying Fortress"), making the Stratoliner the largest commercial airliner in the world. The pressurized plane's ability to fly above bad weather at an incredible twenty-six thousand feet had captured the interest of several airlines and aviation specialists, including the Dutch national carrier KLM, which sent a test pilot to Seattle to conduct the day's trial.[37]

Accompanied by Boeing's chief engineer, its head aerodynamics expert, and several other key employees involved in military aircraft design, the KLM representative took off that morning to put the plane through its paces. At some point, it was apparently agreed to test the aircraft's ability to sustain an engine failure while traveling at low speed. The result was catastrophic. A stall caused the plane to spin out of control, taking it into a fatal dive from ten thousand feet. It crashed into a parking field below Paradise Lodge, less than two hundred yards from where Ralph and Harriet had parked. Although they did not see the impact of the plane, they were among the first on the scene.[38]

According to Harriet, "It was a horrendous crash. The metal of the plane, or what was left of it, was twisted and smoking. You could smell fuel leaking out all over the place. Nobody had any idea if any of the passengers were still alive inside the wreckage, but instead of helping, most of the people in the area were just staring in shock. Everything seemed to be moving in slow motion."[39]

"Ralph's reaction was exactly the opposite," she continued. "He instinctively went sprinting toward the plane, screaming for people not to light any matches or drop any cigarettes. We tried to see if anyone was alive to be

49

rescued. I know Ralph would have gone in and pulled people out if there was any chance at all that someone had lived, but it was pretty obvious when we got up close that no one had survived. Anyone who was there remembers the horror. I was proud over the courage Ralph showed by running in with the intention of saving strangers without regard for his own safety. I'm satisfied that we had both tried to do whatever we could to help under the circumstances."

Whether Ralph was profoundly affected by the carnage he had seen at the crash site is something about which he never spoke to Harriet. She believes, however, that he handled the situation in his stride. "He demonstrated to himself that if there is such a thing as courage under fire, he had it," she said. "I'm sure that in some way, that knowledge helped him to handle all the difficult situations that lay ahead of him."[40]

∞∞∞

Otto Lang arrived at Sun Valley Ski School for the 1939–40 season, joining a staff that now included Dartmouth teammates John Litchfield and Percy Rideout, European champions Sigi Engl and Fred Iselin (the latter a Swiss comedian reputed to have been one of the finest "crud" skiers of all time), Florian "Flokie" Haemmerle of Germany, Joe Duncan of Colorado, and Ralph Bromaghin.[41] According to Litchfield, Bromaghin served with him on the trail crew and did some teaching that season, though not as a featured instructor. "He was quiet," Litchfield remembered. "Some of those guys were real party boys, but not Ralph. He was happy skiing during the day and strumming his guitar at night, painting his watercolors, and generally keeping a very low profile around lots of guys who didn't necessarily take that approach."[42]

Charles McLane, who also made the trip out to Sun Valley, grew to appreciate Bromaghin as a fine ski instructor and musician. His assessment of Ralph's personal life mirrored Litchfield's. According to both, the heady atmosphere of Sun Valley—with the likes of Ernest Hemingway (busy completing his novel *For Whom the Bell Tolls* at the lodge), Clark Gable, Veronica Lake, Claudette Colbert, and Gary Cooper regularly passing on the slopes and in the hallways—did little to affect Ralph's quiet style.[43]

"Even in retrospect," McLane reflected, "it's very hard to pin Bromaghin down. He was self-contained, sort of an introspective type. I don't think he had a huge amount of self-confidence in social situations, and so he tried to stay within certain confines in order to avoid any chance of embarrassment.

Don't get me wrong, he was very amusing, and people liked having him around. But he pursued his own passions, and that didn't include 'worldliness.' Ralph wasn't interested in becoming or in being perceived as a sophisticate. He had skiing, and he had his music, and that satisfied him."[44]

At the end of his first season at Sun Valley, however, Ralph unexpectedly began showing signs of acclimatization to the rarefied social air. In an innocent and revealing letter to his sister Florence, the twenty-two-year-old ski instructor reported with detached cool that he had recently rubbed shoulders with Bing Crosby and film producer Darryl Zanuck on the slopes. Suddenly tipping his hand, though, that perhaps he had not yet developed into one of Sun Valley's truly jaded bon vivants, Ralph added that "I'm learning to dance— so far, so good. . . . I've [also] been [in] on several good parties. One in Ketchum [was] an elk steak dinner and all, with a party of guests among whom were Otto Lang, Friedl, Norma Shearer, and others!"[45]

According to his friend Bob Craig, the shy Bromaghin had also struck up a romantic relationship that winter with 1936 U.S. Women's Olympic Ski Team member Clarita Heath, who had come to Sun Valley to become one of Friedl Pfeifer's first female ski instructors. Craig described her relationship with Ralph as "warm, and I'm sure a learning experience for Brom, though as concerns the depth of it I'm not certain."[46] Sun Valley Ski Patrol director and future Tenth Mountaineer Nelson Bennett similarly noted that dating the pretty and vivacious Heath was probably a good experience for a reticent young man such as Bromaghin, "though he had a lot of competition for her attention."[47]

After the 1939–40 ski season ended at Sun Valley, Ralph Bromaghin perhaps sensed for the first time the wisdom of broadening his formal education to complement his burgeoning social skills. He therefore returned home to Seattle and enrolled at the University of Washington as a liberal arts major for the fall 1940 semester.[48] By then, however, the specter of world war was already intruding upon the normally sedate campus life at U.W.

෨෬

As the end of the decade approached, events in Europe and Asia weighed heavily on the minds of most ordinary Americans, especially those at or nearing draft age. Despite the fact that isolationism still carried the day in the U.S. Congress, each passing week seemed to pull the United States closer to the conflicts already engulfing most of the rest of the world. One such event was the unprovoked invasion of Finland by the Soviet Red Army, a struggle that

51

profoundly captured the attention of—among others—the northwestern U.S. mountaineering community centered in Seattle.

Shortly after signing a nonaggression pact with the Soviet Union, Nazi Germany attacked Poland on September 1, 1939, signaling the start of the Second World War in Europe. Three months later, pursuing expansionistic goals of its own, the Soviets invaded the small Scandinavian country of Finland with a Red Army force of more than a million men supported by tank, air force, and naval units.[49] The Finns, vastly overmatched in equipment and personnel, had one important military element in their favor: well-trained ski troops. For nearly four months, Finnish soldiers in white camouflage uniforms kept the Soviets at bay. Using guerrilla tactics, the Finns ambushed Russian units and blew up convoys before escaping back into the snowy forests on skis. Though finally forced to surrender in March 1940, the Finns succeeded in destroying several Soviet divisions, dramatically illustrating the wartime value of ski troops in cold-weather terrain.[50] Dave Bradley, one of the Wisconsin Bradley boys from Dartmouth, wrote it up just that way for the U.S. government as an on-the-scene observer.[51]

Among those also closely following the events in Finland were the members of the "official" American skiing community. Sensing that the United States was significantly underprepared for a winter war it would inevitably have to fight (perhaps even on its own continental soil), National Ski Patrol founder and chairman Charles Minot "Minnie" Dole wrote to the War Department in July 1940 offering the assistance of the NSP in recruiting U.S. mountain troops. The purpose of this specialized unit, the World War I veteran explained, would be to counter in the most expeditious manner the alpine forces that for centuries had been maintained by the Axis nations of Germany, Austria, and Italy. "I contend that it is more reasonable to make soldiers out of skiers than skiers out of soldiers," Dole advised anyone who would listen.[52]

The persistent Dole finally found a sympathetic ear in army chief of staff General George Marshall. The nation's top general listened to Dole and quickly authorized the formation of ski patrol units within several U.S. Army divisions, most prominent among them the Third Division's Fifteenth Regiment stationed at Fort Lewis near Seattle.[53] Former University of Oregon skiing coach Captain Paul Lafferty (Ralph Lafferty's older brother) and former University of Washington ski team captain John Woodward (a young lieutenant who had become an expert skier by imitating pictures of Hannes Schneider he saw in one of the Arlberg method books) formed the backbone of the Fifteenth

Infantry Regiment's trial ski section.[54] Together, they began to experiment with winter warfare equipment and tactics near Mount Rainier and throughout the Olympic and Cascade Ranges.

౸⦿౸

In early 1941, Lieutenant Woodward led troops on a well-publicized, two-week winter expedition into the rugged Cascade Range to test equipment.[55] By then, the Ptarmigans had gotten wind of the special winter warfare projects being carried out in their backyard, and began to make inquiries as to what the army was up to.

It didn't take long before word was traveling among mountaineers and skiers throughout the Pacific Northwest and the Sierras—including those at Woodward's University of Washington alma mater—that he and Paul Lafferty were putting together the nucleus of a ski regiment for the army. Among those who heard the news was Duke Watson, a Seattle climber and skier who had been drafted after finishing college and assigned to duty in northern California.

According to Watson, he himself was one of the first U.S. Army members to request and receive reassignment to the ski patrol unit at Fort Lewis.[56] The next prospective mountain trooper after Watson to show up that spring at the army post thirty miles from Mount Rainier was a tall guy with a guitar, skis, and a droll sense of humor, whose life would soon become inextricably linked with Watson's. "His name was Ralph Bromaghin," said Watson, "and he had been recruited off the University of Washington campus as a ski instructor by Minnie Dole himself as one of the primary building blocks of the United States ski troops."[57] Bromaghin had, in fact, just completed his second season teaching at Sun Valley, where he had signed on for the 1940–41 season after making the decision to leave U.W. in favor of army enlistment.

"It was the beginning of three years of incredible adventure in some of the most beautiful ski terrain in the world," stated Watson, "followed by some stuff I don't like to recall." Still, in all, the soon-to-be nationally recognized climber remembered his time in the ski troops, especially the period at Fort Lewis and Rainier with Bromaghin, as "the greatest army experience anyone ever had."[58]

In the late spring of 1941, Otto Lang was engaged by the army to produce a military instructional skiing film at Sun Valley. Lang was assigned four men from the Fifteenth Regiment ski patrol unit under the leadership of Lieutenant

Woodward, all of whom accompanied Lang to Idaho.[59] On a second filming trip to Sun Valley, Woodward assembled another team that included Walter Prager, who had recently been drafted away from his job coaching the Dartmouth Ski Team, and Lang's buddy, Ralph Bromaghin.[60]

According to Nelson Bennett, Bromaghin had quite a good time on the film detail. "I remember Prager, Brom, myself, and a few other guys skiing together with [ski school director] Friedl Pfeifer on one of the movie crew's off days. We were all hysterical over how Bromaghin could mimic Friedl's style and mannerisms. He just couldn't quite do it at full speed. No one could. But it was funny to watch a guy that tall—6'4" at least—so closely imitate the style of a much smaller man. . . . He also had Friedl's accent down perfectly, but he kept that quiet in case he wanted to work at Sun Valley again at some point."[61] The resulting films, including the classic military instructional project *Learning to Ski*, contain some of the finest and most artistic film footage of skiing ever shot.[62]

Back at Fort Lewis, Watson, Bromaghin, and Prager were joined in the Fifteenth Regiment Ski Patrol that autumn by another former Sun Valley instructor, Don Goodman (later to be joined by his skiing buddy and brother, Leon). The war in Europe, meanwhile, raged on. During the winter of 1940–41, regulars from the fascist Italian army had been bogged down against Allied troops in the icy, Balkan mountains of Yugoslavia and Albania under conditions for which only the Italian Alpini had trained. The results were catastrophic for Italian dictator Benito Mussolini's troops, who suffered more than forty thousand casualties, including twenty-five thousand dead.[63] If any further impetus was needed by the U.S. War Department to train American mountain troops for combat, the news from the Balkans provided it. Secretary of War Henry Stimson, himself a former mountaineer, approved General Marshall's decision to activate an entire "mountain" regiment at Fort Lewis in the late fall of 1941, and word quickly got around the American ski community that this was *the* outfit to join.[64]

As the story goes, former Dartmouth Ski Team captain Charles McLane showed up straight from Sun Valley in his green letterman's sweater in November, the first of the new volunteers to arrive. When he asked a grizzled Fort Lewis sergeant for help finding his unit, the newly formed Eighty-seventh Mountain Regiment, the reply surprised him. "As far as I can tell, son," he said, "you *are* the Eighty-seventh Mountain Regiment."[65] McLane was assigned to what amounted to his own, semiprivate barracks, and told to wait for his friends.[66]

ജാരു

Snow was already piling up in the Cascades that November when Captain Paul Lafferty began to organize Sunday ski trips to Paradise Lodge on Mount Rainier for his patrollers at Fort Lewis. "Captain Lafferty would show up outside our enlisted men's barracks in his huge Buick convertible, with the top down, of course," remembered Duke Watson, "and all of us privates would pile in with our skis. That didn't go over very well with the regular army types in the Third Division, but we really didn't care if Paul didn't mind, and he didn't."[67]

The first few Sunday trips provided good, early season skiing and warm socializing, but were mainly without incident. Sunday, December 7, 1941, was quite different. "Like everybody alive then, I remember that day so clearly," recalled Watson. "Lafferty and his wife Jean picked us up in the Buick in the very early morning. It was Ralph Bromaghin, Charles McLane, Don Goodman, and myself. By this time, Brom and McLane had discovered that they shared a passion for music and singing, so between the two of them trading songs and making up parodies, we didn't need the radio. It was a beautiful day, and we were all laughing and singing our hearts out."[68]

When the group arrived at Rainier, they split up. "I think Goodman and McLane climbed up to Camp Muir at ten thousand feet, while the rest of us stayed down around Paradise. It was a terrific day of skiing. We had lunch in the sunshine and skied well into the afternoon before heading to the car. While we were waiting for the guys to get back down from Muir, Jean Lafferty absentmindedly switched on the radio. The news just shocked the hell out of us. I mean, it went right through us. Pearl Harbor had been bombed, and hundreds of sailors and airmen had been killed."

It was nearly dark by the time everyone had returned to the car. They set out immediately for Fort Lewis. "The problem was," Watson continued, "that everybody on the West Coast figured the Japanese were on the way, and so everything was a little crazy. We had no way to get in touch with anyone at Lewis, so when we finally made it down to the main road, we stopped at the Green Parrot Restaurant to get the latest news. They were open, but everything was blacked out. By this time, we were starving, but they knew we were army guys and were very reluctant to serve us. I remember the waitress kept asking whether we shouldn't be reporting for duty somewhere. They were all very nervous. So were we. We finally convinced them to feed us so that we could eat and be on our way, but they weren't happy about it."

With the blackout in effect, it took until the middle of the night for the group to creep their way back into Fort Lewis. "We were all pretty keyed up, but Bromaghin was really upset," Watson recalled. "He figured that we might be moved out with the Third Division, and that would be the end of our skiing and climbing for the army. There was also a fear that we might not get to say goodbye to anyone, family or otherwise, before we ended up overseas somewhere. That thought made us all pretty unhappy."[69]

Upon their arrival, the boys were sent immediately out on patrol around Lewis, and spent most of the next two weeks camping outdoors in the snow while guarding roads and military facilities up and down the northern Pacific Coast. They were not, however, shipped out. To the contrary, fresh volunteers rapidly began arriving to join the newly formed mountain troops. The skiing members of the Third Division, including Bromaghin, were quickly transferred to the Eighty-seventh to join McLane, who was forced to surrender his status as a one-man mountain regiment.[70]

The American ski troops, through the dedicated (some in General Marshall's office might say "obsessive") efforts of Minnie Dole and the National Ski Patrol, had finally been born. For many, the experience would prove to be one of the most spectacular and challenging periods of their lives, the good outweighing the bad. For many others, the journey would be filled with terror and anguish, and would not end well. That, however, was all in the future. For now, Ralph Bromaghin could breathe a sigh of relief and write one of the first of his many popular Eighty-seventh Mountain Regiment song parodies, a telling ditty sung to the tune of "I Love to Dance" from the film *Snow White and the Seven Dwarfs*:

A happy lad and just eighteen
They put me in the Army
By official poop to the mountain troops
Where the enemy wouldn't harm me

Ho hum, I'm not so dumb
The mountain troops for me
Men are made in defilade
But I prefer to ski . . .

Every morn at six o'clock
We do our calisthenics
Maidens swoon as we pass by
We are so photogenic

The Sun Valley Serenader (Ralph Bromaghin)

> *Ho hum, I'm not so dumb*
> *The mountain troops for me*
>   *Other guys can fight this war*
> *But I would rather ski.*[71]

The Time of Their Lives

THE CALL WENT OUT IMMEDIATELY AFTER PEARL HARBOR FROM MINNIE DOLE and the National Ski Patrol for skiers and mountain men who wanted to join an alpine combat outfit.[1] The mission of this new regiment would be to fight the Axis powers of Japan, Germany, and Italy (all of whom had declared war on the United States in December 1941) in the mountains of Europe, Asia, and if it came to it, North America. Dole's initiative marked the first and only time a private organization has ever officially recruited for the U.S. military.[2]

Not surprisingly, among the first to answer that call were Privates Rudy Konieczny and Roy Deyle, formerly of the Ski Runners of Adams. They were the initial pair of more than twenty skiers from the small Massachusetts town (the most from any American community of comparable size) to procure the three letters of recommendation necessary for admittance to what the *New Yorker* called "Minnie's Ski Troops."[3]

By March 1942, Rudy and Roy had been transferred from Camp Edwards near Boston to Seattle's Fort Lewis.[4] What the two found when they got there was the answer to a young ski racer's dreams. They were immediately assigned to their new, army-rented "barracks" in the famous Paradise and Tatoosh Lodges on the slopes of Mount Rainier,[5] and within days of their arrival were skiing not only with the former Third Division ski patrol regulars, but also with the likes of legendary Swiss ski mountaineer Peter Gabriel, Austrian-born alpinist Nick Hock, Mount Hood champion Olaf Rodegard of Norway, Steve Knowlton and Paul and Ralph Townsend of the University of New Hampshire, Ralph Lafferty of the University of Oregon, Dick Whittemore and Olympian Robert Livermore of Harvard, army daredevil Ray Zoberski, famed ski film maker John Jay of Williams College, and former U.S. national downhill ski champion Joe Duncan of Colorado.[6]

Rudy Konieczny's passion for the sport was immediately reborn. The boys from Adams were now charter members of what is still considered today to have been one of the most prestigious "ski clubs" in the sport's history. All of Rudy's disappointments over injury and personal defeat on the Thunderbolt, and all of the social complications that had soured him on skiing in general, receded like melting snow on a warm afternoon in the rugged, pristine beauty of the Pacific Northwest.

For those skiers like Rudy who had never experienced life in the mountains outside of the northeastern United States, arrival in the Cascades was a revelation. Used to the shivering cold, gray skies and narrow, icy trails that characterize New England skiing, they were now quartered in luxury digs overlooking the wide-open snowfields of majestic, 14,400-foot Mount Rainier.[7] The minds of Rudy and Roy must have reeled as they stared up into the clouds shrouding the summit, laughing at the thought that they once considered Greylock a monstrous peak.

The differences between East and West didn't stop with terrain or the quality of the on-mountain lodging, either. The surrounding mountains also boasted deep, coastal powder under frequently sunny, spring skies. The snow at Tatoosh Lodge had once again drifted up to the second-floor windows by the time Rudy arrived, giving the troopers a choice of entry by walking through the snow tunnel burrowed to the front door or skiing directly in through the open windows on the second level. They most often chose the more direct route to their rooms upon returning from the slopes. "So did the girls," one member of the Eighty-seventh happily reported.[8] "I'm in snow up to my head," Rudy wrote home excitedly, "and getting paid for it!"[9]

Rudy and Roy, along with the hundreds of other young skiers and climbers who had joined them at Rainier, had found the alpinist's Valhalla they had always imagined. The war seemed very far away, and indeed for the time being, it was. "If this was the army," chuckled Duke Watson, "it was fine by me."[10]

Rudy's rejuvenation of confidence and enthusiasm prompted him to jump into his new situation without concern for the issue of "acceptance" that had haunted him growing up as a mill kid. At this point, not only could he ski with almost anyone, but he and Roy Deyle also had more military experience than practically any other enlisted man in the Eighty-seventh. Rudy's eighteen months of prior army service was the great equalizer for him among the collegiate skiers who were just now showing up, making him in many ways an upperclassman among freshmen.

Although records show that Rudy scored an impressive 92 of 100 in his initial skiing test of April 9, 1942, competition among the world-class downhill racers in the Eighty-seventh was so fierce that his compact and explosive skiing style earned him only a second-rank designation.[11] That stigma, however, would last only as long as the time it took to retest him several months later. After time spent skiing intensively with Walter Prager, he scored a 98 and very definitely moved into the elite class of Eighty-seventh Regimental skiers.[12]

On April 13, 1942, Private Konieczny resumed his racing career, joining dozens of his fellow Eighty-seventh Regiment troopers in the annual Silver Skis Race on Mount Rainier. That competition—the unofficial championship of the Pacific Northwest sponsored by the *Seattle Post-Intelligencer* newspaper—consisted of a wild, top-to-bottom free-for-all from Camp Muir down nearly five thousand vertical feet to Edith Creek Basin (finishing near the Alta Vista run above Paradise Lodge). It usually resulted in a fair amount of chaos, as the country's most aggressive competitors cut one another off and collided. Despite the recent introduction of staggered starting, injuries were still frequent and fatalities, though rare, were by no means unheard of.[13] Rudy was back in his element.

In a race dominated but not won by some of the Eighty-seventh's best skiers, a rusty Rudy Konieczny finished a respectable twelfth.[14] Ironically, considering that Rudy's tough luck in competitions on the Thunderbolt was the stuff of legends, it was a local Seattle firefighter named Matt Broze racing on his own "home" mountain who beat Prager to win the beautiful trophy (a pair of hand-carved, fifteen-inch-high skis leaning on a pillar of solid silver).

By his two-second victory, Broze also bested the rest of an exceptional field that included the Eighty-seventh's McLane and Paul Lafferty. Rudy, who one can imagine might have viewed the fireman's victory with a certain detached satisfaction, himself beat such notable racers to the finish line as Ralph Lafferty and another graceful athlete he had never before skied against, Ralph Bromaghin. Roy Deyle came in thirtieth.[15] Noting that nearly all of the fastest twenty finishers were members of the ski troops, the *Post-Intelligencer* proclaimed the Eighty-seventh "the finest ski team . . . ever put into one lodge."[16]

₧)(Ԓ

While the wide-eyed Rudy Konieczny was probably disappointed over not finishing higher in the race standings, Ralph Bromaghin was certainly satisfied to have finished in the top twenty among such illustrious company. "Like me, Bromaghin was never a great racer," remembered his close friend, Ralph Lafferty. "He was more of a stylist, gliding down with a fluidity you would never expect from a man of his size. Neither of us, though, were racers possessed of the skills and abandon of a Prager, nor did Ralph aspire to that. His goals were strength and grace, and he achieved them."[17] Trooper Richard Whittemore, another top-twenty finisher, described Bromaghin's turns that day as "models of collected elegance."[18]

As graceful a skier as he was, though, "Bromaghin's real gift was teaching," asserted Duke Watson. "He made a skier out of a confirmed climber like me in just a few weeks, with humor and the right amount of cajoling. Even if he wasn't among the very fastest skiers on the mountain, you'd have to say that he was in the highest rank of instructors."[19]

The time Bromaghin spent with Otto Lang had paid off handsomely in developing his Arlberg method teaching skills. According to newly promoted Captain John Woodward, Lang's best-selling instructional manual, *Downhill Skiing*, became the bible for teaching the ski troops, just as it was for the nation's ski schools.[20] Bromaghin probably had as thorough a knowledge of that book as any trooper in the Eighty-seventh, and together with Paul Lafferty, Rodegard, and Gabriel, became one of the four founders of the Regimental Ski School at Rainier.[21] Their job would be to turn hundreds of mountaineers with varying alpine talents and abilities into competent military skiers.

From a technical standpoint, Woodward recalled, the Arlberg method was not the most effective system for skiing with heavy packs and rifles. The smoother, "quieter" Swiss step-turn technique (originated by, among others,

Peter Gabriel and civilians Andre Roch and Austrian Toni Seelos) was far superior to the Arlberg "snowplow/shoulder swing" when it came to soldiering.[22] Also superior, according to Eighty-seventh Regimental ski instructor Nick Hock, was the new "French method" that had been imported from eastern Austria to Chamonix by Emile Allais.[23] As Woodward noted, however, "we only had a few guys who knew the other, up-and-coming methods, while Bromaghin was one among many who were expert in teaching Arlberg. We had to go with the Austrian system, but there was so much concern arguments would break out that we formally agreed to utilize the Lang book as the final arbiter of stylistic disputes. It worked. Nobody killed anyone else over issues of technique."[24]

Aside from ski mountaineering, Ralph Bromaghin was ecstatic about joining the mountain regiment for another reason: he could get back to playing music. Joining the Eighty-seventh gave him a chance to form a regimental glee club with Charles McLane, and the singing group that the two organized quickly became one of the most popularly cited examples of the esprit de corps that characterized the U.S. ski troops. They were joined by Glen Stanley (a mutual friend and racer from Sun Valley) and Charles Bradley (another of the Wisconsin Bradley brothers) in working out parodies and mountain songs in four-part harmony.[25]

"Bromaghin was a fine guitarist, but he was brilliant when it came to vocal arrangement," recalled McLane. "He would come down to a rehearsal with every vocal part worked out, and in between bumming cigarettes from everyone, he'd teach the arrangements to us one by one. Other times he'd work out the parts right on the spot."[26]

John de la Montagne, Jake Nunnemacher's housemate at Dartmouth, was another occasional member of the Eighty-seventh Glee Club. He remembered Bromaghin's instrumental virtuosity more than anything else. "Ralph was an extraordinary amateur guitarist. I had brought my clarinet with me to Fort Lewis, and at Paradise we'd have late-night jam sessions, playing Benny Goodman hits like "Sing Sing Sing" and "Flying Home." Ralph not only knew the full arrangements, he could also throw in all those Charlie Christian guitar rhythms. We had a terrific time."

"What I also remember was his intensity," de la Montagne continued. "He took his skiing seriously, his climbing seriously, and his music seriously. You could see how much he loved those things by the skill that he brought to them, but he was not one for showing unrestrained enthusiasm, even when everything went well. What you saw from him when he was happy was more of a quiet satisfaction, except for those brief glimpses of joy when he was swinging with that guitar. Strange to say, but there was also a vague nervousness about Ralph, as if he were afraid one day he was going to wake up and find out he wasn't really a skier and a musician, but a soldier."[27]

It wasn't long before the Eighty-seventh Regimental Glee Club was entertaining nightly at Paradise Lodge, and making radio appearances throughout the Pacific Northwest on the weekends. The first "important" incident in which the glee club played a prominent role, however, was its immortalizing, in song, of the day the Eighty-seventh was forced to experiment with the dreaded use of snowshoes.

With all of the daily, on-hill activity going on without measurable military results, the Eighty-seventh's commander, Colonel Onslow "Pinky" Rolfe, was soon concerned that there appeared to be more recreational skiing taking place at Paradise than army training. The best skiers often sneaked away from their groups during ski instruction to take unsupervised runs, while those just learning the sport were unable, even after weeks of instruction, to move from place to place with anything that resembled military precision. Moreover, the informality of the training process was decidedly not the "army way," a fact that appalled the few non-skiing officers.[28]

As a result, one spring day, the order came that the Eighty-seventh was to try snowshoes as a potential military alternative to skis. Colonel Rolfe had been charged with training *mountain* troops, not necessarily *ski* troops. If the hickory boards had to go, he announced, so be it. Charles Bradley recalled that the reaction to the order was the sound of 150 jaws, belonging to many of the world's best skiers, dropping.[29]

In the spring of 1942, the members of the Eighty-seventh donned snowshoes for a gloomy day of maneuvers around Paradise. In the process, however, they made a joyful discovery. On steep, snowy hillsides, snowshoes are utterly useless. The troopers made certain that the colonel observed their struggles, demonstrating at every opportunity the dangers posed by the contraptions. At least one man would tip over sideways and slide down the hill whenever the colonel or a member of the Winter Warfare Board wandered by to observe.[30]

By day's end, the snowshoe experiment appeared a disaster. Still, the most paranoid troopers remained concerned that their demonstrations had not driven home the point quite far enough. As a result of this lingering anxiety, Bradley recalled that he, McLane, Glenn Stanley, and Bromaghin called an emergency meeting of the glee club.

"That evening," he wrote, "our singing group gathered in earnest. Before midnight there emerged the ballad of "Sven" in four-part harmony for male voices. Before morning, most of the regiment knew the words and could sing along and, at breakfast, did so mightily."[31]

The four parodists, led by Bromaghin, had concocted new lyrics to the obscure tune "A Bold Bad Man," the gist of which follows in abbreviated form:

Oola had a cousin from the wild and wooly west
While Oola liked the skiing, Sven liked snowshoeing the best
They got into the Mountain Troops to put it to a test
And everywhere they went they gave their war whoop

Oh give me skis and some poles and klister
And let me ski way up on Alta Vista
You can take your snowshoes and burn them sister
And everywhere you go you'll hear my war whoop

Two seconds later Oola finished, in a mighty schuss
Passing on the way poor Sven a-lying on his puss
The moral of the story is that snowshoes have no use
And poor old Sven no longer gives his war whoop.[32]

The creative effort helped both the colonel (who laughed quietly throughout the impromptu breakfast recital) and the troopers make their points. Asking highly skilled ski mountaineers to switch permanently to clumsy snowshoes was a bad idea. So was conveying the impression that while other members of the U.S. Armed Forces were struggling in combat zones from Guadalcanal to North Africa, the members of the Eighty-seventh were engaged in little more than a government-sponsored ski vacation. After the vocal performance that morning, the snowshoes mainly disappeared, and a more serious attitude toward military training was immediately evident among the skiers.[33]

Charles Bradley soon joined regimental ski mountaineers Albert Jackman, Paul Townsend, John Jay, and Peter Gabriel, among others, on a landmark expedition to the top of Rainier led by Captain Paul Lafferty. Making the very first winter-conditions ascent on the nation's most recognizable mountain, they spent two weeks under brutal weather conditions field-testing military mountaineering equipment such as tents and mountain stoves.[34]

Ralph Bromaghin and Rudy Konieczny, meanwhile, spent their time down at Paradise teaching others to ski (Ralph on an official basis and Rudy more informally), and honing their own considerable skills by climbing and schussing for hours each day with heavy packs. According to Eighty-seventh Regiment veteran Gordie Lowe, however, "even though it might sound like it, it really wasn't all fun and games. Yes, we all loved the snow and the mountains, and had volunteered to be there, but the training truly was grueling. Aside from weapons training and marching in every type of foul mountain weather imaginable, we climbed huge distances carrying those ninety-pound rucksacks, and camped in spectacularly frigid conditions. The army wanted to see how much we could take, and believe me, it didn't turn out to be the vacation in the mountains some guys hoped it might be."[35]

Those "ninety-pound rucksacks" (including an M-1 rifle and tent pegs) quickly became the stuff of legend. Corporal Charles Bradley was fond of telling the story of how the men in Company 87-A, under the leadership of Captain Paul Lafferty, pissed and moaned incessantly about the rigorous level of training he was forcing on them at Paradise. After a particularly rugged eight hours of ski touring with heavy packs was followed by a loud bitching session well within the captain's earshot, Lafferty called Bradley into his office.

Rather than the stern rebuke Bradley was expecting, however, the captain matter-of-factly asked him to try out the new rucksack he said he had been experimenting with that afternoon. When Bradley went to pick it up, he reported, "I thought it had been nailed to the floor." He asked what Lafferty was carrying in there. "Oh," Lafferty replied with a shrug, "I always put in a few rocks to keep fit for combat loads." As Bradley related it, "of course he knew I'd pass that news back to the rest of the [guys]. Without saying a word to the company, the bitching faded away on the night wind."[36] "Even with the extra weight in his pack," John Woodward recalled, "Paul Lafferty was still always one hundred to two hundred yards ahead of everyone else heading up into the mountains. The troops [just] couldn't keep up with him."[37]

Captain Lafferty might have been an inspiration, but pity any poor mountain trooper who tipped over in deep snow with one of those rucksacks strapped to his back. "I weighed all of 120 pounds at the time," remembered Earl Clark, another charter member of the Eighty-seventh who reported from Jackson Hole, Wyoming. "When I'd fall over with that heavy pack on, it'd take two guys to get me on my feet again."[38] How does one ski with that much weight on his back? "Slowly," remembered trooper Jeddie Brooks of Adams, "very slowly."[39] "It got you into shape, though," asserted John Woodward, "I can tell you that."[40]

Once again, the Eighty-seventh Mountain Regiment Glee Club sought to commemorate this unique and excruciating aspect of ski trooping in song. Ralph Bromaghin and Charles McLane put pen to paper, and the result was the most famous of all their parodies, "Ninety Pounds of Rucksack." Sung to the tune of the traditional, bawdy ode to the navy, "Bell Bottom Trousers," the new version quickly evolved into the theme song of the American mountain troops:

I was a barmaid in a mountain inn
There I learned the wages, the miseries of sin
Along came a skier, fresh from the slopes
He's the one who ruined me and shattered all my hopes

Singing ninety pounds of rucksack
A pound of grub or two
He'll schuss the mountains
Like his daddy used to do

He asked me for a candle to light his way to bed
He asked me for a kerchief to cover up his head
I being just a foolish maid and thinking it no harm
Jumped into the skier's bed to keep the skier warm

Chorus

Early in the morning before the break of day
He handed me a five-note and with it he did say
Take this my darling for the damage I have done
You may have a daughter, You may have a son
Now if you have a daughter, bounce her on your knee
But if you have a son, send the bastard out to ski

Chorus

The moral of this story, as you can plainly see
Is never trust a skier, an inch above your knee
For I trusted one and now just look at me
I've got a bastard in the Mountain Infantry

Chorus[41]

"Bromaghin's contribution to regimental morale and spirit was extremely significant," said Ralph Lafferty. "The songs he wrote for the glee club were learned and sung by the entire regiment, and later the entire division, and really helped pull us together into a cohesive unit. Ralph Bromaghin was very proud of that. He knew he was putting his music and his sense of humor to good use, and that the guys loved it. Part of the initiation rites into the mountain troops became learning Ralph's songs, and we're still singing them every time we get together."[42]

"We all took a lot of pride in writing and singing for the glee club," recalled Charles McLane. "It's one of my most satisfying memories of the Tenth."[43]

⊱⊰

As intensive and rugged as their "ninety pounds of rucksack" mountain training had become, when it came to military discipline and formality, neither the Eighty-seventh nor the Tenth Mountain Division of which it would become a part ever really adopted "regular army" ways. The shared love for the mountains that its members had in common, regardless of rank, was a primary factor in the relative egalitarianism of the unit. According to the troopers, however, there was more to it than that.[44]

Another factor was that many if not most members of the ski troops had leadership backgrounds, or had achieved levels of skill in sport, which gave *all* of them the shared sense that they were "officer material." In actuality, fully 64 percent of the members of the subsequently formed Eighty-sixth Regiment had test scores that qualified them for Officer's Candidate School.[45] The percentages for the Eighty-seventh and Eighty-fifth were undoubtedly at a similar level, more than double the average of other American divisions. The men knew it, and so did their officers. According to Colonel Robert Works of the Eighty-seventh, he had soldiers serving as corporals who would have been captains in any other infantry outfit.[46] The enlisted men and junior officers, in fact, frequently *taught* the senior officers outdoor skills on a formal basis. (Lieutenant John Jay, for example, became Regimental Commander Pinkie Rolfe's personal ski instructor, and was not above spraying the C.O. with a snow shower from his ski edges just for the fun of it.)[47]

Moreover, the original Tenth Mountain Division as a whole probably had a higher mean level of education among its members than any division in the history of the U.S. Armed Forces.[48] More than 50 percent of the division's volunteers had gone to college, an extraordinary statistic for the Depression era (or any era, for that matter). The percentage was even higher among the original members of the Eighty-seventh Regiment's First Battalion.[49] "It was not an army," concluded Major Bill Bowerman, Tenth Mountain officer and later U.S. Olympic track coach and cofounder of the Nike Shoe Company. "It was a fraternity. It was a brotherhood of outdoorsmen."[50]

Egalitarianism, of course, should not be confused with harmony. Ralph Bromaghin's experience with the "spirited" Ptarmigans served as good preparation for service in the Eighty-seventh. According to Sergeant Peter Wick, "The Eighty-seventh Regiment in particular was unique . . . [A]ll these individuals [alpinists, Nordic skiers, ski mountaineers] would quarrel and fight among themselves about how their various skills would be of more importance. The army, however, had ways of leveling out all the prima donnas. . . ."[51] In the end, it was mutual pride that carried the day, not competition, concluded Charles McLane. Simply being a member of the Eighty-seventh quickly became all that mattered, the chosen discipline of the trooper and the level of his rank notwithstanding.[52]

Perhaps the outlook of the members of the Tenth Mountain Division was best summed up by Eighty-seventh Regiment veteran and former cowboy Oley Kohlman, who said matter-of-factly, "I never met a sonofabitch with a couple of stars I thought was better than me."[53] So, when a set of pictures of Rudy Konieczny, Roy Deyle, and some of their fellow enlistees arrived back home in Adams displaying the whole gang of privates clowning around in "borrowed" Canadian Army officer's jackets, it depicted relatively little out of the ordinary. "I have no idea how they were able to pull that one off," admitted Adolph Konieczny, "but Rudy and the rest of them were always getting busted down a rank or two for pulling crazy stunts like that. They figured they had a skill the army needed, and that it gave them a bit more latitude than normal G.I.s had to express themselves."[54]

According to John Woodward, Rudy got away with most of his shenanigans because he was so well liked. "He was a real go-er," remembered Woodward with a broad smile, "and we took to that."[55]

₭)℁

The year 1942 was a good one for the members of the Eighty-seventh Mountain Regiment. "Bromaghin and the rest of our group just had the greatest time at Rainier," recalled Ralph Lafferty. "The training was rugged, but we had grown up in those mountains, and we loved the idea that we were learning and honing new outdoor skills. Brom, who was a great climber in addition to being such a good skier, was really enjoying life."[56]

68

So much so, in fact, that Bromaghin was reluctant to apply for officer training for fear that he wouldn't get back to the mountain troops. He was one of many in the Eighty-seventh who shared that concern, including Charles McLane. Their fears were assuaged somewhat when the first batch of Eighty-seventh Regiment troopers, among them Duke Watson, returned to Fort Lewis as officers straight from OCS training at Fort Benning, Georgia.[57] Many of those most cautious about maintaining their status as mountain troopers, however, still opted to wait. That included Bromaghin, who busied himself skiing all week for the army, and whenever time permitted, making the nine-hour drive to Alta Ski Resort near Salt Lake City on the weekends.

Ralph Lafferty asserted that he and Bromaghin were crazy enough to drive all the way to Alta because of its abundance of superb powder snow. In addition, because three of the best skiers in the world—Dick Durrance, Friedl Pfeifer, and Alf Engen—took turns managing the mountain, it had become quite a ski scene. Even actor Errol Flynn had become a regular.[58]

Alta had also been chosen in early 1942 as the site of a futile effort by the army to teach warm weather–trained paratroopers how to ski.[59] Civilian Dick Durrance was joined by racing friends Sel Hannah of Dartmouth and Barney McLean, among others, in trying to instruct southern boys (most of whom had never even seen snow) how to run Alta's slopes. "They broke a lot of legs," said Durrance, placidly summing up the project's results.[60] The experiment proved, as Minnie Dole had predicted, that it was a lot easier to teach skiers how to be soldiers than the other way around.

"Brom and I wanted nothing to do with teaching those paratroopers," recalled Lafferty. "We were there to ski the powder. So one day after one of those marathon drives from Rainier, I walked out of the Alta Lodge and found Bromaghin talking to his old friend, Otto Lang. I strutted over, planted my poles in the snow, and shook Otto's hand after Bromaghin introduced us. We all talked skiing for a while. I was pretty impressed with how I handled myself. Then Lang excused himself, and promptly tripped over my gear. Well, I got an earful from him on the proper etiquette of equipment placement, even as he skied away."

"As soon as Otto was out of hearing range, though," Lafferty continued, "Bromaghin went off on a perfect impersonation of him, repeating the entire speech word for word with an exaggerated Austrian accent. He owed Lang a lot, but it didn't stop him from poking fun at that holier-than-thou attitude those Austrians could show you. I'm not sure which one Bromaghin impersonated better, Lang or Friedl Pfeifer, but he wasn't afraid to go off on either one."[61]

"Aside from those who joined the Tenth," according to John Woodward, "the Austrian skiers like Lang didn't mix much with young American skiers for one simple reason: we weren't where the money was. Otto was teaching Nelson Rockefeller's family to ski. Friedl Pfeifer, before he joined the mountain troops, had his movie stars in Sun Valley. It's a fact that their clientele tipped better than kids from Seattle. Bromaghin's good relationship with Lang before the war was the exception, not because the Austrians were especially aloof, but because of ski school economics."[62]

Woodward continued, however, to describe another amusing incident concerning himself and the great Austrian racer and Sun Valley instructor Peter Radacher that more closely fits the stereotype of the cartoonishly arrogant Teutonic skier of that era. The two raced together in the Silver Skis competitions on Rainier in the mid-1930s, and Radacher had won the trophy. Some thirty years following the end of the Second World War, Woodward recognized Radacher's picture in a local restaurant in Zell Am See, Austria, and paid a visit to the hotel at which Radacher was the proprietor. "I introduced myself and told him I had raced against him at Rainier but finished fourth. He said 'ja' and nothing more. I said I was in the Tenth Mountain Division and heard he was opposite us in the Apennines. I said I heard he was captured in our section at the end of the war. He came back and said, 'no, I vasn't.' He paused, and asked 'vas you ever wounded?' I said 'no.' He gruffly replied 'then you vas never against us.' That appeared to end the conversation, and so I left, with him sitting underneath his Silver Skis trophy, and went on my way."[63]

☙〇ლ

In the summer of 1942, ski training trailed off in favor of the usual army miseries of dry-land soldiering back at Fort Lewis. Rudy Konieczny, however, was among a lucky group of troopers chosen as members of the fifty-man detachment that went with Lieutenant Colonel Robert Tillotson, Lieutenant Paul Townsend, and newly minted Lieutenant Duke Watson to the Columbia Ice Fields north of Banff and Lake Louise in the Canadian Rockies. It is an area considered by many to be the most ruggedly beautiful in North America. Their mission was to test in secret (at the direct request of British Prime Minister Winston Churchill) a new, full-track snow vehicle made by the Studebaker Company known as the "weasel."[64]

While in Canada, Rudy and his fellow troopers busied themselves building roads and successfully testing the new equipment, eating great chow paid for by Studebaker, and making first ski descents of the most famous glacial peaks of the Canadian Rockies, including Castleguard, Athabaska, Snow Dome, Kitchener, and Columbia.[65] Private Joe Duncan (soon to be Captain Joe Duncan) made an art form of bridging crevasses with logs, experimenting with adjustments to keep up with the movements of the glaciers.[66] According to Sergeant Pete Wick, if the mission sounded like "a National Geographic deal," that's because it was. "We spent about [four] unbelievable months on the Saskatchewan Glacier working on this project. We also were trained in every phase of glacier mountaineering. . . . When I look back on it now, up there on the Saskatchewan at 8,000 feet with the highest of the Canadian Rockies towering above us, it seems like a fairy tale."[67]

Duke Watson added that though the trip was thoroughly enjoyable and successful, there was one aspect that proved particularly troublesome. "There were grizzly bears all over the damn place," he recalled. "We made the mistake of having our garbage dump out in the open at first, and once the bears figured out there was food to be had, there was no getting rid of them. And those are some fierce animals. I'm not talking about black bears, here. We're talking full-grown Canadian grizzlies." Though no troopers were mauled or eaten, many were left with the thought that perhaps going south again before late autumn, when the bears' food sources grew scarcer, wasn't such a bad idea.

Watson had no clear recollection of Rudy Konieczny's activities in Canada. "To me, that means one of two things," he surmised. "Either Rudy was behaving himself, or he'd gotten better at hiding whatever he was doing that he shouldn't have. Kidding aside, no outdoorsman who was on that mission failed to have a good time, and I'm sure that was true for Rudy."[68]

Like Wick, Rudy had to have felt as though he'd pulled the best duty in the army. Even the trip back home that fall was an adventure. Upon their recall, the men "clamped on their skis, grabbed towing ropes, and were hauled over the snowy highways some *sixty* miles toward the railroad station at Lake Louise."[69] From there, Tillotson's team headed back to the States. They would not, however, be returning to Paradise and Fort Lewis for long.

While they had been away in Canada, the U.S. Army decided it needed a more formal mountain warfare instructional facility. Thus, in September 1942 it activated the Mountain Training Center (MTC) at Camp Carson, Colorado, just south of Colorado Springs. Tillotson's men were quickly directed to Carson for incorporation into the MTC Training Detachment, which was organized there in anticipation of the opening of a brand-new camp in the high mountains to the west. There, teaching units would be needed to help train the ever-increasing numbers of new American mountain troops being recruited by Minnie Dole and the National Ski Patrol.[70]

For those members of the Eighty-seventh who worried about missing the rugged beauty of the Canadian Rockies and the grandeur of Mount Rainier, they needn't have. Troopers arrived at Camp Carson to discover spectacular views and immediate access to another of the Lower 48's most fabled mountains, Pikes Peak, which dominates the horizon of Colorado Springs in a similar manner to the way Rainier exerts supremacy over the Seattle skyline. Rudy and his fellow New Englanders were, once again, awestruck by the majesty of their surroundings in the state that Theodore Roosevelt earlier in the century had called the "Switzerland of America."[71]

Ralph Bromaghin and the rest of the Eighty-seventh Regiment, meanwhile, said their good-byes to Rainier. They then dispersed for training in Jolon, California, before heading to Colorado to join up with the MTC that autumn.[72] At about the same time, a fresh-faced college graduate—one of dozens of Dartmouth students and alumni awaiting induction into the ski troops—also arrived at Camp Carson from Milwaukee for assignment.[73] One of his first tasks was to mail the postcard provided to him by his alma mater telling of his whereabouts. He dutifully explained:

> I am a private in the Mountain Training Center, HQ Co. at Camp Carson, Colorado, soon to be activated as a mountain division at Camp Hale in Pando, Colorado. At present, there are no other Dartmouth men, to my knowledge, at Camp Carson. There will be many at new Camp Hale up in the mountains.
>
> Signed, Jacob Nunnemacher.[74]

Rudy Konieczny in 1935, age seventeen. Courtesy of Konieczny family

The 1940 Eastern U.S. Amateur Downhill Team champions, the legendary Ski Runners of Adams. (left to right) Gerard Gardner, Roy Deyle, Maurice "Greeny" Guertin, Rudy Konieczny, and Bertram Cross. Courtesy of the Adams, Massachusetts, Historical Society

Austrian Skimeister *Hannes Schneider, whose Arlberg method gave birth to modern skiing, arrives with his wife in New Hampshire following his release from imprisonment by the Nazis in 1939. Harvey Gibson, who arranged for Schneider's passage to freedom, stands to the right of Mrs. Schneider. Schneider's top instructor, Benno Rybizka (with cap), stands to the left of the* Meister. *Photographer: Noel Wellman. Courtesy of New England Ski Museum*

Jake Nunnemacher waxing up before a race, circa 1938. Courtesy of Jean Lindemann

Jake Nunnemacher and his future wife, Jean, sailboat racing on Pine Lake, Wisconsin, circa 1938. Courtesy of Jean Lindemann

The 1941 Dartmouth College Ski Team. Jacob Nunnemacher is fourth from the right, back row. Bob Meservey is first on the left, front row. Jack Tobin is fourth from the left, front row. Courtesy of Jean Lindemann

Jake Nunnemacher demonstrates his Arlberg racing technique at the popular Suicide Six ski area in Vermont, circa 1939, where he tied for the top-to-bottom hill speed record. Courtesy Jean Lindemann

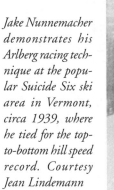

Ralph Bromaghin (left) is presented with the winner's trophy in the "Boys Race" at Paradise Valley on Mount Rainier, circa 1933. Courtesy of Bromaghin family

Ralph Bromaghin, Sun Valley ski instructor, circa 1940. Courtesy of Denver Public Library, Western History Collection

Ralph Bromaghin swinging on upright bass with the lounge band in Sun Valley, circa 1940. Courtesy of Ralph Lafferty

*Joe Duncan, high school
athletic and academic star,
in Estes Park, Colorado,
circa 1931. Courtesy of
Edward Wilkes*

Joe Duncan adopts an Austrian pose shortly after becoming U.S. National Downhill Ski champion of 1934. Courtesy of John Engle

Rocky Mountain Highs

ON THE SECOND EVENING AFTER THE PEARL HARBOR ATTACK, SKI INSTRUCTOR
Friedl Pfeifer was awakened in the middle of the night by federal agents pounding on the door of his Sun Valley home. He and fellow Austrian ski instructors
Hans Hauser and Sepp Froelich were rounded up, handcuffed, and detained
as a preventative security measure against domestic spying until their bona
fides could be proven.[1]

Pfeifer and Froelich were eager to demonstrate their loyalty to America, and
insisted that their hatred for Adolf Hitler had been the principal reason they
had emigrated from Austria in the first place. As a result, they volunteered to
serve in the American army. Hauser, however, remained silent about his politics,
and chose to remain under detention.[2] His friend, Sun Valley "discoverer"
Count Felix Von Schaffgotsch, had—like Peter Radacher—already returned
to Germany to join the Nazi forces. The count later died on the eastern front.[3]

73

In the spring of 1943, Pfeifer reported for duty at Camp Hale, the new American mountain troop training center. Situated at 9,480 feet above sea level in the Pando Valley, the world's highest military training facility and its ski center at Cooper Hill sat astride Tennessee Pass in an isolated section of the Colorado Rockies, roughly between the town of Leadville and the Vail Valley. Hale was built to accommodate fifteen thousand trainees in coal-heated, state-of-the-art redwood barracks. It was surrounded by magnificent ridges, which were buried in even lighter powder snow than the troops of the Eighty-seventh Regiment had experienced in the Cascades, the Olympics, or the Canadian Rockies.[4] The camp newspaper, *The Ski-zette* (later renamed *The Blizzard*), featured pinups in each issue not of Hollywood starlets, but of local mountain peaks.[5]

More than just an army post, Hale was actually a small city set in a mountain enclave. It boasted eight hundred separate buildings, including mess halls, chapels, a hospital, a post office, a stockade, theaters, clubs, day rooms, mule stables, a rifle range, a bayonet drill field, a grenade court, a rock-climbing center, a small camp ski slope, and Cooper Hill ski facility.[6] There was even an artificial glacier, created by spraying a man-made climbing wall with water in winter, for practicing technical ice-climbing.[7]

Pfeifer fell in love immediately. Not with Hale itself, but with a nearby, broken-down mining town in the Roaring Fork River Valley that several of the country's best skiers had already discovered. The town was Aspen, the same locale that American Olympic bobsled champion Billy Fiske had recruited Swiss mountaineer Andre Roch to survey years before. In 1937, Otto Schniebs brought some of his Dartmouth skiers out to see Fiske's playground, and by 1941, Toni Matt was calling the Roch Run on Aspen's Ajax Mountain the best championship downhill course he had ever skied.[8] Even radio personality and ski-area aficionado Lowell Thomas (a native of Victor, Colorado) had jumped on Aspen's rudimentary little bandwagon, and was touting it as the next potential Sun Valley.[9] Tragically, however, Fiske was one of the first Americans killed in the war when he was shot down after joining the British RAF as a fighter pilot prior to Pearl Harbor. With him had died, at least temporarily, the dream of building "the gem of the Roaring Fork" into a major American ski resort.[10]

The first time Pfeifer saw Aspen at the end of a long march from Hale led by Captain John Woodward, he looked up and imagined he was back in St. Anton, with its rounded, ice-cream-scoop hills. In his estimation, Ajax was a near-perfect ski mountain, with the pyramidal rock formation known as Maroon Bells serving as an inspiringly aesthetic backdrop beyond the upper ridges.

"I felt at that moment, an overwhelming sense of my future before me," he wrote.[11] Pfeifer's premonition would play a prominent role in the lives of several of his fellow troopers in the months and years to come, including Ralph Bromaghin, Jake Nunnemacher, and Rudy Konieczny.

By the time of Pfeifer's arrival, word had already spread around Camp Hale of the beauty and potential of Aspen as a world-class ski mountain. That was due in large part to raves from the members of the Eighty-seventh Regiment's Aspen Detachment sent there from Fort Lewis during the summer of 1942 to study mountain bridge-building.[12] Friedl Pfeifer's enthusiasm, however, added to the buzz of excitement about it, and the troopers began making the four-hour wintertime trip in droves. Frank Prejsnar, who had arrived that spring with a mob of other Adams, Massachusetts, skiers and reunited with Roy Deyle and Rudy Konieczny, recalled that after skiing and climbing with heavy packs all week around Hale, the first thing everyone wanted to do on the weekends was ski some more at Aspen.[13]

Because ski-area development in the Colorado Rockies had been progressing at an impressive pace since just after World War I, Aspen wasn't the only choice available to the troopers. It quickly, however, became the runaway favorite. "Once in a while on the weekends," said Prejsnar, "we'd go to Steamboat Springs or Winter Park, which were both a manageable drive away. Some of the really adventurous guys would go all the way up to Alta. After a while, though, we figured, 'why bother?' Aspen was so good, it made no sense going anywhere else. We were all used to climbing, so we'd take the boat tow up and then use skins on our skis to get up to the higher ridges, where the snow and the skiing was absolutely terrific. You could stay at the Jerome Hotel for about fifty cents a night, so we'd treat ourselves to that, and they'd serve these drinks called 'Aspen Cruds,' which were basically alcoholic milkshakes. It was a hell of a good time."[14]

Rudy Konieczny and several of the boys from Adams soon began making inquiries about the availability of options to buy land in Aspen once the war was over.[15] "Rudy was crazy for the place," recounted Prejsnar.[16] In the meanwhile, new recruits continued to pour into Hale, among them some of the world's finest winter athletes.

∞∞

Friedl Pfeifer was assigned immediately to the Tenth Cavalry Reconnaissance Troop (which quickly became known exclusively as the "Tenth Recon"), a detachment of the best skiers and climbers at Hale under the leadership of Captain Woodward and Lieutenants Duke Watson and Ed Link.[17] Its mission, along with a complementary unit known as the Mountain Training Group (MTG), was to impart mountaineering skills to the Tenth's new members, as well as to other specialized army units. Pfeifer was quickly joined by a host of fellow Europeans who had been recruited specifically for their ability to teach the Arlberg skiing method, including old friends from St. Anton and Sun Valley such as Hannes Schneider's son Herbert, Andy Hennig, Luggi Foeger, Flokie Haemmerle, Pepi Tiechner, and Rudy Konieczny's buddy, Toni Matt.[18]

Among some of the other notables who arrived in camp that spring were multidiscipline ski champion Gordy Wrenn from Steamboat Springs, the Schnackenberg brothers from nearby Berthoud Pass, Herb Klein from Sugar Bowl in the Sierras, Dev Jennings from the Wasatch Mountains of Utah, and East Coast racers Percy Rideout, Wendy Cram, and Pete Seibert. America's premier mountaineer, Paul Petzoldt, showed up straight from Jackson Hole, and the U.S. national ski jumping champion, Norwegian immigrant Torger Tokle, strode in from Howelsen Hill, Colorado.[19] Even two members of the von Trapp family, recent escapees from Austria whose story would later be told as *The Sound of Music,* joined up.[20]

"I remember walking down the street at Hale," continued Frank Prejsnar, "and thinking that most of the world's big ski heroes were right there in front of me. That was quite a thrill, knowing that I was right there among them, a member of their same outfit. Rudy never admitted it, but to some degree he probably felt that way, too, though as an MTG member he had his own little following."[21]

As a result of the influx in personnel at Hale, the Eighty-seventh Mountain Regiment was augmented by the formation of the Eighty-sixth and Eighty-fifth Regiments, bringing the total number of troops in the new "Tenth Light Division (Pack, Alpine)" closer to its full complement of more than twelve thousand men.[22] Eventually, there were approximately four thousand members in each regiment, which was further divided into three battalions made up of companies of roughly two hundred troopers each.

Although many if not most of the new recruits had volunteered specifically for duty in the mountain troops, those assigned to the ranks of the Eighty-sixth and Eighty-fifth did not necessarily hail from high alpine regions. Consequently, though several of the division's newest members were as talented and experienced in alpine disciplines as their brethren in the Eighty-seventh, a good number—including the muleskinners—had little such experience and had to be taught mountain skills from scratch. Nor did many of the new recruits possess the famous three letters of recommendation that had been a prerequisite for membership in the Eighty-seventh. Before long, the original members of the division began referring to themselves as "three-letter men" to distinguish themselves from the freshmen, a habit that caused many of the division's "youngsters" to bristle. It was a complicated hierarchy at Hale, where rank, skill, education, experience, personality, and age all played a part in the subtle process of determining status within the brotherhood.

ഇറര

Unquestionably, the biggest "star" in the Tenth Mountain Division was Sergeant Torger Tokle. He was an amazing athletic specimen of rock-solid muscle, with quadriceps the size of small tree trunks that enabled him to make ski jumps of spectacular distances. Lyle Munson, a junior ski jumping champion and close friend and platoon-mate of Tokle's, idolized the Norwegian and was in awe of his ability. "[He] had unbelievable spring in his legs," Munson remembered. "He sometimes demonstrated this by standing near the coal bin at the mess hall or at the rear of an army truck with a light pack on his back, springing up and landing on his feet on top of the bin or on the tailgate of the truck."[23]

Even the legendary Alf Engen of Alta, a simultaneous four-discipline American ski champion and civilian Tenth Mountain Division advisor, was impressed by Tokle's skills.[24] That was especially the case after the national titlist Tokle outdistanced him in several jumping competitions, a result the good-humored Engen was decidedly unused to.[25] "Torger was a champion," concluded Duke Watson, "and he carried himself that way, too. You knew, just looking at him with that big grin of his, how good he felt about just *being* Torger Tokle. He was a hell of a nice guy, too, or seemed to be on the occasions that I met him."[26]

ഇറര

For at least one member of the Eighty-seventh returning with Rudy Konieczny from the Canadian Rockies detail, reporting to Camp Hale was a homecoming of sorts. Joseph Duncan Jr. was a native son of Colorado, having been raised in the town of Estes Park, gateway to Rocky Mountain National Park in the north-central part of the state. According to those who knew him growing up, the scrawny kid with the toothpick legs whom everyone called "Junior" had by high school evolved into the perfect embodiment of the American scholar-athlete, with the added ruggedness of a pioneer survivalist.

Junior Duncan was the son of a colorful, larger-than-life father who styled himself as an "old-time" Colorado justice of the peace.[27] Joe Duncan Sr., known reverentially throughout Estes Park and its surroundings as simply "The Judge," once purportedly had a shoot-out with a fugitive in the Ship's Tavern lounge of the Brown Palace Hotel in Denver. Though there are no official reports of the incident—which could easily have been concocted to increase the legendary status of The Judge as a folk hero—bullet holes supposedly made by the elder Duncan's sidearm in one of the barroom walls were still in evidence when Junior treated Tenth Mountain trooper Roger Eddy (later a company commander with Duncan in the Third Battalion of the Eighty-seventh) to a drink there in 1943.[28]

Growing up, Junior Duncan's talents and popularity were such that he was enabled to move outside of his father's long shadow at an early age. He was honored as the valedictorian of his high school class in 1931, at the same time serving as captain of the football and basketball teams in his senior year. Duncan was also voted the "Best All-Around Boy" at Estes Park High School.[29] Junior, however, did not revel in his toast-of-the-town status. It was in the mountains where he was most comfortable, and as soon as he was able, Duncan got himself a pair of skis and went off to the high country to learn how to use them.[30]

As in the other mountainous, cold-weather regions of the United States, the ski boom had already arrived in Colorado by the early 1930s. Crested Butte, Steamboat Springs, Winter Park, Wolf Creek Pass, and other sites around the state began using the lure of great snow and sunny winter weather to draw area youngsters by the thousands into the new sport.[31] This, in turn, shone a new and heroic light on the hardy breed of local Colorado outdoor enthusiasts who had been using skis to get around the region for decades.

One of those robust ski pioneers was famed Rocky Mountain National Park ranger Jack Moomaw, another Estes Park eccentric whose daring reputation had been earned climbing and skiing the impossibly steep ridges above the town.[32] It was natural that Junior Duncan grew to idolize him. Gradually, Moomaw allowed the aspiring young skier to tag along with him on his backcountry adventures, to the point that Duncan delayed going to college in order to gain greater survival, climbing, and ski mountaineering expertise under the ranger's tutelage.[33]

In 1933, Jack Moomaw decided it was time Rocky Mountain National Park had its own ski run to rival the other, "less exciting" trails around the state. He therefore immediately set about on his own to cut the steep and challenging Hidden Valley Ski Trail. Predictably, the fiercely independent Moomaw failed to go through proper Interior Department channels for permission to remove the trees, and it almost cost him his job.[34] For Duncan, however, the new trail was a godsend from the first moment Moomaw visualized it, and just like the boys on the Thunderbolt in Adams, Massachusetts, he learned every inch by skiing and climbing it nearly every day.

One year later, Moomaw and other local skiing boosters began lobbying to hold the National Downhill Ski Championship on the new Hidden Valley Trail.[35] To the utter amazement of all but Moomaw, national ski officials agreed that the time had come to bring the big race to the Colorado Rockies. And so, on March 24, 1934, Joseph Duncan Jr. became the U.S. National Downhill Champion on the course nicknamed "The Suicide Trail" that his mentor had designed and cut.[36] The *Estes Park Trail* newspaper reported that Duncan "hurtled down the terrifying course . . . before a crowd of open-mouthed spectators," beating Dartmouth's Olympian Linc Washburn and Denver ski legend Frank Ashley by substantial margins, thereby launching his reputation as a western skiing star.[37]

After that, Junior Duncan grabbed life by the throat. He raced all over the east, including the Thunderbolt Trail at Mount Greylock, which he called a tougher run than Hidden Valley.[38] After a brief stint at Dartmouth, the restless student went to Europe as a tour guide, studied hotel management, and later spent two years teaching at Sun Valley Ski School in the late 1930s with Bromaghin, Rideout, Litchfield, and director Friedl Pfeifer.[39]

Growing in sophistication and experience, Duncan next managed one of Sun Valley's main lodges, and served as a mountain escort on behalf of Union Pacific for the rich and famous visiting the ski area. He also met and married a beautiful and popular socialite named Audrey Kilvert, a divorcee who split her time between New York and Paris.[40] Soon, he too was moving in elite social circles.

Duncan's longtime friends speculated, however, that despite the glamorous turns his life had taken, he was and always remained a strong and mostly silent man of the mountains. His heart never lost touch with its Rocky Mountain roots.[41] Thus, in early 1942, Duncan unhesitatingly—perhaps even with relief—put aside the wealthy trappings of his civilian life and answered Minnie Dole's call to war. He became one of the first enlisted members of the Eighty-seventh Mountain Regiment at Fort Lewis, and was quickly recognized as among the most capable and popular troopers on the Canadian Rockies assignment. Now, finally back home in Colorado and serving as an officer with the MTG, the son of The Judge and the protégé of The Ranger began quietly to go about the business of becoming a leader himself.

Lieutenant Victor Eklund recalled traveling with his friend Duncan to Estes Park in 1943 on a weekend pass from Camp Hale. Junior had volunteered to show Eklund and his wife around his hometown and Rocky Mountain National Park. "He was a great tour guide, showed us everything of natural beauty there was to see, but believe it or not he failed to mention that he had won the national ski championship right there at Hidden Valley. He never said a thing. I only found out about it later. He exuded this tough, quiet confidence without ever once bragging about his accomplishments. Bragging? What am I saying? He *wouldn't* talk about them. I remember thinking, after I found out about some of the things he'd done before the war, *this is some guy*. You couldn't get very close to him, but you also couldn't help being impressed by the thought, *here is a leader*. . . . You might say that Joe Duncan was just one of those guys who was made for the ski troops."[42]

৪০৫৪

The wisecracking, street-smart Rudy Konieczny picked up at Hale where he had left off at Paradise and Banff, having the time of his life. According to Sergeant David Burt of Stowe, Vermont, a new and subsequently close friend of Rudy's in Company 87-F and the MTG, Rudy was really coming into his own as a leader when the Eighty-seventh Regiment arrived at Camp Hale.[43] However unobtrusive he might have appeared on the mission to the Columbia Ice Fields, Rudy's personality was pumped back up to its usual size in the thinner air of Colorado.

"Rudy absolutely loved the idea that as a kid who never finished high school," said Burt, "he was now an instructor of college guys trying to learn skills from him. That really tickled him. He turned into a good teacher, too."[44] And teaching in the ski troops was *good* duty. Many of the instructors lived at Cooper Hill far from the watchful eyes of the officers at Camp Hale, skiing by day and helping themselves to the contents of the beer keg hidden in the rafters of their rustic quarters each evening.[45]

Burt also recalled that Rudy suddenly discovered his singing voice as his status and confidence grew. "We all loved to sing our mountain songs, parodies and such that the glee club made up," he continued. "It was part of the bonding and the culture of skiers at that time to sing together as a group. Well, Rudy had some of his own songs, some really bawdy, rough ones. I remember we'd be out driving on an MTG detail, and he'd just start belting them out. He loved to sing, but sometimes I think he was kind of testing me, to see what my reaction would be. I guess he might have wanted to know if I was some stuffed shirt—and believe me, we had a couple of those—or if I was really one of the guys. That's how we became such good friends."[46]

Some of Rudy's other shenanigans left his army buddies shaking their heads. "He sent home close-up photographs from Utah somewhere of a bull moose," recalled his brother Adolph. "Rudy explained in his letter that his friends had warned him not to get too close since it was rutting season and that the animal could easily stomp him to death, but he just laughed at them and told them it was the moose that should be worried if it dared to charge such a well-trained mountain trooper."[47]

Aside from confidence and ability, Rudy was blessed with another attribute that served him well as a member of the Tenth Mountain Division. "The guy didn't need any sleep," said Burt. "He could cram as much activity into one day as anyone I've ever known. And there was plenty to do in Colorado."[48] Without a steady girlfriend, Rudy was free to participate in the Tenth's "weekend bacchanals," as trooper Chuck Hampton referred to them.[49] "As I remember it, the boys from Adams seemed to be really enjoying life," continued Adolph Konieczny. "They were romantic figures with their skis and their uniforms, and the girls loved that."[50]

The ski troops quickly became one of the glamour outfits of the U.S. Army. National magazines and newspapers ran feature stories (including an alluring recruitment piece published in the *New York Times* in December 1942 that listed Rudy Konieczny as among the top international "skiing stars" training in Colorado for service as a "fighting mountaineer").[51] Newsreel appearances of white-clad troopers skiing or marching sharply in formation were common. Hollywood even used Camp Hale as the backdrop for a feature film.[52] And the more attention they got, the crazier the stunts pulled by the troopers seemed to become. That trend was highlighted by the night several Tenth Mountaineers (led by future Olympian Steve Knowlton) used the eight-story atrium lobby of the Brown Palace Hotel in Denver for a spontaneous display of rappelling technique off the high balconies.[53] Hotel management was not enthralled by the fraternity prank, but the bystanders at the bar—who no doubt included several attractive females—probably were.

Not to be outdone, glee-clubber Charles Bradley (now of the Tenth Recon) worked out a routine to end his rock-climbing classes in which a mock struggle would be staged on a high cliff between an instructor and a straw-filled Tenth Mountain trooper uniform. From a distance, it always appeared to horrified students and observers that the instructor had simply lost patience with a trooper, and in a fit of frustration, tossed him off a cliff.[54] Sophomoric as it may have been, it got them every time.

And then there was the crew of mountain troopers who took charge of a flock of carrier pigeons the army had in its wisdom delivered to Camp Hale in 1943. Since the birds experienced difficulties sustaining flight at high altitude, the mountaineers purportedly amused themselves by having the birds walk their messages back and forth across the camp "like miniature Western Union boys."[55] At times, it must have seemed that the only thing missing from the Pando campus was the football stadium.

ഩറ൬

Ralph Bromaghin and Charles McLane, meanwhile, had finally decided to take a leap of faith. The only remaining noncoms from among their friends at Fort Lewis, they at last applied for Officer's Candidate School, and were each lucky enough to find their way back to Camp Hale upon the successful completion of their training. Both were immediately reassigned to the new Eighty-sixth Mountain Regiment, which was being filled out, with members of the Eighty-seventh expected to impart the same espirit de corps to the new recruits as they had developed at Rainier.[56]

According to Paul Kitchen and Dan Pinolini, both of 86-I (one of the record number of units with which roving instructor Ralph Bromaghin served), enduring Lieutenant Bromaghin's learning curve as an officer wasn't always a pleasurable experience for the men serving under him. "In figuring out how to exercise authority over the same guys he had skied with as an enlisted man," said Kitchen, "I think Bromaghin struggled. From my enlisted man's point of view, like any officer, he could come off as—and I'm resorting to the army vernacular here—a real prick. He nailed some guys for picky stuff that he might have let go if he wasn't trying to prove that, if necessary, he could be a hard-ass. Gradually, I think he learned how to balance his new authority with the personal relationships he had with several of the men serving under him. . . . He took himself very seriously, though, and some of the guys really hated that."[57]

"I think that particular problem for guys returning from OCS was universal in the ski troops," added Pinolini. "There was definitely a period of adjustment for many of the officers as they tried to work out how to preserve both protocol and friendships at the same time. For the most part, we worked it all out without too many hard feelings. But there were some."[58]

Bromaghin and McLane were now full-fledged members of the cadre of young officers (many of whom were Tenth Recon or MTG members, including Woodward, Bradley, Watson, and the Laffertys), who would be expected to lead the division into battle. Under such circumstances, considering the weight of their new responsibilities, the two did the most rational thing that occurred to them. They re-formed the glee club and began performing several times a month around the Denver area.[59]

On the weekends, the old Paradise gang would frequently go to Sumers' Ranch, owned by Ralph Lafferty's father-in-law George Sumers, overlooking the Roaring Fork River. There, they could hike, climb, or ski all day, and the unattached could flirt all evening with the young ladies who flocked there knowing that mountain troop officers would be present. The ranch became a popular home away from home for many of them, and served as a warm-weather alternative to nearby Aspen during the summer of 1943.[60]

"Brom really loved the ranch," recalled Ralph Lafferty, who was photographed with his friend as Bromaghin slouched on the front porch, painting a watercolor of a far-off mountain peak. "He could relax there. It was then when that deadpan sense of humor of his really came out." Bromaghin once showed up at Sumers' raving about a beautiful roadside view he had seen on the way over from Hale that had really appealed to his artistic sensibilities. "He described a small boy walking along the road with the glow of the mountains behind him," continued Lafferty, "just as if it were a painting. He was so sincere about it, we were all captivated." The scene had been so compelling, Bromaghin added as an afterthought, that he had been moved to stop the car, get out, and "boot that little boy right in the ass" to make sure he wasn't just dreaming it. Bromaghin's friends roared. In the same fashion that W. C. Fields delivered his diatribes against dogs and children, the big lieutenant never even cracked a smile.[61]

"Naturally, we spent a lot of time in the bars and restaurants around Aspen," Lafferty went on. "Bromaghin loved the places that had pianos, like the pub in Georgetown near Loveland Pass. It gave him a chance to cut loose with his music, and hide from the bar check when it came." In addition to bumming cigarettes, avoiding bar tabs was apparently one of Bromaghin's other great talents. "One time at the Jerome Hotel bar in Aspen, we were really getting on him about that, me especially," said Lafferty. "So Ralph finally volunteered to buy a round of drinks. About halfway through my Aspen Crud, which was a frozen milkshake that I usually ordered with a single or double shot of whiskey, I began to feel a little happier than usual. Bromaghin waited until I'd finished, leaned over, and told me I'd just drank about a twelve-shotter. I don't know how I walked out of there, but I never did ask Ralph to buy me another mixed drink after that."[62]

☙❧

Jake Nunnemacher took to Colorado in the same manner as all the other altitude-starved easterners and midwesterners. Every available moment not spent marching and training at Hale was passed skiing at Cooper Hill, Climax, Winter Park, Loveland, or Aspen with his many new friends, among them John Tripp, Pepi Tiechner, and Jake's frequent University of New Hampshire racing opponent, Steve Knowlton.[63]

Of all Jake's new army buddies, however, one in particular stood out as a truly outstanding mountaineer and outdoorsman. David Brower had come to Camp Carson as a buck private at the advanced age of thirty, already a prominent member of the Sierra Club. At age fifteen, he discovered and had named after him a new species of butterfly in California.[64] Now, fresh from having accomplished the first ascent of the sacred Navajo mountain known as Shiprock in western New Mexico, the northern California native who would later become one of the twentieth century's leading environmentalists was overjoyed to meet a kindred spirit in the form of Jacob Nunnemacher.[65] "We had instant rapport," recalled Brower in his autobiography, especially after Brower learned that Jake had read the book he edited for the University of California Press, *Manual of Ski Mountaineering.*[66]

Despite Brower's climbing experience and expertise, it was Jake who was regarded as the real skiing expert of their little group, which moved together to Camp Hale in early 1943. "One of our great amusements," wrote Brower, became "our weekend opportunities to ski on Cooper Hill, just above Tennessee Pass. I had never been expert in downhill and never learned about skiing on narrow trails through the forest. . . . [My assistant squad leader] Paul Harlow and I became much better than we really were simply by following Jacob Nunnemacher down the forest aisles of Cooper Hill, doing what he did much faster than we would have otherwise dared."[67]

84

Even as Jake adjusted to the excitement of his new environs and the exuberant personalities of his new ski buddies, however, his main preoccupation still remained Jean. That first winter at Pando, he made up his mind that there was no reason to postpone their nuptials, and in May, Jacob and Jean were married.

"The ceremony took place," Jean remembered fondly, "in a small, cozy chapel in Whitefish Bay, Wisconsin. The Saint Monica School Children's Choir, of which I had been a member years earlier, sang beautifully. Jacob's brother Hermann was his best man, and my sister Peggy was my maid of honor. Almost all of our friends had by this time left or graduated from school, many of them already in training or overseas. It was really just a family affair. Owing to the war, it was a strange beginning of a beautiful marriage."

"Jake was so excited by the marriage and the idea that I could now spend all my time with him in the Colorado Rockies," Jean continued, "that we headed straight there after a brief stop in Hot Springs. I agreed we should finish our honeymoon spring skiing at Winter Park, which turned out to be an amusing, if not a very unique choice. We arrived to find several other Tenth Mountain Division couples, including John Tripp and his future wife, Rene, doing the same. Ski mountaineering became the basis for a close friendship among the four of us."[68]

Jean moved to Denver to live with family friends while Jake trained at Hale during the week. The treacherous road conditions between Denver and Pando, however, soon convinced the couple to set up housekeeping in the old mining town of Leadville, just over Tennessee Pass about fifteen miles from Camp Hale. It was there in 1882 that Oscar Wilde claimed to have seen a sign on a saloon wall that quintessentially reflected the spirit of Colorado and the American West. "Please Do Not Shoot the Piano Player," it read in its Americanized form. "He Is Doing His Best."[69]

"What does a twenty-year-old bride do in Leadville, a ghost town full of old mines, while her new husband soldiers?" asked Jean rhetorically. "I read. I hiked up into the abandoned silver and gold mines, I explored the Opera House, a thriving theater in its heyday when Leadville was expected to become the capital of Colorado. I marveled at the treeless little town surrounded by the most beautiful mountains in the country, and read my history books."[70]

Unfortunately, Jean recalled, while Leadville and Aspen remained relatively pristine even with the infusion of wartime traffic, Pando did not. The whistle-stop town with clean air and gorgeous alpine vistas rapidly deteriorated into a high-elevation smog bowl, plagued by coal pollution. "Hale was beautiful, with all those mountains surrounding it," remembered Rudy

Konieczny's buddy David Burt. "But some real problems developed. The coal pollution from the trains and the mountain stoves just hung in that valley, and almost everyone developed a chronic cough known as the 'Pando hack.'"[71]

As colorful and benign as the ailment sounded, the Pando hack was no joke. For some, it was nothing more annoying than a daily morning coughing fit. For others, it was the start of a serious, sometimes life-threatening lung infection. Despite months of acclimation at high elevation, and in spite of being in the best physical condition of his life, Jake Nunnemacher was among those who developed a dangerous respiratory condition at the newly christened "Camp Hell" in the late spring of 1943.

"I moved onto the base to take care of Jacob while he was in the hospital," remembered Jean. "There were so many serious lung cases that I was hired to assist the visiting families of hospital patients in finding their way around the camp." Jake's condition steadily improved as summer approached, "although why the army chose not to bring these sick boys down to a lower altitude for recuperation is beyond my understanding," she continued. Jake remained hospitalized for weeks, as his fellow division members spent their weekdays training and their weekends tramping the Colorado Rockies in search of varying types of adventure.[72]

As had been the case at Rainier, the incongruity of the swashbuckling lifestyle being pursued in Colorado by the ski troopers—compared with the deadly hardships being endured by many other members of the U.S. Armed Forces in 1943—was not lost on the boys at Hale. "We were very well aware of the brutality going on in both the Atlantic and Pacific theaters," recalled Burt. "We didn't feel guilty about our enjoyment of Colorado, however, for two reasons. First, we assumed that we were being readied to face some pretty tough action ourselves at some future point, and we were right. Second, although it sounds in retrospect like it was all just a lot of fun, and the weekends frequently were, the weekly training regimen we went through at Hale would not have been agreeable at all to most members of the service."[73]

In support of Burt's latter point, on a visit to Hale that year, division "founder" Minnie Dole described accompanying troops on maneuvers into the mountains that surrounded the camp. After climbing three thousand vertical feet up Homestake Peak, on skis and loaded down with heavy packs, the men enjoyed an evening under the stars at a temperature of twenty-five degrees below zero. When Dole awoke after a fitful night of sleep, he recalled not being sure if the men with him were sleeping or frozen to death. He was relieved to see them stirring.[74]

The Homestake maneuvers lasted several more days at similar temperatures. While most of the participants handled the conditions well, and in the process advanced the existing body of knowledge regarding high-elevation winter survival, hundreds of cases of frostbite were also reported.[75] The steady trickle of troopers prematurely heading down to Hale to seek treatment for frozen extremities jokingly became known as "the retreat from Moscow," in remembrance of the ignominious withdrawals from frozen Russia of both Napoleon in the prior century and the Nazis in the previous year.[76]

The maneuvers, challenging as they were, also culminated with a most dangerous flourish. Division artillery was used to unleash an avalanche (à la the World War I mountain warfare techniques used in the Dolomites) that sent millions of tons of snow crashing through the ice of Homestake Lake. The resulting cascade of displaced water and ice appeared for a few brief moments as though it might threaten the lives of the troopers and officers camped out near the shore. Luckily—and it may indeed have been a matter of pure luck—no one was injured.[77]

Other, equally painful training exercises took place regularly back down at camp. Marching out to the rifle range on a subzero day, for instance, would invariably result in abject misery for perspiring troops. Once out at the range, their wet clothing would freeze as they stood, knelt, or lay on the snow, frequently resulting in shivering so intense that aim became a remote aspiration. Mountaineer Paul Petzoldt was eventually ordered to give instructional talks on the proper way to layer clothing, minimizing the ordeal, but not eliminating it.[78]

Moreover, mountain training in the Tenth consisted mainly of climbing with enormous loads, whether on skis or with the help of pitons and ropes, up the sides of cliffs. Those activities became quite a chore in arctic-like temperatures. Only true devotees of the outdoors in winter could tolerate such conditions, let alone enjoy them.[79] As Bob Meservey pointed out, many recruits looking for fun and glamour by joining the ski troops "were shocked to find out that it *was* the infantry, but in the cold with a heavier pack."[80]

"The training we received," David Burt continued,

> included several series of physical and mental endurance tests that weeded out those whose biological make-up, regardless of their level of fitness, compromised their ability to operate at altitude and in extreme cold. Those who remained, after a while, became very secure in their physical abilities. We knew what we were capable of handling, although sometimes it took an iron constitution to get through those tests. One night

on top of Homestake, I recall a temperature of about fifty-two degrees below zero.

On the other hand, I want to stress how lucky many of us felt about what we were doing. All in all, we had the good fortune of being able to forget, even for a few hours at a time, that there was a war on. That is a luxury that a lot of our fellow servicemen did not have, and it remains my recollection that most of us appreciated that fact, or should have.[81]

Be that as it may, and despite the introduction of at least a modicum of army discipline into the ski troop regimen since the wild days at Paradise, there was still a feeling among a good many of the new division's members that they had joined a rigorous fraternity of outdoorsmen rather than a wartime military unit. Combat was only a vague abstraction lurking somewhere beyond the horizon, as thoughts of killing and dying do not come easily on the tops of Colorado mountain peaks overlooking vast, untracked fields of powder snow.

Thus, though intellectually aware of the seriousness of being part of an infantry unit, Jake Nunnemacher was itching to get back to being tested and challenging himself as an athlete in the Colorado high country. After a few weeks on his back, the bored patient began pacing the infirmary at Hale, anxious to return to the mountains. "I don't know if I would characterize Jacob's attitude as being disappointed on missing out on the fun," said Jean, "but it is fair to say that he was very eager to resume both his training and his exploration of the Colorado Rockies. Neither of us, of course, had any inkling that his lung condition was about to spare him a very difficult ordeal."[82]

For the rest of the Eighty-seventh Regiment, the days of being so far removed from the war were about to come to a very abrupt end.

From Alaska to Austin

IN JUNE 1943, THE EIGHTY-SEVENTH REGIMENT UNEXPECTEDLY RECEIVED OR-ders to depart Camp Hale for Fort Ord on the California coast, where its members (including Rudy Konieczny) were puzzled over receiving the news that they would now be given training in amphibious landings.[1] Less than two months later, they shipped out to the newly liberated island of Adak in the U.S. territory of Alaska. There, they prepared for an invasion of another rugged island in the Aleutian chain held by the Japanese, Kiska.[2]

The Aleutians were the farthest north that the dagger of Japanese conquest had penetrated, and the continued presence of the Imperial Japanese Army on Kiska was a deep embarrassment to America. The Eighty-seventh was a key part of the task force charged with evicting them.[3]

"After all that time spent training in the mountains, there was an air of unreality over the fact that we were about to enter combat," said David Burt.

"Who knows? Maybe we were just so damn nervous that we were in denial. Whatever the case, we kind of tried to treat the experience like an extension of Camp Hale." For Burt and some other, unnamed members of Rudy's Company 87-F, that effort included surreptitiously dropping CO_2 cartridges down the chimney of a stove in a tent where their captain was giving a combination pep talk and briefing to the enlisted men on Adak. The explosion blew the top off the heater and shot black soot all over the tent, covering the briefing papers and the captain, who nearly jumped through the tent roof after the explosion. "He wasn't too happy with us," admitted Burt. "We paid the price and buckled down to prepare seriously for action after that. That bang sure broke the tension, though."[4]

A few days later, the Eighty-seventh hit the beaches of Kiska in what would prove to be both a brutal and surrealistic introduction to life and death in the combat zone. America's mountain troops were in the war.

"The weather was just awful," Burt continued. "There was cold, bitter-hard rain, dense fog, and absolutely brutal wind. To wash your hair, all you had to do was stand outside for thirty seconds, and nature did the rest." When Burt and Rudy landed, they headed up into the steep, coastal mountains. "As I recall, we ran up those peaks, but when we got up there we couldn't see a thing because of the fog. It was quite eerie. Rudy was a member of a rifle team, and they went out ahead. I don't know what happened out there, and I don't think any members of our group were involved, but we heard shots all night and the next morning we found out what a mess it had been."[5]

The Eighty-seventh had been victimized by bad weather, substandard intelligence information, and the inexperience of its officers. The Japanese were gone, having vacated the island some three weeks prior to the arrival of the Americans, slipping through a supposedly impregnable U.S. naval blockade. They left behind only their mines and booby traps.[6] Meanwhile, patrols had been sent into the fog by officers of the Eighty-seventh to make contact with the enemy. They were given orders to shoot anything that moved, without being told that other members of the Eighty-seventh and elements of the famous Canadian "Devil's Brigade" had been issued similar orders.[7] When two groups of U.S. mountain troops met in the rainy, foggy darkness of Kiska on what they perceived to be opposite sides of the line, the results were tragic.

According to Sergeant Burt, "when dawn broke the next morning, it was still very foggy, and we had all heard rumors of the friendly fire problems. I remember an officer giving one of the members of our light machine gun team, Stan Gosnay, an order to fire on figures he saw moving at the top of the ridge above us. To his credit, Stan refused, even when the officer threatened him with court-martial. He just kept repeating, 'I can't identify them, sir, and I won't fire.' Of course, they turned out to be our own guys. One of them might have been Rudy, for all I know. That was Kiska."[8] The more acerbic troopers would later joke bitterly about some of the officers having suffered from "optical Aleutians."[9]

It was a sobering experience for all who took part. Between the friendly fire and the explosives left behind by the Japanese, nearly two dozen men of the Eighty-seventh died (many of them members of Companies I and K), and many more were wounded.[10] Ruso Perkins of 87-I recalled that "the guy right next to me took a bullet through the helmet that killed him. It was even tougher to find out later that the shot hadn't been fired by the enemy. There's not much to say about that. We were very inexperienced, and it was just a damn shame it happened that way."[11] Captain George Earle summed it up another way: "The enemy on Kiska was Kiska."[12]

Through it all, however, Rudy Konieczny—who was serving at the time under his old skiing nemesis from the days on the Thunderbolt, the mildly eccentric and fun-loving Lieutenant Robert Livermore—retained his sense of humor. Livermore, one of Minnie Dole's original ski troop planners who now amused himself by keeping a tame Arctic blue fox in his tent on Kiska, recalled a strange order that their platoon received from battalion headquarters.[13] During a cold and vicious downpour, as they waited for the Japanese attack that never came, instructions were received to march out and clean the garbage off a ridge recently vacated by two other companies.

"This would have seemed the last straw," said the former Olympian Livermore, until Sergeant Rudy Konieczny laughed and put the detail in perspective. "When I get home and my children ask: What did you do in the war, Daddy," announced Rudy with over-exuberant pride, he would now be able to tell them "I policed up Kiska, son."[14] The laughing troopers proceeded to clean up the ridge in the rain, in much better humor than they would have been had it not been for Rudy's morale boosting. "He was a model sergeant in that way," said Burt, "and both his men and his officers appreciated it, especially under those horrible circumstances we faced on Kiska."[15]

Very little has been written or discussed over the years about the emotional toll inflicted on soldiers who are the instruments of friendly fire deaths. Suffice it to say that some ski troopers returned from the Aleutians profoundly changed and psychologically battered. Even those not directly involved in the incident were deeply affected by having finally experienced the harsh and unpredictable realities of soldiering during wartime. In the correct spirit, all were welcomed back to the United States and to Camp Hale that autumn as heroes who had "taken" Kiska. They arrived on the island ready to do so, and charged headlong into their mission without the knowledge that the Japanese were gone. For those who were there, the lessons learned were in many ways as difficult as if they had faced a well-armed enemy. "We all found out," Burt summed it up succinctly, "how easy it is to get killed in a war zone."[16]

Despite the generosity of most of their comrades in patting the members of the Eighty-seventh on the back for having endured a tough assignment under near-impossible circumstances, however, incidents would occasionally arise demonstrating that the stigma of having served on Kiska still lingered just below the surface, and would continue to do so for years afterward. At least one trooper of the Eighty-sixth, who requested anonymity, recalled tearfully his regret over having used the term "buddy killer" in a heated argument on an unrelated topic with a returning member of the Eighty-seventh that fall. "I don't know why I resorted to saying such a despicable thing," he said, tears welling in his eyes, "but I've regretted doing it for a long, long time. I think it really hurt the guy, and I'm so sorry for that. It was awful, the worst thing I've ever said."[17]

☙℃

Back at Hale, Jake Nunnemacher wrote a letter to his father in late August 1943 explaining that he had finally recovered from his lung ailment, and commenting on the Aleutian mission he had missed. "The fall of Kiska was amazing," he wrote, "but I am so thankful that so many of my friends in the Eighty-seventh were spared thereby."[18]

The overt purposes of Jake's letter appear to have been to say thank you for a substantial cash gift, and to report to Father Nunnemacher that he had at last been accepted as a member of the prestigious Tenth Recon. In conveying this news, Jake took pains to reassure his father that his new assignment was not a dangerous one intended to assuage any guilt over not having gone to Kiska:

> We are solely a non-combat training group organized for the purpose of instructing troops anywhere in the country or Canada in the multi-phased skills of mountain combat. These skills will include such things as rock climbing, mule packing, and skiing. . . . Although we are composed of

about 160 men chosen mostly for knowledge of climbing or skiing, each has to go through much training in all the other unfamiliar fields. Next week we begin training the 10th Light Division recently organized at Hale. A battalion per week (550 men) for at least six weeks. We shall bivouac with each group from Monday until Saturday. Our roster looks like a who's who of skiing and climbing. It's funny to see such names as Pfeifer, Matt, Foegger or Schneider on a K.P. list! Our 1st Sergeant is [my former Dartmouth coach] Walter Prager![19]

In a much more revealing moment, however, Jake took the opportunity to follow up his good news about the Tenth Recon by getting an important issue off his chest. He asserted plainly to his father that he did not believe that he was underachieving by being an enlisted man in the ski troops. This declaration was undoubtedly an answer to his father's concerns that Jake had placed too much emphasis on outdoor activities at the expense of developing his academic skills at Dartmouth, his business experience at Galland Henning, and his leadership credentials in the army. Jake reassured his father—with more than a hint of defensiveness—that his drive for success was very much intact despite having made the decision not to seek an officer's commission in a different and perhaps less dangerous branch of the service. "I like the work a lot, and though I'm still a Pfc., I'd rather be that in the 10th (or the Eighty-seventh) than a Lt. in some ordinary outfit. Don't interpret this to mean that I've lost all initiative to better myself, but rather that I value certain things very highly above rank. The war will end some day, and then these values will again assume their presently maligned positions."[20] The warmth soon returned to Jake's writing, though, as he jokingly promised to send an amphibious jeep to his father for the summer regatta if he could manage it.

When Jean Nunnemacher returned to Colorado in the autumn of 1943 after a summer back in Wisconsin, she and Jake took an apartment in Glenwood Springs, northwest of Aspen and Hale. There, Jean volunteered at the landmark Glenwood Springs Hotel, which had been converted into a troop hospital, as Jake completed his training.[21] Then, with the coming of the first snows that fall, they began a series of adventures together that would prove to be highlights of both their lives.

First came the Tenth Recon trip to Little Cottonwood Canyon near Salt Lake City, where a ski clinic on avalanche safety was held at Alta. "As luck would have it," recalled Jean, "an avalanche came down and blocked the only road out of the canyon as we were preparing to head back to Colorado. We were all forced to ski for two more days in some of the driest, lightest, powder snow I've ever seen. We prayed that the road would stay closed longer, because we had the army's permission to stay as long as it took to clear. It was so beautiful, I still smile thinking about those few days Jacob and I had together in Utah."[22]

When they returned to Hale, Jake was assigned to a special teaching unit with Sergeant Friedl Pfeifer, who had already begun working with the residents of Aspen on plans to develop Ajax Mountain as a ski area.[23] "At the time," remembered Jean, "Aspen was almost completely abandoned as a town. . . . Most of the Victorian homes that were left were crumbling to the ground, and even the Jerome Hotel was in disrepair."[24]

"Friedl and Jacob got to be good friends," she continued. "On the weekends, when the two of them and the rest of their group were surveying the mountain, I went along with my climbing skins, and skied on the ridges above the Roch Run to my heart's content. It was an amazing experience, and one that has stayed fresh in my mind, bringing back wonderful memories each time I go back to Aspen."[25]

So many members of the Tenth Mountain Division recall an intimate affiliation with the efforts to turn Aspen into an international ski resort that it is difficult to discern who really participated in a meaningful way. Indisputably, Pfeifer worked on the project with two Dartmouth alumni he had overseen at the Sun Valley Ski School, Percy Rideout and John Litchfield. It is equally clear that Jake Nunnemacher was allied with Friedl and his fellow Dartmouth grads as they planned the future of the resort with the town fathers, albeit as a junior member of the team.

According to Ralph Lafferty and Percy Rideout, Pfeifer had also tapped another of his Sun Valley compatriots, Ralph Bromaghin, as one of those whose involvement after the war in the development of Aspen would be indispensable. "It is my clear recollection," said Lafferty, "that Ralph Bromaghin was the fourth member of that group of Sun Valley skiers—Pfeifer, Rideout, and Litchfield—who were going to lead the effort to build Aspen into a world-class resort town when the war ended. Friedl himself confirmed that when he approached me after the war on behalf of primary investor Walter Paepcke to see if I would be interested in getting involved."[26]

Rideout offered an even more emphatic confirmation. "Bromaghin was more intimately involved in the project than anyone but Friedl and myself. Ralph wasn't one of the original *four*. He was one of the original *three*."[27]

Moreover, according to Rideout, the Aspen project was extremely important to Bromaghin because it symbolized to him the possibility that he would accomplish something both lasting and personally satisfying. "We were both pretty happy-go-lucky when we were on skis," he recalled, "but both Brom and I had a serious side. We each felt that to that point we hadn't necessarily lived up to our potential, and we wanted to do more with our lives. We discussed those issues quite specifically, and I hope it gets remembered that Ralph Bromaghin was there right from the start. He loved Aspen, and visualized it as this country's premier ski resort in the same way that Friedl and I did."[28] Duke Watson also concurred. "I discussed the future with Bromaghin in 1944, too. In a strange way, Ralph seemed to view the Aspen Mountain project as his best shot at a small piece of immortality, his way to be remembered for doing something special."[29]

There are also those who recall many other members of the ski troops as having been "Aspen visionaries." "Anyone who was part of the Aspen Detachment from Fort Lewis in 1942," asserted Eighty-seventh Regiment officer and Tenth Recon ski instructor Nick Hock, "can claim to have been in on the ground floor. It wasn't hard to spot the potential, and we all kept a close eye on what was going on there over the next two years."[30]

Suffice it to say, during late 1943—as Rudy Konieczny returned from Kiska to rejoin the MTG and explore the Aspen ridges on skis, as Jake Nunnemacher continued his teaching in the Tenth Recon, and as Lieutenant Ralph Bromaghin served as a roving skiing and machine gun instructor for the Eighty-sixth Regiment—all the free time of anyone involved directly or indirectly with the Aspen plan was spent right there in town. "That's where you frequently would have found them," Jean recalled. "At the foot of Ajax Mountain, looking up and dreaming."[31]

෨෭

With so many of their activities centered in Aspen, there arises the intriguing question of whether Ralph Bromaghin, Jake Nunnemacher, and Rudy Konieczny knew one another as comrades. The answer is unquestionably "yes."

Rudy and Jake had skied against one another in New England, and served together in the MTG/Tenth Recon. Jean Nunnemacher had no specific recollection of them being good friends, but she speculated that because of their overlapping racing and teaching activities on the Thunderbolt and at Hale and Cooper Hill, the two were likely familiar with one another. Bob Meservey, who knew each one well, agreed.[32] Jean also suspected that Jake spent time with Ralph Bromaghin in relation to the Aspen project, and had a dim recollection of Friedl Pfeifer having introduced Jake to Bromaghin and several of his other Sun Valley friends.[33]

Similarly, Duke Watson asserted that Rudy Konieczny and Ralph Bromaghin were acquainted with one another, as were almost all of the original troopers assigned to the Eighty-seventh in the earliest days at Fort Lewis. That was especially true in regard to those who raced together in the 1942 Silver Skis competition on Rainier.[34]

Though there is nothing to confirm the sentimental notion that during the first weeks of the 1943–44 ski season, Ralph, Jake, and Rudy shared an afternoon together on the slopes of Aspen or an evening of relaxation in the Jerome Hotel bar, there is likewise nothing to prove that it did not happen just that way. "I knew them all," recalled John Woodward, "and they very well could have spent time together in Aspen."[35] Charles McLane knew all three, as well. "Each had his own circle of friends, but anything is possible. I think their common love for Aspen was the thing that could have brought the three of them together in the same place at the same time, just not in my presence. On the other hand, I'm not the best one to ask."[36] Sadly, since Friedl Pfeifer, Roy Deyle, David Brower, and so many of the others are gone now, the issue is and shall remain only the stuff of wistful speculation.

ℰᗝᑕℛ

As winter arrived and the war intensified, the MTG (along with selected members of the Tenth Recon) increased its profile as a mountain warfare teaching unit for the entire U.S. Army. Having completed the mission of helping to train their own division, members spread out across the United States to give mountaineering and skiing instruction to other specialized units.[37] Jake and Rudy each received assignments to teach winter mountain and survival skills to troops headed overseas, although at different facilities.

Jake Nunnemacher's assignment was to accompany a group that included Friedl Pfeifer, Florian "Flokie" Haemmerle, and his old Dartmouth teammate Bob Meservey to an army post some two hundred miles north of Green Bay in Sidnaw, Michigan, to train soldiers of other divisions en route to the battlefields of Europe.[38] "Frigid and desolate" were the words Jean used to describe the conditions she faced by joining Jake on this detail. They made the best of it, however. "Sidnaw," she wrote, "had little in its favor: one rundown motel, one tiny grocery and dry-goods store, and the daily Chippewa train that shook the two rooms we lived in. We had no running water, no central heat and no plumbing. A beautiful iron stove served us well, [though]. I cooked on it. It heated our pumped water and the furnished rooms. I loved it and the memories of entertaining beside it. But for three months the temperature that winter rarely was above minus twenty. There was so much snow, I [had to] ski down the rail tracks to [get to] the grocery store."[39]

"It was really cold, even by New England standards," recalled Meservey. "At the beginning, Jake, Friedl, and I slept side by side on plank beds with four-inch sides to hold the bushels of corn cobs that served as our mattresses. We were quartered at an abandoned CCC camp that the army had taken over, and the guys we were teaching were even more miserable than we were. It wasn't a particularly good assignment, but we did our best to get them ready to climb, ski, and do whatever else they might be called upon to perform in mountain combat."[40]

"Jacob was okay with the whole trip from the beginning, even before I arrived," Jean continued. "He may have still been smarting over not having gone to Kiska, so I think he figured he was paying his dues in Sidnaw. There was really only one thing that bothered him over everything else about being there. Florian Haemmerle just rubbed him the wrong way."

"Jacob basically got along with *everyone,*" she went on. "But he thought Haemmerle didn't show enough respect for women and was too outspoken about his disdain for the army."[41] The otherwise popular and hard-drinking, German-born Haemmerle made no secret of the fact that he hated Sidnaw with a passion, and was not the happiest or most enthusiastic member of the Tenth Mountain Division. That attitude was still very much in evidence in 1978 when the star instructor of Sun Valley told the *Idaho Mountain Express* that "the Army—those sons of a guns, they teach me nothing, I teach them everything."[42]

Haemmerle would eventually develop jaundice, which he claimed was the result of a yellow fever inoculation he received while teaching at the Seneca Rocks climbing school in West Virginia. He spent the next several years trying to regain his health, never seeing combat.[43] Ironically, Haemmerle returned to Sun Valley and eventually married one of Jean Nunnemacher's closest friends. He became a model husband and father for the remainder of his long life, according to Jean, changing 180 degrees from his days as a Don Juan.[44]

One of the benefits for Jake and Jean being in Michigan for several months was that with a weekend pass, they could drive down to Pine Lake to spend time with their families. "Friedl [Pfeifer] came home with us to Wisconsin on one or two of those weekends," Jean remembered, "and he loved the place.

That was very nice for Jacob, since he admired Friedl so much. He looked up to him, really. Those were some of Friedl's best days in the army, before he returned to Denver and unfortunately endured quite a family tragedy."[45]

Pfeifer returned to Camp Hale during the last week of January 1944, and reunited with his family in Aspen for dinner at the Jerome Hotel that weekend. His five-year-old son, Ricky, had a bad cold. A few days later, the cold had become a serious infection, eventually diagnosed as spinal meningitis. Friedl desperately tried to get a new type of medicine known as antibiotics from the army as his son lay delirious in a hospital bed in Denver, but by the time it was procured, it was too late. The boy died. Pfeifer was crushed.[46]

"Jacob truly did everything he could in trying to help Friedl through his grief," Jean recalled, "and I think Friedl appreciated his empathy. Even though Jacob had never known his own older brother Robert, who died at nine, he was well aware of his parents' suffering, and that was enough to sensitize him to what Friedl was going through."[47] Ralph Bromaghin was also among those who tried to assist the very private Pfeifer in getting back his bearings. Bromaghin, by then serving as the head of the Eighty-sixth Regiment's Second Battalion Ski School at Hale, traveled up to Salt Lake City with Friedl a few weeks following Ricky Pfeifer's death to race in the Alta Cup. Friedl won, at least for a few moments taking his mind off his heartbreaking loss.[48] It was to be the last official race of the Austrian champion's brilliant skiing career.[49]

∞CR

As the war raged on, in February 1944 thirty-three of the division's best ski mountaineers embarked on the legendary "Skier Traverse," a four-day expedition through one of the most rugged portions of the Colorado Rockies, from Leadville to Aspen.[50] Filmmaker John Jay—now a captain—led the party, which included no fewer than five mountaineers who remain among the greatest climbers and outdoorsmen the nation has ever produced: Paul Petzoldt (who had made the first winter ascent of the Grand Teton, and had already established the U.S. elevation record for climbing without oxygen on K-2 in the Himalayas); Ernest "Tap" Tapley (who along with Petzoldt would become one of America's most prominent wilderness survival educators of the twentieth century); Glen Dawson (who made the first ascent of Mount Whitney's treacherous East Face); Fred Beckey (who would be credited with more than one thousand first ascents in North America and set the world elevation record for skiing in 1955 at twenty-two thousand feet on the Khumbu glacier in Nepal);

and Bill Hackett (who accomplished the first ascent of the west buttress of Mount McKinley, and would become the first person to climb the highest peaks on five continents).[51]

According to prominent twenty-first-century ski mountaineer Lou Dawson, who retraced the route of the Skier Traverse on modern ski equipment in 2000, the original trip was "one of the most forward-thinking and aggressive ski traverses ever done in North American mountaineering. . . . [T]he troopers took a direct line and conquered every couloir, ridge and avalanche slope in their path . . . [carrying] 75-pound, steel frame rucksacks, or 90 pounds if you were the guy who hauled one of the group tents."[52] The traverse led through Darling Pass, Lost Man Creek, the jagged Williams Mountains, and down "Trooper Couloir" into Aspen, forty miles of challenging beauty.[53]

Amid all of the celebrated luminaries of ski mountaineering who accomplished the journey in 1944, however, it was a nineteen-year-old kid from upstate New York named Burdell "Bud" Winter who emerged as the detachment's rising star. "He was a big hulk of a guy," recalled fellow Tenth Recon member Bruce Macdonald, "and a *really* good skier."[54] The eager, hyperenergetic private, whom the more experienced troopers (tongues planted firmly in cheek) dubbed "Rugged Winter," still managed to impress the tough group with his skill and high-elevation stamina by spending a good deal of the Traverse cheerfully breaking trail at the head of the column.[55]

One mountaineer on the traverse clearly wasn't surprised by the skills demonstrated by Winter. That was Bill Hackett, whose life Winter had already saved on Mount Democrat, a nearby fourteen-thousand-foot peak. Skiing cautiously across a couloir near Democrat's summit a few weeks before, Hackett's weight had caused a layer of snow known as "wind-slab" to break free and avalanche some twenty-five hundred feet down the mountain. The only thing that prevented Hackett from accompanying the rocketing slab to his death was Bud Winter's ski pole. Winter, standing behind Hackett and seeing what was happening, threw himself to the snow at the base of a rock, held on with one arm, and extended his pole to Hackett with the other. It was an astonishing act of skill and quick thinking by a trooper barely out of high school, but already well on his way to becoming a master mountaineer.[56]

Young Bud Winter hailed from Schenectady, New York, where he grew up fishing, hiking, and skiing the Adirondacks. By age eighteen, he was both an accomplished junior ski racer and an experienced ski patroller, whose exaggerated forward lean on skis and reaching pole plant had earned him the nickname "pole-eater."[57] He joined the Tenth at Camp Hale in 1943 and was immediately assigned to the MTG and Tenth Recon, where he put his youthful enthusiasm to good use.

"What a trip!" Winter wrote in a letter home after the traverse, admitting that he may have "tired some of the other fellows out" by his rapid trail breaking.[58] He told of skiing six-mile runs in new powder, and noted excitedly that the great Petzoldt had invited him to join a Himalayan expedition after the war, his fondest dream come true.[59]

All in all, the assignment had been one of the most exciting adventures of Winter's life. "It was beautiful, and something I will never forget," he concluded.[60] That was likely true not only of the mountaineering and the comradeship, but also of the celebration at the Jerome Hotel bar the boys mounted upon their arrival in Aspen. Before the trip, Winter had admitted not knowing whether Aspen was "on the map or not." He knew it now.[61]

₭₩CC

While Jake Nunnemacher and the grieving Friedl Pfeifer resumed their own explorations of Aspen in the early spring of 1944, Bob Meservey left Sidnaw to join Rudy Konieczny on another Tenth Recon/MTG assignment near Seneca Rocks, West Virginia. There, the army had established its rock-climbing school and populated its ranks of instructors with many of the Tenth's other renowned ski mountaineers, including Duke Watson, David Brower, and Bil Dunaway (who would later achieve fame as a member of the first skiing party to descend Mont Blanc near Chamonix, France).[62]

Rudy Konieczny was by now acting the part of a senior member of the MTG with enormous self-assurance, according to those who knew him. "I can't really say whether Kiska changed Rudy," said David Burt, "but I can say that he seemed to come back even more confident and gung-ho than before. Maybe it was just his increasing maturity. He knew that there were a lot of guys looking up to him, just like it had been for him back home in Massachusetts, and I'm sure he was determined never to let them down. Whatever it was, Rudy became a 'follow me'–type leader, and a lot of people took notice."[63]

One who did was Colonel Robert Works, who was in charge of the MTG training activities in West Virginia.[64] Standing before a group of recruits on the banks of the Blackwater River, which had risen above flood stage, Works asked for a volunteer to demonstrate the proper way to set a line on the far bank. Rudy stepped forward immediately, took a rope, and jumped in. With a fair amount of effort, he crossed to the other side in the freezing, rushing water and came out smiling. "He didn't mind doing dangerous stuff like that," said Burt, who witnessed the incident. "I guess that's what makes a good ski racer, too. He kind of welcomed the challenge of it, the adrenaline, and he inspired a lot of guys to put their own fear aside and take the same attitude."[65]

As Bob Meservey remembered, "Rudy just exuded confidence, and he wore his rank and his experience well. He had developed this good-natured swagger about him. With Rudy, though, you never forgot that there was a very tough kid right under the surface. I distinctly remember thinking to myself that here is a guy you never want to get into a fight with, because no matter what happened, he'd figure a way to beat you."[66]

Corporal Meservey recalled one particular detail that involved hiking the woods of West Virginia with his older New England ski compatriots, Sergeant Konieczny and Lieutenant Livermore, to observe various training exercises. At night, they ate their rations around the campfire, talked over the day's activities, and slept out under the stars.

While Rudy was friendly to Meservey, Livermore was much more stiff and reserved, which the younger man speculated was a result of his concern over breaking officer–enlisted man protocol. Livermore and Rudy, however, were prewar friends and now old comrades from Kiska, and interacted in a much more informal way. The lieutenant, in fact, had grown to appreciate Rudy's wild ways and let Rudy be himself, protocol be damned. "My most lasting memory of that trip," Meservey wrote, "is Rudy singing snatches of popular songs that he used to break into as [the three of us] strode along, occasionally changing the lyrics to reflect his mood. It fitted his exuberant nature and D'Artagnan character . . . though Rudy really was a character unto himself."[67]

⁊◌ℭ

Although some members of the Tenth Recon and the MTG, such as Charles Bradley and Toni Matt, had been permanently assigned to far-flung training facilities in places such as Dutch Harbor, Alaska, many were back at Camp Hale with the rest of the division by March 1944.[68] What they found impressed them. After more than two years of training at high elevation, the Tenth had become one of the best-conditioned forces under Allied command. This was borne out by the division's completion of the "infamous" D-Series maneuvers that spring in the mountains around Pando. It was a "show us what you've got" demonstration for the army brass that tested the ability of soldiers to function outdoors in a high-elevation environment, under blizzard conditions and unrelenting subzero cold, for more than three full weeks. It is generally regarded as the most difficult set of division-wide training exercises the U.S. Army has ever conducted.[69]

"D-Series was just brutal," remembered Ralph Lafferty. "We had temperatures in the minus twenties and lower, several feet of snow on the ground, high winds, and difficult tactical challenges. Most of the boys never got inside for weeks at a time. It really tested you."[70] Of the twelve thousand troops that participated, hundreds suffered weather-related injuries. Frostbite became one of the most common miseries, as no fires were permitted during the maneuvers. On one night alone, more than one hundred cases had to be evacuated.[71]

During usual springs at Hale, snow depths averaged three feet on the flats and eight feet in the timbers. Thirty-foot drifts at the summits encircling the camp were common. In 1944, the snow was even deeper.[72] Under such conditions, the Tenth's mules, the division's principal means of equipment transport, got stuck in the drifts or refused to move. That meant difficulties in getting field rations to the freezing men, who sometimes went hungry for days.[73] "Later on in combat," Lafferty continued, "one of the frequent things you'd hear from an exhausted trooper would be the caustic comment, 'if this gets any worse, it'll be as bad as D-Series.'"[74]

D-Series was mainly a triumph for the members of the division, but a disaster for its top leaders. The vast majority of the superbly trained troops withstood the harsh conditions with few ill effects, prompting one commentator on military training to call the Tenth "the most elite U.S. Division of the Twentieth Century in terms of intelligence, scores, fitness, and training."[75] The evaluation by observers of the Tenth's highest command level, however, was less than stellar. Minnie Dole, who traveled to Colorado to critique the maneuvers for the army, was most disappointed in the lack of leadership exhibited by the division's new commander, the wildly unpopular Major General Lloyd Jones. The general was in ill health and suffering badly at high elevation, thoroughly compromising his ability to inspire confidence among his troops.[76]

Not everyone agreed that the troops had performed up to their capabilities, either. Monty Atwater, one of the division's most respected officers, who would go on to become a leading international expert on avalanche control, criticized many of the sportsmen-turned-officers for failing to recognize military skiing for the simple thing he believed it to be: a means of getting men and materiel from one place to another in difficult terrain and cold weather. No more, no less, and certainly not sport.[77]

Sensing that morale was sinking owing to both endless training with no clear mission in sight and incessant bickering over the division's performance in D-Series, Minnie Dole again went directly to army chief of staff General Marshall. The top American commander assured Dole that he still had confidence in the mountain troops as a valuable component of U.S. military strategy. Once again, however, he pointed out that he had only one mountain division, and wanted to hold it in reserve so that it would be available for deployment only under essential conditions. After nearly three years, Marshall was still counseling patience.[78]

Privately, according to Jean Nunnemacher, disappointment among the troops at Hale over Dole's lack of progress in securing a combat assignment for the division was far from unanimous. On June 6, 1944, the army opted to use rangers rather than mountain troops to scale the Pointe-du-Hoc cliffs above the D-day landing beaches at Normandy. The Tenth was thereby spared appalling casualties. Its members sat in the cool of the Rockies that day, following the news reports of the invasion on their radios along with the rest of the stateside population.

"No one in the division would ever admit that he didn't want to get into the war before it was over," Jean speculated, "but I got the distinct impression being around so many of them that there were those who wouldn't have minded at all if that's the way it worked out. The wives, I can tell you, were overjoyed that things seemed to be going so well in the European theater, and that maybe the boys wouldn't be needed after all."[79]

Jean's hopes in that regard were heightened by the decision that she and Jake had made that spring. Since each adored children and was eager to raise several, waiting to start their family seemed pointless, even considering the hardships that Jean might face were Jake to be called away. By May, she was able to give her husband the happy news that she was pregnant with their first child. "Jacob was absolutely thrilled, although a little apprehensive that he couldn't guarantee he could be with me in person throughout the pregnancy," she recalled. "We both knew, though, that our families would stand in for him if the army needed him elsewhere."[80]

☙❧

Late in the spring of 1944, according to Private Charlie Murphy (86-I), Lieutenant Ralph Bromaghin helped to organize what was to be the last ski race at Camp Hale for the Tenth. It was known optimistically as the First Annual Military Ski Championships, and was won by Clarence "Buster" Campbell, the first sergeant of the Eighty-seventh Regiment's Medical Detachment (and yet another member of the division to serve on the U.S. National and International Ski Federation [FIS] Ski Teams).[81] The remainder of the race standings are lost to history. What remains is additional evidence that Ralph Bromaghin had taken to heart his obligation as an officer to continue to build the division's esprit de corps, just as he had done with his glee club parodies as an enlisted man. "Lieutenant Bromaghin had some conceit about his skiing, I would have to say," recalled Murphy, "but he was good, and his enthusiasm for the sport was contagious. It must have been. I remember it sixty years later."[82]

Bromaghin, however, was still grappling with his "hard-ass" reputation even as he organized the ski race. The race, in fact, may in part have been an effort to overcome grumbling among the enlisted men over a D-Series incident in which Bromaghin had come upon a G.I. machine gunner who had fallen asleep on guard duty at his forward post.

Many would argue that the lieutenant's reaction was justified, in that he was charged with teaching men how to stay alive and to protect one another in future combat. What Bromaghin reportedly did to impress upon the young private the importance of maintaining alertness on the line was quietly to dismantle the gun and spread the pieces over and beneath the deep snow. He then woke the boy up roughly and instructed him to find and reassemble his weapon, and not to bother to report back until the task was completed.[83] In blizzard conditions, the enlisted man experienced a miserable ordeal searching for the gun parts that neither he nor his comrades would soon forget.

A hard lesson was learned from the incident by Bromaghin's platoon, according to Sergeant Don Linscott, another of the Adams, Massachusetts, volunteers.[84] But the machine gun episode and others like it (at least one veteran who preferred anonymity claimed that Bromaghin's indifference to the suffering of his less experienced charges during D-Series resulted in serious and permanent frostbite injuries) did little to endear Bromaghin to his troops. The lieutenant had already come to be viewed by many as—at best— a bewildering dichotomy. Understanding how the skiing watercolorist who had written all the division's parodies, and to whom David Brower referred as "a morale man's morale man," could revert at times to being so "regular army" was difficult.[85]

"Some might say that the machine gun incident was a case of an officer taking his job seriously, and making sure that the failure would not repeat itself for the good of everyone," said Linscott, who later served as an officer himself. "I suppose it could have been done with a trifle more subtlety, though, perhaps with a softer touch. You could easily say he went too far. But we were all learning how to do our jobs at the same time, trying very hard to do our best. Approach, I guess, is a matter of style."[86]

ℬℭ

In the summer of 1944, the division at last received orders to move out from Camp Hale. It was not, however, the assignment that most of its members had been anticipating. No commander in either the Atlantic or Pacific theater seemed to want a specialized, light infantry group like the Tenth, with its six thousand pack mules, dogsled teams, and motorized snow "weasels" but no jeeps or trucks.[87] Rather than a combat mission, therefore, the division was ingloriously ordered from its Colorado high-country home to the hot Texas prairie for regular flatland infantry training at Camp Swift near Austin.[88] This was the mountain man's version of hell, or so many of the men thought upon arriving straight from the Rockies at the dusty outpost in 110-degree heat.

All through the summer and autumn of 1944, as Allied troops swept through Europe toward Berlin and island-hopped across the Pacific toward Tokyo, reversing one fascist conquest after another, the members of the "former" mountain division marched in the unrelenting desert heat of the American Southwest. Morale plummeted further as heatstroke cases multiplied. "Coming down from that altitude," remembered Frank Prejsnar, "the human body is just not equipped to adjust immediately to long desert marches in that heat. Right after we arrived, guys who thought they were among the best-conditioned troops in the army found themselves collapsing along the roadside after just a few miles of marching with full packs."[89]

According to Tom Brooks—a rifleman with the Eighty-fifth Regiment and author of the highly regarded history of the Italian campaign, *The War North of Rome*—after surviving D-Series, being sent to Camp Swift was a stunning disappointment. Even though there were good attempts to revive the spirit of Camp Hale in Texas (such as when twenty-five yodeling troopers rappelled off the roof of the Hotel Stephen Austin, snarling traffic in downtown Austin for hours), the insult of flatland, desert training was simply too much to overcome.[90] When a general call was issued by the army for soldiers

105

wishing to switch to paratrooper units to replace losses in the Eighty-second and 101st Airborne sustained in Normandy, so many members of the Tenth applied that the division was forced to ban all transfers.[91]

More than wounded pride, the serious and growing concern among the deflated mountaineers was that the army was preparing to break up the Tenth in order to utilize its members as replacements for other, depleted divisions.[92] Jean Nunnemacher, who followed Jake down to Austin with Rene Tripp and some of the other army wives, recalled the anxiety that the boys felt as they waited for their next assignment.

"Everyone anticipated that something was going to happen, but there was nothing to be done about it but wait," she remembered. "Would the army really break them up after nearly three years of training together?" The answer was, of course it would if someone of proper rank deemed it advisable, whether Minnie Dole squawked or not. "Jacob found that question very worrisome," Jean continued. "Even those like him who had never seen action knew that one of war's worst-case scenarios is going into combat among strangers. But nobody seemed to need or want the Tenth as a group."[93]

As it turned out, that wasn't exactly the case. For better or worse, there was one general who would decide in the autumn of 1944 that he wanted the help of America's mountain troops after all.

General Clark and the War in Italy

GENERAL MARK CLARK, COMMANDER OF THE AMERICAN FIFTH ARMY FIGHTING its way up the spine of Italy as the back end of a "three front" strategy against the Nazis, remains one of the most controversial figures of the Second World War.[1] Though regarded by some as a good soldier and leader for his perseverance during the difficult and bloody fight to liberate German-controlled Italy, others view him as a selfish blunderer and a notorious waster of American lives.[2] Those in the latter camp often point to the costly Allied victory at Anzio (where confusion and the failure of command leadership resulted in extreme infantry casualties and the utter annihilation of Colonel William Darby's painstakingly trained rangers) and to the Rapido River engagement, an even bloodier fiasco in January 1944.[3]

At the Rapido, in a poorly conceived effort to draw enemy troops away from the Anzio beachhead prior to the Allied landing, Clark ordered the highly

decorated but depleted Thirty-sixth "Texas" Division to engage in two successive days of suicidal attacks against the strongest Nazi positions on the opposite shore.[4] Many members of the Thirty-sixth had been trained in mountain
warfare at schools in Lincoln, New Hampshire, and Buena Vista, Virginia, by
members of the Tenth Recon and MTG.[5] No amount of training, however,
could have prepared them for this assignment. Without provision for an avenue of escape in the event of their failure to secure a breakout, the few men
who made it alive to the other side of the river were overwhelmed and slaugh-
tered.[6] The attack ended when many troops, seeing what lay ahead of them,
eventually refused to move forward to the riverside.[7]

One of Clark's best subordinate commanders, Lieutenant General Lucian
K. Truscott Jr., wrote in his autobiography of the discussions he held with
Clark prior to the Rapido operation:

> Reverting to [the issue of] crossing the Rapido which we had discussed
> previously, General Clarke [sic] asked: "Would you be willing to undertake
> that Rapido crossing if those heights on either flank were under attack
> though not actually in our possession?" After some deliberation, I replied:
> "Yes, but those attacks should be so powerful that every German gun
> would be required to oppose them, for only one or two concealed 88s [a
> devastating Nazi artillery piece] would be able to destroy our bridges. I
> doubt our capability for making any such attacks." The General agreed
> and there our conversation ended. However, these conditions were not
> fulfilled when the 36th Infantry Division made the attempt to cross the
> Rapido a few weeks later, and the attempt was a costly failure.[8]

Reflecting upon the Rapido crossing some years later, Major General Fred
L. Walker—who had direct command over the Thirty-sixth and had argued
with his former War College student General Clark about the plan of battle
before being ordered to send his troops twice across the river[9]—wrote chillingly of Clark's willingness to hurl outnumbered men against an entrenched
enemy holding higher ground: "It was a tragedy that this fine Division had to
be wrecked . . . in an attempt to do the impossible. It was ordered across the
Rapido River . . . under conditions that violated sound tactical principles. The
German observers were on high ground from which they looked down on
every foot of area occupied by the Division. . . . All likely approaches to the
river were mined. . . . My conscience nagged me because I felt I was a party to
an undertaking that would lead to unnecessary losses of many fine men to no
purpose . . . [but] I had to obey the order I had received."[10]

The Thirty-sixth Division took more than fifteen hundred casualties in two days of fighting.[11] After the war, the State of Texas (at the urging of the surviving Texas National Guard members of the division and its officers) went so far as to ask Congress to review the matter to assess the possibility of criminal wrongdoing on the part of General Clark. Hearings were held in 1946, resulting in the general's full exoneration by the Senate Armed Services Committee, and there the matter officially ended.[12]

Accusations against Clark, however, were not limited to incidents relating to the Anzio invasion. He had also earned the animosity of many in the Italian theater when he opted for a triumphal march into Rome on June 4, 1944, swinging his army toward the principally undefended city rather than bottling up tens of thousands of German troops on Italy's western shores near Valmontone.[13]

Though morale was undeniably boosted on the U.S. and Allied home fronts as a result of the liberation of Rome, General Truscott seemed disgusted by both the decision and his commander's actions in seeking the spotlight. After Clark's speech to the people of Rome from Mussolini's old Capitoline Hill balcony, Truscott wrote that he "reckoned" Clark's statement that "this is a great day for the [American] Fifth Army" was correct, "but I was anxious to get out of this posturing and on with the business of war."[14] Clark's immediate superior, British commander of the Fifteenth Army Group General Sir Harold Alexander, was more pointed in his criticism of Clark's decision to ignore his orders to attack Valmontone in favor of moving against the ancient capital: "If he [Clark] had succeeded in carrying out my plan the disaster to the enemy would have been much greater; indeed, most of the German forces [south of Rome] would have been destroyed. . . . [The victory] was not as complete as might have been. . . . I can only assume that the immediate lure of Rome for its publicity value persuaded Mark Clark to switch the direction of his advance."[15]

Clark's triumphal march past the Colosseum got him into the newsreels for but a day or two, after which the Allied D-day invasion of occupied France captured the world's attention. The Nazi troops who were enabled by Clark's move on Rome to flee northward, however, were by the fall of 1944 entrenched in the Apennine Mountains of north-central Italy.[16] There, they were engaged in killing Allied soldiers instead of sitting out the war as prisoners, and effectively blocking the way of the Fifteenth Army Group (of which Clark's Fifth Army was a part) to the Austrian Alpine redoubt where the calculating Goebbels had indicated the Reich intended to make its last stand.[17]

The problems of Clark and Alexander were compounded by the fact that the Soviet Red Army was by that autumn rapidly chasing the Nazis west through Hungary toward Austria and the Italian Alps, as was the Socialist commander of the Yugoslavian forces, Marshal Tito. To allow their communist allies to liberate and possibly to occupy northern Italy and Austria was not a tenable alternative for the United States and Great Britain.[18] Under these bleak circumstances at least partially of their own making (Alexander had in actuality done little to stop Clark from moving on Rome),[19] the two commanders several times during the fall of 1944 sent Allied infantry of the Fifteenth Army Group against the heavily armed German defenders atop Mount Belvedere, one of the Nazis' key Apennine strongholds.[20]

The Allied hope on the Italian front was to produce a northward breakout through the Apennines, into the agriculturally rich Po Valley and up to the Alps. There, they would link up with the British and American forces pushing eastward through Belgium, France, and Bavaria, and with the Soviets moving westward through Poland and central Europe, closing off the redoubt while tightening the noose on Hitler.[21] Each time Clark's understrength combat groups attacked Mount Belvedere, however, they were brutally routed by German troops shooting down from the heights overlooking both the heavily mined approaches and the mountain itself.[22] Shattered Allied tanks and armaments now littered Belvedere's slopes.[23] Comparisons to the Rapido River debacle were sadly compelling.

Moreover, the northward slog of the Fifteenth Army Group to the foot of the Apennines during the summer and fall of 1944 had cost it tens of thousands of casualties.[24] After months of painfully slow progress against an entrenched Nazi force committed to keeping northern Italy for as long as possible, many of the Fifth Army's divisions were now severely depleted. Clark's supply situation had grown so critical that he was now forced to impose restrictions on ammunition.[25] Worse, many of his best troops were being siphoned off by Supreme Allied Command for deployment on the more critical western front across France and Belgium. Those who remained were exhausted and, in the words of historian John P. Delaney, "slipping toward a complete breakdown."[26]

The Allied offensive in Italy was finally and mercifully halted in late fall.[27] What Churchill had predicted would be a sharp thrust through Europe's "soft underbelly" had devolved for Allied troops into a gruesome, yearlong trek through what seemed like the Nazi digestive tract.[28]

In December 1944, there was a shake-up of the Allied command in Italy. General Alexander moved up to command overall operations in the Mediterranean theater, with General Clark taking command of the Fifteenth Army Group in Italy from Alexander, and General Truscott taking command of the American Fifth Army under Clark. However, even as General Clark celebrated his promotion (which some characterized pejoratively as his having been "kicked upstairs"), he remained faced with the fact that despite massive Allied casualties, German troops still held the Italian high ground in the north-central mountain ranges.[29]

As winter approached, it was General Mark Clark who at last decided he could make use of the Tenth Mountain Division in his continuing struggle for northern Italy.[30] General Truscott could only hope that his superior officers had learned something from their prior experiences at Rapido River and Mount Belvedere, as he prepared to incorporate America's mountain troops into the U.S. Fifth Army's fight for the Apennines.

Good-byes

BACK AT CAMP SWIFT IN TEXAS, LIEUTENANT RALPH BROMAGHIN HAD BEEN SERVING as second in command to his buddy Duke Watson in Company 86-I during regular infantry training. When the opportunity arose to head up the Eighty-sixth Regiment's Third Battalion Headquarters Company under one of the best officers in the division, Major John Hay, Bromaghin jumped at the chance. He was promoted to the rank of captain and assigned to serve as one of Hay's key company commanders.[1]

"I'm not sure whether you would call duty in a headquarters company any safer in combat than serving as the ranking officer in a rifle company," said Duke Watson. "Maybe it carried with it a bit lower casualty rate, but I doubt it, considering the aggressiveness of our battalion commanders. I think Bromaghin just saw the chance to move up, and I and everyone else encouraged him to take it."[2]

Ralph Lafferty, who by then was leading the headquarters company of the Eighty-sixth Regiment's Second Battalion, recalled:

> With the way that progress in winning the war had slowed in both theaters that fall, we were pretty sure we were going to get the call soon. I don't recall Bromaghin being any more or less nervous than anyone else regarding where we would be going and when. Our attitude was that staying together as a division was the most important thing, and that we'd worry about the rest later. I subsequently found out, though, that Ralph was having a tough time reconciling the fact that he could survive combat. He had a bad feeling about things even back at Swift, I think. He was a pretty gentle guy underneath that tough officer stuff, and I'm not sure he ever felt totally comfortable in thinking of himself as a soldier. Not that he wasn't both calm and courageous under fire, because it turned out that he certainly was, but I don't believe that he was one of the guys who relished the thought of testing himself in combat. He was ready to do his duty like the rest of us, but I got the idea he also could have done very nicely without that opportunity. He would have been satisfied, say, if the war had ended in victory that fall, and he would have made his contribution to the war effort through his three years of teaching mountain skills.[3]

Ralph Bromaghin, at age twenty-seven, was still very much in the process of sorting things out that autumn at Camp Swift. As an untested officer, he was naturally concerned over his ability to protect the lives of the men serving under him if and when they got into combat, an issue that dominated the thoughts of many of the young officers in the Tenth. That disquiet—among other things—had led to several awkward interactions between Bromaghin and the troopers from whose ranks he had only recently emerged. The divergent reputations Ralph was cultivating among the enlisted men as a regular army bastard, and among his fellow officers as a "morale man's morale man," were a dichotomy with which the young captain likely grappled on a daily basis.

"I don't know how he was with the enlisted men, but to me he was a terrific guy," remembered Lieutenant Victor Eklund, who served under Bromaghin at Swift. "One late Friday night a bit before we shipped out, he saw me on post and asked why I wasn't home with my wife for the weekend," said Eklund. "I told him I'd pulled duty as officer of the guard. All he said to me was 'Go home, I'll take it.' He shoo'd me off base and told me not to come back until Monday. That's the kind of thing I remember about Ralph."[4] On the other hand, according to Sergeant Ross Coppock, who also served under him, "my memories of Captain Bromaghin are not kind ones. The D-Series stuff was extremely harsh, so much so that I prefer not to discuss it."[5]

From a broader perspective, as a shy bachelor dividing his time among several artistic and athletic passions, Ralph Bromaghin clearly had not yet made up his mind where his heart or his future lay. A career in Aspen combining his love for the mountains with a way to earn a living may have beckoned, but Ralph seemed to be having trouble seeing his long-term future with his first likely combat experience looming just ahead.

Then there was the issue of his family. According to his friends, the longer Bromaghin had remained away from home, the further he had drifted from his parents and siblings. Though he regularly corresponded with his sister, Leone, he rarely returned to Seattle after departing Fort Lewis near the end of 1942.[6] Now, more than two years later, it would be easy to speculate that aside from maintaining his close friendships in the Tenth, Ralph Bromaghin had become more of a loner than ever. Then again, suggested Ralph Lafferty, perhaps that was the way he had liked it best since childhood: unattached, with only the music and the mountains as his most intimate companions.[7]

∞⌘

Though it might seem unlikely considering Rudy Konieczny's swaggering style and past combat experience at Kiska, he was apparently experiencing some of the same self-doubts concerning survival as was Bromaghin. That fall, Rudy returned home to New England on leave and talked excitedly to his family about Aspen and the potential of building a life for himself in the ski business there after the war. "He was very impressed with the postwar plans of many of the men he'd met in the Tenth, and I think he probably shared their vision of a major boom in western skiing once life returned to normal," said his younger brother Adolph. "He told us that he, Frank Prejsnar, and a few of the other guys were investigating the purchase of options to buy land in Aspen, and raved about how beautiful it was. He couldn't wait to show me once he got back from wherever overseas they were sending him." And then Rudy said good-bye to his family.

"It was a strange parting, though," Adolph continued, still emotional about it more than fifty-five years later. "It was the one and only time I ever saw Rudy cry. After letting us know about all his plans for the future, acting so optimistically, he pulled our older brother Charlie aside with tears in his eyes and told him that he didn't think he would be coming back. Then he broke down a little bit."

"Charlie told him he was just being crazy," Adolph explained, "that he'd be back home before he knew it. But Rudy said 'no,' that he had a real feeling this was his last time home. I'm guessing, but I think that somewhere inside, Rudy recognized that he was never going to change the way he did things, and after Kiska, he knew that those ways might get him killed. It had suddenly become very real to him that he might never see us, or do the things he loved to do, again. No matter how tough he was, it really broke him up."[8]

Bob Meservey was one among several of Rudy's comrades who agreed with Adolph's assessment. "Rudy knew only one way of doing things when it came to the Tenth," he said, "and that was to commit himself completely. . . . After Kiska, he knew what he'd be getting into as an infantry sergeant in the combat zone."[9]

It is impossible to say for certain, but it is also likely that Rudy remained concerned over living up to expectations, whether his own or those of his neighbors in Adams, an issue with which he had been struggling since his earliest days on the Thunderbolt. "He may have felt pressure to be the hero he thought people had always expected him to be," said his younger brother. "I hope not, because to so many people, he was already a hero. He just didn't realize it."

"When Rudy left the house," Adolph softly concluded, "I went to follow him so we could talk, but he sent me back. He told me he had someone to meet, and that I couldn't go. I didn't really believe him, but out of respect for his privacy, I turned back to the house. When I looked back, he was gone."[10]

ℰↄ◌ℛ

Jake Nunnemacher was most concerned over leaving a pregnant wife behind were he to be sent overseas. "We did our best to enjoy our time together," remembered Jean, "and just hoped for the best. Jacob might have been apprehensive, but he would never allow me to see that. He was eager to prove himself in my eyes, and I'm sure also very much in the eyes of his father. In that way, I think a part of him looked forward to making us all proud of him, and being taken seriously when he returned to Milwaukee after the war to work at Galland Henning, if that's what he chose to do. So we just held each other at every opportunity and waited."[11]

In November 1944, some of the answers to all of the nervous questions began coming. The division, it was announced, would not be broken apart by the army after all. Rather, the Tenth Light Division was officially renamed the Tenth Mountain Division, and reorganized as a regular "heavy" infantry group with the addition of nine heavy weapons companies (one for each battalion) equipped with fixed machine guns and large, 81mm mortars. Division members were also informed that they would soon be issued an arched sleeve patch indicating their special status as "Mountain" troops.[12] This put them in the same elite class as those who wore the rockers of the "Airborne" and the "Rangers," and considerably boosted pride and morale among the members of the division who had now spent nearly six months training on the plains of Texas.[13] Some of the old confidence and swagger from the days at Paradise and Camp Hale returned with just the mention of that little piece of cloth with the word "Mountain" on it.

That month also marked the arrival of a new division commander, General George P. Hays, who had won the Congressional Medal of Honor in the First World War and landed at Omaha Beach on D-day. He had also served in Italy in 1943 under General Clark in the brutal mountain fighting at Mount Cassino.[14] Hays conveyed to his new troops that he considered them to be among the most elite and highly trained in the U.S. Armed Forces, and that he looked forward to leading them. And then he told them that their time had come. The division was to be packed up immediately and taken by rail to Camp Patrick Henry, Virginia, and readied for shipment overseas to a location that would remain secret until nearly the end of their voyage.[15]

The night before departing from Swift, Jean and Jake Nunnemacher had a heart-to-heart talk about their love and their future. "Jacob and I just adored each other, and there was nothing left for us to say in that regard," said Jean. "Wrapped in each other's arms, Jacob then said all the other things he felt he had to say. He told me he expected everything would work out fine, but that he did not want me to underestimate the danger that the Tenth would be facing, and that I had to face the possibility that he might not come home. In that event, he said, he wanted me to remarry someone who would be a good father to our baby, and he made me promise that I would. I suppose so many other couples had that same, heartbreaking conversation. I think Jacob believed he was coming back to me, I really do, but he never would have told me if he thought otherwise. He would not have wanted me to worry."[16]

The next morning, Jake Nunnemacher, Rudy Konieczny, and Ralph Bromaghin went to war.

Rudy Konieczny (center) on maneuvers with two unidentified troopers near Paradise Lodge at Mount Rainier, 1942. Courtesy of Konieczny family

Rudy Konieczny (first on right) and Leo Bartlett of Stowe, Vermont (first on left), clown with two unidentified comrades in "borrowed" Canadian officers' jackets near Paradise Lodge at Mount Rainier, 1942. Photographer presumed to be Roy Deyle. Courtesy of Konieczny family

The 1942 radio debut of the Latrine Quartet, better known as the original Eighty-seventh Mountain Regimental Glee Club. (left to right) Charlie Bradley, Glen Stanley, Charles McLane, and Ralph Bromaghin on guitar. McLane and Bromaghin wrote the lyrics to most of the Tenth Mountain Division's most famous song parodies. According to Bradley, "we yodeled, sang Bavarian ditties, were not at all good according to severe task master Bromaghin, but we were appreciated and enjoyed our debut." Courtesy of Denver Public Library, Western History Collection

Ski troops of the Eighty-seventh Mountain Regiment in formation outside Paradise Lodge on Mount Rainier, 1942. Note that the snow has drifted above the second-story windows of the lodge. Courtesy of Denver Public Library, Western History Collection

facing page: Lieutenant John Woodward takes time out from supervising the military film crew at Sun Valley in April 1942 to pose for a self-portrait with his wife, Verone, on the slopes of Mount Baldy. Photographer: John B. Woodward. Courtesy of Denver Public Library, Western History Collection

The infamous snowshoe maneuvers at Paradise, 1942. That evening, Ralph Bromaghin wrote "The Ballad of Sven," which was performed the following morning by the entire regiment. Photographer: Charles C. Bradley. Courtesy of Denver Public Library, Western History Collection

Camp Hale, located in the Pando Valley roughly between Leadville and the Vail Valley, deep in the Colorado Rockies. Photographer: David B. Allen. Courtesy of Denver Public Library, Western History Collection

The father of the Tenth Mountain Division, Charles Minot "Minnie" Dole (center), at Camp Hale with fellow National Ski Patrol cofounder Roger Langley (left), and Captain Paul Lafferty. Courtesy of Ralph Lafferty

Tenth Recon members set out on the famous Trooper Traverse to Aspen in February 1944. Bud Winter broke trail a good part of the way for a group of famous American ski moun- taineers that included Captain John Jay, Paul Petzoldt, Ernest Tapley, Glenn Dawson, Fred Beckey, and Bill Hackett. Photographer: Richard A. Rocker. Courtesy of Denver Pub- lic Library, Western History Collection

facing page: Austrian downhill ski champion Friedl Pfeifer, who joined the Tenth at Camp Hale in 1943 and became one of the many who fell in love with nearby Aspen. Courtesy of Denver Public Library, Western History Collection

Ski-jumping champion Torger Tokle, who arrived from Norway and joined Company A of the Eighty-sixth Regiment. Courtesy of Ralph Lafferty

Big Bud Winter, the young Adirondack racer and ski patroller, on the rope tow at Cooper Hill, 1943. Courtesy of Denver Public Library, Western History Collection

Young Sergeant Orval McDaniel of Salt Lake City, Utah, prepping his ski gear. Courtesy of McDaniel family.

Sergeant Jake Nunnemacher of the Tenth Recon takes a breather at Cooper Hill, 1943. Courtesy of Jean Lindemann

Jean and Jacob Nunnemacher on their wedding day in May 1943. Courtesy of Jean Lindemann

In front of the Alta Lodge after a long drive and a full day skiing the Utah powder. (left to right) Former Dartmouth Ski Team captain and coach Percy Rideout, Ralph Lafferty, and Ralph Bromaghin. Courtesy of Ralph Lafferty

Best friends Ralph Bromaghin (left) and Ralph Lafferty relax on the porch of Sumers' Ranch near the Roaring Fork River in the summer of 1943. Courtesy of Ralph Lafferty

Captain Joe Duncan and four-year-old daughter Doriane, just prior to Duncan shipping out to Italy as commanding officer of Company L of the Eighty-seventh Regiment. Courtesy of Edward Wilkes

The ski slopes of Ajax Mountain, above Aspen, shortly after the war. This is what the boys had been dreaming about. Photographer: Charles E. Grover. Courtesy of Denver Public Library, Western History Collection

Into the Maelstrom

I must confess that I had an ulterior motive in wanting to join the ski
troops. . . . I can accept nature on her own terms, but it is the wrath of
man I fear. I thought I would be safer engaged in mountain warfare.
Alpine terrain is familiar and comforting. I feel at home there, but war
offers only the terrible unknown conjured up in vivid imagination.

—HARRIS DUSENBERY, *Ski the High Trail: World War II*
Ski Troopers in the High Colorado Rockies

BY EARLY DECEMBER 1944, THE MEMBERS OF THE TENTH MOUNTAIN DIVISION
had completed their move by train to Hampton Roads, Virginia, where they
prepared to sail across the Atlantic. They would be among the very last American combat units to enter the war in Europe.[1] Their secret destination was
Italy.

The members of the Eighty-sixth Regiment were the first to embark on
December 10. They left on the overcrowded SS *Argentina* from Newport News,
docking in the port of Naples on Christmas Eve day after an arduous, two-
week journey punctuated by bad weather and seasickness.[2]

On the way over, reported the regiment's Episcopal chaplain Henry
Brendemihl, his good friend Ralph Bromaghin was baptized and took com-
munion.[3] Although Ralph had never been particularly interested in church
formalities, and according to Duke Watson had proclaimed himself agnostic,

religion apparently had become more of a force in his life.[4] "War prompts many men to seek the comfort of their faith," Chaplain Brendemihl was fond of saying. "There are no atheists in a foxhole" was the more popular expression among the dog faces.[5]

Ralph Lafferty had another explanation. He, Duke Watson, and Bromaghin were discussing their postwar aspirations up on deck during the crossing. When Bromaghin's turn came around, he said "quietly and quite matter-of-factly," according to Lafferty, "you guys can talk about that, but I don't think I'll be around." Lafferty and Watson told him not to say "stupid things like that," but Bromaghin seemed at peace with the notion that he might not be coming home from the war. "I think Ralph might have been preparing himself spiritually in case his premonition came to pass," Lafferty continued. "He was not the only man I personally heard say that he didn't think he'd survive, and oddly, I can't think of another single one who thought that way who did actually come home. It's probably not the best state of mind to be in going into combat, but if that's the way you feel, I think it must be a very hard thing to shake."[6]

As arduous as their crossing was, the men of the Eighty-sixth were in for an even ruder awakening as they finally stepped back onto dry land. On Christmas Day 1944, word arrived that the American Ninety-second Division, a segregated African American outfit suffering from substantial morale problems, had been routed by the Nazis near the northern port city of Livorno. The gap created in the Allied line by their retreat meant ostensibly that the only thing between the German army and the city of Rome to the southeast was the battle-green Eighty-sixth Mountain Regiment.[7]

With the Nazis in the midst of staging a stunning, last-gasp offensive in Belgium popularly known as the "Battle of the Bulge," there was immediate concern among the Italian theater commanders that Hitler might launch a similar attack on their front.[8] The men of the Eighty-sixth were rushed onto a broken-down freighter converted into a troop ship now known as the *Sestriere,* and moved from Naples to Livorno. There they set up a staging area and awaited a potential German offensive as part of a makeshift Allied defensive initiative designated as Task Force 45.[9]

The German offensive never came, but casualties nevertheless mounted quickly. During the first week of January 1945, a mountain soldier assigned to guard a bivouac area deviated from his assigned patrol route along a railroad track and was blown up by a Nazi landmine. The seven troopers who rushed to his aid, including a Catholic chaplain, were also killed when they detonated additional explosives in what turned out to be a large field of enemy mines known as "Bouncing Betties."[10] After the Eighty-seventh Regiment's friendly fire deaths at Kiska, this represented a grimly inauspicious start for the Tenth Mountain Division in Europe.

That same week, the troop ship *West Point*—at the time the largest American oceanliner ever produced and formerly known as the SS *America*—departed Virginia with the Eighty-seventh and Eighty-fifth Mountain Regiments aboard. Rudy Konieczny and Jacob Nunnemacher made the crossing in ten days, docking in Naples harbor on January 13, 1945. The men of the Eighty-seventh Regiment's Second and Third Battalions, including Rudy's 87 Fox Company, were boarded onto unheated railroad cars and transported for twenty-four hours through the cold, devastated Italian countryside to Livorno. From there they joined the members of the Eighty-fifth and Eighty-sixth Regiments on the line.[11]

Nunnemacher and the men of Company B remained in war-torn Naples with the rest of the Eighty-seventh's First Battalion for three days, after which they were loaded onto the *Sestriere* and moved into Livorno through the harbor. Now all three regiments of the Tenth Mountain Division were in place near the Apennine Mountains north of Pisa. There, they tented in the cold, mud, and snow awaiting further orders.[12]

For most of the men on the line, it had been a long road to Italy. Whether from Adams, Massachusetts, or Pine Lake, Wisconsin, or Seattle, Washington, the journey had taken them from some of the most beautiful places in North America to some of the coldest, and then to some of the hottest and dustiest. They had skied and climbed, marched and snowshoed, sung and packed mules, and taught others to do the same. Many had been to college. A number had fought in the awful fog of Kiska. Some had seen their friends killed, and a few unfortunate souls had accidentally killed their friends. And now from the most experienced to the least, they all had one thing in common. They understood how serious a situation they had just entered up on the line, a place where many of them—despite brave assertions to the contrary— never really expected to be.

That is not to say that tension dominated every waking moment. Despite the stresses engendered by being in front-line infantry units for the first time, the men of the Tenth still found time to marvel at the beauty of the Alpine scenery. "I was tremendously impressed by the terrain," recalled trooper Bud Lovett. "It was absolutely gorgeous."[13] Once again, the division newspaper began featuring a "Pin-up Mountain of the Week." The time for reflection on natural wonders, however, was limited. Jake Nunnemacher's battalion was immediately assigned defensive positions and placed on high alert to guard against Nazi patrols.[14] Rudy Konieczny's unit drew the tougher assignment. Its job was to probe the enemy in the area below Mount Belvedere, the terrain that would be the division's first combat objective.[15]

The Nazis, after their successes in repulsing several Allied attacks on Belvedere and its surrounding peaks in November and December, remained convinced that these mountains would serve as key strongholds for the defense of the lush northern Italian plains of the Po Valley. Here, in the Apennines, they would halt the advance of the Allied armies moving northward to push them back through the Italian and Austrian Alps toward their collapsing Fatherland.[16]

Despite the record cold and snowfalls in the French and Belgian lowlands that had plagued the Americans during the Battle of the Bulge, it had been a drier than normal winter in the mountains of northern Italy.[17] As a result, the members of the Tenth who came to Europe expecting to utilize their skiing skills were, for the most part, disappointed. After years of intensive downhill training, America's mountain troops went on only a few risky but uneventful ski patrols into the mountains south of Belvedere in late January and early February, among the only such combat patrols ever undertaken by members of the U.S. Armed Forces in its history. The Tenth Mountaineers then quickly exchanged their snow gear for more conventional implements of war.[18] Wooden skis, it turned out, made too much noise moving over ice and breakable crust to be a serious military tool in any snow conditions other than optimal.[19]

At least as long as the patrols lasted, however, it remained a point of honor for the participants to deny their dangers. "We went out one day on skis," remembered former Dartmouth skier Phil Puchner of 87-G, "and spotted some German gunners in the distance. Most of us got the hell out of there back to our lines. We were confident, but we weren't nuts. But a few of the guys insisted on taking their sweet time on the way home. When we got back, they explained that it had been months since they'd skied, and they were going to make the most of it, German gunners or no German gunners. That attitude changed shortly, believe me."[20]

∽◯◌

By now, Sergeant Rudy Konieczny was a four-and-one-half-year army veteran and one of the most experienced and highly skilled members of the Tenth

Mountain Division. "In Italy, he grew even further into the role of being everyone's big brother," recalled Lieutenant Donald "Mike" Dwyer, Rudy's platoon leader. "That, combined with the fact that he was always willing to lead by example, made him one fine soldier."[21]

"Of all the men of the Eighty-seventh," said Rudy's buddy, Sergeant David Burt, "he was certainly one of the most admired, at least by me." The formerly frail-looking Rudy had filled out considerably in his four years of training, and now chose to carry a powerful Browning Automatic Rifle (BAR) rather than the smaller and lighter standard M-1 Garand. Simply by being a BAR man, his status was further heightened as one of the most respected members of Company 87-F.[22]

After only a short time overseas, according to Lieutenant Dwyer, Rudy appeared to become very relaxed and at peace with himself. "He seemed to have very little fear. At first, a lot of the guys were understandably nervous about going out on night patrols. Rudy would volunteer for them." According to Bob Meservey, the stories about Rudy's lone patrols quickly became legendary in the regiment. "I heard that Rudy used to go out hunting. He'd go off on his own or with the partisans, and from what I understand very quickly became a *serious* soldier."[23] Rudy was either pushing aside or wholly embracing his premonition of a *Rendezvous with Death*.[24]

"The stresses on Rudy and the rest of us in the Second Battalion were pretty high at that point," continued Mike Dwyer. Captain George Earle eloquently described in the *History of the 87th Mountain Infantry* the emotional challenge that those who went out on patrol were facing:

> [Those first patrols] out into the great unknown land of the enemy can be more nerve-wracking to the individual than the mass movements of battle. There is the long strain of silent movement, the breathless waits, the inexorable searching out of him who lies in wait to kill. There is the physical punishment and even torture of alternatively sweating up the rough terrain and lying motionless for hours on the snow, freezing in your own icy sweat. Finally, there is the fast withdrawal, possibly under fire, with no litter bearers for the casualty, and only the desperate loyalty of a comrade to drag the wounded in.[25]

Rudy dealt with the tension not only by meeting it head on, but also by using his sense of humor, recalled Dwyer. "We found a couple of bicycles one day, and Rudy insisted that we use them on patrol through the snow and mud. It was probably a silly thing to do, but with guys starting to get killed and injured from those damn mines and the shelling, Rudy was helping to keep things loose in a very difficult situation. The respect we had for him as a soldier made it possible for him to use humor that way."[26]

As it turned out, Company F commander Captain James Kennett also thought that the bicycle stunt was a great morale builder. According to the regimental history, Sergeant Konieczny and Captain Kennett—two brash peas in a pod—were soon going on reconnaissance missions throughout the Belvedere area together on bicycles, despite being under constant enemy observation.[27] Rudy likely enjoyed an ironic laugh, added his brother Adolph, over memories of being admonished as a kid for recklessness in the way he rode his bike around the hills of Adams.[28]

∞∞

The enemy was not the sole distraction for those Americans new to the Italian front. They were shocked not only at the devastation that had been wreaked on the cities and countryside, but also over the resulting poverty and starvation that were especially hard on the local children. When not out on patrol or actively engaged in defensive activities, many members of the division took time out to assist in whatever way they could the small army of hungry youngsters in the surrounding areas who flocked to them for handouts. Some Tenth Mountain units even set up formal food distribution systems to dispense army leftovers, sparing the locals the indignity of having to pick through military refuse in search of edible meals.[29]

"We went hungry sometimes so we could feed those kids part of our rations," recalled Lieutenant Dwyer.[30] A photo of Rudy Konieczny and David Burt, sitting on a rock in a wooded clearing and laughing with a group of small children surrounding them, is testimony that the men of the Tenth brought the best of what they had to offer to the innocent refugees of the Italian war. Recalling the circumstances of the picture taken that January 1945, Burt joked that he was probably asking the kids in broken phrases if they had older sisters for Rudy and him to meet. "Rudy looks as though he is wondering how Italian can sound so awful, at the same time not wanting to say anything so unkind, and that would be his way."[31] The youngsters did not leave hungry.

The story was the same for Jake Nunnemacher, whose lifelong affection for children had been intensified by his pending fatherhood. "Jacob loved helping kids," said Jean. "It was one of his life's great joys. I'm sure it was a comfort for him to be able to assist in some small way, especially being so far from home and with me expecting any minute. I'm also sure, though, that the suffering of those little ones caused him a great deal of frustration and sadness."[32] According to Private Lewis Hoelscher, also of 87-B, he, Jake, and their platoon mates frequently handed out rations to the local kids during the day, and spent their nights waiting for the enemy to come. On the evening of February 5, it did.

That night, members of Company 87-B detected a patrol in their perimeter and opened fire. The next morning, a wounded German soldier from the Fourth *Gebirgsjäger* (Mountain Troop) Battalion was pulled in from the snow and became the Tenth Mountain Division's first captured prisoner of war.[33] Over the next several weeks, Jake Nunnemacher was kept busy helping to communicate with new prisoners and teaching his buddies potentially useful German phrases. With all the practice, he reported in a letter to Jean, his fluency was coming back to him more quickly than he imagined it would.[34]

Jean soon did some reporting of her own. In early February, Jake received word from home that she had given birth to a healthy baby girl, whom the couple had decided in advance to name Heidi. The ecstatic dad gushed for days about his firstborn, passing around pictures and shaking hands. "We were all really happy for Jake," Lewis Hoelscher recalled. "I dimly recall we had a few toasts on that one. It was a nice little distraction from the task at hand."[35]

୭୦Ო

Ralph Bromaghin, meanwhile, was pulled back in early February with the rest of the Eighty-sixth Regiment to the old walled city of Lucca for training, having served a relatively uneventful month on the line following the January minefield horror near Livorno.[36] During the rest period, several of the Eighty-sixth Regiment's officers were invited into the homes of local Italians, who made them feel welcome by serving sumptuous, peasant-style meals consisting of food they frequently couldn't spare. Inevitably, the dinners would end with the consumption of grappa, the local white lightning.[37]

Ralph wrote home to his sister Leone that he had truly enjoyed one such gathering, at which the grappa was followed by music. He related that the daughter of the family appeared with an accordion, on which she let him play popular songs for the whole family. It reminded him, no doubt, of the evenings so many years before at the Clough home back in Seattle. "He seemed to be very happy that night," his sister wrote, "from the tone of his letter."[38]

Adventures involving accordions seemed to become an odd theme for Ralph Bromaghin in Italy. Bromaghin's Third Battalion intelligence officer, David Brower, Jake Nunnemacher's old friend from Hale who had completed OCS in 1943 and now held the rank of major, recalled his relationship with Captain Bromaghin as one that was greatly enhanced by their shared love of music.

During the February rest period, Brower managed to procure an accordion, which was badly in need of wax to adjust its internal reeds. Setting off to find the elusive substance in order to organize a sing-along with proper accompaniment, Brower and Bromaghin met with little success in conveying to the local Italian shopkeepers the nature of the product they were seeking. Their broken Italian phrases and rudimentary gestures got them nothing but shrugs. Finally, Bromaghin hit upon the way around the language barrier. According to Brower, his friend's stroke of comic genius consisted of illustrating his needs to a merchant by melodramatically "twisting a finger in his ear, pointing to the finger," and deeply intoning the word "*wax.*"[39] Recognition, understanding, and order fulfillment were instantaneous. Through such minor adventures was sanity often preserved among the Tenth's "citizen" officers, whose heightened sense of responsibility was a constant source of stress, whether on or off the line.[40]

The break in Lucca was also a time for serious, technical exchanges among the division's leadership. Bromaghin made sure to keep up his correspondence with Captain Charlie Bradley, his former glee club partner still serving in Alaska on a long-term, survival training assignment. According to Bradley, Bromaghin had a "highly analytical mind" and "took the time to answer my questions and suggest new twists in mountain combat training."[41] Among the innovations that Bromaghin suggested was the incorporation into all mountain warfare training regimes of instruction on the use of a new, light antitank weapon called a "bazooka." Bradley immediately incorporated the suggestion into his recommendations. "Ralph probably figured the best way to keep himself mentally and emotionally ready for what lay ahead," said Captain Percy Rideout, "was to keep himself busy, which he did in a very constructive way."[42]

Despite all the preparations and manufactured distractions in Lucca, however, T4 Charles Wellborn wrote in his *History of the 86th Mountain Infantry* that there was a general air of uneasiness among practically all of the officers and enlisted men during the Eighty-sixth's brief period of rest:

> As the Regiment rested and trained . . . there was a suspenseful and
> somewhat grim expectation in the air. The first short tour of duty on the
> line had been too calm and uneventful. This was not the kind of war that

Ernie Pyle wrote about; there must be something more important, more exciting, more deadly in the future. And most of the men took a hint from their day to day activities that "the future" was not far off. They were right.[43]

ℝ℞

In early February 1945, General Clark called an urgent conference in Florence with his top Fifteenth Army Group generals. According to General Lucian K. Truscott Jr., new commander of the American Fifth Army (of which the Tenth Mountain Division was now a part), the news he conveyed was "depressing."[44] The Allied Combined Chiefs of Staff had decided to transfer more of Clark's divisions and most of his fighter bombers to the western front, and had clarified the southern front mission of the Fifteenth Army Group as follows: "[T]o prevent any German advance south of [its] present positions and to attack at once in case of a German withdrawal from Italy."[45]

It is abundantly clear that Supreme Allied Headquarters, at this late date in the European war, viewed the Italian campaign as a "sideshow" most important for its value as a static front tying up Nazi divisions that might be fighting elsewhere. The only reason to attack would be to force the Nazis to hold in place, were they to attempt a withdrawal in order to reinforce the western front. (The Allies, who had broken the Nazi codes, would likely have learned of such a planned withdrawal well in advance through intercepted communications.)[46] Nevertheless, on the assumption that the war was still far from over and that the southern front might yet prove to be an important strategic battleground in closing out the war in Europe, General Clark ordered his commanders to plan for a spring offensive.[47]

As the date for the beginning phases of the offensive drew near, the danger levels for the members of the Tenth began to increase. More frequent mortar and small-arms fire was exchanged with the Nazis as patrols around the Belvedere foothills became more numerous. The level of physical discomfort for the troops grew as well. A weather pattern of alternating rain and bone-chilling cold made outdoor bivouac conditions miserable, and frostbite-related trench foot became an increasing problem. The men were growing restless even as operational plans were being finalized.[48]

ℝ℞

The Tenth Mountain Division would be going up against the veteran troops of Nazi field marshal "Smiling Al" Kesselring (who was later to be accused of war crimes for summarily executing hundreds of civilians in Rome, but exonerated on the recommendation of General Clark).[49] Kesselring's divisions included several battalions of crack mountain troops.[50] Whether it occurred to Rudy Konieczny and other select members of the Tenth that they might soon be fighting against the same skiers who had raced against them on the Thunderbolt and elsewhere in 1938 is not known. Neither is it clear whether any of the members of the German Universities Skiing Team of Munich who visited the United States that year actually served in Italy. According to German ski historian Dr. Gerd Falkner, many government and university records were lost when Germany was devastated by bombings and overrun by the Allies in 1945, making the tracing of the team members difficult, if not impossible.[51]

Still, since all were from Bavarian colleges (mainly the University of Munich), it is likely that one or more members of the team did in fact serve in the famous Fifth Gebirgs Division formed in 1940 and led by popular mountaineer General Julius "Papa" Ringel. That division, made up predominantly of Bavarian mountaineers and skiers, had fought in Greece at the war's beginning, on the eastern front in 1942–1943, and had been transferred (without Ringel, who was now fighting the Soviet Red Army in Austria) to the mountains of central Italy with elements of the Fourth and Eighth Gebirgs at the beginning of 1944.[52] Its elite members were battle-hardened and experienced, and it cannot be ruled out that some had met their enemy before in the mountains of New England and the American West.

Even the few surviving records of the German military's *Bundesarchive,* however, are silent on the matter, and no definitive proof of service in Italy for any of the German team members has yet been located.[53] In his autobiography, Minnie Dole noted that "not one of the [1938] German team . . . survived the war, I was told," but he gave no indication of the source of such information.[54]

One of the most tantalizing indications that there were extraordinary skiers present on the German side was the description by trooper Bud Lovett of a ski patrol incident in early February. Spotting an enemy military skier standing on a snow dam extending across a ridgeline between two peaks, the Americans called out for him to surrender. "He stood and looked at us," Lovett recalled, "and then he did a jump turn and skied right down that thing as if it were a head wall. Nobody shot at him. I think most of us were impressed by his skiing."[55] Was it Machler? Dehmel? Former U.S. National Downhill champion Ulli Beuter? Probably not, but there will never be a way to know for sure.

In the end, all that really may be concluded with confidence is that the Americans who competed against the German Universities Ski Team in 1938 and who later served in the Tenth Mountain Division had an idea of the confidence and the abilities of the men they would be facing. With that knowledge, they could anticipate that the struggle would be both fierce and deadly.

The Ridges That Could Not Be Taken

THE PLAN OF BATTLE FOR THE TENTH MOUNTAIN DIVISION WAS DEVISED PERSON-
ally by Fifth Army commander General Lucien Truscott and the ski troops' own
commanding officer, General George Hays.[1] Their order, issued by Italian theater
commander General Mark Clark in early 1945, was to prepare for an attack along
the major route known as Highway 65, which connected the Fifth Army's present
position above Florence, north through Bologna, to the targeted Po Valley.[2]

Once again, Clark had plotted a course through the strongest concentration of Nazi firepower, and instructed his subordinates to be ready to imple-
ment it at any moment. After more than six months of brutal but unheralded
fighting through the mud of central Italy that followed the liberation of Rome,
Clark was desperate to be part of the final Allied push to victory. His message
to his commanders was that they would not be sitting out the final months of
the war on a static front.[3]

Truscott was deeply troubled. Though Clark had been successful in moving north along Highway 65 in previous months, his gains had been achieved at enormous human cost.[4] Units under Clark's command had suffered tens of thousands of casualties, and his new plan for a spring offensive would by all indications result in a continuation of the carnage. "An attack through the most heavily defended portion of the German lines under such oppressive conditions of weather and terrain," Truscott wrote in reference to the mountains now sheathed in ice along Highway 65, "would have been an appalling undertaking, and one which would have little prospect of success."[5]

Truscott had another idea. Highway 64, an alternate mountain route into the Po Valley, ran slightly to the west of Highway 65 and had the distinct advantage of substantially fewer entrenched Nazi positions. This was a fact that Truscott believed would help to minimize Fifth Army casualties.[6]

There was one major problem with the Highway 64 alternative. The Allies had been stopped cold along the route in the late autumn of 1944 by Nazi gun emplacements on Mount Belvedere, the huge massif that towered over the highway. Clark had tried and failed on three prior occasions to evict the Germans from this high ground, sustaining substantial casualties.[7] Now, Truscott wanted to try again. The difference, he reasoned, was the presence of American mountain troops. After more than three years of training for such an assignment, Truscott wanted General Hays's Tenth Mountain boys to at least be given the chance of sparing themselves and the rest of the Fifth Army the ordeal of Highway 65.[8]

Not trusting his ability to sway Clark with the facts, however, Truscott obfuscated about the reason for needing to take Belvedere. He told his commander that he believed safe Allied travel along Highway 64 to be an essential prerequisite to implementing a successful attack on Highway 65. Clark wrote back stating he was pleased that Truscott was in agreement with his general plans of operation, and to go ahead with the preliminary action against Belvedere.[9] Truscott later wrote that he was relieved to have succeeded in keeping his options open regarding the Highway 64 plan, in light of the costly slog through Cassino and central Italy that Clark had been boxed into following the Anzio landing.[10]

The Truscott plan for the Tenth Mountain Division called for three distinct phases. The first would be to capture and hold Mount Belvedere and its surrounding peaks, making secure travel possible through the valley below on Highway 64. The second would be to move northeastward and capture the fortified, mountainous area surrounding the town of Castel D'Aiano, straightening the Fifth Army line in preparation for the big April push. Finally, the division would help lead the spring offensive itself, breaking out of the Apennine Mountains through the area dominated by the Rocca di Roffeno massif, and moving into the Po River Valley for a drive northward to the Alps.[11]

Because both Truscott and Hays were acutely aware of the previous failed attempts to take and hold Mount Belvedere, General Hays meticulously reviewed the Fifth Army's past failures when planning the specifics of the new action. He determined that Belvedere could not possibly be taken and held without first capturing the adjacent peak to the west known as Riva Ridge. From Riva on the left, the Nazis looked down onto the entire Belvedere face and the valley below it, from where any Allied assault would have to originate.[12] There was little wonder why the prior attacks on Belvedere had been unmitigated failures.

The real question was, could the steep, icy, two-thousand-foot Riva Ridge be taken from the Nazis entrenched on top? The enemy was certain it could not. General Hays optimistically disagreed. He had, in fact, a more personal stake in the outcome than most field generals. His son was now serving with Jake Nunnemacher in Company B of the Eighty-seventh Regiment, which was scheduled to attack Mount Belvedere on February 19, 1945.[13]

Moreover, in Hays's eyes, failing was not an option. If General Clark was determined to move forward, a failure to take Riva might leave Hays faced with the dual prescriptions for disaster of a naked (and likely abortive) attack against Belvedere followed by a frontal assault by the Fifth Army into the teeth of the strongest Nazi positions along Highway 65. While not overtly disagreeing with the plan to actively engage the enemy, both he and Truscott feared the very worst were those latter scenarios to come to fruition.[14] Their fingers firmly crossed, the two commanders ordered the Tenth Mountain Division back on the line.

₠)ℂℛ

Weeks of reconnaissance, begun in January, were conducted to select the most passable routes up the steep slopes of Riva Ridge. Unfortunately, during the process of preparing for what would prove to be one of the most audacious mountain warfare actions in history, several members of the Tenth gave their lives. It is a sad fact that casualties incurred as the result of small actions undertaken in preparation for big pushes are more often overlooked than those occurring during the push itself. Young private Art Argiewicz is fondly remembered by his fellow soldiers as one whose death in the days prior to the Riva Ridge action might otherwise have been a quiet footnote in the division's history were it not for his extraordinary contribution to the development of mountain training in the U.S. Army.

Argiewicz had joined the California Sierra Club in 1938 as a shy, near-sighted fifteen-year-old. Climbing in Yosemite alongside famed naturalist David Brower and iconic photographer Ansel Adams, however, the youngster quickly developed into an exceptional mountaineer.[15] Within two years, he had pioneered a new climbing technique known as "expansion knee," by which the climber would overcome the lack of a piton large enough to fit a broad crack in the rock by inserting his knee into the crack, bending the leg to anchor, and hoisting himself up to a level where a piton might be inserted. Many soon adopted the new skill, elevating considerably the teenager's status within the Sierra mountaineering community.[16]

Brower and Argiewicz formed strong bonds in the Sierra Club, and when his mentor joined the Tenth Mountain Division, the pupil somehow convinced the army that his poor eyesight was no hindrance to becoming a ski trooper. It wasn't long before Argiewicz's talent for climbing was recognized by the Tenth Recon/MTG, which terminated his efforts to become an expert skier at Cooper Hill by sending him off with Brower, Duke Watson, and the rest of the rappelling experts to teach technical climbing at Seneca Rocks, West Virginia. There, he became one of the unit's leading instructors, developing new techniques and teaching mountain survival skills to thousands of flatlanders.[17]

It was only natural that when Captain John Woodward later tapped Brower to write a new mountain training manual for the division, Brower immediately drafted Argiewicz to assist him. "I could do no better than call on Art," wrote Brower. "He singled out the inconsistencies, found the gaps, wrote the correct doctrine, conceived new tactical training problems, [and] posed for improved diagrams. . . . Finally, the portion on military rock climbing, one-third of the manual, was reorganized, reillustrated and rewritten [by Art], and was published essentially unchanged."[18]

It was on a reconnaissance patrol near the base of Mount Belvedere on January 25, 1945, that things went terribly wrong for young Argiewicz. Assigned to Company L of the Eighty-sixth Regiment, he was helping lead troops near Querciola to reinforce a platoon against Nazi infiltrators. A two-hour firefight erupted, which ended only after American artillery blasted the enemy positions. Argiewicz was killed during the "confusion of a patrol skirmish," as Brower put it, leaving the impression that he may have been killed by friendly fire.[19] The official morning reports are unclear as to the details of his death, but regimental historian Captain George Earle was blunt in his comments on the general subject. "In Italy," he wrote, "we saw so much . . . of all kinds of friendly fire mistakes, that we came to accept it as normal."[20]

In eulogizing his shy, painfully modest friend in the Sierra Club Bulletin in 1945, Brower wrote wistfully that "[Art] was not to know what impact his clear flow of thought and action, in a channel through which the Sierra Club started him, was to have on [the army's mountain training program]. He would, I'm sure, be embarrassed to have Sierra Club members know it, and to remember his story should they happen again to see a fifteen-year-old, bespectacled lad . . . yodeling from Cragmont Cliffs."[21] Art Argiewicz, who gave his life so that others might survive on Riva Ridge and Belvedere, was twenty-two.

જી

With the completion of the planning and reconnaissance phases of the intricate operation, on the evening of February 18, members of the Eighty-sixth Regiment's First and Second Battalions silently emerged from their hiding places at the base of Riva Ridge. During the previous nights, they had been smuggled into every available building and defilade below Riva by antifascist partisans and sympathetic local families, keeping out of sight to avoid alerting the Nazis of the pending action.[22] Among the secreted mountain troopers were Rudy Konieczny's hometown cohorts Frank Prejsnar and Jeddie Brooks, ski racer Pete Seibert, and the good friend of Ralph Bromaghin and Jake Nunnemacher, Captain Percy Rideout.

Sergeant Jacques Parker, an artist who would go on to become the world's best-known ski illustrator, described a highly emotional and poignant moment just before the Eighty-sixth nervously moved out. "Our group was in the attic of one of these homes," he recalled, "and we all knelt together. We had people of various faiths, including this big Austrian who lost part of his family to the Nazis. We all just knelt there. It was one of the most silent, fervent prayers I've ever experienced in my life. Nothing was said. . . . Even though we all thought we were so tough, we knew it was going to be rough on the mountain."[23]

Just after dark, Parker, Brooks, Prejsnar, Seibert, Captain Rideout, and the others silently moved single file, by hand or with the aid of fixed ropes, up the icy peak. Some of the routes passed through freezing waterfalls and rivers that soaked the men, coating their uniforms in layers of ice as they continued toward the summit. They climbed with the knowledge that the discovery of one could easily result in the deaths of all, so closely were they bunched and so vulnerable were their positions along the five difficult climbing routes. After hours of tense movement, they stopped just short of the ridgeline and waited in the cold for first light.[24]

Fortuitously obscured by a dense fog, the climbers attacked the stunned Nazi defenders at dawn. The Germans fell back in confusion as the Tenth Mountaineers charged out of the mist, firing and hurling grenades, and screaming demands for surrender. A number of the enemy capitulated, but the rest quickly regrouped. The Americans then endured fierce counterattacks throughout the following days, as the enemy desperately and unsuccessfully tried to stave off the main attack on Belvedere and its sister peaks by attempting to recapture the heights of Riva.[25] Among the many who would give their lives holding this precious ground was Private Ferdinand LeBrecht of 86-C. He was the big Austrian-born mountaineer who had knelt in prayer with Jacques Parker and the others in the tiny attic at the base of Riva prior to the climb.[26]

As their comrades fought and died to hold Riva Ridge, the rest of the division prepared for the main assault that Nazi commander General Kesselring now assumed was coming. Whether or not General Truscott would have ordered the attack on Mount Belvedere had the Riva operation failed is an intriguing question, and might have set up a major confrontation with General Clark. Truscott's gambit that he needed the ridges above Highway 64 in order to successfully attack Highway 65 could have been used by Clark to hoist him on his own petard, with the troops of the Tenth Mountain Division paying the severe price with an exposed attack on the mountain. The resulting devastation might easily have dwarfed the losses suffered at the Rapido. Suffice it to say that the well-trained alpinists who successfully completed the Riva Ridge action had accomplished an incredible feat of mountain warfare, and by their legendary winter climb had rendered the question moot.

Now it was the turn of the rest of the division to attack and capture Belvedere and the adjacent peaks to its northeast, Mount Gorgolesco and Mount della Torraccia. Rudy and Jake's Eighty-seventh Regiment was assigned the task of taking the lower Belvedere ridges, along with members of the Eighty-fifth who had been designated to capture the mountain's summit and adjoining Mount Gorgolesco. Ralph Bromaghin's Third Battalion of the Eighty-sixth was assigned to the division's right flank, with orders to take Mount della

Torraccia with elements of the Eighty-fifth after the other objectives were secured. The field order received by the men prior to their departure was simple, direct, and frighteningly blunt: "The ground occupied will be held at all costs."[27]

After all of the training and the bravado, for Rudy, Jake, and Ralph—like the marines who landed halfway around the world that day on the beaches of Iwo Jima—the time had finally come to fight. Whether confident, apprehensive, terrified, or all three in tandem, the boys cleared their minds and put one foot in front of the other, moving by sheer force of will toward the objective.

On the evening of February 19, 1945, Sergeant Jacob Nunnemacher's 87 Bravo Company marched three miles to their jump-off point at Querciola (a town that had been quickly and predictably dubbed "Coca Cola" by the Americans) and waited near the foot of Belvedere.[28] Sergeant Rudy Konieczny and the rest of 87 Fox Company moved into position below Belvedere at Case Buio, slightly to the left of Company B.[29] The entire division, except those already deployed on Riva Ridge, was poised to attack or support.

Time stood still for some, and moved much too quickly for others. Prayers were silently offered. Troopers shivered uncontrollably, not knowing whether from cold or fear. "I remember adjusting my helmet and giving the order for fixed bayonets before the march started up the mountain," recalled Lieutenant Morley Nelson of 87-C. "There was a great deal of fright in everyone's eyes."[30] "The bayonet orders snapped everyone to their senses in a hurry," remembered Phil Puchner. "My reactions fluctuated between 'you've got to be kidding' to 'brother, this is serious.'"[31] At 2300 hours, 11 p.m., each soldier drew a deep breath of frigid air and left the line of departure to start his climb.

General Hays, opting once again to utilize surprise insofar as possible, elected to forego an artillery barrage. Instead, the men of the Tenth Mountain Division moved silently over the frozen mud with orders not to fire until first light in order to conceal their positions.[32] A muzzle flash would unmistakably mean enemy fire, to be answered with grenades, because no rounds were permitted to be chambered in American guns. Shortly after midnight, however, the plan of battle went to hell.

Phil Puchner's Company 87-G, slotted between Jake's company on the right and Rudy's on the left, entered a minefield. The ensuing explosions and screams set off a hellacious rain of Nazi mortar and small-arms fire that killed and wounded many and pinned down all three companies for hours.[33] Puchner believed that his company was assigned to the sector at the last minute and had little time for reconnaissance. "We were definitely ready for the push," he remembered with some consternation. "They'd eased us into the situation over a period of weeks, and I really felt prepared for anything. But the mines came as a complete surprise."[34]

Tenth Mountain Division historian Flint Whitlock wrote chillingly of those first moments of terror in combat on Belvedere:

> Fighting their way through the barbed wire, mine fields, mortar and artillery bursts, and the deadly curtain of lead, most of the mountain troops received their first taste of combat. Men were spun to the ground by the impact of bullets, sliced open by whirling, jagged shards of shrapnel, atomized by direct bursts from artillery and mortar shells, catapulted into the air from the force of explosions, or thrown to the ground in agony, screaming with pain, clutching at torn limbs or spilled intestines, at jaws and genitals that had disappeared.[35]

The fighting overnight on Belvedere was desperate and at times confused. At one point, an Italian partisan accompanying the Americans spotted men coming up the mountain from the rear of 87 Fox Company's position and opened fire. To the horror of all, he mistakenly killed Lieutenant John Benson, who was bringing reinforcements to assist Rudy Konieczny's pinned-down squad.[36] The situation grew more chaotic after that incident, as some of Benson's men briefly wanted to take their revenge on the partisans. David Burt recalled it was sometime after dawn that Rudy made his legendary use of two BARs at once, firing both weapons from their bipods simultaneously in an effort to protect his exposed men from the enemy uphill.[37]

At sunrise, communications with Battalion Headquarters were finally re-established by Fox Company, and Allied artillery strikes were ordered in. That effectively ended the battle in the unit's narrow sector, as some fifty-five Germans surrendered soon after the shelling commenced.[38]

Jake Nunnemacher's Bravo Company, meanwhile, fought its way up the nearby slope a few feet at a time throughout the night. T5 Bob Parker, who would later become editor of *Skiing* magazine and serve as an instrumental figure in the establishment of Vail ski resort near Camp Hale in Colorado, helped guide Jake and his men through the minefields.[39] It was a treacherous job that Parker worried seriously throughout the night would get him killed. (The lucky Parker survived the night and the war physically unscratched, despite having Nazi shells land within a yard of him on three separate occasions. In each case, the ordnance failed to detonate.)[40] Private Lewis Hoelscher remembered crawling for hours over freezing ground with Jake toward the summit of Belvedere, feeling ahead for mines and trip wires, not knowing who was still alive among the friends he started up the mountain with. By first light, the men of Company B reached their hillside objective. Miraculously, not a single man in the entire company had been killed, though eleven had been wounded.[41] Nunnemacher came through unhurt.

Not so fortunate were the men of Companies C and D of the Eighty-seventh, who had an unpleasant introduction to Nazi combat tactics. After a dawn firefight near the crest of Belvedere, several Germans came forward from a bunker with their hands up calling out "[Nicht] boom, comrade."[42] Sergeant William F. Murphy walked out to receive the prospective prisoners, when they suddenly dove to the ground. Their Nazi cohorts hiding behind them then opened fire, killing Murphy and wounding several other U.S. mountain troopers before the Americans could shoot them down.[43]

The members of 87-C, serving under newly appointed captain and company commander Morley Nelson (later to become the world's leading expert and trainer of birds of prey), were both horrified and deeply hardened by the incident. One of the troopers was looking off to the side when the Nazis began shooting. According to Nelson, the boy was hit near the temple:

A bullet took out the ridge of his nose and both eyes. [He] screamed and staggered over to the south side of the ridge, trying to get away. . . . We ran over to assist [him], and saw one of the most horrible sights any man will ever see. [He] was trying to go down through the snow with blood coming out of his head and face, and he'd fall down and get up and go some more, and the men were so horrified by his injury that [for a while] they couldn't gather up the strength to help out. . . . So from that day on . . . Company C never took a prisoner.[44]

Nelson's last, chilling comment was more than mere hyperbole. Sergeant Denis Nunan of 87-C wrote to his parents in 1945 that he had been ordered by an officer during a momentary lull in fighting to take six German POWs behind a haystack and execute them with his service revolver. He did. According to his son, Nunan agonized over having done so for the rest of his life.[45]

"That was the level of brutality with which the war was being fought at that point," recalled Captain George Earle. Was it right or wrong? "It just was."[46] The morning after Company C's ordeal on Belvedere, Nunnemacher's Company B had a similar experience with Nazi deception. After a dawn firefight, five Nazis walked out with their hands up, ostensibly to surrender. Luckily, the men of Bravo Company had the benefit of their battalion mates' experience the day before, and were still behind cover when a sixth prospective prisoner suddenly opened fire with a machine gun. Although two Americans were wounded, the six Nazis were quickly dispatched.[47] It would not be the only time in Italy that Jake Nunnemacher would face such a situation.

℘)(℘

The first days of the Belvedere offensive were both an emotional and literal baptism by fire, perhaps felt most acutely by the predominantly young and green members of the Eighty-fifth Regiment that took the Belvedere and Gorgolesco peaks. Sergeant Hugh Evans, a climber and expert skier from the Sierras who earned a Silver Star leading the troops of 85-C to the top of Gorgolesco, wrote of a tragic and poignant moment on the way back down from the captured summit.

In a 1946 article published in the *American Alpine Journal,* Evans recounted, "I met a man from our Company, Eugene Savage, going in the same direction." Sergeant Evans had trained at Hale and Cooper Hill with Gene and Irv Savage, one of the several pairs of ski mountaineering brothers who joined the Tenth together. "As we passed a dead American soldier who had the top of his head blown off," Evans continued, Gene Savage mumbled quietly, "that's my brother." Evans stood stunned as Savage just kept walking, not saying another word.[48] Trooper Dan Kennerly of 85-D recalled that the level of mutilation done to Irv Savage's body "was the most horrible sight I have ever seen."[49] Sergeant Evans made it back to his unit, and after checking in with his wounded captain, recalled that he turned his head away and walked off weeping.[50]

℘)(℘

The enemy counterattacks on Belvedere and Gorgolesco were fierce and continued for days, with the worst fighting yet to come. Artillery and mortars poured into the American positions as the Nazis attempted to repeat past successes in driving the Allied forces off captured high ground. The Americans faced additional danger from mines left behind by the retreating enemy and from the ever-present threat of friendly fire from U.S. artillery and dive bombers.[51]

Through it all, however, the Tenth held on Belvedere and Gorgolesco. For Ralph Bromaghin and the boys on Mount della Torraccia, though, the situation was far more desperate.

137

With the surrealistic specter of hundreds of local Italian civilians watching the battle from the hillsides, Lieutenant Colonel John Stone led the Second Battalion of the Eighty-fifth onto the slopes of della Torraccia on the afternoon of February 21.[52] They were immediately hit with every form of artillery the Nazis had at their disposal, including the dreaded 88mm Flak-41 antitank/antiaircraft shells known reverentially throughout the European theater simply as "eighty-eights." Low on ammunition and food, caring for numerous casualties, and with only sporadic radio communication, Stone received a message from General Headquarters. According to Marty Daneman of Stone's headquarters company, that controversial radio message was to "attack until your battalion is expended."[53]

For two more days, Nazi tree bursts decimated Stone's troops as they dug in, and mortar rounds and small-arms fire tore into them whenever they tried to charge forward. Stone had blundered by having his troops conceal themselves on the forested portion of the hillside, where the Nazi artillery could be utilized to greatest effect. "It was terrible to watch," recalled trooper Tom Brooks. "We could see them taking that beating from our position in the valley below. You'd watch them charge, and have to fall back into the forest to absorb those tree bursts again."[54] Company F of the Eighty-fifth was shredded mercilessly as it tried to advance through an exposed position between two minefields.[55] Finally, on the third day, Stone sent back a message stating that he was low on supplies and had little left but the wounded, and that he could not fight on.[56]

General Hays ordered the reserve Third Battalion of the Eighty-sixth Regiment under Major (soon to be Lieutenant Colonel) John Hay Jr. to relieve Stone, from whom command of his decimated battalion was later taken.[57] After five long days of waiting, Ralph Bromaghin was among those who went into the hell of della Torraccia with Major Hay and the relieving force.

The Eighty-sixth attacked della Torraccia at dawn on February 24. One platoon sergeant from Company 86-K described the jump-off: "We had been told that the objective lay but 700 yards ahead, but I'm sure if we had realized what each of those seven hundred yards held in store for us it would have taken greater force than patriotism, self-pride, and intestinal fortitude to maintain our forward impetus."[58]

Ralph Bromaghin's old Mount Rainier skiing buddy, Captain Duke Watson, led the battalion forward onto the mountain at the head of Company 86-I. His men came under immediate and intense automatic weapons and artillery fire as they struggled up the slope.[59] "It was bad," remembered Major

Hay. "There wasn't a yard of ground that didn't get hit by a mortar or by artillery."[60]

It was so bad, in fact, that General Hays came up to have a look for himself, and to add what inspiration he could by placing himself in harm's way. Major David Brower wrote that the general came through his lower head-quarters post on his way up to make direct contact with the troops. "Things are rough up there," the battalion's intelligence officer made the mistake of telling the general. Before turning away and heading farther up, the general—a Medal of Honor recipient in the previous war—glowered at Brower and shot back, "I don't ever want to hear you talk like that again."[61]

At the end of the charge, the fighting was hand to hand. American fury was especially aroused after some Nazi troops adopted the practice of intentionally killing medics and litter-bearers as they tended to wounded G.I.s. As the *History of the 86th Mountain Infantry* notes, "the men gritted their teeth as they carried aid men [back] who had been shot through their Red Cross . . . helmets," and they vented their rage right back at the enemy.[62]

Duke Watson, three and a half years removed from the fateful day on the slopes of Mount Rainier with Ralph Bromaghin when news of Pearl Harbor arrived, made it to the top of della Torraccia after four hours of vicious fighting. He immediately began to call in coordinates for artillery strikes. Moments later, a huge 170mm Nazi howitzer shell exploded a few feet away, stunning him. "I looked down and saw I'd taken a few pretty good shards in my gut," Captain Watson remembered, "and I must have been a little shocky. I had no idea how bad it was, but I knew intestinal wounds were very dangerous if not treated quickly, and so I started down." Watson walked for a while, staggered for a bit longer, and when the Nazi artillery barrage picked up, he began crawling. By then, his uniform was soaked in red.[63]

"I was really losing blood quickly," Watson remembered, "and there were explosions all around. I figured I was going to die out there, and so did everyone else who saw me. All I remember is this big figure coming over the hill calling to me, 'Stay down, Duke, I'm coming.' He picked me up on his back, and carried me down to the forward observation post." It was Ralph Bromaghin.[64]

Bromaghin had left the relative safety of his hole during the heaviest part of the shelling on della Torraccia, a lone figure moving across open ground to save a friend. "In the midst of all those explosions, and remember that Ralph was a pretty big target, he got me tied onto a mule litter," said Watson. "That's the way I came down off della Torraccia. They took me straight to the aid station, and on to the hospital. Ralph saved my life. There is no doubt in my mind about that. I believe that I would have died up there without his help."[65]

"We took the hill on the morning of the twenty-fourth," recalled Major Hay, "and the enemy decided right away they had to have it back or risk losing the Apennines."[66] The shelling and counterattacks lasted two full days, during which time the outcome was several times in doubt. For infantry troops, bombardments are frequently the worst aspect of combat. "There were times during that shelling that I feared I'd lost most of my men," Hay continued. "We were using captured weapons and ammo, and after a while we had to scrape the blood off German bread and rations with our trench knives because we'd run out of our own food and supplies. But we held on."[67]

Finally, in the late afternoon of the twenty-fifth, things quieted down enough for the Americans to move out of their foxholes. Many of Kesselring's soldiers, realizing that the U.S. mountain troops were not going to surrender this ground, lay down their arms. The rest withdrew.[68] From Riva Ridge on the left to della Torraccia on the right, the Americans now controlled the heights that the Nazis had resolutely believed could not be taken.

How bad had it been on della Torraccia? In his excellent and graphically descriptive book, *Mountain Troops and Medics*, Third Battalion surgeon Dr. Albert Meinke described the reaction of one soldier of the Eighty-sixth carried down from the hill with one of his feet blown off by a mine. Dr. Meinke reported that, rather than cursing his fate, the man was overcome with relief. Through the morphine, the soldier was quite lucid in his rambling assessment of the situation:

> I'm lucky! I'm going home! The war's over for me, and I'm still alive. Losing my foot isn't too much of a price to pay. You guys are the unlucky ones. You have to go out there again. You have to go out there over and over again, but I'm going home. Even the guys who are dead are luckier than you are. They don't have to go out there anymore. But I'm the luckiest, because I'm still alive, and I'm going home.[69]

The most terrifying aspect of the battle for some troopers had been the smell on Belvedere, Gorgolesco, and della Torraccia. "There is a strong scent," wrote trooper Dan Kennerly of 85-D. "At first, I cannot place it. Now it comes to me. The smell is blood. It is the odor of a slaughterhouse. . . . I'm gripped with fear. I feel sick and want to vomit. Now I recognize the terrible nature of infantry warfare. The stark brutality overwhelms me. I feel completely vulnerable . . . like a child wanting its mother."[70]

Private Dan Pinolini of Duke Watson's 86-I remembered lying in a foxhole during the worst of the bombardments and wondering whether it might not be in his best interest to get sent home due to a self-inflicted wound. "A lot of guys told me they had the same thoughts on della Torraccia. You think about these things, especially at night, but then it passes. I mean, it was so bad, and most of us were so young. But you blank out your mind, and you just go on."[71]

Further on that sensitive issue, John Woodward (having been promoted to the rank of major) recalled going forward to investigate an incident in which a young soldier "accidentally" shot off his own trigger finger. "Give the physical logic of that scenario some thought," he said. "But the kid's foxhole mate swore that the gun had accidentally discharged during a shelling, and that's the way I wrote it up."[72]

છગ્ર

That evening at dusk on della Torraccia, Captain Ralph Lafferty showed up at Ralph Bromaghin's forward observation post with a bottle of Regimental scotch and an empty C ration can. The two best friends toasted both their success on somehow surviving the battle and the saving of Duke Watson's life. They talked about Rainier and skiing at Aspen, watercolors and song parodies, anything but the war. "We had some badly needed laughs. I left Ralph standing in the two-foot depth of his foxhole dug into almost solid rock," wrote Lafferty, "and went back down to my . . . command post."[73]

By sunrise the next morning, February 26, 1945, the Nazi shelling had nearly subsided, with only a sporadic burst here and there.[74] The Tenth's first victory was finally at hand. Bromaghin worked with his good friend, Chaplain Brendemihl, in assisting the injured to the aid station. To most of the men who had seen him in action, Bromaghin was no longer the "hard-ass" officer of D-Series, but rather the guy who braved enemy shelling to save his friends and care for his wounded.

Brendemihl and Bromaghin returned to their foxhole and heated up some coffee on a mountain stove, which was placed just outside the front rim of the hole in the bright sunshine. The two sat on the edge with their legs dangling and joked with the men as they passed by, including Captain Rideout, whose Company 86-F would soon be relieving Bromaghin's. Rideout had just come by to check on things, as had Major Brower. Putting aside for the moment the ordeal they had all just been through, everyone was happy simply to be alive. The mood on della Torraccia was good. There were smiles for the first time in days.[75] Bromaghin was busy giving orders to Sergeant Ross Coppock, Coppock's radio man, and a battalion runner as Chaplain Brendemihl looked on, when it happened.[76]

"Mortar shells make no sound when they come in," the chaplain explained in a letter to Ralph Bromaghin's sister, Leone. They leave every soldier equally vulnerable by their randomness. The German ordinance that landed some ten feet in front of the coffeepot, totally unexpectedly, was just a flash of explosive light that blinded the chaplain for a moment. "It was a 'cripple' mortar shell that just dropped straight down on us," recalled Coppock, "totally out of the blue."[77] A stunned Bromaghin blurted out "medic." David Brower remembered hearing the captain repeat the call twice.[78]

The force of the blast blew Coppock backward several yards and over an embankment, where he landed, miraculously unhurt. "I went back to the aid station and bawled like a baby," he recalled. "Everyone there just kind of left me to myself. I suppose they'd seen that reaction before. After about ten minutes, I pulled myself together, stood up, and went back on the line. It was just an overwhelming feeling of anguish and shock, of extreme vulnerability, that caused everything to kind of gush up all of a sudden. But then I was okay."[79]

The blast had also caused the radio man to sustain shrapnel wounds just below the heart, which proved not to be life-threatening, while the runner received a serious head injury.[80] The captain himself, however, took the brunt of the mortar fragments.

"I recovered immediately and caught Ralph as he fell," Brendemihl wrote. "I believe that he knew that it was fatal, for . . . almost as soon as he was hit, he began to say softly the Lord's Prayer."[81]

"The shock of the wound," Brendemihl continued in regard to the eviscerating gash torn into Ralph Bromaghin's abdomen by the fragment, "made it unlikely that he suffered at all. He was very peaceful and relaxed, I would almost say content. There was no pain and no fear. Of all the men I have known, none have been better prepared than Ralph to be received into the loving arms of his Heavenly Father. . . . [He] passed away in my arms" just as he finished the prayer.[82]

Though the story related by Chaplain Brendemihl in his letter to the Bromaghin family seems almost too cinematic, others have confirmed that his description was fact, not merely an account assembled to salve the hurt of bereaved loved ones. According to battalion surgeon Dr. Meinke, "when we were notified of Captain Bromaghin's death, the story was as Chaplain Brendemihl described. He was standing and recited the Lord's Prayer out loud as he died."[83] Henry Brendemihl's embellishments—if there were any—were likely limited to his emphasis on Bromaghin's overall religious faith, which his friends maintain was not an essential part of Ralph's character.[84]

There should be no mistake, however, that the Hollywood overtones created by Bromaghin's dying prayer made this some bloodless, John Wayne–type death. Ralph Bromaghin, the complicated giant of a skier, musician, and watercolorist, died standing up, his knees buckling, with one arm draped over the shoulder of his friend and the other vainly trying to hold in his intestines. Blood poured from his wound onto the dirt in front of him, until Chaplain Brendemihl could finally ease his expired body to the ground.[85] That is frequently how soldiers die in combat. It is one of the reasons why the sacrifice is so dear.

೫೦೦೫

Ralph Bromaghin was carried down the mountain on the back of a mule, in the same manner that so many members of the Tenth returned from their last climb. He was sealed in a dark body bag that swayed hideously on the animal's back with each of its downward movements. Chaplain Brendemihl sent Ralph's family a copy of the memorial service program from the military cemetery where his body was temporarily interred. For his efforts in assisting the wounded on della Torraccia under intense enemy fire, Captain Ralph R. Bromaghin was awarded a Bronze Star, posthumously.[86]

It was a devastated Captain Percy Rideout who came down off della Torraccia to give the bad news to Bromaghin's closest friends, including Ralph Lafferty, that the last explosion had taken him.[87] In the film *Fire on the Mountain,* the award-winning documentary chronicling the history of America's ski troops, Captain Lafferty tried to speak more than fifty years later about that moment. "The worst day for me was when my best friend was killed." He paused to try to regain his composure, smiled, and said with a hoarse, cracking voice, "I still can't talk about it now."[88]

The Brutal Road to Castel d'Aiano

THE NIGHTMARISH EXPERIENCE ON THE BELVEDERE RIDGES, AS ONE MIGHT EXPECT, resulted in a desperate change in attitude among the members of the Tenth Mountain Division. Before being exposed to combat, said trooper Bob Carlson of 86-L, the men of the Tenth believed they were invincible. "They thought they were going to run all over the enemy," he said.[1] After the carnage on Riva Ridge, Belvedere, Gorgolesco, and della Torraccia, all that confidence had been reduced to simple, grim resolve. "We were just a damn ski club," trooper Harry Poschman recalled less politely in regard to the division's prebattle naiveté, "until we got the shit shot out of us in Italy."[2]

For the next few days, in the freezing cold and with sporadic artillery fire still crashing down around them, the men of the Tenth were given time to "rest" in preparation for the next phase of the campaign, the attack on Castel d'Aiano planned to commence on March 3, 1945. Many, like Rudy Konieczny,

144

took time to catch up on reading and writing letters home reassuring loved ones that things would be fine.[3] Some, like Jacob Nunnemacher, reflected long and hard on their own mortality, and wondered how to express such profound feelings and fears in words.

Others, such as the members of the Eighty-sixth who had scaled Riva Ridge, were rewarded with a few hours of recreational skiing outside the village of Vidiciatico near Riva's base. For several, it would be their last, fully healthy time on skis.[4]

As March arrived, Allied troops were already streaming into Germany from both the east and west. It was apparent to all on the German side that the war was lost. Still, Kesselring was determined at the demand of the increasingly incoherent Hitler to hold the line in Italy to the last possible moment. The Waffen SS troops under his command began shooting slackers in a successful effort to stem the tide of desertion.[5] For the time being, the brutal defense by Nazi troops of their "Winter Line" through the Apennines would continue.

On the evening of March 2, only hours before the next phase of battle was to begin, Jake Nunnemacher sat in his foxhole and wrote a lengthy letter to his beloved Jean. It is quite apparent that although he may not have expected the worst from the coming push, after what he had seen on Belvedere he could not risk having failed to say a proper good-bye. Filled with fear and longing, he poured out his heart on subjects ranging from love to philosophy to religion, and got his letter into the mail just before the prebattle curfew. "There will be another period of silence from me soon," he warned her, knowing that with a six-week-old baby, the stress of not hearing from him would be more difficult to bear than ever. The intervening decades have done nothing to diminish the poignancy of the rest:

> Oh, darling, in all the haste and anxiety to turn out as much mail as possible in the short time I have, I think I've neglected to tell you of that old, old subject: my love for you. It bothers me an awful lot to be so completely restrained and checkmated in all efforts to really express my want for you. It was so easy in days gone by when I could count on seeing you every evening knowing you were always ready to fill my outstretched arms. It makes me content in a way now to know that in all the days and nights we've spent together before and after our marriage, we haven't wasted very many opportunities to love each other so completely. When I think of those summer nights at the Lake when I just couldn't say goodnight and let you go, it almost seems as though we had a deep

premonition that some day we were going to be denied completely every chance to be together.

And that is why I am so thankful for our little Heidi. I know she will help you during those lonely, difficult days. And again you must know that she makes my lot less difficult even though so far removed. . . . Of all the things we have done in our lives together—this one little idea to have a baby has been the most providential and fortunate. We must be so thankful, and I guess that is an advantage to having a religion—one is able to give thanks to something specific. I for lack of it give my thanks to you. . . .

It's getting late and unfortunately I must be getting this into the mail. I don't want to say goodnight—I just want to write on and on. Darling, I love you. . . . I want to be able to make you so happy—know always Jeanie that you have been the only inspiration in my life—always it has been *you* and I work tirelessly for the whole great future with you. Oh darling, take me into your arms and let me rest my tired head—I'll dream of you tonight and every night no matter where I might be. Be brave and keep Heidi quiet and loving.

I love you Jeanie—I am yours completely forever—I love you so—

Your own devoted Jacob[6]

Just after dawn on March 3, 1945, the next phase of the offensive was launched. The men of the Tenth Mountain Division immediately absorbed a bombardment the likes of which they had not experienced even on della Torraccia.

Rudy Konieczny's 87 Fox Company had assembled and readied to attack a low hill above a crossroads east of the Belvedere area near Malandrone, their first objective along the route to Castel d'Aiano. That intersection was shortly to become known as "Shrapnel Junction." Before the unit could make a single move toward the hill that had been code-named "Item," enemy artillery fire came blasting in, instantly killing several troopers. Others hit the dirt or scrambled for any available cover as Nazi 105mm howitzer shells and heavy mortars rained down in deadly arcs.[7]

The scene was the same throughout most of the division, although the Third Battalion of the Eighty-seventh received the worst of it at a place so pockmarked by shell holes that it became known as "Punch Board Hill."[8] There, Jake Nunnemacher's close friend and Colorado skiing partner, Sergeant John Tripp, was leading a mortar team with Company 87-L under former U.S. National Downhill champion Captain Joe Duncan. Though struck by shrapnel in both knees, Tripp continued to man his post until the danger of attack had passed, and only then reluctantly agreed to be evacuated.[9] Sergeant Ralph Townsend, formerly of the University of New Hampshire Ski Team, was also seriously wounded in the bombardment as the Third Battalion tried to move up.[10]

Sergeant Pete Seibert of Percy Rideout's Company 86-F, the former East Coast racer and Riva Ridge veteran who would later become the principal founder of the Vail, Colorado, ski resort, was likewise critically injured in the battle. As a result of a tree burst directly overhead, he suffered serious shrapnel wounds to his legs, arms, and torso and one to the jaw that tore out most of his teeth. A second explosion nearly killed the medic giving him aid. Seibert recalled:

> I heard a deafening blast and saw stars in many colors, the predominant one being bright red. . . . The first pain came from my shattered left forearm, which felt as though it had been hit with a baseball bat. I tried to stand up, but my right leg was useless and I fell back. I gazed into the face of Sergeant Hutchens, another platoon leader in F Company [Eighty-sixth Regiment]. He was yelling words I know he didn't believe: "You'll be okay, Pete. Lie back, you're okay." It was about then that I realized that I'd also been hit in the face. I was spitting teeth, gagging and choking on the blood in my throat.[11]

Doctors told Seibert, whose near-fatal wounds that day included the loss of his right kneecap, that he would likely never walk again. After three years of grueling and painful rehabilitation, he was back racing once more. Astonishingly, in 1950, he made the U.S. national ski team.[12]

The greatest of all the Tenth Mountain Division athletes, however, would not recover from wounds received in the battle for Castel d'Aiano. In the nearby town of Iola, U.S. ski-jumping champion Sergeant Torger Tokle—the soldier whom many troopers regarded as the very personification of division pride—was sprinting along the top of a ridgeline with the first platoon of Company 86-A, in pursuit of Germans staging a fighting retreat below them. Sergeant Tokle, as usual, was running back and forth from squad to squad, ensuring that his platoon maintained its forward momentum. They were stopped, however, when a Nazi machine-gun crew set up at the base of the ridge and began firing up at the Americans.[13]

Tokle's company commander, Captain Bill Neidner, was an accomplished ski jumper and mountaineer from Wisconsin, where he grew up as a friend of the Bradley and Nunnemacher families. He adored Tokle not only for his skill but also for his gregarious personality. Many of the men of his company were particularly close because of the bonds they had forged in Nordic skiing stretching back to the first days at Fort Lewis and Camp Hale, and extending to the action on Riva Ridge. As a result, some had formally pledged to lay down their lives for one another, if necessary. Tokle had made such a pact the night before with his good friends and fellow ski jumpers Sergeant Lyle Munson and their platoon leader, Lieutenant Gordon Anderson.[14]

When Sergeant Munson, himself a former junior ski-jumping champion, announced that he was taking his reserve squad over to take out the machine gun, Tokle interjected. He instructed Munson (to whom he always referred with inexplicable but affectionate Norwegian humor as "Ole") to stay put, that he and his bazooka man, Private Arthur Tokola, would move forward and knock it out.[15]

"From about twenty yards away, I watched as Tokle moved to Arthur Tokola's position," remembered Munson. Tokola was an intelligent, serious, and reliable soldier, he wrote, and "probably the best cross-country skier in the division." As usual, Tokola was carrying the bazooka shells on his back, "which meant Tokle would position himself directly behind Arthur, remove a shell from Arthur's pack, load it, prepare the bazooka for firing, and tap Arthur on the shoulder when the bazooka was ready to be fired. Tokola would then aim the bazooka and fire it."[16] Tokle and Tokola got off one round.

Almost simultaneous with the firing of the bazooka, there was an ear-shattering blast. "I heard the explosion," Munson continued. "It was horrendous."[17] Jacques Parker of 86-C was more than a hundred yards away. "Everyone in the battalion area heard and felt that boom," he remembered. "We had no idea what happened."[18] According to Munson and medic Robert Meyerhof, a short round fired by a distant American battery had hit on or near the pack of bazooka rounds Tokola was carrying, setting off the charges all at once.[19] Torger Tokle and Arthur Tokola, the two Scandinavian-born buddies who were among the world's finest Nordic skiers, were killed instantly by the friendly fire.

"I immediately ran to the bazooka position and saw Tokle lying facedown on the slope," said Munson. "There were well over one hundred tufts of pile jacket insulation poking up through holes in the back of Tokle's . . . jacket where the shrapnel tore through his body. All I was able to see of [Arthur] Tokola's remains was a piece of his dog tags and his pants about ten feet up in a tree." A combat boot remained hanging through one of the pants legs. "The sight was devastating. I went to my knees, murmured 'shoot me if you want,' and then proceeded to say some prayers."[20]

"Torger laid down his life for me," Munson concluded of his idol.[21] As it turned out, he and Tokola saved many other American lives as well. The bazooka round they had gotten off just before being struck apparently scored a direct hit on the targeted Nazi MG-42. The advance continued, though dozens of G.I.s were devastated over the deaths of their close friends.[22] Many in the division, in fact, referred to learning of Tokle's death as among the harshest moments of their wartime experiences.

The fact is that Torger Tokle had made a habit of taking extreme risks in combat. "He was always out in front exposing himself to enemy fire, which I thought was a mistake, but that's just the way he was," recalled Fran Limmer, Tokle's friend in Company 86-A and the son of famed ski-boot maker Peter Limmer.[23] "I don't know if there was any fear in the man," added Munson. "He never said 'no' to anything."[24] Tokle also may have been among those who, like Ralph Bromaghin and Rudy Konieczny, shared a fatalistic sense of foreboding. Hours prior to the fateful advance, Tokle was asked if he intended to jump competitively again after the war. "I don't know," he replied to trooper Bart Wolffis. "I might be dead tomorrow."[25] Torger Tokle was twenty-five.

⊱⊰

Rudy Konieczny was himself having quite a time of it with Company F in continued fighting outside of Malandrone. With 105mm artillery shells streaming down and their comrades falling all around them, the members of Fox Company regrouped, struggled forward, and finally assaulted the targeted ridge. This brought even more intense fire and shelling, killing two more members of the company and wounding many others.[26] Finally, Rudy and his mates decided they had had enough and charged uphill. Lugging his BAR and firing madly, Rudy was out in the open on a dead run when a shell landed directly in front of him. It was five years to the day that he had broken his right leg on the Thunderbolt. This time, a hunk of shrapnel tore into the same limb, as other fragments pierced his arms and body, ripping substantial wounds that bled profusely.[27] Those who saw him get hit weren't sure that he could have survived such an explosion, but somehow he did. By now, the days on Greylock must have seemed to Rudy several lifetimes ago.

"Rudy was a real mess, bleeding from several wounds in his arms and side and a real bad one in his leg," recalled friend and aid man Gordie Lowe. "But he kept insisting that he was fine, telling the medics that they needed to fix him up so he could go back out. He just didn't want to leave. Even in his

149

condition, with blood everywhere, he was still full of beans. I'll always remember that."[28]

In a way, Rudy was lucky that his wounds were so serious. He received priority evacuation to Livorno and finally to a surgical hospital in Naples, rather than spending the night in a field station. That evening, a booby trap left by the Nazis exploded in the building chosen to serve as the Eighty-seventh Regimental aid station at Abetaia, killing nearly everyone inside, including two of the three regimental chaplains and at least one medic.[29] "The next few days got even rougher," remembered Lowe.

Captain Morley Nelson of 87-C recalled the difficult process his troops endured over the following days of brutality, attempting to stay focused on their jobs by rationalizing away the deaths of buddies, even as their own lives hung in the balance. "The thing that went through everyone's mind [about the death of a fellow soldier]" he wrote, "was, *ok, he doesn't have to worry anymore.*" Nelson recalled stopping for food and a sip of water during a lull in the fighting for Castel d'Aiano, and looking up into a tree. "Damned if I didn't see a hand hanging there with a sweater on it. We got up and looked closer at the tree, and it was obvious that somebody had been hit by an eighty-eight right there and blown to bits, scattering body parts throughout the tree. We sat down and continued to eat our lunch and said, *well, he doesn't have to worry anymore.*"[30]

ℰᏰℭᎡ

For Jake Nunnemacher's Company 87-B, participation in the first day of fighting for Castel d'Aiano had been mainly in a supporting role, following behind and mopping up after Rudy's Second Battalion.[31] On day two, they were in the thick of it, experiencing some of the many horrors that war can visit on the local population. As the Americans approached the hamlet of Bacucco, a half dozen enemy soldiers emerged from a group of houses on a hill, holding Italian women in front of them as shields. Faced in the heat of battle with the decision of whether to fire despite the presence of the screaming, struggling civilians, the company's leaders were spared a terrible choice when the Nazis began waving white flags. Was it another trick? When one of the soldiers bolted up the hill, he was shot down by an American, who hit him with a round from an M-1 at an impressive four hundred yards. After that, the rest emphatically surrendered for real.[32]

The use of human shields was not the only transgression of the "rules of war" utilized by the Nazis during the battle for Castel d'Aiano. They also continued to evince a startling willingness to target medics. In an incident well-known to every member of the Eighty-seventh Regiment, aid man T5 William R. Conner braved intense fire on the first day of the attack to reach a wounded trooper fifty yards in front of an enemy position. Despite the fact that he carried a Red Cross flag on a pole, which he planted conspicuously in the ground next to the wounded soldier, a German sniper shot and killed him.[33]

In a lesser-known incident, Private Lorenz "Larry" Koehler of 85-L, a refugee European ski mountaineer and one of the many Jewish members of the division, volunteered to go on a dangerous night patrol near Castel d'Aiano with Lieutenant William Lowell Putnam. Putnam, the founder of the Mount Washington Ski Patrol and well-known to Jake Nunnemacher and his Dartmouth cohorts, recalled trying to talk Koehler out of going on yet another risky mission. He relented when Koehler asserted that "my people have special reasons for fighting in this war."[34] On the wooden stock of his Thompson submachine gun, Koehler had carved the slogan of Garibaldi's Red Shirts, *"sempre avanti,"* "always forward," which was later adopted in its formal grammatical form as the unofficial motto of the Eighty-fifth Regiment.[35]

Once out on patrol, Koehler and a scout went ahead. A few moments later, the two were engulfed in a hail of machine-gun fire from a forward Nazi position. They shouted to their comrades to go back because of the suspected strength of the troops in front of them. Putnam knew Koehler and the scout had been severely wounded, but they were lying in a completely exposed area. Any attempt to bring them out would have been suicidal, and Koehler himself instructed them not to try.[36] Under an intense enemy barrage, Putnam was forced to withdraw, losing two more men to friendly fire on the way back.[37]

The next day, having identified Koehler as a Jew, the Nazis hung his dead body from the roof beam of a bombed-out house in the town the patrol had been probing. Putnam wept when he saw the sight. "Those dirty bastards," he wrote. "They couldn't just kill him, they had to hang him out for all to see, too."[38] As time went on, the Nazis were increasingly convincing the Tenth Mountain Division that it did not pay to give the enemy quarter, because none would be given in return.

༓

Like all U.S. Army units at the time, the Tenth Mountain Division was a segregated outfit that had no African American members.[39] Veterans of the ski troops, nevertheless, take great pride in the fact that on the whole their attitude toward race and religion was identical to their point of view on the unimportance of rank. Though always a subject susceptible to historical revisionism, superior relations in the ski troops among soldiers of various ethnic backgrounds (other than African American) appear to have been fact. This is borne out by the confirmed equal treatment of the many Native American and Jewish members of the mountain troops, who were frequently regarded by their fellow troopers and officers as among the highest-skilled and bravest soldiers in the division.

Tenth Mountain Division veteran Luterio Aguilar (87-H), a full-blooded Native of the Santo Domingo Pueblo near Albuquerque, New Mexico, was outspoken about the camaraderie he enjoyed with other members of the Tenth. "Whether in [Washington State] or Colorado, in the Pacific or in Europe, wherever I went as a member of the Tenth Mountain Division I was treated as an equal," he said. "We were all just mountain men. That was the fact, plain and simple."[40]

At a time when even the U.S. Marine Corps was less than evenhanded in its treatment of the now-revered Navajo "Code Talkers," the Tenth Mountain Division was honoring its Indian members in the same manner as it did the rest of its troopers. Among those Native Americans decorated for valor in Italy were Private Sterling Red Eagle of Montana, Sergeant Andreas Vigil and Private José Aguilar of New Mexico, and First Sergeant John R. Winchester of Kalamazoo, Michigan, who was honored with two Silver Stars for service in Italy with Company 86-B.[41]

Ernest Tapley, part Passamaquoddy Indian from Essex County, Massachusetts, was similarly one of the division's most popular and accomplished mountaineers and soldiers.[42] "Ernest was a faithful friend of us all," recalled Bruce Macdonald of 87-L. "We all appreciated his humor, especially when it came to his appreciation for women. [German Jewish refugee skier] Heinz Katzman was also a member of our group, a gang where ethnic origin, religious inclination or family status carried no weight at all. The binding glue was the mountains, skiing and rock climbing."[43]

Norm Gavrin (86-L), awarded a Bronze Star as a volunteer replacement for the Tenth in north Italy, shared the same sentiments and experiences as the others. "As a Jewish member of the armed forces during the 1940s, you expected a certain amount of guff. I experienced it in North Africa, and in the southern Italian campaign. But not when I joined the Tenth. As a replacement, there was that initial distance you felt from the guys who'd served in the division for years, but I never once heard any stuff about religion. That didn't seem to be what they were about. In fact, after the Nazis surrendered, I got invitations all the time from the guys in my outfit to go skiing with them in the Alps. I feel very good about that, because there were some unpleasant incidents in the other units I served with overseas that were not repeated with the Tenth."[44]

Austrian Jewish mountaineer Walter Neuron, one of Hannes Schneider's Arlberg ski instructors, was likewise another of the division's most popular and revered alpinists.[45] "In the mountain troops," concluded Eighty-seventh Regiment trooper Sid Foil who, though not a Native American, was raised in part on the Apache Reservation in southern New Mexico, "race and religion just didn't enter into it. We were all just mountain men and soldiers. It really was that simple."[46] As an odd footnote to this issue, perhaps the most famous skier refused admittance to the Tenth Mountain Division was Ernst Bloch. Years later, having legally changed his name to Ernie Blake, he would found the Taos, New Mexico, ski resort. Bloch attempted to volunteer for the ski troops in 1942, but as a native-born German who had become a Swiss citizen and served in the Swiss army, he was rejected as a potential spy. He went on to distinguish himself behind enemy lines during the war as a member—ironically—of the U.S. intelligence and security branch known as OSS. In applying to the Tenth, Bloch had neglected to reveal the one fact that would have alleviated all suspicions regarding his sympathies and gotten him in for sure. He never mentioned he was Jewish. After the war, Ernie Blake was proudly made an honorary member of the New Mexico chapter of the Tenth Mountain Division Association.[47]

༂༃

On day three of the March offensive, Jake Nunnemacher's 87 Bravo Company continued forward and participated in the capture of the ruined town of Castel d'Aiano. During the fiercest combat, Nazi SS men fired on regular German army troops attempting to surrender.[48]

The next day, Mount della Spe was taken by the Eighty-fifth Regiment after hand-to-hand fighting.[49] With that accomplished, the advance was halted (against the better judgment of many Tenth Mountain officers, including General Hays), and the division given time to rest.[50] In four days of fighting, the Tenth had taken more than six hundred casualties, including 146 dead.[51] Since the attack on Riva Ridge, its members had been in combat for the better part of two weeks, during which time a total of more than 350 of them had been killed and an additional sixteen hundred wounded.[52] It had been brutal. The Nazis, however, had fared far worse, and finally retreated north to set up new defensive positions against the relentless and bloody advance of the Allied armies.

Rest and Recuperation

As THE SMOKE CLEARED AND THE FRONT QUIETED DOWN INTO A ROUTINE OF ONLY occasional shelling, the surviving members of the division had three principal preoccupations. First, they had to come to grips with the horrors they had just experienced. Second, they longed to get away from the front and clear their heads even for a little while. Finally, they had to hope and pray that the war would end before their services were needed again.

Private Harris Dusenbery, in his book *The North Apennines and Beyond*, included a series of diary entries for this period indicative of the fact that the third category was actually the one that drew the sharpest focus of many troopers:

> 3/21 We follow the news closely these days through the Communication Section radio. The Army radio station puts out five minutes of news every hour. . . . 3/24 The news reports good progress being made on all fronts against the Germans, but it seems like it is taking a long time for the war

to end. . . . We read of new progress being made each day in Germany by both the Russian and Allied armies, and we know that in a matter of days or weeks or months there will be nothing left to fight. . . . 3/25 We heard over the radio tonight that the Rhine has been crossed in several places. Even if the news was late, we are surely glad to get it. General Montgomery is quoted as saying that this is the beginning of the final round. I sure hope so, and I hope it is a quick one. We are sitting here with no change of activity. It looks like the war will be won on the north German plain. . . . 3/26 Maybe we will have only a few more weeks of fighting. . . . 3/28 I guess it is a little early to celebrate the end of the War, but the Section is today consuming its bottle of carefully hoarded whiskey. We heard . . . that Patton is now operating under a security blackout in central Germany. That sounds good to us. We do keep hoping.[1]

In mid-March, Jacob Nunnemacher's company was finally pulled off the line and sent to the Fifth Army Rest Area at Monticatini, about thirty miles from the front. There, Jake settled in to write a series of letters home to Jean, describing in detail his life as a combat infantryman during wartime. He began his correspondence in the first days after the battle for Castel d'Aiano with complaints over the slowness of the mails. With uncharacteristic sharpness, he railed against the irresponsibility of the officers who took too much time to censor the enlisted men's letters, substantially delaying delivery to those waiting anxiously at home for news from loved ones.[2] Gradually, however, his tone of frustration gave way to a calm and illuminating narrative.

In setting the parameters of those subjects he was willing to write about, Jacob wrote to Jean explaining that he would rather not dwell on combat in his letters: "I suppose there is much I could write about the big recent push which I was in. Naturally, there are things which I'd like to tell you and which you'd be very much interested in, but dearest you were right in one of your letters in thinking that all in all I'd rather not write of much of what I saw and felt. Instead I'd much rather tell you of the time in the rest area and the inactive life of the present—or best of all I like to write to you of Heidi and of our past and future together."[3]

Jacob then expounded on how the simplest pleasures become the most precious when living in the field. "The main features today," he wrote unselfconsciously on his first day off the line at Monticatini, "have been a glorious shower and change of clothes."[4] The fastidious Jake had been unable to change any article of clothing but his socks for several weeks. The only "luxury" item of clothing he carried with him in his field pack was a pair of slippers Jean had sent him, which he wore at night in his foxhole while waiting for his boots and socks to dry out.

After a few days off the line, Jake began to revert to his former self. Like many of the Tenth Mountain troopers, he had a genuine interest in seeing the art and culture of Italy that he and his comrades had read about all their lives but had never seen in person. After arranging a pass to visit Florence for a day, an amazed Jacob wrote to Jean of the places he had visited after shopping for gifts for her, Heidi, and the family. His words reflected the awe of any young tourist, not that of a soldier, in one of the world's great capitals of art:

[I had] a wonderful trip through the famous Cathedral Del Duomo. Sweet, it was overwhelming in its historical significance and artistic treasure. I had a guide take me through, and then went on my own for a much longer time of the precious day than I had bargained. There were sculptures by Michelangelo and his famous followers, terrific bronze doors and magnificent frescoes—many which I remembered from my art courses at Dartmouth (credit for liberal arts school!). I even climbed 200 odd steps to the very top of the dome and could only think of last December when I made my poor, pregnant wife climb the Capitol Dome [in Austin]! (Won't it be fun to tell Heidi things like that someday—especially when her suitors call on us?) Well, I could have spent days in the vastness . . . of that magnificent space but my desire to do more shopping sent me back out onto the streets. . . .

The last big event in the memorable day in Florence was the movie we saw in a real theater! Even an "Andy Hardy" [picture] seemed terrific cause it was the first one since leaving America! Since then I've seen two more right up here behind the lines. They show them in a small church which has one side half blown out by a shell hit—quite a novel movie house. . . . One thing I can say for the Army in this theater of operations—they go to all limits to give enlisted men everything possible in entertainment. . . . Tomorrow night I think I'm going by truck to a neighboring town to see a U.S.O. performance."[5]

His few days in the rest area over, Jake was returned to the front. Back in the same foxhole he had left only three days before, reality came rushing back, and he began finally to reveal to Jean some of the hardships of life on the line. In one memorable letter, he gave his wife a full explanation—albeit filled with his usual cheerfulness—of how he and the other men lived in the field:

My Sweet Darling—

Still in the same rest area or rather rear area 'cause actually we are "on line" but in a reserve role. The rest area slipped out because this is a pretty easy life we're leading right now. Nothing much to do in the daytime and best of all there isn't so much guard [duty]. . . . Right up front when there's nothing between us and the Germans one of the two men in each foxhole must be awake [at all times]. Each fellow stands 2 hour shifts, usually, so you can see under those conditions a good nights sleep is an up and down proposition.

You asked several times about how and where we live on our meanderings around this countryside. Well, during the drive when everybody is constantly on the move, the troops naturally sleep and live right in the foxholes they dig immediately after stopping. . . . Those holes are essentially defensive positions, and a man digs like a scared mole because the farther underground he gets the safer it is—safer from small arms fire and especially from artillery and mortar shell fragments.

As I said, these holes are large enough for two men, [rectangular,] and the size depends on the quality of the digging (and the state of fright of the digger!). When the hole is completed a roof is put over which is covered by dirt and rocks. This roof is protection against the worst type of artillery of all—"air bursts." That is, they calculate the shell to explode 20 or 30 feet above a man's head and this naturally scatters more fragments than if the shell landed in the ground—hence the roof. I have some pictures of some holes so you and Heidi can see what your hero has been living in for the past two months.

Now when the situation permits and there are enough houses to go around, we do take them over and squeeze as many men as possible into the usually small rooms. The boys, of course, like this better than the holes, even if it happens to be a farmer's kitchen or shed. Four walls and a ceiling have a great attraction to those who live so continuously out of doors. For the past 2 months I should say we have had most of our time outside and not in buildings, but it hasn't been so terribly uncomfortable at all, mainly due to the . . . abundance of straw and hay to sleep on. . . .

One of my greatest post-war aims [is] crawling into that square bed of ours and staying there for days, perhaps! And of course as long as I stay put in bed, why you won't get up, either! So the only one up and around in our house will be Heidi. Do you think she'll mind bringing us our breakfast (as well as dinner and supper)? What a happy household it will be—oh if only it can come fairly soon—it's so hard to wait.[6]

As Jake Nunnemacher dealt with the hardships of life in the field, in a hospital to the south Rudy Konieczny was trying to make the best of a frustrating situation. On March 4, 1945, he wrote a letter home substantially minimizing the extent of his injuries and demonstrating a startling, matter-of-fact optimism that may or may not have been genuine considering that he had been evacuated only the day before on a priority basis:

Dear Sis:

How is everything in Adams? Are you still receiving the snow in the way you have in the past? Cheer up, spring is just around the corner.

Well, you don't have to worry about me being or getting hurt because I've already been hurt as you may have been told by the War Department, and I hope it didn't scare anyone because it really is nothing to worry about.

I was hit by a fragment from a shell and it went clean through my leg but it did not touch the bone, so in a few weeks I will be okay again and ready to go [and] will drop you a line when I am ready. . . . Tell mother and dad not to worry, and at the rate the war has been going lately, we will all be home soon.

Lots of Love & Luck To You All,
Rudy[7]

The fact was that Rudy was already climbing the walls of the hospital the very first week of what he viewed as his incarceration. His daily routine was excruciatingly dull compared with what he had recently been through, and within a short period Rudy's letters began to reveal frustration over a belief that he was somehow missing out on the action while recuperating. He especially bristled over complaints that he was not writing home often enough. "I really have nothing to write because I go no place but the movies, which they hold around here very often. So you see this is another reason why I don't write too often! . . . I am up in the morning between 6:30 and 7:30, eat, wash, and [have] the rest of the morning to myself. Chow again at 12, and maybe movies at 1:30 until supper. There are a great many of the boys here, and we chew the fat [in the evenings]. What else do you want to know?"[8]

According to Frank Prejsnar, one of those boys from Adams recuperating in the ward with him, all Rudy really wanted was to go back to his company. The inactivity was driving him mad. "He was pretty shot up," remembered Prejsnar. "The doctors gave him the option of going home, but he wouldn't even consider it. I had to go back on the line, since my wounds weren't serious enough to warrant a discharge. But Rudy didn't have to. He just wouldn't leave the Tenth. He told me that he had started at the beginning and he intended to see it through to the end. In that way, he hadn't changed at all from the kid on the Thunderbolt. He couldn't wait to go back."[9]

By the beginning of April, Rudy was cracking under the strain of being in the ward. His last letter home to his sister Juliana, written before his escape from the hospital, seems to indicate moods fluctuating between fatalistic bravado and angry frustration. It could have been the painkillers, and it might have been the trauma of having experienced such heavy combat and significant injury. Most likely, all of those factors and others played a role in his rambling and surly expressions of impatience to get back to his unit, interrupted by passing attempts at black humor, superstitious wishes for a safe return home, and stupefying revelations of his recent activities at the front:

Dear Sis:

Everything here is just Ducky. . . . My leg is coming along fine but I will still stay here a while longer. . . . Here every day is about the same (what do you want, blood?). . . . I don't go to town because they don't give us passes, so I haven't seen a thing. [It's] next to being locked up. They treat us as though we are children. . . .

Personally, I would much rather be with my outfit, because there you can always walk around even if you are taking a chance. Up there I would sneak down past our lines and walk through the Jerry dugouts while they were away, and I must say I found some good bottles of wine. I never got drunk because you just can't do something like that on the front lines if you have a brain in your head. . . .

[I've been writing letters, and I'm sorry they don't arrive promptly], so you have nothing to be mad about. . . . Look, I'm not in the states and if I ever get there I won't leave. . . .

If you don't hear from me, it's probably the fault of the mail. . . . I can take care of myself as well as any dog head in the U.S. Army. I should be old enough, don't you think? If something goes wrong I will let someone else write for me (like if my arm goes bad). If I can't do either, I guess the War Department will let you know, so you see no news means good news. . . . This war doesn't have me down and never will because *I ain't no kid.* . . . As a matter of fact I will be 27 years old in two more days. . . .

You may think things are bad over here for me, but they really aren't, [even] as bad as I've seen it. The front lines aren't as bad as you picture them to be. Sometimes, shells [do] crash all around you, and when you push you walk into fire. Some guys are lucky and others aren't. Some die, and others are lucky and just get hurt (like myself, but it's life). Now I am back here and out of danger. Up there . . . I never slept in my foxhole. If you're going to get it, well you get it, so it's just another way of dying regardless of being scared or not.

I love you all. I would like to be home with you. I don't like war [next word unintelligible], but I'm not the only one and I just got here (remember?). Some of these kids have been [here] much longer than I have. . . .

I'm going to close now. I hope I didn't say anything out of the way, but no one knows how it is up here until you've honestly been up front yourself. It's something words or talk can't explain properly. You just have to be here yourself.[10]

Within a few days, Rudy stopped longing to be back with Company F and took matters into his own hands. Hospitals were for the sick and injured. In his mind, he fell into neither category and was sorely needed elsewhere. Whether the doctors liked it or not, if there was to be a next big push, he was going to be there for it.

According to Oley Kohlman of the Eighty-seventh, Rudy Konieczny's attitude was not so far out of the ordinary. "On more than one occasion when we had wounded back in the hospital, they would get to worrying about the outfit, and would go A.W.O.L. [absent without leave] . . . and hitch hike back to the front."[11] That is exactly what Rudy set out to do during the second week of April 1945, hitching an illicit ride on the truck returning Frank Prejsnar to the front.[12]

℘ℜ

By the time of Rudy's escape, Jake Nunnemacher had begun to wander toward the negative in his letters, as well. In a note written just a few days after his own return to the line, Jake allowed himself for one of the very few times in his extensive correspondence with Jean to disclose the true state of his living conditions. At one particularly strained moment, he admitted that the physical discomfort of being at the front was growing wearisome: "My writing is unusually scratchy because my fingers and hand are stiff and cold. They're also quite painful from cracks and sores which develop from the usual cuts and wear and tear. They are always filthy and that doesn't help, either."[13]

Jake also began to reveal in his writing the mental and emotional strain of life on the line. In one such letter, he told Jean that he had been promoted. He used the opportunity to explain to her, albeit with subtlety, that he now had a more dangerous role in the war. As a staff sergeant, he told her, he would serve as a squad leader in the First Platoon of Company B, leading *his* men into battle. "Are you proud of your hubby?" he asked rhetorically. "Well I'm only half excited, 'cause the job has its drawbacks as well as its advantages."[14] He went on to explain that the opportunity had arisen because of a serious combat injury incurred by his predecessor.

Jake took other opportunities to drop hints to Jean of how deadly the situation was in Italy, perhaps attempting to prepare her for the worst, should it happen. In one letter describing a rest area reunion among many former Tenth Recon members whom both he and Jean knew quite well, Jake wrote:

> We . . . got into a terrific argument with Scott [Sgt. Scott G. Osborn]
> which went on and on. You see, Sweet, he has been in the so-called "rear
> echelon" which operates way back in all the many essential jobs which
> keep the front lines supplied and fighting. Well, he was undertaking to
> arrange a transfer from his present job to the 1st Battalion of the 87th—
> my Battalion! At this we were all excited and naturally thought he was nuts
> to trade. More than anything his pride was hurt to think of us up in front,
> and you know what a determined fellow he is. We argued and argued and
> pretty well convinced him to wait at least a while. My main argument was
> that it wasn't his decision to make, for Thelma certainly rated a very
> important consideration. His relatively safe job certainly is a comfort to
> her. I guess we all felt so strongly about it 'cause in the recent operations
> we had heard of more than one of our old group who had fallen. How it
> hurts to hear about those fellows. . . .
>
> Sweet, I love you so very much and during the past few days I think
> I've been more homesick than ever before. I think of you during these
> sunny days and even more at night when I lie in my dugout and gaze at
> the stars. . . . If I could but hold you and look into your eyes. I love you,
> Jeanie, always.[15]

Just as it seemed he was ready to crack just a little bit, however, Jake shook off his fears and loneliness and returned to writing about what made him and so many of his fellow mountaineers happiest. In a March 28 letter to Jean, one of the last she would receive before the next news blackout, he wrote: "The high mountains to the SW of us still have lots of snow on them. They are some of the highest in the Apennines and before the war there were several large ski resorts among them. They seem from here to offer better slopes than the White Mountains [of New Hampshire] and day after day we look longingly at the[m]."[16]

While Jake dreamed in his foxhole of skiing in a place where no one was fighting, Rudy Konieczny was on the road looking for a way back to help the men he had skied and trained with for more than three years, should the fighting continue. Both Rudy and Jake had the same thoughts in mind, as did nearly every other member of the Tenth Mountain Division up on the line. They desperately longed for the comfort and safety of home and the mountains and ski slopes on which they had grown up. They wanted the war to end now. But if it didn't, their commitment to each other was paramount, and they would move forward together if ordered to do so. "It was mountains and skiing that brought us together," concluded Jake's friend Bob Parker. "We were like-minded friends first, and citizen soldiers second, which is why we fought so hard for each other."[17]

The Bloodbath of Spring

Real war [is] tragic and grisly, and its reality, for all intents and purposes,
beyond the power of any literary or philosophic analysis to suggest.

—ROBERT B. ELLIS, *See Naples and Die*

A LITTLE MORE THAN A MONTH AFTER BEING WOUNDED, RUDY KONIECZNY WAS back with 87 Fox Company. "Were we surprised to see him?" pondered David Burt. "Considering that it was Rudy, I'd have to say, no, we weren't. He had gone A.W.O.L. from the hospital to get back to us for the next big push. I wasn't surprised at all. He was more gung-ho than ever."[1]

Rudy Konieczny had returned to a battered but resupplied division, the majority of whose members were hoping more than ever for the end of the war to avoid having to enter what promised to be the bloodiest phase of the campaign.[2] The Tenth had been designated to spearhead the Fifth Army's charge into the Po Valley and up to the Alps, which would mean a sustained assault against the last and least vulnerable of the German outposts in the Apennines, the towering Rocca di Roffeno.

By mid-April, the weather in northern Italy had turned decidedly warmer.

In the five weeks since the end of the Castel d'Aiano offensive, however, the weather wasn't the only condition that had changed in Europe. As flowers sprouted on the mountainsides, news of Allied successes in northern Germany brought to the men of the Tenth Mountain Division even more of a feeling that the surrender of the Nazis was not only inevitable but imminent. American troops had reached the Elbe River just sixty miles west of Berlin on April 11, and the Red Army was already shelling the outskirts of the German capital from the east.[3] The end for Adolf Hitler was unmistakably near.

Moreover, secret discussions between Allied intelligence officers and Nazi SS General Karl Wolff concerning the impending German surrender in Italy had been taking place in Switzerland for several weeks.[4] During those talks, which were attended by representatives of the Allied Command in Italy (including future U.S. joint chief Colonel Lyman Lemnitzer), the enigmatic Wolff debunked as preposterous the theory that Hitler intended to stage a last stand in the "redoubt" of the Austrian and Bavarian Alps near Berchtesgaden. He swore that German surrender in Italy could be arranged without the need for further bloodshed, including, one suspects, his own.[5]

Back in February, the staff of Supreme Allied Commander in Europe, General Dwight D. Eisenhower, had swallowed Joseph Goebbels's final round of baseless Nazi propaganda—the redoubt theory—in its entirety. If, by putting out the story, Goebbels intended to slow the avenging Red Army's advance toward Berlin, he had badly miscalculated. Instead, it was the western Allies who took their eyes off the German capital and headed toward the Obersalzburg and Berchtesgaden from the west, while the Russians continued their sweep toward Hitler's Berlin bunker from the east.[6] Generals Alexander and Clark had taken their cue from Eisenhower, and used the redoubt theory as one of the principal justifications for the recent Tenth Mountain Division attacks on Belvedere and Castel d'Aiano.[7] The real question in mid-April concerned whether the once-plausible redoubt theory truly remained viable.

SS General Wolff's unreliability aside (he carried the baggage of being an enthusiastic mass murderer), his ironic point concerning the preferred course of a peaceful surrender in Italy without the need for further killing was well taken.[8] In southern Germany, the American Seventh Army had entered Bavaria and was headed rapidly for the Austrian Alpine redoubt from the northwest to link up with the Russians, who took Vienna from the east as expected on April 13.[9] Even Allied Mediterranean theater commander Alexander doubted the efficacy of continuing to press the attack from the south under such circumstances, as British Intelligence had already informed him that it was quite skeptical of the redoubt scenario.[10]

After more than a month on the sidelines, however, General Clark desperately wanted his Fifteenth Army Group in Italy to press on. His aim was to cut off the only viable escape route of the Nazi divisions still on Italian soil by beating them (and the advancing U.S. Seventh Army) to the Brenner Pass, the passage leading from the Italian side of the Alps to the Austrian frontier.[11]

The Nazi soldiers that Clark intended to subdue in Italy were some of the same troops who had escaped from the region of Valmontone when he made his fateful decision to occupy Rome nearly a year earlier.[12] Even the remotest possibility that these troops now intended to stage a last stand in the redoubt was considered a threat to him personally. Under the circumstances, General Clark quite probably surmised that he had to act preemptively, lest he risk the harsh judgment of history for his past failures and indulgences. There was also the powerful motivation of personal glory, for which he had already demonstrated a blinding weakness.

The orders given in January to the Fifteenth Army Group, to prevent any Nazi advance and to attack in case of a Nazi withdrawal, had not changed. Still, Clark knew that General Eisenhower and his staff clung to the redoubt scenario, and could not object to an Allied offensive in Italy designed to keep the Nazis bottled up south of the Alps.[13] That would be true whether or not there was a realistic chance of Clark beating the U.S. Seventh Army to the Brenner Pass, because the Fifteenth Army Group would in any event be keeping the Nazis occupied while the remainder of the Allied armies advanced into Austria.

That left Clark needing only to convince his immediate superior, General Alexander. The British commander, Clark was well aware, enthusiastically supported the view of Great Britain's prime minister Winston Churchill that one of the primary aims of the Italian campaign all along had been to keep the communists out of northeastern Italy.[14] Once assured that part of Clark's spring offensive would be a commitment to keep their Soviet and Yugoslavian allies out of Italy's northern tier, Alexander granted Clark his drive to the Alps.[15]

Historian Martin Blumenson, one of the most highly regarded and sympathetic of General Clark's biographers, wrote unflatteringly of his perceptions of the general's thought process in deciding to go forward with the April 1945 attacks. In his book *Mark Clark: The Last of the Great World War II Commanders,* Blumenson wrote that Clark was proceeding principally on the basis of justifying the Italian campaign in its entirety, in essence risking those lives still in his care to justify lives already lost: "With the German military machine crumbling, what should the Allied forces in northern Italy do? Because the Germans were losing power and heart, the longer the Allies waited to attack in Italy, the easier their task would be. The British, Clark suspected, wished to defer an offensive until May, when a crushing Allied blow was likely to be mortal to the Germans. To postpone a final drive, Clark thought, would be a great error. In his opinion, the Fifteenth Army Group had to contribute its full share to the work of destroying the Germans. Otherwise the Italian campaign made little sense."[16]

Ernest F. Fisher Jr. of the U.S. Army's Center of Military History, author of the most authoritative volume on the Italian campaign north of Rome, *Cassino to the Alps,* was startlingly frank in his parallel assessment of Clark's motivations: "Clark was . . . concerned lest the Red Army marching up the Danube and the U.S. Seventh Army advancing through southern Germany should reach Austria's alpine frontier before [his] 15th Army Group should get there. After the long, arduous advance northward from Cassino, Clark was determined to be in on the kill when the war ended and not be left bogged down either in the Northern Apennines or in the Po Valley."[17]

Thus was the fate of the Tenth Mountain Division decided. Whether or not Truscott and Hays agreed with the attack strategy, they would as a matter of course follow Clark and Alexander aggressively if that was the decision of their commanding officers. In fairness to Clark, there is nothing to indicate that either subordinate commander objected in principle to the offensive, only as to where it should be aimed. Truscott was, in fact, with strenuous enthusiasm able to convince Clark that launching the April offensive along the route west of Highway 64, with the Tenth Mountain Division as the spearhead, was a preferable alternative to the Highway 65 plan that Truscott still feared would lead to horrendous losses.[18]

In the end, Clark likely rationalized that the renewed Allied efforts in northern Italy to cut off the Nazi escape route to the redoubt—though not necessarily a military imperative—*might* just end the war a bit sooner, saving lives on other fronts. Who could argue with such a strategy? Perhaps only the boys about to do the fighting in support of that remote possibility. They, however, were not consulted.

As Tenth Mountain Division trainer and historian Hal Burton wrote in his popular treatment of the subject, *The Ski Troops,* "[t]he final battles in Italy epitomized the needless gallantry of war, the compulsiveness that drives generals to commit their troops, the irresistible urge to share in victory that could be earned more prudently by simply standing still."[19]

ౚౚౚ

The men of the Tenth awoke at dawn on April 13, 1945, the scheduled commencement date for the main spring offensive, to shocking news. The only national leader many of them had ever known, President Franklin D. Roosevelt, had died suddenly of a cerebral hemorrhage the previous day.[20] The attack was postponed. "The news about the president was very traumatic for a lot of the guys," recalled Lieutenant Mike Dwyer. "Most of us were really just kids, and the death of the Commander in Chief shook us up a bit."[21] As a result, rumors began to circulate.

One story (the correct one, according to General Truscott) blamed the delay on poor weather at the American air bases to the south, which prevented Allied air strikes in support of the pending attack.[22] Another claimed that uncertainty over command authority created by the president's death was responsible. Some believed that none of the officers wanted to start an operation on Friday the thirteenth.[23] Finally, the more optimistic hoped that General Clark was waiting for the inevitable news of surrender from Germany before committing his troops to a costly operation that might soon prove unnecessary.[24] Trooper Robert Ellis concluded in his diary entry for April 13, the day before the Tenth Mountain Division joined the offensive, that the coming attack reminded him of the film depicting Erich Maria Remarque's novel *All Quiet on the Western Front,* "when the soldier reached for the butterfly on the last day of the war, and was killed by a sniper."[25]

"Today we are on the eve of our last great battle," proclaimed General Truscott to the entire Fifth Army, searching for a way to inspire the more reluctant among his troops. By subduing this "last great enemy force in Italy, we shall . . . prevent withdrawal to oppose our forces on other fronts . . . and prevent further ruin and destruction in this unhappy country."[26] Neither intended motivation rang with particular resonance, but the dog faces—including Jake Nunnemacher and Rudy Konieczny—were going to have to fight, regardless. The "go" order for the spring offensive came at 8:30 a.m. on April 14.[27] Just about everyone expected a bloodbath. They were right for having thought so.

ౚౚౚ

Jake Nunnemacher's Company 87-B was ordered to lead the attack that Saturday morning against Nazi troops then under the command of General Heinrich von Vietinghoff, as Field Marshal Kesselring had been recalled by Hitler to organize the last-ditch defense of Berlin.[28] For 87 Bravo Company, this involved advancing down an exposed road that led directly from the jump-off point to the heavily fortified town of Torre Iussi, a name recalled with bitterness and grief by many Tenth Mountaineers.[29]

The Nazis knew that the Americans were coming as a result of the awesome air and artillery bombardments to which they were subjected immediately prior to the advance. With the enemy dug in after more than a month of preparation, however, the American barrage did little damage.[30] According to Private John Imbrie, "we didn't think there could be anyone alive on the other side by the time that shelling ended, but it's truly amazing what troops with good cover can withstand."[31] When the explosions ceased, the Nazis simply emerged from their bunkers ready to fight.

There was more bad news for the Americans. The Nazi leadership had decided to commit an entire division to stop the Eighty-seventh Regiment that first day. These were not the marginal troops they had used against some of the other Fifteenth Army Group units, either. As the *History of the 87th Mountain Infantry* notes, "they were young, many of them fanatical" Hitlerites more than willing to die for the Fatherland, whether or not the war was already lost.[32]

As a result of these many factors, according to the troopers who were there, some of the American objectives that day were almost tantamount to suicide missions.[33] The assignment given Jake Nunnemacher's Company 87-B appears to have been one such mission, and the members of the regiment seemed to sense it. Shortly before the jump-off, Jake had a chance encounter with his old friend, Major David Brower, whom he had not seen in months. Jake called out to his friend near the staging area, where Brower stopped his Jeep and got out to chat for a moment. "We had time to exchange a few words," recalled Brower. "The feeling of dread was mutual."[34]

Jake's Dartmouth colleague and Riva Ridge veteran, Captain Percy Rideout, was fighting the same feeling. "The night before the big push," Rideout remembered, "I suddenly started thinking about a relative of mine who'd been killed in the First World War. I'm sure Bromaghin was in the back of my mind, too. In order to knock those thoughts out of my head, I must have walked around for three-quarters of the night, talking to anyone who'd talk back to me. Other officers, privates, anyone. I was determined to stay positive, even though I knew how tough it was going to be. Jake knew and so did everyone else."[35]

The brutality of the Allied air and artillery salvo that morning was matched immediately afterward by the well-prepared Nazi gun batteries. Jake Nunnemacher's company came under withering fire even before reaching its line of departure, because the Germans could clearly observe their movements from positions across the valley.[36] On the long, narrow road leading directly into Torre Iussi, the Americans were hit with their worst shelling yet. "A thunder of fire smashed into the men," according to Captain George Earle, pinning them down on the road for nearly an hour and causing numerous casualties.[37] When the troops finally reached the town, with Jake's squad in the lead, the enemy's resolve grew even stronger. Torre Iussi had been virtually untouched by the American bombardment, the result of an intelligence failure to recognize the town as a fortified Nazi stronghold.[38] German snipers and machine gunners seemed to be firing from every building.[39]

Jake led his men to the side of the first building at the edge of town, which was situated below an ancient monastery. Heavy fire burst from several windows and doorways of the old house, instantly killing two other sergeants, Wayne Clark and Harry Shevchik.[40] If Jean and Heidi had been in the back of Jake's mind before, renewed surges of adrenaline focused him entirely on dealing with what was rapidly degenerating into a desperate situation. Pinned down again and left with little choice—even a withdrawal would have been exceedingly risky—Jake dodged a fusillade of bullets in order to toss a hand grenade through one of the building's windows. It detonated.[41]

Calling out in German to those inside, Sergeant Nunnemacher demanded their surrender. The firing diminished. A few moments later, several Nazis emerged with their hands up. The house was quiet. Jake called out in German again, asking if there were others inside. There was an exchange during which the enemy soldiers apparently said "no."[42]

According to Lewis Hoelscher, who had been with Jake in Company B since the first days at Camp Hale, "I was five feet or so away from him when he went by those prisoners and into the house to check things out. I think he suspected they were lying to him because we'd seen this kind of thing before, but Jake was a very brave guy, and you never know how you're going to react in a situation like that until it happens. He went ahead."[43]

John de la Montagne, Jake's close friend from Dartmouth, remained mystified over why such an otherwise meticulous and deliberate person with so much to live for would choose to place himself in such extreme danger, especially against his own instincts. "In heavy combat," he explained, "I think anger sometimes plays a part, and at times so does the disorientation of battle. Whatever it was, Jake took a calculated risk in doing his job that we all wish he hadn't taken. That house probably should have been cleared with artillery and explosives."[44]

Jacob Nunnemacher slipped into the building while the others, including Hoelscher, Sergeant John Sugden (Jake's friend since the MTG days who would later marry Jake's sister Audrey), and first scout Private Leon Burrows waited for his word at the doorway. Jake was their ranking noncom. He spoke German fluently, and he made clear to them that he regarded this search as his responsibility.[45]

Jake quietly moved inside the building and cautiously started up the stairs. The momentary calm was broken by a single rifle shot, which rang in the ears of the soldiers standing frozen in the doorway. Profanities were blurted in anguish.

Fired from behind by a Nazi sniper who had remained secreted on the first floor, the bullet went straight through the back of Jacob's head, entering below the rim of his helmet. He probably never knew what hit him.

ℰↃ☙

The men in Jake's squad wept openly, in grief and in rage. "We took care of the man who killed him," John Sugden wrote bitterly to Jean, informing her that he and Jake had been inseparable since arriving in Italy. "I cried when he died. . . . He was [such a] wonderful guy. . . . What [more] can I say? Grief stops me."[46]

Leon Burrows, who also lost his twin brother in the Italian campaign, was hit in the hand by the same gunner who killed Jake. He similarly took the time to write to Jean after recovering: "I slept [in the same foxhole] with Jake all the time we were over in Italy. I knew him as well as I knew my own brothers. I knew that he was one of the finest and swellest fellows that I have ever met on the face of the earth. He was smart and intelligent and every bit of a man—a man that will live with me for the rest of my life. . . . He never will be here physically and neither will my twin brother, but within our hearts they have not died—they will live for ever and ever."[47]

And an anonymous soldier nicknamed "Bud" (most likely an officer to whom Jean had once been introduced) wrote to her adding his thoughts concerning the affection and respect Jake had earned from his men in Italy: "I talked to most of the men in Jake's squad, just to substantiate what I knew must be true. I have never in my life heard any group of men give such unanimous and sincere praise to a fellow soldier."[48]

Lewis Hoelscher, the plainspoken man from the cotton country of central Texas, who has for his entire life remained baffled as to why he was assigned to Camp Hale and the mountain troops, gave the most concise of all the assessments of Jake. "We knew his background, about Dartmouth and the ski team, and that he could have tried to hold all that stuff over people. Instead, he was just a regular guy with a lot of guts. He used his brains to help you, not to try to embarrass anyone. He was that kind of guy." Hoelscher and Jake each won a Silver Star that day for their efforts to protect the men with whom they had gone into battle.[49]

Jake Nunnemacher's body was removed by the graves detail and buried temporarily in the nearby U.S. Military Internment Site at Garanglione. His surviving brother, Hermann, who taught Jake to ski back home in Milwaukee, remained distressed and angry over Jake's death more than half a century later. "I was told that the guy who killed him was also trying to kill his own buddies who had just surrendered. He was one of those SS guys, a real rabid Nazi. It's ironic, but my brother looked more like their damn posters of Aryan supermen than they did. You have to understand that at that point with the SS, our boys were fighting against mad dogs. We had to send some very good kids to get rid of those guys, including my brother. I'm just still not sure that at that point in the war we needed to keep risking them that way, but I guess it's too late to think like that now. Isn't it?"[50]

Bad Times

GENERAL HAYS HAD PROMISED HIS BOYS "GOOD TIMES AND BAD TIMES." APRIL 14, 1945, and the days that immediately followed fell hard into the latter category.

After Jake Nunnemacher's death, Company 87-B continued to take a terrific pounding at Torre Iussi. From an adjacent mound designated as Hill 860, the troopers were being raked by heavy machine-gun fire from German MG-42s. Sergeant Beta Fotas, judged by Major John Woodward as one of the division's most promising young ski mountaineers, died in a barrage of fire with four others as they attempted to take out one of the gun crews.[1] "It was a real mess," recalled Lewis Hoelscher. "The Krauts had several weeks to prepare, and they knew we were coming. It was no damn good at all."[2]

The preparedness of the Nazis quickly became a source of anger and consternation for many members of the Tenth on the front lines. As Captain Albert Meinke (86-Med-3) put it: "It was most discouraging for our troops to

173

stage an attack, pass through artillery and mortar fire, pass through enemy mine fields, watch the enemy withdraw and leave their side of the front wide open and undefended, only to be ordered to 'stop and dig in.' [After the attacks in February and March], our men would watch as the enemy soldiers reorganized, returned to the front, created new mortar and artillery emplacements, and planted new mines, only to be ordered to attack again through the newly installed defenses."[3]

Some have suggested that this situation had been created by the bizarre strategic conundrum that favored the Nazis. Had the Allies in Italy advanced too quickly, the result might have been a complete and rapid disengagement and withdrawal of the Nazis to the Alpine redoubt, exactly the scenario Commanding Generals Alexander and Clark were seeking to avoid.[4] Whether fact or mere theory, after Torre Iussi and the other bloody gains achieved in the earliest stages of the spring offensive, the Tenth Mountain Division's commander General Hays determined that there would be no more stopping. He had been charged with the responsibility of fighting a war, and he was going to fight it.[5]

By the late morning of the fourteenth, Rudy Konieczny's Fox Company was one of the Second Battalion units of the Eighty-seventh that had been ordered to follow Jake Nunnemacher's Company B into Torre Iussi to lend a hand. Moving north through a draw between the foothills near the Rocca di Roffeno (a mountain that bears more than a passing resemblance to Rudy's beloved Greylock), they were immediately showered with all manner of Nazi artillery.[6] As the *History of the 87th Mountain Infantry* puts it, "the road to Torri Iussi was a grim sight with men and mules scattered. Parts of mules were everywhere. The hardest soldier was shocked by broken and dismembered bodies in his own familiar uniform."[7]

Jim Merritt of 87-I described the shock of moving through Torre Iussi after the initial attack by the First Battalion of the Eighty-seventh. "Things were pretty normal until we got well along a dirt road that side-hilled down into [the town]. Here the [troops] must have come under severe artillery and mortar fire. The ditch was filled with American dead, many blown in half. Some with only the top half there, some who were only there from the [bottom] half down. Many of these faces we might have recognized had we stopped to look. We didn't."[8] Merritt's platoon-mate Ray Garlock added, "this was the town or spot that really lives vividly in my memory as to the destruction and death that are a part of war. It was total devastation for men and animals. What made it tough for me was the fact that I was once in [the First Battalion] that had led the attack through this area a short while before and I didn't want to look too close at some of my old buddies."[9]

Mines and small-arms fire made the going even more treacherous for Rudy's Company F as it moved through the bombardment into the town, resulting in several deaths and injuries and one small miracle. Mike Dwyer was knocked sprawling by a bullet that struck him flush on the lieutenant's bars of his jacket. Other than a significant bruise and, by fellow officers, the permanent addition to his name of the phrase "you lucky sonofabitch," he was unhurt.[10]

Others were not so lucky. Lieutenant Bob Dole—the future Senate majority leader—and the famed Friedl Pfeifer were among those who suffered near-fatal wounds that day serving with other division outfits.[11] Dole, a replacement serving with Company I of the Eighty-fifth Regiment and leading a squad that included future U.S. Olympic skier Dev Jennings, was hit in the back while pulling his wounded runner into a shell depression west of Torre Iussi near Pra del Bianco.[12] Whatever hit him fragmented, breaking his right shoulder, collarbone, and arm and crushing some of his spinal vertebrae, which displaced his spinal cord and rendered him temporarily quadriplegic. The surgeon who pieced him back together did not think he'd recover. He did, though permanently losing the use of his right arm.[13]

Jacob Nunnemacher's friend, Aspen visionary Friedl Pfeifer, was hit nearby at about the same time. In Pfeifer's autobiography, the division's best downhill skier and quite possibly the world's greatest ski racer described the agony of being wounded in combat: "Artillery ripped through the trees and we heard the sounds of bullets clipping branches over our heads. Men started falling everywhere. Artillery fire intensified. Clouds of drifting smoke filled the woods and every explosion sprayed hot metal through the haze. . . . I could see the mule train panic as explosions burst all around. Then a shell exploded right in the middle of the train, animals falling away, braying wildly. So close to the impact, I was twisted and thrown, and felt like I had been slammed in the back with the butt of a rifle. I fell to the ground, paralyzed."[14]

Sergeant Pfeifer was given a shot of morphine and carried back to the aid station by two young German POWs, who dropped his stretcher at least once to avoid incoming artillery. A medic at the aid station nearly made the mistake of giving him another shot of morphine, which might have killed him. Friedl was barely conscious enough to refuse the injection. The POWs then placed him onto a Jeep, which transported him to a field hospital.

When Pfeifer awoke, he was in a silent room. A nurse heard him moaning and walked over. "You're supposed to be dead," she said flatly, before having him loaded into an ambulance. Friedl ended up on the operating table at the military hospital in Pistoia, where most of his left lung, shredded by shrapnel, was removed. He recovered, due in part to the diligent attention of a physician, Major Tom Buford, who recognized him as the man who had taught him to ski at Sun Valley. It would be five months before Pfeifer was up and around, and much longer before he was back to the mountains.[15] He would carry the scars—and some of the shrapnel—with him for the rest of his life.

❧❦

One of Pfeifer's partners in the dream of establishing Aspen Ski Resort, Captain Percy Rideout of Dartmouth, had survived Riva Ridge without a scratch. On the night before the spring offensive, he had devoted every ounce of energy to staying positive, despite knowing what a difficult fight lay ahead. Now, moving his company forward from Torre Iussi north onto Hill 868, they suddenly came under heavy sniper and machine-gun fire from the ridges above the village. At the same time, they were meeting fierce resistance from Germans on the hilltop. Pinned down, Rideout got a call on the field telephone from General Hays himself. "I told him we couldn't move, and that the Torre Iussi ridges still needed to be cleared of snipers," Rideout remembered. "His reply was a two-word order: *'Get moving.'* So we got moving."

A few moments later, Rideout turned to scream an order to his lieutenant, and felt something slam into the side of his head. The bullet passed through his cheek and exited in front of his ear on the opposite side. "It's one of those strange things in war," he continued. "If I hadn't turned at that precise instant, that bullet goes straight through my skull, just like my friend Jake Nunnemacher. Instead, I received pretty much a sew-up wound that I'm able to describe fifty-seven years later."[16] Forty-six mountain troopers became casualties taking Hill 868,[17] including Captain Ralph Lafferty—Ralph Bromaghin's best friend and skiing buddy—who was wounded coming to relieve Rideout.[18] Rideout and Lafferty—both of whom were awarded Silver Stars to go with their more highly prized Combat Infantry Badges ("no one had to put you in for a CIB, you earned it yourself")[19]—would later join Pfeifer in the hospital at Pistoia. There, they settled in for a long period of recuperation.[20]

Regrettably, there were also many less fortunate division members that day. Private Richard D. Johnston, a Winter Park, Colorado, skiing star who joined Company A of the Eighty-seventh at Camp Hale in 1943, had seen his unit battered on the road into Torre Iussi as it moved in behind Jake Nunnemacher's bloodied Bravo Company. Its members eventually charged north to capture Hill 903 in bitter fighting, complicated by the unfortunate overlap of field radio frequencies with elements of the Eighty-sixth Regiment moving on their right.

To alleviate the confusion being caused by the garbled communications, Private Johnston was selected (doubtlessly owing to his physical conditioning) to run a crucial set of instructions forward to the company's first sergeant, who was awaiting instructions near the town of Le Coste. On the way, states the regimental history, Johnston was struck by an enemy bullet in the chest, "but climbed back to his feet and continued on."[21] Somehow, he struggled to Le Coste, located the sergeant, and delivered the message. His mission accomplished, Private First Class Richard D. Johnston then collapsed at the sergeant's feet. He was awarded a Silver Star, posthumously, for his tenacious bravery on behalf of his company-mates.[22]

And then there was big Bud Winter, the energetic young Adirondack ski patroller who had saved Bill Hackett's life during the Mount Democrat avalanche and thoroughly impressed his more senior climbing colleagues on the celebrated Tenth Mountain Ski Traverse between Leadville and Aspen. Now one of the division's youngest officers, the irrepressible Lieutenant Winter had recently written home requesting that his mother forward to him his fly rod and fishing tackle in anticipation of the war's end.[23]

On the morning of April 14, Winter found himself in heavy fighting with the Eighty-fifth Regiment's Third Battalion west of Torre Iussi, close to where Bob Dole had been hit a short time before. Attached to a rifle company as a forward mortar observer near Hill 913, Winter suddenly discovered in the midst of the pitched battle that he was the unit's sole remaining radio operator. The lieutenant, who had only recently returned to action after several weeks in the hospital recovering from wounds received on Mount Belvedere, moved forward without hesitation.[24]

"Courageously," notes his commendation, "he followed the company commander through [the] mines and . . . the most intense artillery and mortar barrages, relaying messages and directing the fire of his mortars."[25] Bud Winter was just twenty years old when, moments later, a mortar shell brutally ended his life, leaving his dream to climb and ski in the Himalayas with his friend and idol Paul Petzoldt forever unrealized.

"Uncle Bud's Cabin" on the Tenth Mountain Division Hut Route in Colorado was erected and named in honor of Burdell Winter. His father, however, soon after the posthumous presentation of Bud's Bronze Star, penned a personal tribute that remains a greater and more loving monument to his short life than any edifice or medal ever could be:

> Sleep peacefully my buddy boy, beneath Italian skies . . .
>   And may God give you silver skis,
> To ski celestial hills,
>   And fishing rods and lines and reels
> To fish those streams and rills.[26]

April 14, 1945, remains by far the single worst day of combat for the Tenth Mountain Division in its history. The division took well more than five hundred casualties in the twelve-hour battle, the world's greatest skiers and climbers well represented in that group. And the advance was just getting started.

❧✦☙

By nightfall on the fourteenth, Rudy Konieczny's Fox Company and the rest of the Eighty-seventh Regiment's Second Battalion had helped take Torre Iussi and the adjacent town of Tabole, and settled in for a night of shelling that "landed mostly on Company F."[27] As a result, Rudy and his company-mates received neither rations nor water and got no sleep.[28]

At 9:00 on the following morning, they were ordered back into action on Mount Pigna just to the north of Tabole, which was captured under intense fire.[29] That accomplished, the company moved west to take Mount Sette Croci under mortar attack. At 9 p.m., after an arduous day of almost nonstop combat, Company F was ordered to make a long and difficult night march down through the valley to Le Coste (the town in which Richard Johnston had given his life the previous day), where Phil Puchner's Company 87-G was pinned down and in desperate trouble. Upon their arrival, the members of Rudy's exhausted company—who by now had not slept or eaten for more than forty hours—went immediately back into combat and extricated their comrades.[30]

Elsewhere, the fighting of April 15 was equally intense. Thunderbolt ski trail veteran Jeddie Brooks had survived the climb up Riva Ridge and the shellacking taken by Percy Rideout's Company 86-F at Torre Iussi and on Hill 868. Now, the young sergeant from Rudy Konieczny's hometown of Adams, Massachusetts, was caught in heavy fighting on the hills near Mount Sette Croci. When his buddy, Ed Ketchledge, was raked by machine-gun fire from gut to shoulder, Brooks went out to get him.[31]

178

"The medics told us he had no chance unless we got to him right away," Brooks recalled, "so I went. Almost as soon as I got out into the open, though, there was an explosion, and down I went. I knew that something had gone through my ankle, and wasn't sure I could get up." Lying out in the open, Brooks could hear the pop of bullets all around him. "That's the sound they make when they whiz past your ears and hit the ground around you. 'Pop, pop, pop.' I said to myself, 'Jed, you're going to move or you're going to die,' and somehow I managed to jump up and get back to cover."[32]

His ankle mangled, Brooks struggled back up the hill to a barn where the wounded, including Captain Rideout, were being tended to on their stretchers. Moments after his arrival, a Nazi shell knocked out one of the building's walls. Medics dove gingerly on the wounded to protect them from flying debris. "I figured that this wasn't such a great place to be, either," Brooks recalled. "So another guy took a rifle, I took a bandoleer of ammo, and with two boards as crutches we helped each other back toward the woods and the rear. When we got to those woods, though, we were really just shocked by what we saw. The tree bursts that hit our guys in that forest caused indescribable damage. It was heartbreaking, seeing the men and the mules just broken into pieces that way."

As Brooks stood gaping at a scene of utter carnage, enemy artillery started up again. "There was nothing we could do but dive into foxholes on top of guys that had already been killed. It hurts you to have to do that, but we had no choice, or even time to think about it." The two soldiers finally made it back to an aid station, where shouting and the screaming of the wounded kept them up all night. Finally, after a shot of morphine to dull the pain in his ankle, Brooks was carried to the rear by Nazi POWs. "I worried they'd kill me when we went into the woods again on the way back," he recalled, "but they wanted to get out of there as much as I did."

Jeddie Brooks underwent surgery and months of rehabilitation, which culminated with his return to the slopes as a civilian ski instructor after the war. It was an avocation he practiced for decades, teaching countless youngsters of southern New England the joys of winter sports. He also went on to become one of the longtime leaders of the Tenth Mountain Division Ski Troop Demonstration Team, the "Pando Commandos." "I'll never forget what I saw those two days in April, though," he concluded. "Never."[33]

Edwin H. Ketchledge was eventually dragged from the field by other members of 86-F under intense fire. When Brooks, who was awarded a Bronze Star for his actions, met up with him in the hospital months later, he was astonished that his friend had survived his frightful wounds.[34] He was also taken aback when Ketchledge asked, with apparent innocence, what foolish thing Brooks had done to get himself shot up. "That's the last time I try to do something nice for you," sputtered Brooks, before the two looked at one another and broke into the reassuring laughter of survivors.[35]

Following the war, Ketchledge returned to his beloved Adirondack Mountains in northern New York State to teach forestry and biology in the New York State University system. Dr. Ketchledge would eventually be honored as one of the pioneering leaders of the American ecology movement for his groundbreaking educational programs developed in conjunction with the Association for the Protection of the Adirondacks.[36]

೫)ೕ

For the night of April 15, 1945, as Jeddie Brooks, Percy Rideout, Ralph Lafferty, and hundreds of other wounded G.I.s waited on stretchers to be evacuated to hospitals in the rear, it is not difficult to imagine a division of men traumatized by what they had experienced over a two-day period of bloody, nonstop combat. At some time during the evening, however, Rudy Konieczny pushed aside any lingering fears or premonitions and rallied himself one more time.

Speculating on what Rudy might have been going through as he tried to gather his thoughts, Sergeant David Burt suggested that "sometimes in combat, you reach a point of exhaustion and fatalism where you stop being frightened of anything. You just want to know the outcome, to get things over with. I'm not saying that's what happened to Rudy, but he may have felt he had seen and done so many things on the battlefield that he no longer felt he had anything to lose, that his fate was out of his own hands. So he just concentrated on doing his job, which for Rudy meant protecting all those around him, the friends he considered his younger brothers."[37]

Lieutenant Mike Dwyer added that "Rudy surely never changed the way he did things, even if he had some secret doubts about getting out of there alive. His injuries might have killed another man, and here he was a month later and guys could barely keep up with him. It was incredible." What was driving him? "Maybe it was as simple as feeling he had found a place in this world with the Tenth, and he wasn't going to give that up willingly."[38]

The next morning, April 16, Fox Company was asked to take the town of Torre. Sergeant Konieczny's squad led the way. According to the *History of the*

87th Mountain Infantry, "Rudolph Konieczny led a bazooka team . . . as usual toting his powerful BAR. The sergeant got so far ahead that the rest of the men were running trying to keep up with him." Rudy was the first Allied soldier into Torre by a wide margin.[39] Was it courage or recklessness? Determination or resignation? "It was just typical Rudy," said David Burt. "No more, no less."[40]

୫୦ଔ

A few hundred yards east of Torre, while Rudy and Company F were absorbing an intense mortar attack, Company 87-I had its hands full trying to hold Mount Croce. Having taken the hill and dug in on the near side of the summit, a terrific Nazi artillery barrage commenced, indicating that a counterattack up the reverse slope might be imminent.[41] Company commander Adrian Riordan asked for volunteers to establish a forward observation post on the exposed, reverse slope to protect against a surprise enemy attack. Sergeant Orval McDaniel stepped forward.

A young skier from Salt Lake City who had grown up on the slopes of Alta and Brighton, McDaniel arrived at Camp Hale in 1943 barely sporting peach fuzz on his eighteen-year-old cheeks. Two years later, a veteran of Cooper Hill, Kiska, and Italy (where he had already been awarded a Bronze Star), McDaniel now led a squad of five others through blinding fog and 120mm artillery fire onto the reverse slope. When they reached their objective, however, they found the ground rock-hard. Out in the open and desperately trying to dig into the rocky earth, McDaniel and his comrades quickly realized that the process was taking too long. Still, they worked madly in hope of protecting the rest of their company.[42]

Moments later, Nazi gunners placed a shell directly on the Americans. "His heroic sacrifice inspired all who witnessed it to maintain their precarious position in spite of the heaviest enemy fire," read McDaniel's Silver Star commendation. The five troopers with him were wounded, but managed to pull through. Company I held on Mount Croce.[43] Sergeant Orval R. McDaniel was twenty-one.

୫୦ଔ

The troops of Rudy Konieczny's 87-F spent the remainder of April 16 scrambling over rough terrain on their way from Torre to Casa Bacucchi, a farm

181

where they arrived at midnight and dug in.[44] Once again, though, there would be no rest.

Lieutenant Dwyer, on a reconnaissance patrol to evaluate the company's new position, walked only a short distance in the pitch black before finding himself surrounded by German-speaking voices. Dwyer returned, gathered Rudy Konieczny's depleted squad, and moved forward in the direction of the noise. There, they waited tensely for dawn.[45] In seventy-two hours of fierce combat, the members of Company 87-F had managed less than six hours of sleep, and now another day of bloodletting awaited.

At first light on Tuesday, April 17, 1945, Dwyer and Konieczny realized that they were now positioned at the edge of a minefield less than one hundred yards from the enemy lines. When Nazi soldiers began moving forward, oblivious to the presence of the American squad, a firefight broke out. Despite the advantage of surprise, the Americans soon found themselves dangerously pinned down by a sniper firing from a protected position on their left. Rudy told Dwyer he was going out to get him.[46]

"Rudy would never send someone else to do a job like that," said Lieutenant Dwyer. "I saw him go off on his own so many times in those situations. He believed it was his responsibility to go out there to protect his men, in part because he was so good at it. He just said to me what he always said: 'I'll find a way.'"[47]

He did. The sniper silenced, Rudy reported back to Dwyer.[48] A subsequent patrol outflanked the remaining Nazis, who surrendered after their officer was killed.[49] And for a few precious moments, Company F stopped to regroup.

⟡

The Third Battalion of the Eighty-seventh, meanwhile, was engaged that morning in a mop-up operation in the nearby town of Madna di Rodiano, where fierce fighting had taken the lives of dozens of Americans. Captain Joseph Duncan Jr., commander of Company 87-L and the former U.S. National Downhill Ski champion from Estes Park, Colorado, organized a reconnaissance patrol through the adjacent area of Casa Costa. The mission was to locate a big Nazi gun that was sporadically harassing Third Battalion troops as they attempted to move into the open fields that led down to the Po Valley.[50]

Since his instructor days at Camp Hale, the colorful Junior Duncan—the mountain man who moved in elite circles with his socialite wife in Sun Valley,

New York, and Europe before the war—had developed into one of the regiment's most admired combat leaders.[51] Battalion commander Colonel Robert Works, one of Duncan's high-ranking admirers, wrote of observing him leading his troops onto "Punch Board Hill" on the night of February 27, 1945, while under heavy mortar fire. "In the glare of a star shell," wrote the colonel, "I saw Captain Duncan on an exposed ledge above the trail exhorting his men to greater speed to avoid this dangerous area. . . . [He] was a soldier with great loyalty to his men . . . [and] an outstanding combat leader."[52]

Sergeant (later Lieutenant) Walter Stillwell Jr. added that Duncan, though he had only taken command of Company L that November, was personally affected each time he lost one of *his* boys in combat. "During a lull in battle," wrote Stillwell, "I saw him many times walk over to the body of one of his men killed in action, pause, and show his respect. . . . It hurt him."[53] As Lieutenant Victor Eklund had noted back in Colorado, *"here was a leader."*[54]

Duncan's company the previous day had taken a vicious pounding to the south of Madna di Rodiano, even worse than the sustained artillery barrage it endured on Punch Board Hill in March. Assigned to clear the Mt. Mosca ridge leading into the town in preparation for a sweep forward by the Eighty-sixth Regiment, Company L had been victimized by the failure of the Eighty-sixth to move up at the designated time because of the wounding of its commander, Colonel Tomlinson.[55] Left to fight its way up the ridge and hold it alone in a swirling, disorienting fog, the company was three times beaten back by heavy small-arms fire and fearsome shelling. At last, its Second Platoon mounted a "Banzai Charge" to the top during which some thirty of the unit's forty men were killed or wounded.[56]

The fighting on what became known as "Banzai Ridge" was "as desperate as any the 87th experienced," according to the regimental history. "The pitiful sight of helpless wounded and smashed dead comrades will never be forgotten by the survivors of that charge."[57] It did not appear possible for Company 87-L to prevail, but it did. For that, Joe Duncan deserves a great deal of the credit.

"The entire area was under direct enemy observation," reads his commendation, "which made any exposure hazardous. But Captain Duncan, disregarding his personal safety completely, made his way among his platoon, reorganizing the men and bolstering their courage. When orders came to resume the attack, he personally issued instructions to each of his platoon leaders, and led the company through the heaviest fire to storm the strong enemy positions."[58]

The fighting ended beyond the ridge in a churchyard on the outskirts of Madna di Rodiano, where young Private Lee Norris—one of the very few members of the Second Platoon who had survived the final charge with Duncan—was hit in the stomach by a sniper. He died in the arms of a German medic attempting to save him, adding a sense of ironic absurdity to the day's bitter fighting that had decimated Duncan's company.[59]

Duncan's radio man, Private Al Soria, recalled the captain expressing to him in an unguarded moment "how terrible war was and his concern about casualties. 'Soria,' he would say, 'you and I are not made for this war.' "[60] "What he meant," said Soria (who grew up skiing the southern Alpine slopes of Sestriere prior to emigrating as a teenager to New England, where he would later become a renowned ski patroller), "was that the captain knew we were living an experience that would haunt us for the rest of our lives. He was saddened by that."[61]

The stress of combat appeared to be taking its toll on Duncan. Photographs of him taken shortly before the commencement of the spring offensive reveal a man who seems to have aged fifteen years in a matter of weeks. Gone completely was his striking resemblance to film star Gary Cooper, replaced by the countenance of an aging warrior. "Regardless," recalled a fellow officer, "he was handling things like a soldier. Everyone was under stress, and it showed in our faces, but Duncan was a very gifted leader and he kept his company positive and moving forward."[62] Now, however, with so many of his young troopers lying dead on Banzai Ridge, even a man who had become as accustomed to the horrors of combat in his three bloody engagements as Joe Duncan must have wondered how he had survived against such odds, and perhaps even why.

Over the years, there has been much talk of Captain Duncan's extraordinary leadership and humanity. There has also been a controversial suggestion that the intense combat experienced by Company 87-L in Italy had also, somewhat paradoxically, turned Joe Duncan into a very hard man. That allegation, however, has been vehemently and persuasively rebutted by those who knew Duncan best.

In a 2001 draft of his memoirs posted for a short time on the Tenth Mountain Division Association Internet Web site, retired career United Nations diplomat Bruce Macdonald—a former Tenth Recon and 87-L member living in France—suggested that a disturbing incident took place in Italy involving himself, Captain Duncan, a misidentified corporal, and several German POWs. The alleged incident, which the good-humored and sincere Macdonald asserted still upsets him, was said to have taken place at the time of the bloody March push against Castel d'Aiano. According to Macdonald, it concerned a statement Duncan supposedly made to a particular corporal, which resulted in the execution of a group of about a dozen young enemy prisoners of war.

As the group of prisoners stood under guard near the top of a hill after the day's fighting had ended, Duncan reputedly made the statement at the direction of his battalion commander, "Men, we don't take prisoners. Do I have any volunteers?" Macdonald asserted that a corporal (whom he named) stepped forward and led the prisoners behind a huge rock. "Ten to fifteen shots rang out in the evening twilight," wrote Macdonald, and the corporal returned to report "mission completed" to Duncan.[63]

Several veterans of 87-L immediately disputed Macdonald's account, asserting that such an incident would have been completely antithetical to everything battalion commander Robert Works and Captain Joe Duncan stood for and did throughout their time in Italy. "It makes no sense at all," said Bruce Berends of Duncan's company. "We're talking about two officers of the highest moral character, who demonstrated that repeatedly in combat. I've spoken to many of the surviving members of our company, none of whom recall anything even resembling such a terrible event. We safely processed literally hundreds of prisoners, before, during, and after the March push. Obviously, there was no such policy, and in my opinion, absolutely no such incident. It simply did not happen."[64] "Those are the facts," echoed John Engle, a self-described "spear carrier" in 87-L. "I'd say so if something like that happened, and it didn't."[65]

Albert Soria was equally baffled by Macdonald's account. "As Captain Duncan's radio man, I spent a great deal of time with him. I never witnessed or heard of such an event, and it seems to me it would have been totally out of character for him to have done such a thing. We were always taking prisoners. Duncan would never, never, never give such an order."[66] Berends further pointed out that the enlisted man named by Macdonald as the perpetrator was in actuality killed in action several days *prior* to the date of the alleged incident.[67]

Macdonald, nevertheless, remained steadfast in his belief that his recollections are accurate insofar as an incident having taken place. "I certainly do not want to disparage any memories of Captain Duncan," he wrote in reply to a letter from Berends and other members of 87-L. "He was, in my view, an excellent Captain. [But as to those who say] 'that never happened,' I respectfully disagree. . . . I stand by my recollection, which remains embedded in my memory to eternity, except for the name of the Corporal who went behind the rocks. 'We take no prisoners' came from many brave and compassionate quarters during the war. I do believe that we should see war as it really is."[68]

As Duncan's close friend, Captain George Earle, posited generally and not in regard to this alleged incident, the mists of time should not obscure the fact that in the last, desperate days of the war in Italy, situational brutality on both sides was simply part of the equation. Captain Duncan should and must be presumed innocent of wrongdoing, especially in light of both his well-earned reputation as a compassionate and intelligent officer and the resolute testimony of those who knew him best and accompanied him constantly. Likewise, Company 87-L deserves no blemishes on its substantial records of accomplishment.

It remains impossible, however, to avoid the conclusion that the rage and carnage engendered by late fighting in the Apennines drove many moral men to commit acts against other combatants that under ordinary circumstances would have been personally unthinkable. Prisoners were sometimes "not taken," as Captain Morley Nelson noted in regard to his own company's distressed reaction over murderous Nazi combat tactics on Belvedere.[69] That is war, as Bruce Macdonald pointed out, as it really is.

In the early afternoon of April 17, Captain Joe Duncan finally located the German battery firing on his battalion, and sent a patrol under Sergeant Stillwell to knock it out. "It was either an 88 or a 105 [mm gun]," remembered George Earle, who was next to Duncan in a foxhole when they figured out where the flat-trajectory firing was coming from. "It was annoying the hell out of him, really irritating him, and he wanted it silenced."[70] Whether the captain's subsequent actions were affected by the anger, grief, and fatigue of battle over the previous twenty-four hours is impossible to say. Duncan, however, next climbed to a highly exposed observation post, positioning himself to call in help if the patrol ran into trouble.[71] Everything was quiet as the captain crawled into the open with Al Soria and two others, observing through his field glasses Stillwell's movements toward the gun. The calm in combat activity made the shell's explosion that much more shocking.

Enemy gunners had spotted Duncan in the clear, and placed a single shell on the presighted rock ledge above his position. The massive concussion caused a torrent of rock and steel shrapnel to rain down, killing the captain instantly along with Lieutenant Harrison King and Private Walter Smith. Al Soria was the lone survivor.[72] "It was absolute luck that I survived," Soria remembered. "I got some dirt and rocks thrown across the shoulders of my jacket. That's the way it happens in combat. Just a few yards, sometimes just an inch or two, is the difference between living and dying."[73]

According to Captain Hal Ekern, the troops were devastated by the deaths of their captain and comrades. "Joe Duncan's soldiers, who by that time had seen death in all its forms, were stunned," he wrote. "Some wept, and it was told to me second hand that some were driven by such fury that they charged the enemy gunners and shot them down *without a chance to surrender.*"[74]

"How the gods must have chortled," wrote Captain Earle in 2002, who named a son after his fallen friend. "Duncan for the past three days always out in front of his men, surrounded by every imaginable kind of fire—everyone of the enemy in sight and beyond his sight trying to get him—and then to be knocked off by a single shot, and with all the war around him momentarily at rest. . . . I was more deeply hurt by this than any other one thing in the war."[75]

Earle's *History of the 87th Mountain Infantry* noted that "Captain Duncan's death removed a brilliant and inspiring combat leader from our ranks; his continual regard for his men's welfare and his repeated heroism won not merely the respect, but the love of his men and associates. His loss was mourned by all, even at a time when there were so many fine men to mourn for."[76] Joe Duncan Jr., who was awarded a Silver Star for his leadership on Banzai Ridge and two Bronze Stars for bravery in prior actions, left a wife and a young daughter. He is buried in the American Cemetery near Florence, Italy. The Army Reserve Center at Fort Carson, Colorado, the Estes Park American Legion Post, and a mountain peak near Sun Valley, Idaho, are all named in his honor. He was thirty-three.

സ∞ൽ

Back at Casa Bacucchi, after only a brief period of inaction following their intense firefight earlier that morning, Rudy Konieczny's Company 87-F received yet another combat order: attack a small ridge known as Mount Serra. It looked like an easy assignment, considering all the high ground the company had already captured. Unfortunately, the action quickly deteriorated into the most desperate struggle Fox Company would face in Italy.[77]

"It was just a bad day," recalled David Burt. "The Germans on Serra had made up their minds that they weren't leaving alive."[78] The *History of the 87th Mountain Infantry* describes the fighting on the slope as both "furious" and "savage," with many men dying in hand-to-hand combat as Americans moved forward one Nazi-occupied foxhole at a time. Fire literally came from every direction.[79] Sergeant Burt saved his own life with a pistol against an enemy standing just three or four yards away.[80] According to Gordie Lowe, the action on Serra, as at Torre Iussi on the previous Saturday and Monday on Banzai Ridge, "was some of the worst action the entire Tenth Mountain Division saw. It was extremely chaotic, and very bloody." Lieutenant Dwyer added quietly, "close combat is something too intense and frightening to describe adequately to someone who hasn't experienced it. It's kind of useless to even try."[81]

At some point during the awful struggle up the Serra Ridge, notes the regimental history, "Sergeant Konieczny went off on another of his frequent solo missions to clear out a bunker."[82] "Things were so confused," remembered Mike Dwyer, "that it was impossible to track the movements of every soldier on the ridge. Rudy went off to do his job, and that was all there was to it. Nobody saw what happened."[83]

Only his helmet was found, lying between two German dugouts.[84] Rudy had simply vanished.

෨෬

That evening, the heavy-hearted men of Company 87-F finally got to rest. "As it got dark," recalled David Burt, "we were really worried about Rudy being missing. We all kind of feared the worst, but you never really know, especially in fighting that intense. That's a day I started trying to forget before it was over. I'm still working on it."[85]

So stressed were Rudy's friends that Burt and Sergeant Kelly Oechsli nearly fired on one another when each mistook a goat banging around in a barn for an enemy soldier. "We came face-to-face with this poor animal between us," Burt remembered, "the two of us with our rifles pointed and ready, and the insanity of it all hit us both. That was the comic relief following the tragedy, but it illustrates how frayed we had all become. We were being pushed very, very hard."[86]

The week of combat on and around the Rocca di Roffeno in April 1945 was barbarous. The cream of America's youth—its scholar athletes, future leaders, and just plain citizen soldiers—had been thrown wholesale into the meat grinder of what war correspondent Ernie Pyle described as "the forgotten front" less than three weeks before the inevitable Nazi surrender. More than thirteen hundred of them were killed or wounded in the vicious fighting.[87] (Pyle himself was killed on April 18, not in Italy where he had spent so much of the war, but near Okinawa covering G.I.s in the Pacific theater.)[88]

Mountain troops fighting on foreign soil are, by definition, expected to attack uphill against entrenched enemy forces. Nevertheless, it is difficult to imagine that the members of the Tenth could have anticipated either the horrors that awaited them in Italy or the level of bravery with which they would respond in spite of the knowledge that the war in Europe was clearly in its final stages. As one commentator graphically described the final battle for the Apennines: "The Tenth moved out, and the Germans watched them come, and they wondered how they would ever cross that [open] ground and climb the incredible heights [of Rocca di Roffeno]. . . . The Americans wept as they crawled, and they screamed, and the Germans who saw them thought they were crazy. And the Germans cried, too. Some out of pity. Some out of fear. And some out of disbelief."[89]

Pursuit to the Alps

AT TERRIBLE COST, GENERAL HAYS'S TENTH MOUNTAIN DIVISION BROKE THROUGH to the Po Valley on the evening of April 20, 1945. General Clark offered his congratulations. As Hays prepared to exploit the breach and chase the Nazis across the Po River, however, Clark informed him that he was to cease forward movement until the remainder of the Fifth Army could catch up.[1] The commanding general wanted others to assume the lead in the offensive, an order that again may have stemmed from his fear of pushing the Nazis into a full-scale retreat into the redoubt if Hays moved too quickly. Once more, the enemy would be given time to regroup and the opportunity to set up a new line of defensive positions that the Tenth had just sacrificed the lives of hundreds of mountain troops to knock out.[2]

A troubled General Hays sensed that the German army in Italy had been broken and that this was the time to press forward, but he was in no position to challenge Clark directly by continuing the offensive—that is, until General Truscott and his top subordinate, General Crittenberger, showed up at Hays's headquarters a short time later.[3] "This is no time to relax, George," Truscott told Hays, and departed to exhort the rest of the Fifth Army to get the lead out.[4] Hays pounced. He regarded Truscott's statement as a revised order, and immediately launched his now-legendary drive that left the Nazis in northern Italy reeling in confusion and the remainder of the American troops in the sector well behind.

The Tenth quickly became the first unit of the Fifteenth Army Group to cross the Po River, commandeering boats intended for use by other divisions still far to the rear.[5] Those Nazis in the path of the mountain troops were forced to swim across if they wished to avoid capture or worse. Dozens of towns were liberated by the Tenth, including Carpi, the site of Italy's most notorious concentration camp, where a small number of remaining Jews and state enemies had still been suffering and dying.[6]

Inevitably, the Tenth also experienced numerous casualties along the way, especially upon reaching Lake Garda at the foot of the Alps. There, Nazi artillery continued to shell American troops until the final minutes of the war in Italy, causing numerous deaths in and around the tunnels along the shoreline.[7]

It is one of the great ironies of the Second World War that among the last Allied soldiers to be killed in action in the European theater was Colonel William Darby. The man who had founded the U.S. Army ranger program and had seen his own ranger battalion shattered at Anzio had still volunteered to serve under Clark and Truscott in the last weeks of the war with the Tenth Mountain Division.[8] On the early evening of April 30, a German artillery shell burst nearby as he stood next to his Jeep on an embankment above Lake Garda. The explosion caused him severe shrapnel wounds, to which he succumbed less than an hour later from internal bleeding.[9] Killed with him was Sergeant Major John Evans of Colorado.[10] Unknown to Darby and Evans and to the Nazi gunners who had fired on them, at the time the Americans were struck, Adolf Hitler was already dead. He had taken his life in the Berlin Chancellery bunker earlier that afternoon.[11]

By the end of the campaign and the official Nazi surrender in Italy two days later on May 2, the Tenth Mountain Division had sustained nearly one thousand fatalities.[12] Among them were the world-class skiers, jumpers, climbers, and instructors Torger Tokle, Arthur Tokola, Beta Fotas, Joseph Duncan, Art Argiewicz, Bud Winter, Orval McDaniel, Richard Johnston, Ralph Bromaghin, and Jacob Nunnemacher. Nearly another four thousand mountain troops, including Friedl Pfeifer, Paul and Ralph Townsend, Percy Rideout, Ralph Lafferty, John Imbrie, Pete Seibert, Jeddie Brooks, Frank Prejsnar, Lyle Munson, Ed Ketchledge, Al Soria, and John Tripp, had been wounded. For the comparatively short time in which they served on the line, the Tenth amassed one of the highest casualty rates per combat day of any American division during the entire war.[13] Overall, roughly one of every three infantrymen who came ashore with the Tenth at Naples was either killed or wounded in action, principally during the last three months of war on the Italian front.[14] And yet, it could have been even worse, if not for the willingness of Generals Truscott and Hays to ignore the instructions of General Clark to slow down.

For that reason, the members of the Tenth by and large regard General Hays as a fine commander who did an excellent job under difficult circumstances. According to battalion surgeon Captain Albert Meinke, M.D., far more wounded were expected to come through the division's aid stations than actually did as a result of the unorthodox approach taken by Hays in his pursuit of rapid victory. His race to the Alps was exhausting for his troops, but it probably kept more of them alive than if a conventional campaign had been conducted against fixed Nazi positions, as Clark had envisioned.[15]

Ultimately, General Clark never achieved the glory he was seeking in the Alps. The general arrived in Austria to find that a sign had already been erected welcoming G.I.s to the Brenner Pass, gateway to the Austrian redoubt, "courtesy of" General George S. Patton's Seventh Army.[16] Nevertheless, the victories achieved by the Fifteenth Army Group and its Tenth Mountain Division (to which Clark referred as "the finest Army Division I have ever seen")[17] served to rehabilitate the general's reputation at the very end of the hostilities in Italy. One can easily speculate that this may have been the real prize Clark was seeking all along by launching the spring offensive. As important as that issue is, however, it is one that can never be resolved.

The war in Europe ended officially on May 8, 1945, with the Tenth Mountain Division tattered in victory, with General Clark's reputation restored and enhanced, and with Rudy Konieczny still unaccounted for.

Lieutenants Donald "Mike" Dwyer (left) and John Benson of 87-F days prior to the Riva Ridge and Mount Belvedere assaults. Benson was killed on Belvedere by friendly fire from partisans, who mistook him for the enemy as he tried to assist Rudy Konieczny's pinned-down squad. Courtesy of Donald Dwyer

Sergeants Rudy Konieczny (left) and David Burt (right) entertain a group of young Italian friends a few days prior to going into action. The members of all three regiments of the Tenth Mountain Division took considerable time to assist the local population, especially the children, by distributing food and offering medical aid. Photographer presumed to be Sergeant Kelly Oechsli. Courtesy of David Burt

During a momentary lull, the troops of 85-C move up Mount Gorgolesco. The Mount Belvedere flank is in the background on the middle right. Riva Ridge is in the background on the middle left. Mount della Torraccia is the next ridge behind the vantage point of the photographer. Army Signal Corps photograph. Courtesy of Denver Public Library, Western History Collection

Tenth Mountain Division commander General George Hays (foreground) receives instructions from Italian theater commander General Mark Clark prior to the controversial spring offensive. Photographer: Roy O. Bingham. Courtesy of Denver Public Library, Western History Collection

Chaplain Henry Brendemihl, who was with Captain Ralph Bromaghin on Mount della Torraccia when a mortar shell landed close by. Courtesy of Brendemihl family

Trooper Norman Gavrin of 86-L, just prior to the spring offensive. Courtesy of Gavrin family

Captain Joe Duncan of 87-L (center, back row) and some of his boys before the spring offensive. Flanking their commanding officer are Lieutenants William Wolfgram (back row, left) and Willard Dora (back row, right), both of whom were killed during the assault on Madna di Rodiano on April 16, 1945. (Front row, left to right) First Sergeant John Campbell and Technical Sergeant Ervin Lord. Photographer: Walter Stillwell. Courtesy John Engle

facing page: The infamous house below the monastery at Torre Iussi, which Jake Nunnemacher's squad was charged with clearing on the first day of the spring offensive. Photographer: Richard A. Rocker. Courtesy of Denver Public Library, Western History Collection

The Allied generals, including Tenth Mountain Division C.O. General George Hays and British Field Marshal Sir Harold Alexander, celebrate their victories in Italy at the foot of the Alps, June 1945. Photographer: Roy O. Bingham. Courtesy of Denver Public Library, Western History Collection

Home

On March 8, 1945, a Western Union boy on a bicycle—the central fig-ure in millions of American nightmares both real and imagined during the 1940s—stopped at the front door of the Bromaghin home in Seattle. The news he delivered broke four hearts. Whether in spite of or more likely because of the distance that had grown between Ralph and his family during his four years of service, the grief of his parents and two sisters seems to have been particu-larly acute. It was leavened by remorse over time not spent and things unsaid.

A few days after learning of Ralph's death, his sister Leone Hutchinson wrote to her brother's close friend and spiritual confidant, Chaplain Henry Brendemihl. On behalf of her mother, father, and younger sister, she thanked him for having shown so much devotion to their Ralphie. The poignant ques-tions and requests related in the rest of the letter remain timeless in their re-flection of the emotions felt by those closest to the casualties in any war.

"I feel you are a friend to me," she wrote, "for you were my brother's friend, and he mentioned your kindness many times in his letters. There are a thousand and one questions that we'd be so appreciative if you could give us the answers. Did he suffer? Were you at his side? We'd treasure always the smallest detail you could send to us. Reading it would heal a bit the sorrow, the aches, in our hearts.

"It would mean so much to our mom," she continued. "She said this evening if she knew that he was buried on a mountainside that he loved, amidst the snow that he cherished of its pure beauty, [she would feel so much more at peace]. She said she knew that if there was even one kind of flower placed upon his grave, it would mean so much to her. Friend, could you for mom's sake, place one there? Ralphie loved flowers, and all growing things touched only by God."[1]

Chaplain Brendemihl replied immediately, providing the details of his friend's death. "While at the cemetery [for the memorial service]," he added, "I visited and as your mother wished, placed a flower on Ralph's grave. The mountains do look down upon the cemetery, and I know Ralph would love the view."[2] Whether the chaplain's kind gesture helped ease the pain of premature death and unsaid good-byes in the Bromaghin household is impossible to say. What is clear is that Henry Brendemihl, like so many chaplains not only in the Tenth Mountain Division but throughout the U.S. Armed Forces, was not only a brave man, but a very good and compassionate one as well.

Ralph Bromaghin's body was eventually returned to Seattle, its final resting place. There is no record of a subsequent memorial service (Bromaghin's friend Bob Craig recalled only that a military funeral did take place) or of what might have been said there.[3] Captain Ralph Lafferty, however, had a very clear idea of what his best friend would have wanted.

"Bromaghin was a sentimentalist at heart," he remembered. "Of all the songs in his repertoire, his personal favorite was 'When It's Twilight on the Trail.' I remember his telling me once that he would be very pleased to have that played at his funeral. If you had known Ralph, you would appreciate why it was his favorite."[4] Harriet Clough Waldron, Bromaghin's childhood friend, emphatically agreed.[5]

The words of the old western folk song reflect the ideals of a man who found his peace—and himself—in the spirituality of the natural world, not in material wealth.

Twilight on the Trail*

When it's twilight on the trail
and I jog along, the world is like a dream
and the ripple of the stream is my song
When it's twilight on the trail
and I rest once more, my ceiling is the sky
and the grass on which I lie is my floor
Never ever have a nickel in my jeans
Never ever have a debt to pay
Still I understand what real contentment means
Guess I was born that way
When it's twilight on the trail
and my voice is still, please plant this heart of mine
underneath the lonesome pine on the hill
You can plant this heart of mine upon the hill

෪ඏ

At Pine Lake, Wisconsin, there was a heartfelt celebration on May 8, 1945, "V.E." (Victory in Europe) Day. Of the more than fifty young men who had entered the service from the area, not a single one had been reported missing or killed in action during the entire war, a happenstance extraordinary enough on its own to merit a commemoration. Among the Nunnemachers, however, there was uneasiness. Even as neighbors hugged and congratulated them on behalf of Jake, and then shifted their full attention to the boys still serving in the Pacific (where the Japanese war would rage until late summer), the family was quietly holding its breath with apprehension.[6]

By mid-May, it had been more than a month since Jean received a letter from her husband, and that one had been written on March 31. It was decidedly unlike Jacob to allow even a few days to go by without composing a long letter, let alone six weeks, especially since his daughter Heidi had been born. The family tried to focus on believing there was some rational explanation for the silence other than a serious injury, but it got harder with each passing day to remain optimistic.

---

*Written by Sidney D. Mitchell and Louis Alter. Copyright, Famous Music Corporation, all rights reserved. Used by permission.

"I had no choice but to hold myself together for Heidi's sake," Jean remembered, "but as each day went by without word, my heart sank a little lower. After a while, you know something is wrong, and you just hope against hope that it's not your worst fears come true."[7] More weeks dragged by.

Finally, late in May, news came to the Nunnemachers. It arrived by telephone, not via telegram, in answer to the persistent and urgent inquiries to the War Department by Jean and Father Nunnemacher. According to Jake's sister Audrey: "I remember it so vividly. The phone rang and my father, who was one of the . . . most stoic people I've ever known, answered it. He listened for a moment, and he let out a sound I have never heard before or since. It was like the muffled cry of a wounded animal. His face went white, and he just started weeping, saying very softly, 'my son.' My mother came into the room, and she knew immediately. She just sank into a chair, put her head in her hands, and said in German, 'God has taken my replacement gift, too.' She was referring to the death of my eldest brother Robert a few months before Jacob was born. That may have been the saddest moment of my life, thinking about Jean and Heidi, and my parents, and my poor brother Jacob."[8]

"Jean is absolutely one of the strongest people I've ever had the pleasure of knowing," said Rene Tripp, Jean's neighbor and traveling companion back in the days of Camp Hale and Camp Swift. "She was stricken with grief, of course, but she never once that I saw conveyed anything but resiliency during that entire, terrible period of mourning. She knew she had to go on, even though everyone knew she had lost the love of her life, her soul mate. She's been that way for her whole life, through every difficult situation she has had to face over the years."[9]

Like the family of Ralph Bromaghin, the Nunnemachers chose to bring Jacob home from Italy for burial. He was laid to rest at Forest Home Cemetery in Milwaukee in 1946. A ceremony was held at about the same time to present Jean with his posthumous Silver Star. As it turned out, the Nunnemachers were, in fact, the only Gold Star family at Pine Lake. Every single one of the community's other fifty-odd boys in the service returned home after the war, though it is unclear how many actually served in active combat.[10]

"Mother Nunnemacher never really recovered from losing Jacob," Jean said. She died a few short years later. Father Nunnemacher, who according to Jean mellowed in his later years, never stopped mourning for his youngest son, either. "My parents, especially my mother," maintained Jake's brother Hermann, "were casualties of that war just as sure as my brother was."[11]

෩ଚ

Back in Adams, Massachusetts, the Konieczny family also celebrated the end
of the war in Europe, rejoicing in the fact that their Rudy would finally be
coming home after nearly five years in the service. There might have been
some lingering anxiety among family members over not having had word from
him for several weeks, but Rudy was notorious for permitting such gaps in his
correspondence. Besides, as he had written in his last letter from the hospital
in early April, "no news is good news." The family had not been contacted by
the army, and the assumption was that everything was just fine.

Two days after V.E. Day, however, any cause for celebration was abruptly
extinguished. The telegram from the War Department that arrived at the home
of Charles and Sophie Konieczny bluntly informed them that their son, Rudy,
was missing in action.[12] It gave no further details.

For eleven agonizing days, the Konieczny family waited for additional
news. "It was torturous for my parents," remembered Adolph Konieczny, "getting news like that *after* the end of the war, thinking Rudy would be coming
home safely. Actually, it was excruciating for all of us. All we could do, though,
was wait. Rudy just seemed so indestructible, it was hard to think of even the
possibility of him not coming back."[13]

Rudy's platoon leader, Lieutenant Mike Dwyer, recalled, "we simply don't
know what happened out there on that ridge near the bunkers. But the boys
finally found him at the base of the hill at Serra, in all that thick foliage."[14]
According to one story, Rudy's remains were discovered surrounded by the
bodies of eight Nazis.[15] Exaggeration or not, there can be no doubt of one
thing. Rudy Konieczny went down swinging.

On May 21, a second telegram coldly and concisely delivered the bad
news to the Konieczny family and Adams: "The Secretary of War desires me to
express his deept [sic] regret that your son T/Sgt Rudolph W. Konieczny was
killed in action in Italy 17 April 45. He had previously been reported missing
in action. Confirming letter follows."[16]

"My mother and father were just shattered," said Adolph. "We all were,
but my father really took it hard. He regretted having supported Rudy's decision to join the infantry, rather than influencing him to try to find a safer place
for himself in the service. He just kept repeating over and over to himself, 'I
never should have let him join the army.' I'm not sure he ever got over that."

"Mother, being very religious," Adolph went on, "wanted to make sure he
got home for a Catholic burial. That was very important to her. It was a lot for

us to come to grips with. The war was so close to over when it happened. But what can you do? He was just so full of life, it was hard to imagine him gone forever."[17]

The *History of the 87th Mountain Infantry* notes that the details of Rudy Konieczny's death are simply not known. Summing up his time in the Tenth, however, the narrative continued: "With the death of Konieczny, the 87th lost one of its oldest and most colorful members. From his exploits on skis at Rainier to the two BARs he managed to fire simultaneously in the Apennines, Konieczny's exploits were legendary. He might have been safe in a hospital bed from his previous wound; but no hospital could hold him when his outfit was jumping off."[18]

After four years of red tape, which according to his brother included the failure of the army to properly process the recommendation for a Silver Star that had been written up for him, Rudy Konieczny returned to the Berkshires for the final time.[19] On March 9, 1949, after a Catholic Mass attended by both of his parents and his family, Rudy was buried with full military honors at Veterans' Memorial Plot in Adams's Bellevue Cemetery.[20] Among the honor guard was Roy Deyle, who had traveled with him from boyhood to the Ski Runners to the Tenth Mountain Division, and now back to Adams.[21] Much of the little town wept.

It is more than fitting that from Rudy Konieczny's gravesite, the ski trail that runs from just below the War Memorial Tower atop Mount Greylock down to the old Thiel farm is clearly visible. The hero of the Thunderbolt— like the heroes of Pine Lake and of Paradise Ridge—had finally come home.

Legacy

Great men are rarely isolated mountain peaks;
they are the summits of ranges.

—Thomas Wentworth Higginson[1]

The atomic bombs that fell on Japan in August 1945 kept the surviving members of the Tenth Mountain Division from being annihilated on the beaches of Honshu, where they were scheduled to attack the Japanese homeland had such an assault been necessary. "I saw those beaches and the Japanese batteries above them," said Tenth Mountain Division artillery officer and lifetime army intelligence analyst Colonel Bill Gall, "and I can truly assure you that none of us would have been coming home."[2] Many veterans of the Tenth agree that it is possible both to feel sorry for the noncombatant victims of those bombs and to be thankful that President Harry Truman opted to drop them. As an anonymous veteran of Okinawa standing by to invade the mainland once said with resounding clarity, "we had mothers, too, you know."

༄༅༄

So the Tenth Mountain Division's survivors returned home from Italy (after a few weeks of climbing and skiing in the Italian Dolomites and on the *Grossglockner* in the Austrian Alps following the Nazi surrender), and set about establishing a peacetime legacy to rival their fabled wartime contributions. After months in military hospitals, Friedl Pfeifer and Percy Rideout returned to Aspen, and along with John Litchfield and others shaped the old mining town into a world-class ski resort. Pete Seibert and Bob Parker did the same at Vail, as did Larry Jump at Arapahoe Basin, in Colorado. Duke Watson and Ed Link set up shop at Crystal Mountain in the Cascades, and Nelson Bennett helped establish White Pass, each not far from Fort Lewis and Mount Rainier. A hut system was created in Colorado by a group of Tenth Mountain alumni (headed by Frank Lloyd Wright–trained architect Fritz Benedict) to approximate the Haute Route between France and Switzerland in the Alps. Bob Lewis pioneered hiking and skiing programs for the handicapped while becoming a well-known filmmaker and environmental activist in the Roaring Fork Valley. John Jay continued as the leader of the North American ski film community.

The Tenth's old stomping grounds weren't the only places its influence reached. Bob Nordhaus founded both the Sandia Peak and Ski Santa Fe resorts in New Mexico while becoming one of the nation's foremost legal advocates for Native American rights. George Fleming, who lost a leg in the Apennines, helped put Jackson Hole Ski Area on the Wyoming map. Jack Murphy founded Sugarbush in Vermont, and Bill Healey established Mount Bachelor in Oregon.

Five members of the division skied on the 1948 U.S. Ski Team: Steve Knowlton, Gordy Wren, Dev Jennings, Wendy Broomhall, and Joe Perrault. Sergeant Walter Prager was their coach.[3] Jennings later served as executive director of Ski Utah and Ski New England, while Steve Knowlton became the first director of Colorado Ski Country USA.

David Brower became president of the Sierra Club, founded Friends of the Earth, was three times nominated for the Nobel Peace Prize, and is widely revered as one of the twentieth century's greatest environmental naturalists. Ed Ketchledge became one of the leaders of the American ecology movement as a professor of forest biology in New York State and as a leading member of the Association for the Protection of the Adirondacks. Albert Jackman helped lay out the Appalachian Trail in Maine. Ome Daiber cofounded the National Mountain Rescue Council in Seattle. Paul Petzoldt founded the National Outdoor Leadership School in Jackson Hole, Wyoming, with Tap Tapley, who also founded the American Outward Bound program.

Bill Bowerman coached the U.S. Olympic Track Team and cofounded the Nike shoe company. Charles McLane (Dartmouth), John Imbrie (Brown and Columbia), George Earle (Syracuse), and Charlie Bradley and John Montagne (both at the University of Montana) were among the many who became professors at prestigious colleges. Montagne also founded the Montana Wilderness Association. The great mountaineer Fred Beckey became a renowned adventure writer, and his climbing buddy Glen Dawson a famous book publisher.

Don Coryell led the San Diego Chargers football team. Frank Sergeant led the state of Massachusetts. Bob Dole led the United States Senate. And the entire division led the way toward peaceful reconciliation among all combatants with the formation of the International Federation of Mountain Soldiers, an organization dedicated to world peace ostensibly pursuant to the basic principle *if everyone skied, there would be no more war.*

According to Tenth Mountain veteran Dick Wilson, founding editor of *Skiing* magazine, overall some two thousand members of the division went to work in the U.S. ski industry when they returned home. More than sixty American ski resorts were founded, directed, or managed by ski troop veterans.[4] "Not even the Army could kill my love for the mountains," joked Carlton Miller, a seventy-seven-year-old Tenth Mountain veteran, as he climbed a particularly difficult rock trail near Mount Washington in 2002.[5] That seems to be the attitude of nearly every Tenth Mountain veteran, as each tries to maintain in his golden years the same affection for the high alpine that he carried with him in his youth. Many are succeeding in that endeavor as they reach their eighties and beyond.

For the families of those men who did not return, however, things have naturally been quite different. Like many of those killed in action, Rudy Konieczny and Ralph Bromaghin left no wives or children. It has therefore fallen to their siblings and friends to forge remembrances, a tiring job that Adolph Konieczny spent decades pursuing on behalf of his brother. "I organized ski races in Rudy's honor after the war and helped prompt the town of Adams to do the same, but community interest in that kind of thing fades. After a while, I realized I'd feel just as satisfied to impart to the new generations of our own family the pride they should take in the sacrifice Rudy made, and inspire them to remember him with affection even if they never had the pleasure of meeting him. I think I'm accomplishing that, and it makes me happy."[6]

Sadly, as he was a youngest child, there is no one left in Ralph Bromaghin's family who had personal contact with him during his brief life. It has been his comrades in mountaineering and in arms who have seen to it that his contributions may be remembered by future generations. Among others, historian Harvey Manning paid tribute to Ralph in his legendary article on mountain climbing in the Pacific Northwest, "The Ptarmigans and Their Ptrips." "So unobtrusive yet effective was [Ralph Bromaghin's] leadership and well-beloved his personality," wrote Manning, "that some Ptarmigans are confident the club would have survived the war had he also done so."[7]

As for Jean Nunnemacher, it has not been an easy life since she lost Jacob, but it has been a rewarding one. "There is scarcely a day that passes that I don't think of him, forever young at 26," she wrote in 2002. "My choice of being with him was a good one, and it required love and courage, things I learned about that have made my life in the continuing years very special—no demand too great."[8]

Jean remarried and was widowed twice more, but she has been blessed with a large brood of children and grandchildren who visit her at Pine Lake quite often. Jacob's daughter Heidi is married, has two children, and skis around the world. So does her mother, who still makes very few concessions to the calendar.

Heidi's two children, Robyn and Jason, are grown. Each is a superior skier and athlete, imbued with their grandfather Jacob's spirit of adventure. Among their other exploits, Robyn and her husband have bicycled the Himalayas in Tibet and Nepal, photographing and documenting local mountain people and culture. Jason has likewise biked from Oregon to New Hampshire alone, as a test of his endurance and resourcefulness.[9] Jacob Nunnemacher, who never got to see his daughter, Heidi, undoubtedly would be a very proud man.

℘℧

And so, finally, there arises the question of what sense can be made of all this. What can be drawn from the ultimate sacrifice of these boys who really wanted only to ski and climb amid the serenity of the mountains, but who ended up as leaders of other young men struggling through the savagery of war?

The answers are both simple and crucial to our survival as a nation: appreciation and responsibility. More specifically, appreciation of what it truly means for a fellow citizen to have made the ultimate sacrifice in war, and as a result of such understanding, an acceptance of our responsibility to protect those who would serve and who are serving in harm's way on our behalf. As Supreme Allied Commander in Europe and president of the United States Dwight D.

Eisenhower said at perhaps his most eloquent moment, "Men acquainted with the battlefield will not be found among the numbers that glibly talk of another war."[10]

Rudy Konieczny, Jacob Nunnemacher, and Ralph Bromaghin are symbols of that special selflessness called heroism. With everything to live for, they laid down their skis and then their lives to stop perhaps the most brutal form of tyranny the world has ever known. By virtue of their willingness to risk all for the safety of others in the pursuit of an overwhelmingly just cause, they are role models for all future generations of Americans. Beyond that, however, through the example of their lives and deaths, we are also given the opportunity to comprehend more deeply the personal nature of sacrifice, and the fact that the saddest aspect of any war is the loss of so many with such enormous potential.

It is self-evident that the members of the Tenth Mountain Division who gave their lives in the Second World War are no more special than any other of the nearly three hundred thousand Americans killed in the service of their country during those bitter years. The ski troops are emblematic, however, through the vitality so easily demonstrated in their pre- and postwar civilian lives, of what nations and individuals place at risk in war. Gauging by the accomplishments achieved by those who returned, there is no telling what the world was denied by the loss of men such as Rudy, Jake, and Ralph, but our society is a poorer place by reason of their absence.

In evaluating the wisdom of any future call to war, that is a fact worthy of the highest consideration. While there are things in this world worth fighting for, the choice to fight must be viewed in the context of what we risk. The precious cargo returned from the combat zone in a flag-draped coffin is not a statistic. It is the lifeless, flesh-and-blood remains of shattered dreams and unfulfilled aspirations that might have brought much light into the world. The cure for cancer, the solution to world hunger, the greatest work of art, or perhaps just the world's best father—all might have been lost to us forever on della Torraccia, or in Torre Iussi, or north of Hill 807 at Serra. We can never know for sure.

Moreover, when circumstances dictate that we must fight, it is likewise our collective responsibility to learn from the past in shaping the future. One of the most lamentable aspects of American life at the beginning of the twenty-first century—even in our post–9/11 world—is that we tend to throw our history away with the morning paper. That is not the sign of a healthy society. A nation without history is one without conscience, and ultimately one without a soul. Eventually, it is also a nation without citizens properly able to differentiate fact from falsehood, prone to committing the same mistakes and indulgences that in the past have resulted in needless suffering and loss.

There is simply no answer to the question of whether the 1945 spring offensive in the Apennines was a military imperative. What is clear, however, is what we owe to all of those who have sacrificed their futures on our behalf. It is our sacred pledge to ensure that in our democracy, the commander in chief and the military will always answer to the people for their conduct, and take every reasonable precaution to prevent avoidable casualties in combat. Part of protecting our communal sons and daughters in the armed services is living up to that duty, in our capacity as what Justice Felix Frankfurter once called the highest office in this land: that of citizen.[11]

There is a mountain close to Sun Valley named for Ralph Bromaghin. There is an island on Pine Lake and a Dartmouth Outing Club cabin near the Appalachian Trail that bear the name of Jacob Nunnemacher. At the top of Mount Greylock, in the warming hut above the Thunderbolt trail, is a plaque dedicating the structure in memory of Rudy Konieczny.

The real honor, however, to Rudy Konieczny, Jacob Nunnemacher, Ralph Bromaghin, and all of the others who have failed to return home from war over the years is the one that we carry in our hearts. It is the knowledge we take with us every time we go to the mountains—whether actually or metaphorically—that once someone stood exactly where we are now standing, understood exactly the joy that we are now feeling, and gave it all up to make *our* time here possible. To forget that is to deny ourselves their other most precious gift: the honor of being a part of their legacy, with all of the joys and responsibilities that such an honor brings.

Sempre Avanti.

Notes

CHAPTER 1

1. Deborah E. Burns and Lauren R. Stevens, *Most Excellent Majesty* (Pittsfield, Massachusetts: Berkshire County Land Trust and Conservation Fund/The Studley Press, 1988), p. 3.

2. Burns and Stevens, *Most Excellent Majesty,* p. 47.

3. Adolph Konieczny, in-person interview, March 7, 2003, Pando, Colorado, and telephone interviews, November 23, 2001, and December 26, 2001 ("Konieczny Interviews").

4. Konieczny Interviews.

5. Konieczny Interviews.

6. Konieczny Interviews.

7. Filmed interview of Maurice "Greeny" Guertin in *Purple Mountain Majesty* (Film), Blair Mahar (Producer), Hurricane Productions, 1999. This excellent documentary film chronicling the history of the Thunderbolt is highly recommended to all those interested in U.S. ski history.

8. Konieczny Interviews.

9. Burns and Stevens, *Most Excellent Majesty,* p. 67.

10. The Thunderbolt Ski Trail is no longer officially maintained by the State of Massachusetts, but remains accessible to those willing to climb and bushwhack the difficult Mount Greylock terrain, when snow conditions permit. Mount Greylock is regarded by the International Ski History Association (ISHA) as the largest "lost" ski area in the United States. Letter to author from Morten Lund of ISHA dated February 19, 2002.

11. Burns and Stevens, *Most Excellent Majesty,* p. 68.

12. Robert Meservey, telephone interviews, July 30, 2002, and September 13, 2002 ("Meservey Interviews").

13. Burns and Stevens, *Most Excellent Majesty,* p. 68.

14. Konieczny Interviews.

15. Konieczny Interviews. Filmed interview of Maurice "Greeny" Guertin in *Purple Mountain Majesty.*

16. Konieczny Interviews.

17. Filmed interview of Lester Horton in *Purple Mountain Majesty.*

18. Filmed interview of Bill Linscott in *Purple Mountain Majesty.*

19. Konieczny Interviews.

20. Konieczny Interviews.

21. Konieczny Interviews.

22. Konieczny Interviews.

23. Norman H. Ransford, "McLane and Dartmouth Team Sweep Massachusetts Ski Meet," *Berkshire Evening Eagle,* February 3, 1941, p. 10.

24. Filmed interview of Adolph Konieczny in *Purple Mountain Majesty.*

25. Konieczny Interviews.

26. "Konieczny Paces 52 Entrants in Thunderbolt Time Trials," *Berkshire Evening Eagle,* January 17, 1938, p.10.

27. Konieczny Interviews.

28. *Berkshire Evening Eagle,* January 17, 1938, p. 10.

29. Frank Elkins, "Eastern Tourney Tops Ski Program," *New York Times,* February 5, 1938, p. 11.

30. Norman H. Ransford, "Adams Develops Youngster Who's Going Places in Skiing," *Berkshire Evening Eagle,* January 27, 1938, p. 10.

31. Konieczny Interviews.

32. Konieczny Interviews.

33. Filmed interview of Dick Durrance in *Legends of American Skiing* (Film), Richard Moulton (Producer), Keystone Productions, 1982.

34. Meservey Interviews.

35. Charles McLane, telephone interview, July 26, 2002 ("McLane Interview").

36. Letter to author from Robert Meservey dated October 8, 2002.

37. Konieczny Interviews.

38. Ransford, *Berkshire Eagle,* January 27, 1938, p. 10.

39. Ransford, *Berkshire Eagle,* January 27, 1938, p. 10.

40. Ransford, *Berkshire Eagle,* January 27, 1938, p. 10.

41. *Of Pure Blood* (Film), Clarissa Henry and Marc Hillel (Producers/Directors), Agence de Presse Film Television/Agence Française d'Images Paris (Adaptation for the BBC), 1974.

42. *Of Pure Blood.* The films produced and directed by Leni Riefenstahl, who began work as an actress in the ski films of Dr. Arnold Fanck and ended up being the "unofficial" filmmaker of the Third Reich, are particularly instructive on these points. See, for example, her "documentary" film depicting the 1936 Summer Olympic Games, *Olympia.*

43. "The Brown Bomber," in *The American Heritage History of the 20s and 30s* (Ralph K. Andrist, Editor) (New York: American Heritage Publishing Co., 1970), p. 303. Schmeling defeated Louis at Yankee Stadium in June 1936.

44. Max Schmeling, *Max Schmeling: An Autobiography* (George B. Von Der Lippe, Translator/Editor) (Chicago: Bonus Books, 1998), pp. 86–87, 144–47. Goebbels developed such an abiding hatred of Schmeling for his refusal to cooperate that, following the

boxer's subsequent defeat in a midsummer 1938 rematch with Joe Louis, he convinced Hitler to make sure that Schmeling was drafted into the paratroopers and sent on a series of suicide missions during World War II. See Hans Otto Meissner, *Magda Goebbels: The First Lady of the Third Reich* (Gwendole Mary Keeble, Translator) (New York: The Dial Press, 1980), p. 145. Schmeling survived into old age. Goebbels did not. William L. Shirer, *The Rise and Fall of the Third Reich* (New York: MJF/Simon & Schuster 1959), p. 1136.

45. Westbrook Pegler, "The Olympic Army (1936)," in David Halberstam and Glenn Stout (Eds.), *The Best American Sports Writing of the Century* (Boston: Houghton Mifflin Company, 2001), pp. 136–37. Pegler wrote: "Soldiers are everywhere. . . . [A]rmy transports go tearing through the streets . . . giv[ing] a strange suggestion of war in the little mountain resort. . . . Ten thousand swastikas stir faintly in the light winter wind along the streets. . . . Such shoving around as the populace received at the hands of the strong-armed squad of Hitler bodyguards appropriately, though ingenuously, named the Black Guards, was never seen in the United States. . . . They are a special corps, . . . all young, athletic, tall and of overbearing demeanor. The Olympics were of secondary importance, if any, [to these displays]."

46. *The British Ski Yearbook VIII,* 17 (1936): 434–45.

47. David Wallechinsky, *The 20th Century* (Boston: Little, Brown and Company, 1995), p. 655.

48. Wallechinsky, *The 20th Century,* p. 655.

49. "German Skiers Honored," *New York Times,* February 1, 1938, p. 14B.

50. "Snow Flurries Elevate Hopes for Championship Ski Events," *Berkshire Evening Eagle,* January 31, 1938, pp. 1–2; flyer advertisement for the "Bavarian Ski Boys," dated March 21, 1938, from the archives of Ralph Lafferty.

51. "German Skiers Honored," *New York Times,* February 1, 1938, p. 14B.

52. Elkins, *New York Times,* February 5, 1938, p. 11.

53. Elkins, *New York Times,* February 5, 1938, p. 11.

54. Konieczny Interviews.

55. Filmed interview of Maurice "Greeny" Guertin in *Purple Mountain Majesty.*

56. Norman H. Ransford, "Fritz Dehmel, Doctor of Philosophy, Wins Eastern Downhill Ski Title," *Berkshire Evening Eagle,* February 7, 1938, p. 12.

57. Ransford, *Berkshire Evening Eagle,* February 7, 1938, p. 12.

58. Konieczny Interviews.

59. Ransford, *Berkshire Evening Eagle,* February 7, 1938, p. 12.

60. Frank Elkin, "Dehmel Annexes Eastern Ski Race," *New York Times,* February 7, 1938, p. 14.

61. E. John B. Allen, *New England Skiing* (Dover, New Hampshire: Arcadia Publishing, 1997), p. 44.

62. Frank Prejsnar, telephone interview, November 27, 2001 ("Prejsnar Interview").

63. Konieczny Interviews.

64. Ralph Lafferty, telephone interviews, May 29, 2002, and December 15, 2002 ("Lafferty Interviews").

65. Minot (Minnie) Dole, *Adventures in Skiing* (New York: Franklin Watts, 1965), p. 62.

66. Lafferty Interviews.

67. Konieczny Interviews.

68. Konieczny Interviews.

69. Norman H. Ransford, "Toni Matt Winner in First Greylock Trophy 'No Fall' Ski Race," *Berkshire Evening Eagle,* February 27, 1939, p. 8.

70. Konieczny Interviews.

71. Konieczny Interviews.

72. Norman H. Ransford, "Berkshire Had Best Ski Racing Year," *Berkshire Evening Eagle,* December 31, 1938, p. 10.

73. David Burt letter to Donald Dwyer, May 10, 2000 (on file in Tenth Mountain Division Collection, Western History Department, Denver Public Library, Denver, Colorado) ("Burt Letter to Dwyer, 5/10/00").

74. Norman H. Ransford, "Ted Hunter's Bold Ride Wins Massachusetts Downhill Ski Championship," *Berkshire Evening Eagle,* January 30, 1939, p. 10.

75. Ransford, *Berkshire Evening Eagle,* January 30, 1939, p. 10.

76. Filmed interview of Adolph Konieczny in *Purple Mountain Majesty.*

77. Joe Ski, "Alex Bright Sets New Thunderbolt Ski Record to Win State Title," *Berkshire Evening Eagle,* February 19, 1940, p. 10.

78. Konieczny Interviews.

79. Norman H. Ransford, "Three Break Thunderbolt Ski Record in Eastern Championship Race," *Berkshire Evening Eagle,* February 26, 1940, p. 12.

80. Konieczny Interviews.

81. "Skier Injured on Thunderbolt," *North Adams Transcript,* March 4, 1940, p. 3.

82. Konieczny Interviews.

83. "Skiing Star Among Seven to Join Army," *Berkshire County Eagle,* September 25, 1940, p. 1.

84. "Skiing Star Among Seven to Join Army," *Berkshire Country Eagle,* September 25, 1940, p. 1.

CHAPTER 2

1. Jean (Schmidt/Nunnemacher) Lindemann, in-person interview at Pine Lake, Wisconsin, September 5, 2002, and numerous telephone interviews throughout 2002–2004 ("Lindemann Interviews"). She is Jacob Nunnemacher's widow.

2. Lindemann Interviews.

3. Lindemann Interviews. This point was verified by all subsequent, numerous interviews with those who knew, served with, or competed against Jake Nunnemacher throughout his life.

4. Lindemann Interviews.

5. William F. Stark, *Pine Lake* (Sheboygan, Wisconsin: Zimmermann Press, 1984), p. 204.

6. Audrey Pertl, telephone interviews, September 20, 2002, and November 4, 2002 ("Pertl Interviews"). She is Jacob Nunnemacher's sister.

7. Lindemann Interviews.

8. Pertl Interviews.

9. Lindemann Interviews and Nunnemacher family archives. Another reason for the trip was to seek expert medical advice from physicians in Vienna regarding a persistent infection suffered by young Audrey. The family visited several doctors, none of whom could offer the relief that the simple administration of antibiotics eventually would; Pertl Interviews.

10. Pertl Interviews.

11. Lindemann Interviews.

12. Lindemann Interviews.

13. Fritz Trubshaw, in-person interview at Pine Lake, Wisconsin, September 5, 2002 ("Trubshaw Interview").

14. Trubshaw Interview.

15. Lindemann Interviews.

16. Trubshaw Interview.

17. Pertl Interviews.

18. Trubshaw Interview.

19. Stark, *Pine Lake,* p. 209.

20. Lindemann Interviews.

21. Filmed interview of Ted Ryan, Fiske's friend and business partner, in *Legends of American Skiing.*

22. Filmed interview of Alf Engen in *Thrills and Spills in the North Country* (Film), Rick Moulton (Producer), New England Ski Museum, 1998.

23. Lindemann Interviews.

24. Ezra Bowen, *The Book of American Skiing* (New York: Bonanza Books, 1963), pp. 162–63.

25. Heiliger Huegel Ski Club 2001–2002 Roster and Club History.

26. Lindemann Interviews.

27. Telephone Interview with Hermann Nunnemacher, July 14, 2002 ("Nunnemacher Interview"). Hermann Nunnemacher is Jake Nunnemacher's older brother.

28. Lindemann Interviews.

29. Lindemann Interviews; Records of the University of Wisconsin at Madison.

30. Lindemann Interviews.

31. As for Professor Bradley, he was still whooping it up as he skied *off-piste* with members of the Sun Valley ski patrol—including Tenth Mountain Division veteran Nelson Bennett—on Bald Mountain at the age of ninety-two, six years before he passed away in 1976. Nelson Bennett, in-person interviews in New York City, New York, September 21, 2002, and in Mohonk, New York, March 23, 2003 ("Bennett Interviews").

32. Lindemann Interviews.

33. Lindemann Interviews.

34. Lindemann Interviews.

35. *Dartmouth Aegis* (Hanover, New Hampshire: Dartmouth College, 1938), Volume 66, p. 75.

36. *Dartmouth Aegis* (Hanover, New Hampshire: Dartmouth College, 1939), Volume 67, p. 80.

37. Lindemann Interviews.

38. Lindemann Interviews.

39. American National Red Cross, *New York–New England Hurricane and Floods 1938: Official Report of Relief Operation* (Washington: The American National Red Cross, 1939), p. 2.

40. Charles F. Brooks, "Wind," *The Mount Washington Observatory News Bulletin* 4 (December 1938), p. 20.

41. Lindemann Interviews.

42. Lindemann Interviews.

43. John C. Tobin, *The Fall Line: A Skier's Journal* (New York: Meredith Press, 1969), p. 29.

44. Stan Cohen, *A Pictorial History of Downhill Skiing* (Missoula, Montana: Pictorial Histories Publishing Company, 1985), p. 28.

45. Hal Burton, *The Ski Troops* (New York: Simon and Schuster, 1971), p. 34.

46. Friedl Pfeifer with Morten Lund, *Nice Goin'—My Life on Skis* (Missoula, Montana: Pictorial Histories Publishing Company, 1993), p. 58; See C. Lester Walker, "A Way of Life," in *The Ski Book* (Morten Lund, Robert Gillen and Michael Bartlett, Editors) (New York: Arbor House, 1982), p. 204.

47. E. John B. Allen, *From Skisport to Skiing* (Amherst: The University of Massachusetts Press, 1993), p. 98.

48. Burton, *The Ski Troops,* p. 33. The influential Arlberg instructor Sig Buchmayr of Peckett's-on Sugar-Hill, New Hampshire, was not an "official" member of the Schneider gang, but is deserving of mention as well.

49. Cohen, *A Pictorial History of Downhill Skiing,* p. 28. As an interesting footnote to the saga of Hannes Schneider, soon after his arrival in America he was able to exact a small measure of revenge against his former captors with the assistance of Harvey Gibson. When the German ambassador to the United States arrived on holiday from New York at Gibson's famous Eastern Slope Inn in Cranmore, New Hampshire, with three important guests in tow, Gibson and his wife gave instructions to his dining room orchestra leader. With a wink to Schneider, they ordered that only music written by Jewish composers was to be played during dinner. After about an hour, the Nazi guests apparently had had all the Felix Mendelsohn, Sig Romberg, and Kurt Weill they could handle, and made a show of storming out of the room. Only then did Mrs. Gibson allow the orchestra to return to its full repertoire. Burton, *The Ski Troops,* p. 45.

50. Tobin, *The Fall Line,* pp. 43–44.

51. Meservey Interviews.

52. McLane Interview.

53. Lindemann Interviews.

54. Tobin, *The Fall Line,* p. 35.

55. Tobin, *The Fall Line,* p. 35.

56. Lindemann Interviews.

57. Lindemann Interviews.

58. Lindemann Interviews.

59. Lindemann Interviews.

60. *Dartmouth Aegis* (Hanover, New Hampshire: Dartmouth College, 1940), Volume 68, pp. 72–73.

61. Letter to author from Robert Meservey dated October 8, 2002.

62. Joe Ski, "Matt Retains Mt. Greylock Trophy Ski Title in Brilliant Run on Thunderbolt," *Berkshire Evening Eagle,* January 29, 1940.

63. Ski, *Berkshire Evening Eagle,* February 19, 1940, p. 10.

64. Letter to author from Bob Meservey dated October 8, 2002; Meservey Interviews.

65. Ransford, *Berkshire Evening Eagle,* February 26, 1940, p. 12.

66. Meservey Interviews.

67. Tobin, *The Fall Line,* p. 57.

68. *Dartmouth Aegis* (Hanover, New Hampshire: Dartmouth College, 1941), Volume 69, pp. 71–72.

69. *Dartmouth Aegis* (Hanover, New Hampshire: Dartmouth College, 1942), Volume 70, pp. 71–72.

70. Lindemann Interviews.

71. Meservey Interviews.

72. Lindemann Interviews.

73. Lindemann Interviews.

74. Lindemann Interviews.

75. Meservey Interviews.

76. Tobin, *The Fall Line,* p. 43.

77. Pertl Interviews.

78. David Hooke, *A Brief History of the Dartmouth Outing Club* (unpublished, circa 2001), p. 1 (on file in Tenth Mountain Division Collection, Western History Department, Denver Public Library, Denver, Colorado).

79. Lindemann Interviews.

80. Lindemann Interviews.

81. "Lead Big Green in All-Important ISU Meet at Middlebury," *The Dartmouth,* February 20, 1942, p. 7; *Dartmouth Aegis* (1942), p. 71.

82. *Dartmouth Aegis* (1942), pp. 71–72.

83. *Dartmouth Aegis* (1942), p. 72.

84. Meservey Interviews.

85. Meservey Interviews.

86. Phil Puchner, telephone interview, September 24, 2002 ("Puchner Interview").

87. Jacob Nunnemacher's records at Dartmouth College (on file in Tenth Mountain Division Collection, Western History Department, Denver Public Library, Denver, Colorado).

88. Pertl Interviews.

89. Lindemann Interviews.

90. Lindemann Interviews.

91. See, for example, Joyce Milton, *Loss of Eden—A Biography of Charles and Anne Morrow Lindbergh* (New York: HarperCollins, Publishers, 1993), pp. 374–402.

92. Lindemann Interviews.

93. John de la Montagne, now known as John Montagne, telephone interviews, November 12, 2002, and December 15, 2002 ("Montagne Interviews").

94. Lindemann Interviews.

CHAPTER 3

1. Harvey Manning, "The Ptarmigans and Their Ptrips," *Mountaineer Annual,* 1958, pp. 48–49.

2. Manning, *Mountaineer Annual,* p. 51.

3. Manning, *Mountaineer Annual,* p. 63.

4. Ray Clough, telephone interview, August 10, 2002 ("Ray Clough Interview").

5. Ralph Clough, telephone interview, August 10, 2002 ("Ralph Clough Interview").

6. Ray Clough Interview.

7. Robert Craig, in-person interview, February 25, 2004, and telephone interview, March 21, 2004 ("Craig Interviews").

8. Harriet Clough Waldron, telephone interview, August 21, 2002 ("Waldron Interview").

9. Theresa Frees, telephone interview, September 27, 2002 ("Frees Interview"). She is a niece of Ralph Bromaghin's.

10. Waldron Interview.

11. Waldron Interview.

12. Manning, *Mountaineer Annual,* p. 63.

13. Manning, *Mountaineer Annual,* p. 63.

14. Waldron Interview.

15. Joel Connelly, "Turbulent Years Turned Out Lasting Leaders," *Seattle Post-Intelligence Reporter,* November 19, 1999, p. 1.

16. Waldron Interview.

17. McLane Interview.

18. Waldron Interview.

19. Ray Clough Interview.

20. Pfeifer, *Nice Goin',* p. 62.

21. Cohen, *A Pictorial History of Downhill Skiing,* p. 190.

22. Pfeifer, *Nice Goin',* p. 63.

23. Pfeifer, *Nice Goin',* p. 63.

24. British actor David Niven recalled meeting Schaffgotsch on the count's return voyage to the United States with his band of instructors. Niven wrote of Schaffgotsch: "A handsome and affable Graf, he was also a dyed-in-the-wool Nazi. He spent hours extolling the virtues of Hitler, sympathizing with his problems and enthusing over his plans. . . . Felix said that he was bringing over a dozen good ski instructors from his home in Austria—'all Nazis too.'" David Niven, *The Moon's a Balloon* (New York: G.P. Putnam's Sons, 1972), p. 215.

25. Cohen, *A Pictorial History of Skiing,* p. 196.

26. Cohen, *A Pictorial History of Skiing,* p. 187.

27. Allen, *From Skisport to Skiing,* p. 171.

28. Pfeifer, *Nice Goin',* pp. 51–52.

29. Otto Lang, *A Bird of Passage—The Story of My Life* (Helena, Montana: Sky House Publishers/Falcon Press, 1994), p. 149.

30. Lang, *A Bird of Passage,* p. 154.

31. Pfeifer, *Nice Goin',* p. 70.

32. Denny Pace, telephone interview, August 22, 2002.

33. John Woodward, in-person interview, Valley Forge, Pennsylvania, November 9, 2002; telephone interviews, August 28, 2002, and December 19, 2002 ("Woodward Interviews").

34. Lang, *A Bird of Passage,* pp. 192–93.

35. Waldron Interview.

36. Waldron Interview.

37. "New Craft Crumples on Routine Test Flight," *Seattle Times,* March 19, 1939, p. 1; James Wallace, "Aerospace Notebook: Veteran Test Pilot Links Boeing's Past and Future," *Seattle Post-Intelligencer,* March 30, 2002, p. B-1.

38. Waldron Interview.

39. Waldron Interview. By coincidence, Harriet Clough first met her husband that day at Rainier. In 2003, they celebrated their sixtieth wedding anniversary.

40. Waldron Interview.

41. Pfeifer, *Nice Goin',* p. 79.

42. John Litchfield, telephone interview, July 28, 2002 ("John Litchfield Interview").

43. Joe Cutts, "Sun Valley," *New York Times,* January 25, 2004, Section 5, p. 12.

44. McLane Interview.

45. Ralph Bromaghin letter on stationery of the Challenger Inn in Sun Valley to his sister Florence and her husband David, undated, approximately March 1940 (on file in Tenth Mountain Division Collection, Western History Department, Denver Public Library, Denver, Colorado).

46. Clarita Heath later married fellow 1936 Olympic Ski Team member Alex Bright. Her first husband, William Reiter, was a navy pilot killed in action in the Pacific during World War II. "Olympian Clarita Heath Bright Dies at 87," *U.S. Alpine Team News,* October 19, 2003, p. 1.

47. Bennett Interviews.

48. Records of the University of Washington.

49. John Imbrie, *A Chronology of the 10th Mountain Division* (Watertown, New York: The National Association of the Tenth Mountain Division, 2001), p. 1 (hereinafter *Chronology*); William R. Trotter, *A Frozen Hell: The Russo-Finnish War of 1939–40* (Chapel Hill, North Carolina: Algonquin, 1991), pp. 36–37.

50. Imbrie, *Chronology,* p. 1.

51. McKay Jenkins, *The Last Ridge: The Epic Story of the U.S. Army's 10th Mountain Division and the Assault on Hitler's Europe* (New York: Random House, 2003), p. 16.

52. Imbrie, *Chronology,* p. 1; Dole, *Adventures in Skiing,* pp. 90–93.

53. Imbrie, *Chronology,* p. 1; Dole, *Adventures in Skiing,* pp. 100–102.

54. Woodward Interviews.

55. Jeffrey Leich, "Tales of the 10th" (Part 1 of 2) in *New England Ski Museum Newsletter* (Winter 2001, Issue 52), p. 9.

56. Roe "Duke" Watson, telephone interviews, July 22, 2002, and December 15, 2002 ("Watson Interviews").

57. Watson Interviews; Richard F. W. Whittemore, *For the Love of Skiing* (Stowe, Vermont: Self-Published, 1998), p. 75.

58. Watson Interviews.

59. Woodward Interviews.

60. Letter to author from John Woodward dated December 6, 2002.

61. Bennett Interviews.

62. Woodward Interviews.

63. Burton, *The Ski Troops*, p. 74; Thomas P. Govan, *The Army Ground Forces Training for Mountain and Winter Warfare, Study No. 23* (Washington: Historical Section, Army Ground Forces, 1946), text accompanying note 18.

64. Govan, *The Army Ground Forces Training for Mountain and Winter Warfare, Study No. 23*, note 18, citing Apt. No. 6910 of Lieutenant Colonel Norman E. Fiske, Military Attaché, jib: Italy–Military operations; Burton, *The Ski Troops*, p. 92.

65. Whittemore, *For the Love of Skiing*, p. 73.

66. In the meanwhile, McLane trained with the Coast Artillery. McLane Interview; Jeffrey R. Leich, *Tales of the 10th: The Mountain Troops and American Skiing* (Franconia, New Hampshire: The New England Ski Museum, 2003), p. 32.

67. Watson Interviews.

68. Watson Interviews.

69. Watson Interviews.

70. Imbrie, *Chronology*, p. 2.

71. Whittemore, *For the Love of Skiing*, p. 75.

CHAPTER 4

1. Govan, *The Army Ground Forces Training for Mountain and Winter Warfare, Study No. 23*, text accompanying note 10.

2. Govan, *The Army Ground Forces Training for Mountain and Winter Warfare, Study No. 23*, note 10. The National Ski Patrol at the time was officially known as the National Ski Association; George F. Earle, *History of the 87th Mountain Infantry, Italy 1945* (Denver: Bradford Robinson Printing Co., 1945), p. 6 (hereinafter *87th Regimental History*).

3. Dole, *Adventures in Skiing*, p. 103; *Fire on the Mountain* (Film), Beth Gage and George Gage (Producers/Directors), First Run Features, 1995.

4. "Adams Ski Trooper Missing in Action," *North Adams Transcript*, May 11, 1945, p. 3.

5. Govan, *The Army Ground Forces Training for Mountain and Winter Warfare, Study No. 23*, text accompanying note 26.

6. Flint Whitlock and Bob Bishop, *Soldiers on Skis* (Boulder, Colorado: Paladin Press, 1992), pp. 5–7. See also Records of the Tenth Mountain Division (on file in Tenth Mountain Division Collection, Western History Department, Denver Public Library, Denver, Colorado).

7. Jeffrey Leich, *New England Ski Museum Newsletter* (Winter 2001, Issue 52), p. 16.

8. Filmed interview of Lieutenant Colonel Ross Wilson, *Soldiers of the Summit* (Film), Tom Feliu (Producer), KRMA-TV/Total Communications Company for The Council for Public Television, 1987. See also *Winter Warriors* (Film), Martin Gillam (Producer), Greystone Communications, 2001.

9. John Hitchcock, "Ski Shelter on Greylock Will Be Dedicated in Memory of Rudy Konieczny of Adams," *The Advocate* (Adams, Massachusetts), May 25, 1999, p. 8.

10. Watson Interviews.

11. Records of the Tenth Mountain Division (on file in Tenth Mountain Division Collection, Western History Department, Denver Public Library, Denver, Colorado).

12. Records of the Tenth Mountain Division (on file in Tenth Mountain Division Collection, Western History Department, Denver Public Library, Denver, Colorado).

13. "One Killed, 2 Hurt in Ski Race," *Seattle Post-Intelligencer,* April 14, 1940, p. 1.

14. Mike Donahoe, "City Fireman Wins Silver Skis Trophy," *Seattle Post-Intelligencer,* April 13, 1942, pp. 1, 15.

15. Donahoe, *Seattle Post-Intelligencer,* April 13, 1942, p. 15.

16. Donahoe, *Seattle Post-Intelligencer,* April 13, 1942, p. 15.

17. Lafferty Interviews.

18. Whittemore, *For the Love of Skiing,* p. 102.

19. Watson Interviews.

20. Woodward Interviews.

21. Whittemore, *For the Love of Skiing,* p. 84.

22. Woodward Interviews.

23. Nick Hock, telephone interview, January 20, 2004 ("Hock Interview").

24. Woodward Interviews.

25. McLane Interview.

26. McLane Interview.

27. Montagne Interviews.

28. Whittemore, *For the Love of Skiing,* p. 88.

29. Charles C. Bradley, *Aleutian Echoes* (Anchorage: The University of Alaska Press, 1994), p. 11.

30. Bradley, *Aleutian Echoes,* pp. 11–12.

31. Bradley, *Aleutian Echoes,* pp. 12–13.

32. Bradley, *Aleutian Echoes,* pp. 13–14.

33. Bradley, *Aleutian Echoes,* pp. 14–17.

34. Bradley, *Aleutian Echoes,* pp. 14–17.

35. Gordon Lowe, telephone interview, December 3, 2001 ("Lowe Interview").

36. Bradley, *Aleutian Echoes,* p. 11.

37. Letter to author from John Woodward dated June 6, 2002.

38. Filmed interview of Earl Clark in *Fire on the Mountain.*

39. Jeddie Brooks, in-person interviews, March 4–7, 2003, Summit County, Colorado ("Jeddie Brooks Interviews").

40. Woodward Interviews.

41. *Songs of the 10th Mountain Division,* compiled for the 1989 Tenth Mountain Division Reunion at French Lick, Indiana, p. 1 (on file in Tenth Mountain Division Collection, Western History Department, Denver Public Library, Denver, Colorado).

42. Lafferty Interviews.

43. McLane Interview.

44. Filmed interview of Bill Bowerman, Earl Clark, and others in *Fire on the Mountain.*

45. Records of the Tenth Mountain Division (on file in Tenth Mountain Division Collection, Western History Department, Denver Public Library, Denver, Colorado);

Burton, *The Ski Troops,* p. 136; Thomas R. Brooks, *The War North of Rome—June 1944– May 1945* (Edison, New Jersey: Castle Books, 1996), p. 351.

46. Brower, *For Earth's Sake,* p. 89.

47. Minnie Dole, *Birth Pains of the 10th Mountain Division* (unpublished), 1955, p. 4 (on file in Tenth Mountain Division Collection, Western History Department, Denver Public Library, Denver, Colorado).

48. Robert B. Ellis, *See Naples and Die* (Jefferson, North Carolina: McFarland & Company, 1996), p. 35.

49. Robert Wallace, *The Italian Campaign* (Alexandria, Virginia: Time-Life Books, 1978), p. 184.

50. Filmed interview of Bill Bowerman in *Fire on the Mountain.*

51. Peter Wick, "Reflections on Fort Lewis," in *Good Times and Bad Times* (John Imbrie and Hugh W. Evans, Editors) (Quechee, Vermont: Vermont Heritage Press, 1995), p. 188.

52. McLane Interview.

53. Filmed interview of Oley Kohlman in *Fire on the Mountain.*

54. Konieczny Interviews.

55. Woodward Interviews.

56. Lafferty Interviews.

57. Watson Interviews.

58. Duane Shrontz, *Alta, Utah: A People's Story* (Alta, Utah: Two Doors Press, 2002), p. 75.

59. Dick Durrance as told by John Jerome, *The Man on the Medal: The Life & Times of America's First Great Ski Racer* (Aspen, Colorado: Durrance Enterprises, 1995), p. 81.

60. Durrance, *The Man on the Medal,* p. 81.

61. Lafferty Interviews.

62. Woodward Interviews.

63. Letter to author from John Woodward dated December 6, 2002.

64. Burton, *The Ski Troops,* p. 101.

65. Burton, *The Ski Troops,* p. 101.

66. Burton, *The Ski Troops,* p. 101.

67. Wick, *Reflections on Fort Lewis,* p. 188.

68. Watson Interviews.

69. Burton, *The Ski Troops,* p. 103.

70. Watson Interviews.

71. Gorton Carruth and Eugene Erlich, *American Quotations* (New York: Wings Books, 1988), p. 147.

72. Whitlock and Bishop, *Soldiers on Skis,* p. 9.

73. Montagne Interviews.

74. Archives of Dartmouth College (information on file in Tenth Mountain Division Collection, Western History Department, Denver Public Library, Denver, Colorado).

CHAPTER 5

1. Pfeifer, *Nice Goin',* p. 9.

2. Rudy Abramson, *Spanning the Century: The Life of W. Averell Harriman 1891– 1986* (New York: William Morrow and Company, 1992), p. 231; Myrna Hampton, "The

10th Mountain Division—A Legacy to American Skiing," *Idaho Mountain Express,* March 9, 1978, p. C5; Burton, *The Ski Troops,* p. 144.

3. Abramson, *Spanning the Century,* pp. 231–32. *The Sun Valley Skiers* (Film), David Butterfield (Producer), Centennial Entertainment, 2000.

4. Whitlock and Bishop, *Soldiers on Skis,* pp. 8–9.

5. Whitlock and Bishop, *Soldiers on Skis,* p. 31.

6. Whitlock and Bishop, *Soldiers on Skis,* pp. 8–9.

7. Bob Parker, in-person interview March 7, 2003, Pando, Colorado, and telephone interview April 29, 2003 ("Bob Parker Interviews").

8. Sally Barlow-Perez, *A History of Aspen* (Basalt, Colorado: Who Press, 2000), pp. 40–42.

9. Barlow-Perez, *A History of Aspen,* p. 41. Starting in the 1930s, Thomas annually broadcast his popular radio show for several days from the Jerome Hotel in Aspen.

10. Abbott Fay, *A History of Skiing in Colorado* (Ouray, Colorado: Western Reflections, 2000), p. 50.

11. Pfeifer, *Nice Goin',* p. 111.

12. Hock Interview.

13. Prejsnar Interview.

14. Prejsnar Interview.

15. Konieczny Interviews.

16. Prejsnar Interview.

17. Watson Interviews.

18. Hampton, *Idaho Mountain Express,* p. C-5.

19. Whitlock and Bishop, *Soldiers on Skis,* pp. 6–7. See also Records of the Tenth Mountain Division (on file in Tenth Mountain Division Collection, Western History Department, Denver Public Library, Denver, Colorado).

20. Whitlock and Bishop, *Soldiers on Skis,* p. 124.

21. Prejsnar Interview.

22. Whitlock and Bishop, *Soldiers on Skis,* p. 31.

23. Whitlock and Bishop, *Soldiers on Skis,* p. 7.

24. Alan K. Engen, *For the Love of Skiing: A Visual History* (Salt Lake City: Gibbs-Smith, Publisher, 1998), pp. 70–71.

25. Engen, *For the Love of Skiing,* pp. 68–70.

26. Watson Interviews.

27. Edward Wilkes telephone interview, July 17, 2003 ("Wilkes Interview"). Wilkes is the nephew of Joseph Duncan Jr. and grandnephew of Joseph Duncan Sr.

28. Letter to John M. Engle from Roger W. Eddy, dated March 11, 2002. On file in Tenth Mountain Division Collection, Western History Department, Denver Public Library, Denver, Colorado. It is possible that Duncan was pulling Eddy's leg about the gun battle, but Eddy claimed to have seen the bullet holes in the wall behind a curtain. The Brown Palace Hotel could not verify that the shooting incident had ever taken place. Letter to author from John M. Engle dated May 15, 2003.

29. *The Whispering Pine 1930* (Estes Park, Colorado: The Estes Park High School, 1930), Vol. II, p. 13.

30. Wilkes Interview.

31. Fay, *A History of Skiing in Colorado,* pp. 47–56.

32. George Peck Jr., *Winter Sports in the Estes Park Area: An Address at the Estes Park Historical Museum, April 15, 1982.* Transcript on file in the Oral History Project Section of the Estes Park Public Library, Estes Park, Colorado. Peck was a contemporary of Junior Duncan's.

33. Jack C. Moomaw, *Recollections of a Rocky Mountain Ranger* (Estes Park, Colorado: The YMCA of the Rockies, 1963, 2001), p. 176.

34. Moomaw, *Recollections of a Rocky Mountain Ranger,* p. 175.

35. Peck, *Winter Sports in the Estes Park Area.*

36. Moomaw, *Recollections of a Rocky Mountain Ranger,* p. 176.

37. "Local Youth Is New National Ski Champion," *Estes Park Trail,* March 30, 1934, p. 1.

38. Burns and Stevens, *Most Excellent Majesty,* p. 68.

39. Uncredited press release, "Post Named in Honor of Captain Joseph J. Duncan, an Estes Park Native," prepared by the Estes Park American Legion Post. On file at the Estes Park Public Library, Estes Park, Colorado.

40. "Captain J. J. Duncan Killed in Action in Italy," *Estes Park Trail,* June 22, 1945, p. 2.

41. Victor Eklund, telephone interview, June 28, 2003 ("Eklund Interview").

42. Eklund Interview.

43. David Burt, telephone interviews, November 24, 2001, December 23, 2001, December 14, 2002 ("Burt Interviews").

44. Burt Interviews.

45. Peter Shelton, *Climb to Conquer* (New York: Scribner, 2003), p. 67.

46. Burt Interviews.

47. Konieczny Interviews.

48. Burt Interviews.

49. Charles Hampton letter to author dated December 27, 2003.

50. Konieczny Interviews.

51. Frank Elkin, "Nation's Skiing Stars Prepare for Mountaineer Troop Service: Torger Tokle Heads List of Those on the Army Roster—Prager, Percy Rideout, Litchfield at Colorado Camp," *New York Times,* December 15, 1942, p. 16.

52. Whitlock and Bishop, *Soldiers on Skis,* pp. 31–32: "The film . . . *I Love a Soldier* . . . gave the general public the idea that, in spite of the glamorous, ski resort atmosphere, training in the Rockies was a tough, often serious business."

53. Whitlock and Bishop, *Soldiers on Skis,* p. 42. Filmed interview of Steve Knowlton describing balcony rappelling technique utilized in *Soldiers of the Summit.*

54. Burton, *The Ski Troops,* p. 103.

55. Burton, *The Ski Troops,* p. 103.

56. Watson Interviews.

57. Paul Kitchen, in-person interview, Valley Forge, Pennsylvania, November 9, 2002.

58. Dan Pinolini, in-person interview, Valley Forge, Pennsylvania, November 9, 2002 ("Pinolini Interview").

59. Watson Interviews.

60. Lafferty Interviews.

61. Lafferty Interviews.

62. Lafferty Interviews.

63. Lindemann Interviews.

64. John McPhee, *Encounters with the Archdruid* (New York: Farrar, Straus and Giroux, 1971), p. 27.

65. Brower, *For Earth's Sake,* p. 84.

66. Brower, *For Earth's Sake,* p. 88.

67. Brower, *For Earth's Sake,* p. 89.

68. Letter to author from Jean (Nunnemacher) Lindemann dated October 30, 2002.

69. Carruth and Erlich, *American Quotations,* p. 147.

70. Jean S. Lindemann, "An Army Wife," *The Blizzard* (the Newsletter of the 10th Mountain Division Association), 2nd Quarter 2002, p. 4.

71. Burt Interviews.

72. Lindemann Interviews.

73. Burt Interviews.

74. Dole, *Adventures in Skiing,* pp. 123–24.

75. Shelton, *Climb to Conquer,* pp. 62–64; Bob Parker Interviews.

76. Shelton, *Climb to Conquer,* pp. 62–64; John Woodward Interviews.

77. Shelton, *Climb to Conquer,* p. 64.

78. Filmed interview of Paul Petzoldt in *Fire on the Mountain.*

79. Letter to author from Robert Meservey dated October 8, 2002.

80. Letter to author from Robert Meservey dated October 8, 2002.

81. Burt Interviews.

82. Lindemann Interviews.

CHAPTER 6

1. Whitlock and Bishop, *Soldiers on Skis,* p. 19.

2. Whitlock and Bishop, *Soldiers on Skis,* p. 29.

3. Govan, *The Army Ground Forces Training for Mountain and Winter Warfare, Study No. 23,* text accompanying note 45, citing Statement of Maj Gen. Lloyd Jones to AGF Hist. Office, 2 Jun 45.

4. Burt Interviews.

5. Burt Interviews.

6. Whitlock and Bishop, *Soldiers on Skis,* p. 29.

7. Whitlock and Bishop, *Soldiers on Skis,* p. 26.

8. Burt Interviews.

9. George F. Earle, *Birth of a Division* (Syracuse, New York: Signature Publications, 1995), p. 22.

10. Whitlock and Bishop, *Soldiers on Skis,* p. 29; Imbrie, *Chronology,* p. 5; Records of the Tenth Mountain Division (on file in Tenth Mountain Division Collection, Western History Department, Denver Public Library, Denver, Colorado).

11. Ruso Perkins, in-person interview, Valley Forge, Pennsylvania, November 10, 2002.

12. George Earle, telephone interview, May 30, 2003 ("Earle Interview").

13. Burton, *The Ski Troops,* p. 117.

14. Burton, *The Ski Troops,* p. 117.

15. Burt Interviews.

16. Burt Interviews.

17. Anonymous source, in-person interview, March 2002.

18. Letter to H. J. Nunnemacher from Jacob Nunnemacher, August 25, 1943. On file in Tenth Mountain Division Collection, Western History Department, Denver Public Library, Denver, Colorado.

19. Letter to H. J. Nunnemacher from Jacob Nunnemacher, August 25, 1943.

20. Letter to H. J. Nunnemacher from Jacob Nunnemacher, August 25, 1943.

21. Lindemann, *The Blizzard* (2nd Quarter 2002), p. 4.

22. Lindemann Interviews; Lindemann, *The Blizzard* (2nd Quarter 2002), p. 4.

23. Lindemann Interviews; Pfeifer, *Nice Goin',* pp. 116–18.

24. Lindemann Interviews; Lindemann, *The Blizzard* (2nd Quarter 2002), p. 4.

25. Lindemann Interviews; Lindemann, *The Blizzard* (2nd Quarter 2002), p. 4.

26. Lafferty Interviews.

27. Percy Rideout, telephone interview, December 15, 2002 ("Rideout Interview").

28. Rideout Interview.

29. Watson Interviews.

30. Hock Interview.

31. Lindemann Interviews.

32. Meservey Interviews.

33. Lindemann Interviews.

34. Watson Interviews.

35. Woodward Interviews.

36. McLane Interview.

37. Burt Interviews; Records of the Tenth Mountain Division (on file in Tenth Mountain Division Collection, Western History Department, Denver Public Library, Denver, Colorado).

38. Records of the Tenth Mountain Division (on file in Tenth Mountain Division Collection, Western History Department, Denver Public Library, Denver, Colorado).

39. Lindemann, *The Blizzard* (2nd Quarter 2002), p. 4.

40. Meservey Interviews.

41. Lindemann Interviews.

42. Hampton, *Idaho Mountain Express,* March 9, 1978, pp. C-4–5.

43. Hampton, *Idaho Mountain Express,* March 9, 1978, p. C-5.

44. Lindemann Interviews.

45. Lindemann Interviews.

46. Pfeifer, *Nice Goin',* p. 116.

47. Lindemann Interviews.

48. Pfeifer, *Nice Goin',* p. 118.

49. Pfeifer, *Nice Goin',* p. 116.

50. Lou Dawson, "Trooper Traverse," *Skiing,* March/April 2002, p. 70.

51. Records of the Tenth Mountain Division (on file in Tenth Mountain Division Collection, Western History Department, Denver Public Library, Denver, Colorado).

52. Dawson, *Skiing,* March/April 2002, pp. 70–72.

53. Dawson, *Skiing,* March/April 2002, pp. 70–72.

54. Letter to author from Bruce Macdonald dated September 25, 2003.

55. Dawson, *Skiing,* March/April 2002, p. 71.

56. Shelton, *Climb to Conquer,* pp. 100–101.

57. Lou Dawson, "Eulogy: Burdell S. 'Bud' Winter 1925–1945" (unpublished, circa 1999). On file in Tenth Mountain Division Collection, Western History Department, Denver Public Library, Denver, Colorado.

58. Dawson, *Skiing,* March/April 2002, pp. 70–72; Dawson, "Eulogy: Burdell S. 'Bud' Winter 1925–1945."

59. Shelton, *Climb to Conquer,* pp. 98–101.

60. Dawson, *Skiing,* March/April 2002, pp. 70–72; Dawson, "Eulogy: Burdell S. 'Bud' Winter 1925–1945."

61. Shelton, *Climb to Conquer,* p. 101.

62. Brower, *For Earth's Sake,* p. 95; *Fire on the Mountain.*

63. Burt Interviews.

64. Burt Letter to Dwyer dated May 10, 2000.

65. Burt Interviews.

66. Meservey Interviews.

67. Letter to author from Robert Meservey dated October 8, 2002.

68. Bradley, *Aleutian Echoes,* pp. 43, 49.

69. Ellis, *See Naples and Die,* pp. 68–71.

70. Lafferty Interviews.

71. Whitlock and Bishop, *Soldiers on Skis,* p. 42; Records of the Tenth Mountain Division (on file in Tenth Mountain Division Collection, Western History Department, Denver Public Library, Denver, Colorado).

72. Govan, *The Army Ground Forces Training for Mountain and Winter Warfare, Study No. 23,* p. 18.

73. Whitlock and Bishop, *Soldiers on Skis,* p. 42.

74. Lafferty Interviews.

75. McKay Jenkins, *The White Death* (New York: Anchor Books, 2000), pp. 29–30.

76. Burton, *The Ski Troops,* pp. 137–38.

77. Burton, *The Ski Troops,* 137–39.

78. Dole, *Birth Pains of the 10th Mountain Division,* p. 6; Burton, *The Ski Troops,* p. 139.

79. Lindemann Interviews. According to John Woodward, "the Division was divided about half and half between those hoping to see combat and those who preferred otherwise." Woodward Interviews.

80. Lindemann Interviews.

81. Robert Parker, "Roadrunner Report," *The Blizzard,* 3rd Quarter 2003, p. 13.

82. Charlie Murphy, in-person interview, Nyack, New York, December 11, 2002.

83. Don Linscott, telephone interview, January 25, 2003, and in-person interview, March 7, 2003, Pando, Colorado ("Linscott Interviews").

84. Linscott Interviews.

85. Brower, *For Earth's Sake,* p. 101.

86. Linscott Interviews.

87. Whitlock and Bishop, *Soldiers on Skis,* p. 52.

88. Whitlock and Bishop, *Soldiers on Skis,* p. 46.

89. Prejsnar Interview.

90. Earle, *Birth of a Division,* p. 25.

91. Brooks, *The War North of Rome,* p. 352.

92. Govan, *The Army Ground Forces Training for Mountain and Winter Warfare, Study No. 23,* text accompanying notes 55 and 56; Whitlock and Bishop, *Soldiers on Skis,* p. 51.

93. Lindemann Interviews.

CHAPTER 7

1. George Botjer, *Sideshow War* (College Station: Texas A&M University Press, 1996), pp. 14–15.

2. Jenkins, *The Last Ridge,* p. 137.

3. Botjer, *Sideshow War,* pp. 76–77.

4. Martin Blumenson, *Bloody River* (College Station: Texas A & M University Press, 1970), p. 125.

5. Govan, *The Army Ground Forces Training for Mountain and Winter Warfare, Study No. 23,* text accompanying note 41.

6. Botjer, *Sideshow War,* pp. 70–71.

7. Blumenson, *Bloody River,* pp. 90–92.

8. Lucian Truscott, *Command Mission* (Novato, California: Presidio Press/E.P. Dutton and Co., 1954), p. 295.

9. Botjer, *Sideshow War,* p. 71.

10. Blumenson, *Bloody River,* pp. 125–26.

11. Blumenson, *Bloody River,* p. 110.

12. Botjer, *Sideshow War,* p. 71; Wallace, *The War in Italy,* p. 117; Blumenson, *Bloody River,* p. 135.

13. Botjer, *Sideshow War,* pp. 104–5; Jenkins, *The Last Ridge,* pp. 122–23.

14. Truscott, *Command Missions,* p. 380.

15. Ernest F. Fisher Jr., *Cassino to the Alps* (Washington: Center of Military History, United States Army, 1993), pp. 221–22, citing John North, ed., *Memoirs, Field Marshal Alexander of Tunis, 1939–45* (New York: McGraw-Hill, 1962).

16. Fisher, *Cassino to the Alps,* p. 199.

17. Shirer, *Rise and Fall,* p. 1105: "The National Redoubt was a phantom. It never existed except in the propaganda blasts of Dr. Goebbels."

18. Fisher, *Cassino to the Alps,* pp. 444–45; Ellis, *See Naples and Die,* p. 171.

19. Martin Blumenson, *Mark Clark—The Last of the Great World War II Commanders* (New York: Congdon & Weed, 1984), p. 218.

20. Jenkins, *The Last Ridge,* 135–36. See also *Soldiers of the Summit* (Film), Tom Feliu (Producer/PBS Documentary), Denver: KRMA-TV, 1987.

21. Fisher, *Cassino to the Alps,* p. 449.

22. Imbrie, *Chronology,* p. 9.

23. Earle, *87th Regimental History,* p. 19.

24. Brooks, *The War North of Rome,* p. 303.

25. Brooks, *The War North of Rome,* p. 303.

26. Brooks, *The War North of Rome,* p. 303.

27. Brooks, *The War North of Rome,* p. 303.

28. Brooks, *The War North of Rome,* p. 2.

29. Botjer, *Sideshow War,* p. 185; Fisher, *Cassino to the Alps,* p. 406.

30. Jenkins, *The Last Ridge,* pp. 137–38; Whitlock and Bishop, *Soldiers on Skis,* p. 53.

CHAPTER 8

1. Watson Interviews; Records of the Tenth Mountain Division (on file in Tenth Mountain Division Collection, Western History Department, Denver Public Library, Denver, Colorado).

2. Watson Interviews.

3. Lafferty Interviews.

4. Eklund Interview.

5. Ross Coppock, telephone interview, February 24, 2003 ("Coppock Interview").

6. Watson Interviews.

7. Lafferty Interviews.

8. Konieczny Interviews.

9. Meservey Interviews.

10. Konieczny Interviews.

11. Lindemann Interviews.

12. Whitlock and Bishop, *Soldiers on Skis,* p. 52.

13. Whitlock and Bishop, *Soldiers on Skis,* p. 53.

14. Whitlock and Bishop, *Soldiers on Skis,* p. 53.

15. Albert H. Meinke Jr., M.D.*, Mountain Troops and Medics* (Kewadin, Michigan: Rucksack Publishing Company, 1993), p. 17.

16. Lindemann Interviews.

CHAPTER 9

1. Fisher, *Cassino to the Alps,* pp. 417–18.

2. Meinke, *Mountain Troops and Medics,* p. 16.

3. Letter from Henry Brendemihl to Leone Hutchinson, undated, approximately April 1, 1945. On file in Tenth Mountain Division Collection, Western History Department, Denver Public Library, Denver, Colorado (hereinafter "Brendemihl Letter").

4. Watson Interviews.

5. Fred Brendemihl, telephone interview, August 20, 2002. Fred is the late Chaplain Henry Brendemihl's son.

6. Lafferty Interviews.

7. Meinke, *Mountain Troops and Medics,* p. 25.

8. Truscott, *Command Missions,* p. 454.

9. Charles Wellborn, *History of the 86th Mountain Infantry, Italy 1945* (Denver: Bradford Robinson Printing Co., 1945), pp. 2–3 (hereinafter *86th Regimental History*).

10. Whitlock and Bishop, *Soldiers on Skis*, p. 64. This particular mine was built to launch the explosive charge to the crotch level of its victim prior to detonating.

11. Earle, *87th Regimental History*, pp. 9–10.

12. Earle, *87th Regimental History*, p. 10.

13. Whitlock and Bishop, *Soldiers on Skis*, p. 67.

14. Earle, *87th Regimental History*, p. 13.

15. Earle, *87th Regimental History*, p. 13.

16. Imbrie, *Chronology*, p. 8; Fisher, *Cassino to the Alps*, p. 426.

17. Fisher, *Cassino to the Alps*, p. 449.

18. Puchner Interview.

19. Woodward Interviews.

20. Puchner Interview.

21. Donald "Mike" Dwyer, telephone interviews, December 3, 2001, and January 11, 2002 ("Dwyer Interviews").

22. Burt Interviews.

23. Meservey Interviews, quoting Peter Wick; Earle, *87th Regimental History*, p. 89: "Sergeant Konieczny . . . was piling up a large score of personal victims."

24. The poem "I Have a Rendezvous with Death," written by American Alan Seeger (1888–1916), was morbidly popular among troops during both world wars. "I have a rendezvous with death, at some disputed barricade . . . On some scarred slope of battered hill," wrote Seeger prophetically. He died serving with the French Foreign Legion in World War I. Ellis, *See Naples and Die*, p. 97.

25. Earle, *87th Regimental History*, p. 12.

26. Dwyer Interviews.

27. Earle, *87th Regimental History*, pp. 128–29. Tragically, Captain Kennett was killed in the Po Valley on a similar bicycle reconnaissance mission just days prior to the end of the war in Italy.

28. Konieczny Interviews.

29. Stephen Stuebner, *Cool North Wind: Morley Nelson's Life with Birds of Prey* (Caldwell, Idaho: Caxton Press, 2002), pp. 76–77.

30. Dwyer Interviews.

31. David Burt letter to Mike Dwyer, dated June 9, 2000.

32. Lindemann Interviews.

33. Earle, *87th Regimental History*, p. 14.

34. Lindemann Interviews.

35. Lewis Hoelscher, telephone interviews, August 15, 2002, December 15, 2002, and July 4, 2003 ("Hoelscher Interviews").

36. Wellborn, *86th Regimental History*, p. 7.

37. Lafferty Interviews.

38. Letter from Leone Hutchinson to Henry Brendemihl, undated, approximately March 10, 1945 ("Hutchinson Letter").

39. Brower, *For Earth's Sake*, p. 158.

40. Rideout Interview.

41. Bradley, *Aleutian Echoes,* pp. 222–23.

42. Rideout Interview.

43. Wellborn, *86th Regimental History,* p. 7.

44. Truscott, *Command Missions,* p. 477.

45. Truscott, *Command Missions,* p. 477.

46. Fisher, *Cassino to the Alps,* p. 440.

47. Truscott, *Command Missions,* pp. 476–77.

48. Dwyer Interviews.

49. Botjer, *Sideshow War,* p. 110.

50. Fisher, *Cassino to the Alps,* p. 442.

51. Dr. Gerd Falkner, telephone interview conducted in German by Sabina Wolf (Munich, Germany), November 10, 2001 ("Falkner Interview"). Substance of interview confirmed in English to author by Dr. Falkner, Salt Lake City, Utah, January 24, 2002.

52. Gordon Williamson, *German Mountain & Ski Troops 1939–45* (Oxford: Osprey Publishing, 1996), p. 9.

53. Falkner Interview.

54. Dole, *Adventures in Skiing,* p. 64.

55. Whitlock and Bishop, *Soldiers on Skis,* p. 67.

CHAPTER 10

1. John Imbrie and Thomas Brooks, *10th Mountain Division Campaign in Italy 1945* (Forest Hills, New York: National Association of the Tenth Mountain Division, 2002), p. 9.

2. Truscott, *Command Missions,* p. 451.

3. Truscott, *Command Missions,* p. 476.

4. Brooks, *The War North of Rome,* p. 303; Truscott, *Command Missions,* p. 466.

5. Truscott, *Command Missions,* p. 477.

6. Truscott, *Command Missions,* pp. 477–78.

7. Jenkins, *The Last Ridge,* pp. 135–36; Thomas R. Brooks and John Imbrie, "Deny Belvedere Ridge to the Enemy," *The Blizzard,* 3rd Quarter 2003, p. 4.

8. Truscott, *Command Missions,* p. 478.

9. Truscott, *Command Missions,* p. 478.

10. Truscott, *Command Missions,* pp. 478–79.

11. Whitlock and Bishop, *Soldiers on Skis,* p. 60; Truscott, *Command Missions,* pp. 478–79.

12. Brooks, *The War North of Rome,* pp. 352–53 (citing Hays's unpublished diaries); Burton, *The Ski Troops,* p. 150.

13. Earle, *87th Regimental History,* p. 19.

14. Truscott, *Command Missions,* p. 477; Burton, *The Ski Troops,* p. 150.

15. Jennifer Hattam, "First on Top," *Sierra Magazine,* May/June 2001, p. 27.

16. Hattam, *Sierra Magazine,* May/June 2001, p. 27.

17. Brower, *For Earth's Sake,* p. 97.

18. Brower, *For Earth's Sake,* p. 99.

19. Brower, *For Earth's Sake,* p. 96.

20. Earle, *Birth of a Division,* p. 21.

21. Brower, *For Earth's Sake,* p. 99.

22. Whitlock and Bishop, *Soldiers on Skis,* p. 60; Rideout Interview.

23. Whitlock and Bishop, *Soldiers on Skis,* p. 77.

24. Rideout Interview.

25. Imbrie, *Chronology,* p. 6; Prejsnar Interview.

26. Jacques Parker, telephone interview, January 14, 2004 ("Jacques Parker Interview"). Private LeBrecht was awarded a Silver Star for valor, posthumously. SSM GO#173. Records of the Tenth Mountain Division (on file in Tenth Mountain Division Collection, Western History Department, Denver Public Library, Denver, Colorado).

27. Earle, *87th Regimental History,* p. 19.

28. Earle, *87th Regimental History,* p. 20.

29. Earle, *87th Regimental History,* p. 20.

30. Stuebner, *Cool North Wind,* p. 78.

31. Puchner Interview.

32. Whitlock and Bishop, *Soldiers on Skis,* pp. 90–91; Imbrie and Brooks, *10th Mountain Division Campaign in Italy 1945,* p. 7.

33. Earle, *87th Regimental History,* pp. 21–22.

34. Puchner Interview.

35. Whitlock and Bishop, *Soldiers on Skis,* p. 91.

36. Earle, *87th Regimental History,* pp. 21–22; Burt Interviews.

37. Earle, *87th Regimental History,* p. 90; Burt Interviews.

38. Earle, *87th Regimental History,* p. 22.

39. Earle, *87th Regimental History,* p. 20.

40. Bob Parker Interviews. He credits sabotage in Nazi munitions factories by antifascist workers, some of whom were trained by OSS members dropped behind enemy lines, for his good fortune.

41. Earle, *87th Regimental History,* p. 21.

42. Stuebner, *Cool North Wind,* p. 81.

43. Earle, *87th Regimental History,* p. 21.

44. Stuebner, *Cool North Wind,* p. 82.

45. Jenkins, *The Last Ridge,* p. 216. In another incident described by trooper Dick Nebeker of Company 85-A, "when eight or ten prisoners were brought into the little saddle below Hill 916, Boston Blackie, a lieutenant newly assigned to the 2nd platoon, took a B.A.R. and killed all of the disarmed prisoners at 25 foot range. He was relieved of command the following day, or week." Dick Nebeker, *My Experience in the Ski Troops* (unpublished article, circa 1990), p. 12. On file in Tenth Mountain Division Collection, Western History Department, Denver Public Library, Denver, Colorado.

46. Earle Interview.

47. Earle, *87th Regimental History,* pp. 26–27.

48. Hugh Evans, "Baptism on Belvedere," in *Good Times and Bad Times,* p. 50.

49. Dan Kennerly, "Following C Company up Mt. Belvedere," in *Good Times and Bad Times,* p. 233.

50. Evans, *Good Times and Bad Times,* p. 50.

51. Burt Interviews.

52. Wellborn, *86th Regimental History,* p. 15.

53. Whitlock and Bishop, *Soldiers on Skis,* p. 101; Marty Daneman, telephone interview, December 14, 2003 ("Daneman Interview"). Daneman said that he also saw a written transcription of the order. He likewise reported that Lieutenant Colonel Stone had lost the confidence of his troops during their stateside training period, and never really regained their trust. This added to Stone's difficulties on della Torraccia.

54. Thomas R. Brooks, in-person interview, March 27, 2003, New York City. Unless otherwise noted, all further quotes attributed to Tom Brooks were made during the foregoing interview ("Tom Brooks Interview").

55. Whitlock and Bishop, *Soldiers on Skis,* p. 102.

56. Whitlock and Bishop, *Soldiers on Skis,* p. 103.

57. Whitlock and Bishop, *Soldiers on Skis,* p. 103.

58. David Brower, *Remount Blue* (Berkeley, California: Self-Published, 1948), p. 19.

59. Wellborn, *86th Regimental History,* p. 19; Watson Interviews.

60. Filmed interview of John Hay Jr. in *Fire on the Mountain.*

61. David Brower, *Insight of the Archdruid* (unpublished article dated January 5, 2000). On file in Tenth Mountain Division Collection, Western History Department, Denver Public Library, Denver, Colorado.

62. Wellborn, *86th Regimental History,* p. 20. Battalion surgeon Dr. Albert Meinke has written that he believes at least one such injury to have been caused by a "lucky" shot from great distance. Meinke, *Mountain Troops and Medics,* pp. 114–15.

63. Watson Interviews.

64. Brower, *For Earth's Sake,* p. 101; Watson Interviews.

65. Watson Interviews.

66. Filmed interview of John Hay Jr. in *Fire on the Mountain.*

67. Filmed interview of John Hay Jr. in *Fire on the Mountain.*

68. Wellborn, *86th Regimental History,* p. 20.

69. Meinke, *Mountain Troops and Medics,* p. 128.

70. Kennerly, *Good Times and Bad Times,* p. 233.

71. Pinolini Interview.

72. Woodward Interviews. According to trooper Bruce Macdonald of 87-L, "the common way of getting sent back to the rear was for the GI to put the barrel of his M-1 between his big toe and the others and pull the trigger. The result: a bad burn, but no lost toes and a ticket to the rear." Letter to author from Bruce Macdonald, dated September 25, 2003.

73. Letter to author from Ralph Lafferty, dated December 7, 2002.

74. Lafferty Interviews.

75. Rideout Interview.

76. Ross Coppock, "No Snow Atop Mount Della Torraccia," *The Blizzard,* 4th Quarter 2002, p. 8.

77. Coppock Interview. A "cripple" round is one with a defective launching charge.

78. Brower, *For Earth's Sake,* p. 101.

79. Coppock Interview. He also sustained a slight shrapnel wound to the arm in the blast.

80. Coppock Interview.

81. Brendemihl Letter.

82. Brendemihl Letter.

83. Letter to author from Dr. Albert Meinke, dated October 2, 2002.

84. Watson Interviews; Rideout Interview.

85. Letter to author from Dr. Albert Meinke, dated October 2, 2002.

86. Records of the Tenth Mountain Division (on file in Tenth Mountain Division Collection, Western History Department, Denver Public Library, Denver, Colorado).

87. Lafferty Interviews.

88. Filmed interview of Ralph Lafferty in *Fire on the Mountain.*

CHAPTER 11

1. Whitlock and Bishop, *Soldiers on Skis,* p. 107.

2. Shelton, *Climb to Conquer,* p. 172.

3. Konieczny Interviews.

4. Peter W. Seibert with William Oscar Johnson, *Vail—Triumph of a Dream* (Boulder, Colorado: Mountain Sports Press, 2000), p. 56.

5. Meinke, *Mountain Troops and Medics,* pp. 216–17.

6. Letter to Jean Nunnemacher (Lindemann) from Jake Nunnemacher, dated March 2, 1945. On file in Tenth Mountain Division Collection, Western History Department, Denver Public Library, Denver, Colorado.

7. Earle, *87th Regimental History,* p. 41.

8. Earle, *87th Regimental History,* p. 33.

9. Earle, *87th Regimental History,* p. 37.

10. Earle, *87th Regimental History,* p. 37.

11. Seibert, *Vail—Triumph of a Dream,* p. 58.

12. Seibert, *Vail—Triumph of a Dream,* p. 69.

13. Whitlock and Bishop, *Soldiers on Skis,* p. 112; Letter to author from Lyle Munson, dated May 26, 2004 ("Munson Letter [5/26/04]").

14. Whitlock and Bishop, *Soldiers on Skis,* p. 112.

15. Whitlock and Bishop, *Soldiers on Skis,* p. 112; Munson Letter (5/26/04).

16. Munson Letter (5/26/04).

17. Whitlock and Bishop, *Soldiers on Skis,* p. 112.

18. Jacques Parker Interview.

19. According to Lyle Munson, "only one shell came in and it was an artillery shell. . . . I am positive that it was a short round." Munson Letter (5/26/04). Robert Meyerhoff (86-I-Med) stated that it was the impression of the medics on the scene that Tokle's wounds had been sustained as the result of an American artillery round falling short. Robert Meyerhoff, in-person interview, February 26, 2004, Keystone, Colorado. Highly respected Tenth Mountain Division Artillery Officer Lt. Colonel William Gall stated in 2004 that although it was never definitively established where the round came from, "it appeared from the direction and flight of the shell that it was probably friendly fire that killed Tokle and Tokola." William Gall, telephone interview, July 18, 2004.

20. Munson Letter (5/26/04).

21. Whitlock and Bishop, *Soldiers on Skis,* p. 112.

22. Wellborn, *86th Regimental History,* p. 26.

23. Whitlock and Bishop, *Soldiers on Skis,* p. 113.

24. Whitlock and Bishop, *Soldiers on Skis,* p. 112.

25. Whitlock and Bishop, *Soldiers on Skis,* p. 113.

26. Earle, *87th Regimental History,* pp. 41–42.

27. Letter to sister from Rudy Konieczny, dated March 4, 1945. On file in Tenth Mountain Division Collection, Western History Department, Denver Public Library, Denver, Colorado.

28. Lowe Interview.

29. Earle, *87th Regimental History,* p. 42.

30. Stuebner, *Cool North Wind,* p. 84.

31. Earle, *87th Regimental History,* p. 43.

32. Earle, *87th Regimental History,* p. 43.

33. Earle, *87th Regimental History,* p. 37.

34. William Lowell Putnam, *Green Cognac* (New York: The AAC Press, 1991), p. 108.

35. Putnam, *Green Cognac,* p. 108.

36. Putnam, *Green Cognac,* pp. 108–9.

37. Putnam, *Green Cognac,* pp. 108–9.

38. Putnam, *Green Cognac,* p. 110.

39. Truscott, *Command Missions,* pp. 473–74 (describing the morale problems of the segregated African American Ninety-second Division).

40. Luterio Aguilar, in-person interview at Santo Domingo Pueblo, New Mexico, November 10, 2000.

41. Records of the Tenth Mountain Division (on file in Tenth Mountain Division Collection, Western History Department, Denver Public Library, Denver, Colorado).

42. Shelton, *Climb to Conquer,* p. 82.

43. Letter to author from Bruce Macdonald, dated September 25, 2003.

44. Norman Gavrin, telephone interview, July 28, 2000.

45. Jeffrey R. Leich, *Tales of the 10th: The Mountain Troops and American Skiing* (Franconia, New Hampshire: New England Ski Museum, 2003), p. 115.

46. Sid Foil, in-person interview in Albuquerque, New Mexico, November 11, 2000.

47. Rick Richards, *Ski Pioneers: Ernie Blake, His Friends, and the Making of Taos Ski Valley* (Helena, Montana: Dry Gulch/Sky House Publishers, 1992), pp. 27–35.

48. Earle, *87th Regimental History,* pp. 45–47.

49. Whitlock and Bishop, *Soldiers on Skis,* p. 123.

50. Brooks, *The War North of Rome,* p. 359.

51. Imbrie and Brooks, *10th Mountain Division Campaign in Italy 1945,* p. 12.

52. Imbrie and Brooks, *10th Mountain Division Campaign in Italy 1945,* pp. 7, 12.

CHAPTER 12

1. Harris Dusenberry, *The North Apennines and Beyond* (Portland, Oregon: Binford & Mort Publishing, 1998), pp. 244–51.

2. Letter to Jean Nunnemacher (Lindemann) from Jacob Nunnemacher, dated March 18, 1945. On file in Tenth Mountain Division Collection, Western History Department, Denver Public Library, Denver, Colorado.

3. Letter to Jean Nunnemacher (Lindemann) from Jacob Nunnemacher, dated March 18, 1945.

4. Letter to Jean Nunnemacher (Lindemann) from Jacob Nunnemacher, dated March 13, 1945. On file in Tenth Mountain Division Collection, Western History Department, Denver Public Library, Denver, Colorado.

5. Letter to Jean Nunnemacher (Lindemann) from Jacob Nunnemacher, dated March 18, 1945.

6. Letter to Jean Nunnemacher (Lindemann) from Jacob Nunnemacher, dated March 21, 1945. On file in Tenth Mountain Division Collection, Western History Department, Denver Public Library, Denver, Colorado.

7. Letter to sister from Rudy Konieczny, dated March 4, 1945. On file in Tenth Mountain Division Collection, Western History Department, Denver Public Library, Denver, Colorado.

8. Letter to sister from Rudy Konieczny, dated March 18, 1945. On file in Tenth Mountain Division Collection, Western History Department, Denver Public Library, Denver, Colorado.

9. Prejsnar Interview.

10. Letter to sister from Rudy Konieczny, dated April 1, 1945. On file in Tenth Mountain Division Collection, Western History Department, Denver Public Library, Denver, Colorado.

11. Oley Kohlman, *Uphill with the Ski Troops* (Cheyenne, Wyoming: Self-Published, 1985), p. 97.

12. Prejsnar Interview.

13. Letter to Jean Nunnemacher (Lindemann) from Jacob Nunnemacher, dated March 27, 1945. On file in Tenth Mountain Division Collection, Western History Department, Denver Public Library, Denver, Colorado.

14. Letter to Jean Nunnemacher (Lindemann) from Jacob Nunnemacher, dated March 13, 1945. On file in Tenth Mountain Division Collection, Western History Department, Denver Public Library, Denver, Colorado.

15. Letter to Jean Nunnemacher (Lindemann) from Jacob Nunnemacher, dated March 18, 1945.

16. Letter to Jean Nunnemacher (Lindemann) from Jacob Nunnemacher, dated March 28, 1945. On file in Tenth Mountain Division Collection, Western History Department, Denver Public Library, Denver, Colorado.

17. "Fixed Bayonets—The Fighting 10th Mountain Division," *Ski Press USA,* Spring 2001, p. 1 (quoting Tenth Mountain Division veteran Bob Parker).

CHAPTER 13

1. Burt Interviews.

2. Whitlock and Bishop, *Soldiers on Skis,* p. 131.

3. Shirer, *The Rise and Fall of the Third Reich,* p. 1107.

4. Peter Grose, *Gentleman Spy: The Life of Allen Dulles* (New York: Houghton Mifflin Company, 1994), p. 241; Fisher, *Cassino to the Alps,* pp. 514–17.

5. Grose, *Gentleman Spy,* p. 241; Fisher, *Cassino to the Alps,* pp. 514–17.

6. Shirer, *The Rise and Fall of the Third Reich,* p. 1105–6.

7. Fisher, *Cassino to the Alps,* p. 446; Burton, *The Ski Troops,* p. 150.

8. Christopher Simpson, *The Splendid Blond Beast——Money, Law and Genocide in the Twentieth Century* (New York: Grove Press, 1993), pp. 201–5.

9. Shirer, *The Rise and Fall of the Third Reich,* p. 1107.

10. Fisher, *Cassino to the Alps,* p. 443; Burton, *The Ski Troops,* p. 149.

11. Fisher, *Cassino to the Alps,* p. 444.

12. These included members of the dreaded XIV Panzer Corps and the German Ninety-fourth Division. Fisher, *Cassino to the Alps,* p. 442.

13. Fisher, *Cassino to the Alps,* pp. 483–84.

14. Fisher, *Cassino to the Alps,* pp. 444–45.

15. Fisher, *Cassino to the Alps,* pp. 444–45.

16. Blumenson, *Mark Clark,* pp. 242–43.

17. Fisher, *Cassino to the Alps,* p. 449.

18. Truscott, *Command Missions,* 445. It should not be ignored that the prevailing view of many soldiers and officers who had spent months and sometimes years on the bloody Italian front was that it was time for the Tenth Mountain Division to do its "fair share." After all, this was a specialized infantry group, most of whose members had *volunteered* for dangerous duty. Why shouldn't they be called upon finally to face the enemy after spending most of the war stateside? Rideout Interview; Bob Parker Interviews. For a scathing recollection of the animosity felt toward the members of the Tenth upon its arrival by veterans of the Fifth Army's long and bitter campaign in Italy, see Roy Livengood, "The Myths of the Tenth Mountain Division," *The Powder River Journal of the 91st Infantry Division Association, Inc.* (Summer 1985), p. 1.

19. Burton, *The Ski Troops,* p. 168.

20. Whitlock and Bishop, *Soldiers on Skis,* p. 132.

21. Dwyer Interviews.

22. Earle, *87th Regimental History,* pp. 57–58.

23. Earle, *87th Regimental History,* pp. 57–58.

24. Burt Interviews.

25. Ellis, *See Naples and Die,* p. 171.

26. Ellis, *See Naples and Die,* p. 176, quoting Truscott's written message to the troops.

27. Earle, *87th Regimental History,* p. 58.

28. Fisher, *Cassino to the Alps,* p. 437.

29. Earle, *87th Regimental History,* pp. 58–59.

30. Earle, *87th Regimental History,* pp. 58–59.

31. Filmed interview with John Imbrie, *Winter Warriors.*

32. Earle, *87th Regimental History,* p. 65.

33. Filmed interview with John Imbrie, *Winter Warriors.*

34. Brower, *For Earth's Sake,* p. 103.

35. Rideout Interview.

36. Earle, *87th Regimental History,* p. 58.

37. Earle, *87th Regimental History,* pp. 58–59.

38. Letter to author from John Woodward, dated February 16, 2004.

39. Hoelscher Interviews.

40. Earle, *87th Regimental History,* p. 59.

41. Hoelscher Interviews.

42. Hoelscher Interviews.

43. Hoelscher Interviews.

44. Montagne Interviews.

45. Hoelscher Interviews.

46. Letter to Jean Nunnemacher (Lindemann) from John Sugden, dated May 4, 1945. On file in Tenth Mountain Division Collection, Western History Department, Denver Public Library, Denver, Colorado.

47. Letter to Jean Nunnemacher (Lindemann) from Leon Burrows, undated, approximately June 1, 1945. On file in Tenth Mountain Division Collection, Western History Department, Denver Public Library, Denver, Colorado.

48. Letter to Jean Nunnemacher (Lindemann) from anonymous soldier signed "Bud," dated May 19, 1945. On file in Tenth Mountain Division Collection, Western History Department, Denver Public Library, Denver, Colorado.

49. Records of the Tenth Mountain Division (on file in Tenth Mountain Division Collection, Western History Department, Denver Public Library, Denver, Colorado).

50. Nunnemacher Interview.

CHAPTER 14

1. Earle, *87th Regimental History,* p. 59.

2. Hoelscher Interviews.

3. Letter to author from Dr. Albert Meinke, dated December 8, 2002.

4. Fisher, *Cassino to the Alps,* p. 446.

5. Jenkins, *The Last Ridge,* p. 227; Whitlock, *Soldiers on Skis,* 155, quoting Ken Templeton Jr., aide to assistant division commander Colonel Robinson Duff; Fisher, *Cassino to the Alps,* p. 446; Shelton, *Climb to Conquer,* p. 184; *Fire on the Mountain.*

6. Earle, *87th Regimental History,* p. 64.

7. Earle, *87th Regimental History,* p. 64.

8. Ross J. Wilson, *History of the First Battalion 87th Mountain Infantry* (Kalispell, Montana: Self-Published, 1991), p. 36.

9. Wilson, *History of the First Battalion 87th Mountain Infantry,* p. 36.

10. Earle, *87th Regimental History,* p. 66.

11. Pfeifer, *Nice Goin',* pp. 122–23.

12. Jenkins, *The Last Ridge,* p. 222.

13. Ellis, *See Naples and Die,* pp. 178–79, quoting Richard Ben Cramer, *What It Takes: The Way to the White House* (New York: Random House, 1992), pp. 102–5.

14. Pfeifer, *Nice Goin',* p. 120.

15. Pfeifer, *Nice Goin',* pp. 120–21.

16. Rideout Interview.

17. Whitlock and Bishop, *Soldiers on Skis,* p. 139.

18. Wellborn, *86th Regimental History,* pp. 41–42.

19. Rideout Interview; SSM GO#87 (Lafferty); SSM GO#21 (Rideout). Rideout also received a Bronze Star, BSM GO#111. Records of the Tenth Mountain Division (on file in Tenth Mountain Division Collection, Western History Department, Denver Public Library, Denver, Colorado).

20. Pfeifer, *Nice Goin',* p. 121; Wellborn, *86th Regimental History,* p. 41.

21. Earle, *87th Regimental History,* p. 62.

22. SSM GO#85. Records of the Tenth Mountain Division (on file in Tenth Mountain Division Collection, Western History Department, Denver Public Library, Denver, Colorado); Earle, *87th Regimental History,* p. 62.

23. Shelton, *Climb to Conquer,* p. 183.

24. Shelton, *Climb to Conquer,* pp. 155–56.

25. BSM GO#92. Records of the Tenth Mountain Division (on file in Tenth Mountain Division Collection, Western History Department, Denver Public Library, Denver, Colorado).

26. Shelton, *Climb to Conquer,* p. 251.

27. Earle, *87th Regimental History,* p. 67.

28. Earle, *87th Regimental History,* p. 73.

29. Earle, *87th Regimental History,* pp. 69–70.

30. Earle, *87th Regimental History,* pp. 69–70.

31. Jeddie Brooks Interviews.

32. Jeddie Brooks Interviews.

33. Jeddie Brooks Interviews.

34. BSM GO#132. Records of the Tenth Mountain Division (on file in Tenth Mountain Division Collection, Western History Department, Denver Public Library, Denver, Colorado).

35. Jeddie Brooks Interviews.

36. Jeddie Brooks Interviews.

37. Burt Interviews.

38. Dwyer Interviews.

39. Earle, *87th Regimental History,* pp. 85–86.

40. Burt Interviews.

41. Earle, *87th Regimental History,* p. 84.

42. SS #GO-104. On file in Tenth Mountain Division Collection, Western History Department, Denver Public Library, Denver, Colorado.

43. Earle, *87th Regimental History,* p. 84.

44. Earle, *87th Regimental History,* p. 86.

45. Earle, *87th Regimental History,* pp. 88–89.

46. Earle, *87th Regimental History,* p. 89.

47. Dwyer Interviews.

48. Earle, *87th Regimental History,* p. 89.

49. Earle, *87th Regimental History,* p. 89.

50. Earle, *87th Regimental History,* p. 94.

51. Uncredited press release, "Post Named in Honor of Captain Joseph J. Duncan, an Estes Park Native," prepared by the Estes Park American Legion Post. On file at the Estes Park Public Library, Estes Park, Colorado.

52. Statement of Colonel Robert Works, dated March 7, 1985. On file in Tenth Mountain Division Collection, Western History Department, Denver Public Library, Denver, Colorado.

53. Statement of Walter Stillwell Jr., undated (approximately January 1985). On file in Tenth Mountain Division Collection, Western History Department, Denver Public Library, Denver, Colorado.

54. Eklund Interview.

55. Earle, *87th Regimental History,* p. 80.

56. Earle, *87th Regimental History,* p. 80.

57. Earle, *87th Regimental History,* p. 81.

58. SS #GO-35. Records of the Tenth Mountain Division (on file in Tenth Mountain Division Collection, Western History Department, Denver Public Library, Denver, Colorado).

59. Earle, *87th Regimental History,* p. 81.

60. Letter to Bruce Berends from Al Soria, dated August 31, 2001. On file in Tenth Mountain Division Collection, Western History Department, Denver Public Library, Denver, Colorado.

61. Albert Soria, telephone interview, October 2, 2003 ("Soria Interview").

62. Earle Interview.

63. A copy of the draft memoir is on file with the author. At Bruce Macdonald's request, it was removed from the Tenth Mountain Division Association Web site in October 2003.

64. Bruce Berends, telephone interviews, September 10 and 15, 2003 ("Berends Interviews").

65. John Engle, telephone interviews, April 16, 2003, and January 13, 2004 ("Engle Interviews").

66. Soria Interview; Letter to author from Al Soria, dated October 22, 2003.

67. Berends Interviews.

68. Letter to Bruce Berends from Bruce Macdonald, dated September 26, 2003.

69. Stuebner, *Cool North Wind,* pp. 81–82.

70. Earle Interview.

71. Earle, *87th Regimental History,* p. 94.

72. Earle, *87th Regimental History,* p. 94.

73. Soria Interview.

74. Letter to Colonel Frank Romano from Halvor O. Ekern, dated January 24, 1985. On file in Tenth Mountain Division Collection, Western History Department, Denver Public Library, Denver, Colorado. Bruce Macdonald denied that this possible incident was the alleged prisoner "execution" that he had described. Bruce Macdonald telephone interview, July 15, 2003. Macdonald stated that he had already been evacuated, because of wounds, by the time of Captain Duncan's death, and that he knew nothing about the circumstances surrounding it. Another alleged execution similar to the one described by Macdonald is noted in Jenkins, *The Last Ridge,* p. 216, as previously cited in footnotes.

Selected Bibliography

BOOKS

Abramson, Rudy. *Spanning the Century: The Life of W. Averell Harriman 1891–1986.* New York: William Morrow and Company, 1992.

Allen, E. John B. *From Skisport to Skiing.* Amherst: The University of Massachusetts Press, 1993.

The American Heritage History of the 20s and 30s. Edited by Ralph K. Andrist. New York: American Heritage Publishing Co., 1970.

American Quotations. Edited by Gorton Carruth and Eugene Erlich. New York: Wings Books, 1988.

Barlow-Perez, Sally. *A History of Aspen.* Basalt, Colorado: Who Press, 2000.

The Best American Sports Writing of the Century. Edited by David Halberstam and Glenn Stout. Boston: Houghton Mifflin Company, 2001.

Blumenson, Martin. *Bloody River.* College Station: Texas A & M University Press, 1970.

Blumenson, Martin. *Mark Clark—The Last of the Great World War II Commanders.* New York: Congdon & Weed, 1984.

Botjer, George. *Sideshow War.* College Station: Texas A & M University Press, 1996.

Bowen, Ezra. *The Book of American Skiing.* New York: Bonanza Books, 1963.

Bradley, Charles C. *Aleutian Echoes.* Anchorage: The University of Alaska Press, 1994.

Brooks, Thomas R. *The War North of Rome—June 1944–May 1945.* Edison, New Jersey: Castle Books, 1996.

Brower, David R. *For Earth's Sake: The Life and Times of David Brower.* Salt Lake City: Peregrine Smith Books/Gibbs Smith Publisher, 1990.

Burns, Deborah E., and Lauren R. Stevens. *Most Excellent Majesty.* Pittsfield, Massachusetts: Berkshire County Land Trust and Conservation Fund/The Studley Press, 1988.

Burton, Hal. *The Ski Troops.* New York: Simon and Schuster, 1971.

Cohen, Stan. *A Pictorial History of Downhill Skiing.* Missoula, Montana: Pictorial Histories Publishing Company, 1985.

Dole, Minot (Minnie). *Adventures in Skiing.* New York: Franklin Watts, 1965.

Durrance, Dick, as told by John Jerome. *The Man on the Medal: The Life & Times of America's First Great Ski Racer.* Aspen, Colorado: Durrance Enterprises, 1995.

Dusenberry, Harris. *Ski the High Trail: World War II Ski Troopers in the High Colorado Rockies.* Illustrated by Wilson P. Ware. Portland, Oregon: Binford & Mort Publishing, 1991.

Earle, George F. *Birth of a Division.* Syracuse, New York: Signature Publications, 1995.

Earle, George F. *History of the 87th Mountain Infantry, Italy 1945.* Denver: Bradford Robinson Printing Co., 1945.

Ellis, Robert B. *See Naples and Die.* Jefferson, North Carolina: McFarland & Company, 1996.

Engen, Alan K. *For the Love of Skiing: A Visual History.* Salt Lake City, Utah: Gibbs-Smith, Publisher, 1998.

Fay, Abbott. *A History of Skiing in Colorado.* Ouray, Colorado: Western Reflections, 2000.

Fisher, Ernest F. *Cassino to the Alps.* Washington: Center of Military History, United States Army, 1993.

Good Times and Bad Times. Edited by John Imbrie and Hugh W. Evans. Quechee, Vermont: Vermont Heritage Press, 1995.

Govan, Thomas P. *The Army Ground Forces Training for Mountain and Winter Warfare, Study No. 23.* Washington: Historical Section, Army Ground Forces, 1946.

Grose, Peter. *Gentleman Spy: The Life of Allen Dulles.* New York: Houghton Mifflin Company, 1994.

Imbrie, John. *A Chronology of the 10th Mountian Division.* Watertown, New York: National Association of the Tenth Mountain Division, 2001.

Imbrie, John, and Thomas Brooks. *10th Mountain Division Campaign in Italy 1945.* Forest Hills, New York: National Association of the Tenth Mountain Division, 2002.

Jenkins, McKay. *The Last Ridge: The Epic Story of the U.S. Army's 10th Mountain Division and the Assault on Hitler's Europe.* New York: Random House, 2003.

Lang, Otto. *A Bird of Passage—The Story of My Life.* Helena, Montana: Sky House Publishers/ Falcon Press, 1994.

Leich, Jeffrey R. *Tales of the 10th: The Mountain Troops and American Skiing.* Franconia, New Hampshire: New England Ski Museum, 2003.

McPhee, John. *Encounters with the Archdruid.* New York: Farrar, Straus and Giroux, 1971.

Meinke, Albert H., M.D. *Mountain Troops and Medics.* Kewadin, Michigan: Rucksack Publishing Company, 1993.

Meissner, Hans Otto. *Magda Goebbels: The First Lady of the Third Reich.* Translated by Gwendole Mary Keeble. New York: The Dial Press, 1980.

Milton, Joyce. *Loss of Eden—A Biography of Charles and Anne Morrow Lindbergh.* New York: HarperCollins, 1993.

Moomaw, Jack C. *Recollections of a Rocky Mountain Ranger.* Estes Park, Colorado: The YMCA of the Rockies, 1963 and 2001.

New York–New England Hurricane and Floods 1938: Official Report of Relief Operation. Washington: The American National Red Cross, 1939.

Pfeifer, Friedl, with Morten Lund. *Nice Goin'—My Life on Skis.* Missoula, Montana: Pictorial Histories Publishing Company, 1993.

Putnam, William Lowell. *Green Cognac.* New York: The AAC Press, 1991.

Reporting World War II, Part Two: American Journalism 1944–1946. Edited by Samuel Hynes, Anne Matthews, Nancy Caldwell-Sorel, and Roger J. Spiller. New York: The Library of America, 1995.

Richards, Rick. *Ski Pioneers: Ernie Blake, His Friends, and the Making of Taos Ski Valley.* Helena, Montana: Dry Gulch/Sky House Publishers, 1992.

Schmeling, Max. *Max Schmeling: An Autobiography* (George B. Von Der Lippe, Translator/Editor). Chicago: Bonus Books, 1998.

Shelton, Peter. *Climb to Conquer.* New York: Scribner, 2003.

Shirer, William L. *The Rise and Fall of the Third Reich.* New York: MJF/Simon and Schuster, 1959.

Shrontz, Duane. *Alta, Utah: A People's Story.* Alta, Utah: Two Doors Press, 2002.

The Ski Book. Edited by Morten Lund, Robert Gillen, and Michael Bartlett. New York: Arbor House, 1982.

Stark, William F. *Pine Lake.* Sheboygan, Wisconsin: Zimmermann Press, 1984.

Stuebner, Stephen. *Cool North Wind: Morley Nelson's Life with Birds of Prey.* Caldwell, Idaho: Caxton Press, 2002.

Thomas, Lowell. *Book of the High Mountains.* New York: Julian Messner, 1964.

Tobin, John C. *The Fall Line: A Skier's Journal.* New York: Meredith Press, 1969.

Trotter, William R. *A Frozen Hell: The Russo-Finnish War of 1939–40.* Chapel Hill, North Carolina: Algonquin, 1991.

Truscott, Lucian K., Jr. *Command Mission.* Novato, California: Presidio Press/E.P. Dutton and Co., 1954.

Vance, Thomas J. *Elliot Richardson and the Virtue of Politics: A Brief Biography.* Washington: The Council for Excellence in Government, 2000.

Wallace, Robert. *The Italian Campaign.* Alexandria, Virginia: Time-Life Books, 1978.

Wallechinsky, David. *The 20th Century.* Boston: Little, Brown and Company, 1995.

Wellborn, Charles. *History of the 86th Mountain Infantry, Italy 1945.* Denver: Bradford Robinson Printing Co., 1945.

The Whispering Pine 1930, Vol. II. Estes Park, Colorado: Estes Park High School, 1930.

Whitlock, Flint, and Bob Bishop. *Soldiers on Skis.* Boulder, Colorado: Paladin Press, 1992.

Whittemore, Richard F. W. *For the Love of Skiing.* Stowe, Vermont: Self-Published, 1998.

Williamson, Gordon. *German Mountain & Ski Troops 1939–45.* Oxford: Osprey Publishing, 1996.

Wilson, Ross J. *History of the First Battalion 87th Mountain Infantry.* Kalispell, Montana: Self-Published, 1991.

UNPUBLISHED WORKS

(on file in the Tenth Mountain Division Collection,
Western History Department, Denver Public Library, Denver, Colorado)

Brower, David. *Insight of the Archdruid,* 2000.

Dawson, Lou. *Eulogy: Burdell S. "Bud" Winter 1925–1945,* circa 1999.

Dole, Minnie. *Birth Pains of the 10th Mountain Division,* 1955.

Earle, George F. *Heroes: Fourth Day—Across the Line—The Joe Duncan Story,* 2002.

Nebeker, Dick. *My Experience in the Ski Troops,* circa 1990.

Peck, George, Jr. *Winter Sports in the Estes Park Area: An Address at the Estes Park Historical Museum,* April 15, 1982.

FILMS

Climb to Glory. (An episode of the series *The Big Picture*), United States Army Film Archives, 1960. Rereleased in edited form as *The 10th Mountain Division: Ridge Runners,* OnDeck Home Entertainment, 1997.

Fire on the Mountain. Produced and directed by Beth Gage and George Gage. First Run Features, 1995.

Legends of American Skiing. Produced by Richard Moulton. Keystone Productions, 1982.

Of Pure Blood. Produced and directed by Clarissa Henry and Marc Hillel. Agence de Presse Film Television/Agence Française d'Images Paris (Adaptation for the BBC), 1974.

Purple Mountain Majesty. Produced by Blair Mahar. Hurricane Productions, 1999.

Soldiers of the Summit. Produced by Tom Feliu. KRMA-TV/Total Communications Company for the Council for Public Television, 1987.

The Sun Valley Skiers. Produced by David Butterfield. Centennial Entertainment, 2000.

Thrills and Spills in the North Country. Produced by Rick Moulton. The New England Ski Museum, 1998.

Winter Warriors. Produced by Martin Gillam. Greystone Communications, 2001.

About the Author

CHARLES J. SANDERS IS THE NEPHEW OF A TENTH MOUNTAIN DIVISION WORLD WAR II veteran, and has been privileged to ski with and study under Camp Hale alumni since childhood. As a dedicated skier and mountain photographer, he has so far descended the slopes of one hundred different mountains on three continents, and hopes to ski on one hundred more with his son, Jackson. In his "other life," he is an attorney in the music industry, an adjunct professor of ethics at New York University, a professional musician with numerous album credits, and cofounder of The James Madison Project, an advocacy group for freedom of information rights. He lives on Pocantico Lake, New York, with his wife and son, where they are supervised by an Australian shepherd named Puck.

Index

Contents

Alternate Table
of Contents

Description

Examples

Preface:
To the Instructor

How often have you, as a reading or writing teacher, asked yourself questions such as these:

- Why must I spend so much time looking for timely selections that students will *want* to read?

- Where can I find a book of essays that also helps me teach the reading and writing skills my students need to know?

- Is there a reader out there devoted to old-fashioned human values— ones that can inspire and motivate even today's students?

If you've asked any of the above questions, *Voices and Values* may be the book for you. Suitable for reading and/or writing classes, the book provides a series of forty lively and thought-provoking essays that will compel student attention. Each selection is accompanied by a set of activities to help students read, understand, and write about the essay. By providing instruction and practice in the skills necessary for close and thoughtful reading, the text will help all those teachers whose students say, "I read it, but I didn't understand it." And by providing a wide number and range of writing assignments, as well as help with getting started on these assignments, the text will help all those teachers whose students say, "I don't know what to write about."

Distinguishing Features of the Book

Readings that celebrate human values. The book contains forty essays chosen for their celebration of significant human values. For example, in the first selection, "Bird Girl," an author describes the guilt he feels for doing nothing when his high school classmates behaved cruelly toward a student who was different. The story becomes a plea for the importance of courage—speaking up in defense of another—and the need for kindness. Other essays—in a style that never preaches—cover such values as gratitude, personal growth, fairness, responsibility, love and compassion, common sense, and moderation.

Emphasis on clear thinking. A basic truth that is at the heart of both the reading and the writing process is that any thoughtful communication of ideas has two basic parts: (1) a point is made and (2) that point is supported. As they work their way through this book, students learn to apply this principle of point and support. They are encouraged when *reading* an essay to look for a central idea as well as for the reasons, examples, facts, and details that support that idea. They are reminded when *writing* to follow the same basic principle—to make a point and then provide support for that point. And they discover that clear *thinking* (which they also do when actively reading or writing) involves both recognizing ideas and deciding whether there is solid support for those ideas.

Frequent skills practice. Accompanying the high-interest selections is a series of high-quality activities that truly help students improve their reading, thinking, and writing. As we have already stated, the book assumes that reading and writing are interrelated skills. Work on reading can improve writing; work on writing can improve reading. Extensive practice in reading, thinking, and writing follows each of the forty selections. Here is the sequence of activities—prepared by two authors who have themselves been teachers—for each essay:

- *First Impressions* Following each reading is a freewriting activity titled "First Impressions" that encourages students to come to terms with what they have read. The activity consists of three questions that permit students to respond on different levels of feeling and opinion. For example, the first question is always "Did you enjoy reading this selection? Why or why not?" The two other questions focus on particular issues raised by the essay—issues about which every student should have something to say. Students can respond to one or all of these questions at the beginning of a class session, or, alternatively, students can record their responses in a "reading journal."

  The "First Impressions" activity provides at least two additional benefits. First, it lays the groundwork for oral participation; many more students can contribute intelligently to classroom discussion after they have collected their thoughts on paper in advance. Second, as an integral step in the writing process, freewriting or journal keeping can supply students with raw material for one or more of the paragraph and essay assignments that follow the selections.

- *Words to Watch* **and** *Vocabulary Check* Students need to strengthen their vocabularies in order to succeed in school—and they know it. *Voices and Values* builds vocabulary in the most research-proven and interesting way, by providing hundreds of useful words in context. The most challenging words and phrases in each selection are defined in the "Words to Watch" section that precedes each reading, and four of these words are tested in the "Vocabulary Check" activity that follows each reading. Other words from the reading that may be unfamiliar to students also appear in the Vocabulary Check. Students thus have frequent opportunities to sharpen their skill at deriving meaning from context.

- *Reading Check* Practice in reading skills is provided through an activity titled "Reading Check," a series of comprehension questions that follow the Vocabulary Check. The questions involve four key skills: finding the central point and main ideas, recognizing key supporting details, making inferences, and understanding the writer's craft. The craft questions include such elements as introduction and conclusion strategies; types of support; patterns of organization and the transitions that indicate these patterns; tone; purpose; intended audience; and titles. As students sharpen these crucial reading skills, they will become better, more insightful readers—and they will be ready to use the same techniques in their own writing.

- *Discussion Questions* Four discussion questions follow the Reading Check. These questions provide a final chance for students to deepen their understanding of an essay and the issues and values that it contains. They also function as a helpful intermediate step between reading a selection and writing about it. If the teacher chooses, these discussion questions can serve as additional writing topics.

- *Paragraph Assignments and Essay Assignments* Four writing topics—two paragraph assignments and two essay assignments— conclude the activities for each selection. The assignments emphasize the basic principle of clear communication: that a student make a point and support that point. Numerous sample topic sentences and thesis statements, along with specific suggestions for supporting these points, help students to succeed on these assignments. Twenty additional topics on pages 461–468 invite students to read pairs of essays and write papers inspired by both.

Versatility. Since it is "a reader for writers," *Voices and Values* can be used in a number of teaching and learning situations:

- As a reader in a writing course covering paragraphs, essays, or both
- As an anthology in an English course studying the essay as a *genre*
- As the core text in a reading course employing a whole-language approach
- As a collection of inspiring motivational readings

Ease of use and helpful support. The book is designed to be simple for both teachers and students to use. The activities already listed are easy to present in class and convenient to correct. Answers to the activities appear in two places. First, an annotated *Instructor's Edition* of the book—chances are you are holding it in your hand—includes answers to the Vocabulary Checks and Reading Checks, making the book very easy for teachers to use. Second, an *Instructor's Manual* provides complete answers on letter-sized sheets for these activities. At the teacher's option, these sheets can easily be duplicated and distributed to students so they can check their own answers. The manual also contains teaching suggestions, suggested answers to the "Discussion Questions" that follow each reading, and ten additional guided writing assignments.

In short, *Voices and Values* contains an appealing collection of readings and an exceptional series of activities that will give students extensive guided practice in reading and writing. We believe the book's value lies in the humanistic quality of the selections, the variety of activities that follow each essay, and the integrated approach to reading and writing that is maintained throughout.

Acknowledgments

We owe thanks to Eleanor Tauber for her typing and Barbara Solot for her proofreading. We are also grateful to Eliza Comodromos, John Langan, and Carole Mohr for their helpful editing of the manuscript. On a personal note, our gratitude goes to our husbands, Martin Goldstein and Bob Anderson, for their enthusiasm and support as we worked on this project. In addition, Beth wishes to thank her children, Samuel, Isaac, and Madeleine. Their love of reading and writing is a steady source of pleasure and inspiration.

Janet M. Goldstein
Beth Johnson

Becoming a
Better Reader

Voices and Values consists of this introductory chapter, a brief chapter on writing, and forty high-interest essays. This introduction will describe the format of the forty essays. It will then explain how understanding the concept of *point and support* can make you a better reader and writer. Finally, it will offer specific strategies for effective reading of the essays. The chapter that follows. "Becoming a Better Writer," will then present in a nutshell what you need to know to write effectively.

FORMAT OF THE FORTY READING SELECTIONS

Each of the forty essays begins with a *Preview* that presents helpful background information and arouses your interest in the piece. What information, for example, do you learn about the first essay, "Bird Girl," by reading the preview (page 31)?   *(Answers may vary.)*

The essay is about the lasting damage teasing can do. It was originally

published as three separate columns in the <u>Philadelphia Inquirer</u>.

Following the preview is a list of *Words to Watch*, which gives the definitions of difficult words taken from the reading. In parentheses next to each word is the number of the paragraph in which it appears. Also, each word is marked in the reading itself with a small circle (°).

- How many "Words to Watch" are provided for "Bird Girl" (page 31)?

  _13_

Following every essay is a series of activities. The initial activity, *First Impressions,* asks you to write for ten minutes about the piece you have just finished reading.

- Turn to "First Impressions" (page 35) and note how many writing choices you are given: __3__

Next there is a series of questions titled *Vocabulary Check.* Half of these questions will help you learn words in a research-proven way: by seeing how they are actually used in the selection. The other questions will help reinforce the meanings of selected words learned in "Words to Watch."

- Turn to the "Vocabulary Check" (pages 35–38) and record how many vocabulary questions appear: __8__

The vocabulary material is followed by a *Reading Check.* The questions here will help you to practice and develop several important reading skills.

- Turn to "Reading Check" (pages 38–41) to note the number of skill questions that are asked: __10__

- Complete the list below of the kinds of comprehension questions provided:

Central Point and Main Ideas

Key Supporting Details
_____

Inferences
_____

The Writer's Craft

Next, there are *Discussion Questions* about the essay. These questions provide a final chance for you to deepen your understanding of a reading.

- Turn to page 42 and note how many discussion questions are provided for "Bird Girl": __4__

Two *Paragraph Assignments* and two *Essay Assignments* follow each essay. To get you started, the first paragraph assignment and the first essay assignment include sample central points (called *topic sentences* in paragraphs and *thesis statements* in essays).

- What is the sample topic sentence provided for the paragraph assignment on "Bird Girl"? *Gordon was bullied a lot by my eighth-grade classmates because of his unusual behavior.*

junk food. They encourage little children to crave sugary snacks and breakfast cereals made of tiny chocolate doughnuts or cookie nuggets. In addition, these commercials urge children to be greedy. At the same time parents are teaching their children to share what they have with others, TV commercials make them want more expensive toys and other products for themselves. The worst thing about these ads, however, is that they take advantage of children who have not yet learned what advertising is or how it works. If a beloved cartoon character tells a child that a cereal or a toy is great, the child believes it. Children can't see how advertisers trick them into wanting a product or how ads make toys or games look better than they really are. Aiming ads at little children is unfair.

Can you find the central point and the three key supporting details in this paragraph? Answer the questions below, and then read the explanations that follow them.

1. Which sentence best expresses the central point of "TV Commercials and Children"?
   a. All television commercials should be banned.
   (b.) TV commercials aimed at young children should be banned.
   c. Commercials make young children want to eat junk food.
   d. Advertisers do not care what children eat.

   In this selection, the central point is *b,* "TV commercials aimed at young children should be banned." Answer *a* is *too broad*—it refers to all television commercials, not just those aimed at youngsters. Answer *c* is *too narrow*—it is actually one of the supporting details for the central point. Answer *d* may or may not be true, but it is not what the whole paragraph is about. Only answer *b* states the central point of the paragraph.

2. On the lines below, write the three key supporting details for the central point. (Ask yourself, "What specific reasons does the author give for why TV ads are harmful to children?")
   a. *They promote junk food.*
   b. *They encourage greed.*
   c. *They take advantage of children.*

If you wrote answers similar to "They promote junk food," "They encourage greed," and "They take advantage of children," you are correct.

Strategy 4: Make Inferences.

Inferences are the reasonable guesses we make based on the facts presented. For example, if a crowd of people is smiling and talking after leaving a movie, we would probably assume that the movie is an enjoyable one. And if rolled-up newspapers accumulate on a neighbor's porch over a holiday weekend, we could conclude that the family is away on a brief vacation. Or if trucks that usually race along the highway are suddenly observing the speed limit, we could infer that a police radar trap is nearby. We make the same kinds of judgments when we draw conclusions about what we read. In this book, you'll be answering several inference questions each time you read a selection. Look again at the paragraph on "TV Commercials and Children" (pages 6–7) and answer the following question. Then read the explanation that follows it.

____T____ TRUE OR FALSE? We can infer from the paragraph that young children think that ads tell the truth.

You can find the answer to this question near the end of the paragraph, when the writer explains that young children haven't learned what advertising is. The paragraph goes on to state that if a cartoon character praises a cereal or toy, the child believes that character. Therefore, the author is suggesting that young children believe everything they see on TV—including ads. The inference is true.

Strategy 5: Be Aware of the Writer's Craft.

"Writer's craft" refers to techniques an author uses to communicate ideas. Being aware of these strategies will increase your understanding of what you read as well as improve your own writing. In this book, questions on the writer's craft cover the following:

1   **Introductions and Conclusions.** What does an author do to interest you in reading what he or she has written? Four common kinds of introductions include (1) an entertaining story (sometimes called an *anecdote*), (2) one or more questions, (3) an idea that is the opposite of what will be written about, or (4) a broad statement that narrows down to the central point. Examples of all four introductions are on pages 16–17. Conclusions may include a summary and perhaps a final thought or two.

2   **Type of Support.** How has the author supported his or her central point? As already mentioned, common methods of support include reasons, examples, details, facts, quotations, and personal experiences.

3 **Patterns of Organization.** How have the supporting details been arranged? Authors often use a *time order*—telling the parts of a story in the order that they happened. Common word signals (also called *transitions*) that mark time order are *first, then, before, as, after, next,* and *last.*

An equally popular pattern of organization is a *listing order*— providing a series of reasons, examples, or details. Common word signals or transitions that mark listing order are *first of all, another, in addition, also,* and *finally.*

Another pattern of organization is *comparison-contrast*—showing how two things are alike or (more often) different. Typical transitions for this pattern are *like, just as, similarly, but, however, in contrast,* and *on the other hand.*

A final pattern worth noting is *cause-effect*—explaining the reasons why something happened or the results of something. Typical transitions for this pattern are *because, therefore, effect, consequently,* and *as a result.*

4 **Tone.** Just as a speaker's tone of voice reveals how he or she feels, a writer's tone also communicates feelings. You should be able to tell how an author feels about his or her subject by looking at the wording of the selection. It will often indicate whether a selection's tone is humorous or serious, angry or friendly, formal or informal, self-pitying or sarcastic, encouraging or discouraging, or simply objective (factual).

5 **Purpose.** Decide what type of writing you are reading. Is it intended to inform (give people information), to entertain (give people pleasure), or to persuade (change people's minds about an issue)? Or does it have a combination of these purposes?

6 **Audience.** Decide for what kind of reader the selection was probably written. Was it meant for the general reader (anyone)? Or was the author writing for a smaller audience, such as major-league baseball players, a group of fellow researchers, or parents of high-school students?

7 **Titles.** Most authors choose their titles very carefully. Many times, a title clearly describes the topic of the essay, and sometimes it is the shortest possible summary of the central point of an essay. Look closely at titles for excellent clues about authors' ideas and their attitudes toward their topics.

FINAL THOUGHTS ABOUT READING THE ESSAYS

Read each selection first to enjoy whatever it may have to say about human nature and life today. Then reread the selection and work on the activities with the intention of learning as much as you can.

To help you learn, answers to the questions on the first selection, "Bird Girl," appear immediately following the questions themselves. Read these answers and the explanations that follow them *after* you have worked through the activities. Be sure you understand why each answer is correct. This information will help prepare you to do well on the remaining selections, for which answers are not given.

Finally, remember that learning is, in the end, up to you. If you have the intention of gaining as much as you can from this book, then *Voices and Values* will offer you a great deal. As you learn to consistently apply the questions "What is the point?" and "What is the support for that point?" you will acquire a powerful learning and reasoning tool—a tool that can make you a skilled and independent learner for the rest of your life. Just as important, you will find that reading the essays will not only improve your mind but also touch your heart. The essays will help you connect with others and realize that all people have the same shared humanity. Someone once wrote, "We read in order to know that we are not alone." We become less isolated as we share the common experiences, emotions, and thoughts that make us human.

Becoming a
Better Writer

What, in a nutshell, do you need to become a better writer? You need to know the basic goals in writing and to understand the writing process—as explained on the pages that follow.

TWO BASIC GOALS IN WRITING

When you write a paper, your two basic goals should be (1) to make a point and (2) to support that point. Look for a moment at the following cartoon:

See if you can answer the following questions:

- What is Snoopy's point in his paper?

  Your answer: His point is that _____*dogs are superior to cats.*_____

- What is his support for his point?

  Your answer: _____*No support is given.*_____

Explanation:

Snoopy's point, of course, is that dogs are superior to cats. But he offers no support whatsoever to back up his point! There are two jokes here. First, he is a dog and so is naturally going to believe that dogs are superior. The other joke is that his evidence ("They just are, and that's all there is to it!") is a lot of empty words. His somewhat guilty look in the last panel suggests that he knows he has not proved his point. To write effectively, you must provide *real* support for your points and opinions.

WRITING PARAGRAPHS

A *paragraph* is a series of sentences about one main idea, or *point*. A paragraph typically starts with a point (also called the *topic sentence*), and the rest of the paragraph provides specific details to support and develop that point.

Look at the following paragraph, written by a student named Carla.

Three Kinds of Bullies

There are three kinds of bullies in schools. First of all, there are the physical bullies. They are the bigger or meaner kids who try to hurt kids who are smaller or unsure of themselves. They'll push other kids off swings, trip them in the halls, or knock books out of their hands. They'll also wait for kids after school and slap them or yank their hair or pull out their shirts or throw them to the ground. They do their best to frighten kids and make them cry. Another kind of bully is the verbal bully. This kind tries to hurt with words rather than fists. Nursery-school kids may call each other "dummy" or "weirdo" or "fatty," and as kids get older, their words carry even more sting.

(continued)

Second Supporting Paragraph

Perhaps even worse than physical attack is verbal bullying, which uses words, rather than hands or fists, as weapons. We may be told that "sticks and stones may break my bones, but names can never harm me," but few of us are immune to the pain of a verbal attack. Like physical bullies, verbal bullies tend to single out certain targets. From that moment on, the victim is subjected to a hail of insults and put-downs. These are usually delivered in public, so the victim's humiliation will be greatest: "Oh, no; here comes the nerd!" "Why don't you lose some weight, blubber boy?" "You smell as bad as you look!" "Weirdo." "Fairy." "Creep." "Dork." "Slut." "Loser." Verbal bullying is an equal-opportunity event, with girls as likely to be verbal bullies as boys. Meanwhile, the victim retreats further and further into his or her shell, hoping to escape further notice.

Third Supporting Paragraph

As bad as verbal bullying is, many would agree that the most painful type of bullying is social bullying. Many students have a strong need for the comfort of being part of a group. For social bullies, the pleasure of belonging to a group is increased by the sight of someone who is refused entry into that group. So, like wolves targeting the weakest sheep in a herd, the bullies lead the pack in isolating people who they decide are different. They roll their eyes and turn away in disgust if those people try to talk to them. They move away if a victim sits near them at lunch or stands near them in a school hallway or at a bus stop. No one volunteers to work with these victims on class activities, and they are the ones that no one wants as part of gym teams. They make sure the unwanted ones know about the games and parties they aren't invited to. As the victims sink further into isolation and depression, the social bullies—who seem to be female more often than male—feel all the more puffed up by their own popularity.

Concluding Paragraph

Whether bullying is physical, verbal, or social, it can leave deep and lasting scars. If parents, teachers, and other adults were more aware of the types of bullying, they might help by stepping in before the situation becomes too extreme. If students were more aware of the terrible pain that bullying causes, they might think twice about being bullies themselves.

- Which sentence in the introductory paragraph expresses the central point of the essay? _____*The final sentence*_____
- How many supporting paragraphs are provided to back up the central point? __*3*__

THE PARTS OF AN ESSAY

Each of the parts of an essay is explained below.

Introductory Paragraph

A well-written introductory paragraph will normally do the following:

- Gain the reader's interest by using one of several common methods of introduction.
- Present the thesis statement. The thesis statement expresses the central point of an essay, just as a topic sentence states the main idea of a paragraph. The central idea in Carla's essay is expressed in the last sentence of the introductory paragraph.

Four Common Methods of Introduction

Four common methods of introduction are (1) telling a brief story, (2) asking one or more questions, (3) shifting to the opposite, or (4) going from the broad to the narrow. Following are examples of all four.

1 **Telling a brief story.** An interesting anecdote is hard for a reader to resist. In an introduction, a story should be no more than a few sentences, and it should relate meaningfully to the central idea. The story can be an experience of your own, of someone you know, or of someone you have read about. Carla uses this method of introduction for her essay on bullying:

> Eric, a new boy at school, was shy and physically small. He quickly became a victim of bullies. Kids would wait after school, pull out his shirt, and punch and shove him around. He was called such names as "Mouse Boy" and "Jerk Boy." When he sat down during lunch hour, others would leave his table. In gym games he was never thrown the ball, as if he didn't exist. Then one day he came to school with a gun. When the police were called, he told them he just couldn't

THE WRITING PROCESS

Even professional writers do not sit down and write a paper in a single draft. Instead, they have to work on it one step at a time. Writing a paper is a process that can be divided into the following five steps:

Step 1: Getting Started through Prewriting
Step 2: Preparing a Scratch Outline
Step 3: Writing the First Draft
Step 4: Revising
Step 5: Editing

Step 1: Getting Started through Prewriting

What you need to learn, first, are methods that you can use to start working on a writing assignment. These techniques will help you think on paper. They'll help you figure out both the point you want to make and the support you need for that point. Here are three helpful prewriting techniques:

- Freewriting
- Questioning
- List making

Freewriting

Freewriting is just sitting down and writing whatever comes into your mind about a topic. Do this for ten minutes or so. Write without stopping and without worrying in the slightest about spelling, grammar, and the like. Simply get down on paper all the information that occurs to you about the topic.

Below is part of the freewriting done by Carla for her paragraph about bullies. Carla had been given the assignment, "Write about the types of bullying that go on in school." She began prewriting as a way to explore her topic and generate details about it.

Example of Freewriting

Bullying is part of school most of the time teachers dont have a clue. I really never thought about it and was just glad I wasn't part of it. At least for the most part. I'd see some phisikal stuff now and then but kind of turned my head not wanting to look at it. The worst thing with girls was words, they meant more than phisikal stuff. I rember once being called a name and it stung me so bad and it bothered me for weeks. . . .

Notice that there are lots of problems with spelling, grammar, and punctuation in Carla's freewriting. Carla is not worried about such matters, nor should she be—at this stage. She is just concentrating on getting ideas and details down on paper. She knows that it is best to focus on one thing at a time. At this point, she just wants to write out thoughts as they come to her, to do some thinking on paper.

You should take the same approach when freewriting: explore your topic without worrying at all about writing "correctly." Figuring out what you want to say should have all your attention in this early stage of the writing process.

Activity: Freewriting

On a sheet of paper, freewrite for at least ten minutes on the best or worst job or chore you ever had. Don't worry about grammar, punctuation, or spelling. Try to write—without stopping—about whatever comes into your head concerning your best or worst job or chore.

Questioning

Questioning means that you generate details about your topic by writing down a series of questions and answers about it. Your questions can start with words like *what, when, where, why,* and *how.*

Here are just some of the questions that Carla might have asked while developing her paper:

Example of Questioning

- Who was bullied?
- Who were the bullies?
- When did bullying take place?
- Where did it happen?
- Were there different kinds of bullying?
- Why were some kids teased and bullied?

Activity: Questioning

On a sheet of paper, answer the following questions about your best or worst job or chore.

- When did you have the job (or chore)?
- Where did you work?

- What did you do?
- Whom did you work for?
- Why did you like or dislike the job? (Give one reason and some details that support that reason.)
- What is another reason you liked or disliked the job? What are some details that support the second reason?
- Can you think of a third reason you liked or did not like the job? What are some details that support the third reason?

List Making

In *list making* (also known as *brainstorming*), you make a list of ideas and details that could go into your paper. Simply pile these items up, one after another, without worrying about putting them in any special order. Try to accumulate as many details as you can think of.

After Carla did her freewriting about bullies, she made up a list of details, part of which is shown below.

Example of List Making

some bullies were phisikal
boys would push kids around
kids would be tripped in hallways
some kids would cry
names would be used
"dummy" or "creep" or "fairy"
no one would sit near some kids
some kids never chosen for games
. . . .

One detail led to another as Carla expanded her list. Slowly but surely, more supporting material emerged that she could use in developing her paper. By the time she had finished her list, she was ready to plan an outline of her paragraph and to write her first draft.

Activity: List Making

On separate paper, make a list of details about the job (or chore). Don't worry about putting them in a certain order. Just get down as many details about the job as occur to you. The list can include specific reasons you liked or did not like the job and specific details supporting those reasons.

Step 2: Preparing a Scratch Outline

A *scratch outline* is a brief plan for a paragraph. It shows at a glance the point of the paragraph and the support for that point. It is the logical framework on which the paper is built.

This rough outline often follows freewriting, questioning, list making, or all three. Or it may gradually emerge in the midst of these strategies. In fact, trying to outline is a good way to see if you need to do more prewriting. If a solid outline does not emerge, then you know you need to do more prewriting to clarify your main point or its support. And once you have a workable outline, you may realize, for instance, that you want to do more list making to develop one of the supporting details in the outline.

In Carla's case, as she was working on her list of details, she suddenly discovered what the plan of her paragraph could be. She realized she could describe different kinds of bullies.

Example of a scratch outline

There are three kinds of bullies.
1. Physical
2. Verbal
3. Social

After all her preliminary writing, Carla sat back pleased. She knew she had a promising paper—one with a clear point and solid support. Carla was now ready to write the first draft of her paper, using her outline as a guide.

Activity: Scratch Outline

Using the list you have prepared, see if you can prepare a scratch outline made up of the three main reasons you liked or did not like the job.   *(Answers will vary.)*

_____ was the best (*or* worst) job (*or* chore) I ever had.

Reason 1: _____

Reason 2: _____

Reason 3: _____

Step 3: Writing the First Draft

When you do a first draft, be prepared to put in additional thoughts and details that didn't emerge in your prewriting. And don't worry if you hit a snag. Just leave a blank space or add a comment such as "Do later" and press on to finish the paper. Also, don't worry yet about grammar, punctuation, or spelling. You don't want to take time correcting words or sentences that you may decide to remove later. Instead, make it your goal to develop the content of your paper with plenty of specific details.

Here are a few lines of Carla's first draft:

First Draft

There are different kinds of bullies that can be seen in schools. One kind of bullying that goes on is done by phisikal bullies. You see kids who will get pushed around on the playground. You see kids getting shoved into lockers and that kind of stuff. There was a girl I knew who was a real bully and a bit crazy because of a really bad home life. She would shove gum into another girl's hair and would also pull her hair. Other bullying went on with words and the calling of names. There were awful names that kids would use with each other, words included "creep" and "wierdo" and names that I don't even want to write here. . . .

Activity: First Draft

Now write a first draft of your paper. Begin with your topic sentence stating that a certain job (or chore) was the best or worst one you ever had. Then state the first reason why it was the best or the worst, followed by specific details supporting that reason. Use a transition such as *First of all* to introduce the first reason. Next, state the second reason, followed by specific details supporting that reason. Use a transition such as *Secondly* to introduce the second reason. Last, state the third reason, followed with support. Use a transition such as *Finally* to introduce the last reason.

Don't worry about grammar, punctuation, or spelling. Just concentrate on getting down on paper the details about the job.

Step 4: Revising

Revising is as much a stage in the writing process as prewriting, outlining, and doing the first draft. *Revising* means that you rewrite a paper, building upon what has been done, to make it stronger and better. One writer has said about revision, "It's like cleaning house—getting rid of all the junk and putting things in the right order." A typical revision means writing at least one or two more drafts, adding and omitting details, organizing more clearly, and beginning to correct spelling and grammar.

Here are a few lines of Carla's second draft.

Second Draft

> There are three kinds of bullies in schools. First of all, there are the physical bullies. They are the bigger kids who try to hurt smaller kids. They'll push kids off of swings in the playground or shove them into lockers. Other examples are knocking books out of the hands of kids or waiting for them after school and slapping them around or yanking their hair. Another kind of bullying is by verbal bullies. The aim here is to hurt with words rather than with fists. A victim will be called a "creep" or "weirdo" or "fatty" or will be told "You are such a loser." . . .

Notice that in redoing the draft, Carla started by more concisely stating the point of her paragraph. Also, she inserted transitions ("First of all" and "Another") to clearly set off the kinds of bullies. She omitted the detail about the crazy girl she knew because it was not relevant to a paragraph focusing on bullies. She added more details, so that she would have enough supporting examples for the types of bullies.

Carla then went on to revise the second draft. Since she was doing her paper on a computer, she was able to print it out quickly. She double-spaced the lines, allowing room for revisions, which she added in longhand as part of her third draft, and eventually the paragraph on pages 12–13 resulted. (Note that if you are not using a computer, you may want to skip every other line when writing out each draft. Also, write on only one side of a page, so that you can see your entire paper at one time.)

Activity: Revising the Draft

Ideally, you will have a chance to put the paper aside for a while before doing later drafts. When you revise, try to do all of the following:

- Omit any details that do not truly support your topic sentence.
- Add more details as needed, making sure you have plenty of specific support for each of your three reasons.
- Be sure to include a final sentence that rounds off the paper, bringing it to a close.

Step 5: Editing

Editing, the final stage in the writing process, means checking a paper carefully for spelling, grammar, punctuation, and other errors. You are ready for this stage when you are satisfied that your point is clear, your supporting details are good, and your paper is well organized.

At this stage, you must **read your paper out loud**. Hearing how your writing sounds is an excellent way to pick up grammar and punctuation problems in your writing. Chances are that you will find sentence mistakes at every spot where your paper does not read smoothly and clearly. This point is so important that it bears repeating: *To find mistakes in your paper, read it out loud!*

At this point in her work, Carla read her latest draft out loud. She looked closely at all the spots where her writing did not read easily. She used a grammar handbook to deal with the problems at those spots in her paper, and she made the corrections needed so that all her sentences read smoothly. She also used her dictionary to check on the spelling of every word she was unsure about. She even took a blank sheet of paper and used it to uncover her paper one line at a time, looking for any other mistakes that might be there.

Activity: Editing

When you have your almost-final draft of the paper, edit it in the following ways:

- Read the paper aloud, listening for awkward wordings and places where the meaning is unclear. Make the changes needed for the paper to read smoothly and clearly. In addition, see if you can get another person to read the draft aloud to you. The spots that this person has trouble reading are spots where you may have to do some revision and correct your grammar or punctuation mistakes.

- Using your dictionary (or a spell-check program if you have a computer), check any words that you think might be misspelled.

- Finally, take a sheet of paper and cover your paper, so that you can expose and carefully proofread one line at a time. Use your handbook to check any other spots where you think there might be grammar or punctuation mistakes in your writing.

FINAL THOUGHTS

You have a paper to write. Here in a nutshell is what to do:

1 Write about what you know. If you don't know much about your topic, go onto the Internet by using the helpful search engine Google. You can access it by typing:

www.google.com

A screen will then appear with a box in which you can type one or more keywords. For example, if you were thinking about doing a paper on some other topic involving bullies, you could type in the keyword *bullies*. Within a second or so you will get a list of over 80,000 articles on the Web about bullies!

You would then need to narrow your topic by adding other keywords. For instance, if you typed *bullies in schools,* you would get a list of over 20,000 items. If you narrowed your potential topic further by typing *solutions to bullies in schools,* you would get a list of 2,500 items. You could then click on the items that sound most promising to you.

2 Use prewriting strategies to begin to write about your topic. Look for a point you can make, and make sure you have details to support it.

3 Write several drafts, aiming all the while for three goals in your writing: a **clear point**, **strong support** for that point, and **well-organized support**. Use transitions to help organize your support.

4 Then read your paper out loud. It should read smoothly and clearly. Look closely for grammar and punctuation problems at any rough spots. Check a grammar handbook or a dictionary as needed.

Unit One

Overcoming Obstacles

1

Bird Girl
Clark DeLeon

Preview

"Sticks and stones can break my bones, but names can never hurt me." Is this old saying true? Or can teasing hurt, and hurt deeply? In the following selection, made up of three columns first published in the *Philadelphia Inquirer*, Clark DeLeon writes about the lasting scars—and the tragedies—that can result from childhood teasing, and his readers respond.

Words to Watch

sallow (1): sickly, pale yellow
tacitly (1): silently
lest (2): for fear that
greasers (3): tough, bullying teenagers
defiant (5): bold
unrelenting (7): not stopping
contend (8): struggle
malicious (8): mean
taunts (8): insults
encounter (9): meeting
eluded (10): escaped
mobile (11): movable
instigators (11): leaders

Targets: A Lesson in Life

There was a weird girl in my high school whom we all called the Bird. We called her that because of her nervous, birdlike movements and the way she would hunch her shoulders toward her ears as if she was hoping her head would disappear into her body. She had sallow° skin that looked as if it had never felt the sun, and there was usually a blotchy red rash in the middle of her forehead. She had fine black hair on her arms long enough to comb, and she wore clothes that had been out of fashion since Shirley Temple was singing "The Good Ship Lollipop." She was also the object of such contempt and scorn, such cruel ridicule, that it shames me to this day to think I was part of it, even tacitly°.

Oh, I was never one to say anything to her face. I wasn't that brave. I'd wait until she hurried by with her books held tightly to her chest and join in the chorus of birdcalls with the other guys. She was always good for a laugh. And it's important when you're a teenager to join the laughter, lest° the laughter turn on you.

I remember one day when the Bird was surrounded by three or four suburban-variety greasers° who had stopped her in the corridor between classes. They were flapping their arms and screeching in her ear. She was terrified. Her eyes darted in panic. A couple of her books fell to the floor. When she stopped to pick them up, they bent over her in a circle, closing in, screeching, screeching.

Then this girl came out of nowhere. I'd never seen such anger in a girl before. She went up to the leader of the tormentors and ripped into him with a hot fury. "Stop it!" she shouted. "Can't you see what you're doing?" The guys backed off, stunned. Then the girl went over to the Bird and put her arm around her shoulder and walked her to class.

I thought about the Bird when I read about Nathan Faris, the little boy who shot a classmate and killed himself after being the target of teasing by the kids in his school. I thought of how I had been a part of her misery, how more than 20 years later it still bothers me. But I also think of what I learned that day about decency and bravery, about being a human being, from a girl whose name I don't even know. And I wonder if that one act of defiant° kindness may have saved another girl's life.

Targets: Why Are Kids So Cruel?

"I just had to write to you in regard to your item 'Targets' that appeared in today's (March 8) *Inquirer*," wrote Ray Windsor of Lansdowne.

I received several letters about that piece, which concerned a girl I knew in high school who was the victim of cruel and unrelenting° ridicule because she was unattractive, uncool and unable to defend herself. That piece touched a chord in people, and I think Ray's story will, too. Here it is:

"Back in high school I had to contend° with many of the malicious°   8
deeds and taunts° from my 'fellow students,' similar but different. With me, however, I was a victim of gross physical immaturity. . . . I actually didn't start shaving regularly until I was 25 or so.

"This problem was very hard for me to deal with, even though it was   9
out of my control. The class 'bullies' and insensitive and uncaring types never hesitated for one moment to knock me around, having read my problems like a book. Gym class, especially, was my psychological encounter° with hell—twice weekly. Because of my outward appearance, I always skipped showering with the rest of the class. Eventually, they caught on to this and many of the guys would either throw me in the showers, or if they didn't do this, they would spit in my underwear or socks or shoes and then (usually) chuck them out of the window to the ground two stories below.

"Is it no wonder I was sick as often as I could be on Gym Day? Oh,   10
all the wonderful FUN they had at my emotional expense. I once mustered the courage to talk to my 'guidance counselor' about the problems I was contending with, and all he was able to tell me was that this was the type of thing that students like myself go through to become a man. How I was to become a man through all this eluded° me, primarily because I was being treated as less than human by these jerks.

"Once this pattern was set up, I easily became a target for much the   11
same outside of gym. Often I was pushed and shoved in the hallway. On occasion, I was tripped or punched, and on special occasions, I would even be tossed into the mobile° trash cans and rolled into classrooms that weren't even mine. I may have been bigger than some of these instigators°, but I could never seem to get the courage to bring a fist up to their ugly faces. It was always THEM against ME. How often I broke down and cried out of sheer frustration is uncountable. What really gets me is that I let this happen. Is it any wonder that I turned to alcohol and had two major ulcer operations before I was 25?

"As I suspect you know by now, I have picked up the shattered pieces   12
of my adolescence and have gotten my life back together again. The HATE and RAGE I once felt for these ne'er-do-wells has since turned to pity. In fact, they are no doubt half-decent guys now. But if they only knew how much harm they'd caused me, they'd become a little upset with themselves. At least I hope so, anyway. I only wish that someone had yelled, 'Stop it! Can't you see what you're doing?' back at school. It may have saved me from much of the misery I was forced to endure until I graduated from that hell hole."

That's Ray's story. I've got my own, and you probably have yours.   13

How did we survive those years? How did we endure the anger, the   14
shame, the emotional brutality? And we're talking middle-class suburban
kids, here. We're talking the seeds of the promised land. If parents only
knew what their kids were going through, what their kids *are* going
through.

I don't know if there's an answer. How can we make teenagers treat   15
each other like human beings? How can we penetrate that closed society
of adolescence? How can we let the victims know that life gets better?
How can we shame the bullies with what they will feel about their
actions, if they ever grow up?

Kids: Lessons Learned Early

I want to share something with you, something nice.   16

It's what some kids have had to say in letters to me about the column   17
about the Bird, the girl I knew in high school who was teased and
tormented by everyone, until one day another girl stood up to a group of
guys who were picking on the Bird. You wonder when you write something like this about growing up, how kids will receive your message.
Here are some of their reactions:

"I read your article about the weird girl called the Bird," wrote   18
Stephanie K. "I am in the sixth grade, and one of my classmates is weird
like in your article, and we too make fun of him. We don't make fun of
him as much anymore. We used to make fun of him all day long. . . . I
really thought about what you've said and I want to thank you for taking
time to write something that will prevent other people from feeling bad."

"I have read your story about the girl that was called the Bird because   19
she had pale skin and acted weird. In the story, you said that you were one
of the ones who teased the Bird," wrote Cuong N. "You also spoke highly
of the girl who came up to you and your friends and told you guys to stop
teasing the Bird. If you spoke highly of that girl, why didn't you do the
same thing, or were you scared of being teased too? If I was in your place,
I would have done the same thing you did and prevented myself from
being teased. Please write back to me if you can."

"I would probably have done the same thing as you did," wrote Katie   20
M. "Now that I read the story and understand the problem going on, I
wonder why more people aren't like the kid who came and helped the
Bird."

"I think the girl who stood up for the Bird was very brave," wrote   21
Nicole G. "She could have been beaten up or teased, but she did it
anyway. I really look up to and respect people like that."

"I think that you shouldn't have held back what you thought about the 22
other kids teasing the Bird, because that makes you in a way worse than
the others," wrote Michael C. "If you felt that the girl reacted bravely for
sticking up for the Bird and that she was a good person for doing what
she did, why didn't you at least find out who she was?"

I wish I had found out her name, Michael. And I respect people like 23
that too, Nicole. And I too wonder why more people aren't like the girl
who helped the Bird, Katie. And the reason I spoke highly of the girl is
that I was afraid to do what she did, and her bravery inspired me, Cuong.
And I'm especially glad that you've stopped teasing your sixth-grade
classmate, Stephanie. Thank you all for thinking about the story the way
you did.

FIRST IMPRESSIONS

To the Student: The three "First Impressions" questions that follow each
selection allow you to write freely about your first reactions to what you
have read. Normally, you won't be handing in this writing to your instructor. It is personal writing that focuses your ideas about the selection and
its relationship to your own life. Don't worry about making mistakes. Just
get your reactions down on paper.

Freewrite for ten minutes on one of the following.

1. Did you enjoy reading this selection? Why or why not?

2. Who do you remember being teased at your school? Why was this
    person teased? How did you respond when you saw the teasing?

3. Why do you think teasing is so common among children and
    teenagers?

VOCABULARY CHECK

The explanations below each question on the following pages are
provided to help you understand how to answer the questions and
complete the other items in this book. Try to figure out each answer yourself first. Then check your answer. Study the explanation, especially if
your response wasn't correct. As you work on the exercises, cover the
explanations below the items with a card or piece of paper so you're not
tempted to look at them until *after* you've tried the items yourself.

The vocabulary words covered in the first four items are not defined in "Words to Watch," so it's up to you to figure out what they mean. But that doesn't mean you have to guess the answers blindly. First, read each item to see if you already know the answer. If you don't, start by crossing off one or more of the words that you're sure are wrong. Then try replacing the *italicized* word in the item with each answer that's left. The word that fits best is right.

A. Circle the letter of the word or phrase that best completes each of the following four items.

1. In the sentence below, the word *contempt* means
   a. praise.
   (b.) disgust.
   c. envy.
   d. love.

   > "She was also the object of such contempt and scorn, such cruel ridicule, that it shames me to this day. . . ." (Paragraph 1)

   The sentence suggests that *contempt* has a meaning similar to that of "scorn" and "cruel ridicule." Knowing this should help you rule out "praise" and "love." Then you can try "disgust" and "envy" in place of *contempt* in the sentence. "Envy" doesn't make sense, so your answer is "disgust" *(b)*.

2. In the sentence below, the word *insensitive* means
   a. intelligent.
   b. friendly.
   (c.) unfeeling.
   d. far away.

   > "The class 'bullies' and insensitive and uncaring types never hesitated for one moment to knock me around, having read my problems like a book." (Paragraph 9)

   To answer this item, ask yourself how bullies would feel about someone else's problems. The sentence says they are "uncaring," a clue that the answer is *c,* "unfeeling."

3. In the sentence on the next page, the word *mustered* means
   a. fought.
   (b.) gathered.
   c. refused.
   d. ignored.

"I once mustered the courage to talk to my 'guidance counselor' about the problems I was contending with. . . ." (Paragraph 10)

Here, the question to ask yourself is what Ray would do to his courage before talking to someone about his problems. Discussing personal problems would take courage for anyone and would probably have been especially difficult for Ray. He would not want to fight or refuse or ignore his courage. So the right answer is *b,* "gathered."

4. In the sentence below, the word *endure* means
   a. commit.
   b. enjoy.
   c. borrow.
   (d.) put up with.

   "It may have saved me from much of the misery I was forced to endure until I graduated from that hell hole." (Paragraph 12)

What would the writer be forced to do with misery he couldn't avoid? He would have to "put up with" it, so the correct answer to this one is *d.*

B. Circle the letter of the answer that best completes each of the following four items. Each item uses a word (or form of a word) from "Words to Watch."

The second set of vocabulary items checks your understanding of terms from "Words to Watch." Each item requires you to choose the word from "Words to Watch" that best fits the situation. If you need to, look back at the definitions that appear before the essay on page 31. Then try each possible definition to see how well it fits. Cover the answers at the end of this exercise while you do the items. Then check to see how well you did.

5. If a girl has a very *sallow* complexion, you might conclude that she
   (a.) spends a lot of time inside.
   b. comes from a wealthy family.
   c. spends a great deal of time in the sun.

6. When the enemy captain demanded, "Surrender!" the leader of the rebels *defiantly*
   a. put down their weapons.
   b. burst into tears.
   (c.) shouted, "Never!"

7. A *malicious* answer to the question "How do I look?" would be
   a. "You look lovely."
   b. "Have you lost weight?"
   ⓒ "Really ugly."

8. Little Johnny reached for a cookie. His mother gave her *tacit* approval by
   a. shouting, "Don't you dare!"
   ⓑ smiling at him as he took it.
   c. saying, "Go ahead, Johnny. You can have one."

Check your answers: 5. *a*   6. *c*   7. *c*   8. *b*

READING CHECK

The next ten questions check your understanding of the selection's content. You'll be asked to identify the central point, or thesis, of the entire selection and then the main idea of at least one of its paragraphs. Next come questions on the key supporting details. After the detail questions are questions on inferences—ideas that are not directly stated in the selection but are clearly suggested. The final questions focus on the writer's craft, and they concern techniques the author used in writing the selection.

Central Point and Main Ideas

1. Which sentence best expresses the central point of the entire selection?
   a. Gym class is the worst place for teenagers who are victims of teasing.
   b. Childhood and adolescence are difficult times for many people.
   c. A classmate's courageous action may have saved a girl's life.
   ⓓ Teenagers should learn to stop being cruel to people who are different.

Sometimes all of the possible answers for an item like this one are true, but some are *too narrow*, which means they give only details, not main ideas. Others are *too broad*, giving ideas that are more like the subjects of whole books than the central points of essays. If you can't find the correct answer right away, cross out the sentences that give details instead of general ideas. Here, sentences *a* and *c* give supporting details, so they're definitely wrong —they are too narrow. That leaves sentences *b* and *d*. Can you tell which of these two sentences is too broad? It's sentence *b*, which contains a bigger subject than the selection does, a subject that could have a whole book devoted to it instead of just three newspaper columns. So, by eliminating the wrong answers, you've found the right one, sentence *d*.

2. Which sentence best expresses the main idea of paragraph 11?
    a. Ray was teased a great deal while in school.
    (b.) Once the teasing started, it took over Ray's life.
    c. Ray eventually began drinking and had two major ulcer operations.
    d. Ray didn't have the courage to fight back.

To answer an item like this one, look back at the paragraph it covers (11) to remind yourself of what it's about. Then, try to choose the correct answer. If you can't, go back to read the paragraph again. Sometimes the paragraphs you'll look back at will have topic sentences that state the main idea, but this one doesn't. Therefore, you'll have to decide for yourself what the main idea of the paragraph is. A good way to start is by crossing out the sentences that are too narrow, *c* and *d*. These sentences both give details. Two general sentences, *a* and *b*, remain. Sentence *b* is the better choice of the two because it includes the idea that the teasing affected Ray's life.

3. Which sentence best expresses the main idea of paragraph 19?
    a. Cuong had read the story of the Bird.
    b. Cuong thought the author should not have admitted being scared.
    c. Cuong wanted the author to write back.
    (d.) Cuong would not have stopped the teasing but wondered why the author had not tried to stop it either.

Again, look back at the paragraph (19). Then cross out the sentences that state details rather than main ideas—*a* and *c*. (Notice that although sentence *a* refers to the first sentence of the paragraph, which is often the topic sentence, this time that sentence is not broad enough to be a topic sentence.) To choose between the remaining sentences, *b* and *d*, look for the one that does a better job of stating the overall idea of the paragraph. The sentence that does the best job of stating the main idea is sentence *d*.

Key Supporting Details

Questions about key details give you a chance to check your understanding of the information the author provides to back up the central point and main ideas. To answer this type of question, you may need to look back at the selection to check on details you've forgotten.

4. The girl in the article had gotten the nickname of "the Bird" because of
    (a.) her movements and posture.
    b. the hair on her arms.
    c. the whistling sounds she made.
    d. her high voice.

Did you look back at the description of the Bird in paragraph 1? It says that the Bird's nickname was based on "her nervous, birdlike movements and the way she would hunch her shoulders," so the answer is *a*.

5. The most humiliating experiences for Ray Windsor took place in
   a. math class.
   b. the lunch room.
   c. gym class.
   d. English class.

This question is answered in paragraphs 9 and 10, where Ray calls gym class "my psychological encounter with hell" and goes on to describe the other boys' throwing him into the shower or tossing his clothing out the window. He was treated so badly, in fact, that he "was sick as often as [he] could be on Gym Day." Thus the answer is *c*.

6. After reading DeLeon's article, a student named Stephanie K. wrote that
   a. she thought DeLeon was in a way worse than the other students who had teased the Bird.
   b. she looked up to people like the girl who had defended the Bird.
   c. DeLeon should have found out the name of the girl who had defended the Bird.
   d. she and her friends are now teasing a "weird" classmate less often.

The paragraph in which DeLeon mentions Stephanie is paragraph 18. Stephanie says that she also has a weird classmate whom she and the other kids used to make fun of, but they "don't make fun of him as much anymore." She does not say that DeLeon was worse than the others or should have found out the name of the other girl. Nor does she say that she admires the girl. These statements are made by other students in paragraphs 21 and 22. So the correct answer must be *d*.

Inferences

For this group of questions, you will be drawing conclusions about what the author means but does not state directly.

7. The author suggests that Nathan Faris
   a. might have been helped like the Bird if someone had stood up for him.
   b. was probably very different from the Bird.
   c. was justified in shooting one of his classmates.
   d. was too weak to defend himself.

You can find the answer to this question by skimming rapidly to find Nathan Faris's name. It's mentioned in paragraph 5. Reading the whole paragraph will give you some clues to the answer, but the best clue is in the last sentence: "And I wonder if that one act of defiant kindness may have saved another girl's life." This means that DeLeon thinks the girl who spoke up to protect the Bird may have prevented her suicide. If that's the case, just one person speaking up might have kept Nathan Faris from shooting another person and killing himself, so the answer to this question is *a*.

8. ___*F*___ TRUE OR FALSE? The author implies that the problem of teasing in adolescence is not very important.

You have to think about the whole selection to answer this item. Think back to the examples of the Bird, Ray Windsor, and Nathan Faris. Would you call the teasing and problems they had to put up with "not very important"? No, especially when you consider the effects the teasing had on their lives. So the answer is FALSE.

The Writer's Craft

This group of items asks about the way the selection was written. It includes questions about topics such as how the author organized the selection and supported general ideas.

9. As the signal words *when* and *then* indicate, paragraphs 3 and 4 present
   a. items in no particular order.
   b. events in time order.
   c. comparisons and contrasts.
   d. examples.

Think about the words *when* and *then* in each of the types of situations mentioned in the answers. *When* and *then* wouldn't be needed if details were given in no special order *(a)*, nor do they point out similarities and differences *(c)* or examples *(d)*, so you've found the right answer: *b*.

10. The author's purpose in writing these columns is to
    a. entertain readers with stories of schoolchildren.
    b. inform readers of ways to combat teasing.
    c. persuade readers that childhood is an important time of life.
    d. persuade readers that young people's cruelty to each other must be stopped.

Was this selection meant just as entertainment? If you look back, you'll see that the ideas in it are rather serious, so you can eliminate *a*. Among the answers that are left, *b* can be dropped because DeLeon is more emotional about his subject than someone who was just giving information would be. Between *c* and *d, d* is the better choice because it is about the topic of the piece, young people's cruelty toward each other.

DISCUSSION QUESTIONS

The four questions that follow provide you and your classmates with a final opportunity to further your understanding of the selection. Your teacher may ask you to respond to these questions individually or in small groups as well as in a large classroom setting.

1. Many centuries ago the Greek philosopher Philo of Alexandria made the following observation: "Be kind, for everyone you meet is fighting a great battle." What do you think he meant by this statement? How might it apply to "Bird Girl"?

2. In paragraph 2, DeLeon says that "it's important when you're a teenager to join the laughter, lest the laughter turn on you." What does he mean? Is he correct?

3. Why do you think so many readers wrote to DeLeon about the story of the Bird?

4. DeLeon asks, "How can we make teenagers treat each other like human beings?" How would you answer this question?

PARAGRAPH ASSIGNMENTS

Your teacher may ask you to write a paragraph or an essay on any of the following topics. Notice that the first topic in each set helps you get started by suggesting a possible central point for your paper.

1. Write your own paragraph about a person who was teased or bullied in your school or neighborhood. Describe the person and then explain how others treated him or her. Make your description detailed enough so that your readers can picture the person clearly and understand what happened. Use a topic sentence such as "Gordon was bullied a lot by my eighth-grade classmates because of his unusual behavior."

2. Considering the social pressures for teenagers to be "part of the crowd," the girl who helped the Bird was especially brave. Even under less difficult circumstances, people do not always go out of their way to help others through an act of kindness. Write a paragraph about a time someone you know did go out of his or her way to help another person. Possible examples might include caring for a sick person, taking in a foster child, doing volunteer work, acting as a family peacemaker, or providing financial or moral support at a time of crisis. Include vivid details so your readers can clearly picture what happened.

ESSAY ASSIGNMENTS

1. DeLeon admits that he regrets two things: taking part in teasing the Bird and not finding out who the girl was who stepped in to stop the teasing. Write an essay about three regrets in your life. They might be things you did and later wished you hadn't, or things you didn't do and later wished you had done. Explain what happened in each case, and then tell why you wish you had handled things differently. Try to support your general idea with details as interesting as the ones DeLeon uses. Your thesis statement might be similar to the following: "I can think of three regrets I have about some of my past behavior."

2. When Ray Windsor went to his school guidance counselor to talk about being teased, he didn't receive much help. What would you do if you were a counselor who had been asked to come up with ideas to help students treat one another better? Write an essay in which you make detailed suggestions for what teachers and students could do to make your school a friendlier, gentler place. You might want to include such ideas as buddy systems, in which seniors act as personal counselors to younger students; discussion groups of students and teachers; or an anti-teasing education campaign.

2

The Scholarship Jacket
Marta Salinas

Preview

All of us have suffered disappointments and moments when we have felt we've been treated unfairly. In "The Scholarship Jacket," originally published in *Growing Up Chicana: An Anthology*, Marta Salinas writes about one such moment in her childhood in southern Texas. By focusing on an award that school authorities decided she should not receive, Salinas shows us the pain of discrimination as well as the need for inner strength.

Words to Watch

scholarship (1): acknowledgment of academic excellence
agile (2): able to move quickly
despaired (3): lost hope
eavesdrop (4): secretly listen
filtered (7): passed through
muster (12): call forth
mesquite (15): a sweet-smelling thorny tree
clod (15): lump of earth or clay
gaunt (25): thin and bony
vile (29): very unpleasant
adrenaline (31): a hormone that raises the blood pressure and stimulates
the heart

The small Texas school that I attended carried out a tradition every year   1
during the eighth grade graduation: a beautiful gold and green jacket, the
school colors, was awarded to the class valedictorian, the student who had
maintained the highest grades for eight years. The scholarship° jacket had
a big gold *S* on the left front side, and the winner's name was written in
gold letters on the pocket.

My oldest sister, Rosie, had won the jacket a few years back, and I   2
fully expected to win also. I was fourteen and in the eighth grade. I had
been a straight-A student since the first grade, and the last year I had
looked forward to owning that jacket. My father was a farm laborer who
couldn't earn enough money to feed eight children, so when I was six I
was given to my grandparents to raise. We couldn't participate in sports
at school because there were registration fees, uniform costs, and trips out
of town; so even though we were quite agile° and athletic, there would
never be a sports school jacket for us. This one, the scholarship jacket,
was our only chance.

In May, close to graduation, spring fever struck, and no one paid any   3
attention to class; instead we stared out the windows and at each other,
wanting to speed up the last few weeks of school. I despaired° every time
I looked in the mirror. Pencil thin, not a curve anywhere, I was called
"Beanpole" and "String Bean," and I knew that's what I looked like. A flat
chest, no hips, and a brain, that's what I had. That really isn't much for a
fourteen-year-old to work with, I thought, as I absentmindedly wandered
from my history class to the gym. Another hour of sweating during
basketball and displaying my toothpick legs was coming up. Then I
remembered my P.E. shorts were still in a bag under my desk where I'd
forgotten them. I had to walk all the way back and get them. Coach
Thompson was a real bear if anyone wasn't dressed for P.E. She had said
I was a good forward and once she even tried to talk Grandma into letting
me join the team. Grandma, of course, said no.

I was almost back at my classroom door when I heard angry voices   4
and arguing. I stopped. I didn't mean to eavesdrop°; I just hesitated, not
knowing what to do. I needed those shorts and I was going to be late, but
I didn't want to interrupt an argument between my teachers. I recognized
the voices: Mr. Schmidt, my history teacher, and Mr. Boone, my math
teacher. They seemed to be arguing about me. I couldn't believe it. I still
remember the shock that rooted me flat against the wall as if I were trying
to blend in with the graffiti written there.

"I refuse to do it! I don't care who her father is, her grades don't even   5
begin to compare to Martha's. I won't lie or falsify records. Martha has a
straight-A-plus average and you know it." That was Mr. Schmidt, and he
sounded very angry. Mr. Boone's voice sounded calm and quiet.

"Look, Joann's father is not only on the Board, he owns the only store   6
in town; we could say it was a close tie and—"

The pounding in my ears drowned out the rest of the words, only a   7
word here and there filtered° through. ". . . Martha is Mexican . . . resign
. . . won't do it. . . ." Mr. Schmidt came rushing out, and luckily for me
went down the opposite way toward the auditorium, so he didn't see me.
Shaking, I waited a few minutes and then went in and grabbed my bag
and fled from the room. Mr. Boone looked up when I came in but didn't
say anything. To this day I don't remember if I got in trouble in P.E. for
being late or how I made it through the rest of the afternoon. I went home
very sad and cried into my pillow that night so Grandmother wouldn't
hear me. It seemed a cruel coincidence that I had overheard that
conversation.

The next day when the principal called me into his office, I knew what   8
it would be about. He looked uncomfortable and unhappy. I decided I
wasn't going to make it any easier for him, so I looked him straight in the
eye. He looked away and fidgeted with the papers on his desk.

"Martha," he said, "there's been a change in policy this year regarding   9
the scholarship jacket. As you know, it has always been free." He cleared
his throat and continued. "This year the Board decided to charge fifteen
dollars—which still won't cover the complete cost of the jacket."

I stared at him in shock and a small sound of dismay escaped my   10
throat. I hadn't expected this. He still avoided looking in my eyes.

"So if you are unable to pay the fifteen dollars for the jacket, it will be   11
given to the next one in line."

Standing with all the dignity I could muster°, I said, "I'll speak to my   12
grandfather about it, sir, and let you know tomorrow." I cried on the walk
home from the bus stop. The dirt road was a quarter of a mile from the
highway, so by the time I got home, my eyes were red and puffy.

"Where's Grandpa?" I asked Grandma, looking down at the floor so   13
she wouldn't ask me why I'd been crying. She was sewing on a quilt and
didn't look up.

"I think he's out back working in the bean field."   14

I went outside and looked out at the fields. There he was. I could see   15
him walking between the rows, his body bent over the little plants, hoe in
hand. I walked slowly out to him, trying to think how I could best ask him
for the money. There was a cool breeze blowing and a sweet smell of
mesquite° in the air, but I didn't appreciate it. I kicked at a dirt clod°. I
wanted that jacket so much. It was more than just being a valedictorian
and giving a little thank-you speech for the jacket on graduation night. It
represented eight years of hard work and expectation. I knew I had to be
honest with Grandpa; it was my only chance. He saw me and looked up.

He waited for me to speak. I cleared my throat nervously and clasped   16
my hands behind my back so he wouldn't see them shaking. "Grandpa, I
have a big favor to ask you," I said in Spanish, the only language he knew.
He still waited silently. I tried again. "Grandpa, this year the principal said
the scholarship jacket is not going to be free. It's going to cost fifteen
dollars and I have to take the money in tomorrow, otherwise it'll be given
to someone else." The last words came out in an eager rush. Grandpa
straightened up tiredly and leaned his chin on the hoe handle. He looked
out over the field that was filled with the tiny green bean plants. I waited,
desperately hoping he'd say I could have the money.

He turned to me and asked quietly, "What does a scholarship jacket   17
mean?"

I answered quickly; maybe there was a chance. "It means you've   18
earned it by having the highest grades for eight years and that's why
they're giving it to you." Too late I realized the significance of my words.
Grandpa knew that I understood it was not a matter of money. It wasn't
that. He went back to hoeing the weeds that sprang up between the
delicate little bean plants. It was a time-consuming job; sometimes the
small shoots were right next to each other. Finally he spoke again.

"Then if you pay for it, Marta, it's not a scholarship jacket, is it? Tell   19
your principal I will not pay the fifteen dollars."

I walked back to the house and locked myself in the bathroom for a   20
long time. I was angry with Grandfather even though I knew he was right,
and I was angry with the Board, whoever they were. Why did they have
to change the rules just when it was my turn to win the jacket?

It was a very sad and withdrawn girl who dragged into the principal's   21
office the next day. This time he did look me in the eyes.

"What did your grandfather say?"   22

I sat very straight in my chair.   23

"He said to tell you he won't pay the fifteen dollars."   24

The principal muttered something I couldn't understand under his   25
breath, and walked over to the window. He stood looking out at
something outside. He looked bigger than usual when he stood up; he was
a tall, gaunt° man with gray hair, and I watched the back of his head while
I waited for him to speak.

"Why?" he finally asked. "Your grandfather has the money. Doesn't   26
he own a small bean farm?"

I looked at him, forcing my eyes to stay dry. "He said if I had to pay   27
for it, then it wouldn't be a scholarship jacket," I said and stood up to
leave. "I guess you'll just have to give it to Joann." I hadn't meant to say
that; it had just slipped out. I was almost to the door when he stopped me.

"Martha—wait."   28

I turned and looked at him, waiting. What did he want now? I could   29
feel my heart pounding. Something bitter and vile° tasting was coming up
in my mouth; I was afraid I was going to be sick. I didn't need any
sympathy speeches. He sighed loudly and went back to his big desk. He
looked at me, biting his lip, as if thinking.

"Okay, damn it. We'll make an exception in your case. I'll tell the   30
Board, you'll get your jacket."

I could hardly believe it. I spoke in a trembling rush. "Oh, thank you,   31
sir!" Suddenly I felt great. I didn't know about adrenaline° in those days,
but I knew something was pumping through me, making me feel as tall as
the sky. I wanted to yell, jump, run the mile, do something. I ran out so I
could cry in the hall where there was no one to see me. At the end of the
day, Mr. Schmidt winked at me and said, "I hear you're getting a
scholarship jacket this year."

His face looked as happy and innocent as a baby's, but I knew better.   32
Without answering I gave him a quick hug and ran to the bus. I cried on
the walk home again, but this time because I was so happy. I couldn't wait
to tell Grandpa and ran straight to the field. I joined him in the row where
he was working and without saying anything I crouched down and started
pulling up the weeds with my hands. Grandpa worked alongside me for a
few minutes, but he didn't ask what had happened. After I had a little pile
of weeds between the rows, I stood up and faced him.

"The principal said he's making an exception for me, Grandpa, and   33
I'm getting the jacket after all. That's after I told him what you said."

Grandpa didn't say anything; he just gave me a pat on the shoulder and   34
a smile. He pulled out the crumpled red handkerchief that he always
carried in his back pocket and wiped the sweat off his forehead.

"Better go scc if your grandmother needs any help with supper."   35

I gave him a big grin. He didn't fool me. I skipped and ran back to the   36
house whistling some silly tune.

FIRST IMPRESSIONS

Freewrite for ten minutes on one of the following.

1. Did you enjoy reading this selection? Why or why not?

2. Have you ever felt that you were treated unfairly simply because of
   your gender, age, ethnicity, or financial situation? Explain.

3. Which person in this story do you admire the most? Why?

VOCABULARY CHECK

A. Circle the letter of the word or phrase that best completes each of the following four items.

1. In the sentences below, the word *falsify* means
   a. write down.
   b. make untrue.
   c. keep track of.
   d. sort alphabetically.

   "I won't lie or falsify records. Martha has a straight-A-plus average and you know it." (Paragraph 5)

2. In the sentences below, the words *fidgeted with* mean
   a. folded neatly.
   b. fussed nervously with.
   c. played happily with.
   d. calmly examined.

   "He looked uncomfortable and unhappy. . . . He looked away and fidgeted with the papers on his desk." (Paragraph 8)

3. In the sentences below, the word *dismay* means
   a. joy.
   b. comfort.
   c. relief.
   d. disappointment.

   "I stared at him in shock and a small sound of dismay escaped my throat. I hadn't expected this." (Paragraph 10)

4. In the sentence below, the word *withdrawn* means
   a. not healthy.
   b. curious.
   c. amused.
   d. not responsive.

   "It was a very sad and withdrawn girl who dragged into the principal's office the next day." (Paragraph 21)

B. Circle the letter of the answer that best completes each of the following four items. Each item uses a word (or form of a word) from "Words to Watch."

5. Because Michael is not particularly *agile*, he does not do well in
   a. English.
   b. math.
   (c.) sports.

6. After two weeks of looking for a job, Rita *despaired* when
   (a.) none of her interviews led to a job.
   b. a friend told her of an opening in a new shoe store.
   c. the owner of a bookstore said, "You're hired."

7. My cousin looked particularly *gaunt* after he
   a. won a scholarship to college.
   (b.) lost fifty pounds.
   c. finally got a good night's sleep and ate a hearty breakfast.

8. Laverne took one sip of the *vile*-tasting tomato juice and exclaimed,
   a. "Give me a big glass of this!"
   b. "Is this plain tomato juice, or are there other vegetables in it?"
   (c.) "Yuck!"

READING CHECK

Central Point and Main Ideas

1. Which sentence best expresses the central point of the selection?
   a. It is more important to be smart than good-looking or athletic.
   b. People who are willing to pay for awards deserve them more than people who are not.
   (c.) By refusing to give in to discrimination, the author finally received the award she had earned.
   d. Always do what the adults in your family say, even if you don't agree.

2. Which sentence best expresses the main idea of paragraph 2?
   a. Marta wanted to win the scholarship jacket to be like her sister Rosie.
   (b.) The scholarship jacket was especially important to Marta because she was unable to earn a jacket in any other way.
   c. The scholarship jacket was better than a sports school jacket.
   d. Marta resented her parents for sending her to live with her grandparents.

3. Which sentence best expresses the main idea of paragraph 7?
   a. Marta didn't want her grandmother to know she was crying.
   b. Marta was shocked and saddened by the conversation she overheard.
   c. Mr. Schmidt didn't see Marta when he rushed out of the room.
   d. Marta didn't hear every word of Mr. Schmidt's and Mr. Boone's conversation.

Key Supporting Details

4. Marta was raised by her grandparents because
   a. she wanted to learn to speak Spanish.
   b. her father did not earn enough money to feed all of his children.
   c. she wanted to learn about farming.
   d. her parents died when she was six.

5. __T__ TRUE OR FALSE? Marta was called by a different name at school.

Inferences

6. We can infer from paragraph 8 that the principal was "uncomfortable and unhappy" because
   a. the students had not been paying attention in class during the last few weeks before graduation.
   b. his office was very hot.
   c. he was ashamed to tell Marta that she had to pay fifteen dollars for a jacket that she had earned.
   d. Mr. Boone and Mr. Schmidt were fighting in the hallway.

7. The author implies that the Board members were not going to give Marta the scholarship jacket because
   a. she was late for P.E. class.
   b. they wanted to award the jacket to the daughter of an important local citizen.
   c. another student had better grades.
   d. they didn't think it was fair to have two members of the same family win the jacket.

8. __T__ TRUE OR FALSE? The author implies that the Board's new policy to require a fee for the scholarship jacket was an act of discrimination.

The Writer's Craft

9. The author begins her story with a description of the scholarship jacket in order to
   a. get readers interested in who will win the jacket.
   b. show that the jacket is desirable.
   c. let readers see exactly what the jacket looks like.
   d. do all of the above.

10. The tone, or emotion, that the author conveys in paragraph 31 is best described as
    a. contentment.
    b. anger.
    c. joy.
    d. disappointment.

DISCUSSION QUESTIONS

1. In her first meeting with the principal, Marta could have challenged him by telling what she had overheard the two teachers saying. Why do you think she stayed silent? What do you think the principal would have said or done if she'd told him she knew the real reason she wasn't being given the jacket?

2. Why do you think the principal gave in during his second meeting with Marta? What do you think will happen when he has to face the Board again? If you were the principal, what would you say to the Board?

3. What values did Marta learn from her grandfather? Where in the story do they demonstrate similar values?

4. Marta implies that she was discriminated against because of her racial background (she was Mexican) and her family's economic condition (they were poor). Have you ever experienced discrimination, or do you know of a friend who has experienced it? Explain.

PARAGRAPH ASSIGNMENTS

1. Write a paragraph about a time when you experienced or witnessed an injustice. Describe the circumstances surrounding the incident and why you think the people involved acted as they did. In your paragraph, describe how you felt at the time and any effect the incident has had on you. Your topic sentence could be something like one of the following:

- I was angry when my supervisor promoted his nephew even though I was more qualified.

- A friend of mine recently got in trouble with authorities even though he was innocent of any wrongdoing.

2. Marta stresses again and again how important the scholarship jacket was to her and how hard she worked to win it. Write a paragraph about something you worked hard to achieve when you were younger. How long did you work toward that goal? How did you feel when you finally succeeded? Or as an alternative, write about not achieving the goal. How did you cope with the disappointment? What lessons, if any, did you learn from the experience?

ESSAY ASSIGNMENTS

1. This story contains several examples of authority figures— specifically, the two teachers, the principal, and Marta's grandfather. Write an essay describing three qualities that you think an authority figure should possess. Such qualities might include honesty, fairness, compassion, and knowledge, among others.

   Devote each of the supporting paragraphs in the body of your essay to one of those qualities. Within each paragraph, give an example or examples of how an authority figure in your life has demonstrated that quality.

   You may write about three different authority figures that have demonstrated those three qualities to you. Alternatively, one authority figure may have demonstrated all three.

   Your thesis statement might be similar to one of these:

   - My older brother, my grandmother, and my football coach have been models of admirable behavior for me.

   - My older brother's honesty, courage, and kindness to others have set a valuable example for me.

2. In paragraph 3, Marta recalls her self-consciousness about her skinny body, which made the other students call her "Beanpole" and "String Bean." Her reaction reflects the importance placed on physical appearance in our society.

   Think about the messages teenagers receive regarding their appearance ("appearance" could include their bodies, dress, hairstyles, among other things). These messages can come from any of the following:

- other students
- music videos
- magazine advertisements
- television commercials
- talk shows
- television shows and movies
- sports figures

Write an essay about the types of pressure that teenagers face to look or act a certain way. Examine the consequences—for example, low self-esteem, eating disorders, steroid use—when these ideals are not achieved.

Focus your essay on three different influences—for example, fashion magazines, popular TV shows, and professional sports—and the consequences of each.

3

Life Over Death
Bill Broderick

Preview

A small, furry body lies on the pavement. It's a daily reality for most of us, living as we do in a world where the automobile rules the road. But in this case, something moved the author to stop and investigate. What he found reminded him that the chance to save a life doesn't come along every day.

Words to Watch

grimaced (2): made a twisted face to express pain or disgust
immobile (2): not moving
ligament (5): a band of tissue which connects bones or supports organs
tendon (5): a tissue which connects muscles to bones and other parts of
 the body
good Samaritan (6): someone who helps others unselfishly
kinked (7): twisted
resignation (9): acceptance without resistance
dejected (11): depressed
pathetic (11): pitiful

My reaction was as it always is when I see an animal lying in the   1
roadway. My heart sank. And a lump formed in my throat at the thought
of a life unfulfilled. I then resolved to move him off the road, to ensure
that one of God's creations did not become a permanent part of the

pavement. Some might ask what difference it makes. If it's already dead, why not just leave it there? My answer is that I believe in death with dignity, for people and for animals alike.

So I pulled my car over to the side of the road and walked back to where the cat lay motionless. Two cars passed over him, managing to avoid running him over. With no other cars in sight, I made my way to the lifeless form just as a jogger went by. The jogger grimaced° at the sight of the immobile° cat, blood dripping from his mouth. "How'd it happen?" he asked. I replied that I didn't know; he probably got hit by some careless driver. I just wanted to get him off the road. I reached down for the cat and got the surprise of my life. The little creature lifted his head ever so slightly and uttered a pitiful, unforgettable little "meow." He was still alive.

What was I going to do now? I was already late for work. All I had intended to do was move the cat off the road. I didn't need this. But I knew I had no choice. I sighed deeply, then reached down and carefully cradled the cat in my hands. I asked the jogger to open my car trunk and remove the things from a small box. Then I gently placed the cat in the box. He was in shock, so he probably could not feel the pain from his obvious injuries. "Kinda funny lookin', isn't he?" asked the jogger. I was annoyed by his question, but I had to admit that he was right. This cat looked peculiar. Not ugly, mind you. But he seemed to have a comical look on his face, even at such a dreadful time.

"What are you gonna do with him?" the jogger asked. I told him I would take the cat to the local vet and let him decide what to do.

The vet was only five minutes away. My wife and I had been bringing our animals to him for several years, and I knew I could rely on him to do what was best for the cat. I brought the cat into the reception room and placed it on the counter. As this was an emergency, the vet was summoned right away. He examined the cat thoroughly, listing the injuries for his assistant to write down. "Broken jaw, that'll have to be set. Two teeth broken. A couple more loose. Possible internal injuries, but they don't look too bad. Uh-oh. This doesn't look good. He doesn't appear to have any movement in his right front leg. Possible break, definite ligament° and tendon° damage."

The vet completed his examination, then looked at me and asked what I wanted to do. I knew what he meant. Did I want to have the cat "put to sleep"? I became uneasy. I clumsily explained that I was hoping to get advice from him on what to do. Fair enough. The jaw would have to be wired shut for six weeks, and the cat would have to wear a cast on its leg for three months. There was no way of knowing if the damage to the leg was permanent. He could have the cast removed and still not be able to use the leg. The cost of all the surgery would be high, but I would get a 50 percent "good Samaritan°" discount if I went ahead with it.

Now I was really at a loss. If I went ahead with the surgery, I'd be 7
paying for a cat which wasn't mine, whose owner I'd probably never find,
and who might end up with the use of only three legs. And on top of it,
this was one of the funniest-looking cats ever born. Black and white,
spotted where it shouldn't be, kinked° tail, and a silly half-smile on its
face. I chuckled at that and the entire situation.

"What do you want to do, Bill?" asked the vet. 8

I shrugged my shoulders in resignation°. "Dan, I'll choose life over 9
death every time. Let's give it our best shot."

I called back later in the day and learned that the surgery had been 10
successful. "You can pick up your cat tomorrow morning," I was told. My
cat. I started to say that he was not my cat, but I knew otherwise.

The next morning, my wife and I drove to the vet and picked up the 11
cat. He looked ghastly. His jaw was now bandaged, and a cast covered
one leg entirely and wrapped around his midsection. We were dejected°.
But, as we drove him home, we began thinking that perhaps this cat was
not as pathetic° as he looked. As frightened as he must have been, as
much pain as he must have felt, he sat calmly in my wife's lap. He purred
and stared out the window with his curious half-smile.

When we got home, we introduced him to our two Siamese cats, who 12
stared in disbelief at this strange creature. They sensed it might be a cat,
but they had never seen one like this. It took him very little time to get used
to his new surroundings. It took him longer to get used to the cast, which
made even walking a chore. Surely he must have been embarrassed. After
all, an animal normally able to glide around quietly should not make a
resounding thump every time he moves.

In due time, the cast came off. To our relief, Pokey, as we now called 13
him, had about 90 percent mobility in the leg. He got around okay, but he
limped whenever he tried to move any faster than a slow walk.

All this occurred four years ago. Pokey is still with us today. In fact, 14
he has become our most beloved cat. Because of his injury, he is strictly
an indoor cat. This does not seem to bother him at all. It is hard to believe
that any cat has ever enjoyed himself more. Maybe it's because he had
been slowed after being hit by a car, or perhaps he just has a special
individuality. He is never bored. At times he will race around the house
like he is leading the Indy 500. Or he'll leap into the air at an imaginary
foe. Or he'll purr loudly at the foot of our bed, staring into space with that
silly grin on his face. And he couldn't care less that he still looks funny.

It would have been easy to let Pokey lie in the middle of the road. And 15
it would have been just as simple to have the vet put him to sleep. But
when I think of all the pleasure this cat has given us, and of how much
fun he has living with us, I know the right decision was made. And I'd do
it again in a second. I'll take life over death every time.

FIRST IMPRESSIONS

Freewrite for ten minutes on one of the following.

1. Did you enjoy reading this selection? Why or why not?

2. Would you ever stop to remove an animal's dead body from the road? Under what circumstances?

3. Do you consider yourself an animal lover? Explain.

VOCABULARY CHECK

A. Circle the letter of the word or phrase that best completes each of the following four items.

1. In the sentence below, the word *resolved* means
   a. forgot.
   b. hid.
   (c.) decided.
   d. drove.

   > "I then resolved to move him off the road, to ensure that one of God's creations did not become a permanent part of the pavement." (Paragraph 1)

2. In the sentences below, the word *summoned* means
   a. paid.
   (b.) called for.
   c. telephoned.
   d. ignored.

   > "As this was an emergency, the vet was summoned right away. He examined the cat thoroughly. . . ." (Paragraph 5)

3. In the sentences below, the word *ghastly* means
   a. threatening.
   b. appealing.
   (c.) terrible.
   d. marvelous.

   > "He looked ghastly. His jaw was now bandaged, and a cast covered one leg entirely and wrapped around his midsection." (Paragraph 11)

4. In the sentence below, the word *resounding* means
   a. soft.
   b. brave.
   c. relaxed.
   (d.) loud.

   > "After all, an animal normally able to glide around quietly should not make a resounding thump every time he moves." (Paragraph 12)

B. Circle the letter of the answer that best completes each of the following four items. Each item uses a word (or form of a word) from "Words to Watch."

5. Naturally, I *grimaced* when
   a. my sister handed me a bouquet of roses.
   (b.) the doctor poked me with the needle.
   c. I smelled the aroma of my favorite pizza.

6. A car would be *immobile* if
   (a.) its engine had burned out.
   b. it was very dirty.
   c. it had a full tank of gas.

7. The employees were *dejected* to learn that
   a. they were each receiving a raise in their next paycheck.
   b. the employee cafeteria was being redecorated.
   (c.) there would be no Christmas bonus this year.

8. A *pathetic* scene in a movie is intended to make people
   a. amused.
   (b.) sad.
   c. angry.

READING CHECK

Central Point and Main Ideas

1. Which sentence best expresses the central point of the selection?
   a. Drivers need to be alert to dangers on the road.
   (b.) Every life is valuable.
   c. Cats make wonderful pets.
   d. Pokey is strictly an indoor cat because of his injury.

2. Which sentence best expresses the main idea of paragraphs 3 and 4?
    a. The author didn't know what to do.
    (b.) The author was willing to take responsibility for the cat.
    c. The author was annoyed at the jogger's questions.
    d. The cat was funny-looking.

3. Which sentence best expresses the main idea of paragraph 6?
    a. The author wanted to know if the damage to the cat's leg was permanent.
    b. The vet didn't know what to do with the cat.
    (c.) To help the author decide what to do, the vet explained what could be done for the cat and what it would cost.
    d. The author expected the vet to say that the cat should be "put to sleep."

4. Which sentence best expresses the main idea of paragraph 14?
    (a.) Pokey is beloved and enjoys life a great deal now.
    b. Pokey sometimes leaps into the air at imaginary enemies.
    c. Pokey must spend the rest of his life indoors.
    d. Pokey was injured four years ago.

Key Supporting Details

5. The author
    a. saw a car hit the cat.
    (b.) was very surprised that the cat was still alive.
    c. was surprised that the jogger came by.
    d. thought that the cat was ugly.

6. The author
    a. had heard about the vet.
    b. looked for the nearest vet.
    (c.) knew and trusted the vet.
    d. drove for hours till he found a vet.

7. For Pokey's surgery, the vet charged the author
    a. nothing.
    b. extra, because of the emergency circumstances.
    (c.) half the usual cost.
    d. the usual cost.

Inferences

8. It is reasonable to conclude that
    a. Pokey would have lived if the author had not picked him up.
    (b.) this was not the first time the author had moved the body of an animal off the road.
    c. the author was angry that the vet charged him for Pokey's surgery.
    d. the author's wife does not like cats as much as he does.

9. We can conclude from paragraph 3 that the author
    a. would have left the cat there if the jogger hadn't been watching.
    b. was frequently late to work.
    (c.) knew the cat would not recover without medical attention.
    d. knew that the cat's injuries were not very severe.

The Writer's Craft

10. The author's purpose in writing this selection was to
    a. entertain readers with a charming story about adopting a cat.
    b. teach readers that animals can be helped to recover from serious injuries.
    c. persuade readers that doing the right thing has its own rewards.
    (d.) do all of the above.

DISCUSSION QUESTIONS

1. In the first paragraph, the author uses the expression "death with dignity." What do you think he means by that expression?

2. When the vet told Broderick that he could pick up his cat at the vet's office, the author began to protest but then stopped. Why do you think Broderick decided the cat was really his?

3. Why do you think that Pokey has become, in Broderick's words, "our most beloved cat"? Do you think Pokey's injuries had an effect on how the author ended up feeling about him? Why or why not?

4. Can and should something be done to make the world a better place for hurt and homeless animals like Pokey? Or should our priorities lie elsewhere? Explain your answer.

PARAGRAPH ASSIGNMENTS

1. Think of an animal that has played a role in your life. Perhaps it was a pet in your own home or in the home of someone you visited frequently. Perhaps it was a neighborhood animal that you often observed. Write a paragraph about the animal in which you emphasize one of that animal's characteristics. Such characteristics might include, for example, playfulness, bad temper, stupidity, energy, and intelligence. Start your paragraph with a topic sentence that identifies the animal and names the characteristic, like this: "Rags, the dog I had when I was a child, was very comical." Continue your paragraph by giving two or three examples that illustrate the characteristic you have chosen.

2. The author of "Life Over Death" felt he "had no choice"—that he *had* to help the injured cat. For this assignment, write a one-paragraph letter to the author telling him about a time you also did something because you thought it was the only right thing to do. A topic sentence for this letter could be worded something like this: "When I realized my brother was shoplifting, I felt I had no choice but to tell our parents."

   After your topic sentence, describe the situation that faced you, and then explain the decision you made. Conclude by telling what finally happened.

ESSAY ASSIGNMENTS

1. Why do people own pets? What do pets contribute to people's lives? Write an essay about some of the reasons people choose to keep pets. For each reason, provide specific details or examples that help illustrate that reason. An effective thesis statement for this essay might be one of the following:

   - Pets are important to people for several reasons.

   - Owning a pet guarantees a steady supply of amusing anecdotes, satisfying responsibilities, and—best of all—unconditional love.

2. Bill Broderick acted as a "good Samaritan" when he saved Pokey—in other words, he unselfishly helped another creature without expecting any reward. Write an essay about one or more good Samaritans you have known and what they have done to help others. In your essay, be sure to answer the following questions:

   - Who was the good Samaritan?
   - Who was the person (or animal) in need?
   - Exactly what did the person do to help?
   - What might have happened if the Samaritan had *not* provided help?

4

A Small Victory
Steve Lopez

Preview

There are a million small miseries in a big city, and most of them go unnoticed and unrepaired. But when *Philadelphia Inquirer* columnist Steve Lopez wrote about Ruby Knight, a gracious woman caught in a nightmarish tangle of medical red tape, he touched a nerve in his readers. You may or may not be surprised to learn of the outpouring of response to Lopez's article.

Words to Watch

dog days (1): the hot, humid summer days between early July and early
              September
metropolis (2): big city
glances (2): flashes
shimmer (2): shine
bureaucracy (6): a system in which complex rules interfere with effective
              action
inventory (15): the amount of goods on hand
exclusively (40): entirely
sprawling (44): spread out (and therefore hard to deal with)
cynical (53): distrustful of people's motives

First column, written on July 22:

On the dog days° of summer, ten floors above Camden [New Jersey], 1
Ruby Knight sets the fan at the foot of her bed and aims it at Philadelphia.
Then she sits in the window, breeze at her back, and lets her thoughts
carry her across the river to the city where she grew up.

She is 71 and has lived—since her husband passed on—in a high-rise 2
near the Ben Franklin Bridge toll plaza. The neighborhood isn't the
greatest, but from the tenth floor, Philadelphia is a gleaming metropolis°.
The city sprouts above the river, and the sun glances° off skyscrapers that
shimmer° in the July heat.

Mrs. Knight watches the boats and ships on the river, the cars on the 3
bridge. She looks to North Philly and thinks back on her eighteen proud
years as a crossing guard at 17th and Ridge. And she worries about
tomorrow.

Mrs. Knight, in the quiet of her home, is slowly starving. 4

She beat cancer: Her doctor calls it a near miracle. But now she's 5
wrestling a worse kind of beast.

Bureaucracy°. 6

Joseph Spiegel, a Philadelphia surgeon, tells the story: 7

In 1986, a tumor filled Mrs. Knight's throat. Spiegel removed her 8
voice box and swallowing mechanism. Mrs. Knight was fed through a
tube to her stomach. It was uncomfortable and painful, but she was happy
to be alive.

Although she couldn't speak, she learned to write real fast and took to 9
carrying a note pad around. She gets help from an older sister, Elizabeth
Woods, who herself beat a form of lung cancer that's often a quick killer.

The doctor was impressed by Mrs. Knight's fight. "She said she was 10
placing her faith in my hands and the Lord's," he says.

Mrs. Knight had several more operations. But over the years, no sign 11
of cancer. And five months ago—she smiles at the memory—Spiegel
removed the tube. She was able to swallow again. After four years.

Little did she know the end of one problem was the start of another. 12

Instead of pouring her liquid nutrition down the tube, Mrs. Knight 13
now drank it. The same exact liquid.

But Medicare, which paid when it went down the tube, refused to pay 14
when it went down her throat.

Mrs. Knight, who lives on a fixed and meager income, kept the liquid 15
cans in the corner of her living room, an open inventory°. She would look
at those cans as if they represented the days left in her life. And she began
rationing.

Mrs. Knight says her fighting weight is close to 100. When it dropped 16
noticeably, she went to the doctor, but had trouble making her point.

"I think she was a little embarrassed that she couldn't afford to buy the 17
stuff," Spiegel says.

She had lost about ten pounds since her last visit, down to the high 18
eighties. She was on her way, Spiegel says, to starving herself to death.

Spiegel got an emergency supply of the liquid—she goes through 19
about six cans a day at one dollar a can—and began calling Medicare. If
she ends up in the hospital, Spiegel argued, it'll cost Medicare a lot more
than six dollars a day.

But Medicare, with built-in safeguards against intentional or 20
accidental use of common sense, wouldn't budge.

"This is a federally funded program and we have specific guidelines 21
for what we can pay for and can't pay for," Jan Shumate said in an
interview. She's director of "Medicare Part B Services" in the Columbia,
South Carolina claims office.

But it's the same liquid. 22

"Yes, I understand that." 23

It costs less than hospitalization. 24

"Yes, I understand that, but we're mandated to go by the rules." 25

Even if it costs more money? 26

"My only solution I can suggest is if she files again and it gets denied, 27
she can request an informal review."

The reasoning is Medicare can't pay for every substance somebody 28
claims to need for survival.

Spiegel says Mrs. Knight needs this drink. She can't eat or drink much 29
of anything else. He has told her he may have to put the tube back in her
stomach, so Medicare will pay again.

At the mere suggestion, Mrs. Knight loses it. No way. Her sister is 30
with her, the two of them confused by it all. They've beaten cancer,
cheated the days, and now this.

Mrs. Knight hustles to the bathroom and returns with the scale. She 31
puts it by her bed, gets on. The needle hits 83. She stands at the window,
frail against the Philadelphia skyline, grace and dignity showing through
her despair.

The two sisters look at the cans in the corner. There's enough for one 32
month, but Mrs. Knight will try to stretch it. On her pad, she writes:

"My trial. God's got to do something." 33

(Dr. Spiegel is at 215-545-3322.) 34

Follow-up column, written on July 29:

It's the kind of thing I don't get around to often enough. But today, I think 35
some thanks are in order.

The problem is, I won't be able to get to everyone. I don't even know 36 where to begin.

Maybe with last week's column. 37

Those who looked in this corner last Sunday saw a story about Ruby 38 Knight, a retired crossing guard in North Philadelphia. She had throat cancer real bad at one time, but Dr. Joseph Spiegel removed a tumor and Mrs. Knight has gone nearly five years without a recurrence.

It took four years for Mrs. Knight, now 71, to learn how to swallow 39 again. And it was a big day for her about six months ago when Spiegel removed the feeding tube from her stomach. Finally, she could swallow.

Problem was, she couldn't eat or drink regular food because of 40 discomfort. Her diet was still, exclusively°, a nutritional supplement called Ensure Plus.

Now here's the deal. 41

When Mrs. Knight poured it down the tube, it was covered by 42 Medicare. When she drank the same stuff, Medicare refused to cover it.

Medicare reasons that if you don't need a tube, you don't need a 43 special diet. The rule exists to avoid abuse.

"The idea is a good one," Spiegel says. "But Medicare is the biggest, 44 most sprawling° bureaucracy of all." He says its inability to make reasonable exceptions often hurts the elderly poor.

Spiegel tried to get Medicare to change its mind, arguing that it would 45 cost the government a lot more if he had to surgically implant the tube back in Mrs. Knight's stomach. But he got nowhere.

"We're mandated to go by the rules," a Medicare spokeswoman told 46 me when I asked for an explanation.

Meanwhile, Mrs. Knight, without anyone's knowledge, was working 47 on her own solution. She had begun rationing her Ensure Plus.

She kept a careful count of the cans, figuring she needed at least four 48 a day to survive. Mrs. Knight stacked the fifty-one cans in her Camden living room, measuring the supply each day against her fixed income.

As Spiegel put it, "she was slowly starving herself." She went from 49 nearly one hundred pounds to eighty-three.

When I went to visit, I found one of the sweetest, most unassuming 50 people I have met. Mrs. Knight's sister, Elizabeth Woods, is the same way. She's 76 and also beat cancer. They live in the same high-rise apartment house with a fabulous view of Philadelphia, and they help each other through the days.

Mrs. Knight can't speak, but she gets her points across just fine. She 51 writes almost as fast as you can talk and she has a world-class hug.

The day after the column, Spiegel and his staff got to their Pine Street 52 office at 8 a.m. There were seventy-four messages on the machine. By noon, there were 150. By closing time Monday, more than four hundred people had called.

"You can get cynical° about things," Spiegel says, "but then there's 53 this outpouring of help from people. It's just astounding."

People called for two reasons. Compassion and anger. Everyone 54 knows somebody who's been seriously ill. Everyone has had trouble with bureaucracy.

Ruby Knight hit the daily double.   55

And I would like to begin now with the thank-yous. First to Dr. 56 Spiegel for his sense of compassion and outrage. To his staff—Lori, Gina, Maria, Sally, Laura, Monica and Mike—for patiently handling calls, letters and donations. "It was kind of fun," Maria says.

And thanks to readers whose names fill thirteen typed pages compiled 57 by Spiegel's staff. One person gave a year's supply of Ensure Plus. One donated twenty cases. Some sent prayers, holy cards, religious medals.

Some thanked Mrs. Knight for her years as a crossing guard at 17th 58 and Ridge. Some people sent as much as four hundred dollars. One sent three one-dollar bills and a note: "I wish I could send more."

One sent ten dollars and this note: "May God bless you. I lost my dear 59 husband to leukemia two and a half years ago."

Some called Medicare to complain. Some called Ensure Plus, where 60 spokeswoman Sharon Veach said she thought the company could arrange to provide a lifetime supply, if needed.

Friday at noon, Spiegel, Maria and Mike drove to Camden and 61 dropped in on Mrs. Knight with thirty cases of Ensure Plus and a list of donors.

Mrs. Knight was beside herself, humble, gracious, overwhelmed. She 62 and her sister kept looking at each other, shaking their heads.

"I'm speechless," Mrs. Knight wrote on her pad, and then laughed. 63

She said she would pray for everyone. She kept scribbling that she 64 wishes there were some way she could express thanks and love for the kindness of strangers.

And I told her that she had.   65

FIRST IMPRESSIONS

Freewrite for ten minutes on one of the following.

1. Did you enjoy reading this selection? Why or why not?

2. Think of someone you know who has gotten involved in a frustrating struggle with a bureaucracy. What happened to this person?

3. Why do you think people responded so strongly to Mrs. Knight's story?

VOCABULARY CHECK

A. Circle the letter of the word or phrase that best completes each of the following four items.

1. In the sentence below, the word *meager* means
   a. stolen.
   b. avoidable.
   c. very small.
   d. enormous.

   > "Mrs. Knight . . . lives on a fixed and meager income." (Paragraph 15)

2. In the sentences below, the word *mandated* means
   a. not allowed.
   b. scared.
   c. mistaken.
   d. required.

   > "'This is a federally funded program and we have specific guidelines for what we can pay for and can't pay for. . . . [W]e're mandated to go by the rules.'" (Paragraphs 21 and 25)

3. In the sentence below, the word *recurrence* means
   a. regret.
   b. reduction.
   c. reappearance.
   d. review.

   > "She had throat cancer real bad at one time, but Dr. Joseph Spiegel removed a tumor and Mrs. Knight has gone nearly five years without a recurrence." (Paragraph 38)

4. In the sentence below, the word *compiled* means
   a. put together.
   b. paid for.
   c. delayed.
   d. remembered.

   > "And thanks to readers whose names fill thirteen typed pages compiled by Spiegel's staff." (Paragraph 57)

B. Circle the letter of the answer that best completes each of the following four items. Each item uses a word (or form of a word) from "Words to Watch."

5. Every year, we wait until the *dog days* arrive, and then we
   a. take our German shepherd to the vet for a checkup.
   b. take advantage of the after-Christmas sales in all the local stores.
   c. take a break from work and go to the beach.

6. A shoe store's *inventory* would consist of
   a. the bricks, cement, and other materials used to construct the building.
   b. athletic shoes, dress shoes, sandals, and maybe socks.
   c. a manager, an assistant manager, and several part-time clerks.

7. "Don't *sprawl* on the couch," Renee warned her teenage son. "Instead,
   a. sit up straight."
   b. take your bag of potato chips into the kitchen and eat there."
   c. go for a run if you want some exercise."

8. A person who takes a *cynical* view of marriage would say,
   a. "In a marriage, each person is just looking to use the other one and get as much as he or she can get."
   b. "Marriage is a holy partnership that should never be dissolved."
   c. "There is one perfect partner out there for every man and woman in the world."

READING CHECK

Central Point and Main Ideas

1. Which sentence best expresses the central point of the entire selection?
   a. The elderly poor usually suffer unnecessarily.
   b. Individuals were able to solve a problem that bureaucracy failed to handle.
   c. Mrs. Knight's diet is made up almost completely of a liquid supplement.
   d. Ruby Knight lost her voice box to throat cancer.

2. Which sentence best expresses the main idea of paragraph 15?
   a. Mrs. Knight lives on a fixed income.
   b. Mrs. Knight kept her supply of Ensure Plus in her living room.
   c. Mrs. Knight looked every day at the cans of Ensure Plus in her living room.
   (d.) Since Mrs. Knight could not afford more Ensure Plus, she began rationing the cans she had.

3. Which sentence best expresses the main idea of paragraph 52?
   a. Only four hundred people read the author's column.
   b. Dr. Spiegel and his staff begin their work day at 8 a.m.
   c. Dr. Spiegel's office is a busy one.
   (d.) Many people called Dr. Spiegel in response to the author's column.

Key Supporting Details

4. __T__ TRUE OR FALSE? Both Ruby Knight and her sister have been cured of cancer.

5. Even though she could now swallow, Mrs. Knight
   (a.) could comfortably take only Ensure Plus.
   b. had lost her taste for regular food.
   c. preferred to feed herself through a tube.
   d. wanted to go to the hospital.

6. Dr. Spiegel's argument to Medicare was that
   a. the government should pay for whatever a person needs to survive.
   b. Mrs. Knight had suffered greatly because of her cancer.
   (c.) it would cost the government more if he had to re-insert the tube in Mrs. Knight's stomach.
   d. keeping Mrs. Knight out of the hospital would be helpful because the hospitals are already too full.

Inferences

7. We can assume that Lopez included Dr. Spiegel's phone number
   a. with Dr. Spiegel's permission.
   b. to encourage people to help Mrs. Knight.
   c. because he believed people would want to help Mrs. Knight.
   (d.) for all of the above reasons.

8. Which of the following statements would the author of this selection
   be most likely to agree with?
   a. All Medicare rules should be eliminated.
   b. People helped Mrs. Knight because they knew they would be
      praised in the newspaper.
   c. Ensure Plus is too expensive.
   d. The Medicare system should find a way to make reasonable
      exceptions to its rules.

The Writer's Craft

9. When the author refers to Mrs. Knight, his tone is
   a. humorous and amused.
   b. totally objective.
   c. admiring and affectionate.
   d. critical and disbelieving.

10. Lopez titles this selection "A Small Victory." Which of the following
    best explains his choice of a title?
    a. Medicare won a small victory over Mrs. Knight.
    b. Mrs. Knight and her sister, Mrs. Woods, each won a small victory
       over cancer.
    c. By helping Mrs. Knight, people joined together to win a small
       victory over bureacracy.
    d. Steve Lopez won a small victory by writing such a popular story.

DISCUSSION QUESTIONS

1. If Steve Lopez hadn't written about Mrs. Knight, what do you think
   might have happened to her? Do you think anyone else in the story
   would have continued to try to help her?

2. What do you think Lopez means when he says in paragraph 20 that
   Medicare has "built-in safeguards against intentional or accidental use
   of common sense"? What is Lopez implying by his choice of words?

3. Lopez writes, "Medicare reasons that if you don't need a tube, you
   don't need a special diet. The rule exists to avoid abuse." What kind of
   abuse do you think Medicare might be trying to avoid by having such
   a rule? How might Medicare be taken advantage of by people who
   wanted to do so?

4. Lopez writes, "People called for two reasons. Compassion and anger" (paragraph 54). Why do you think so many people reacted with such depth of feeling? What events have you read or heard about recently that provoked a similar response in you?

PARAGRAPH ASSIGNMENTS

1. Lopez writes, "Everyone knows somebody who's been seriously ill. Everyone has had trouble with bureaucracy." Write a paragraph about one of those topics: either someone who has dealt with a serious illness or someone who has struggled with bureacracy. In your paragraph, describe the illness or the trouble with a bureacratic agency. Then explain what was done to cope with this problem.

   Your topic sentence for the paragraph might be a sentence like one of the following:

   • When my father was out of work with a back injury, it was a difficult time for him and the rest of the family.

   • Trying to get an insurance settlement after my car was damaged by a hit-and-run driver turned into a bureacratic nightmare.

   • Applying for a grant to help pay for my education has taught me the true meaning of "red tape."

   To make clear the sequence of events in your paragraph, remember to use some time transition words such as *first, next, after,* and *finally*.

2. Steve Lopez makes the humorous claim that Medicare has "safeguards against intentional or accidental use of common sense." Think about what "common sense" means to you, then write a paragraph about a time someone you know displayed a *lack* of common sense. In your paragraph, describe the situation, indicate what a sensible response to the situation *would* have been, and tell what the person did instead. Your paragraph may be serious or humorous. A topic sentence for this paragraph might be something like this:

   • When my little sister's kitten got stuck in a tree, my sister's attempt to rescue it showed a real lack of common sense.

   • The first time my brother did his own laundry, his lack of common sense created some colorful problems.

ESSAY ASSIGNMENTS

1. In his first column, Steve Lopez wrote about a problem he hoped his readers would help solve. Write an essay for your school newspaper discussing a problem at your school and offering solutions.

   Your thesis statement might be something like any of these:

   • "Students, teachers, and administrators could all work together to make our campus a more pleasant place."

   • "Our campus could be made safer if a few simple steps were taken."

   • "Steps should be taken to help students at our school have a better educational experience."

   Your essay will be richer and more interesting if you provide examples to emphasize your point. For instance, if you are writing about making the campus more attractive, you could provide specific examples of places that are currently unattractive.

2. Lopez emphasizes in his columns that Mrs. Knight is a proud, independent woman who wants to live her life with dignity. But it is also clear that Mrs. Knight's age, income, and physical condition all make it difficult for her to maintain that dignity.

   Write an essay about the challenges that face people who are growing old in America today: physical, mental, social, financial, or other kinds of challenges. Choose any three challenges and provide specific examples of each type.

5

Joe Davis: A Cool Man
Beth Johnson

Preview

Drugs and guns, crime and drugs, drugs and lies, liquor and drugs. If there was one constant in Joe Davis's life, it was drugs, the substance that ruled his existence. Personal tragedy was not enough to turn him off the path leading to the brink of self-destruction. Finally Joe was faced with a moment of decision. The choice he made has opened doors into a world that the old Joe barely knew existed.

Words to Watch

option (6): choice
rehabilitated (10): brought back to a good and healthy life
encountered (20): met
unruly (26): disorderly
hushed (27): quiet

J oe Davis was the coolest fourteen-year-old he'd ever seen.   1

He went to school when he felt like it. He hung out with a wild crowd.   2
He started drinking some wine, smoking some marijuana. "Nobody could tell me anything," he says today. "I thought the sun rose and set on me." There were rules at home, and Joe didn't do rules. So he moved in with his grandmother.

Joe Davis was the coolest sixteen-year-old he'd ever seen.   3

Joe's parents gave up on his schooling and signed him out of the tenth   4
grade. Joe went to work in his dad's body shop, but that didn't last long.
There were rules there, too, and Joe didn't do rules. By the time he was in
his mid-teens, Joe was taking pills that got him high, and he was even
using cocaine. He was also smoking marijuana all the time and drinking
booze all the time.

Joe Davis was the coolest twenty-five-year-old he'd ever seen.   5

He was living with a woman almost twice his age. The situation   6
wasn't great, but she paid the bills, and certainly Joe couldn't pay them.
He had his habit to support, which by now had grown to include heroin.
Sometimes he'd work at a low-level job, if someone else found it for him.
He might work long enough to get a paycheck and then spend it all at
once. Other times he'd be caught stealing and get fired first. A more
challenging job was not an option°, even if he had bothered to look for
one. He couldn't put words together to form a sentence, unless the
sentence was about drugs. Filling out an application was difficult. He
wasn't a strong reader. He couldn't do much with numbers. Since his drug
habit had to be paid for, he started to steal. First he stole from his parents,
then from his sister. Then he stole from the families of people he knew.
But eventually the people he knew wouldn't let him in their houses, since
they knew he'd steal from them. So he got a gun and began holding
people up. He chose elderly people and others who weren't likely to fight
back. The holdups kept him in drug money, but things at home were
getting worse. His woman's teenage daughter was getting out of line. Joe
decided it was up to him to discipline her. The girl didn't like it. She told
her boyfriend. One day, the boyfriend called Joe out of the house.

BANG.   7

Joe Davis was in the street, his nose in the dirt. His mind was still   8
cloudy from his most recent high, but he knew something was terribly
wrong with his legs. He couldn't move them; he couldn't even feel them.
His mother came out of her nearby house and ran to him. As he heard her
screams, he imagined what she was seeing. Her oldest child, her first
baby, her bright boy who could have been and done anything, was lying
in the gutter, a junkie with a .22 caliber bullet lodged in his spine.

The next time Joe's head cleared, he was in a hospital bed, blinking up   9
at his parents as they stared helplessly at him. The doctors had done all
they could; Joe would live, to everyone's surprise. But he was a
paraplegic—paralyzed from his chest down. It was done. It was over. It
was written in stone. He would not walk again. He would not be able to
control his bladder or bowels. He would not be able to make love as he
did before. He would not be able to hold people up, then hurry away.

Joe spent the next eight months being moved between several   10
Philadelphia hospitals, where he was shown the ropes of life as a
paraplegic. Officially he was being "rehabilitated°"—restored to a
productive life. There was just one problem: Joe. "To be *re*habilitated,
you must have been *habilitated* first," he says today. "That wasn't me."
During his stay in the hospitals, he found ways to get high every day.

Finally Joe was released from the hospital. He returned in his   11
wheelchair to the house he'd been living in when he was shot. He needed
someone to take care of him, and his woman friend was still willing. His
drug habit was as strong as ever, but his days as a stickup man were over.
So he started selling drugs. Business was good. The money came in fast,
and his own drug use accelerated even faster.

A wheelchair-bound junkie doesn't pay much attention to his health   12
and cleanliness. Eventually Joe developed his first bedsore: a deep, rotting
wound that ate into his flesh, overwhelming him with its foul odor. He was
admitted to Magee Rehabilitation Hospital, where he spent six months on
his stomach while the ghastly wound slowly healed. Again, he spent his
time in the hospital using drugs. This time his drug use did not go
unnoticed. Soon before he was scheduled to be discharged, hospital
officials kicked him out. He returned to his friend's house and his business.
But then police raided the house. They took the drugs, they took the
money, they took the guns.

"I really went downhill then," says Joe. With no drugs and no money   13
to get drugs, life held little meaning. He began fighting with the woman
he was living with. "When you're in the state I was in, you don't know
how to be nice to anybody," he says. Finally she kicked him out of the
house. When his parents took him in, Joe did a little selling from their
house, trying to keep it low-key, out of sight, so they wouldn't notice. He
laughs at the notion today. "I thought I could control junkies and tell
them, 'Business only during certain hours.'" Joe got high when his
monthly Social Security check came, high when he'd make a purchase for
someone else and get a little something for himself, high when a visitor
would share drugs with him. It wasn't much of a life. "There I was," he
says, "a junkie with no education, no job, no friends, no means of
supporting myself. And now I had a spinal cord injury."

Then came October 25, 1988. Joe had just filled a prescription for pills   14
to control his muscle spasms. Three hundred of the powerful muscle
relaxants were there for the taking. He swallowed them all.

"It wasn't the spinal cord injury that did it," he says. "It was the   15
addiction."

Joe tried hard to die, but it didn't work. His sister heard him choking   16
and called for help. He was rushed to the hospital, where he lay in a coma
for four days.

Joe has trouble finding the words to describe what happened next.   17

"I had . . . a spiritual awakening, for lack of any better term," he says.   18
"My soul had been cleansed. I knew my life could be better. And from
that day to this, I have chosen not to get high."

Drugs, he says, "are not even a temptation. That life is a thing that   19
happened to someone else."

Joe knew he wanted to turn himself around, but he needed help in   20
knowing where to start. He enrolled in Magee Hospital's vocational
rehabilitation program. For six weeks, he immersed himself in
discussions, tests, and exercises to help him determine the kind of work
he might be suited for. The day he finished the rehab program, a nurse at
Magee told him about a receptionist's job in the spinal cord injury unit at
Thomas Jefferson Hospital. He went straight to the hospital and met
Lorraine Buchanan, coordinator of the unit. "I told her where I was and
where I wanted to go," Joe says. "I told her, 'If you give me a job, I will
never disappoint you. I'll quit first if I see I can't live up to it.'" She gave
him the job. The wheelchair-bound junkie, the man who'd never been able
to hold a job, the drug-dependent stickup man who "couldn't put two
words together to make a sentence" was now the first face, the first voice
that patients encountered° when they entered the spinal cord unit. "I'd
never talked to people like that," says Joe, shaking his head. "I had
absolutely no background. But Lorraine and the others, they taught me to
speak. Taught me to greet people. Taught me to handle the phone." How
did he do in his role as a receptionist? A huge smile breaks across Joe's
face as he answers, "Excellent."

Soon, his personal life also took a very positive turn. A month after   21
Joe started his job, he was riding a city bus to work. A woman recovering
from knee surgery was in another seat. The two smiled, but didn't speak.

A week later, Joe spotted the woman again. The bus driver sensed   22
something was going on and encouraged Joe to approach her. Her name
was Terri. She was a receptionist in a law office. On their first date, Joe
laid his cards on the table. He told her his story. He also told her he was
looking to get married. "That about scared her away," Joe recalls. "She
said she wasn't interested in marriage. I asked, 'Well, suppose you did
meet someone you cared about who cared about you and treated you well.
Would you still be opposed to the idea of marriage?' She said no, she
would consider it then. I said, 'Well, that's all I ask.'"

Four months later, as the two sat over dinner in a restaurant, Joe   23
handed Terri a box tied with a ribbon. Inside was a smaller box. Then a
smaller box, and a smaller one still. Ten boxes in all. Inside the smallest
was an engagement ring. After another six months, the two were married
in the law office where Terri works. Since then, she has been Joe's
constant source of support, encouragement, and love.

After Joe had started work at Jefferson Hospital, he talked with his   24
supervisor, Lorraine, about his dreams of moving on to something bigger,
more challenging. She encouraged him to try college. He had taken and
passed the high-school general equivalency diploma (GED) exam years
before, almost as a joke, when he was recovering from his bedsores at
Magee. Now he enrolled in a university mathematics course. He didn't do
well. "I wasn't ready," Joe says. "I'd been out of school seventeen years.
I dropped out." Before he could let discouragement overwhelm him, he
enrolled at Community College of Philadelphia (CCP), where he signed
up for basic math and English courses. He worked hard, sharpening study
skills he had never developed in his earlier school days. Next he took
courses toward an associate's degree in mental health and social services,
along with a certificate in addiction studies. Five years later, he graduated
from CCP, the first member of his family ever to earn a college degree.
He went on to receive a bachelor's degree in mental health from
Hahnemann University in Philadelphia.

Now Joe is in his final year in the University of Pennsylvania's Master   25
of Social Work program. Besides being a student, he is employed as a
psychotherapist at John F. Kennedy Mental Health Center in
Philadelphia. His dream now is to get into the "real world," the world of
young men and women immersed in drugs, violence, and crime. In fact,
in his field-placement work for school, Joe mentors a group of at-risk
adolescent boys. Also, whenever he can, he speaks at local schools
through a program called Think First. He tells young people about his
drug use, his shooting, and his experience with paralysis.

At a presentation at a disciplinary school outside of Philadelphia, Joe   26
gazes with quiet authority at the unruly° crowd of teenagers. He begins to
speak, telling them about speedballs and guns, fast money and bedsores,
even about the leg bag that collects his urine. At first, the kids snort with
laughter at his honesty. When they laugh, he waits patiently, then goes on.
Gradually the room grows quieter as Joe tells them of his life and then
asks them about theirs. "What's important to you? What are your goals?"
he says. "I'm still in school because when I was young, I chose the dead-
end route many of you are on. But now I'm doing what I have to do to get
where I want to go. What are you doing?"

He tells them more, about broken dreams, about his parents' grief,   27
about the former friends who turned away from him when he was no
longer a source of drugs. He tells them of the continuing struggle to
regain the trust of people he once abused. He tells them about the desire
that consumes him now, the desire to make his community a better place
to live. His wish is that no young man or woman should have to walk the

path he's walked in order to value the precious gift of life. The teenagers are now silent. They look at this broad-shouldered black man in his wheelchair, his head and beard close-shaven, a gold ring in his ear. His hushed° words settle among them like gentle drops of cleansing rain. "What are you doing? Where are you going?" he asks them. "Think about it. Think about me."

Joe Davis is the coolest forty-four-year-old you've ever seen.   28

FIRST IMPRESSIONS

Freewrite for ten minutes on one of the following.

1. Did you enjoy reading this selection? Why or why not?

2. Why do you think Joe tried to kill himself?

3. Have you ever known someone who has turned his or her life around, as Joe has? What were the circumstances?

VOCABULARY CHECK

A. Circle the letter of the word or phrase that best completes each of the following four items.

1. In the sentence below, the word *restored* means
   a. held back.
   b. punished.
   c. returned.
   d. paid.

   "Officially he was being 'rehabilitated'—restored to a productive life." (Paragraph 10)

2. In the sentence below, the word *accelerated* means
   a. increased.
   b. grown less serious.
   c. disappeared.
   d. helped.

   "The money came in fast, and his own drug use accelerated even faster." (Paragraph 11)

3. In the sentence below, the word *ghastly* means
   a. quite small.
   b. very unpleasant.
   c. caused by a gun.
   d. illegal.

   > "He was admitted to Magee Rehabilitation Hospital, where he spent six months on his stomach while the ghastly wound slowly healed." (Paragraph 12)

4. In the sentence below, the word *immersed* means
   a. totally ignored.
   b. greatly angered.
   c. deeply involved.
   d. often harmed.

   > "For six weeks, he immersed himself in discussions, tests, and exercises to help him determine the kind of work he might be suited for." (Paragraph 20)

B. Circle the letter of the answer that best completes each of the following four items. Each item uses a word (or form of a word) from "Words to Watch."

5. The usual *options* after graduating from high school include
   a. happiness mixed with sadness for leaving a familiar place.
   b. going to college, getting a job, or joining the army.
   c. looking forward to your first high-school reunion.

6. "I *encountered* a poisonous snake on my camping trip," David announced. Chris responded,
   a. "Who was more afraid when you met—it or you?"
   b. "Why in the world would you eat a poisonous animal?"
   c. "Why did you kill it?"

7. Because their twin boys are so *unruly*, the Millers
   a. have a hard time finding anyone willing to baby-sit for them.
   b. teach a parenting class to help other parents raise similarly well-behaved children.
   c. worry about why the boys are so quiet and inactive.

8. One place that does not usually have a *hushed* atmosphere is a
   a. church.
   b. circus.
   c. library.

READING CHECK

Central Point and Main Ideas

1. Which sentence best expresses the central point of the selection?
    a. Most people cannot improve their lives once they turn to drugs and crime.
    b. Joe Davis overcame a life of drugs and crime and a disability to lead a rich, meaningful life.
    c. The rules set by Joe Davis's parents caused him to leave home and continue a life of drugs and crime.
    d. Joe Davis's friends turned away from him once they learned he was no longer a source of drugs.

2. A main idea may cover more than one paragraph. Which sentence best expresses the main idea of paragraphs 21–23?
    a. The first sentence of paragraph 21
    b. The second sentence of paragraph 21
    c. The first sentence of paragraph 22
    d. The first sentence of paragraph 23

3. Which sentence best expresses the main idea of paragraph 24?
    a. It was difficult for Joe to do college work after being out of school for so many years.
    b. Lorraine Buchanan encouraged Joe to go to college.
    c. Joe's determination enabled him to overcome a lack of academic preparation and eventually succeed in college.
    d. If students would stay in high school and work hard, they would not have to go to the trouble of getting a high-school GED.

Key Supporting Details

4. Joe Davis quit high school
    a. when he was 14.
    b. when he got a good job at a hospital.
    c. when he was in the tenth grade.
    d. after he was shot.

5. Joe tried to kill himself by
    a. swallowing muscle-relaxant pills.
    b. shooting himself.
    c. overdosing on heroin.
    d. not eating or drinking.

6. According to the selection, Joe first met his wife
   a. in the hospital, where she was a nurse.
   (b.) on a city bus, where they were both passengers.
   c. on the job, where she was also a receptionist.
   d. at Community College of Philadelphia, where she was also a student.

7. Joe decided to stop using drugs
   a. when he met his future wife.
   b. right after he was shot.
   (c.) when he awoke from a suicide attempt.
   d. when he was hired as a receptionist.

Inferences

8. We can conclude from paragraph 26 that
   (a.) Joe is willing to reveal very personal information about himself in order to reach young people with his story.
   b. Joe was angry at the Philadelphia students who laughed at parts of his story.
   c. Joe is glad he did not go to college directly from high school.
   d. Joe is still trying to figure out what his life goals are.

The Writer's Craft

9. When the author writes "Joe Davis was the coolest fourteen- [or sixteen- or twenty-five-] year-old he'd ever seen," she is actually expressing
   a. her approval of the way Joe was living then.
   b. her envy of Joe's status in the community.
   c. her mistaken opinion of Joe at these stages in his life.
   (d.) Joe's mistaken opinion of himself at these stages in his life.

10. To conclude her article, Johnson uses
    a. a series of statistics.
    (b.) an anecdote followed by a personal comment.
    c. a summary of her main idea.
    d. a prediction of what will happen to Joe in the future.

DISCUSSION QUESTIONS

1. When speaking of his suicide attempt, Joe said, "It wasn't the spinal cord injury that did it. It was the addiction." What do you think Joe meant? Why do you think he blamed his addiction, rather than his disability, for his decision to try to end his life?

2. Why do you think the students Joe spoke to laughed as he shared personal details of his life? Why did they later quiet down? What effect do you think his presentation had on these students?

3. Joe speaks of wanting to "regain the trust of people he once abused." In other words, he hopes they will give him a second chance. Have you ever given a second chance to someone who had abused your trust? Alternatively, have you ever sought a second chance from someone you had wronged? What happened?

4. Joe wants young people to learn the lessons he has learned without having to experience his hardships. What lessons have you learned in your life that you would like to pass on to others?

PARAGRAPH ASSIGNMENTS

1. Like Joe Davis, many of us have learned painful lessons from life. And like him, we wish we could pass those lessons on to young people to save them from making the same mistakes.

   Write a one-paragraph letter to a young person you know. In it, use your experience to pass on a lesson you wish he or she would learn. Begin with a topic sentence in which you state the lesson you'd like to teach, as in these examples:

   - My own humiliating experience taught me that shoplifting is a very bad idea.
   - I learned the hard way that abandoning your friends for the "cool" crowd will backfire on you.
   - The sad experience of a friend has taught me that teenage girls should not give in to their boyfriends' pressure for sex.
   - Dropping out of high school may seem like a great idea, but what happened to my brother should convince you otherwise.

   Your letter should describe in detail the lesson you learned and how you learned it.

2. Although Joe's parents loved him, they weren't able to stop him from using drugs, skipping school, and doing other self-destructive things. Think of a time that you have seen someone you cared about doing something you thought was bad for him or her. What did you do? What did you *want* to do?

   Write a paragraph in which you describe the situation and how you responded. In it, make sure you answer the following questions:

- What was the person doing?
- Why was I concerned about him or her?
- Did I feel there was anything I could do?
- Did I take any action?
- How did the situation finally turn out?

ESSAY ASSIGNMENTS

1. One of Joe's goals is to regain the trust of the friends and family members he abused during his earlier life. Have you ever given a second chance to someone who treated you poorly? Write an essay about what happened. You could begin with a thesis statement something like this: "Although my closest friend betrayed my trust, I decided to give him another chance."

   You could then go on to structure the rest of your essay in this way:

   - In your first supporting paragraph, explain what the person did to lose your trust. Maybe it was an obviously hurtful action, like physically harming you or stealing from you. Or perhaps it was something more subtle, like insulting or embarrassing you.
   - In your second supporting paragraph, explain why you decided to give the person another chance.
   - In your third supporting paragraph, tell what happened as a result of your giving the person a second chance. Did he or she treat you better this time? Or did the bad treatment start over again?
   - In your concluding paragraph, provide some final thoughts about what you learned from the experience.

   Alternatively, write an essay about a time that you were given a second chance by someone whose trust you had abused. Follow the same pattern of development.

2. Obviously, young people often do not learn from the experiences of others. For example, despite all the evidence about how harmful smoking is to health, young people continue to smoke. The same can be said for careless driving, drug and alcohol abuse, and other reckless behaviors.

   Write an essay in which you explore possible reasons why young people often disregard the experience of others and, instead, learn their lessons the hard way.

6

From Horror to Hope
Phany Sarann

Preview

The horrors of war had made Phany Sarann's existence in Cambodia terribly difficult. She came to the United States full of optimism, believing she was leaving behind her life of hardship. To her despair, she found a new kind of nightmare waiting. Phany's account of her search for a better life won a major award in a college writing contest.

Words to Watch

communal (3): public
trudged (3): walked in a slow, struggling manner
stalks (3): stems
guerrillas (5): rebel fighters
bribe (8): an illegal payoff
forbade (12): would not allow

For the hundredth time, I closed my bedroom door, collapsed on the bed, and started to sob. Covering my face, I tried to cry silently, so my aunt and uncle wouldn't hear. Once again I asked myself why they were so cruel to me. Didn't they remember that they had invited me to work for them in America in exchange for my college education? Since my uncle had gone to college in Cambodia, why didn't he understand that education was so important to me, too? My life had already been too full of challenges. Having gone through so much and come so far, would I be defeated now?

When Pol Pot's Khmer Rouge soldiers* took charge of my life and my   2
country in 1975, they forced people like my family, who lived in the city of Phnom Penh, to move to the countryside. My father understood that we would be gone for a long time, so he made sure we took everything possible with us. Somehow, somewhere, he found a tractor and trailer. Since my three sisters and I were little, we rode on the wagon while my older brother and the adults walked behind. The horrible April weather cooked us and turned the dirt roads to dust. We settled first in a remote mountainous region near the Cambodian-Thai border, where we had to carry all our water from a muddy canal about half an hour's walk away. Later the Khmer Rouge moved us to a site along a river. There, at least, we could catch fish to eat. Soon my father was trading smoked fish for oranges, coffee, rice, and medicine.

After a year, the local authorities sent an oxcart to move our family   3
again. They said it was because our settlement was too crowded, but my mom said the real reason was that my dad would not respect their authority. Dad hated having the uneducated local people control everything. The crops we grew, the chickens we raised, the people we talked to, the places we could and could not go, and even the family's children—all were controlled not by us, but by the authorities. After we were moved, we were all together for a few months, but then the Khmer Rouge began to separate our family. My brother and oldest sister were sent to a labor camp to dig canals by hand. My father was sent away for months to cut wood for the communal° kitchens. While I missed him, I was too hungry to feel much of anything but emptiness. My mother had to work in the rice fields all day, but thankfully she could come home at night. There were no schools and no hospitals. Many of our companions died of starvation, disease, and exhaustion. Even tiny children worked: as soon they were big enough to walk, they joined us in the rice fields. Day after day we trudged° behind the rice cutters, collecting the stalks° that they had missed. All our dreams were about finding food. The rice we harvested was hidden away or exported while we were given only one cup of watery porridge a day. To survive, we ate whatever we could find: rats, crickets, caterpillars, snakes, frogs, and boiled banana tree bark. Our only hope was that some day our country would be rescued from the Khmer Rouge.

---

*The murderous dictator Pol Pot and his military group, the Khmer Rouge, ruled the country of Cambodia for four years and were responsible for the deaths of over one million people.

The horror grew worse when my father was accused of stealing one of   4
our own chickens. My parents heard that my father would soon be
"taken," which we knew meant executed, so he decided to escape. On the
day he ran away, my sister and I met him on our way back from the fields.
"Look after yourselves and tell your mother that I am leaving," he said. "I
do not know when I will see you again."

In March of 1979, Vietnamese and Cambodian troops came to set us   5
free. It took us two days to walk from the village back to town, and since
I did not have shoes, I tried to make some from layers of leaves. When
they fell apart, I cried and limped along on blistered feet. At first, we
thought our nightmare was over because there were no more killings and
nobody was forcing us to work. But we were starving. My mother
exchanged her diamond ring for rice to feed our hungry family. After the
rice was gone, we began a series of moves, trying to find a place where
life would be better. But there was no peace, because the Khmer Rouge
guerrillas° and the new government troops were at war. Finally we arrived
again in our old home of Phnom Penh.

All this time we kept hoping to see my father's face again. But in late   6
1981 we all wept to learn of his death. He had been shot by the Khmer
Rouge as he swam across a river to escape them. There would be no more
support from the man who was the most important part of our family. My
mother was very sad; nevertheless, she struggled hard to bring up four
daughters by herself.

That same year, we three younger girls began school. My sisters   7
eventually quit in favor of going to work, but I felt that getting an
education was the most important goal in my life. Struggling through
high school was especially difficult because my family did not understand
why I was doing it. Traditionally, Cambodians believe that education is
important only for boys, so daughters are not encouraged to go to school.
Many times when I came home from school, exhausted from studying,
my mom would complain. "What makes you tired?" she would ask. "You
just go there, sit and listen, but do nothing! But I have to carry heavy loads
and move all the time!" My mother also kept reminding me that she could
not support me past high school. How could I continue my education?
Then, after I graduated from high school in 1989 and my mother offered
to buy me a small stall at the local market, I had an idea. I told her, "I will
not sell things at the market, but if I do all the housework and all the
cooking for the whole family, can I keep on studying? If I study English
now, I can find a good job to support myself later." While she did not give
me an answer, she did not make me go to the market either.

Even without my mother's support, I kept trying to get into college.   8
However, I soon found how corrupt the educational system was. If I didn't

have the money to pay a bribe°, I would not be admitted even though my test scores were adequate. I sadly gave up the thought of college, but I started studying English in a private class. I would wake up every morning at 4:30 and ride my bicycle through the cold, dark streets to my class. I never wanted to get out of bed and go out into the cold. I was also scared people might hurt me and take my bike. But I went anyway. Soon, I found four Cambodians who wanted to speak English, so I began teaching them what I was learning. Life was full of challenges, but I was learning English and earning money too.

I realized how much more I had to learn when I took a job working for   9
the United States Agency for International Development (USAID). After each staff meeting, I left the room with an aching head and an unsure feeling about what I was supposed to do. Having to make presentations in English was like a nightmare for me. Writing reports in English was the worst of all. The simplest report took me hours and hours because I spent so much time checking words in a dictionary.

After a year my uncle, who had immigrated to Houston, Texas, asked   10
me to come to work in his doughnut shop. In exchange, he promised to pay for my education in America. In great excitement, I quit my good job at USAID, said farewell to my family and friends, and came to Texas. This seemed like a dream come true—not only would I receive a good education, but I would meet many new people and have wonderful new experiences.

But the reality of my life in America was nothing like my dreams.   11
Before school began, I worked hard seven days a week. When the school term started, I worked every weekend. I arranged hot doughnuts on the shelves, filled napkin boxes, made coffee, cleared tables, and sold doughnuts. Many times each day I washed all the trays we used for displaying and serving doughnuts. The hot water burned my hands, but my uncle and aunt refused to let me wear gloves, for fear they would slow me down.

Instead of treating me like a member of their family, my uncle and   12
aunt regarded me with great suspicion. Because they were afraid I would steal money from the registers, they gave me working clothes with no pockets. Regularly, they searched my room, went through my belongings, and even opened and read my mail. Even my little bit of free time was not my own. I was allowed to go only to classes. When I asked to go to the Buddhist temple to honor my father on Cambodian New Year's Day and the Day of the Dead, the answer was "no." My dreams of making new friends evaporated too. My uncle and aunt forbade° me to say anything but "hi" or "good morning" to people who came in the doughnut shop. I felt I was living in a prison with no walls.

Once the shop was closed, the work continued. My uncle and aunt 13
expected me to keep house for their family. I had to prepare their main
meal every day and clean up after it. Three times a week, I mopped the
floors and scrubbed the fixtures. I also swept and dusted all through the
house once a week. How could they have forgotten to tell me that they
also expected me to do all of this? But I swallowed my anger, gritted my
teeth, and kept quiet.

After ten months of this life, my uncle announced that he could not 14
pay for my tuition anymore and that I had to go back to Cambodia. The
excuse was a lie; I knew his business was making money. This sad
experience with my aunt and uncle taught me not to trust people just
because they are relatives.

While I felt angry, used, and scared, I also felt the freedom of the 15
decision before me. Would I let my uncle force me to return to
Cambodia? I decided the answer was no. I left my uncle's house and
moved in with Nancy Dean, my former English teacher. Hearing of my
plight, my former boss at USAID offered me a plane ticket to Michigan,
where I could live with her parents and continue my education.

How excited I was to travel to Michigan, and how nervous—I had 16
never met the people I was going to live with. However, the minute I got
off the plane and met Gale and Roberta Lott, I knew a new life was about
to begin. Gale and Roberta treat me as one of their children. The special
attention they give me makes me feel complete for the first time in my
life. Good things have continued to happen since I enrolled at Lansing
Community College. I like all my classes, people are very friendly, and I
have found a part-time job in the Student and Academic Support office.

My past has been full of challenges; some of these I could control, and 17
some I could not. Learning to deal with challenges has made me a
stronger person with the confidence to pursue my dreams. I plan to
transfer to a university and graduate with a bachelor of arts degree and
then return to my homeland. I hope that a degree from an American
university will help me move into a leadership role in Cambodia. Since
education for women is still not valued there, my next challenge will be
to make my culture understand that educating women will make my
country a better place for everyone.

FIRST IMPRESSIONS

Freewrite for ten minutes on one of the following.

1. Did you enjoy reading this selection? Why or why not?

2. Which details of Phany's life in Cambodia impressed or surprised you the most? Why?

3. Do you know people who think education is a waste of time—especially for girls? Why do you think they feel this way?

VOCABULARY CHECK

A. Circle the letter of the word or phrase that best completes each of the following four items.

1. In the sentence below, the word *harvested* means
   (a.) gathered.
   b. stole.
   c. ate.
   d. lost.

   "The rice we harvested was hidden away or exported while we were given only one cup of watery porridge a day." (Paragraph 3)

2. In the sentences below, the word *corrupt* means
   a. modern.
   b. difficult.
   (c.) dishonest.
   d. strong.

   "I soon found how corrupt the educational system was. If I didn't have the money to pay a bribe, I would not be admitted. . . ." (Paragraph 8)

3. In the sentences below, the word *evaporated* means
   a. came true.
   b. made good sense.
   (c.) disappeared.
   d. were similar.

   "My dreams of making new friends evaporated too. My uncle and aunt forbade me to say anything but 'hi' or 'good morning' to people who came in the doughnut shop." (Paragraph 12)

4. In the sentence below, the word *gritted* means
   a. cleaned.
   b. displayed proudly.
   (c.) closed tightly.
   d. bared fiercely.

   > "But I swallowed my anger, gritted my teeth, and kept quiet."
   > (Paragraph 13)

B. Circle the letter of the answer that best completes each of the following four items. Each item uses a word (or form of a word) from "Words to Watch."

5. *Communal* baths, such as those popular in Japan, are
   a. filled with icy cold water.
   (b.) shared by many people at once.
   c. very shallow.

6. From the way that Allan *trudged* through the door after his date with Ellie, I concluded that
   (a.) the date had not gone well.
   b. they had eaten at his favorite restaurant.
   c. he was happy and excited.

7. Which of these situations would be considered a *bribe*?
   a. Gary sends in an annual contribution to the Montgomery County Police Association.
   b. Gary pays a parking ticket.
   (c.) Gary offers a police officer twenty dollars to "forget" that Gary had been speeding.

8. It is understandable that Mrs. Oliver *forbade* her son to use her car because
   a. he is an especially careful, responsible driver.
   b. he washes the car every time it gets the least bit dirty.
   (c.) he has had three accidents in the last two weeks.

READING CHECK

Central Point and Main Ideas

1. Which sentence best expresses the central point of the selection?
    a. People would have a better life if they stayed in the country where they were born.
    b. Phany Sarann overcame extreme difficulties and succeeded in getting an education.
    c. People never know what challenges they will face in life.
    d. When the Khmer Rouge soldiers took charge of Cambodia, life became horrible for the author and her family.

2. The main idea of paragraph 9 is expressed in its
    a. first sentence.
    b. second sentence.
    c. next-to-last sentence.
    d. last sentence.

3. The main idea of paragraph 17 is expressed in its
    a. first sentence.
    b. second sentence.
    c. third sentence.
    d. last sentence.

Key Supporting Details

4. Phany's father decided to run away after he was accused of
    a. joining the Khmer Rouge.
    b. stealing a chicken.
    c. illegally studying English.
    d. cutting wood that didn't belong to him.

5. According to the selection, the author
    a. did not believe her uncle when he said he could not pay for her tuition.
    b. was fired from her job at USAID.
    c. never went to school in Houston.
    d. was forced to move back to Cambodia from the United States.

6. __F__ TRUE OR FALSE? The author moved from Houston to Cambodia to Michigan.

Inferences

7. Phany implies that her uncle
    a. was actually stealing money from her.
    b. greatly respected Phany's dead father.
    c. was himself uneducated.
    (d.) saw Phany only as a source of cheap labor.

8. We can conclude that
    (a.) Phany's former employer at USAID thought highly of her.
    b. Phany never intends to return to Cambodia.
    c. Gale and Roberta Lott used to live in Cambodia.
    d. Phany's uncle was a devout Buddhist.

The Writer's Craft

9. The tone of this essay is
    (a.) serious and determined.
    b. bitter and vengeful.
    c. optimistic and humorous.
    d. hopeless and despairing.

10. In paragraph 3, the author
    a. gives the history of the Khmer Rouge.
    b. quotes a well-known expert who has written about the Khmer Rouge.
    (c.) gives examples of the horrible conditions of life under the Khmer Rouge.
    d. provides statistics about the Khmer Rouge.

DISCUSSION QUESTIONS

1. Can you understand why Phany's mother might not have supported her daughter's desire to continue her education? How did Phany's point of view regarding education differ from her mother's? Why do you think their views were so different?

2. What were the actual reasons Phany's uncle wanted her to come to the United States? Why do you think he changed his mind and wanted to send her back to Cambodia?

3. Phany's job at her uncle's doughnut shop turned out to be a nightmare. What is the worst job you have ever had? What made it so terrible?

4. What challenges have you faced in getting to college? Describe one or two obstacles and how you overcame them.

PARAGRAPH ASSIGNMENTS

1. If you had a chance to meet Phany, what would you like to say to her? Write her a one-paragraph letter in response to her story. In your letter, you might do one or more of the following:

    *   Tell her what parts of her story you think were most memorable, touching, or troubling.

    *   Share an experience of your own that you think she could relate to because it is in some way similar to something she has gone through.

    *   Tell her what you think of her plan to return to Cambodia to work on behalf of women's education there.

    *   Tell her what kind of person you think she must be, judging from her story.

    You might begin with a topic sentence similar to one of the following:

    *   Phany, I think you would understand the difficulties I have had in trying to get a good education.

    *   After reading your story, I think you are a person with very high standards.

    *   For several reasons, I admire your decision to return to Cambodia and work for women's rights.

2. Both in Cambodia and in Houston, Phany encountered cruel people. Write a paragraph in which you describe a cruel person you have known. In it, be sure to provide specific details that illustrate the person's cruelty.

ESSAY ASSIGNMENTS

1. At first, Phany's uncle's invitation to work in his doughnut shop seemed kind. Later, though, Phany felt that her uncle and aunt had only wanted to use her. Have you ever found that someone who seemed friendly or helpful really wished to take advantage of you? Write an essay about the incident. Begin with a thesis statement, like this one, that tells in general how you were used: "At first I thought Manny was a genuine friend, but I then realized that what he really liked about me was that I would lend him money and help him with his assignments."

    Your essay will probably be organized by time order—explaining what happened first, next, and at the end. Be sure your essay includes the following information:

- Who was involved in the incident?
- What was your first impression of that person's behavior toward you?
- How did you realize you were being taken advantage of?
- What did the person really want of you?
- How did you respond after you realized what the person really wanted?
- As a result of the experience, how did you feel and what did you learn?

2. Write an essay about the worst job or chore that you have ever had. You will need to provide very specific details in order to make your reader understand just how unpleasant it was. Here are some questions you might ask yourself in order to generate such details:

   - Where did I work?
   - What was my position?
   - Exactly what were my duties?
   - What were the physical conditions where I worked?
   - Whom did I work with?
   - Whom did I work for?
   - What was my supervisor like?
   - What were my coworkers like?
   - What aspects of the job (*or* chore) were particularly awful?

7

Migrant Child to College Woman
Maria Cardenas

Preview

Maria Cardenas grew up in a family of migrant workers. As the family moved from state to state, following the fruit and vegetable harvest, Maria became used to backbreaking labor, poverty, and violence. The brutality she encountered, as well as her own lack of education, could have snuffed out her hopes for a better life. But, as this selection will show, Maria has found the courage both to dream and to make her dreams become reality.

Words to Watch

abducted (18): taken away by force
taunted (22): cruelly teased
overwhelmed (24): overcame
briskly (24): in a lively manner
GED (24): general equivalency diploma (equal to a high-school diploma)
eligible (27): qualified

As I walk into the classroom, the teacher gazes at me with her piercing 1
green eyes. I feel myself shrinking and burning up with guilt. I go straight
to her desk and hand her the excuse slip. Just like all the other times, I say,
"I was sick." I hate lying, but I have to. I don't want my parents to get in
trouble.

I'm not a very good liar. She makes me hold out my hands, inspecting   2
my dirty fingernails and calluses. She knows exactly where I've been the
past several days. When you pick tomatoes and don't wear gloves, your
hands get rough and stained from the plant oils. Soap doesn't wash that
out.

In the background, I can hear the students giggling as she asks her   3
usual questions: "What was wrong? Was your brother sick, too? Do you
feel better today?" Of course I don't feel better. My whole body aches
from those endless hot days spent harvesting crops from dawn to dusk. I
was never absent by choice.

That year, in that school, I think my name was "Patricia Rodriguez,"   4
but I'm not sure. My brother and I used whatever name our mother told
us to use each time we went to a new school. We understood that we had
to be registered as the children of parents who were in the United States
legally, in case Immigration ever checked up.

My parents had come to the States in the late '60s to work in the fields   5
and earn money to feed their family. They paid eight hundred dollars to
someone who smuggled them across the border, and they left us with our
aunt and uncle in Mexico. My five-year-old brother, Joel, was the oldest.
I was 4, and then came Teresa, age 3, and baby Bruno. The other kids in
the neighborhood teased us, saying, "They won't come back for you."
Three years later, our parents sent for us to join them in Texas. My little
heart sang as we waved good-bye to those neighbor kids in Rio Verde. My
father did love us!

My parents worked all the time in the fields. Few other options were   6
open to them because they had little education. At first, our education was
important to them. They were too scared to put us in school right away,
but when I was 8 they did enroll us. I do remember that my first-grade
report card said I was "Antonietta Gonzales." My father made sure we had
everything we needed—tablets, crayons, ruler, and the little box to put
your stuff in. He bragged to his friends about his children going to school.
Now we could talk for our parents. We could translate their words for the
grocer, the doctor, and the teachers. If Immigration came by, we could tell
them we were citizens, and because we were speaking English, they
wouldn't ask any more questions.

In the years to come, I often reminded myself that my father had not   7
forgotten us like the fathers of so many kids I knew. It became more
important for me to remember that as it became harder to see that he loved
us. He had hit my mother once in a while as I was growing up, but when
his own mother died in Mexico in 1973, his behavior grew much worse.
My uncles told me that my father, the youngest of the family, had often
beaten his mother. Maybe it was the guilt he felt when she died, but for

whatever reason, he started drinking heavily, abusing my mother emotionally and physically, and terrorizing us kids. The importance of our education faded away, and now my papa thought my brother and I should work more in the fields. We would work all the time—on school vacations, holidays, weekends, and every day after school. When there were lots of tomatoes to pick, I went to school only every other day.

If picking was slow, I stayed home after school and cooked for the   8
family. I started as soon as I got home in the afternoon. I used the three large pots my mother owned: one for beans, one for rice or soup, and one for hot salsa. There were also the usual ten pounds of flour or maseca, ground corn meal, for the tortillas. I loved this cooking because I could eat as much as I wanted and see that the little kids got enough before the older family members finished everything. By this time there were three more children in our family, and we often went to bed hungry. (My best subject in school was lunch, and my plate was always clean.)

Other than lunchtime, my school life passed in a blur. I remember a   9
little about teachers showing us how to sound words out. I began to stumble through elementary readers. But then we'd move again, or I'd be sent to the fields.

Life was never easy in those days. Traveling with the harvest meant   10
living wherever the bosses put us. We might be in little houses with one outdoor toilet for the whole camp. Other times the whole crew, all fifty or one hundred of us, were jammed into one big house. Working in the fields meant blistering sun, aching muscles, sliced fingers, bug bites, and my father yelling when we didn't pick fast enough to suit him.

But we were kids, so we found a way to have some fun. My brother   11
and I would make a game of competing with each other and the other adults. I never did manage to pick more than Joel, but I came close. One time I picked 110 baskets of cucumbers to Joel's 115. We made thirty-five cents a basket.

Of course, we never saw any of that money. At the end of the week,   12
whatever the whole family had earned was given to my father. Soon he stopped working altogether. He just watched us, chatted with the field bosses, and drank beer. He began to beat all of us kids as well as our mother. We didn't work fast enough for him. He wanted us to make more money. He called us names and threw stones and vegetables at us. The other workers did nothing to make him stop. I was always scared of my father, but I loved him even though he treated us so badly. I told myself that he loved us, but that alcohol ruled his life.

I knew what controlled my father's life, but I never thought about   13
being in control of my own. I did as I was told, spoke in a whisper, and tried not to be noticed. Because we traveled with the harvest, my brothers

and sisters and I attended three or four different schools in one year. When picking was good, I went to the fields instead of school. When the little kids got sick, I stayed home to watch them. When I did go to school, I didn't understand very much. We spoke only Spanish at home. I don't know how I got through elementary school, much less to high school, because I only knew how to add, subtract, and multiply. And let's just say I got "introduced" to English writing skills and grammar. School was a strange foreign place where I went when I could, sitting like a ghost in a corner alone. I could read enough to help my mother fill out forms in English. But enough to pick up a story and understand it? Never. When a teacher told the class, "Read this book, and write a report," I just didn't do it. I knew she wasn't talking to me.

In 1978, my mother ran away after two weeks of terrible beatings. Joel and I found the dime under the big suitcase, where she had told us it would be. We were supposed to use it to call the police, but we were too scared. We stayed in the upstairs closet with our brothers and sisters. In the morning, I felt guilty and terrified. I didn't know whether our mother was alive or dead. Not knowing what else to do, I got dressed and went to school. I told the counselor what had happened, and she called the police. My father was arrested. He believed the police when they said they were taking him to jail for unpaid traffic tickets. Then the police located my mother and told her it was safe to come out of hiding. My father never lived with us again although he continued to stalk us. He would stand outside the house yelling at my mother, "You're gonna be a prostitute. Those kids are gonna be no-good drug addicts and criminals. They're gonna end up in jail." 14

My father's words enraged me. I had always had a hunger for knowledge, always dreamed of a fancy job where I would go to work wearing nice clothes and carrying a briefcase. How dare he try to kill my dream! True, the idea of that dream ever coming true seemed unlikely. In school, if I asked about material I didn't understand, most of the teachers seemed annoyed. My mother would warn me, "Please, don't ask so many questions." 15

But then, somehow, when I was 14, Mrs. Mercer noticed me. I don't remember how my conversations with this teacher started, but it led to her offering me a job in the Western clothing store she and her husband owned. I helped translate for the Spanish-speaking customers who shopped there. I worked only Saturdays, and I got paid a whole twenty-dollar bill. Proudly, I presented that money to my mother. The thought "I can actually do more than field work" began to make my dreams seem like possibilities. I began to believe I could be something more. The month of my sixteenth birthday, Mrs. Mercer recommended me for a 16 cashier's job in the local supermarket. I worked there for six weeks, and on Friday, January 16, 1981, I was promoted to head cashier. I was on top of the world! I could not believe such good things were happening to me. I had a good job, and I was on my way to becoming my school's first Spanish-speaking graduate. I thought nothing could go wrong, ever again.

But that very night, my dreams were shattered again—this time, I   17
thought, permanently. The manager let me off at nine, two hours early. I didn't have a ride because my brother was not picking me up until 11:00 p.m. But I was in luck! I saw a man I knew, a friend of my brother's, someone I had worked with in the fields. He was a trusted family friend, so when he offered me a lift, I said, "Of course." Now I could go home and tell everybody about the promotion.

I never made it home or to my big promotion. The car doors were   18
locked; I could not escape. I was abducted° and raped, and I found myself walking down the same abusive road as my mother. My dreams were crushed. I had failed. In my old-fashioned Mexican world, I was a "married woman," even if I wasn't. To go home again would have been to dishonor my family. When I found I was pregnant, there seemed to be only one path open to me. I married my abductor, dropped out of tenth grade, and moved with him to Oklahoma.

"My father was right," I thought. "I am a failure." But dreams die hard.   19
My brother Joel was living in the same Oklahoma town as I was. He would see me around town, my face and body bruised from my husband's beatings. But unlike the workers in the fields who had silently watched our father's abuse, Joel spoke up. "You've got to go," he would urge me. "You don't have to take this. Go on, you can make it."

"No!" I would tell him. I was embarrassed to have anyone know what   20
my life had become. I imagined returning to my mother, only to have her reprimand me, saying, "What's the matter with you that you can't even stay married?"

But Joel wouldn't give up. Finally he told me, "I don't care what you   21
say. I am going to tell Mother what is going on."

And he did. He explained to our mother that I had been forced to go   22
with that man, that I was being abused, and that I was coming home. She accepted what he told her. I took my little girl and the clothes I could carry, threw everything into my car, and left Oklahoma for Florida. My husband taunted° me just as my father had my mother: "You'll be on food stamps! You can't amount to anything on your own!" But I proved him wrong. I worked days in the fields and nights as a cashier, getting off work at midnight and up early the next day to work again. I don't know how I did it, but I kept up the payments on my little car, I didn't go on food stamps, and I was happy.

But as Antonietta grew up and started school, I began to think my little 23 triumphs were not enough. I was thrilled to see her learning to read, doing well in school. And when she would bring me her simple little books and trustingly say, "Read with me!" it filled me with joy. But I realized the day would come, and come soon, that I would be unable to read Antonietta's books. What would she think of me when I said, "I can't"? What would I think of myself?

Teaching myself to read became the most important goal in my life. I 24 began with Antonietta's kindergarten books. I thought sometimes how people would laugh if they saw me, a grown woman, a mother, struggling through *The Cat in the Hat*. But with no one to watch me, I didn't care. Alone in my house, after my daughter was asleep, I read. I read everything we had in the house—Antonietta's books, cereal boxes, advertisements that came in the mail. I forced myself through them, stumbling again and again over unfamiliar words. Eventually I began to feel ready to try a real story, a grown-up story. But my fears nearly stopped me again. We lived near a library. Antonietta had asked again and again to go there. Finally I said "all right." We walked in, but panic overwhelmed° me. All those people, walking around so briskly°, knowing where to find the books they wanted and how to check them out! What was someone like me doing there? What if someone asked me what I wanted? Too intimidated to even try, I insisted that we leave. I told Antonietta to use the library at her school. I struggled on in private, eventually earning my GED°.

The years passed, and I married a wonderful man who loved me and 25 my daughter. He was proud that I had some real education, and he knew that I wanted more. But I couldn't imagine that going on in school was possible.

Then, in 1987, I was working for the Redlands Christian Migrant 26 Association. They provided services for migrant children. One day, in the office, I spotted something that made my heart jump. It was a book called *Dark Harvest*. It was filled with stories about migrant workers. Although my reading skills had improved, I had still never read a book. But this one was about people like me. I began reading it, slowly at first, then with more and more interest. Some of the people in it had gone back for a GED, just as I had! Even more—some had gone on to college and earned a degree in education. Now they were teaching. When I read that book, I realized that my dream wasn't crazy.

My husband and I took the steps to become legally admitted residents 27 of the United States. Then, my husband found out about a federal program that helps seasonal farm workers go to college. I applied and found I was eligible°. When I took my diagnostic tests, my reading,

English, and math levels turned out to be seventh-grade level. Not as bad as I thought! The recruiter asked if I would mind attending Adult Basic Education classes to raise my scores to the twelfth-grade level. Mind? I was thrilled! I loved to study, and in spite of a serious illness that kept me out of classes for weeks, my teacher thought I was ready to try the ABE exams early. Her encouragement gave my confidence a boost, and I found my scores had zoomed up to a 12.9 level.

Then, in the fall of 1994, I took the greatest step of my academic life.   28
Proud and excited, I started classes at Edison Community College in Florida. Of course, I was also terrified, trembling inside almost like that scared little girl who used to tiptoe up to the teacher's desk with her phony absence excuses. But I'm not a scared little kid anymore. My self-confidence is growing, even if it's growing slowly.

I laugh when I look back at that day I fled in terror from the library.   29
My family and I might as well live there now. We walk in with me saying, "Now, we have other things to do today. Just half an hour." Three hours later, it's the kids saying to me, "Mom, are you ready yet?" But it's so exciting, knowing that I can learn about anything I want just by picking up a book! I've read dozens of how-to books, many of them about gardening, which has become my passion. I can't put down motivational books, like Ben Carson's *Gifted Hands* and *Think Big*. I love Barbara Kingsolver's novels. One of them, *The Bean Trees*, was about a young woman from a very poor area in Kentucky whose only goal, at first, was to finish school without having a child. I could understand her. But my favorite author is Maya Angelou. Right now, I'm re-reading her book *I Know Why The Caged Bird Sings*. She writes so honestly about the tragedy and poverty she's lived with. She was raped when she was little, and she had a child when she was very young. And now she's a leader, a wonderful writer and poet. When I see her—she read a poem at President Clinton's inauguration—I am very moved. And I can't talk about my life now without mentioning Kenneth and Mary Jo Walker, the president of Edison Community College and his wife. They offered me a job in their home, but so much more than that: they have become my friends, my guardian angels. I am constantly borrowing books from them, and they give me so much encouragement that I tell them, "You have more faith in me than I do myself."

Sometimes I have to pinch myself to believe that my life today is real.   30
I have a hard-working husband and three children, all of whom I love very much. My son Korak is 11. Whatever he studies in school—the Aztecs, the rainforest, Mozart—he wants to find more books in the library about it, to learn more deeply. Jasmine, my little girl, is 7, and is reading through the *Little House on the Prairie* books. Like me, the children have

worked in the fields, but there is little resemblance between their lives and mine as a child. They are in one school the whole year long. They work at their own pace, learning the value of work and of money—and they keep what they earn. Antonietta, who inspired me to begin reading, is 17 now. Although she's only a junior in high school, she's taking college calculus classes and planning to study pre-med in college, even though her teachers have encouraged her to become a journalist because of her skill in writing.

And guess what! My teachers compliment my writing too. When I 31 enrolled in my developmental English class at Edison, my teacher, Johanna Seth, asked the class to write a narrative paragraph. A narrative, she explained, tells a story. As I thought about what story I could write, a picture of a scared little girl in a schoolroom popped into my head. I began writing:

> *As I walk into the classroom, the teacher gazes at me with her* 32
> *piercing green eyes. I feel myself shrinking and burning up with guilt.*
> *I go straight to her desk and hand her the excuse slip. Just like all the*
> *other times, I say, "I was sick." I hate lying, but I have to. I don't want*
> *my parents to get in trouble.*

I finish my narrative about giving my phony excuses to my grade- 33 school teachers and hand it in. I watch Mrs. Seth read it and, to my horror, she begins to cry. I know it must be because she is so disappointed, that what I have written is so far from what the assignment was meant to be that she doesn't know where to begin to correct it.

"Did you write this?" she asks me. Of course, she knows I wrote it, 34 but she seems disbelieving. "You wrote this?" she asks again. Eventually I realize that she is not disappointed. Instead, she is telling me something incredible and wonderful. She is saying that my work is good, and that she is very happy with what I've given her. She is telling me that I can succeed here.

And now I know she's right. I'm graduating from Edison as a member 35 of Phi Theta Kappa, the national academic honors society for junior colleges. I'll enroll in the fall at Florida Gulf Coast University to finish my degree in elementary education. I will spend the summer working, maybe picking crops once again. But in the fall, when my children return to school, so will I. I have a goal: to teach migrant children to speak English, to stand on their own two feet, to achieve their dreams. In helping them, I will be making my own dream come true.

FIRST IMPRESSIONS

Freewrite for ten minutes on one of the following.

1. Did you enjoy reading this selection? Why or why not?

2. Have you ever known anyone who frequently moved from one town (or school) to another? What effects did all that moving have on the person?

3. Why do you think Maria didn't immediately leave her first husband when he began to beat her? If you were in Maria's situation, what would you have done?

VOCABULARY CHECK

A. Circle the letter of the word or phrase that best completes each of the following four items.

1. In the sentences below, the word *options* means
   a. opinions.
   b. pleasures.
   c. gifts.
   d. choices.

   "My parents worked all the time in the fields. Few other options were open to them because they had little education." (Paragraph 6)

2. In the sentence below, the word *reprimand* means
   a. scold.
   b. ignore.
   c. compliment.
   d. support.

   "I imagined returning to my mother, only to have her reprimand me, saying, 'What's the matter with you that you can't even stay married?'" (Paragraph 20)

3. In the sentences on the next page, the word *intimidated* means
   a. thoughtful.
   b. bored.
   c. fearful.
   d. critical.

"We walked in, but panic overwhelmed me. . . . What was someone like me doing there? What if someone asked me what I wanted? Too intimidated to even try, I insisted that we leave." (Paragraph 24)

4. In the sentence below, the word *resemblance* means
    a. difference.
    b. similarity.
    c. confusion.
    d. pride.

    "Like me, the children have worked in the fields, but there is little resemblance between their lives and mine as a child." (Paragraph 30)

B. Circle the letter of the answer that best completes each of the following four items. Each item uses a word (or form of a word) from "Words to Watch."

5. "Aliens *Abduct* Movie Star!" read the headline. I read the story, eager to know how the aliens had
    a. imitated the movie star.
    b. kidnapped the movie star.
    c. hired the movie star.

6. Lucy *taunted* Marcia about her clothes, saying,
    a. "Did you get that dress out of the garbage?"
    b. "That color looks pretty on you."
    c. "My sister has a dress like that."

7. Which animal is most likely to move *briskly*?
    a. A snail.
    b. A racehorse.
    c. A turtle.

8. Which of the following would not be *eligible* to enter the Miss America contest?
    a. An unmarried woman.
    b. A woman from Ohio.
    c. An Italian citizen.

READING CHECK

Central Point and Main Ideas

1. Which sentence best expresses the central point of the entire selection?
    a. Maria's goal is to graduate from college and teach migrant children to achieve their dreams.
    b. With hard work and courage, Maria was able to overcome great difficulties to build a wonderful family and go to college.
    c. Some books are filled with inspirational stories that can help us all.
    d. Maria shows that certain skills, including writing and mathematical abilities, are necessary if we want to succeed in college.

2. The topic sentence of paragraph 10 is its
    a. first sentence.
    b. second sentence.
    c. third sentence.
    d. last sentence.

3. Which sentence best expresses the main idea of paragraph 26?
    a. In 1987, Maria worked for the Redlands Christian Migrant Association.
    b. The book *Dark Harvest* convinced Maria that her dream for a better education wasn't crazy.
    c. The Redlands Christian Migrant Association provided services for migrant children.
    d. The book *Dark Harvest* contained stories about migrant workers, including some who had gone on to college and became teachers.

Key Supporting Details

4. Maria's father began to drink heavily and abuse his wife more than ever after
    a. he lost his job.
    b. his children began going to school.
    c. Immigration came to the house.
    d. his mother died.

5. To see if Maria had been working in the fields, her teacher inspected her
    a. clothing.
    b. homework.
    c. shoes.
    d. hands.

6. Maria was encouraged to leave her abusive husband by her
   a. mother.
   b. daughter.
   c. brother.
   d. employer.

Inferences

7. ___F___ TRUE OR FALSE? Maria and her parents immigrated to the United States at the same time.

8. From the article, we can conclude that
   a. none of Maria's high school teachers thought she would ever amount to anything.
   b. at least one of Maria's teachers, Mrs. Mercer, realized that Maria was intelligent and hard-working.
   c. Maria would have done better in school if she had followed her mother's advice and not asked any questions.
   d. when Maria was promoted to head cashier, she immediately made plans to quit high school.

The Writer's Craft

9. The author introduces her article by
   a. describing the life of a migrant worker.
   b. telling a story about her experience in school.
   c. discussing the need for better schools for migrant children.
   d. imagining herself as a teacher.

10. The relationship of the second sentence below to the first is one of
    a. addition.
    b. time order.
    c. comparison.
    d. conclusion.

    "Proud and excited, I started classes at Edison Community College in Florida. Of course, I was also terrified. . . ." (Paragraph 28)

DISCUSSION QUESTIONS

1. Maria's children work in the fields, as their mother had. In what ways are those children's lives different from Maria's life when she was a child working in the fields?

2. Why might it have been so important to Maria to learn to read after her daughter began school? What do you think she imagined might happen if she did *not* learn to read?

3. Why do you think Mrs. Seth cried upon reading Maria's narrative about giving phony excuses to her grade-school teacher? Why might Maria have thought that Mrs. Seth was disappointed with what she had written?

4. What do you think Maria means when she says she wants to teach migrant children to "stand on their own two feet"? What do you think all children must learn in order to "stand on their own two feet"?

PARAGRAPH ASSIGNMENTS

1. All through her adult life, Maria Cardenas has made herself do things that were very scary or difficult for her. For example, she left an abusive husband, despite not knowing how she would cope on her own. She made herself learn to read. She forced herself to begin college. She did all these things because she believed the long-term benefits would outweigh the short-term difficulties.

   When have you made yourself do something difficult, even though it would have been easier not to? Maybe it was one of these:

   - Apologizing for something you did wrong
   - Starting a new class or job
   - Moving to a new town
   - Speaking up for yourself to someone who was treating you badly

   Write a paragraph about what you did and why. In it, answer these questions:

   - What did I do that was difficult?
   - Why did I find doing it so hard or frightening?
   - Why did I think doing it would be worthwhile?
   - How did I feel about myself after I'd done it?

   You might begin with a topic sentence similar to one of the following:

   - One of the hardest things I've ever had to do was to transfer to a new school halfway through my freshman year.

- Apologizing to my sister for playing a cruel trick on her was a difficult moment for me.

2. Maria feels a strong drive to help migrant children learn to speak English and to "stand on their own two feet."

   If you were offered the chance to help a particular group of people, who would it be? Write a paragraph in which you explain what group you would help and why and, finally, what you would do to help the people in this group.

   Or instead, if you are now a volunteer with a particular group, write a paragraph about your experiences with that group. Tell why you decided to volunteer, what you actually do, and what the rewards are. Remember to give specific examples from your volunteering experience to support your general points.

ESSAY ASSIGNMENTS

1. Like Maria, many people reach adulthood without having learned to read well. Unlike Maria, many of those people live the rest of their lives as non-readers.

   Learning to read as an adult is challenging for a number of reasons. Some of those reasons are as follows:

   - Easy-to-read material is often written for small children, and such material may seem boring or insulting to adults.
   - Adults are often ashamed of being poor readers, and they may fear they will be further humiliated if they seek help.
   - Adults often have work and family commitments that make attending classes difficult.

   Keeping those challenges in mind, write an essay in which you describe a plan for teaching adults in your community to read. You could begin with a thesis statement something like this: "For our adult-literacy program to succeed, it will have to deal with several challenges." Then go on to organize your essay by addressing a specific challenge in each paragraph and explaining how you would overcome it.

2. Many people would describe Maria as courageous. She is courageous not because she goes out and performs dramatic, heroic acts, but because she has faced her fears and made brave choices, not easy ones.

   Think of someone you know whom you would consider courageous. Write an essay in which you describe this person and explain why you see him or her as brave. Include specific examples that demonstrate this person's courage.

8

He Was First
John Kellmayer

Preview

Jackie Robinson is widely known as the superb athlete who broke major-league baseball's "color line" in 1947. But as this story shows, it is worth remembering just what Robinson went through to achieve that breakthrough. The Robinson story also shows how professional baseball's white establishment, spurred both by self-interest and a growing distaste for racism, pinned its hopes on Robinson, his skills, and—most of all—his character.

Words to Watch

transition (3): change
exclusion (4): restriction from participating
bigotry (6): prejudice
rampant (6): widespread
staunch (7): strong
conclave (14): meeting
cantankerous (21): ill-tempered
prestigious (29): highly respected
tumultuous (31): noisy
adulation (31): great admiration

Today few people remember what it was like *not* to see blacks in 1 professional baseball.

But until April 15, 1947, when Jackie Robinson played his first game 2 with the Brooklyn Dodgers, the world of major-league baseball was a whites-only world.

The transition° was not an easy one. It took place largely because 3 Branch Rickey, owner of the Dodgers, held on to a dream of integrating baseball and because Jackie Robinson had the character, talent, and support to carry him through an ugly obstacle course of racism.

Even before he arrived in professional baseball, Robinson had to 4 combat discrimination. Robinson entered the army with a national college reputation as an outstanding athlete. Still, he was denied permission to play on the football and baseball teams at Fort Riley, Kansas, where he was stationed. He had been allowed to practice with the football team, but when the first game against an opposing team came up, Robinson was sent home on a pass. His exclusion° from the baseball team there was more direct. A member of that team recalls what happened: "One day we were out at the field practicing when a Negro lieutenant tried out for the team. An officer told him, 'You have to play with the colored team.' That was a joke. There was no colored team." Robinson walked silently off the field.

Eventually, Robinson was granted an honorable discharge, and soon 5 after he signed a contract to play baseball in the Negro American League.

At this time Branch Rickey was waiting for his opportunity to sign a 6 black ballplayer and to integrate major-league baseball. He understood not only that the black ballplayer could be good box office but that bigotry° had to be fought. While involved with his college baseball team, he had been deeply moved by a nasty scene in which his star catcher, an outstanding young black man, was prohibited from registering at a hotel with the rest of the team. Rickey then became determined to do something about the rampant° racism in baseball.

By 1944, the social climate had become more accepting of integration, 7 in large part because of the contribution of black soldiers in World War II. Also, when the commissioner of baseball, a staunch° opponent of integration, died in 1944, he was replaced by a man named Happy Chandler. Chandler was on record as supporting integration of the game—"If a black man can make it at Okinawa and go to Guadalcanal, he can make it in baseball."

Rickey knew the time had come. He began searching for the special 8 black ballplayer with the mix of talent and character necessary to withstand the struggles to follow. When he learned about a star player in the Negro American League named Jackie Robinson, he arranged to meet with him.

At their meeting, Rickey said, "Jack, I've been looking for a great   9
colored ballplayer, but I need more than a great player. I need a man who
will accept insults, take abuse, in a word, carry the flag for his race. I want
a man who has the courage not to fight, not to fight back. If a guy slides
into you at second base and calls you a black son of a bitch, I wouldn't
blame you if you came up swinging. You'd be right. You'd be justified.
But you'd set the cause back twenty years. I want a man with courage
enough not to fight back. Can you do that?"

Robinson thought for a few minutes before answering, "If you want to   10
take this gamble, I promise you there'll be no incidents." The promise was
not easily made. Robinson had encountered plenty of racism in his life,
and he was accustomed to fighting for black rights. He was known by his
teammates in the Negro American League to have a fast temper.
Consequently, keeping his promise to Rickey was going to require great
personal will.

After signing with the Dodgers in October 1945, Robinson did not   11
have to wait long to put his patience to the test. Even before he began to
play with the Dodger organization, he and his wife, Rachel, encountered
the humiliation of Southern racism.

It began when the Robinsons flew from Los Angeles to spring training   12
in Florida, two weeks after they got married. On a stop in New Orleans,
they were paged and asked to get off the plane. They later learned that, in
the South, whites who wanted seats on a flight took preference over
blacks already seated. Their places had been given to a white couple.
They had to wait a day to get another flight and then were told to get off
for yet another white couple at a stop in Pensacola, Florida. The
Robinsons then had to take a segregated bus the rest of the way to
Jacksonville, where Branch Rickey had a car waiting for them. Of that
trip, Rachel Robinson later said, "It sharpened for us the drama of what
we were about to go into. We got a lot tougher thereafter."

Soon after, during an exhibition game in Florida, Jackie suffered   13
another humiliation, the first of many more to come on the diamond.
During the first inning of that game, a police officer came onto the field
and told Jackie, "Your people don't play with no white boys. Get off the
field right now, or you're going to jail." Jackie had no choice but to walk
quietly off the field. Not one of his teammates spoke up for him then.

Robinson's assignment to the Dodger minor-league team in Montreal   14
was evidence of Rickey's careful planning for the breaking of the color
barrier, as there was little racism in the Canadian city. That fact became
important in supporting the spirits of Jackie and Rachel against the
horrible outpouring of hate that greeted him at each stop on the road.
Baseball historian Robert Smith wrote that when Robinson first appeared
in Syracuse, "the fans reacted in a manner so raucous, obscene, and

disgusting that it might have shamed a conclave° of the Ku Klux Klan."
It was during this game that a Syracuse player threw a black cat at Jackie
and yelled, "Hey, Jackie, there's your cousin." In Baltimore, the players
shouted racist insults, threw balls at his head, and tried to spike him. In
addition, as would be the case at many stops through the years, Jackie
wasn't allowed to stay at the same hotel as the rest of the team.

Robinson's manager at Montreal was Clay Hopper, a Mississippi   15
native adamantly opposed at first to the presence of Robinson on his ball
club. Rickey once stood near Hopper during a game when Robinson made
a superb dive to make an out, and Rickey commented that Robinson
seemed "superhuman." Hopper's reply was, "Do you really think he's a
human being?"

No civil rights legislation could have turned Clay Hopper around the   16
way Jackie Robinson did. By the end of a season in which Robinson led
his team to the minor-league World Series, Hopper told Robinson,
"You're a great ballplayer and a fine gentleman. It's been wonderful
having you on the team." Hopper would later remark to Rickey, "You
don't have to worry none about that boy. He's the greatest competitor I
ever saw, and what's more, he's a gentleman."

It was clear that Jackie Robinson's next stop was the big leagues, the   17
Brooklyn Dodgers. Not surprisingly, though, the prospect of a black
major-league player was not met by all with open arms. Just how much
resistance there was, however, could be seen in the meeting of the
baseball club owners in January of 1947 in which every owner but Rickey
voted against allowing Jackie to play.

Fortunately, commissioner Happy Chandler had another point of view.   18
He later told Rickey, "Mr. Rickey, I'm going to have to meet my maker
some day. If He asked me why I didn't let this man play, and I answered,
'Because he's a Negro,' that might not be a sufficient answer. I will
approve of the transfer of Robinson's contract from Montreal to
Brooklyn." So the color barrier was broken, and Robinson became a
member of the Brooklyn Dodgers.

Robinson's talent meant less to some of the Brooklyn players than   19
race. The prospect of a black teammate prompted a Dodger outfielder, a
Southerner by the name of Dixie Walker, to pass among the other
Southern players a petition urging Rickey to ban Robinson from their
team. Walker gathered signatures and his petition gained momentum until
he approached shortstop Pee Wee Reese, a Kentucky native. Robinson
had originally been signed on as a shortstop and could have posed a real
threat to Reese's job. Nonetheless, Reese refused to sign the petition.
Reese was one of the leaders of the Brooklyn "Bums," so his acceptance
of Robinson was of great importance in determining how the rest of the
Dodgers would react.

As expected, Robinson's presence triggered an ugly racial response. It 20
began with hate mail and death threats against him and his wife and baby
boy. In addition, some of his teammates continued to oppose him. Some
even refused to sit near him.

The opposing teams, however, were much worse, and the hatred was 21
so intense that some of the Dodger players began to stand up for Jackie.
In Philadelphia, players cried out such insults as, "They're waiting for
you in the jungles, black boy," and "Hey, snowflake, which one of you
white boys' wives are you dating tonight?" The first Dodger to stand up
for Robinson on the field was a Southerner, the cantankerous° Eddie "The
Brat" Stankey. When the Phillies pointed their bats at Robinson and made
machine-gun-like noises in a cruel reference to the threats on his and his
family's lives, Stankey shouted, "Why don't you yell at someone who can
answer back?"

Other opposing teams were no better. In an early-season game in 22
Cincinnati, for instance, players yelled racial epithets at Jackie. Rex
Barney, who was a Dodger pitcher then, described Pee Wee Reese's
response: "While Jackie was standing by first base, Pee Wee went over to
him and put his arm around him, as if to say, 'This is my man. This is the
guy. We're gonna win with him.' Well, it drove the Cincinnati players
right through the ceiling, and you could have heard the gasp from the
crowd as he did it."

In the face of continuing harassment, Jackie Robinson, a hot-tempered 23
young man who had struggled against racism all his life, chose to fight his
toughest battle, not with his fists or foul language, but with the courage
not to fight back. Instead, he answered his attackers with superior play
and electrifying speed.

Within the first month of the 1947 season, it became apparent that 24
Robinson could be the deciding factor in the pennant race. His speed on
the base paths brought an entirely new dimension to baseball. Robinson
used bunts and fake bunts and steals and fake steals to distract opposing
pitchers and force basic changes in strategy in the game.

Undoubtedly, one reason many Dodger players rallied around 25
Robinson was that they saw him as a critical, perhaps *the* critical, factor
in their pursuit of the pennant. Like Rickey's, their motives reflected a
mixture of personal ambition and a genuine concern for doing what was
right.

And many did do what was right, even off the field. For example, 26
Robinson at first waited until all his teammates had finished their showers
before he would take his. One day, outfielder Al Gionfriddo patted
Robinson on the butt and told him to get into the showers with everybody
else, that he was as much a part of the team as anyone. Robinson smiled
and went to the showers with Gionfriddo.

The ballplayers' wives also extended the hand of friendship to 27
Robinson and his wife. Pitcher Clyde King related an incident that was
typical of the efforts put forth to make the Robinsons feel part of the
Dodger family. At Ebbets Field, an iron fence ran from the dugout to the
clubhouse, keeping the fans from the players. After the games, the
Dodger wives would be allowed inside the fence to wait for their
husbands. Rachel Robinson, reluctant to join the other wives, would wait
for Jackie outside the fence among the fans. King remembers that his own
wife, Norma, a North Carolina girl, insisted that Rachel join her and the
other Dodger wives inside.

For Jackie, a series of such small but significant events may have 28
meant the difference between making it and exploding under the
enormous pressure that followed him throughout that first baseball
season.

As the season passed, he gained the support not only of many of his 29
teammates but of much of the baseball world in general. On September
12, *Sporting News*, the bible of baseball, selected Robinson as its Rookie
of the Year—the first of many prestigious° awards he would receive
during his term with the Dodgers.

In the article announcing the award, there was a quote from none other 30
than Dixie Walker, the same Dodger who had started the petition in the
spring to ban Robinson from playing for Brooklyn. Walker praised
Robinson for his contributions to the club's success, stating that Robinson
was all that Branch Rickey had said and more.

On September 22, the Dodgers defeated the St. Louis Cardinals to 31
clinch the National League pennant—against a team in whose town
Jackie had to stay in a "colored" hotel. Fittingly enough, the following
day was proclaimed Jackie Robinson Day at the Dodger ballpark.
Robinson was honored with a tumultuous° outpouring of affection from
the Brooklyn fans, an unbroken peal of adulation° that shook the very
foundations of Ebbets Field.

Americans learned something that year about competition and 32
excellence, about character and race. The fire that Jackie Robinson fanned
swept across the years to follow, resulting in a permanent change in the
makeup of the game. He had demonstrated that not only could blacks play
on the same field with white players; they could excel. People brought
their families hundreds of miles to see him play. The floodgates opened
for the signing of the black ballplayer. The same major-league team
owners who had voted against hiring blacks soon followed Rickey's lead.
In the next few years came Willie Mays, Ernie Banks, Henry Aaron, and
more—an endless list of black stars.

For some, Jackie Robinson is simply one of the greatest second 33
basemen of all time. For others, he is much more. He is an individual who

stood up and opposed the ugliness of racism with a relentless intensity. He was the first to brave the insults and the ignorance, the first to show that major-league baseball could be raised from the depths of segregation. His victory is a model of what one determined person can accomplish.

FIRST IMPRESSIONS

Freewrite for ten minutes on one of the following.

1. Did you enjoy reading this selection? Why or why not?

2. Were you already familiar with who Jackie Robinson was and what he had done? Were you surprised by any of the details revealed in this story? Explain.

3. In what ways do you think that attitudes have changed since Jackie Robinson's day? In what ways have they perhaps *not* changed?

VOCABULARY CHECK

A. Circle the letter of the word or phrase that best completes each of the following four items.

1. In the sentence below, the word *raucous* means
    a. cold and silent.
    b. loud and disorderly.
    c. warm and welcoming.
    d. shocked and confused.

    "Baseball historian Robert Smith wrote that when Robinson first appeared in Syracuse, 'the fans reacted in a manner so raucous, obscene, and disgusting that it might have shamed a conclave of the Ku Klux Klan.'" (Paragraph 14)

2. In the sentence below, the word *adamantly* means
    a. weakly.
    b. stubbornly.
    c. secretly.
    d. pleasantly.

    "Robinson's manager at Montreal was Clay Hopper, a Mississippi native adamantly opposed at first to the presence of Robinson on his ball club." (Paragraph 15)

3. In the sentences below, the word *momentum* means
   a. money.
   b. opposition.
   c. forward movement.
   d. defeat.

   "Walker gathered signatures and his petition gained momentum until he approached shortstop Pee Wee Reese. . . . Reese refused to sign the petition." (Paragraph 19)

4. In the sentences below, the word *epithets* means
   a. insults.
   b. poetry.
   c. encouragements.
   d. questions.

   "As expected, Robinson's presence triggered an ugly racial response. . . . In an early-season game in Cincinnati, for instance, players yelled racial epithets at Jackie." (Paragraphs 20–22)

B. Circle the letter of the answer that best completes each of the following four items. Each item uses a word (or form of a word) from "Words to Watch."

5. The little boy's *exclusion* from his classmate's birthday party
   a. pleased him.
   b. made him realize how much the classmate liked him.
   c. hurt his feelings badly.

6. My uncle is a *staunch* Democrat. He
   a. will vote for anyone who is a Democrat.
   b. can't bear to even be in the same room as a Democrat.
   c. votes Democratic sometimes, Republican sometimes, and sometimes doesn't vote at all.

7. Our cat is so *cantankerous* that she
   a. jumps on any stranger's lap and purrs loudly.
   b. hides under the bed most of the time, afraid to show her face.
   c. will bite and claw me even while I'm trying to feed her.

8. Which place would you expect to have the most *tumultuous* atmosphere?
   a. A church during silent worship
   b. A bowling alley with several kids' birthday parties going on
   c. A classroom during a final exam

READING CHECK

Central Point and Main Ideas

1. Which sentence best expresses the central point of the entire selection?
   a. Until 1947, there were no blacks in professional baseball.
   b. Jackie Robinson, a man of principle and courage, became the best second baseman in baseball.
   c. Baseball became integrated because of the courage of Branch Rickey and Jackie Robinson, who proved blacks could excel in major-league baseball.
   d. The integration of American society was not easily accomplished.

2. Which sentence best expresses the main idea of paragraph 7?
   a. Happy Chandler became baseball commissioner in 1944.
   b. Black soldiers fought for the United States during World War II.
   c. A commissioner of baseball who was opposed to integration died in 1944.
   d. By 1944, society and the commissioner of baseball had become more open to integrating major-league baseball.

3. Which sentence best expresses the main idea of paragraph 12?
   a. In the South at that time, blacks who were already seated on an airplane had to give up their seats for whites who wanted them.
   b. Although the Robinsons' trip to Florida was marked by irritating incidents of racism, what was to come later was worse.
   c. While on their way to Florida, the Robinsons were forced off two planes because white passengers wanted their seats.
   d. Branch Rickey was waiting for the Robinsons in Jacksonville, Florida.

Key Supporting Details

4. Robinson encountered racism
   a. on and off the field in both the North and the South.
   b. only during baseball games.
   c. mainly in Canada.
   d. until he joined the major leagues.

5. ___F___ TRUE OR FALSE? During Robinson's first year with the Dodgers, none of his teammates accepted him.

6. Branch Rickey had wanted to do something about racism in baseball
   ever since
   a. he saw Jackie Robinson denied a chance to play sports in the army.
   b. he himself had been a victim of racism.
   c. he saw a member of his college baseball team denied a room in a
      whites-only hotel.
   d. he saw Pee Wee Reese's acceptance of a black teammate.

Inferences

7. __T__ TRUE OR FALSE? The author implies that the Dodgers won the
   1947 National League pennant largely because of Jackie Robinson.

8. Which of the following inferences is best supported by paragraph 19?
   a. All Southern players were racist.
   b. Pee Wee Reese felt no threat from Jackie Robinson.
   c. Pee Wee Reese put principle ahead of personal concern.
   d. Without Pee Wee Reese, baseball would never have become
      integrated.

The Writer's Craft

9. In which paragraph does the author, through his choice of words, first
   begin to reveal his attitude towards Jackie Robinson?
   a. Paragraph 1
   b. Paragraph 3
   c. Paragraph 8
   d. Paragraph 9

10. The main purpose of this selection is to
    a. inform readers about how major-league baseball became integrated,
       thanks in large part to Branch Rickey and Jackie Robinson.
    b. simply entertain readers with an account of Jackie Robinson's first
       major-league season.
    c. persuade readers that Branch Rickey deserves all the credit for
       integrating baseball.
    d. persuade readers that Jackie Robinson was the greatest second
       baseman of all time.

DISCUSSION QUESTIONS

1. Kellmayer writes, "By 1944, the social climate had become more accepting of integration, in large part because of the contribution of black soldiers in World War II." Why might the contribution of black soldiers in World War II have affected how people felt about integration in the United States?

2. Why do you think the idea of integrating professional sports inspired such strong feelings in people? Would the integration of another profession—medicine or law, for example—have gotten people so excited? Why or why not?

3. Do you think Branch Rickey was right to ask Robinson "not to fight back"? Was Robinson right to agree? Explain your answers.

4. Robinson had to face a great deal of racism. Unfortunately, despite the greater integration of today, racism still exists. Have you experienced any racial insults yourself or seen anyone else treated badly because of the racial or ethnic group he or she belongs to? Describe what happened and how you or the other person reacted.

PARAGRAPH ASSIGNMENTS

1. Pee Wee Reese used his position as a team leader to stop the anti-Robinson momentum. When have you seen an individual stand up to a group and speak up for another point of view? Write a paragraph that describes what happened. Your topic sentence could be similar to one of the following:

   • I'll never forget the day my shy sister finally spoke up for herself.

   • When my cousin heard his parents criticizing a family of another race that had moved onto their street, he stood up for the new family.

   • By inviting several unpopular kids to his party, my friend Peter showed he wouldn't go along with the crowd and its cruelty.

   Be sure to include details such as what the mood of the group was, what actions you or the individual took, and how the group responded.

2. If you had been Jackie Robinson, do you think you could have agreed to Branch Rickey's request not to fight back when you were insulted? If so, do you believe you could have honored that request in the face of what Robinson experienced? Write a paragraph in which you tell what your response to Rickey would have been and how you believe you would have handled the pressures of Robinson's experience.

ESSAY ASSIGNMENTS

1. Why do some people react with such violent hatred to others whom they perceive as "different?" Write an essay in which you discuss several possible explanations for hate crimes. A thesis statement for this paper could be something like the following: "I believe that people who commit hate crimes are driven by their upbringing, their fears, and their desire to impress their friends."

2. Because of his great skill and his inner strength, Jackie Robinson became a national hero. But every community, school, and even family has its "everyday heroes"—people who have quietly and courageously dealt with obstacles in their lives. Write an essay about an everyday hero with whom you are familiar. Perhaps it is a single mother who has done a great job raising her children. Or maybe it is a young man who has achieved an education, despite receiving little support at home. In your essay, make it clear in what way this person is an everyday hero, what obstacles stood in his or her way, and what effect you think his or her actions have had on others.

Unit Two

Understanding Ourselves

9

Night Watch
Roy Popkin

Preview

How often have you seen the advice, "Practice random acts of kindness"? The following story belongs in this category. It proves, in the words of its author, that "there are people who care what happens to their fellow human beings."

Words to Watch

smudged (2): dirty with streaks or stains
relayed (3): passed along
boondocks (3): a rural region
maneuvers (3): military exercises
sedated (5): drugged with a pain reliever
oblivious (7): unaware
condolence (9): sympathy

The story began on a downtown Brooklyn street corner. An elderly man   1
had collapsed while crossing the street, and an ambulance rushed him to
Kings County Hospital. There, during his few returns to consciousness,
the man repeatedly called for his son.

From a smudged°, oft-read letter, an emergency-room nurse learned   2
that the son was a Marine stationed in North Carolina. Apparently, there
were no other relatives.

Someone at the hospital called the Red Cross office in Brooklyn, and   3
a request for the boy to rush to Brooklyn was relayed° to the Red Cross
director of the North Carolina Marine Corps camp. Because time was
short—the patient was dying—the Red Cross man and an officer set out
in a jeep. They located the sought-after young man wading through
marshy boondocks° on maneuvers°. He was rushed to the airport in time
to catch the one plane that might enable him to reach his dying father.

It was mid-evening when the young Marine walked into the entrance   4
lobby of Kings County Hospital. A nurse took the tired, anxious
serviceman to the bedside.

"Your son is here," she said to the old man. She had to repeat the   5
words several times before the patient's eyes opened. Heavily sedated°
because of the pain of his heart attack, he dimly saw the young man in the
Marine Corps uniform standing outside the oxygen tent. He reached out
his hand. The Marine wrapped his toughened fingers around the old
man's limp ones, squeezing a message of love and encouragement. The
nurse brought a chair, so the Marine could sit alongside the bed.

Nights are long in hospitals, but all through the night the young   6
Marine sat there in the poorly lighted ward, holding the old man's hand
and offering words of hope and strength. Occasionally, the nurse
suggested that the Marine move away and rest a while. He refused.

Whenever the nurse came into the ward, the Marine was there. His full   7
attention was on the dying man, and he was oblivious° of her and of the
night noises of the hospital—the clanking of an oxygen tank, the laughter
of night-staff members exchanging greetings, the cries and moans and
snores of other patients. Now and then she heard him say a few gentle
words. The dying man said nothing, only held tightly to his son through
most of the night.

Along toward dawn, the patient died. The Marine placed on the bed the   8
lifeless hand he had been holding, and went to tell the nurse. While she did
what she had to do, he relaxed—for the first time since he got to the hospital.

Finally, she returned to the nurse's station, where he was waiting. She   9
started to offer words of condolence° for his loss, but the Marine
interrupted her. "Who was that man?" he asked.

"He was your father," she answered, startled.   10

"No, he wasn't," the Marine replied. "I never saw him before in my life."   11

"Why didn't you say something when I took you to him?" the nurse   12
asked.

"I knew right off there'd been a mistake, but I also knew he needed his   13
son, and his son just wasn't here. When I realized he was too sick to tell
whether or not I was his son, I figured he really needed me. So I stayed."

With that, the Marine turned and left the hospital. Two days later a   14
routine message came in from the North Carolina Marine Corps base

informing the Brooklyn Red Cross that the real son was on his way to Brooklyn for his father's funeral. It turned out there had been two Marines with the same name and similar serial numbers in the camp. Someone in the personnel office had pulled out the wrong record.

But the wrong Marine had become the right son at the right time. And   15 he proved, in a uniquely human way, that there are people who care what happens to their fellow human beings.

FIRST IMPRESSIONS

Freewrite for ten minutes on one of the following.

1. Did you enjoy reading this selection? Why or why not?

2. Have you ever spent time with an ill or injured person in the hospital? What do you remember most about the experience? How did it affect you?

3. Why do you think the young Marine did not immediately tell the people at the hospital that the old man wasn't his father?

VOCABULARY CHECK

A. Circle the letter of the word or phrase that best completes each of the following four items.

1. In the sentence below, the words *enable him* mean
   a. stop him.
   b. encourage him.
   c. delay him.
   d. make it possible for him.

   "He was rushed to the airport in time to catch the one plane that might enable him to reach his dying father." (Paragraph 3)

2. In the sentences below, the word *dimly* means
   a. clearly.
   b. unclearly.
   c. rarely.
   d. often.

   "She had to repeat the words several times before the patient's eyes opened. Heavily sedated because of the pain of his heart attack, he dimly saw the young man. . . . " (Paragraph 5)

3. In the sentence below, the word *condolence* means
   a. excuse.
   b. bitterness.
   c. surprise.
   (d.) sympathy.

   > "She started to offer words of condolence for his loss, but the Marine interrupted her." (Paragraph 9)

4. In the sentence below, the words *uniquely human* mean
   a. impossible for humans.
   b. scary to humans.
   (c.) done only by humans.
   d. not human.

   > "And he proved, in a uniquely human way, that there are people who care what happens to their fellow human beings." (Paragraph 15)

B. Circle the letter of the answer that best completes each of the following four items. Each item uses a word (or form of a word) from "Words to Watch."

5. My mother's car window got *smudged* when my uncle
   a. washed and waxed her car as a birthday surprise.
   b. batted a baseball right through it.
   (c.) accidentally pushed his ice-cream cone against it.

6. Katrina *relayed* her brother's message by
   a. plugging her ears with her fingers.
   b. sneaking into his bedroom and reading it before he came home.
   (c.) bringing his note to his girlfriend across the street.

7. A *sedative* is a medication intended to make people
   (a.) become quiet and calm.
   b. lose their appetite for food.
   c. become lively and energetic.

8. A juggler is putting on a show on a street corner. Which of the following people is *oblivious* to his performance?
   a. The one putting money in the basket at the juggler's feet
   (b.) The one walking by without noticing the show
   c. The one trying to make the juggler drop one of his plates

READING CHECK

Central Point and Main Ideas

1. Which sentence best expresses the central point of the entire selection?
   a. A mistake led to the wrong Marine being sent to the bedside of a dying man.
   b. In order to comfort a dying man, a young Marine pretended to be the old man's son.
   c. Because the dying man was heavily sedated, he did not realize that the young man at his bedside was not his son.
   d. A young Marine sat all night at the bedside of a dying old man.

2. Which sentence best expresses the main idea of paragraph 6?
   a. The Marine refused the nurse's suggestion to rest.
   b. Nights are long in a hospital.
   c. The hospital ward where the dying man lay was poorly lighted.
   d. The Marine spent the whole night keeping the old man company.

3. Which sentence best expresses the main idea of paragraph 14?
   a. Two days after the man died, the mixup was explained.
   b. The real son and the Marine shared the same name.
   c. Someone in the Marine personnel office had pulled the wrong Marine's record.
   d. The real son was on his way to his father's funeral.

Key Supporting Details

4. People at the hospital learned the son's name
   a. when the son called the hospital, looking for his father.
   b. from the elderly man, who told them his son's name and that he was in the Marines.
   c. from a Marine Corps officer.
   d. from a letter the old man had with him.

5. The Marine realized the old man was not his father
   a. after the man had died.
   b. midway through the night.
   c. as soon as he saw him.
   d. when he was on maneuvers.

Inferences

6. We can conclude that the author learned most of the details of this story from the
   a. Marine.
   b. old man.
   c. officer who located the Marine.
   d. nurse on duty at the hospital.

7. We can assume that
   a. the Marine also had an elderly father.
   b. the Marine was glad to be relieved of his military duties for a while.
   c. the Marine did not get along well with his own father.
   d. the Marine's father was dead.

8. In paragraph 5 the author implies that
   a. the old man's poor vision led him to believe the Marine was his son.
   b. the old man did not want to embarrass the Marine by saying he wasn't his son.
   c. the old man was growing stronger.
   d. the nurse realized that the Marine was not the old man's son.

The Writer's Craft

9. Which of the following best describes the author's purpose in writing this story?
   a. To inform readers of the type of people who join the Marines
   b. To inform readers that careless mistakes are made in hospital and Marine offices
   c. To entertain readers with an inspirational story of a young man's compassion for a dying man
   d. To persuade readers to provide clear instructions about how to contact relatives in case of emergency

10. In the final paragraph of the story, the author
    a. quotes the nurse.
    b. gives his own thoughts about the Marine's actions.
    c. suggests that Americans should be proud of the Marines.
    d. predicts what will happen to the Marine.

DISCUSSION QUESTIONS

1. At what point do you think the Marine realized that the man was not his father? How can you tell?

2. Why didn't the Marine immediately reveal that a mistake had been made? Do you think his decision was the right one? Why or why not?

3. If you had been the man's son, how might you have felt when you learned what had happened?

4. The author refers to the "uniquely human way" in which the Marine showed "that there are people who care what happens to others." Have you seen other examples of people going out of their way to help strangers? What do you think motivates people to help people they don't know?

PARAGRAPH ASSIGNMENTS

1. The Marine said he stayed with the old man because "I figured he really needed me." Write a paragraph about a time that you felt needed. Explain who needed you and in what way, how you responded to the person's need, and the positive or negative feelings you had about being needed. Here's a sample topic sentence for such a paragraph: "When my mom took a full-time job, she really needed me to help out more at home."

2. Imagine that you are the son of the old man in the story. The day after your father died, you arrive and hear the story of the other Marine who had been with him when he died. How do you think you would feel about the situation? Would you feel primarily one emotion, or a mixture of several?

   Write a one-paragraph letter to the other Marine. In it, express your feeling or feelings about what happened. Be sure to tell the other man not only how you feel, but why.

ESSAY ASSIGNMENTS

1. When people are facing death, they often realize what is most important to them in life. In the case of the old man in this story, for example, he wanted more than anything else to see his son.

   If you knew that your life would end soon, what are some things that you would want to accomplish while you still had time? Maybe there are adventures or experiences that you would make a priority. For example, you may have always wanted to learn to snowboard, but have never gotten around to it. Or maybe there is unfinished business between you and a loved one that you would want to resolve. You might, for instance, want to patch up an argument with an old friend, or see a relative that you've lost touch with. Write an essay about several things that you would want to do before you died. Explain not only what those actions are, but why they are so important to you. Possible thesis statements for such an essay might be like these:

   - If I knew that I had only a short time left on earth, I would want to see the Pacific Ocean and go deep-sea fishing there with my brother.

   - Three things that I would want to accomplish before my life ended would be to visit the Grand Canyon, to read a great book such as George Eliot's *Middlemarch*, and to spend more time with my grandparents.

2. Sometimes when one is faced with a decision, there is pretty clearly a right choice and a wrong choice. But other times, the choice isn't so black and white. For example, the young Marine in this story decided that it was right to say nothing about the mistake that had been made until after the old man died. But another person faced with the same situation might have decided it was wrong to let everyone think he was the old man's son—and might have continued to try to locate the true son.

   Write an essay about a time when it was difficult for you to decide what was the right thing to do. In your essay, describe the problem you were facing. Then explain the alternatives you considered. Describe the good points and the bad points of each of those alternatives. Then, tell the reader what decision you finally made. End your essay by saying how you now feel about your decision.

10

Thank You
Alex Haley

Preview

For most of us, Thanksgiving has become a day marked by overeating, football, and sleepy conversation with similarly overstuffed relatives. Rarely do people observe the day by acting out its meaning. For Alex Haley, the celebrated author of *Roots*, the inspiration to do just that came on an unusual Thanksgiving spent far from home. This story of how Haley practiced true thanksgiving was first published in *Parade* magazine.

Words to Watch

destination (1): the place toward which something or someone is going
fo'c'sle (3): short for *forecastle*, the front part of a ship where the crew's
        quarters are located
afterdeck (4): the part of a ship's deck located towards the rear of the ship
draughts (4): inhalations
reflex (5): automatic reaction
waning (6): coming to an end
nostalgia (16): a longing for something or someone remembered fondly
jostling (19): pushing and shoving
nigh (25): nearly
yearning (25): desiring
buoyant (27): light-hearted

It was 1943, during World War II, and I was a young U.S. coast-guardsman, serial number 212-548, a number we never seem to forget. My ship, the USS *Murzim*, had been under way for several days. Most of her holds contained thousands of cartons of canned or dried foods. The other holds were loaded with five-hundred-pound bombs packed delicately in padded racks. Our destination° was a big base on the island of Tulagi in the South Pacific.   1

I was one of the *Murzim*'s several cooks and, quite the same as for folk ashore, this Thanksgiving morning had seen us busily preparing a traditional dinner featuring roast turkey.   2

Well, as any cook knows, it's a lot of hard work to cook and serve a big meal, and clean up and put everything away. But finally, around sundown, with our whole galley crew just bushed, we finished at last and were free to go flop into our bunks in the fo'c'sle°.   3

But I decided first to go out on the *Murzim*'s afterdeck° for a breath of open air. I made my way out there, breathing in great, deep draughts° while walking slowly about, still wearing my white cook's hat and the long apron, my feet sensing the big ship's vibrations from the deep-set, turbine diesels and my ears hearing that slightly hissing sound the sea makes in resisting the skin of a ship.   4

I got to thinking about Thanksgiving. In reflex°, my thoughts registered the historic imagery of the Pilgrims, Indians, wild turkeys, pumpkins, corn on the cob and the rest.   5

Yet my mind seemed to be questing for something else—some way that I could personally apply to the waning° Thanksgiving. It must have taken me a half hour to sense that maybe some key to an answer could result from reversing the word "Thanksgiving"—at least that suggested a verbal direction, "Giving thanks."   6

Giving thanks—as in praying, thanking God, I thought. Yes, of course. Certainly.   7

Yet my mind continued nagging me. Fine. But something else.   8

After awhile, like a dawn's brightening, a further answer did come—that there were people to thank, people who had done so much for me that I could never possibly repay them. The embarrassing truth was I'd always just accepted what they'd done, taken all of it for granted. Not one time had I ever bothered to express to any of them so much as a simple, sincere "Thank you."   9

At least seven people had been particularly and indelibly helpful to me. I realized, with a gulp, that about half of them had since died—so they were forever beyond any possible expression of gratitude from me. The more I thought about it, the more ashamed I became. Then I pictured the three who were still alive and, within minutes, I was down in the fo'c'sle.   10

Sitting at a mess table with writing paper and memories of things each   11 had done, I tried composing genuine statements of heartfelt appreciation and gratitude to my dad, Simon A. Haley, a professor at the old AMNC (Agricultural Mechanical Normal College) in Pine Bluff, Arkansas, now a branch of the University of Arkansas; to my grandma, Cynthia Palmer, back in our little hometown of Henning, Tennessee; and to the Rev. Lonual Nelson, my grammar school principal, retired and living in Ripley, six miles north of Henning.

I couldn't even be certain if they would recall some of their acts of 12 years past, acts that I vividly remembered and saw now as having given me vital training, or inspiration, or directions, if not all of these desirables rolled into one.

The texts of my letters began something like, "Here, this 13 Thanksgiving at sea, I find my thoughts upon how much you have done for me, but I have never stopped and said to you how much I feel the need to thank you—" And briefly I recalled for each of them specific acts performed in my behalf.

For instance, something uppermost about my father was how he had 14 impressed upon me from boyhood to love books and reading. In fact, this graduated into a family habit of after-dinner quizzes at the table about books read most recently and new words learned. My love of books never diminished and later led me toward writing books myself. So many times I have felt a sadness when exposed to modern children so immersed in the electronic media that they have little to no awareness of the wondrous world to be discovered in books.

I reminded the Reverend Nelson how each morning he would open 15 our little country town's grammar school with a prayer over his assembled students. I told him that whatever positive things I had done since had been influenced at least in part by his morning school prayers.

In the letter to my grandmother, I reminded her of a dozen ways she 16 used to teach me how to tell the truth, to be thrifty, to share, and to be forgiving and considerate of others. (My reminders included how she'd make me pull switches from a peach tree for my needed lesson.) I thanked her for the years of eating her good cooking, the equal of which I had not found since. (By now, though, I've reflected that those peerless dishes are most gloriously flavored with a pinch of nostalgia°.) Finally, I thanked her simply for having sprinkled my life with stardust.

Before I slept, my three letters went into our ship's office mail sack. 17 They got mailed when we reached Tulagi Island.

We unloaded cargo, reloaded with something else, then again we put 18 to sea in the routine familiar to us, and as the days became weeks, my little personal experience receded. Sometimes, when we were at sea, a mail ship would rendezvous and bring us mail from home, which, of course, we accorded topmost priority.

Every time the ship's loudspeaker rasped, "Attention! Mail call!" two-   19
hundred-odd shipmates came pounding up on deck and clustered about
the raised hatch atop which two yeomen, standing by those precious
bulging gray sacks, were alternately pulling out fistfuls of letters and
barking successive names of sailors who were, in turn, hollering "Here!
Here!" amid the jostling°.

One "mail call" brought me responses from Grandma, Dad and the   20
Reverend Nelson—and my reading of their letters left me not only
astounded, but more humbled than before.

Rather than saying they would forgive that I hadn't previously thanked   21
them, instead, for Pete's sake, they were thanking me—for having
remembered, for having considered they had done anything so exceptional.

Always the college professor, my dad had carefully avoided anything   22
he considered too sentimental, so I knew how moved he was to write me
that, after having helped educate many young people, he now felt that his
best results included his own son.

The Reverend Nelson wrote that his decades as a "simple, old-   23
fashioned principal" had ended with grammar schools undergoing such
swift changes that he had retired in self-doubt. "I heard more of what I
had done wrong than what I did right," he said, adding that my letter had
brought him welcome reassurance that his career had been appreciated.

A glance at Grandma's familiar handwriting brought back in a flash   24
memories of standing alongside her white wicker rocking chair, watching
her "settin' down" some letter to relatives. Frequently touching her
pencil's tip to pursed lips, character by character, each between a short,
soft grunt, Grandma would slowly accomplish one word, then the next, so
that a finished page would consume hours. I wept over the page
representing my Grandma's recent hours invested in expressing her
loving gratefulness to me—whom she used to diaper!

Much later, retired from the Coast Guard and trying to make a living   25
as a writer, I never forgot how those three "thank you" letters gave me an
insight into something nigh° mystical in human beings, most of whom go
about yearning° in secret for more of their fellows to express appreciation
for their efforts.

I discovered in time that, even in the business world, probably no two   26
words are more valued than "thank you," especially among people at
stores, airlines, utilities and others that directly serve the public.

Late one night, I was one of a half-dozen passengers who straggled   27
weary and grumbling off a plane that had been forced to land at the huge
Dallas/Fort Worth Airport. Suddenly, a buoyant°, cheerful, red-jacketed
airline man waved us away from the regular waiting room seats, saying,
"You sure look bushed. I know a big empty office where you can stretch
out while you wait." And we surely did. When the weather improved

enough for us to leave, "Gene Erickson" was in my notebook and, back home, I wrote the president of that airline describing his sensitivity and his courtesy. And I received a thank you!

I travel a good deal on lecture tours and I urge students especially to   28
tell their parents, grandparents, and other living elders simply "thank you" for all they have done to make possible the lives they now enjoy. Many students have told me they found themselves moved by the response. It is not really surprising, if one only reflects how it must feel to be thanked after you have given for years.

Now, approaching Thanksgiving of 1982, I have asked myself what   29
will I wish for all who are reading this, for our nation, indeed for our whole world—since, quoting a good and wise friend of mine, "In the end we are mightily and merely people, each with similar needs." First, I wish for us, of course, the simple common sense to achieve world peace, that being paramount for the very survival of our kind.

And there is something else I wish—so strongly that I have had this   30
line printed across the bottom of all my stationery: "Find the good—and praise it."

FIRST IMPRESSIONS

Freewrite for ten minutes on one of the following.

1. Did you enjoy reading this selection? Why or why not?

2. If you've traveled, did being far from home affect your feelings about the people and things in your life? In what ways?

3. Who are some people whom you would like to thank for making a special contribution to your life? What did each of these people do for you?

VOCABULARY CHECK

A. Circle the letter of the word or phrase that best completes each of the following four items.

1. In the sentence below, the word *indelibly* means
    a. unwillingly.
    b. permanently.
    c. foolishly.
    d. cruelly.

    "At least seven people had been particularly and indelibly helpful to me." (Paragraph 10)

2. In the sentence below, the words *immersed in* mean
   a. disgusted with.
   b. improved by.
   c. uninterested in.
   (d.) deeply involved in.

   > "So many times I have felt a sadness when exposed to modern children so immersed in the electronic media that they have little to no awareness of the wondrous world to be discovered in books." (Paragraph 14)

3. In the sentence below, the word *rendezvous* means
   a. sink.
   (b.) meet at a prearranged time and place.
   c. pass without stopping.
   d. speed up.

   > "Sometimes, when we were at sea, a mail ship would rendezvous and bring us mail from home. . . ." (Paragraph 18)

4. In the sentence below, the word *paramount* means
   a. an unneeded luxury.
   b. similar.
   c. not possible.
   (d.) of greatest importance.

   > "First, I wish for us, of course, the simple common sense to achieve world peace, that being paramount for the very survival of our kind." (Paragraph 29)

B. Circle the letter of the answer that best completes each of the following four items. Each item uses a word (or form of a word) from "Words to Watch."

5. If you were taking a bus trip from Chicago to New York, your *destination* would be
   a. Chicago.
   (b.) New York.
   c. a thousand miles.

6. When an object comes flying toward one's face, the natural *reflex* is to
   a. not notice.
   (b.) blink.
   c. carefully consider what the object might be.

7. As we walked along the bank of the creek, Grandpa's *nostalgic* comment was,
    a. "Be sure you don't fall in."
    b. "I'm getting cold; let's go back."
    c. "I wish you could have seen this place forty years ago."

8. Before Christmas, the children *yearned* over pictures of their favorite toys in catalogs. In other words, they
    a. fought over the pictures.
    b. longed for the toys in the pictures.
    c. scribbled over the pictures.

READING CHECK

Central Point and Main Ideas

1. Which sentence best expresses the central point of the entire selection?
    a. Haley was ashamed to realize that he had never gotten around to thanking several important people in his life who were now dead.
    b. By writing letters of thanks to three important people in his life, Haley demonstrated his belief that we should be more appreciative of one another.
    c. When Haley's father, grammar school principal, and grandmother received their letters, they in turn thanked Haley for writing them.
    d. Haley believes he owes much of his success to his father, his grammar school principal, and his grandmother.

2. Which sentence best expresses the main idea of paragraph 23?
    a. Reverend Nelson was an old-fashioned man.
    b. Haley's letter reassured Reverend Nelson that he had been a good principal.
    c. Reverend Nelson had retired filled with self-doubts.
    d. People had complained about the things Reverend Nelson had done wrong.

3. Which sentence best expresses the main idea of paragraph 27?
    a. Haley's plane was forced to land at the Dallas/Fort Worth airport.
    b. An airline representative, Gene Erickson, was kind to Haley and his fellow passengers.
    c. Airline representatives can be helpful in an emergency.
    d. Haley's letter to the airline president describing Gene Erickson's kindness to him and his fellow passengers was appreciated.

Key Supporting Details

4. As Haley thought about Thanksgiving, his very first thoughts were of
   a. the need to thank God.
   b. the need to thank people who had helped him.
   c. Pilgrims, Indians, turkey, and pumpkins.
   d. his grandmother.

5. Haley's father had been
   a. a college professor.
   b. a member of the Coast Guard.
   c. a school principal.
   d. an author.

6. Haley writes that the people who appreciate words of thanks most are
   a. people who directly serve the public.
   b. college students.
   c. people serving in the military.
   d. retired teachers.

Inferences

7. In paragraph 16, the author implies that
   a. he disliked his grandmother's cooking.
   b. he feels his grandmother was abusive to him.
   c. his grandmother spent little time with him as a child.
   d. his grandmother was both loving and strict.

8. From reading paragraph 19, we can conclude that
   a. few sailors on the *Murzim* received letters from home.
   b. mail calls happened every day on the *Murzim*.
   c. Haley got more mail from home than anyone else on board ship.
   d. getting mail from home was of great importance to the sailors.

The Writer's Craft

9. In paragraphs 14–16, Haley
   a. describes the personalities of his father, principal, and grandmother.
   b. explains how his father, principal, and grandmother each taught him about gratitude.
   c. contrasts the positive and negative characteristics of each of the people he wrote to.
   d. lists the specific reasons he was thanking his father, principal, and grandmother.

10. In the final paragraph of this article, Haley
    a. quotes his grandmother's favorite saying.
    b. restates his central idea.
    c. predicts what will happen if readers follow his advice.
    d. asks a question.

DISCUSSION QUESTIONS

1. What did the three replies that Haley received have in common? Why do you think Haley was surprised by what they said? What did these replies teach him about human nature?

2. Do you ever write personal letters or e-mail? To whom? And do you, like Haley and his shipmates, enjoy receiving mail? Is receiving a letter or e-mail better than receiving a telephone call? Why or why not?

3. Haley believes we need to say "thank you" more often. But most of us say and hear "thanks" many times a day. What's the difference between everyday "thank you's" and the kind of thanks that Haley is talking about? Give an example of each.

4. Haley urges readers, "Find the good—and praise it." Some people can do this easily; others cannot. Why do you think people might have difficulty expressing gratitude or praise? Do you experience this difficulty? Explain.

PARAGRAPH ASSIGNMENTS

1. Alex Haley didn't have to write those thank-you letters. He decided to simply because he felt it was the right and kind thing to do. Write a paragraph about a time you did something kind, not because anyone told you to do it but just because you wanted to. Maybe you stopped in to visit a friend you knew was feeling depressed, or surprised someone with a gift, or did some chores around the house without being asked. In your paragraph, explain what you did, how you felt about it, and any response you received. You might want to start the paragraph with a sentence like "I felt real satisfaction the day I decided to _____."

2. When have you received a significant letter (or e-mail)? It might have been significant because it brought good news, bad news, or surprising news. Write a paragraph about this occasion. Provide details that make clear to your readers who wrote the letter, what your relationship to that person was, and why the letter was important to you.

ESSAY ASSIGNMENTS

1. As you look back on your life, to which three persons are you especially grateful? Write an essay showing exactly how these persons have made a difference in your life. Devote each supporting paragraph to one of these persons, including one especially dramatic example or several smaller examples of what that person has done. In either case, provide plentiful details to illustrate each person's influence on you. Alternatively, you may write your entire essay about one person, devoting each supporting paragraph to an aspect of that person's important role in your life.

    An effective thesis statement for this essay might be one of the following:

    - I will never forget my best friend in first grade, my sixth-grade English teacher, and my wonderful grandmother.

    - My grandmother's constant physical presence and her financial and emotional support have made a real difference in my life.

2. Most people, Haley writes, "go about yearning in secret for more of their fellows to express appreciation." Select three categories of people who you think deserve more appreciation than they generally receive. Write an essay in which you explain, for each category, why these people deserve thanks and how the people whose lives they affect could show appreciation. Some categories of people you might write about are these:

    - Parents
    - Teachers
    - Waiters and waitresses
    - Store clerks
    - Police officers
    - Cleaning people
    - Church volunteers
    - School volunteers

11

Winners, Losers, or Just Kids?
Dan Wightman

Preview

For a lucky few, high school is four years of fun and accomplishment. For most of the rest of us, though, the high-school experience is—or was— marred by anxiety over grades, envy of our better-looking or more athletically-skilled classmates, and a general feeling that happiness and success are things that happen to other people. Author Dan Wightman, a high school "loser," looks back from a fifteen-year vantage point. To his fellow losers, he has a message: "A" students sometimes earn D's in life, and high-school losers can turn out to be winners.

Words to Watch

coyly (1): with pretended shyness
flaunted (1): showed off
blotto (2): very drunk
swank (3): ritzy
metamorphoses (4): great changes
morose (7): gloomy
fare (8): make out
endeared (9): made dear
sheepish (11): shamefaced

presumptuous (11): taking too much for granted
regressed (13): gone backward
quick (15): the sensitive flesh under the fingernails
finding their stride (17): achieving a natural, effective pace

If I envied anyone in high school, it was the winners. You know who I 1
mean. The ones who earned straight A's and scored high on their
Scholastic Aptitude Tests. The attractive ones who smiled coyly°, drove
their own sport cars and flaunted° those hard, smooth bodies that they
kept tan the year round.

By contrast, my high-school friends were mostly losers. We spent a lot 2
of time tuning cars and drinking beer. Our girlfriends were pale and
frumpy, and we had more D's than B's on our report cards. After
graduation, many of us went into the Army instead of to a university; two
of us came back from Vietnam in coffins, three more on stretchers. On
weekends, when we drank Colt 45 together in my father's battered Ford,
we'd laughingly refer to ourselves as the "out crowd," But, unless we
were thoroughly blotto°, we never laughed hard when we said it. And I,
for one, rarely got blotto when I was 16.

The reason I mention this is that last month 183 winners and losers 3
from my Northern California high-school graduating class got together at
a swank° country club for a revealing fifteen-year reunion.

Predictably, only happy and successful people attended. The strange 4
thing, though, was that the people I once pegged as losers outnumbered
the winners at this reunion by a visible margin. And, during a long session
at the bar with my informative friend Paula, I got an earful about the
messy lives of people I'd once envied, and the remarkable
metamorphoses° of people I'd once pitied.

Paula reported that Len, a former class officer, was now a lost soul in 5
Colorado, hopelessly estranged from his charming wife. Tim, one of the
sorriest students I'd ever known, was a successful sportswriter, at ease
with himself.

Estelle, who was modestly attractive in her teens, was now a part-time 6
stripper in the Midwest, working to support her young son. Connie, a
former car-club "kitten," had become a sophisticated international flight
attendant.

Paula told me that Gary, a college scholarship winner, was overweight, 7
underemployed, and morose°. Ron, who had shown little flair for music,
had become a symphony violinist.

Sipping a piña colada, I thought to myself how terribly mistaken my 8
senior counselor had been when she told me that high-school
performance indicates how one will fare° later.

I looked at Paula, a high-school troublemaker with a naughty smile, 9
whose outgoing personality and rebellious spirit had endeared° her to me
so long ago. Together, we once stole a teacher's grade book, changed
some of our low marks, then dropped the book in the lost-and-found box.
The savvy teacher never said a word about the incident, but at the end of
the year, when report cards were issued, gave us the D's we deserved.

Now Paula was a housewife, a volunteer worker, and the mother of two 10
sons. She wore a modest dress and sat at the bar tippling Perrier on ice.

She shook her head when I reminded her of the grade-book escapade, 11
and the sheepish° look on her face reminded me how presumptuous° it is
to predict the lives of others.

It also got me thinking about my own life since high school—how I'd 12
gradually shaken my loser's image, gotten through college, found a
decent job, married wisely, and finally realized a speck of my potential.

I thought about numerous situations where I could have despaired, 13
regressed°, given up—and how I hadn't, though others had—and I
wondered why I was different, and had more luck, less guilt.

"The past is fiction," wrote William Burroughs. And, although I don't 14
subscribe to that philosophy entirely, the people I admire most today are
those who overcome their mistakes, seize second chances and fight to pull
themselves together, day after day.

Often they're the sort of people who leave high school with blotchy 15
complexions, crummy work habits, fingernails bitten down to the quick°.
And of course they're bitterly unsure of themselves, and slow to make
friends.

But they're also the ones who show up transformed at fifteen-year 16
reunions, and the inference I draw is that the distinction between winners
and losers is often slight and seldom crucial—and frequently overrated.

In high school especially, many people are slow getting started. But, 17
finding their stride°, they quickly catch up, and in their prime often return to
surprise and delight us—their lives so much richer than we'd ever imagined.

FIRST IMPRESSIONS

Freewrite for ten minutes on one of the following.

1. Did you enjoy reading this selection? Why or why not?

2. What makes high school such a difficult time and place for so many
   people?

3. From your observation, does high-school popularity make much of a
   difference in people's later lives? Explain your answer.

VOCABULARY CHECK

A. Circle the letter of the word or phrase that best completes each of the following four items.

1. In the sentence below, the word *pegged* means
    a. feared.
    b. labeled.
    c. admired.
    d. envied.

    "The strange thing, though, was that the people I once pegged as losers outnumbered the winners at this reunion by a visible margin." (Paragraph 4)

2. In the sentence below, the word *flair* means
    a. dislike.
    b. inability.
    c. talent.
    d. money.

    "Ron, who had shown little flair for music, had become a symphony violinist." (Paragraph 7)

3. In the sentences below, the word *savvy* means
    a. foolish.
    b. cruel.
    c. misled.
    d. wise.

    "Together, we once stole a teacher's grade book, changed some of our low marks, then dropped the book in the lost-and-found box. The savvy teacher . . . at the end of the year, when report cards were issued, gave us the D's we deserved." (Paragraph 9)

4. In the sentences below, the words *subscribe to* mean
    a. agree with.
    b. disagree with.
    c. understand.
    d. pay for.

    "'The past is fiction,' wrote William Burroughs. And although I don't subscribe to that philosophy entirely, the people I admire . . . are those who overcome their mistakes. . . ." (Paragraph 14)

B. Circle the letter of the answer that best completes each of the following four items. Each item uses a word (or form of a word) from "Words to Watch."

5. Right after her engagement, Janice *flaunted* her diamond ring because
   a. it didn't fit well and she had to have it re-sized.
   b. she and her fiancé had agreed to keep the engagement secret for a while.
   (c.) she wanted everyone to notice it.

6. Superman's famous *metamorphosis* occurs whenever he
   a. does battle with the forces of evil.
   (b.) steps into a phone booth as Clark Kent and emerges as a superhero.
   c. flirts shyly with Lois Lane.

7. I understood why Chris seemed so *morose* after I learned that
   (a.) his beloved cat had died.
   b. he'd been admitted to his first-choice college.
   c. he had been working out in the gym every day for months.

8. Tiffany quickly *endeared* herself to her boss by
   a. coming into work late and with a hangover.
   (b.) volunteering to take on several tasks that no one else would do.
   c. losing an important file.

READING CHECK

Central Point and Main Ideas

1. Which sentence best expresses the central point of the entire selection?
   a. High-school winners always end up being losers in life.
   b. Only happy and successful people attend school reunions.
   c. The author attended his fifteen-year reunion.
   (d.) High-school performance doesn't necessarily show how well a student will do later in life.

2. The main idea of paragraph 2 is best expressed in the
   (a.) first sentence.
   b. second sentence.
   c. third sentence.
   d. last sentence.

3. A single main idea may cover several paragraphs. Which sentence best expresses the main idea of paragraphs 4–7?
   a. Only happy and successful people attended the reunion.
   b. The author learned that many former losers were now winners and people he once envied were troubled.
   c. Paula provided many details about the author's former classmates.
   d. The author learned that Len, a former class officer, was separated from his charming wife.

Key Supporting Details

4. The author's old friend Paula, a troublemaker in high school,
   a. had become a part-time stripper.
   b. had become a housewife, mother, and volunteer worker.
   c. had remained a troublemaker.
   d. told the author nothing about their classmates' lives.

5. Since graduating from high school, the author had
   a. been following the careers of his former classmates.
   b. become estranged from his wife.
   c. gone to college, found a good job, and married.
   d. become a successful sportswriter.

Inferences

6. From the article, we can conclude that in high school, the author
   a. knew the winners would not always be winners.
   b. thought the winners did not deserve their grades.
   c. eventually became part of the popular crowd.
   d. might have wanted to trade places with the winners.

7. The author implies that
   a. people often mistakenly think that high-school losers will remain losers.
   b. high-school winners succeed in life more often than high-school losers do.
   c. fifteen-year reunions change losers to winners.
   d. everyone knows that high-school losers often become winners.

8. The author implies that people who attend high-school reunions
   a. generally do so because they feel good about their lives.
   b. are living in the past, unable to get on with their lives.
   c. are those who were most popular in high school.
   d. don't want to, but go out of a sense of obligation.

The Writer's Craft

9. The author's main purpose in writing this piece is to
   a. inform readers of the usual path successful people take in life.
   b. entertain readers with stories about the people with whom he went to school.
   c. persuade readers to be kinder to one another in high school.
   (d.) persuade readers that their success in high school does not determine their success in life.

10. To back up his point that high-school losers often turn out to be winners, the author relies on
    a. expert opinions.
    b. statistics and studies.
    (c.) his personal experience and a friend's evidence.
    d. letters he's received from former classmates.

DISCUSSION QUESTIONS

1. What does Wightman really mean by "winners" and "losers"? Why does the title also say, "or Just Kids"?

2. What do the first two paragraphs of this selection accomplish? Why do you think Wightman chose to begin his essay with these instead of with the story of his fifteen-year reunion?

3. Since their high-school experiences were so negative, why might Wightman and Paula have decided to attend the reunion? Do you think you will attend *your* high-school reunion? Why or why not?

4. Wightman and many of the people whose stories he tells have shaken their self-image as "losers." What does Wightman say are the reasons for this transformation? What are some other factors that might determine whether a person can change his or her self-image?

PARAGRAPH ASSIGNMENTS

1. What positive changes have occurred in your life? Write a paragraph about one way you have changed that you are happy about. Give specific details or examples of that change and how it has affected your life. Your opening sentence could be similar to this one: "Now that I'm studying more, I feel much better about myself."

2. Most of us have heard or read some inspirational story about a highly successful person who was not at all successful at some point earlier in life. Such a person might be an entertainer, athlete, businessperson, artist, or educator. Write a paragraph in which you contrast what you know about a person's earlier lack of success with the success he or she later achieved. Include any conclusions you can draw about what made that person turn his or her life around and become successful.

ESSAY ASSIGNMENTS

1. Write an essay about someone you know who has changed a great deal during the time you have known him or her. The change could be for the good—or not so good. Describe what that person was like when you were first acquainted, how he or she is today, and what you think might have caused the changes. You might, for instance, write about one of the following:

   - A person who was once a successful student who is now having problems in school or in life

   - A person you thought would never achieve anything who is now doing well

   - A person who once was mean or unfriendly but is now pleasant

   An effective thesis statement for this essay might be: "My friend Kenyon is very different today from the way he was when we first met."

2. As Wightman suggests in this article, school is often a difficult, frustrating experience. What factors make school hard for so many people? Write an essay in which you isolate several kinds of pressures that, in your experience, make school so unpleasant. You might consider including some of the following:

   - Pressure to conform
   - Pressure to be part of a particular group
   - Pressure to get good grades
   - Pressure to be popular
   - Pressure to have a boyfriend/girlfriend
   - Pressure to look/dress/act in certain ways
   - Pressure from parents

   As you write your essay, be sure to include specific details about how the pressures you have chosen affect students.

12

Responsibility
M. Scott Peck

Preview

The Road Less Traveled, a well-known book by psychiatrist and author M. Scott Peck, begins with this famous line: "Life is difficult." Unlike most "self-help" authors, Dr. Peck does not suggest that once his readers do A and B, they will permanently lose weight, find the perfect mate, never again feel depressed, or suddenly become rich. Instead, Peck encourages people to embrace the messy difficulties that make up life, stressing that growth and development are achieved only through hard work. The following excerpt from *The Road Less Traveled* emphasizes one of Peck's favorite themes: personal responsibility.

Words to Watch

self-evident (1): not requiring any explanation
ludicrous (2): laughable because of being obviously ridiculous
clarified (19): made clear
amenable (23): agreeable
glared (37): stared angrily

We cannot solve life's problems except by solving them. This statement may seem idiotically self-evident°, yet it is seemingly beyond the comprehension of much of the human race. This is because we must accept responsibility for a problem before we can solve it. We cannot solve a problem by saying, "It's not my problem." We cannot solve a problem by hoping that someone else will solve it for us. I can solve a problem only when I say, "This is my problem and it's up to me to solve it." But many, so many, seek to avoid the pain of their problems by saying to themselves: "This problem was caused by other people, or by social circumstances beyond my control, and therefore it is up to other people or society to solve this problem for me. It is not really my personal problem."

The extent to which people will go psychologically to avoid assuming   2
responsibility for personal problems, while always sad, is sometimes almost ludicrous°. A career sergeant in the army, stationed in Okinawa and in serious trouble because of his excessive drinking, was referred for psychiatric evaluation and, if possible, assistance. He denied that he was an alcoholic, or even that his use of alcohol was a personal problem, saying, "There's nothing else to do in the evenings in Okinawa except drink."

"Do you like to read?" I asked.   3

"Oh yes, I like to read, sure."   4

"Then why don't you read in the evening instead of drinking?"   5

"It's too noisy to read in the barracks."   6

"Well, then, why don't you go to the library?"   7

"The library is too far away."   8

"Is the library farther away than the bar you go to?"   9

"Well, I'm not much of a reader. That's not where my interests lie."   10

"Do you like to fish?" I then inquired.   11

"Sure, I love to fish."   12

"Why not go fishing instead of drinking?"   13

"Because I have to work all day long."   14

"Can't you go fishing at night?"   15

"No, there isn't any night fishing in Okinawa."   16

"But there is," I said. "I know several organizations that fish at night   17
here. Would you like me to put you in touch with them?"

"Well, I really don't like to fish."   18

"What I hear you saying," I clarified°, "is that there are other things to   19
do in Okinawa except drink, but the thing you like to do most in Okinawa
is drink."

"Yeah, I guess so."   20

"But your drinking is getting you in trouble, so you're faced with a   21
real problem, aren't you?"

"This damn island would drive anyone to drink."   22

I kept trying for a while, but the sergeant was not the least bit   23
interested in seeing his drinking as a personal problem which he could

solve either with or without help, and I regretfully told his commander that he was not amenable° to assistance. His drinking continued, and he was separated from the service in mid-career.

A young wife, also in Okinawa, cut her wrist lightly with a razor blade   24
and was brought to the emergency room, where I saw her. I asked her why she had done this to herself.

"To kill myself, of course."   25

"Why do you want to kill yourself?"   26

"Because I can't stand it on this dumb island. You have to send me   27
back to the States. I'm going to kill myself if I have to stay here any longer."

"What is it about living on Okinawa that's so painful for you?" I   28
asked.

She began to cry in a whining sort of way. "I don't have any friends   29
here, and I'm alone all the time."

"That's too bad. How come you haven't been able to make any   30
friends?"

"Because I have to live in a stupid Okinawan housing area, and none   31
of my neighbors speak English."

"Why don't you drive over to the American housing area or to the   32
wives' club during the day so you can make some friends?"

"Because my husband has to drive the car to work."   33

"Can't you drive him to work, since you're alone and bored all day?"   34
I asked.

"No. It's a stick-shift car, and I don't know how to drive a stick-shift   35
car, only an automatic."

"Why don't you learn how to drive a stick-shift car?"   36

She glared° at me. "On these roads? You must be crazy."   37

FIRST IMPRESSIONS

Freewrite for ten minutes on one of the following.

1. Did you enjoy reading this selection? Why or why not?

2. Do you agree with Peck that many people refuse to take responsibility for their own problems? Explain your answer.

3. What do you think of the sergeant and young wife that Peck describes? How do you think either could improve his or her situation?

VOCABULARY CHECK

A. Circle the letter of the word or phrase that best completes each of the following four items.

1. In the sentence below, the word *comprehension* means
   a. definition.
   (b.) understanding.
   c. confusion.
   d. absence.

   > "This statement . . . is seemingly beyond the comprehension of much of the human race." (Paragraph 1)

2. In the sentence below, the word *extent* means
   (a.) lengths.
   b. fright.
   c. surprise.
   d. humor.

   > "The extent to which people will go psychologically to avoid assuming responsibility for personal problems, while always sad, is sometimes almost ludicrous." (Paragraph 2)

3. In the sentence below, the word *excessive* means
   a. good-natured.
   b. unwilling.
   c. moderate.
   (d.) beyond what is normal.

   > "A career sergeant . . . in serious trouble because of his excessive drinking. . . ." (Paragraph 2)

4. In the sentence below, the word *evaluation* means
   (a.) examination.
   b. help.
   c. punishment.
   d. entertainment.

   > "A career sergeant . . . was referred for psychiatric evaluation and, if possible, assistance." (Paragraph 2)

B. Circle the letter of the answer that best completes each of the following four items. Each item uses a word (or form of a word) from "Words to Watch."

5. Dressed for the party, my father looked quite *ludicrous* in
   a. a well-tailored tuxedo.
   (b.) a diaper and baby's bonnet.
   c. jeans and a sweater.

6. The teacher *clarified* the homework assignment by
   a. doubling the number of pages we had to read.
   b. refusing to answer questions about the assignment.
   (c.) explaining the assignment again in different words.

7. Rita showed that she was *amenable* to Rob's marriage proposal by
   (a.) jumping up, kissing him, and shouting "Yes!"
   b. staring at him in astonishment and saying not a word.
   c. muttering "I don't think so" and leaving the room.

8. Sitting on the couch with his date, Eddie began to *glare* at his little sister as she
   (a.) continued chattering on, refusing to leave the two of them alone.
   b. offered them a couple of sodas.
   c. left the house to visit a friend.

READING CHECK

Central Point and Main Ideas

1. Which sentence best expresses the central point of the entire selection?
   a. In Okinawa, Peck met two people who refused to take responsibility for their own problems.
   b. People demonstrate healthy creativity in the excuses they make for their irresponsibility.
   (c.) Many people, like the sergeant and the young wife, won't solve their problems because they refuse to take responsibility for them.
   d. The sergeant and the young wife would rather see their careers and lives ruined than take responsibility for their problems.

2. Which sentence best expresses the main idea of paragraphs 2–22?
   a. A career sergeant was in trouble because of his drinking.
   b. The sergeant denied that he had a problem with alcohol.
   c. Peck was expected to evaluate the sergeant and, if possible, help him.
   (d.) People will go to ridiculous lengths to avoid responsibility for their problems.

3. Which sentence best expresses the main idea of paragraph 23?
   a. Peck tried for some time to help the sergeant.
   b. Drinking has destroyed the lives of many people.
   c. The sergeant was completely unwilling to help himself.
   (d.) Peck had to tell the sergeant's commander that he could not help.

Key Supporting Details

4. The author claimed that the sergeant "was not amenable to assistance." What evidence did he have for that statement?
   a. The sergeant did not like to fish.
   b. The sergeant did not like to read.
   (c.) The sergeant refused every one of Peck's suggestions.
   d. All of the above

5. The young wife first saw Peck because she
   a. was drinking too much.
   (b.) had cut her wrist.
   c. had tried to return to the States.
   d. wanted to learn to drive.

6. The young wife said she could not drive to the wives' club because
   (a.) she could not drive a stick-shift car.
   b. she had to be away at work all day.
   c. none of the other wives spoke English.
   d. she and her husband did not own a car.

Inferences

7. Which statement would Peck be most likely to make to the young wife?
   (a.) "Your unwillingness to learn to drive a stick-shift car indicates that you don't really want to help yourself."
   b. "Your neighbors really should learn English so that they can communicate with you."
   c. "No one could be expected to be happy living in your circumstances."
   d. "The military should make better arrangements for spouses who are living far away from home."

8. We can infer that the sergeant and the young wife
   (a.) wanted someone else to take responsibility for their problems.
   b. knew each other.
   c. were good at taking responsibility for themselves back in the States.
   d. became happier and better adjusted after their meetings with Peck.

The Writer's Craft

9. The author states, "The extent to which people will go psychologically to avoid assuming responsibility for personal problems . . . is sometimes almost ludicrous" (paragraph 2). He supports this statement with
   a. evidence from psychological textbooks.
   b. examples from his own practice.
   c. statistics and other figures from sociological studies.
   d. examples from news stories.

10. Peck's tone as he describes people who refuse responsibility for their problems can best be described as
    a. supportive.
    b. humorous.
    c. annoyed.
    d. approving.

DISCUSSION QUESTIONS

1. Peck refers to the "ludicrous"—that is, ridiculous—lengths people will go to to avoid taking responsibility for their problems. What do you think he finds ludicrous about the sergeant's behavior? The young wife's? Do you find their behavior ridiculous? Why or why not?

2. What problems—big or small—do you observe around you that result from people refusing to take responsibility for their own behavior?

3. What do you think Peck means when he says that "we must accept responsibility for a problem before we can solve it"? Can you give an example from your (or someone else's) experience to illustrate the meaning of his statement?

4. Why do you think so many people find it difficult to take responsibility for their own problems? How might they be helped to do so?

PARAGRAPH ASSIGNMENTS

1. Write a paragraph about a time you have seen someone avoiding responsibility for his or her own problem. Begin with this topic sentence: "Just like M. Scott Peck, I have seen someone refuse to take responsibility for his (*or* her) own problem." Then go on to develop your paper by explaining who the person is, what the person's problem was, how he or she helped to create it, and how he or she blamed others or circumstances rather than accept responsibility.

2. Peck is drawing examples of irresponsible behavior from his practice as a military psychiatrist. But you can find examples of people dodging responsibility everywhere. What kinds of responsibility do students often avoid? Write a paragraph giving details about two or three ways students try to escape their responsibilities. Explain what kind of excuses they frequently make for their behavior.

ESSAY ASSIGNMENTS

1. Peck explains that the only way to solve a problem is to solve it—in other words, to take responsibility for the problem and find a solution. Write an essay about a time in your own life when you had to accept responsibility for a problem and figure out a solution for it. As you decide on a topic, you might list areas in which you have experienced problems. Here is one imaginary student's list:

   - Getting along with parents
   - Breaking off with friends who were a bad influence
   - Managing money
   - Holding a job
   - Keeping up with schoolwork

   Once you have decided on a topic to write about, you might begin with a statement like this: "After blaming my teachers for my problems in school, I finally accepted responsibility for my own poor grades."

   Alternatively, write about two or three problems you've had to face and solve.

2. How could this country be improved through people accepting more responsibility for themselves? Write an essay in which you show how several of this country's big problems are related to a lack of personal responsibility. Indicate how those problems would be lessened or eliminated if people were more willing to act responsibly. If you prefer, instead of focusing on the whole country, you can write about problems in your state, city, neighborhood, or school.

13

Anxiety: Challenge by Another Name
James Lincoln Collier

Preview

What makes the difference between people who live boring, unadventurous lives, and those whose lives are filled with excitement and new discoveries? Is it luck? Is it some sort of special ability? Is it courage? According to writer James Lincoln Collier, it isn't any of those things. In this essay, first published in *Reader's Digest*, Collier tells the story of an exciting opportunity, an unhappy choice, and the lessons he learned from both.

Words to Watch

fabled (2): very famous
prospect (2): mental picture of something to come
proposition (3): offer
wavered (7): went back and forth between alternatives
inevitably (8): unavoidably
venture (10): uncertain task

Between my sophomore and junior years at college, a chance came up   1
for me to spend the summer vacation working on a ranch in Argentina.
My roommate's father was in the cattle business, and he wanted Ted to
see something of it. Ted said he would go if he could take a friend, and he
chose me.

The idea of spending two months on the fabled° Argentine Pampas*   2
was exciting. Then I began having second thoughts. I had never been very
far from New England, and I had been homesick my first weeks at
college. What would it be like in a strange country? What about the
language? And besides, I had promised to teach my younger brother to
sail that summer. The more I thought about it, the more the prospect°
daunted me. I began waking up nights in a sweat.

In the end I turned down the proposition°. As soon as Ted asked   3
somebody else to go, I began kicking myself. A couple of weeks later I
went home to my old summer job, unpacking cartons at the local
supermarket, feeling very low. I had turned down something I wanted to
do because I was scared, and had ended up feeling depressed. I stayed that
way for a long time. And it didn't help when I went back to college in the
fall to discover that Ted and his friend had had a terrific time.

In the long run that unhappy summer taught me a valuable lesson out   4
of which I developed a rule for myself: *Do what makes you anxious; don't
do what makes you depressed.*

I am not, of course, talking about severe states of anxiety or   5
depression, which require medical attention. What I mean is that kind of
anxiety we call stage fright, butterflies in the stomach, a case of nerves—
the feelings we have at a job interview, when we're giving a big party,
when we have to make an important presentation at the office. And the
kind of depression I am referring to is that downhearted feeling of the
blues, when we don't seem to be interested in anything, when we can't
get going and seem to have no energy.

I was confronted by this sort of situation toward the end of my senior   6
year. As graduation approached, I began to think about taking a crack at
making my living as a writer. But one of my professors was urging me to
apply to graduate school and aim at a teaching career.

I wavered°. The idea of trying to live by writing was scary—a lot more   7
scary than spending a summer on the Pampas, I thought. Back and forth
I went, making my decision, unmaking it. Suddenly, I realized that every
time I gave up the idea of writing, that sinking feeling went through me;
it gave me the blues.

The thought of graduate school wasn't what depressed me. It was   8
giving up on what deep in my gut I really wanted to do. Right then I
learned another lesson. To avoid that kind of depression meant,
inevitably°, having to endure a certain amount of worry and concern.

---

*A vast plain in south-central South America.

The great Danish philosopher Soren Kierkegaard believed that anxiety   9
always arises when we confront the possibility of our own development.
It seems to be a rule of life that you can't advance without getting that old,
familiar, jittery feeling.

Even as children we discover this when we try to expand ourselves by,   10
say, learning to ride a bike or going out for the school play. Later in life we
get butterflies when we think about having that first child, or uprooting the
family from the old hometown to find a better opportunity halfway across
the country. Any time, it seems, that we set out aggressively to get
something we want, we meet up with anxiety. And it's going to be our
traveling companion, at least part of the way, into any new venture°.

When I first began writing magazine articles, I was frequently   11
required to interview big names—people like Richard Burton, Joan
Rivers, sex authority William Masters, baseball great Dizzy Dean. Before
each interview I would get butterflies and my hands would shake.

At the time, I was doing some writing about music. And one person I   12
particularly admired was the great composer Duke Ellington. On stage
and on television, he seemed the very model of the confident,
sophisticated man of the world. Then I learned that Ellington still got
stage fright. If the highly honored Duke Ellington, who had appeared on
the bandstand some ten thousand times over thirty years, had anxiety
attacks, who was I to think I could avoid them?

I went on doing those frightening interviews, and one day, as I was   13
getting onto a plane for Washington to interview columnist Joseph Alsop,
I suddenly realized to my astonishment that I was looking forward to the
meeting. What had happened to those butterflies?

Well, in truth, they were still there, but there were fewer of them. I had   14
benefited, I discovered, from a process psychologists call "extinction." If
you put an individual in an anxiety-provoking situation often enough, he
will eventually learn that there isn't anything to be worried about.

Which brings us to a corollary to my basic rule: *You'll never eliminate*   15
anxiety by avoiding the things that cause it. I remember how my son Jeff
was when I first began to teach him to swim at the lake cottage where we
spent our summer vacations. He resisted, and when I got him into the
water he sank and sputtered and wanted to quit. But I was insistent. And
by summer's end he was splashing around like a puppy. He had
"extinguished" his anxiety the only way he could—by confronting it.

The problem, of course, is that it is one thing to urge somebody else   16
to take on those anxiety-producing challenges; it is quite another to get
ourselves to do it.

Some years ago I was offered a writing assignment that would require   17
three months of travel through Europe. I had been abroad a couple of

times on the usual "If it's Tuesday this must be Belgium"* trips, but I hardly could claim to know my way around the continent. Moreover, my knowledge of foreign languages was limited to a little college French.

I hesitated. How would I, unable to speak the language, totally 18 unfamiliar with local geography or transportation systems, set up interviews and do research? It seemed impossible, and with considerable regret I sat down to write a letter begging off. Halfway through, a thought—which I subsequently made into another corollary to my basic rule—ran through my mind: *You can't learn if you don't try.* So I accepted the assignment.

There were some bad moments. But by the time I had finished the trip 19 I was an experienced traveler. And ever since, I have never hesitated to head for even the most exotic of places, without guides or even advance bookings, confident that somehow I will manage.

The point is that the new, the different, is almost by definition scary. 20 But each time you try something, you learn; and as the learning piles up, the world opens to you.

I've made parachute jumps, learned to ski at 40, flown up the Rhine in 21 a balloon. And I know I'm going to go on doing such things. It's not because I'm braver or more daring than others. I'm not. But I don't let the butterflies stop me from doing what I want. Accept anxiety as another name for challenge, and you can accomplish wonders.

FIRST IMPRESSIONS

Freewrite for ten minutes on one of the following.

1. Did you enjoy reading this selection? Why or why not?

2. In general, do you find decision-making easy—or difficult? Explain.

3. Have you ever turned down an opportunity that you later wished you had taken? Why do you think you turned it down?

---

*Reference to a film comedy about a group of tourists who visited too many countries in too little time.

VOCABULARY CHECK

A. Circle the letter of the word or phrase that best completes each of the following four items.

1. In the sentences below, the word *daunted* means
   a. interested.
   b. bored.
   c. soothed.
   d. discouraged.

   "The more I thought about it, the more the prospect daunted me. I began waking up nights in a sweat." (Paragraph 2)

2. In the sentence below, the word *confront* means
   a. face.
   b. loosen.
   c. calm.
   d. develop.

   "The great Danish philosopher Soren Kierkegaard believed that anxiety always arises when we confront the possibility of our own development." (Paragraph 9)

3. In the sentence below, the word *corollary* means
   a. an idea that is false.
   b. an idea that follows from another idea.
   c. an idea that has not yet been tested.
   d. an idea that cannot be proven.

   "Which brings us to a corollary to my basic rule: *You'll never eliminate anxiety by avoiding the things that cause it.*" (Paragraph 15)

4. In the sentence below, the word *subsequently* means
   a. previously.
   b. later.
   c. unsuccessfully.
   d. mistakenly.

   "Halfway through, a thought—which I subsequently made into another corollary to my basic rule—ran through my mind: *You can't learn if you don't try.*" (Paragraph 18)

B. Circle the letter of the answer that best completes each of the following four items. Each item uses a word (or form of a word) from "Words to Watch."

5. A woman's *prospective* husband is
   a. the man she used to be married to.
   b. a man she expects to marry in the future.
   c. her current husband.

6. An example of a *proposition* is
   a. "You're fired."
   b. "If you take the job, I'll pay you $30,000 a year."
   c. "Why do you think we should hire you?"

7. When I was asked what I wanted to do Saturday night, I *wavered*. I
   a. immediately replied, "Let's see the new Jim Carrey movie!"
   b. explained that I was too busy to go out.
   c. couldn't decide between seeing the new Jim Carrey movie and renting a video.

8. The famous saying "Only death and taxes are *inevitable*" means that
   a. death and taxes are very much alike.
   b. death and taxes are two undesirable things.
   c. death and taxes are two things we can't avoid.

READING CHECK

Central Point and Main Ideas

1. Which sentence best expresses the central point of the entire selection?
   a. There are two kinds of anxiety: the normal anxiety that one feels when confronted with a new situation, and abnormal, disabling anxiety, which requires medical attention.
   b. The author turned down an exciting opportunity in college and almost immediately wished he had accepted it.
   c. Accepting challenges that make you anxious helps you to learn and grow in beneficial ways.
   d. The author accepted a writing assignment that required that he spend three months in Europe, even though the idea made him very anxious.

2. The topic sentence of paragraph 10 is its
   a. first sentence.
   b. second sentence.
   c. third sentence.
   d. last sentence.

3. Which sentence best expresses the main idea of paragraph 15?
   a. When Jeff wanted to quit swimming lessons, his father insisted that he keep at it.
   b. Jeff's experience in learning to swim demonstrates that you can "extinguish" a fear by confronting it.
   c. Jeff was at first afraid to try to swim, but he soon got over his fear.
   d. Avoiding things that cause anxiety is never a good idea.

Key Supporting Details

4. Once the author's friend asked another young man to go with him to Argentina, the author felt
   a. relieved.
   b. hurt and insulted.
   c. regretful and depressed.
   d. anxious.

5. The philosopher Soren Kierkegaard believed that
   a. people should do whatever is necessary to avoid feeling anxious.
   b. even very well-known people often suffer from stage fright.
   c. anxiety is an abnormal condition.
   d. anxiety results when we face the possibility of our own development.

6. Which of the following is *not* one of the reasons the author was hesitant about accepting the European assignment?
   a. He did not speak any European languages.
   b. He had promised to teach his brother to sail that summer.
   c. He was unfamiliar with the geography of the places he would be traveling.
   d. He did not know the transportation systems of the cities where he would be staying.

Inferences

7. We can conclude that the author
    a. no longer feels anxiety about new experiences.
    b. wishes that he had not accepted the European writing assignment.
    (c.) in some ways welcomes the feeling of anxiety when he faces a new task.
    d. thought less of Duke Ellington after learning that he suffered from stage fright.

8. In paragraph 19, the author implies that
    a. his European trip was a disaster.
    (b.) after his European trip, he felt pleased with his ability to deal with the challenges he found there.
    c. he realizes now that he was reckless to head off to Europe without a better idea of what he was doing.
    d. since his European trip, he has traveled a good deal for pleasure, but not on writing assignments.

The Writer's Craft

9. For the most part, Collier relies on which of the following to illustrate his points?
    a. Statistics
    b. Theoretical examples involving characters he has invented
    c. Quotations from experts on human development
    (d.) Examples from his personal experience

10. Collier's piece is organized around which of the following?
    a. Three rules
    (b.) A rule and two corollary rules
    c. Two rules and one corollary rule
    d. Three corollary rules

DISCUSSION QUESTIONS

1. Can you understand why Collier turned down the chance to go to Argentina? Would you have felt some of the same fears he felt? Explain.

2. Do you agree with Collier that anxiety has a positive side? Can you give an example from your own life of a decision that has made you feel anxious, as opposed to a decision that has left you feeling depressed?

3. The same situations that make some people anxious do not affect others at all. What are some particularly anxiety-provoking situations for you? Possibilities include speaking in public, meeting new people, eating alone in a restaurant, driving in an unfamiliar city. What strategies have you developed for dealing with your particular anxieties?

4. Like most people, at one time or another, you have probably decided not to take on a challenge because it made you feel too anxious. How did you feel about yourself and your decision? In the long run, do you think the decision worked out for the best, or would you do it differently if you had another chance?

PARAGRAPH ASSIGNMENTS

1. By explaining how his life experiences have made him view the term "anxiety" in a new way, Collier is actually redefining the term. Write a paragraph in which you, too, redefine a term in light of your personal experience. You might want to write about a term such as "regret," "success," "unselfishness," or "homesickness." Begin your paragraph with a sentence that includes the term, like this: "Since I've started running regularly, I think of the term 'physical fitness' in a whole new way."

2. Write a paragraph in which you describe the process you went through when you were faced with a difficult decision. Be sure to discuss the following: what the decision was; why it was particularly difficult for you; the pros and cons of the options you considered; and, of course, the decision you finally made. Conclude by explaining how you feel now about the wisdom of your decision.

ESSAY ASSIGNMENTS

1. Collier is writing about two approaches to life: one in which a person shies away from new experiences and the anxiety they cause, and the other in which a person embraces new challenges. Write an essay in which you contrast two types of people who live their lives in very different ways. You might choose to contrast, for instance, a spendthrift with a miser, or an emotionally expressive person with someone who keeps feelings to himself or herself. In your essay, provide plenty of specific examples that illustrate the different ways the two types of people react to similar situations. At some point in the essay, you should state briefly which type of behavior you find preferable, and why. Focus your essay with a thesis statement similar to one of the following:

   - While my mother (*or* other relative) never lets people know what's on her mind, my father (*or* other relative) is very emotional and finds it easy to share his feelings.

   - Adventurous people and timid people lead very different everyday lives.

2. From the example involving Collier and his son, it is clear that Collier wants to pass on to his children what he has learned about facing challenges. What are two or three "rules for life" that you'd like your children (if you were to have any) to learn? Write an essay in the form of a letter to your child. In it, state the two or three rules that you would like to pass on. Explain, using vivid examples, why and how you believe following these rules would benefit your child.

14

The Bystander Effect
Dorothy Barkin

Preview

Most of us think of ourselves as decent, helpful people. We certainly wouldn't turn our backs on someone in obvious need of help . . . or would we? Sociologists' experiments confirm what occasional, shocking news stories suggest: Many of us, when faced with a person who seems to be in desperate trouble, do absolutely nothing. In this article, Dorothy Barkin explores some of the possible explanations for this troubling "bystander effect."

Words to Watch

intervene (2): interfere
phenomena (4): facts
apathy (23): indifference
diffusion (32): spreading thin
paralysis (32): inability to act

I t is a pleasant fall afternoon. The sun is shining. You are heading toward   1
the parking lot after your last class of the day. All of a sudden, you come
across the following situations. What do you think you'd do in each case?

Situation One: A man in his early twenties dressed in jeans and a T-
shirt is using a coat hanger to pry open a door of a late-model Ford

sedan. An overcoat and a camera are visible on the back seat of the car. You're the only one who sees this.

Situation Two: A man and woman are wrestling with each other. The woman is in tears. Attempting to fight the man off, she screams, "Who are you? Get away from me!" You're the only one who witnesses this.

Situation Three: Imagine the same scenario as in Situation Two except that this time the woman screams, "Get away from me! I don't know why I ever married you!"

Situation Four: Again imagine Situation Three. This time, however, there are a few other people (strangers to you and each other) who also observe the incident.

Many people would choose not to get involved in situations like these. 2
Bystanders are often reluctant to intervene° in criminal or medical emergencies for reasons they are well aware of. They fear possible danger to themselves or getting caught up in a situation that could lead to complicated and time-consuming legal proceedings.

There are, however, other, less obvious factors which influence the 3
decision to get involved in emergency situations. Complex psychological factors, which many people are unaware of, play an important part in the behavior of bystanders; knowing about these factors can help people to act more responsibly when faced with emergencies.

To understand these psychological phenomena°, it is helpful to look at 4
what researchers have learned about behavior in the situations mentioned at the beginning of this article.

Situation One: Research reveals a remarkably low rate of bystander intervention to protect property. In one study, more than 3,000 people walked past 214 staged car break-ins like the one described in this situation. The vast majority of passers-by completely ignored what appeared to be a crime in progress. Not one of the 3,000 bothered to report the incident to the police.

Situation Two: Another experiment involved staging scenarios like this and the next situation. In Situation Two, bystanders offered some sort of assistance to the young woman 65 percent of the time.

Situation Three: Here the rate of bystander assistance dropped down to 19 percent. This demonstrates that bystanders are more reluctant to help a woman when they believe she's fighting with her husband. Not only do they consider a wife in less need of help; they think interfering with a married couple may be more dangerous. The husband, unlike a stranger, will not flee the situation.

Situation Four: The important idea in this situation is being a member of a group of bystanders. In more than fifty studies involving many different conditions, one outcome has been consistent: bystanders are much less likely to get involved when other witnesses are present than when they are alone.

In other words, membership in a group of bystanders lowers the 5 likelihood that each member of the group will become involved. This finding may seem surprising. You might think there would be safety in numbers and that being a member of a group would increase the likelihood of intervention. How can we explain this aspect of group behavior?

A flood of research has tried to answer this and other questions about 6 bystanders in emergencies ever since the infamous case of the murder of Kitty Genovese.

In 1964 in the borough of Queens in New York City, Catherine "Kitty" 7 Genovese, 28, was brutally murdered in a shocking crime that outraged the nation.

The crime began at 3 a.m. Kitty Genovese was coming home from her 8 job as manager of a bar. After parking her car in a parking lot, she began the hundred-foot walk to the entrance of her apartment. But she soon noticed a man in the lot and decided instead to walk toward a police call box. As she walked by a bookstore on her way there, the man grabbed her. She screamed.

Lights went on and windows opened in the ten-story apartment building. 9

Next, the attacker stabbed Genovese. She shrieked, "Oh, my God, he 10 stabbed me! Please help me! Please help me!"

From an upper window in the apartment house, a man shouted, "Let 11 that girl alone!"

The assailant, alarmed by the man's shout, started toward his car, 12 which was parked nearby. However, the lights in the building soon went out, and the man returned. He found Genovese struggling to reach her apartment—and stabbed her again.

She screamed, "I'm dying! I'm dying!" 13

Once more lights went on and windows opened in the apartment 14 building. The attacker then went to his car and drove off. Struggling, Genovese made her way inside the building.

But the assailant returned to attack Genovese yet a third time. He 15 found her slumped on the floor at the foot of the stairs and stabbed her again, this time fatally.

The murder took over a half hour, and Kitty Genovese's desperate 16 cries for help were heard by at least thirty-eight people. Not a single one of the thirty-eight who later admitted to having witnessed the murder bothered to pick up the phone during the attack and call the police. One man called after Genovese was dead.

Comments made by bystanders after this murder provide important 17
insight into what group members think when they consider intervening in
an emergency.

These are some of the comments: 18

"I didn't want my husband to get involved." 19

"Frankly, we were afraid." 20

"We thought it was a lovers' quarrel." 21

"I was tired." 22

The Genovese murder sparkcd a national debate on the questions of 23
public apathy° and fear and became the basis for thousands of sermons,
editorials, classroom discussions, and even a made-for-television movie.
The same question was on everybody's mind—how could thirty-eight
people have done so little?

Nine years later, another well-publicized incident provided additional 24
information about the psychology of a group witnessing a crime.

On a summer afternoon in Trenton, New Jersey, a twenty-year-old 25
woman was brutally raped in a parking lot in full view of twenty-five
employees of a nearby roofing company. Though the workers witnessed
the entire incident and the woman repeatedly screamed for help, no one
came to her assistance.

Comments made by witnesses to the rape were remarkably similar to 26
those made by the bystanders to the Genovese murder. For example, one
witness said, "We thought, well, it might turn out to be her boyfriend or
something like that."

It's not surprising to find similar excuses for not helping in cases 27
involving a group of bystanders. The same psychological principles apply to
each. Research conducted since the Genovese murder indicates that the
failure of bystanders to get involved can't be simply dismissed as a symptom
of an uncaring society. Rather, the "bystander effect," as it is called by social
scientists, is the product of a complex set of psychological factors.

Two factors appear to be most important in understanding the 28
reactions of bystanders to emergencies.

First is the level of ambiguity involved in the situation. Bystanders are 29
afraid to endanger themselves or look foolish if they take the wrong
action in a situation they're not sure how to interpret. A person lying face
down on the floor of a subway train may have just suffered a heart attack
and be in need of immediate medical assistance—or he may be a
dangerous drunk.

Determining what is happening is especially difficult when a man is 30
attacking a woman. Many times lovers do quarrel, sometimes violently.
But they may strongly resent an outsider, no matter how well-meaning,
intruding into their affairs.

When a group of bystanders is around, interpreting an event can be   31
even more difficult than when one is alone. Bystanders look to others for
cues as to what is happening. Frequently other witnesses, just as
confused, try to look calm. Thus bystanders can mislead each other about
the seriousness of an incident.

The second factor in determining the reactions of bystanders to   32
emergencies is what psychologists call the principle of moral diffusion°.
Moral diffusion is the lessening of a sense of individual responsibility
when someone is a member of a group. Responsibility to act diffuses
throughout the crowd. When a member of the group is able to escape the
collective paralysis° and take action, others in the group tend to act as
well. But the larger the crowd, the greater the diffusion of responsibility,
and the less likely someone is to intervene.

The more social scientists are able to teach us about how bystanders   33
react to an emergency, the better the chances that we will take appropriate
action when faced with one. Knowing about moral diffusion, for example,
makes it easier for us to escape it. If you find yourself witnessing an
emergency with a group, remember that everybody is waiting for
someone else to do something first. If you take action, others may also
help.

Also realize that any one of us could at some time be in desperate need   34
of help. Imagine what it feels like to need help and have a crowd watching
you suffer and do nothing. Remember Kitty Genovese.

FIRST IMPRESSIONS

Freewrite for ten minutes on one of the following.

1. Did you enjoy reading this selection? Why or why not?

2. Have you ever encountered someone who seemed to be in an
   emergency situation? How did you respond?

3. In your experience, is it true that people take less responsibility when
   they are in a group than when they are alone? What examples can you
   think of to support this idea?

VOCABULARY CHECK

A. Circle the letter of the word or phrase that best completes each of the following four items.

1. In the sentence below, the word *scenario* means
   a. question.
   b. relationship.
   c. sequence of events.
   d. quotation.

   > "Imagine the same scenario as in Situation Two except that this time the woman screams, 'Get away from me! I don't know why I ever married you!'" (Paragraph 1)

2. In the sentences below, the word *assailant* means
   a. observer.
   b. bystander.
   c. victim.
   d. attacker.

   > "Next, the attacker stabbed Genovese. . . . From an upper window in the apartment house, a man shouted, 'Let that girl alone!' . . . The assailant, alarmed by the man's shout, started toward his car. . . ." (Paragraphs 10–12)

3. In the sentences below, the word *ambiguity* means
   a. argument.
   b. uncertainty.
   c. lack of interest.
   d. crowding.

   > "First is the level of ambiguity involved. . . . Bystanders are afraid to endanger themselves or look foolish . . . in a situation they're not sure how to interpret." (Paragraph 29)

4. In the sentence below, the word *cues* means
   a. laughs.
   b. hints.
   c. blame.
   d. danger.

   > "Bystanders look to others for cues as to what is happening." (Paragraph 31)

B. Circle the letter of the answer that best completes each of the following four items. Each item uses a word (or form of a word) from "Words to Watch."

5. "I resent your parents' *intervention* in our marriage problems," Alan told Susan. He meant that he resented the way
   a. her parents ignored their problems.
   b. her parents always sided with her when the couple had problems.
   c. her parents interfered in the couple's problems.

6. When I asked where we should go for dinner, I received this *apathetic* response from my daughter:
   a. "Who cares?"
   b. "I can't decide—pizza and Chinese food both sound so good."
   c. "Please, please, please let's go to the Tex-Mex Cafe!"

7. Caught cheating on the test, the student tried to *diffuse* his guilt by
   a. saying, "I am really, truly ashamed of myself."
   b. insisting that he had not been cheating.
   c. saying, "I can name eight other people who were cheating on it, too."

8. Permanent physical *paralysis* is often caused by
   a. chicken pox.
   b. a broken arm.
   c. a severe spinal cord injury.

READING CHECK

Central Point and Main Ideas

1. Which sentence best expresses the central point of the entire selection?
   a. People don't want to get involved in emergencies.
   b. Kitty Genovese was murdered because no one came to her assistance or called the police.
   c. People don't care what happens to others.
   d. Understanding why bystanders react as they do in a crisis can help people act more responsibly.

2. Which sentence best expresses the main idea of paragraph 27?
   a. A number of factors, not a simple lack of caring, keeps bystanders from getting involved.
   b. Bystanders always have the same excuses for not helping.
   c. There has been research on bystanders since the Genovese murder.
   d. The "bystander effect" is a symptom of an uncaring society.

3. The sentence that makes up paragraph 28 states the main idea of
   a. paragraph 29.
   b. paragraphs 29–30.
   c. paragraphs 29–31.
   d. paragraphs 29–32.

Key Supporting Details

4. Bystanders are most likely to help
   a. a woman being attacked by her husband.
   b. a woman being attacked by a stranger.
   c. when property is being stolen.
   d. in any emergency when others are around.

5. According to the author, when there is a group of bystanders,
   a. everyone is more likely to help.
   b. it is easier to understand what is happening.
   c. the people in the group do not influence each other at all.
   d. each is more likely to act after someone else takes action.

6. The author supports her statement that "bystanders are much less likely to get involved when other witnesses are present" (paragraph 4) with
   a. opinions.
   b. quotations from experts.
   c. research and examples.
   d. no evidence.

Inferences

7. The reading suggests that people tend to believe
   a. theft is justified.
   b. loss of property is worse than bodily harm.
   c. bodily harm is worse than loss of property.
   d. rape is worse than murder.

8. From the article, we can conclude that Kitty Genovese's killer
   a. knew his victim.
   b. was unaware of the witnesses.
   c. stabbed her too quickly for her to get help.
   (d.) kept attacking when he realized no one was coming to help her.

9. In which of the following situations can we conclude that a bystander is most likely to get involved?
   a. A man passes a clothing store with a smashed window from which people are carrying away clothes.
   (b.) A college student sees a man collapsing on a street where no one else is present.
   c. A neighbor sees a father and son fighting in their yard.
   d. A softball team sees the coach angrily yelling at and shoving his wife.

The Writer's Craft

10. The main purpose of this article, as suggested in the closing paragraphs, is to
    a. inform people of the existence of the phenomenon called "the bystander effect."
    b. inform readers that Kitty Genovese and others like her could have been saved if bystanders had taken action.
    c. entertain readers with vivid stories involving crisis situations.
    (d.) persuade people to recognize the bystander effect and be on guard against it in their own lives.

DISCUSSION QUESTIONS

1. Have you ever been influenced by the bystander effect? What was the situation? How did you explain your own response?

2. In paragraph 31, the author writes, "Bystanders look to others for cues as to what is happening. Frequently other witnesses, just as confused, try to look calm." Have you seen examples of this happening? Why would people try to look calm during an emergency?

3. One witness to the Trenton rape said, "We thought, well, it might turn out to be her boyfriend or something like that." If the rapist had been her boyfriend—or her husband—should that have affected whether witnesses interfered? Why or why not?

4. Judging from your experience, are there ways other than those described in this article that people act differently in groups than they act when they are alone? What other effects can being in a group have on individuals?

PARAGRAPH ASSIGNMENTS

1. Barkin's article suggests that people act differently when they're alone and when they're part of a group. Select an individual you know (for example, "My friend Reba") and write a paragraph that contrasts that person's behavior when he or she is alone versus when he or she is in a particular public setting. Examples of public settings might be a party, a basketball game, a dance, a family gathering, or a shopping mall. Your paragraph may be serious or humorous in tone. Provide lively examples to illustrate your points. You could begin with a topic sentence such as the following: "My friend Reba behaves very differently depending on whether she is with others or alone."

   Alternatively, write the paragraph about yourself.

2. Barkin writes about the impact of emergency situations on people's behavior. Selecting a lighter, less serious topic, write a paragraph in which you show the effects of some other factor on the way people act. You might, for example, write about the effects of final exams on college students, the impact of football season on family life, or the influence of the remote control on people's television-viewing habits. Discuss at least two ways in which the factor you have chosen affects behavior, illustrating each with lively examples from your own experiences or those of people you know. Title your paragraph something like "The Football Effect" or "The Remote-Control Effect."

ESSAY ASSIGNMENTS

1. "The Bystander Effect" is filled with anecdotes of people who stood back when help was needed, preferring to wait for someone else to act. Think of an individual you know of who has acted in the opposite way, someone who perceived a need and offered assistance. Then write an essay showing how this person went out of his or her way to help someone in need. Explain specifically what the problem was (perhaps it was a crime, a car accident, or a health emergency; or perhaps it was a more long-term need such as an illness or financial problem); what the individual did; and how the situation turned out. Include clear, striking details to help your reader picture the sequence of events. In your conclusion, you may wish to explain what might have happened if help had not been given. A possible thesis statement for this essay might be: "When I had to miss several weeks of school recently, my cousin Oscar came to my rescue in more ways than one."

2. Crises such as those described in "The Bystander Effect" are *not* the only events in which people behave inappropriately. Think of another situation in which people sometimes fail to act responsibly. Then write an essay exploring the possible reasons for this failure. You could, for example, write about why some parents avoid disciplining their children, why some college students fail to pay back their academic loans, or why some teachers are careless in grading student work. Come up with several explanations for the behavior, and be sure to provide convincing examples to illustrate your points.

15

Don't Let Stereotypes Warp Your Judgments
Robert L. Heilbroner

Preview

"A priest, a rabbi, and a minister were playing golf . . ."
"After the minor traffic accident, this Italian got out of his car . . ."
"She's a typical blonde, you know the type . . ."

We've all heard—or made—jokes and comments that begin with phrases like these. What they have in common is that each plays on or involves a stereotype, a kind of mental shorthand that allows us to believe we "know" what certain categories of people are like. Stereotypes can produce some amusing jokes. But, as this selection shows, they can also produce effects that are anything but funny.

Words to Watch

delve (4): search deeply
yokels (8): awkward or unsophisticated country people
dinned (8): repeated forcefully
stock (8): typical
perpetuated (8): caused to continue
synchronized (9): occurring at the same time
semantics (11): the study of word meanings
preconceptions (11): judgments made ahead of time
impoverish (12): make poor
reactionaries (12): opponents of change
inimitable (12): not able to be copied

lapse (15): end

chastening (18): humbling

edifice (18): structure

Is a girl called Gloria apt to be better-looking than one called Bertha? Are criminals more likely to be dark than blond? Can you tell a good deal about someone's personality from hearing his voice briefly over the phone? Can a person's nationality be pretty accurately guessed from his photograph? Does the fact that someone wears glasses imply that he is intelligent? 1

The answer to all these questions is obviously, "No." 2

Yet from all the evidence at hand, most of us believe these things. Ask any college boy if he'd rather take his chances with a Gloria or a Bertha, or ask a college girl if she'd rather blind-date a Richard or a Cuthbert. In fact, you don't have to ask: college students in questionnaires have revealed that names conjure up the same images in their minds as they do in yours—and for as little reason. 3

Look into the favorite suspects of persons who report "suspicious characters" and you will find a large percentage of them to be "swarthy" or "dark and foreign-looking"—despite the testimony of criminologists that criminals do not tend to be dark, foreign or "wild-eyed." Delve° into the main asset of a telephone stock swindler and you will find it to be a marvelously confidence-inspiring telephone "personality." And whereas we all think we know what an Italian or a Swede looks like, it is the sad fact that when a group of Nebraska students sought to match faces and nationalities of 15 European countries, they were scored wrong in 93 percent of their identifications. Finally, despite the fact that horn-rimmed glasses have now become the standard television sign of an "intellectual," optometrists know that the main thing that distinguishes people with glasses is just bad eyes. 4

Stereotypes are a kind of gossip about the world, a gossip that makes us prejudge people before we ever lay eyes on them. Hence it is not surprising that stereotypes have something to do with the dark world of prejudice. Explore most prejudices (note that the word means "prejudgment") and you will find a cruel stereotype at the core of each one. 5

For it is the extraordinary fact that once we have typecast the world, we tend to see people in terms of our standardized pictures. In another demonstration of the power of stereotypes to affect our vision, a number of Columbia and Barnard students were shown thirty photographs of pretty but unidentified girls, and asked to rate each in terms of "general liking," 6 "intelligence," "beauty" and so on. Two months later, the same group were shown the same photographs, this time with fictitious Irish, Italian, Jewish and "American" names attached to the pictures. Right away the ratings changed. Faces which were now seen as representing a national group went down in looks and still farther down in likability, while the "American" girls suddenly looked decidedly prettier and nicer.

Why is it that we stereotype the world in such irrational and harmful   7
fashion? In part, we begin to typecast people in our childhood years. Early in life, as every parent whose child has watched a TV Western knows, we learn to spot the Good Guys from the Bad Guys. Some years ago, a social psychologist showed very clearly how powerful these stereotypes of childhood vision are. He secretly asked the most popular youngsters in an elementary school to make errors in their morning gym exercises. Afterwards, he asked the class if anyone had noticed any mistakes during gym period. Oh, yes, said the children. But it was the unpopular members of the class—the "bad guys"—they remembered as being out of step.

We not only grow up with standardized pictures forming inside of us,   8
but as grown-ups we are constantly having them thrust upon us. Some of them, like the half-joking, half-serious stereotypes of mothers-in-law, or country yokels°, or psychiatrists, are dinned° into us by the stock° jokes we hear and repeat. In fact, without such stereotypes, there would be a lot fewer jokes. Still other stereotypes are perpetuated° by the advertisements we read, the movies we see, the books we read.

And finally, we tend to stereotype because it helps us make sense out   9
of a highly confusing world, a world which William James once described as "one great, blooming, buzzing confusion." It is a curious fact that if we don't know what we're looking at, we are often quite literally unable to see what we're looking at. People who recover their sight after a lifetime of blindness actually cannot at first tell a triangle from a square. A visitor to a factory sees only noisy chaos where the superintendent sees a perfectly synchronized° flow of work. As Walter Lippmann has said, "For the most part we do not first see, and then define; we define first, and then we see."

Stereotypes are one way in which we "define" the world in order to   10
see it. They classify the infinite variety of human beings into a convenient handful of "types" toward whom we learn to act in stereotyped fashion. Life would be a wearing process if we had to start from scratch with each and every human contact. Stereotypes economize on our mental effort by covering up the blooming, buzzing confusion with big recognizable cut-outs. They save us the "trouble" of finding out what the world is like— they give it its accustomed look.

Thus the trouble is that stereotypes make us mentally lazy. As S. I.   11
Hayakawa, the authority on semantics°, has written: "The danger of
stereotypes lies not in their existence, but in the fact that they become for
all people some of the time, and for some people all the time, substitutes
for observation." Worse yet, stereotypes get in the way of our judgment,
even when we do observe the world. Someone who has formed rigid
preconceptions° of all Latins as "excitable," or all teenagers as "wild,"
doesn't alter his point of view when he meets a calm and deliberate
Genoese, or a serious-minded high-school student. He brushes them aside
as "exceptions that prove the rule." And, of course, if he meets someone
true to type, he stands triumphantly vindicated. "They're all like that," he
proclaims, having encountered an excited Latin, an ill-behaved adolescent.

Hence, quite aside from the injustice which stereotypes do to others,   12
they impoverish° ourselves. A person who lumps the world into simple
categories, who typecasts all labor leaders as "racketeers," all
businessmen as "reactionaries°," all Harvard men are "snobs," and all
Frenchmen as "sexy," is in danger of becoming a stereotype himself. He
loses his capacity to be himself—which is to say, to see the world in his
own absolutely unique, inimitable° and independent fashion.

Instead, he votes for the man who fits his standardized picture of what   13
a candidate "should" look like or sound like, buys the goods that someone
in his "situation" in life "should" own, lives the life that others define for
him. The mark of the stereotype person is that he never surprises us, that
we do indeed have him "typed." And no one fits this strait-jacket so
perfectly as someone whose opinions about other people are fixed and
inflexible.

Impoverishing as they are, stereotypes are not easy to get rid of. The   14
world we typecast may be no better than a Grade B movie, but at least we
know what to expect of our stock characters. When we let them act for
themselves in the strangely unpredictable way that people do act, who
knows but that many of our fondest convictions will be proved wrong?

Nor do we suddenly drop our standardized pictures for a blinding   15
vision of the Truth. Sharp swings of ideas about people often just
substitute one stereotype for another. The true process of change is a slow
one that adds bits and pieces of reality to the pictures in our heads, until
gradually they take on some of the blurriness of life itself. Little by little,
we learn not that Jews and Negroes and Catholics and Puerto Ricans are
"just like everybody else"—for that, too, is a stereotype—but that each
and every one of them is unique, special, different and individual. Often
we do not even know that we have let a stereotype lapse° until we hear
someone saying, "All so-and-so's are like such-and-such," and we hear
ourselves saying, "Well—maybe."

Can we speed the process along? Of course we can.   16

First, we can become aware of the standardized pictures in our heads,   17
in other people's heads, in the world around us.

Second, we can become suspicious of all judgments that we allow   18
exceptions to "prove." There is no more chastening° thought than that in
the vast intellectual adventure of science, it takes but one tiny exception
to topple a whole edifice° of ideas.

Third, we can learn to be chary of generalizations about people. As   19
F. Scott Fitzgerald once wrote: "Begin with an individual, and before you
know it you have created a type; begin with a type, and you find you have
created—nothing."

Most of the time, when we typecast the world, we are not in fact   20
generalizing about people at all. We are only revealing the embarrassing
facts about the pictures that hang in the gallery of stereotypes in our own
heads.

FIRST IMPRESSIONS

Freewrite for ten minutes on one of the following.

1. Did you enjoy reading this selection? Why or why not?

2. What do you think of when you picture each of the following?
    - Someone named Helga
    - A professional wrestler
    - A funeral director
    - A computer programmer
    - Someone named Percy
    - An accountant
    - A hair stylist
    - Someone who rides a motorcycle

    Write about as many of these as you can in the time provided. Tell
    what they look like and how they speak and act. When you finish, look
    at what you have written. Does any of it contain the kind of
    stereotyped thinking Heilbroner describes in his article?

3. Have you ever felt that someone stereotyped you? If so, explain what
    happened and how it felt. Did you do anything about it?

VOCABULARY CHECK

A. Circle the letter of the word or phrase that best completes each of the following four items.

1. In the sentence below, the words *conjure up* mean
   a. destroy.
   (b.) produce.
   c. shrink.
   d. reward.

   "In fact, you don't have to ask: college students in questionnaires have revealed that names conjure up the same images in their minds as they do in yours." (Paragraph 3)

2. In the sentence below, the word *typecast* means
   a. left.
   b. grown tired of.
   c. forgiven.
   (d.) judged ahead of time.

   "For it is the extraordinary fact that once we have typecast the world, we tend to see people in terms of our standardized pictures." (Paragraph 6)

3. In the sentences below, the word *vindicated* means
   a. amazed.
   b. world-famous.
   c. silly.
   (d.) proved right.

   "He brushes them [a calm Genoese or a serious-minded high-school student] aside as 'exceptions that prove the rule.' And of course, if he meets someone true to type, he stands triumphantly vindicated." (Paragraph 11)

4. In the sentences below, the words *chary of* mean
   a. encouraging about.
   (b.) cautious about.
   c. optimistic about.
   d. proud of.

   "Can we speed the process [of getting rid of stereotypes] along? Of course we can. . . . [W]e can learn to be chary of generalizations about people." (Paragraphs 16 and 19)

B. Circle the letter of the answer that best completes each of the following four items. Each item uses a word (or form of a word) from "Words to Watch."

5. The researchers *delved* into the question of family violence
   a. for a few minutes.
   (b.) for months.
   c. carelessly.

6. The mayor's *stock* response, "We'll form a committee to investigate that," was one we'd
   a. never heard before.
   (b.) heard over and over.
   c. been hoping, but not expecting, to hear.

7. The *reactionaries* on our club's board of directors
   a. are constantly suggesting new activities.
   (b.) want to go back to the old ways of doing things.
   c. agree with whatever the majority wants.

8. Since my subscription to *Newsweek* has *lapsed*, I
   (a.) haven't gotten any copies.
   b. read it every week.
   c. get two copies every week.

READING CHECK

Central Point and Main Ideas

1. Which sentence best expresses the central point of the entire selection?
   (a.) Stereotyping, which is common for various reasons, harms our thinking, but we can learn to avoid it.
   b. We stereotype in order to make sense of the world.
   c. There are several ways to get rid of stereotyped thinking.
   d. We can learn to stereotype better.

2. Which sentence best expresses the main idea of paragraph 8?
   a. Many jokes are based on stereotypes.
   b. Stereotypes make growing up difficult.
   (c.) As adults, we are surrounded by stereotypes.
   d. Advertisements, movies, and books use stereotypes.

3. Which sentence best expresses the main idea of paragraph 15?
   a. Minority groups are not "just like everybody else."
   b. We need to stop depending on stereotypes.
   c. Changes in our thinking about people often involve the substitution of one stereotype for another.
   d. Learning not to stereotype is a gradual process.

Key Supporting Details

4. According to the article, which of the following does *not* encourage stereotyping?
   a. Childhood influences
   b. Careful observation
   c. Advertisements, movies, and books
   d. The urge to make sense of the world

5. When asked to guess people's nationalities from their photographs, a group of Nebraskan students
   a. were right 93 percent of the time.
   b. were wrong 93 percent of the time.
   c. correctly identified most of the people from European countries.
   d. reported a higher "general liking" of those who had fictitious Irish and Italian names.

6. According to the author, stereotyping
   a. is rare.
   b. is often accurate.
   c. makes us mentally lazy.
   d. broadens our view of the world.

Inferences

7. __T__ TRUE OR FALSE? The author implies that prejudice is based on stereotypes.

8. From the experiment with Columbia and Barnard students (paragraph 6), we can infer that
   a. names have nothing to do with stereotypes.
   b. college students are good judges of beauty.
   c. the students tended to prefer nationalities different from their own.
   d. the students tended to prefer people who were not members of minority groups.

The Writer's Craft

9. The author begins this selection with a series of questions on familiar stereotypes because
   a. he doesn't know the answers.
   b. he thinks readers won't know the answers.
   (c.) he wants to show readers that they may be relying on stereotypes.
   d. he wants to show his dislike for foreign-looking people with strange names.

10. What audience did Heilbroner seem to have in mind when he wrote this essay?
    a. Psychologists who study the effect of stereotypes.
    b. College instructors teaching courses about stereotypes.
    (c.) General readers who may not be aware of how they are affected by stereotypes.
    d. Witnesses to crimes, who are often influenced by stereotypes.

DISCUSSION QUESTIONS

1. What are some of the stereotypes you have heard or seen in jokes, ads, movies, books, or television shows? Did you think they were stereotypes when you first encountered them?

2. What stereotyped attitudes towards men and women have you come across? Are these stereotypes harmful in any way?

3. What stereotypes do you find particularly harmful or offensive? What are some good ways to respond to people who reveal prejudiced or stereotyped attitudes?

4. The author states, "Explore most prejudices (note that the word means 'prejudgment') and you will find a cruel stereotype at the core of each one." What do you think he means? How is a prejudice similar to a stereotype? How is it different?

PARAGRAPH ASSIGNMENTS

1. Have you ever felt that someone was stereotyping you? Perhaps someone thought he or she knew all about you because of a stereotyped image of your race, nationality, sex, age, appearance, or job. Write a paragraph about what it is like to be stereotyped. Your topic sentence might be similar to this: "I was once the victim of stereotyping because of my _____."

2. Think of a name you would (or would *not*) name your child. Then explain why you would or would not choose this name for your son or daughter. Support your point by discussing what qualities, abilities, or characteristics you and other people might associate with this name. You might want to mention:

   - Famous people who have the same name
   - How "masculine" or "feminine" the name sounds
   - The personal qualities that this name suggests
   - What the name really means (for example, Leo means "lion")
   - The fact that the name has been in your family for generations

ESSAY ASSIGNMENTS

1. Stereotypes frequently appear in popular media. Write an essay in which you show how TV programs, movies, or books stereotype one or more groups of people. For instance, you might examine how teenagers or single mothers are portrayed in TV sitcoms. Or you might show how Latinos, Asians, African Americans, or people from a particular region of the country are stereotyped in movies. Your thesis might be similar to one of these:

   - In several recent movies, Latin men are stereotyped as hot-tempered criminals.

   - Single adult females are often portrayed as stupid and superficial on prime-time TV shows.

2. Write an essay entitled "All _____ Aren't _____," in which you tell how you discovered that all members of a certain group are not what the stereotype says they are. For example, you might write about one or more redheads who turned out to be gentle and patient, not hot-headed or temperamental. Or you might write about a "jock" who is sensitive, likes classical music, or writes poetry. Or perhaps you know an eighty-year-old person who likes rock music. Your essay should tell about two or three incidents (that you observed or that you heard or read about) which proved the stereotype wrong.

16

Dealing with Feelings
Rudolph F. Verderber

Preview

When you are angry, are you inclined to "get it off your chest" or to "bite your tongue"? When you're happy, do you let the world know it, or keep it to yourself? How does the way you express your emotions make you feel about yourself? How does it make the people around you feel? In this excerpt from the college textbook *Communicate!*, Sixth Edition (Wadsworth), the author explores three ways of dealing with feelings and the consequences of each.

Words to Watch

self-disclosure (1): revealing oneself
decipher (2): interpret
seethe (2): boil with emotion
perceived (3): seen
undemonstrative (3): tending not to express feelings
inconsequential (4): unimportant
interpersonally (7): involving relations between people
potential (12): possible
net (14): final
triggered (16): set off
elated (17): very happy

An extremely important aspect of self-disclosure° is the sharing of   1
feelings. We all experience feelings such as happiness at receiving an
unexpected gift, sadness about the breakup of a relationship, or anger
when we believe we have been taken advantage of. The question is
whether to disclose such feelings, and if so, how. Self-disclosure of
feelings usually will be most successful not when feelings are withheld or
displayed but when they are described. Let's consider each of these forms
of dealing with feelings.

Withholding Feelings

Withholding feelings—that is, keeping them inside and not giving any   2
verbal or nonverbal cues to their existence—is generally an inappropriate
means of dealing with feelings. Withholding feelings is best exemplified
by the good poker player who develops a "poker face," a neutral look that
is impossible to decipher°. The look is the same whether the player's cards
are good or bad. Unfortunately, many people use poker faces in their
interpersonal relationships, so that no one knows whether they hurt inside,
are extremely excited, and so on. For instance, Doris feels very nervous
when Candy stands over her while Doris is working on her report. And
when Candy says, "That first paragraph isn't very well written," Doris
begins to seethe°, yet she says nothing—she withholds her feelings.

Psychologists believe that when people withhold feelings, they can   3
develop physical problems such as ulcers, high blood pressure, and heart
disease, as well as psychological problems such as stress-related neuroses
and psychoses. Moreover, people who withhold feelings are often
perceived° as cold, undemonstrative°, and not much fun to be around.

Is withholding ever appropriate? When a situation is inconsequential°,   4
you may well choose to withhold your feelings. For instance, a stranger's
inconsiderate behavior at a party may bother you, but because you can
move to another part of the room, withholding may not be detrimental. In
the example of Doris seething at Candy's behavior, however, withholding
could be costly to Doris.

Displaying Feelings

Displaying feelings means expressing those feelings through a facial   5
reaction, body response, and/or spoken reaction. Cheering over a great
play at a sporting event, booing the umpire at a perceived bad call, patting
a person on the back when the person does something well, or saying,
"What are you doing?" in a nasty tone of voice are all displays of feelings.

Displays are especially appropriate when the feelings you are   6
experiencing are positive. For instance, when Gloria does something nice for

you, and you experience a feeling of joy, giving her a big hug is appropriate; when Don gives you something you've wanted, and you experience a feeling of appreciation, a big smile or an "Oh, thank you, Don" is appropriate. In fact, many people need to be even more demonstrative of good feelings. You've probably seen the bumper sticker "Have you hugged your kid today?" It reinforces the point that you need to display love and affection constantly to show another person that you really care.

Displays become detrimental to communication when the feelings you   7
are experiencing are negative—especially when the display of a negative feeling appears to be an overreaction. For instance, when Candy stands over Doris while she is working on her report and says, "That first paragraph isn't very well written," Doris may well experience resentment. If Doris lashes out at Candy by screaming, "Who the hell asked you for your opinion?" Doris's display no doubt will hurt Candy's feelings and short-circuit their communication. Although displays of negative feelings may be good for you psychologically, they are likely to be bad for you interpersonally°.

Describing Feelings

Describing feelings—putting your feelings into words in a calm,   8
nonjudgmental way—tends to be the best method of disclosing feelings. Describing feelings not only increases chances for positive communication and decreases chances for short-circuiting lines of communication; it also teaches people how to treat you. When you describe your feelings, people are made aware of the effect of their behavior. This knowledge gives them the information needed to determine whether they should continue or repeat that behavior. If you tell Paul that you really feel flattered when he visits you, such a statement should encourage Paul to visit you again; likewise, when you tell Cliff that you feel very angry when he borrows your jacket without asking, he is more likely to ask the next time he borrows a jacket. Describing your feelings allows you to exercise a measure of control over others' behavior toward you.

Describing and displaying feelings are not the same. Many times   9
people think they are describing when in fact they are displaying feelings or evaluating.

If describing feelings is so important to communicating effectively,   10
why don't more people do it regularly? There seem to be at least four reasons why many people don't describe feelings.

1. Many people have a poor vocabulary of words for describing the   11
various feelings they are experiencing. People can sense that they are angry; however, they may not know whether what they are feeling might best be described as annoyed, betrayed, cheated, crushed, disturbed, furious, outraged, or shocked. Each of these words

describes a slightly different aspect of what many people lump together as anger.

2. Many people believe that describing their true feelings reveals too 12 *much about themselves.* If you tell people when their behavior hurts you, you risk their using the information against you when they want to hurt you on purpose. Even so, the potential° benefits of describing your feelings far outweigh the risks. For instance, if Pete has a nickname for you that you don't like and you tell Pete that calling you by that nickname really makes you nervous and tense, Pete may use the nickname when he wants to hurt you, but he is more likely to stop calling you by that name. If, on the other hand, you don't describe your feelings to Pete, he is probably going to call you by that name all the time because he doesn't know any better. When you say nothing, you reinforce his behavior. The level of risk varies with each situation, but you will more often improve a relationship than be hurt by describing feelings.

3. Many people believe that if they describe feelings, others will make 13 *them feel guilty about having such feelings.* At a very tender age we all learned about "tactful" behavior. Under the premise that "the truth sometimes hurts" we learned to avoid the truth by not saying anything or by telling "little" lies. Perhaps when you were young your mother said, "Don't forget to give Grandma a great big kiss." At that time you may have blurted out, "Ugh—it makes me feel yucky to kiss Grandma. She's got a mustache." If your mother responded, "That's terrible—your grandma loves you. Now you give her a kiss and never let me hear you talk like that again!" then you probably felt guilty for having this "wrong" feeling. But the point is that the thought of kissing your grandma made you feel "yucky" whether it should have or not. In this case what was at issue was the way you talked about the feelings—not your having the feelings.

4. Many people believe that describing feelings causes harm to others 14 *or to a relationship.* If it really bothers Max when his girlfriend, Dora, bites her fingernails, Max may believe that describing his feelings to Dora will hurt her so much that the knowledge will drive a wedge into their relationship. So it's better for Max to say nothing, right? Wrong! If Max says nothing, he's still going to be bothered by Dora's behavior. In fact, as time goes on, Max will probably lash out at Dora for others things because he can't bring himself to talk about the behavior that really bothers him. The net° result is that not only will Dora be hurt by Max's behavior, but she won't understand the true source of his feelings. By not describing his feelings, Max may well drive a wedge into their relationship anyway.

If Max does describe his feelings to Dora, she might quit or at   15
least try to quit biting her nails; they might get into a discussion in
which he finds out that she doesn't want to bite them but just can't
seem to stop, and he can help her in her efforts to stop; or they might
discuss the problem and Max may see that it is a small thing really and
not let it bother him as much. The point is that in describing feelings
the chances of a successful outcome are greater than they are in not
describing them.

To describe your feelings, first put the emotion you are feeling into   16
words. Be specific. Second, state what triggered° the feeling. Finally,
make sure you indicate that the feeling is yours. For example, suppose
your roommate borrows your jacket without asking. When he returns, you
describe your feelings by saying, "Cliff, I [indication that the feeling is
yours] get really angry [the feeling] when you borrow my jacket without
asking [trigger]." Or suppose that Carl has just reminded you of the very
first time he brought you a rose. You describe your feelings by saying,
"Carl, I [indication that the feeling is yours] get really tickled [the feeling]
when you remind me about that first time you brought me a rose
[trigger]."

You may find it easiest to begin by describing positive feelings: "I   17
really feel elated° knowing that you were the one who nominated me for
the position" or "I'm delighted that you offered to help me with the
housework." As you gain success with positive descriptions, you can try
negative feelings attributable to environmental factors: "It's so cloudy; I
feel gloomy" or "When the wind howls through the cracks, I really get
jumpy." Finally, you can move to negative descriptions resulting from
what people have said or done: "Your stepping in front of me like that
really annoys me" or "The tone of your voice confuses me."

FIRST IMPRESSIONS

Freewrite for ten minutes on one of the following.

1. Did you enjoy reading this selection? Why or why not?

2. What do you normally do when you have strong feelings—withhold
   them, display them, or describe them? Give an example.

3. When have you been on the receiving end of a negative display of
   feelings? A positive display? How did you respond to either of them?

VOCABULARY CHECK

A. Circle the letter of the word or phrase that best completes each of the following four items.

1. In the sentence below, the word *exemplified* means
   a. contradicted.
   b. illustrated.
   c. surprised.
   d. ignored.

   "Withholding feelings is best exemplified by the good poker player who develops a 'poker face,' a neutral look. . . ." (Paragraph 2)

2. In the sentence below, the word *detrimental* means
   a. useful.
   b. private.
   c. helpless.
   d. harmful.

   "For instance, a stranger's inconsiderate behavior at a party may bother you, but because you can move to another part of the room, withholding may not be detrimental." (Paragraph 4)

3. In the sentence below, the word *premise* means
   a. question.
   b. surprise.
   c. belief.
   d. disagreement.

   "Under the premise that 'the truth sometimes hurts' we learned to avoid the truth by not saying anything or by telling 'little' lies." (Paragraph 13)

4. In the sentence below, the word *wedge* means
   a. something that divides.
   b. loyalty.
   c. friendship.
   d. greater attraction.

   "Max may believe that describing his feelings to Dora will hurt her so much that the knowledge will drive a wedge into their relationship." (Paragraph 14)

B. Circle the letter of the answer that best completes each of the following four items. Each item uses a word (or form of a word) from "Words to Watch."

5. Although he didn't say anything during the meeting, it was clear Aaron was *seething*; he
   a. just sat there looking bored.
   (b.) was frowning and holding his pen so tightly his knuckles were turning white.
   c. nodded and smiled at everything that was said.

6. "I *perceive* that you have already had dinner," Dad said. He might instead have said,
   (a.) "I see that you have already had dinner."
   b. "I hope that you have already had dinner."
   c. "I fear that you have already had dinner."

7. A *potentially* dangerous situation is one that
   a. is not dangerous.
   b. was dangerous at one time, but is no longer dangerous.
   (c.) could be dangerous.

8. Ramon felt *elated* when
   a. another driver pulled into the parking place he was about to take.
   b. he realized he would be over an hour late for his job interview.
   (c.) his supervisor told him that she was recommending him for promotion.

READING CHECK

Central Point and Main Ideas

1. Which sentence best expresses the central point of the entire selection?
   a. Everyone has feelings.
   (b.) There are three ways to deal with feelings; describing them is most useful for educating others about how you want to be treated.
   c. Withholding feelings means not giving verbal or nonverbal clues that might reveal those feelings to others.
   d. Expressing feelings often leads to problems with others.

2. Which sentence best expresses the main idea of paragraphs 2 and 3?
   a. Withholding negative feelings may lead to physical problems.
   b. Withholding negative feelings may lead to psychological problems.
   c. Withholding positive feelings can make one seem cold.
   (d.) Withholding feelings has several disadvantages.

3. Which sentence best expresses the main idea of paragraph 6?
   (a.) When people have positive feelings, they should display them.
   b. Giving someone a hug is appropriate when he or she does something nice for you.
   c. Women are usually more demonstrative of positive feelings than men are.
   d. In order to reassure others of your love, you need to constantly demonstrate that love.

Key Supporting Details

4. According to the author, you are more likely to create physical problems for yourself by
   (a.) withholding your feelings.
   b. displaying your positive feelings.
   c. describing your positive feelings.
   d. describing your negative feelings.

5. When Doris screams at Candy, Doris is
   a. withholding feelings.
   b. displaying positive feelings.
   (c.) displaying negative feelings.
   d. describing negative feelings.

6. __*F*__ TRUE OR FALSE? Withholding feelings is never appropriate.

Inferences

7. From the reading, we can conclude that consistently displaying negative feelings
   a. is often the best way to solve problems.
   (b.) will probably alienate those around you.
   c. will make those around you feel better about themselves.
   d. is a good way to deal with superiors.

8. Which of the following can we conclude is an example of describing a feeling?
    a. Rachel moves to a different table in the library rather than ask nearby students to stop talking.
    (b.) Mrs. Hawkins tells her husband, "It annoys me when you leave your dirty socks on the floor."
    c. The football fan jumps out of his seat and shouts "YES!" as his team makes a touchdown.
    d. "You dumb jerk!" Hal shrieks at another driver who cut him off in traffic.

The Writer's Craft

9. The author's tone in this selection is best described as
    a. critical.
    b. humorous.
    (c.) matter-of-fact.
    d. sentimental.

10. The main purpose of this article is to
    a. inform readers that displaying feelings is often harmful to interpersonal relations.
    (b.) inform readers of the different ways to deal with feelings and when each way is appropriate.
    c. entertain readers with stories of how people deal with their feelings.
    d. persuade people that they should always describe their feelings.

DISCUSSION QUESTIONS

1. What is the difference between describing feelings and displaying them? How might Doris describe her feelings (rather than displaying them) to Candy after Candy says, "That first paragraph isn't very well written" (paragraph 2)?

2. In paragraph 13, Verderber discusses "tactful" behavior, also known as "little lies." Do you think Verderber approves of these "little lies"? Why or why not?

3. Why do you think Verderber goes into more detail about describing feelings than the other two methods of dealing with feelings?

4. What are some examples from your own experience of withholding, displaying, and describing feelings? How useful was each?

PARAGRAPH ASSIGNMENTS

1. Write a paragraph about a time when you (or someone else) withheld or displayed feelings when describing them might have been the better choice. Tell about the event from beginning to end, showing how the feelings were withheld or displayed and what happened as a result. Conclude by explaining how the situation would have been changed if the feelings had been described. Your topic sentence might be something like this: "After I withheld my feelings during a conversation with my boyfriend last week, I realized that describing them would have been a healthier thing to do."

2. What was the usual way of expressing feelings in your home as you were growing up? Were you encouraged to describe your feelings? Or were your family members more inclined to display or withhold them? Write a paragraph in which you describe the atmosphere regarding feelings in your home. In your topic sentence, state which way (or ways) of expressing feelings was most common in your home. Here are sample topic sentences for this assignment:

    •   When it came to expressing feelings, my family definitely fell into the "displaying" category.

    •   In my home, my father usually withheld his feelings, while my mother was more able to describe hers.

    Include specific examples of the behavior or behaviors you have chosen to write about.

ESSAY ASSIGNMENTS

1. "Dealing With Feelings" lists and discusses several ways to handle emotions. Write a paper in which you present three ways to do something else. Your tone may be serious or humorous. For example, you might write about three ways to . . .

    •   cut expenses.
    •   ruin a meal.
    •   meet people.
    •   embarrass your friends.
    •   criticize in a helpful manner.
    •   hurt a relationship.

    Here is a possible opening sentence for this assignment: "In order to ruin a meal, you must follow three simple steps."

2. Write an essay in which you show yourself dealing with one situation three different ways. To begin, invent a situation that you know would stir up negative emotions in you. Examples of such a situation might be these:

- An encounter with a very critical relative
- Dealing with a difficult customer at work
- Sitting near a table full of very noisy people in a restaurant
- Being called a nickname that you really hate
- Discussing a bad grade on a test or paper with a teacher

In your essay, describe the annoying situation in enough detail to show your reader just how it would make you feel. Then write out three scenes in which you deal with the situation in each of the ways explained in this selection—by withholding, displaying, and describing your feelings. End your essay by saying which of the three approaches you think would work best in that situation and why.

Unit Three

Relating to Others

17

All the Good Things
Sister Helen Mrosla

Preview

Teachers must often wonder if their efforts on behalf of their students are appreciated—or even noticed. In this article, Sister Helen Mrosla, a Franciscan nun from Little Falls, Minnesota, tells the story of a moment when she learned the answer to that question in a most bittersweet way. Since its publication in 1991, this simple but powerful story has been reprinted many times, as well as widely circulated on the Internet.

Words to Watch

mischievousness (1): minor misbehavior
novice (3): new
deliberately (5): slowly and on purpose
concept (8): idea
crankiness (8): grouchy mood
lull (13): silence
taps (16): a bugle call sounded at night and at a military funeral
sheepishly (20): with embarrassment
frazzled (20): worn-out; ragged

He was in the first third-grade class I taught at Saint Mary's School in   1
Morris, Minnesota. All thirty-four of my students were dear to me, but
Mark Eklund was one in a million. He was very neat in appearance but

had that happy-to-be-alive attitude that made even his occasional mischievousness° delightful.

Mark talked incessantly. I had to remind him again and again that   2
talking without permission was not acceptable. What impressed me so much, though, was his sincere response every time I had to correct him for misbehaving—"Thank you for correcting me, Sister!" I didn't know what to make of it at first, but before long I became accustomed to hearing it many times a day.

One morning my patience was growing thin when Mark talked once   3
too often, and then I made a novice° teacher's mistake. I looked at him and said, "If you say one more word, I am going to tape your mouth shut!"

It wasn't ten seconds later when Chuck blurted out, "Mark is talking   4
again." I hadn't asked any of the students to help me watch Mark, but since I had stated the punishment in front of the class, I had to act on it.

I remember the scene as if it had occurred this morning. I walked to   5
my desk, very deliberately° opened my drawer, and took out a roll of masking tape. Without saying a word, I proceeded to Mark's desk, tore off two pieces of tape and made a big X with them over his mouth. I then returned to the front of the room. As I glanced at Mark to see how he was doing, he winked at me.

That did it! I started laughing. The class cheered as I walked back to   6
Mark's desk, removed the tape, and shrugged my shoulders. His first words were, "Thank you for correcting me, Sister."

At the end of the year I was asked to teach junior-high math. The years   7
flew by, and before I knew it Mark was in my classroom again. He was more handsome than ever and just as polite. Since he had to listen carefully to my instruction in the "new math," he did not talk as much in ninth grade as he had talked in the third.

One Friday, things just didn't feel right. We had worked hard on a new   8
concept° all week, and I sensed that the students were frowning, frustrated with themselves—and edgy with one another. I had to stop this crankiness° before it got out of hand. So I asked them to list the names of the other students in the room on two sheets of paper, leaving a space after each name. Then I told them to think of the nicest thing they could say about each of their classmates and write it down.

It took the remainder of the class period to finish the assignment, and as   9
the students left the room, each one handed me the papers. Charlie smiled. Mark said, "Thank you for teaching me, Sister. Have a good weekend."

That Saturday, I wrote down the name of each student on a separate   10
sheet of paper, and I listed what everyone else had said about that individual.

On Monday I gave each student his or her list. Before long, the entire 11
class was smiling. "Really?" I heard whispered. "I never knew that meant
anything to anyone!" "I didn't know others liked me so much!"

No one ever mentioned those papers in class again. I never knew if the 12
students discussed them after class or with their parents, but it didn't
matter. The exercise had accomplished its purpose. The students were
happy with themselves and one another again.

That group of students moved on. Several years later, after I returned 13
from a vacation, my parents met me at the airport. As we were driving
home, Mother asked me the usual questions about the trip—the weather,
my experiences in general. There was a slight lull° in the conversation.
Mother gave Dad a sideways glance and simply said, "Dad?" My father
cleared his throat as he usually did before something important. "The
Eklunds called last night," he began. "Really?" I said. "I haven't heard
from them in years. I wonder how Mark is."

Dad responded quietly. "Mark was killed in Vietnam," he said. "The 14
funeral is tomorrow, and his parents would like it if you could attend." To
this day I can still point to the exact spot on I-494 where Dad told me
about Mark.

I had never seen a serviceman in a military coffin before. Mark looked 15
so handsome, so mature. All I could think at that moment was, Mark, I
would give all the masking tape in the world if only you would talk to me.

The church was packed with Mark's friends. Chuck's sister sang "The 16
Battle Hymn of the Republic." Why did it have to rain on the day of the
funeral? It was difficult enough at the graveside. The pastor said the usual
prayers, and the bugler played taps°. One by one those who loved Mark
took a last walk by the coffin and sprinkled it with holy water.

I was the last one to bless the coffin. As I stood there, one of the 17
soldiers who had acted as pallbearer came up to me. "Were you Mark's
math teacher?" he asked. I nodded as I continued to stare at the coffin.
"Mark talked about you a lot," he said.

After the funeral, most of Mark's former classmates headed to 18
Chuck's farmhouse for lunch. Mark's mother and father were there,
obviously waiting for me. "We want to show you something," his father
said, taking a wallet out of his pocket. "They found this on Mark when he
was killed. We thought you might recognize it."

Opening the billfold, he carefully removed two worn pieces of 19
notebook paper that had obviously been taped, folded and refolded many
times. I knew without looking that the papers were the ones on which I
had listed all the good things each of Mark's classmates had said about
him. "Thank you so much for doing that," Mark's mother said. "As you
can see, Mark treasured it."

Mark's classmates started to gather around us. Charlie smiled rather   20
sheepishly° and said, "I still have my list. It's in the top drawer of my desk
at home." Chuck's wife said, "Chuck asked me to put his list in our wedding
album." "I have mine too," Marilyn said. "It's in my diary." Then Vicki,
another classmate, reached into her pocketbook, took out her wallet, and
showed her worn and frazzled° list to the group. "I carry this with me at all
times," Vicki said without batting an eyelash. "I think we all saved our lists."

That's when I finally sat down and cried. I cried for Mark and for all   21
his friends who would never see him again.

FIRST IMPRESSIONS

Freewrite for ten minutes on one of the following.

1. Did you enjoy reading this selection? Why or why not?

2. Do you have any special keepsake or souvenir that you have saved for
   a long time? What is it? Why is it special to you?

3. Name one teacher you are likely to remember years from now. What
   is it that you will remember about him or her?

VOCABULARY CHECK

A. Circle the letter of the word or phrase that best completes each of the
following four items.

1. In the sentences below, the word *incessantly* means
   a. slowly.
   b. constantly.
   c. quietly.
   d. pleasantly.

   "Mark talked incessantly. I had to remind him again and again that
   talking without permission was not acceptable." (Paragraph 2)

2. In the sentence below, the words *blurted out* mean
   a. said suddenly.
   b. watched for.
   c. ran away.
   d. looked at.

   "It wasn't ten seconds later when Chuck blurted out, 'Mark is
   talking again.'" (Paragraph 4)

3. In the sentences below, the phrase *proceeded to* means
    a. stayed at.
    b. went on to.
    c. wrote on.
    d. threw.

> "I walked to my desk, very deliberately opened my drawer, and took out a roll of masking tape. Without saying a word, I proceeded to Mark's desk, tore off two pieces of tape and made a big X with them over his mouth." (Paragraph 5)

4. In the sentence below, the word *edgy* means
    a. funny.
    b. calm.
    c. easily annoyed.
    d. happy.

> "We had worked hard on a new concept all week, and I sensed that the students were frowning, frustrated with themselves—and edgy with one another." (Paragraph 8)

B. Circle the letter of the answer that best completes each of the following four items. Each item uses a word (or form of a word) from "Words to Watch."

5. My new puppy is *mischievous*. She enjoys
    a. chewing on my bedroom slippers.
    b. sleeping for six hours at a time.
    c. learning to sit and shake hands.

6. It was clear that our waiter was a *novice*; he
    a. remembered our orders perfectly without writing them down.
    b. spoke with a slight foreign accent.
    c. was very nervous and had to ask another waiter where the menus were kept.

7. Bill's *crankiness* today is understandable. He
    a. just won a two-week trip to Hawaii.
    b. has a very bad headache.
    c. is looking forward to his date tonight.

8. My roommate looked *sheepish* as she
    a. told me she had gotten a perfect score on her history final.
    b. asked me if I needed a ride to play practice.
    c. admitted she had worn my sweater without asking and had torn it.

READING CHECK

Central Point and Main Ideas

1. Which sentence best expresses the central point of the entire selection?
    a. Mark Eklund was a charming, talkative student who appreciated Sister Helen's efforts to teach him.
    b. Sister Helen found out that an assignment she had given years ago had been very important to a beloved former student and his classmates.
    c. When Sister Helen was a young teacher, she had some unusual classroom techniques.
    d. A promising young man, whom Sister Helen had taught and loved, lost his life in Vietnam.

2. Which sentence best expresses the main idea of paragraphs 1–2?
    a. Mark Eklund was in the first third-grade class Sister Helen taught at Saint Mary's School.
    b. Mark Eklund was the most talkative of all Sister Helen's students.
    c. Although Mark Eklund was talkative and mischievous, he was also very sweet-natured.
    d. Although Sister Helen kept reminding Mark that talking without permission was not permitted, she was unable to stop him from talking.

3. Which sentence best expresses the main idea of paragraphs 8–12?
    a. A difficult math concept had made Sister Helen's students irritable.
    b. The "good things" assignment made the students feel happy with themselves and others.
    c. Sister Helen gave up part of her weekend to write out a list of good things about each student.
    d. At the end of Friday's class, both Charlie and Mark seemed to be in good moods.

Key Supporting Details

4. When the students didn't mention the lists after the day they received them, Sister Helen
    a. assumed that the assignment had been a failure.
    b. didn't mind, because the assignment had done what she hoped.
    c. called a few students to ask what they thought of the lists.
    d. felt angry that the students didn't appreciate what she had done.

5. Sister Helen learned of Mark's death
   a. when her parents called her while she was on vacation.
   b. from Chuck, Mark's old friend.
   (c.) in the car on the way home from the airport.
   d. from a story in the local newspaper.

6. At the funeral, Sister Helen learned that
   a. Mark was the only student who had saved his list.
   b. Vicki and Mark were the only students who had saved their lists.
   c. the lists were more important to the male students than the female students.
   (d.) all the students in attendance at Mark's funeral had saved their lists.

Inferences

7. The author implies that
   a. she had known all along how important the lists were to her students.
   b. she did not support the war in Vietnam.
   (c.) the lists meant more to the students than she had ever realized.
   d. Mark's parents were jealous of her relationship with him.

8. It is reasonable to conclude that Mark
   (a.) cared as much for Sister Helen as she cared for him.
   b. never talked much about his past.
   c. planned to become a math teacher himself.
   d. had not stayed in touch with his classmates.

9. __F__ TRUE OR FALSE? The author implies that Mark had gotten married.

The Writer's Craft

10. At the beginning of paragraph 18, the word *after* signals which kind of transition?
    a. Addition (the author is adding a detail to a list of items)
    (b.) Time (the author is telling the next part of the story)
    c. Contrast (the author is showing that what follows is different from what has gone before)
    d. Illustration (the author is giving an example of what she has just explained)

DISCUSSION QUESTIONS

1. In this story, we read of two classroom incidents involving Sister Helen and her students. In one, she briefly taped a third-grader's mouth closed. In another, she encouraged junior-high students to think of things they liked about one another. In your opinion, what do these two incidents tell about Sister Helen? What kind of teacher was she? What kind of person?

2. Why do you think so many of Sister Helen's students kept their lists for so long? Why were the lists so important to them—even as adults?

3. At the end of the story, Sister Helen tells us that she "cried for Mark and for all his friends who would never see him again." Do you think she might have been crying for other reasons, too? Explain what they might be.

4. "All the Good Things" has literally traveled around the world. Not only has it been reprinted in numerous publications, but many readers have sent it out over the Internet for others to read. Why do you think so many people love this story? Why do they want to share it with others?

PARAGRAPH ASSIGNMENTS

1. Do you have any souvenir that, like Sister Helen's lists, you have kept for years? Write a paragraph about that souvenir. Start your paragraph with a topic sentence such as "_____ is one of my oldest and proudest possessions." Then describe just what the item is, how you originally obtained it, and where you keep it now. Most importantly, explain why the souvenir is precious to you.

2. Although Sister Helen didn't want to do it, she felt she had to tape Mark's mouth shut after announcing that she would do so. When have you done something you didn't really want to do because others expected it? Write a paragraph about that incident. Explain why you didn't want to do it, why you felt pressure to do it, and how you felt about yourself afterward. Here are sample topic sentences for such a paragraph:

   - Even though I knew it was wrong, I told my friend's parents a lie to keep my friend out of trouble.

   - Last year, I pretended I didn't like a girl that I really did like because my friends convinced me she wasn't cool enough.

ESSAY ASSIGNMENTS

1. If Mark hadn't been killed, Sister Helen might never have found out how much her students appreciated her work with them. Write an essay about someone to whom you are grateful. Begin by explaining who that person is and why you are thankful to him or her. Your thesis statement should be something like any of these:

    -   I owe a lot to my Aunt Lydia, who has been like a second mother to me.

    -   My best friend, Theresa, has been a constant source of love and support to me.

    -   If it wasn't for my seventh-grade science teacher, Mr. Kosinski, I don't think I would be in school today.

    Then tell in detail what that person has done for you and why it has been important in your life.

2. Mark Eklund obviously stood out in Sister Helen's memory. She paints a vivid "word portrait" of Mark as a third grader. Write an essay about three fellow students who, for positive or negative reasons, you have always remembered. The three may have been your classmates at any point in your life. Your essay should be confined to your memories of those students *in the classroom*—not on the playground, in the cafeteria, or outside of school. As you describe your memories of those three classmates in that setting, include details that appeal to as many senses as possible—hearing, sight, touch, smell—to make your readers vividly picture those individuals and that time and place in your history.

    Alternatively, you may write an essay about three teachers whom you will always remember.

18

The Yellow Ribbon
Pete Hamill

Preview

When America is involved in overseas military actions, U.S. communities often display yellow ribbons to symbolize the hope that their sons and daughters will return home safely. That practice was probably inspired by this story, which first appeared as a column in the *New York Post*. Read it to learn what message a yellow handkerchief conveyed to a worried, lonely man.

Words to Watch

cocoon (2): protective covering
bluntness (13): abruptness
parole (19): the early release of a prisoner on certain conditions
solitude (21): the state of being alone
exaltation (22): joy

They were going to Fort Lauderdale, the girl remembered later. There 1
were six of them, three boys and three girls, and they picked up the bus at
the old terminal on 34th Street, carrying sandwiches and wine in paper
bags, dreaming of golden beaches and the tides of the sea as the gray cold
spring of New York vanished behind them. Vingo was on board from the
beginning.

As the bus passed through Jersey and into Philly, they began to notice 2
that Vingo never moved. He sat in front of the young people, his dusty
face masking his age, dressed in a plain brown ill-fitting suit. His fingers
were stained from cigarettes and he chewed the inside of his lip a lot,
frozen into some personal cocoon° of silence.

Somewhere outside of Washington, deep into the night, the bus pulled 3
into a Howard Johnson's, and everybody got off except Vingo. He sat
rooted in his seat, and the young people began to wonder about him,
trying to imagine his life: Perhaps he was a sea captain, maybe he had run
away from his wife, he could be an old soldier going home. When they
went back to the bus, the girl sat beside him and introduced herself.

"We're going to Florida," the girl said brightly. "You going that far?" 4

"I don't know," Vingo said. 5

"I've never been there," she said. "I hear it's beautiful." 6

"It is," he said quietly, as if remembering something he had tried to 7
forget.

"You live there?" 8

"I did some time there in the Navy. Jacksonville." 9

"Want some wine?" she said. He smiled and took the bottle of Chianti 10
and took a swig. He thanked her and retreated again into his silence. After
a while, she went back to the others, as Vingo nodded in sleep.

In the morning they awoke outside another Howard Johnson's, and 11
this time Vingo went in. The girl insisted that he join them. He seemed
very shy and ordered black coffee and smoked nervously, as the young
people chattered about sleeping on the beaches. When they went back on
the bus, the girl sat with Vingo again, and after a while, slowly and
painfully and with great hesitation, he began to tell his story. He had been
in jail in New York for the last four years, and now he was going home.

"Four years!" the girl said. "What did you do?" 12

"It doesn't matter," he said with quiet bluntness°. "I did it and I went 13
to jail. If you can't do the time, don't do the crime. That's what they say
and they're right."

"Are you married?" 14

"I don't know." 15

"You don't know?" she said. 16

"Well, when I was in the can I wrote to my wife," he said. "I told her, 17
I said, Martha, I understand if you can't stay married to me. I told her that.
I said I was gonna be away a long time, and that if she couldn't stand it,
if the kids kept askin' questions, if it hurt her too much, well, she could
just forget me. Get a new guy—she's a wonderful woman, really
something—and forget about me. I told her she didn't have to write me
or nothing. And she didn't. Not for three and a half years."

"And you're going home now, not knowing?"   18

"Yeah," he said shyly. "Well, last week, when I was sure the parole°   19
was coming through I wrote her. I told her that if she had a new guy, I
understood. But if she didn't, if she would take me back, she should let me
know. We used to live in this town, Brunswick, just before Jacksonville,
and there's a great big oak tree just as you come into town, a very famous
tree, huge. I told her if she would take me back, she should put a yellow
handkerchief on the tree, and I would get off and come home. If she didn't
want me, forget it, no handkerchief, and I'd keep going on through."

"Wow," the girl said. "Wow."   20

She told the others, and soon all of them were in it, caught up in the   21
approach of Brunswick, looking at the pictures Vingo showed them of his
wife and three children, the woman handsome in a plain way, the children
still unformed in a cracked, much-handled snapshot. Now they were
twenty miles from Brunswick and the young people took over window
seats on the right side, waiting for the approach of the great oak tree. Vingo
stopped looking, tightening his face into the ex-con's mask, as if fortifying
himself against still another disappointment. Then it was ten miles, and
then five and the bus acquired a dark hushed mood, full of silence, of
absence, of lost years, of the woman's plain face, of the sudden letter on
the breakfast table, of the wonder of children, of the iron bars of solitude°.

Then suddenly all of the young people were up out of their seats,   22
screaming and shouting and crying, doing small dances, shaking clenched
fists in triumph and exaltation°. All except Vingo.

Vingo sat there stunned, looking at the oak tree. It was covered with   23
yellow handkerchiefs, twenty of them, thirty of them, maybe hundreds, a
tree that stood like a banner of welcome blowing and billowing in the
wind, turned into a gorgeous yellow blur by the passing bus. As the young
people shouted, the old con slowly rose from his seat, holding himself
tightly, and made his way to the front of the bus to go home.

FIRST IMPRESSIONS

Freewrite for ten minutes on one of the following.

1. Did you enjoy reading this selection? Why or why not?

2. Have you ever gotten into an interesting conversation with a stranger?
    What did you learn about him or her?

3. Why do you think the young people were so excited when they saw
    the tree? What did it mean to them? If you had been on the bus, how
    would you have reacted?

VOCABULARY CHECK

A. Circle the letter of the word or phrase that best completes each of the following four items.

1. In the sentence below, the word *retreated* means
   a. became talkative.
   b. began a new activity.
   c. drew back.
   d. was ungrateful.

   "He thanked her and retreated again into silence." (Paragraph 10)

2. In the sentence below, the word *fortifying* means
   a. strengthening.
   b. watching.
   c. hurrying.
   d. losing.

   "Vingo stopped looking, tightening his face into the ex-con's mask, as if fortifying himself against still another disappointment." (Paragraph 21)

3. In the sentence below, the word *acquired* means
   a. needed.
   b. took on.
   c. stopped.
   d. lost.

   "Then it was ten miles, and then five and the bus acquired a dark hushed mood. . . ." (Paragraph 21)

4. In the sentence below, the word *hushed* means
   a. quiet.
   b. evil.
   c. surprising.
   d. pleasant.

   "[T]he bus acquired a dark hushed mood, full of silence, of absence, of lost years, of the woman's plain face, of the sudden letter on the breakfast table. . . ." (Paragraph 21)

B. Circle the letter of the answer that best completes each of the following four items. Each item uses a word (or form of a word) from "Words to Watch."

5. "In response to today's harsh, fast-paced world," said the newspaper article, "more and more young couples report that they spend their weekends *cocooning*. They define 'cocooning' as
   (a.) spending time quietly within the privacy of their homes."
   b. going out to parties and dances."
   c. becoming involved in charitable causes."

6. A *blunt*-spoken man is one who
   a. speaks in beautiful, poetic phrases.
   b. talks too much.
   (c.) says what he means in very few words.

7. A *parolee* is someone
   a. who has escaped from prison and is being hunted by authorities.
   b. who is a prison guard responsible for keeping count of prisoners.
   (c.) who has been released from prison, but must check in with authorities regularly.

8. If a friend a year ahead of you in school reported that the English course she had taken had filled her with *exaltation*, you would probably
   (a.) sign up for that course.
   b. ask her what about the course had confused her.
   c. avoid that course by any means necessary.

READING CHECK

Central Point and Main Ideas

1. Which sentence best expresses the central point of the entire selection?
   a. Prison sentences can ruin marriages.
   b. If you commit a crime, you must pay for it.
   c. Vingo did not know what to expect.
   (d.) Vingo returned from prison to find that his wife still loved him.

2. Which sentence best expresses the main idea of paragraph 3?
   a. The bus stopped at a Howard Johnson's.
   (b.) The young people began to be curious about Vingo.
   c. Vingo might have been a sea captain.
   d. Everyone got off the bus except Vingo.

3. Which sentence best expresses the main idea of paragraph 21?
    a. The young people watched out the window more than Vingo did as the bus neared Brunswick.
    b. Vingo showed the young people photographs of his wife and children.
    c. Vingo tightened his face as if to prepare himself for a disappointment.
    d. The suspense built as the bus neared Brunswick and the oak tree.

Key Supporting Details

4. When the young girl asks what he was in prison for, Vingo answers that
    a. it is none of her business.
    b. it doesn't matter.
    c. he is too ashamed to tell her.
    d. he was imprisoned for a crime he didn't commit.

5. Vingo describes his wife as
    a. not much of a letter writer.
    b. a wonderful woman.
    c. an ex-convict like himself.
    d. very beautiful.

Inferences

6. We can infer that the young people were going to Florida
    a. on business.
    b. to visit relatives.
    c. on vacation.
    d. to get married.

7. The author implies that Vingo thought
    a. he would someday be in prison again.
    b. there might be no yellow handkerchief on the tree.
    c. his wife was wrong for not writing to him in prison.
    d. his wife was sure to want him back.

8. By writing, "[Vingo] slowly rose from his seat, holding himself tightly" (paragraph 23), the author implies that Vingo
    a. has suffered a physical injury.
    b. does not want to get off the bus.
    c. is trying to control his emotions.
    d. is angry about something.

9. By telling us that the picture of Vingo's family was a "cracked, much-handled snapshot," the author implies that
   a. Vingo didn't know how to take good care of photos.
   b. the pictures were not really of Vingo's family.
   (c.) Vingo had looked at the snapshot a great deal while in jail.
   d. the photo was relatively new.

The Writer's Craft

10. The introductory paragraph indicates that Hamill
    a. was one of the young people on the bus.
    b. heard the story from Vingo years later.
    (c.) interviewed one of the young girls who had been on the bus.
    d. knew Vingo personally.

DISCUSSION QUESTIONS

1. According to the information in the selection, what is Vingo's attitude toward his wife? What else do you learn about her at the conclusion of the story?

2. Why do you think the young people first became interested in Vingo? How do you think their attitude about him changed after they'd learned his story?

3. While there is much we don't learn about Vingo in this very short narrative, Hamill does provide us with clues to some important aspects of his personality. What evidence is there that he is a decent man, a person who we could feel deserves a second chance?

4. Many people are thrilled, some even to tears, by this story. How did you and your classmates react when you first read it? Why do you think "The Yellow Ribbon" has such a powerful effect on readers?

PARAGRAPH ASSIGNMENTS

1. In "The Yellow Ribbon," Hamill suggests strongly that although Vingo has been in jail, he is still a decent man. Such clues are found in Vingo's attitude towards his fellow passengers, in what he says about his past and his family, and in his behavior as the bus nears his hometown. Write a paragraph that begins with this topic sentence: "Details in 'The Yellow Ribbon' suggest that Vingo is a good man who deserves to be welcomed home by his family." Find and include specific evidence from the story to back up that statement.

2. For some reason, it is not unusual for fellow passengers in a bus, train, or airplane to enter into quite personal conversations. The same thing sometimes happens in public waiting spaces, like a doctor's office. Perhaps it is because people feel free to confide in someone they do not expect to ever see again. Write a paragraph about a personal conversation you have had with a stranger. As Hamill does, include details that make your reader able to picture where you were, how you started talking with the person, and what your first impression was of him or her. Then narrate the conversation that occurred. Include non-verbal information, such as body language, to paint the most vivid word picture that you can.

ESSAY ASSIGNMENTS

1. Most people like to "people watch." It can be fascinating to watch strangers, notice their appearance, observe their characteristics, and overhear bits of their conversations. The young people on the bus are doing such people-watching when they first notice Vingo. They study his appearance and characteristics, then imagine who he is and where he is going.

   Taking a notebook along, go to a public place, such as a park, coffee shop, mall, or ball game. Pick out a stranger who catches your interest—someone whom you can observe for at least ten or fifteen minutes. Trying not to be too obvious about it (pretend you're doing ordinary homework!), jot down notes about that person. Your notes should cover not only physical characteristics (such as the person's features, build, hair color and style, clothing), but also anything you notice about his or her nervous habits, gestures, tone of voice, way of moving, mood, and so on.

Once you are back home with your notes, write a descriptive essay about this person. In it, give as rich and detailed a description as you can of him or her. Describe not only what the person looked like, but what your observations suggested about his or her personality. End your essay by telling your reader what you imagine about this person. Let your imagination run wild! You might imagine what the person does for a living, what his or her home life is like, or what he or she was thinking during the time you were watching.

In your thesis statement, you could mention the overall impression the person made on you, like this:

- The heavy-set man eating scrambled eggs in Mel's Diner caught my attention because he looked so deeply unhappy.

- The young woman sitting on the park bench, reading a paperback novel, looked to me like a person without a problem in the world.

2. Vingo had to wait in suspense to discover something important about his future. When have you had the experience of waiting a long time (or what seemed like a long time) to find out something important? Such situations might have involved a grade for a project or a class, an award for which you were in the running, a part in a play, a question concerning your (or a loved one's) health, or an acceptance or rejection by a college or another important program. Write an essay about the situation. Tell the story a little at a time, as Hamill does, in order to keep the reader in suspense until the end. Begin by explaining what you were waiting for and why it was important. Continue by describing the wait and the emotions you experienced as time went by. Finish by telling how the wait finally ended and how you felt once it was over.

19

What Do Children Owe Their Parents?
Ann Landers

Preview

"I don't owe anybody anything," teenagers sometimes claim. According to Ann Landers, the famous advice columnist, they are mistaken. But what, exactly, do teenagers owe their parents? And what do adult children owe? The answers Ann Landers gives to these questions may surprise you.

Words to Watch

punitive (2): punishing
injunction (4): command
bestow (6): give
brittle (6): easily broken
stemming from (6): arising out of
chronic (6): lasting for a long period of time; occuring repeatedly
obsolescence (6): becoming out of date
muster (11): gather
gumption (14): boldness
exploit (14): take advantage of
outset (15): beginning
incontinent (17): unable to control bodily waste functions
implore (17): beg

"What is your mother doing these days?" I asked a friend who recently   1
returned from a visit with her family in New York. "Mother is very busy
doing what she does best," was the reply. "She's the East Coast distributor
for guilt."

I often hear this sentiment expressed by young marrieds, who are   2
irritated and resent their invisible burden. There's a tremendous amount
of guilt around these days, and many of the victims don't know if it is
being laid on them by self-centered, punitive° parents—or if they really
are rotten kids.

What do children owe their parents, anyway? Not just married   3
children, but all children—from six years of age to sixty-six. No one can
speak for everyone, but since this question has been raised by many
people groping for answers, I shall try to respond.

First, let's start with teenagers. Here are the basics: You owe your   4
parents consideration, loyalty, and respect. The Biblical injunction°
"Honor thy father and thy mother" is simple and clear. "But what if they
are drunks and abusive and failures, not only as parents but as human
beings? Are we still supposed to 'honor' them? Do we still owe them
consideration, loyalty, and respect?" This question is often put to me.
"Yes," is my answer. Honor them because they gave you life. Give them
consideration and loyalty for the same reason.

Consideration is a word that needs no definition, but loyalty as it   5
relates to the family is sometimes vague. What does it mean? It means
hanging in there when things go wrong. It means keeping family matters
inside the family. The child who speaks ill of his parents and runs them
down to outsiders says more about himself than he says about them.

Respect is difficult to bestow° when it hasn't been earned—and sad to   6
say, some parents have not earned it. If you feel your parents have not
earned your respect, try to find it in your heart to substitute understanding
and compassion. Granted, this is a great deal to ask of a teenager, but if
you can do it, it will help you grow as a person. Look beyond the brittle°
facade and you'll see people who are bitterly ashamed of their inability to
measure up. They're insecure and shaky—struggling with unresolved
problems stemming from° their childhood. To fail as a parent is extremely
painful. They suffer a lot. But most parents are not drunks, nor are they
abusive. They are plain, ordinary people with good intentions and feet of
clay—trying desperately to survive in a dangerous, untidy world. They
are out there every day, on the front lines, battling inflation, obesity,
chronic° fatigue, obsolescence°, and crabgrass.

Nearly 48 percent of the work force in America today is female. This   7
means great numbers of mothers are wearing two hats, or three. They're
working at part-time (or full-time) jobs, trying to run a house, raise

children, and participate in community activities. What do children owe parents who fit this description? Here are the fundamentals. They owe them prompt and honest answers to the following questions:

- Where are you going?
- Who are your companions?
- How do you plan to get there?
- When will you be home?

Teenagers frequently write to complain that their parents want to pick   8
their friends. Do they have a right to do this? The answer is, "No." I never fail to point out, however, that when parents are critical of a teenager's friends, they usually have a good reason. Bad company can be bad news. But in the final analysis, the choice of friends should be up to the individual. If he or she makes poor selections, he or she will have to pay for it.

Parents have the right to expect their children to pick up after   9
themselves and perform simple household chores. For example, every member of the family over six years of age should clean the bathtub and the sink so they will be in respectable condition for the next person. He or she should also run errands and help in the kitchen if asked—in other words, carry a share of the load without feeling persecuted. The days of "hired help" are, for the most part, gone. And this is good. Boys as well as girls should be taught to cook and clean, do laundry, and sew on buttons. This is not "sissy stuff." It makes for independence and self-reliance.

What do teenagers and college students owe their parents in terms of   10
time and attention? There's no pat answer. Some parents are extremely demanding; others are loose hangers. Some children can't wait to move out of the house; others must be pushed out. A college student shouldn't be expected to write home every day, but certainly a postcard once a week isn't asking too much if parents wish this. A phone call (collect, of course) on Sunday should not be impossible to manage if parents want it. What about vacations? Do children owe it to their parents to come home, rather than go to Fort Lauderdale or to a ski resort? Yes, they do, if the parents want them home and are footing the bills for education and transportation.

What do working children who live at home owe their parents in terms   11
of financial compensation? The following letter is typical of what I read at least two dozen times a week:

Dear Ann Landers:

Our daughter is twenty-six years old. She chose business school over college and is now number-one secretary to the president of a large firm. We are pleased that Terry still lives with us and doesn't want an apartment of her own, but I feel we are being taken advantage of.

Terry has no savings account. She buys expensive clothes, has her own car, vacations in Europe, and doesn't give us one cent for room and board. She pays the telephone bill, because the long-distance calls are hers. I do her laundry, clean her room, fix her breakfast every morning, and dinner whenever she wants it.

Our home is paid for and Terry knows we are not hard up for money, but it would be awfully nice to have a little extra coming in. My husband says not to 'rock the boat' or she might move. What do you say? If you believe she should pay—how much? Thanks for your help, Ann.

A Pittsburgh Mom

I replied,

Dear Mom:

Terry should give you 20 percent of her paycheck. If she thinks she can get lodging, breakfast, laundry, and maid service elsewhere for less—let her try it.

The fact that you are not hard up for money is no excuse for your daughter's selfishness. Share this letter with your husband; and I hope together you will muster° up the courage to talk to Terry promptly.

When sons and daughters marry, things change considerably. Even 12
though parents have a tendency to forever think of their children as
"children," they should be granted a totally different status when they
establish a family unit of their own. Should Mom be forever and always
the number-one woman in Sonny's life? Not at all. A loving mother
willingly relinquishes that place to her daughter-in-law. She remembers
how she felt about her husband's mother when she married. By the same
token, a kind and thoughtful daughter-in-law will be considerate of her
husband's mother so she will not feel displaced. Life's cycles have an
ironic way of evening up the score. The woman who finds herself with a
mother-in-law problem might do well to think ahead a few years when her
son will marry and she will become the mother-in-law.

Getting down to specifics, what do married children owe their parents 13
in terms of time and attention? According to my readers, this is a major
problem among marrieds in their thirties and forties. Here are some
questions from this week's mailing:

From Lubbock, Texas:

My mother telephones me at least four times a day. She wants to know if the children ate a good breakfast, who wore what at a party last night, what am I fixing for supper, has my husband's boss said anything about a raise . . . ?

From Nashville, Tennessee:

> *My husband's mother asks me every two weeks if I am pregnant yet. She keeps reminding me that I'm not getting any younger and she would give anything to have a grandchild. The woman is getting on my nerves.*

From Richmond, Virginia:

> *My husband's parents are in their mid-seventies. He spends at least five hours every Saturday driving them to the supermarket, the dentist, the doctor, the pharmacy, the optometrist, the greenhouse, the dry cleaners, and so on. My in-laws have two daughters who live in town, but they never bother them—my husband is the one they run ragged. Does he owe them this kind of service?*

From San Diego, California:

> *My mother is 64, a widow, attractive, and well-read. When we have guests for an evening, she's hurt if she isn't included. I love her dearly, but Mom has strong opinions and I have the feeling our friends resent her. Am I obligated to include her because she is my mother?*

There are no rules to cover every situation, but here are suggestions 14
that can be tailored to fit a great many:

- Countless people are also victims of friends who have black-cord fever—also known as telephonitis. The best protection against these types is to develop a technique for getting off the phone after a reasonable period of time. The victim should have prepared sentences handy and read them when the need arises. Sample: "Sorry, dear. I have a million things to do this morning and I must hang up now. We'll talk again soon."

- People have no right to complain about being trapped or taken advantage of if they don't have the gumption° to assert themselves. I tell them repeatedly, "No one can exploit° you without your permission." This includes refusing to answer "nun-uvyer-bizniz" type questions. Sample comeback: "Now why in the world would you be interested in that?"

- No woman owes her in-laws grandchildren. Any person who pressures a woman to "give us a grandchild" should be put in her place.

- Running errands and chauffeuring aged parents can be time- and energy-consuming, but it may be essential when no alternatives exist. If there are other children (or nieces and nephews) who might help out, they certainly should be asked to do so. Where time is more valuable than money, a paid driver may relieve a lot of tension.

• Including parents in social activities is not essential, and parents should not expect it. No excuses are necessary.

Perhaps the most anxiety-producing problem is one that hits in the late   15
forties or early fifties—about the same time some adults are going through the mid-life crisis: what to do with Mama when Papa dies. Or, if Mama goes first, what should be done with Papa? Circumstances alter cases. Some mamas wouldn't live with their children on a bet. The same goes for some papas. Many factors should be considered at the outset°— first, how would Grandma or Grandpa fit in with the family? Is she or he too bossy? Would there be trouble in the kitchen? Would the children feel that too many people are telling them what to do? Finances are another major consideration. Does the surviving parent have sufficient money to maintain his or her own place? The issue of health is also important. Is Mama or Papa well enough to live alone? The answers to these questions should be carefully reviewed before a decision.

Strictly from a standpoint of morality and decency, do you owe your   16
parent a place in your home if he or she would like to move in? I say, "No." If parents need housing or care, it goes without saying you should provide it, but you do not owe them a place under your roof if it would create dissension and conflict in your family. The ideal solution is to keep the surviving parent in his or her own home if it is economically feasible. When money is a problem, all the children should ante up and share the cost. (Often this is easier said than done.) Endless family fights have resulted because brother George or sister Mabel say they can't help out with the old folks because they have kids in college. Yet they go to Florida or Arizona every winter, belong to the country club, and drive new cars.

The most serious crisis arises when Mama or Papa becomes ill or too   17
old to take care of themselves. Nursing homes are expensive, and many old people don't want to go there. What then? Some heroic women have taken in a parent or an in-law (or both) at tremendous personal sacrifice. This can be the most physically exhausting and emotionally draining job in the world, since old folks tend to be senile, incontinent°, ill-tempered, and in need of constant watching. Implore° daughters and daughters-in-law not to feel guilty if they are unable to do it. The woman who does make this sacrifice, in my opinion, deserves a place at God's right hand, come reckoning time.

In the final analysis, none of us goes through life debt-free. We all owe   18
something to somebody. But the most noble motivation for giving in is not prompted by a sense of duty—it flows freely from unselfish love.

FIRST IMPRESSIONS

Freewrite for ten minutes on one of the following.

1. Did you enjoy reading this selection? Why or why not?

2. Do you ever read advice columns such as the one Ann Landers writes? Do you think these columns contain good advice? Explain your answer.

3. Do (or did) your parents sometimes make you feel guilty? If so, about what? Have you ever changed your behavior because of the guilt you felt?

VOCABULARY CHECK

A. Circle the letter of the word or phrase that best completes each of the following four items.

1. In the sentence below, the word *facade* means
   a. outer layer.
   b. candy.
   c. honesty.
   d. inner self.

   > "Look behind the brittle facade and you'll see people who are bitterly ashamed of their inability to measure up." (Paragraph 6)

2. In the sentences below, the word *relinquishes* means
   a. keeps back.
   b. fights for.
   c. gives up.
   d. stands in.

   > "Should Mom be forever and always the number-one woman in Sonny's life? Not at all. A loving mother willingly relinquishes that place to her daughter-in-law." (Paragraph 12)

3. In the sentence below, the word *dissension* means
   a. strong disagreement.
   b. great generosity.
   c. harmless fear.
   d. shared goals.

   > "If parents need housing and care, . . . you should provide it, but you do not owe them a place under your roof if it would create dissension and conflict in your family." (Paragraph 16)

4. In the sentence below, the word *feasible* means
   a. difficult.
   b. possible.
   c. wrong.
   d. careful.

   "The ideal solution is to keep the surviving parent in his or her own home if it is economically feasible." (Paragraph 16)

B. Circle the letter of the answer that best completes each of the following four items. Each item uses a word (or form of a word) from "Words to Watch."

5. When Eddie brought home a bad report card, his mother took *punitive* action: she
   a. gave him ten dollars.
   b. made him stay in the house for a week.
   c. pretended that nothing was wrong.

6. The twig was very *brittle*—
   a. nothing could break it.
   b. it snapped at the slightest touch.
   c. there were small buds all over it.

7. When the doctor told Martha her illness was *chronic*, she knew she would
   a. have it for a long time.
   b. never have it again.
   c. have to spend the next week in a hospital.

8. The workers in our company feel *exploited* because the management pays them
   a. very high salaries.
   b. nothing for the overtime hours they are required to work.
   c. exactly what they are worth.

READING CHECK

Central Point and Main Ideas

1. Which sentence best expresses the central point of the entire selection?
   a. Children of all ages owe their parents something.
   b. Parents and children would get along better if they just ignored their problems.
   c. All parents deserve their children's respect.
   d. Parents have ways of making their children feel guilty.

2. Which sentence best expresses the main idea of paragraph 15?
   a. Many factors must be considered when an elderly parent is widowed.
   b. People sometimes are dealing with a mid-life crisis when one of their parents dies.
   c. It's important for adult children to consider whether their parent will fit in with the family before inviting the parent to share their home.
   d. Elderly people have more problems than young people do.

Key Supporting Details

3. According to Landers, teenagers should *not*
   a. be allowed to pick their own friends.
   b. criticize their parents to outsiders.
   c. have to write home from college once a week.
   d. tell their parents where they are going.

4. __T__ TRUE OR FALSE? Landers thinks bad parents are likely to be ashamed of their failures.

5. Landers feels that married children owe their parents
   a. grandchildren.
   b. a daily phone call.
   c. help with errands when necessary.
   d. invitations to social events.

Inferences

6. The author implies in paragraph 11 that parents should accept money from working children who live at home
   a. because it is the best way to get them to move out.
   b. only if they need it.
   c. only if the children are over 21.
   d. as a fair exchange for room, board, laundry, and maid service.

7. __T__ TRUE OR FALSE? Landers implies that it is often people's own fault when others take advantage of them.

8. Landers uses letters from her readers
   a. to make the writers feel ashamed of themselves.
   b. because the people who wrote them are friends of hers.
   c. to show the kinds of problems real people face.
   d. so that readers have a chance to give her advice for a change.

The Writer's Craft

9. Landers's main method of organizing her essay is according to the
   a. difficulty of the problems.
   b. kinds of solutions.
   c. ages of the children.
   d. dates when she got the letters.

10. To conclude her essay, the author uses
   a. a prediction.
   b. a series of questions.
   c. an anecdote.
   d. a summary and final thought.

DISCUSSION QUESTIONS

1. Which parts of Landers's advice do you agree with? Which letter (or letters) would you have answered differently? What advice would you have given instead?

2. Assume that you are a parent whose child has chosen a friend you do not approve of. How would you handle this situation?

3. What do you think college students living at home owe their parents?

4. If you had children of your own, what do you think they would owe you? Why?

PARAGRAPH ASSIGNMENTS

1. Landers writes in paragraph 18 that "none of us goes through life debt-free. We all owe something to somebody." Think of a person to whom you owe something. Write a paragraph in which you tell who this person is, what he or she has done for you, and what you feel you owe in return. Use a topic sentence such as "If it hadn't been for Miss Lee, my high-school guidance counselor, I would never have decided to go to college."

2. Write a one-paragraph letter to Ann Landers describing a real or imagined problem in your life (or a friend's life) and asking for advice. Use specific details, and provide one or two clear examples to illustrate the problem. You might even suggest some solutions and ask what Landers thinks of them. Choose a problem similar to one of the following:

- Telling a classmate or coworker that he or she has made a mistake
- Refusing to lend money to a friend
- Getting rid of unwanted house guests
- Coping with friends who insist on telling you their problems
- Dealing with an overly demanding teacher or boss

ESSAY ASSIGNMENTS

1. Would you raise your children the same way you were raised? Write an essay comparing and contrasting the way you would raise your children with the way you were brought up. In your essay, argue that children either should or should not be raised as you were. Support your points with explanations and specific examples. You might use a thesis statement such as "When I have children, I hope I can spend as much time with them, listen as carefully to their problems, and show them as much affection as my parents did for me."

2. In paragraph 8, Landers writes that if a teenager makes a poor choice of friends, "he or she will have to pay for it." Write an essay about a time when you chose a friend and later regretted your choice. Tell what the friend was like, what he or she did to you, and how you felt afterwards. If you learned a useful lesson from the experience, explain what it was. As an alternative, write about someone who proved to be a true friend. Devote a separate paragraph of your essay to each quality you admire in your friend. Whichever topic you choose, be sure to supply specific examples of your friend's behavior and your reactions to it.

20

Shame
Dick Gregory

Preview

Although he was famous first as a comedian, Dick Gregory became equally well known as a social activist. In this excerpt from his autobiography, Gregory gives a glimpse into two incidents from his early life, incidents that helped shape his commitment to aiding the oppressed without insulting their dignity.

Words to Watch

light-complected (1): fair-complexioned, or having light-colored skin
symbol (2): something that stands for something else
nappy (2): kinky, or tightly curled
stoop (2): an outside stairway, porch, or platform at the entrance to a house
squirmed (6): wriggled and twisted around like a snake
worthy (28): deserving
mackinaw (28): a short, plaid coat or jacket
numbness (29): lack of feeling
googobs (29): Gregory's slang for gobs, a large amount

I never learned hate at home, or shame. I had to go to school for that. I was about seven years old when I got my first big lesson. I was in love with a little girl named Helene Tucker, a light-complected° little girl with pigtails and nice manners. She was always clean and she was smart in school. I think I went to school then mostly to look at her. I brushed my hair and even got me a little old handkerchief. It was a lady's handkerchief, but I didn't want Helene to see me wipe my nose on my hand. The pipes were frozen again, there was no water in the house, but I washed my socks and shirt every night. I'd get a pot, and go over to Mister Ben's grocery store, and stick my pot down into his soda machine. Scoop out some chopped ice. By evening the ice melted to water for washing. I got sick a lot that winter because the fire would go out at night before the clothes were dry. In the morning I'd put them on, wet or dry, because they were the only clothes I had.

Everybody's got a Helene Tucker, a symbol° of everything you want. I loved her for her goodness, her cleanness, her popularity. She'd walk down my street and my brothers and sisters would yell, "Here comes Helene," and I'd rub my tennis sneakers on the back of my pants and wish my hair wasn't so nappy° and the white folks' shirt fit me better. I'd run out on the street. If I knew my place and didn't come too close, she'd wink at me and say hello. That was a good feeling. Sometimes I'd follow her all the way home, and shovel the snow off her walk and try to make friends with her Momma and her aunts. I'd drop money on her stoop° late at night on my way back from shining shoes in the taverns. And she had a Daddy, and he had a good job. He was a paper hanger.

I guess I would have gotten over Helene by summertime, but something happened in that classroom that made her face hang in front of me for the next twenty-two years. When I played the drums in high school it was for Helene and when I broke track records in college it was for Helene and when I started standing behind microphones and heard applause I wished Helene could hear it, too. It wasn't until I was twenty-nine years old and married and making money that I finally got her out of my system. Helene was sitting in that classroom when I learned to be ashamed of myself.

It was on a Thursday. I was sitting in the back of the room, in a seat with a chalk circle drawn around it. The idiot's seat, the troublemaker's seat.

The teacher thought I was stupid. Couldn't spell, couldn't read, couldn't do arithmetic. Just stupid. Teachers were never interested in finding out that you couldn't concentrate because you were so hungry, because you hadn't had any breakfast. All you could think about was noontime, would it ever come? Maybe you could sneak into the cloakroom and steal a bite of some kid's lunch out of a coat pocket. A bite of something. Paste. You can't really make a meal of paste, or put it on bread for a sandwich, but sometimes I'd scoop a few spoonfuls out of the big paste jar in the back of the room. Pregnant people get strange tastes.

2

3

4

5

I was pregnant with poverty. Pregnant with dirt and pregnant with smells that made people turn away, pregnant with cold and pregnant with shoes that were never bought for me, pregnant with five other people in my bed and no Daddy in the next room, and pregnant with hunger. Paste doesn't taste too bad when you're hungry.

The teacher thought I was a troublemaker. All she saw from the front   6
of the room was a little black boy who squirmed° in his idiot's seat and made noises and poked the kids around him. I guess she couldn't see a kid who made noises because he wanted someone to know he was there.

It was on a Thursday, the day before the Negro payday. The eagle   7
always flew on Friday. The teacher was asking each student how much his father would give to the Community Chest. On Friday night, each kid would get the money from his father, and on Monday he would bring it to the school. I decided I was going to buy a Daddy right then. I had money in my pocket from shining shoes and selling papers, and whatever Helene Tucker pledged for her Daddy I was going to top it. And I'd hand the money right in. I wasn't going to wait until Monday to buy me a Daddy.

I was shaking, scared to death. The teacher opened her book and   8
started calling out names alphabetically.

"Helene Tucker?"   9

"My Daddy said he'd give two dollars and fifty cents."   10

"That's very nice, Helene. Very, very nice indeed."   11

That made me feel pretty good. It wouldn't take too much to top that. I   12
had almost three dollars in dimes and quarters in my pocket. I stuck my hand in my pocket and held onto the money, waiting for her to call my name. But the teacher closed her book after she called everybody else in the class.

I stood up and raised my hand.   13

"What is it now?"   14

"You forgot me."   15

She turned toward the blackboard. "I don't have time to be playing   16
with you, Richard."

"My Daddy said he'd . . ."   17

"Sit down, Richard, you're disturbing the class."   18

"My Daddy said he'd give . . . fifteen dollars."   19

She turned around and looked mad. "We are collecting this money for   20
you and your kind, Richard Gregory. If your Daddy can give fifteen dollars you have no business being on relief."

"I got it right now, I got it right now, my Daddy gave it to me to turn   21
in today, my Daddy said . . ."

"And furthermore," she said, looking right at me, her nostrils getting   22
big and her lips getting thin and her eyes opening wide, "we know you don't have a Daddy."

Helene Tucker turned around, her eyes full of tears. She felt sorry for 23
me. Then I couldn't see her too well because I was crying, too.

"Sit down, Richard." 24

And I always thought the teacher kind of liked me. She always picked 25
me to wash the blackboard on Friday, after school. That was a big thrill,
it made me feel important. If I didn't wash it, come Monday the school
might not function right.

"Where are you going, Richard!" 26

I walked out of school that day, and for a long time I didn't go back 27
very often. There was shame there.

Now there was shame everywhere. It seemed like the whole world had 28
been inside that classroom, everyone had heard what the teacher had said,
everyone had turned around and felt sorry for me. There was shame in
going to the Worthy° Boys Annual Christmas Dinner for you and your
kind, because everybody knew what a worthy boy was. Why couldn't they
just call it the Boys Annual Dinner, why'd they have to give it a name?
There was shame in wearing the brown and orange and white plaid
mackinaw° the welfare gave to three thousand boys. Why'd it have to be
the same for everybody so when you walked down the street the people
could see you were on relief? It was a nice warm mackinaw and it had a
hood, and my Momma beat me and called me a little rat when she found
out I stuffed it in the bottom of a pail full of garbage way over on Cottage
Street. There was shame in running over to Mister Ben's at the end of the
day and asking for his rotten peaches, there was shame in asking Mrs.
Simmons for a spoonful of sugar, there was shame in running out to meet
the relief truck. I hated that truck, full of food for you and your kind. I ran
into the house and hid when it came. And then I started to sneak through
alleys, to take the long way home so the people going into White's Eat
Shop wouldn't see me. Yeah, the whole world heard the teacher that day,
we all know you don't have a Daddy.

It lasted for a while, this kind of numbness°. I spent a lot of time 29
feeling sorry for myself. And then one day I met this wino in a restaurant.
I'd been out hustling all day, shining shoes, selling newspapers, and I had
googobs° of money in my pocket. Bought me a bowl of chili for fifteen
cents, and a cheeseburger for fifteen cents, and a Pepsi for five cents, and
a piece of chocolate cake for ten cents. That was a good meal. I was eating
when this old wino came in. I love winos because they never hurt anyone
but themselves.

The old wino sat down at the counter and ordered twenty-six cents 30
worth of food. He ate it like he really enjoyed it. When the owner, Mister
Williams, asked him to pay the check, the old wino didn't lie or go
through his pocket like he suddenly found a hole.

He just said: "Don't have no money."   31

The owner yelled: "Why in hell you come in here and eat my food if   32
you don't have no money? That food cost me money."

Mister Williams jumped over the counter and knocked the wino off his   33
stool and beat him over the head with a pop bottle. Then he stepped back
and watched the wino bleed. Then he kicked him. And he kicked him again.

I looked at the wino with blood all over his face and I went over.   34
"Leave him alone, Mister Williams. I'll pay the twenty-six cents."

The wino got up, slowly, pulling himself up to the stool, then up to the   35
counter, holding on for a minute until his legs stopped shaking so bad. He
looked at me with pure hate. "Keep your twenty-six cents. You don't have
to pay, not now. I just finished paying for it."

He started to walk out, and as he passed me, he reached down and   36
touched my shoulder. "Thanks, sonny, but it's too late now. Why didn't
you pay it before?"

I was pretty sick about that. I waited too long to help another man.   37

FIRST IMPRESSIONS

Freewrite for ten minutes on one of the following.

1. Did you enjoy reading this selection? Why or why not?

2. When you were in elementary school did you, like Gregory, ever have
   a crush on a classmate? What was it about this person that you liked
   so much?

3. Were you ever badly embarrassed by a teacher (or did you witness
   someone else embarrassed by a teacher)? What happened?

VOCABULARY CHECK

A. Circle the letter of the word or phrase that best completes each of the
following four items.

1. In the sentences below, the words *pregnant with* mean
   a. full of.
   b. empty of.
   c. sick of.
   d. pleased with.

   > "Pregnant people get strange tastes. I was pregnant with poverty . . .
   > and pregnant with hunger. Paste doesn't taste too bad when you're
   > hungry." (Paragraph 5)

2. In the sentence below, the word *pledged* means
   a. repeated.
   b. studied.
   c. promised to give.
   d. brought home.

   > "I had money in my pocket . . . and whatever Helene Tucker pledged for her Daddy, I was going to top it." (Paragraph 7)

3. In the sentences below, the word *function* means
   a. enjoy itself.
   b. do its job.
   c. sound.
   d. shut down.

   > "And I always thought the teacher kind of liked me. She always picked me to wash the blackboard on Friday, after school. That was a big thrill, it made me feel important. If I didn't wash it, come Monday the school might not function right." (Paragraph 25)

4. In the sentence below, the word *hustling* means
   a. complaining.
   b. relaxing.
   c. studying hard.
   d. working energetically.

   > "I'd been out hustling all day, shining shoes, selling newspapers, and I had googobs of money in my pocket." (Paragraph 29)

B. Circle the letter of the answer that best completes each of the following four items. Each item uses a word (or form of a word) from "Words to Watch."

5. A well-known *symbol* for a proud, vain person is
   a. bragging.
   b. the peacock.
   c. looking in the mirror.

6. When Teresa asked Bill an embarrassing question, Bill *squirmed* like a
   a. rock.
   b. carpet on the floor.
   c. worm on a hook.

7. Elaine thought she was *worthy* of receiving a bonus at work because
   a. the boss was her uncle.
   b. she had been working at the company for only a month.
   c. she had the best sales record of anyone in her department.

8. My fingers were *numb* after I
   a. scraped snow off the car with my bare hands.
   b. played the piano for five minutes.
   c. accidentally touched a very hot plate.

READING CHECK

Central Point and Main Ideas

1. Which sentence best expresses the central point of the entire selection?
   a. Dick Gregory had a long-standing crush on a girl named Helene Tucker.
   b. The charity Gregory received was given in a way that labeled him as poor, which made him ashamed.
   c. As both a receiver and a giver, Gregory learned that giving something the wrong way can cause shame.
   d. Gregory grew up in a fatherless, poor family.

2. Which sentence best expresses the main idea of paragraph 2?
   a. The author adored Helene Tucker, a symbol of everything he wanted.
   b. Everybody has a symbol of everything he or she wants.
   c. Helene Tucker made the author feel ashamed of his looks.
   d. Unlike the author, Helene Tucker had a father.

3. Which sentence best expresses the main idea of paragraph 5?
   a. Gregory liked to eat paste.
   b. The teacher assumed that Gregory was stupid.
   c. The teacher never realized that Gregory was hungry all the time.
   d. The teacher assumed that Gregory was stupid and never realized that his poor work was the result of hunger.

Key Supporting Details

4. After the teacher told the class that Gregory was the type of person the Community Chest helped and that he was fatherless, Gregory
   a. never went back to school.
   b. felt sorry for himself for a while.
   c. stopped working.
   d. felt that Helene Tucker did not feel sorry for him.

5. Gregory could afford to contribute to the Community Chest because he had
   a. worked as a paperhanger.
   b. stolen money out of the pockets of coats in the school cloakroom.
   c. earned money by cleaning the blackboard for the teacher.
   (d.) earned money by shining shoes and selling papers.

6. Gregory's mother beat him when he
   (a.) threw away the jacket that he'd gotten from welfare.
   b. dropped his money on Helene's stoop.
   c. didn't stop Mister Williams from beating the wino.
   d. walked out of school.

Inferences

7. __F__ TRUE OR FALSE? In the classroom scene, the author implies that Helene is not sensitive.

8. In paragraph 5, the author implies that
   a. he is stupid.
   b. teachers understood him well.
   (c.) it was difficult for him to concentrate in school.
   d. the only way he ever got food was to steal it.

9. When the wino says, "I just finished paying for [the food]," he is implying that he
   a. had found some money to give Mister Williams.
   (b.) had paid for it by taking a beating.
   c. had paid for the meal before he ate.
   d. would work for Mister Williams to pay for the meal.

The Writer's Craft

10. The word that best describes the tone of the last paragraph of the selection is
    a. angry.
    b. objective.
    c. sentimental.
    (d.) regretful.

DISCUSSION QUESTIONS

1. Why do you think Gregory included both the classroom story and the restaurant story in his article? In what ways are the two incidents similar? What is the difference between the shame he felt in the first incident and the shame he felt in the second?

2. We say that something is *ironic* when it has an effect that is the opposite of what might be expected. In this reading, Gregory uses irony in several places. In what ways are the following quotations from "Shame" ironic?

   - "I never learned hate at home, or shame. I had to go to school for that."

   - "If I knew my place and didn't come too close, she'd wink at me and say hello. That was a good feeling."

   - "I looked at the wino with blood all over his face and I went over. 'Leave him alone, Mister Williams. I'll pay the twenty-six cents.'

     "The wino got up. . . . He looked at me with pure hate."

3. Has anyone ever tried to help you in a way that embarrassed or hurt you, instead of pleasing you? If so, how did you feel toward that person? Explain.

4. The Community Chest incident could have had very different results if Gregory's teacher had handled the situation in another way. What do you think she should have done when Gregory said, "You forgot me"? Or could she have used a different method of collecting money from students? Explain.

PARAGRAPH ASSIGNMENTS

1. When have you, like Gregory, regretted the way you acted in a particular situation? Perhaps you didn't speak up when someone was being teased, or perhaps you spoke harshly to someone because you were in a bad mood. Write a paragraph that describes the situation and how you acted. You might want to start the paragraph with a sentence like "I still regret the way I acted when _____."
Conclude by explaining why you feel you acted wrongly and what you wish you had done instead.

2. Teachers are powerful figures in children's lives. At times—perhaps because of impatience, poor judgment, a misunderstanding, or anger—a teacher may hurt a student's feelings. Write a paragraph about a situation you witnessed (or experienced yourself) in which you believe a teacher acted inappropriately and made a student feel bad. Be sure to explain not only what the teacher did but also how the student was affected.

ESSAY ASSIGNMENTS

1. A dictionary defines a word by briefly explaining its meaning. But in an essay, an author can define a term in a different, more personal manner. In this reading, Dick Gregory defines *shame* by describing two incidents in his life in which shame played a central part.

   Write an essay in which you define a powerful word by narrating one or more personal experiences. Some words to consider include *gratitude, fear, jealousy, pride, joy, anger, kindness,* and *disappointment.* Your central point might be stated something like this: "Two experiences in my childhood taught me the real meaning of joy." Be sure to focus on those parts of the incidents that illustrate the meaning of the word. Your essay will be most powerful if, like Gregory, you include significant bits of description and dialogue.

2. By embarrassing him in front of the class, Gregory's teacher demonstrated the negative effect that a teacher can have on a student. But teachers also have the potential to be very positive figures in their students' lives. Write an essay about three qualities that you think a good teacher should possess. Some of these qualities might be patience, a sense of humor, insight into students' feelings, and the ability to make a lesson interesting. Illustrate each of those qualities with examples of behavior you have witnessed from real-life teachers. Include your observations on how students benefit when a teacher has the qualities you're writing about.

21

Rowing the Bus
Paul Logan

Preview

If you could go back in time and undo one thing you are sorry for, what would it be? Such a long-regretted moment is the focus of Paul Logan's essay. While we can never turn back the clock, this story illustrates how we can do the next best thing: we can turn our regrets into valuable lessons in living.

Words to Watch

musty (3): stale or moldy in odor
trudge (5): walk in a heavy, tired way
brunt (6): greatest part
taunted (6): mocked and insulted
gait (7): manner of moving on foot
sinister (7): evil
distracted (9): interested in something else
stoic (13): emotionless
stricken (25): affected by painful emotions

When I was in elementary school, some older kids made me row the   1
bus. Rowing meant that on the way to school I had to sit in the dirty bus
aisle littered with paper, gum wads, and spitballs. Then I had to simulate
the motion of rowing while the kids around me laughed and chanted,

"Row, row, row the bus." I was forced to do this by a group of bullies who spent most of their time picking on me.

I was the perfect target for them. I was small. I had no father. And my mother, though she worked hard to support me, was unable to afford clothes and sneakers that were "cool." Instead she dressed me in outfits that we got from "the bags"—hand-me-downs given as donations to a local church.

Each Wednesday, she'd bring several bags of clothes to the house and pull out musty°, wrinkled shirts and worn bell-bottom pants that other families no longer wanted. I knew that people were kind to give things to us, but I hated wearing clothes that might have been donated by my classmates. Each time I wore something from the bags, I feared that the other kids might recognize something that was once theirs.

Besides my outdated clothes, I wore thick glasses, had crossed eyes, and spoke with a persistent lisp. For whatever reason, I had never learned to say the "s" sound properly, and I pronounced words that began with "th" as if they began with a "d." In addition, because of my severely crossed eyes, I lacked the hand and eye coordination necessary to hit or catch flying objects.

As a result, footballs, baseballs, soccer balls and basketballs became my enemies. I knew, before I stepped on the field or court, that I would do something clumsy or foolish and that everyone would laugh at me. I feared humiliation so much that I became skillful at feigning illnesses to get out of gym class. Eventually I learned how to give myself low-grade fevers so the nurse would write me an excuse. It worked for a while, until the gym teachers caught on. When I did have to play, I was always the last one chosen to be on any team. In fact, team captains did everything in their power to make their opponents get stuck with me. When the unlucky team captain was forced to call my name, I would trudge° over to the team, knowing that no one there liked or wanted me. For four years, from second through fifth grade, I prayed nightly for God to give me school days in which I would not be insulted, embarrassed, or made to feel ashamed.

I thought my prayers were answered when my mother decided to move during the summer before sixth grade. The move meant that I got to start sixth grade in a different school, a place where I had no reputation. Although the older kids laughed and snorted at me as soon as I got on my new bus—they couldn't miss my thick glasses and strange clothes—I soon discovered that there was another kid who received the brunt° of their insults. His name was George, and everyone made fun of him. The kids taunted° him because he was skinny; they belittled him because he had acne that pocked and blotched his face, and they teased him because his voice was squeaky. During my first gym class at my new school, I wasn't the last one chosen for kickball; George was.

George tried hard to be friends with me, coming up to me in the   7
cafeteria on the first day of school. "Hi. My name's George. Can I sit with
you?" he asked with a peculiar squeakiness that made each word high-
pitched and raspy. As I nodded for him to sit down, I noticed an
uncomfortable silence in the cafeteria as many of the students who had
mocked George's clumsy gait° during gym class began watching the two
of us and whispering among themselves. By letting him sit with me, I had
violated an unspoken law of school, a sinister° code of childhood that
demands there must always be someone to pick on. I began to realize two
things. If I befriended George, I would soon receive the same treatment
that I had gotten at my old school. If I stayed away from him, I might
actually have a chance to escape being at the bottom.

Within days, the kids started taunting us whenever we were together.   8
"Who's your new little buddy, Georgie?" In the hallways, groups of
students began mumbling about me just loud enough for me to hear,
"Look, it's George's ugly boyfriend." On the bus rides to and from school,
wads of paper and wet chewing gum were tossed at me by the bigger,
older kids in the back of the bus.

It became clear that my friendship with George was going to cause me   9
several more years of misery at my new school. I decided to stop being
friends with George. In class and at lunch, I spent less and less time with
him. Sometimes I told him I was too busy to talk; other times I acted
distracted° and gave one-word responses to whatever he said. Our
classmates, sensing that they had created a rift between George and me,
intensified their attacks on him. Each day, George grew more desperate as
he realized that the one person who could prevent him from being
completely isolated was closing him off. I knew that I shouldn't avoid
him, that he was feeling the same way I felt for so long, but I was so afraid
that my life would become the hell it had been in my old school that I
continued to ignore him.

Then, at recess one day, the meanest kid in the school, Chris, decided   10
he had had enough of George. He vowed that he was going to beat up
George and anyone else who claimed to be his friend. A mob of kids
formed and came after me. Chris led the way and cornered me near our
school's swing sets. He grabbed me by my shirt and raised his fist over
my head. A huge gathering of kids surrounded us, urging him to beat me
up, chanting "Go, Chris, go!"

"You're Georgie's new little boyfriend, aren't you?" he yelled. The hot   11
blast of his breath carried droplets of his spit into my face. In a complete
betrayal of the only kid who was nice to me, I denied George's friendship.

"No, I'm not George's friend. I don't like him. He's stupid," I blurted   12
out. Several kids snickered and mumbled under their breath. Chris stared
at me for a few seconds and then threw me to the ground.

"Wimp. Where's George?" he demanded, standing over me. Someone 13
pointed to George sitting alone on top of the monkey bars about thirty yards
from where we were. He was watching me. Chris and his followers sprinted
over to George and yanked him off the bars to the ground. Although the
mob quickly encircled them, I could still see the two of them at the center
of the crowd, looking at each other. George seemed stoic°, staring straight
through Chris. I heard the familiar chant of "Go, Chris, go!" and watched
as his fists began slamming into George's head and body. His face bloodied
and his nose broken, George crumpled to the ground and sobbed without
even throwing a punch. The mob cheered with pleasure and darted off into
the playground to avoid an approaching teacher.

Chris was suspended, and after a few days, George came back to 14
school. I wanted to talk to him, to ask him how he was, to apologize for
leaving him alone and for not trying to stop him from getting hurt. But I
couldn't go near him. Filled with shame for denying George and angered
by my own cowardice, I never spoke to him again.

Several months later, without telling any students, George transferred 15
to another school. Once in a while, in those last weeks before he left, I
caught him watching me as I sat with the rest of the kids in the cafeteria.
He never yelled at me or expressed anger, disappointment, or even
sadness. Instead he just looked at me.

In the years that followed, George's silent stare remained with me. It 16
was there in eighth grade when I saw a gang of popular kids beat up a
sixth-grader because, they said, he was "ugly and stupid." It was there my
first year in high school, when I saw a group of older kids steal another
freshman's clothes and throw them into the showers. It was there a year
later, when I watched several seniors press a wad of chewing gum into the
hair of a new girl on the bus. Each time that I witnessed another awkward,
uncomfortable, scared kid being tormented, I thought of George, and
gradually his haunting stare began to speak to me. No longer silent, it told
me that every child who is picked on and taunted deserves better, that no
one—no matter how big, strong, attractive or popular—has the right to
abuse another person.

Finally, in my junior year when a loudmouthed, pink-skinned bully 17
named Donald began picking on two freshmen on the bus, I could no
longer deny George. Donald was crumpling a large wad of paper and
preparing to bounce it off the back of the head of one of the young
students when I interrupted him.

"Leave them alone, Don," I said. By then I was six inches taller and, 18
after two years of high-school wrestling, thirty pounds heavier than I had
been in my freshman year. Though Donald was still two years older than
me, he wasn't much bigger. He stopped what he was doing, squinted and
stared at me.

"What's your problem, Paul?"   19

I felt the way I had many years earlier on the playground when I   20
watched the mob of kids begin to surround George.

"Just leave them alone. They aren't bothering you," I responded   21
quietly.

"What's it to you?" he challenged. A glimpse of my own past, of   22
rowing the bus, of being mocked for my clothes, my lisp, my glasses, and
my absent father flashed in my mind.

"Just don't mess with them. That's all I am saying, Don." My   23
fingertips were tingling. The bus was silent. He got up from his seat and
leaned over me, and I rose from my seat to face him. For a minute, both
of us just stood there, without a word, staring.

"I'm just playing with them, Paul," he said, chuckling. "You don't   24
have to go psycho on me or anything." Then he shook his head, slapped
me firmly on the chest with the back of his hand, and sat down. But he
never threw that wad of paper. For the rest of the year, whenever I was on
the bus, Don and the other troublemakers were noticeably quiet.

Although it has been years since my days on the playground and the   25
school bus, George's look still haunts me. Today, I see it on the faces of a
few scared kids at my sister's school—she is in fifth grade. Or once in a
while I'll catch a glimpse of someone like George on the evening news, in
a story about a child who brought a gun to school to stop the kids from
picking on him, or in a feature about a teenager who killed herself because
everyone teased her. In each school, in almost every classroom, there is a
George with a stricken° face, hoping that someone nearby will be strong
enough to be kind—despite what the crowd says—and brave enough to
stand up against people who attack, tease or hurt those who are vulnerable.

If asked about their behavior, I'm sure the bullies would say, "What's   26
it to you? It's just a joke. It's nothing." But to George and me, and
everyone else who has been humiliated or laughed at or spat on, it is
everything. No one should have to row the bus.

FIRST IMPRESSIONS

Freewrite for ten minutes on one of the following.

1. Did you enjoy reading this selection? Why or why not?

2. What do you think would have happened if Paul had stood up for
   George? Would it have made any difference?

3. Did your elementary or high school have bullies and victims similar
   to the ones in this story? How did they behave?

VOCABULARY CHECK

A. Circle the letter of the word or phrase that best completes each of the following four items.

1. In the sentence below, the word *simulate* means
   a. sing.
   b. ignore.
   (c.) imitate.
   d. stop.

   "Then I had to simulate the motion of rowing while the kids around me laughed and chanted, 'Row, row, row the bus.'" (Paragraph 1)

2. In the sentence below, the word *feigning* means
   a. escaping.
   (b.) faking.
   c. recognizing.
   d. curing.

   "I feared humiliation so much that I became skillful at feigning illnesses to get out of gym class." (Paragraph 5)

3. In the sentences below, the word *rift* means
   a. friendship.
   b. agreement.
   (c.) break.
   d. joke.

   "I decided to stop being friends with George. . . . Our classmates, sensing that they had created a rift between George and me, intensified their attacks on him." (Paragraph 9)

4. In the sentence below, the word *vulnerable* means
   (a.) easily wounded.
   b. courageous.
   c. cruel.
   d. physically large.

   "In each school, in almost every classroom, there is a George . . . hoping that someone nearby will be . . . brave enough to stand up against people who attack, tease, or hurt those who are vulnerable." (Paragraph 25)

B. Circle the letter of the answer that best completes each of the following four items. Each item uses a word (or form of a word) from "Words to Watch."

5. When I looked over my teacher's comments on my essay, I saw that my spelling had received the *brunt* of her criticism. I had
   a. not made a single spelling error.
   b. made a great many spelling errors.
   c. made few spelling errors, but many grammatical errors.

6. The audience shouted *taunts* at the band, such as
   a. "You guys rule!"
   b. "More! More!"
   c. "Get off the stage and let a real band play!"

7. We could tell from the woman's *gait* that she
   a. had not eaten all day.
   b. was in a hurry.
   c. was about to be interviewed for a job.

8. My dad is so *stoic* that
   a. no matter how tough his workday was, he always looks perfectly calm when he gets home.
   b. he loses his temper and screams at parking meters, television sets, and computers.
   c. he cries over sad scenes in movies, and even touching commercials.

READING CHECK

Central Point and Main Ideas

1. Which sentence best expresses the central point of the entire selection?
   a. Although Paul Logan was a target of other students' abuse when he was a young boy, their attacks stopped as he grew taller and stronger.
   b. When Logan moved to a different school, he discovered that another student, George, was the target of more bullying than he was.
   c. Logan's experience of being bullied and his shame at how he treated George eventually made him speak up for someone else who was teased.
   d. Logan is ashamed that he did not stand up for George when George was being attacked by a bully on the playground.

2. Which sentence best expresses the main idea of paragraphs 2–4?
   a. The first sentence of paragraph 2
   b. The second sentence of paragraph 2
   c. The first sentence of paragraph 3
   d. The first sentence of paragraph 4

3. Which sentence best expresses the implied main idea of paragraph 5?
   a. Because of Logan's clumsiness, gym was a miserable experience for him in elementary school.
   b. Because Logan hated gym so much, he made up excuses to avoid it.
   c. The gym teacher caught on to Logan's excuses.
   d. Other students did not want Logan to be a member of their team when games were played.

Key Supporting Details

4. When Chris attacked George, George reacted by
   a. fighting back hard.
   b. shouting for Logan to help him.
   c. running away.
   d. accepting the beating.

5. Logan finally found the courage to stand up for abused students when he saw
   a. Donald about to throw paper at a younger student.
   b. older kids throwing a freshman's clothes into the shower.
   c. seniors putting bubble gum in a new student's hair.
   d. a gang beating up a sixth-grader whom they disliked.

6. Which of the following was *not* a reason Logan was teased?
   a. He had crossed eyes.
   b. He wore hand-me-down clothes.
   c. He had a foreign accent.
   d. He spoke with a lisp.

Inferences

7. We can conclude that when Logan began sixth grade at the new school, he
   a. became quite popular.
   b. began to dress more fashionably.
   c. was relieved to find someone who was more unpopular than he was.
   d. became a bully himself.

8. The author implies that
    a. the kids who picked on George did not really intend to be cruel.
    b. bullying can lead to terrible tragedies at schools.
    c. his sister is the victim of teasing, much as he was.
    d. George grew up to be a confident, well-adjusted person.

9. ___F___ TRUE OR FALSE? The author implies that as adults, he and George talked together about what had happened at their school.

The Writer's Craft

10. Logan begins his essay with
    a. an anecdote that illustrates the humiliation he suffered.
    b. a description of his elementary school.
    c. a series of questions about the nature of bullying.
    d. a comparison of his school experience with George's.

DISCUSSION QUESTIONS

1. Paul Logan titled his selection "Rowing the Bus." Yet very little of the essay actually deals with the incident the title describes—only the first and last paragraphs. Why do you think Logan chose that title?

2. Logan wanted to be kind to George, but he wanted even more to be accepted by the other students. Have you ever found yourself in a similar situation—where you wanted to do the right thing but felt that it had too high a price? Explain what happened.

3. Logan refers to "a sinister code of childhood that demands there must always be someone to pick on." What does the phrase "a sinister code of childhood" mean to you? Why do children need someone to pick on?

4. The novelist Henry James once said, "Three things in human life are important. The first is to be kind. The second is to be kind. And the third is to be kind." Are there things that teachers, school administrators, parents, and other concerned adults can do to encourage young people to treat one another with kindness rather than cruelty?

PARAGRAPH ASSIGNMENTS

1. Logan writes, "In each school, in each classroom, there is a George with a stricken face." Think of a person who filled the role of George in one of your classes. In a paragraph, describe why he or she was the target of bullying and what form that bullying took. Include a description of your own thoughts and actions regarding the student who was bullied. Your topic sentence could be something like the following: "In my eighth-grade class, _____ was a student who was often bullied."

2. Because he was afraid that his life would be made miserable, the author decided to stop being friends with George. How do you feel about that decision? Do you think it was cruel? Understandable? Were there other options Logan might have tried? Write a paragraph in which you explain what you think of Logan's decision and why. Suggest at least one other way he could have acted, and tell what you think the consequences might have been.

ESSAY ASSIGNMENTS

1. From reading this essay, and from your own observations, can you pick out several characteristics that many bullies share? Write an essay that supports this thesis statement: "Most bullies share certain characteristics." In your essay, mention two or three qualities of bullies. Support your claim with evidence from the essay or from your own experience. In your concluding paragraph, you might discuss what these characteristics tell us about bullies.

2. Some students, like the author and George, are singled out as targets for bullying. But other students are singled out for different reasons, positive as well as negative. For instance, besides "The Target," a school might have "The Brain," "The Troublemaker," "The Actor," "The Jock," "The Beauty," "The Clown," and other categories. Write an essay in which you describe two or three students in your school that have been singled out and labeled in this way. Explain what about each of them resulted in their unique status.

22

Bullies in School
Kathleen Berger

Preview

Tragically, more and more incidents of bullying are making their way into news headlines. School shootings, student suicides, and other fatal attacks have all been linked to kids' harassment of one another. This excerpt from a college textbook, *The Developing Person: Through the Life Span,* Fourth Edition (Worth Publishers), explores the causes and effects of bullying and what one nation has done to combat it.

Words to Watch

developmental (1): having to do with human development
typified (2): represented
systematically (2): methodically; step by step
shun (2): avoid
implicit (5): understood though not openly stated
abet (7): to encourage (usually in doing something illegal or wrong)
longitudinal study (7): a study that follows people or groups over time
demean (9): to put down; to injure in reputation or social standing
cognitive (10): relating to knowing, awareness, reasoning, or judgment
fruitful (10): productive; useful
fatalistic (10): thinking that something is "fate" and so cannot be avoided
slights (10): discourtesies
proactive (13): acting in advance to deal with an expected difficulty
reprisal (13): retaliation; getting hurt in return for having inflicted injury

Bullying was once commonly thought to be an unpleasant but normal part 1
of child's play, not to be encouraged, of course, but of little consequence
in the long run. However, developmental° researchers who have looked
closely at the society of children consider bullying to be a very serious
problem, one that harms both the victim and the aggressor, sometimes
continuing to cause suffering years after the child has grown up.

One leading researcher in this area is Dan Olweus, who has studied 2
bullying in his native country of Norway and elsewhere for twenty-five
years. The cruelty, pain, and suffering that he has documented in that time
are typified° by the examples of Linda and Henry:

> *Linda was systematically° isolated by a small group of girls, who*
> *pressured the rest of the class, including Linda's only friend, to shun°*
> *her. Then the ringleader of the group persuaded Linda to give a party,*
> *inviting everyone. Everyone accepted; following the ringleader's*
> *directions, no one came. Linda was devastated, her self-confidence*
> *"completely destroyed."*

> *Henry's experience was worse. Daily, his classmates called him*
> *"Worm," broke his pencils, spilled his books on the floor, and mocked*
> *him whenever he answered a teacher's questions. Finally, a few boys*
> *took him to the bathroom and made him lie, face down, in the urinal*
> *drain. After school that day he tried to kill himself. His parents found*
> *him unconscious, and only then learned about his torment.*

Following the suicides of three other victims of bullying, the 3
Norwegian government asked Olweus in 1983 to determine the extent and
severity of the problem. After concluding a confidential survey of nearly
all of Norway's 90,000 school-age children, Olweus reported that the
problem was widespread and serious; that teachers and parents were
"relatively unaware" of specific incidents of bullying; and that even when
adults noticed bullying, they rarely intervened. Of all the children Olweus
surveyed, 9 percent were bullied "now and then"; 3 percent were victims
once a week or more; and 7 percent admitted that they themselves
sometimes deliberately hurt other children, verbally or physically.

As high as these numbers may seem, they are equaled and even 4
exceeded in research done in other countries. For instance, a British study
of 8- and 9-year-olds found that 17 percent were victims of regular
bullying and that 13 percent were bullies. A study of middle-class children
in a university school in Florida found that 10 percent were "extremely
victimized." Recently, American researchers have looked particularly at
sexual harassment, an aspect of childhood bullying ignored by most
adults. Fully a third of 9- to 15-year-old girls say they have experienced
sexual teasing and touching sufficiently troubling that they wanted to

avoid school, and, as puberty approaches, almost every boy who is perceived as homosexual by his peers is bullied, sometimes mercilessly.

Researchers define bullying as repeated, systematic efforts to inflict 5 harm on a particular child through physical attack (such as hitting, punching, pinching, or kicking), verbal attack (such as teasing, taunting, or name-calling), or social attack (such as deliberate social exclusion or public mocking). Implicit° in this definition is the idea of an unbalance of power: victims of bullying are in some way weaker than their harassers and continue to be singled out for attack, in part because they have difficulty defending themselves. In many cases, this difficulty is compounded by the fact that the bullying is being carried out by a group of children. In Olweus's research, at least 60 percent of bullying incidents involved group attacks.

As indicated by the emphasis given to it, the key word in the preceding 6 definition of bullying is "repeated." Most children experience isolated attacks or social slights from other children and come through them unscathed. But when a child must endure such shameful experiences again and again—being forced to hand over lunch money, or to drink milk mixed with detergent, or to lick someone's boots, or to be the butt of insults and practical jokes, with everyone watching and no one coming to the child's defense—the effects can be deep and long-lasting. Not only are bullied children anxious, depressed, and underachieving during the months and years of their torment, but even years later, they have lower self-esteem as well as painful memories.

The picture is somewhat different, but often more ominous, for 7 bullies. Contrary to the public perception that bullies are actually insecure and lonely, at the peak of their bullying they usually have friends who abet°, fear, and admire them, and they seem brashly unapologetic about the pain they have inflicted, as they often claim, "all in fun." But their popularity and school success fade over the years, and especially if they are boys, they run a high risk of ending up in prison. In one longitudinal study° done by Olweus, by age 24, two-thirds of the boys who had been bullies in the second grade were convicted of at least one felony, and one-third of those who had been bullies in the sixth through the ninth grades were already convicted of three or more crimes, often violent ones. International research likewise finds that children who are allowed to regularly victimize other children are at high risk of becoming violent offenders as adolescents and adults.

Unfortunately, bullying during middle childhood seems to be universal: 8 it occurs in every nation that has been studied, is as much a problem in small rural schools as in large urban ones, and is as prevalent among well-to-do majority children as among poor immigrant children. Also quite common, if not universal, is the "profile" of bullies and their victims. Contrary to popular belief, victims are not distinguished by their external traits: they are no more likely to be fat, skinny, or homely, or to speak with an accent, than nonvictims are. But they usually are "rejected" children, that is, children who have few friends because they are more anxious and less secure than most children and are unable or unwilling to defend themselves. They also are more often boys than girls and more often younger children.

Bullies have traits in common as well, some of which can be traced to   9
their upbringing. The parents of bullies often seem indifferent to what their children do outside the home but use "power-assertive" discipline on them at home. These children are frequently subjected to physical punishment, verbal criticism, and displays of dominance meant to control and demean° them, thereby giving them a vivid model, as well as a compelling reason, to control and demean others. Boys who are bullies are often above average in size, while girls who are bullies are often above average in verbal assertiveness. These differences are reflected in bullying tactics: boys typically use force or the threat of force; girls often mock or ridicule their victims, making fun of their clothes, behavior, or appearance, or revealing their most embarrassing secrets.

What can be done to halt these damaging attacks? Many psychologists   10
have attempted to alter the behavior patterns that characterize aggressive or rejected children. Cognitive° interventions seem particularly fruitful°: some programs teach social problem-solving skills (such as how to use humor or negotiation to reduce a conflict); others help children reassess their negative assumptions (such as the frequent, fatalistic° view of many rejected children that nothing can protect them, or the aggressive child's typical readiness to conclude that accidental slights° are deliberate threats); others tutor children in academic skills, hoping to improve confidence and short-circuit the low self-esteem that might be at the root of both victimization and aggression.

These approaches sometimes help individuals. However, because they   11
target one child at a time, they are piecemeal, time-consuming, and costly. Further, they have to work against habits learned at home and patterns reinforced at school, making it hard to change a child's behavior pattern. After all, bullies and their admirers have no reason to learn new social skills if their current attitudes and actions bring them status and pleasure. And even if rejected children change their behavior, they still face a difficult time recovering accepted positions in the peer group and gaining friends who will support and defend them. The solution to this problem must begin, then, by recognizing that the bullies and victims are not acting in isolation but, rather, are caught up in a mutually destructive interaction within a particular social context.

Accordingly, a more effective intervention is to change the social 12
climate within the school, so that bully-victim cycles no longer spiral out
of control. That this approach can work was strikingly demonstrated by a
government-funded awareness campaign that Olweus initiated for every
school in Norway. In the first phase of the campaign, community-wide
meetings were held to explain the problem; pamphlets were sent to all
parents to alert them to the signs of victimization (such as a child's having
bad dreams, having no real friends, and coming home from school with
damaged clothes, torn books, or unexplained bruises); and videotapes
were shown to all students to evoke sympathy for victims.

The second phase of the campaign involved specific actions within the 13
schools. In every classroom, students discussed reasons for and ways to
mediate peer conflicts, to befriend lonely children, and to stop bullying
attacks whenever they saw them occur. Teachers were taught to be
proactive°, organizing cooperative learning groups so that no single child
could be isolated, halting each incident of name-calling or minor assault
as soon as they noticed it, and learning how to see through the bully's
excuses and to understand the victim's fear of reprisal°. Principals were
advised that adequate adult supervision during recess, lunch, and
bathroom breaks distinguished schools where bullying was rare from
those where bullying was common.

If bullying incidents occurred despite such measures, counselors were 14
urged to intervene, talking privately and seriously with bullies and their
victims, counseling their parents, and seeking solutions that might
include intensive therapy with the bully's parents to restructure family
discipline, reassigning the bully to a different class, grade, or even school,
and helping the victim strengthen skills and foster friendships.

Twenty months after this campaign began, Olweus resurveyed the 15
children in forty-two schools. He found that bullying had been reduced
overall by more than 50 percent, with dramatic improvement for both
boys and girls at every grade level. Developmental researchers are excited
because results such as these, in which a relatively simple, cost-effective
measure has such a decided impact on a developmental problem, are rare.
Olweus concludes, "It is no longer possible to avoid taking action about
bullying problems at school using lack of awareness as an excuse . . . it
all boils down to a matter of will and involvement on the part of the
adults." Unfortunately, at the moment, Norway is the only country to have
mounted a nationwide attack to prevent the problem of bullying. Many
other school systems, in many other nations, have not even acknowledged
the harm caused by this problem, much less shown the "will and
involvement" to stop it.

FIRST IMPRESSIONS

Freewrite for ten minutes on one of the following.

1. Did you enjoy reading this selection? Why or why not?

2. Researcher Dan Olweus's findings suggest that bullies are actually popular and admired, at least for a while. Why do you think anyone would admire a bully?

3. Is bullying a major problem in your school (or was it when you were younger)? Who tended to get bullied, and why?

VOCABULARY CHECK

A. Circle the letter of the word or phrase that best completes each of the following four items.

1. In the sentences below, the word *compounded* means
   a. reduced.
   b. increased.
   c. solved.
   d. forgiven.

   > "[V]ictims of bullying . . . continue to be singled out for attack, in part because they have difficulty defending themselves. In many cases, this difficulty is compounded by the fact that the bullying is being carried out by a group of children." (Paragraph 5)

2. In the sentences below, the word *unscathed* means
   a. unharmed.
   b. unpleasant.
   c. unknown.
   d. uncertain.

   > "Most children experience isolated attacks . . . from other children and come through them unscathed. But when a child must endure such shameful experiences again and again . . . the effects can be deep and long-lasting." (Paragraph 6)

3. In the sentence below, the word *brashly* means
   a. shyly.
   b. ashamedly.
   c. boldly.
   d. secretly.

   > "[A]t the peak of their bullying they . . . seem brashly unapologetic about the pain they have inflicted, as they often claim, 'all in fun.' " (Paragraph 7)

4. In the sentence below, the word *intervene* means
   a. ignore a situation.
   b. step in.
   c. make a joke.
   d. give up.

   > "If bullying incidents occurred despite such measures, counselors were urged to intervene, talking privately and seriously with bullies and their victims. . . ." (Paragraph 14)

B. Circle the letter of the answer that best completes each of the following four items. Each item uses a word (or form of a word) from "Words to Watch."

5. Since they've broken up, Teresa has *shunned* Peter. She
   a. leaves any room that he walks into.
   b. treats him as a close friend, but not as a romantic partner.
   c. follows him everywhere to spy on him.

6. The shoplifter was *abetted* by
   a. the person who reported him to the store detective.
   b. the person who distracted the clerk so that the shoplifter could steal more.
   c. the shoplifter's mother, who didn't know that her son was a thief.

7. The professor *demeaned* her students by
   a. arriving early to class.
   b. calling them "stupid" and "worthless."
   c. addressing them as "Mr." and "Miss."

8. The meeting was unusually *fruitful*. We
   a. came up with solutions to a number of problems.
   b. talked for hours, but accomplished very little.
   c. ate bananas, orange slices, and apples.

READING CHECK

Central Point and Main Ideas

1. Which sentence best expresses the central point of the entire selection?
    a. Certain types of children are likely to become either bullies or victims.
    b. To combat the problem of bullying, a Norwegian researcher designed an innovative program for all schools in Norway.
    c. Developmental researchers consider bullying a very serious problem, one that harms both victims and aggressors.
    (d.) Developmental researchers have concluded that bullying is a very serious problem that can be addressed only by changing the social climate within a school.

2. The main idea of paragraph 9 is
    (a.) stated in the first sentence of the paragraph.
    b. stated in the second sentence of the paragraph.
    c. stated in the last sentence of the paragraph.
    d. unstated.

3. Which of the following sentences expresses the main idea of paragraph 10?
    a. Victims of bullying often feel that nothing can be done to help them.
    (b.) Several approaches have been used to try to halt bullying.
    c. Tutoring children in academic skills sometimes helps both victims and bullies.
    d. Problem-solving skills include using humor to reduce conflict.

Key Supporting Details

4. __F__ TRUE OR FALSE? Victims of bullies tend to be physically unattractive.

5. Olweus found that by age 24, two-thirds of the boys who had been bullies in second grade had
    a. expressed regret for their behavior.
    b. been convicted of three or more violent crimes.
    c. become parents of bullies themselves.
    (d.) been convicted of at least one felony crime.

6. Twenty months after Olweus's anti-bullying campaign began,
   a. it was halted because of lack of funding.
   b. bullying had decreased significantly among boys, but not among girls.
   (c.) incidents of bullying had dropped by more than 50 percent.
   d. a number of former victims had become bullies themselves.

Inferences

7. It is reasonable to conclude that
   a. bullying is more of a problem in Norway than in most other countries.
   b. Dan Olweus was raised outside of Norway.
   (c.) the Norwegian government takes the problem of bullying seriously.
   d. the problem of bullying in Norway has disappeared.

8. From the reading, we can infer that
   a. the parents of bullies are generally very worried about their children's bullying.
   (b.) bullies frequently "learn" to become bullies from their parents.
   c. gentle, loving parents often raise children who are bullies.
   d. parents have little influence over whether or not their children become bullies.

The Writer's Craft

9. Which of the following best describes the writer's attitude towards her subject?
   (a.) Objective
   b. Light-hearted
   c. Confused
   d. Sentimental

10. The article ends with the author's
    a. personal anecdote about having been the victim of bullying.
    (b.) criticism that so few schools and nations have addressed the problem of bullying.
    c. prediction of what will happen if more nations do not address the problem of bullying.
    d. restatement of what bullying is and how it affects children.

DISCUSSION QUESTIONS

1. As a child, were you ever involved in bullying—either as the aggressor or as the victim? What effect did this involvement have on you? If you could live those years over again, would you do anything differently?

2. How does, or how did, your school deal with bullying? After reading this article, what suggestions for stopping bullying would you make to your school?

3. Do you feel the job of controlling aggressive behavior in children should be left to the schools? How can others—parents, religious leaders, the larger community, and the media—be involved?

4. Based on your own observations, what do victims of bullies seem to have in common? What could be done—at home, in the school, in the neighborhood—to help these children feel better about themselves and relate more easily to others?

PARAGRAPH ASSIGNMENTS

1. If you were a teacher in a classroom and you became aware that one child was being bullied, how would you respond? Write a paragraph that tells what you would do and why. A possible topic sentence for this paragraph is "If a child in my classroom was being bullied, I would respond in the following ways."

2. As the author points out in paragraph 5, bullying does not always involve physical violence. Bullies may attack other people verbally or socially. Write a paragraph about a time you witnessed (or were involved in) a verbal or social attack. What happened? How did the bully and victim each behave? If there were witnesses, how did they respond to what was happening?

ESSAY ASSIGNMENTS

1. Write an essay describing three forms of bullying. You may want to read first the model student essay on bullying on pages 14–15. You also can focus on physical, verbal, and social bullying, and you can use the thesis statement in the model essay. All of the examples in your essay, however, should be based on your own personal observation of bullying behavior during your school years. Do your best to provide specific, vivid examples and details that will help others clearly "see" the bullying behavior that you or students you know experienced. Your thesis statement can simply be "Every member of a school community should be aware of bullying and the three hateful forms that it takes: physical, verbal, and social bullying."

2. Read (or re-read) "Bird Girl" (page 31) and "Rowing the Bus" (page 242). Write an essay in which you support one of the following thesis statements:

   • The bullies and victims in "Bird Girl" and "Rowing the Bus" share certain similarities with the bullies and victims described in "Bullies in School."

   • The victims in "Bird Girl" and "Rowing the Bus" could have been helped if their schools had followed the program described in "Bullies in School."

   In your essay, support your points with specific evidence from the articles you are discussing.

23

Seven Ways to Keep the Peace at Home
Daniel Sugarman

Preview

Families aren't like machines—you can't just flip the "on" switch and expect them to work. Unfortunately, many of us seem to expect our families to function well automatically, and we often blame one another when that doesn't happen. Here, psychologist Daniel Sugarman points out seven ways people may contribute to family tensions, and how they can reverse those behaviors to make their families more peaceful and happy.

Words to Watch

full-fledged (1): fully developed
hypochondriac (1): a person who has frequent imaginary physical illnesses
chronic (2): lasting for a long time
perpetuate (3): to cause (something) to last a long time
ingrained (4): deeply rooted
sanitized (5): made clean by removing any unpleasant features
bolster (7): support
solicitous (16): attentive and caring
wary (16): cautious
distorted (17): twisted in form or meaning
blatantly (22): openly

promiscuous (22): lacking standards of selection in sexual partners
confidante (22): one to whom secrets are entrusted
engendered (23): produced
placate (25): to calm
aptitudes (27): natural abilities
bravado (29): false show of courage
vicissitudes (32): changes in one's life or surroundings; life's ups and downs
vex (32): bother
niggling (33): annoying
embezzlement (35): theft from one's employer

Not long ago, the parents of a seven-year-old girl consulted me because   1
their daughter was on her way to becoming a full-fledged° hypochondriac°.
The girl's father was a physician, and both parents were busy, involved
people. During an early session with the family, the reasons behind the
girl's problems became clear. Dad arrived late and was preoccupied and
worried. He started to speak to me when his daughter interrupted: "My
throat hurts a lot. I feel sick." Automatically he produced a tongue
depressor and looked into her throat. As he reassured her about her health,
I realized the girl's complaints represented the *only* way that she could
engage her father's full attention.

When I pointed out that it was *he* who was unconsciously turning his   2
daughter into a chronic° complainer, the father altered his behavior. He
began giving her more attention when she was *not* complaining about her
health, and treating her physical complaints very lightly when they did
occur. The girl began to improve. Soon, she hardly complained about her
health at all.

In the course of my clinical practice, I have seen hundreds of families   3
in conflict, and I am astounded at how frequently families unwittingly
perpetuate° tension-causing behavior. Explosions just seem to happen
again and again, until family members can be helped to understand their
interactions and learn to meet their mutual needs in less destructive ways.

Although conflicts may be so ingrained° for some families that   4
outside professional help is needed, certain principles of Family First Aid
can go a long way in reducing friction for most families. Here are seven
steps that I have found to be helpful for diminishing family tension.

1. Give Up the Myth of the Perfect Family. A couple of years ago,   5
an unhappy teenager came to my office with her family and announced,
"Well, here we are! The *Shady*, not the *Brady*, Bunch!" I find that many
people, like this girl, resent their own families for not living up to some
romanticized notion of family life that can be found only on television. In

contrast to TV families, *real* families go through periods of crisis that strain everyone's nerves. During these trying times, most families' feelings and actions bear little resemblance to the sanitized°, prepackaged half-hour comedy routines on TV.

Some months ago, for example, Grace and Lew Martin* brought their sixteen-year-old son to me. Frank was an angry, sullen boy who had been doing poorly in school and been caught smoking pot there. When Frank took his father's car out and was caught speeding at ninety miles per hour, his parents insisted he come for treatment. 6

During our first session, it became evident that Frank's problem was certainly not the only one in the family. Mr. Martin had been consistently passed over for promotion at work. Mrs. Martin worked long hours trying to sell real estate, but because of high mortgage rates she was having little success. Frank's fourteen-year-old sister had fractured her leg the previous winter, and several operations had been required before it was set properly. Mr. Martin had become angry and withdrawn, and was criticizing Mrs. Martin's ability to manage the household. She, in turn, spent more time away from home and began to drink heavily. Family fights became more and more frequent. Everyone tried to bolster° his or her own tottering sense of self-esteem by shattering the self-esteem of a loved one. 7

As I listened to this troubled family, I became aware that it wasn't the real problems that were about to do them in. It was their self-hate. Mr. Martin was furious at himself for not having gotten his promotion and because his wife had to work. Mrs. Martin was furious with herself because she wasn't selling houses and because she couldn't stay at home and care for her daughter. Frank was angry at them all, and so guilty about his angry feelings that I suspect his ninety-mile-per-hour ride partially represented an attempt at self-execution. 8

Once the Martin family understood how they were punishing themselves for not being a perfect family, they began to show compassion toward themselves. They rapidly began to solve the real problems. 9

The idea of the typical happy family is becoming an anachronism. As the national divorce rate approaches 50 percent, increasing numbers of people will live in single-parent families. Should these people hate themselves because they aren't part of a typical family? Unfortunately, too many do just that. As high interest rates nibble away at the American dream of owning one's own home, should people hate themselves because they don't have a "typical" single-family dwelling—or because everyone in the family has to work to support this home? Unfortunately, too many do that, too. 10

---

*All names in this article have been changed to protect patients' privacy.

I often wonder if the perfect American family ever did exist. If it did, 11
I haven't met it often in the past few years. As a matter of fact, research
suggests that growing up in a perfectly happy family is not as important
as psychologists once thought. In one continuing study of 248 children,
Jean Macfarlane at the University of California Institute of Human
Development has found that children who grew up in troubled homes do
not necessarily grow up to be troubled adults. Children who grew up in
happy homes are *not* necessarily better adjusted by the age of thirty.

When you give up the myth of the perfect family and deal with your 12
real problems in a spirit of compassion, psychological growth begins to
take place.

2. Tell It Like You Feel It. Have you heard the story of the fifteen-year- 13
old boy who had never said a word in his whole life? He came to breakfast
one day and suddenly yelled, "This oatmeal is cold!" His astounded
mother replied, "You can *talk!* Why haven't you spoken before?" The boy
shrugged and said, "Before this, everything was OK."

Funny story. Not so funny when situations like this occur in real 14
families. And they do. All too frequently I encounter people in families
who, for one reason or another, feel they must hide their feelings.

A few months ago, I saw an unhappy couple. Mrs. Raymond was 15
almost always depressed. Sometimes she couldn't even take care of her
home and children. Mr. Raymond was quite protective of his wife—but at
the same time he was having an affair.

Together in my office, the Raymonds had little to say to each other. 16
Each was very solicitous°, but wary° of saying something that might
upset the other. By not saying what they felt, they managed to upset each
other more than if they had communicated their feelings directly.

It's odd how many people believe that when they stop verbalizing, 17
communication ceases. Nothing, of course, is further from the truth,
because communication consists of much more than words. Angry
silence, sighs, headaches, impotence and arrests for drunken driving can
often be forms of distorted° communication.

For his vacation, Mr. Raymond made plans to take his family on a 18
two-week camping trip. Mrs. Raymond told me she *dreaded* the idea of
camping. When I urged her to express her displeasure so a mutually
satisfying vacation could be arranged, she replied, "But he works so hard.
He deserves to go where he wants for vacation." Once at the campsite, she
developed headaches and nausea. After two days of misery, she went to a
local doctor, who failed to find any physical reason for her discomfort.
During the rest of the vacation she tortured both herself and her husband
with her physical complaints. It would have been much kinder had she
told him how she felt before they left home.

Each time we conceal something from someone close to us, the 19
relationship becomes poorer. So, if you want to reduce family tensions,
one of the most important ways to start is to send honest communications
to those you love.

3. Don't Play Telephone. Do you remember the game "Telephone"? A 20
message gets passed from person to person, and everyone laughs at how
distorted it becomes. As a game, "Telephone" can be fun. In real life,
sending messages through third parties fouls things up. It's important for
family members who have "business" with other family members to take
it up *directly*.

When tension mounts in a relationship between two people, a frequent 21
way of dealing with this is to send messages through a third person.
Family therapists refer to the process as "triangulation." Following a spat,
a mother may say to her son, "Tell your father to pass the salt," which may
be answered by, "Tell your mother to get her own salt." In many chronic
cases of triangulation, the middleman becomes severely disturbed.

Two years ago, Ruth and Ralph Gordon brought their seventeen-year- 22
old daughter for treatment. Lucille was not doing well in school, using
drugs heavily and becoming blatantly° promiscuous°. When I began to
work with her, she was uncommunicative and hostile. After some time,
however, she opened up and told me her parents rarely talked to each
other—but both used her as a confidante°. Mrs. Gordon was sexually
unsatisfied and suggested to Lucille that she ask her father to go for
marital counseling. Mr. Gordon told Lucille that he was seeing another
woman, and he urged Lucille to speak to her mother about improving her
grooming. Caught in this tangle of feelings, Lucille became more and
more troubled. It wasn't until she refused to play middleman that she
began to improve. When either parent began to send a message through
her, she learned to say, "Tell him/her yourself!"

You'll find that when family members learn to dial each other directly, 23
there's rarely a busy signal or wrong number. With direct dialing, a sense
of freshness is engendered°.

4. Make Your Blueprints Flexible. Almost all parents have a secret 24
master plan for their children. Sometimes this calls for a child to grow up
exactly like a parent—or, more often, for the child to become an
improved version of the parent. In our culture, with its emphasis on
getting ahead and self-fulfillment, it's tempting to hope that our children
will realize many of our own desires. Whether we like it or not, though,
children have a habit of spinning their own dreams. When a child's plans
become different from his parents' blueprint, the family is on a collision
course that can be avoided only by understanding and flexibility.

Most parents don't even realize how much they push and pull. I think   25
you would be surprised, too, at how frequently children will say things to
their parents only to placate° them.

One teenage girl assured her parents that she was going to study harder   26
and prepare for college. This girl told me, "I don't plan to go to college, but
I can't tell them yet. They are disappointed enough, and I don't want to rip
up any more of their dreams for me." Caught in a web of parental
expectations, this girl was miserable, and didn't feel free enough to explore
her own potential and channel her abilities into realistic vocational goals.

An experienced parent knows that different children require different   27
handling. When we become wise and willing enough to revise our
blueprints so that they incorporate the child's realistic needs and
aptitudes°, we are on the road to a less tension-filled family life.

5. Learn to Use Contracts. Psychologists say that when two people   28
marry, they agree to a contract. Sometimes, a couple has a strong
emotional investment in keeping the not-so-pretty clauses of the contract
hidden from everyone—including themselves. Gina and Tom Butler were
married twenty-five years before their hidden contract caused problems.

When Tom met Gina, he was a skinny kid from a poor family who had   29
a burning desire to become financially successful. He was, under his
bravado°, painfully anxious and felt very inadequate. Gina was the
prettiest girl in town. She was also desperately unhappy at home and
couldn't wait to get away from the constant bickering there. When she
was sixteen, she had an abortion. At seventeen, she met Tom. As they
dated, they unwittingly began to draft their contract. Gina, unconsciously,
agreed to make Tom feel adequate to reduce his anxieties. Tom, for his
part, agreed never to discuss Gina's abortion, and to remove her from her
hostile home situation by marrying her.

For many years their contract worked well. Gina massaged Tom's ego.   30
She encouraged, reassured, supported him. When the children went off to
college, however, she felt she needed to grow. She attended a local
college, graduated with honors, and accepted a position with a well-
known company. As Gina became successful, Tom became irritable and
angry. He accused her of not being interested in the family. Eventually, he
accused her of having a lover and of being "a tramp, like you were when
I met you and like you'll always be." With these words their contract was
breached, and both sought the services of attorneys. Fortunately, Gina's
lawyer suggested counseling before divorce. Once in treatment, the
hidden aspects of Gina and Tom's contract were uncovered, and they
negotiated a more mature contract based upon mutual respect.

Many family contracts, like the Butlers', tend to disintegrate when one   31
member of the family begins to grow. And that's really all right, if the

family can use the anxiety that inevitably results as a catalyst to foster healthy mutual growth.

I find it helps a lot if you can face up to your hidden contracts and then [32] update them. It's also fruitful when you set clear provisions for the many minor vicissitudes° of daily living that can vex° the family. Coats not hung up in the closet, hedges left untrimmed—these are the raw materials that fuel family explosions. Frequently, an annoying, persistent source of tension can be cleared away by drafting a new contract, whose terms are clearly understood by all parties.

One teenager agreed to wash the dishes in exchange for transportation [33] to cheerleading practice. One husband agreed not to smoke when he was with his wife, in exchange for her maintaining her weight loss. In these cases, all involved felt they had gotten a good deal, and niggling° sources of family tension were eliminated by negotiation.

6. Stop the "Good Guy"–"Bad Guy" Routine. Sometimes, the greatest [34] problems in families arise when people classify children as Good Guys and Bad Guys. These families tend to make a scapegoat of one of their members, who from that point on becomes "it" in a never-ending game of tag.

The Freemonts had four children. Brett, the third child, resembled [35] Mrs. Freemont's uncle Mark, who was serving time for embezzlement°. "He's just like Uncle Mark," the Freemonts proclaimed when Brett came home from nursery school with a toy giraffe that he had taken, and again when Brett was eight and got into a fight with another third-grader. By the time Brett was fifteen, he had far more serious problems. "I'm just like my Uncle Mark," he told me: the label had become a self-fulfilling prophecy. Brett felt doomed to replicate his uncle's life. But once you realize that no two people are exactly alike, you can free members of your family to be themselves.

Curiously, sometimes the Bad Guy of the family really serves to hold [36] that family together. I once worked with an eighteen-year-old girl who was constantly involved in mischief. As I began to understand her family situation, I realized that this girl's parents were emotionally estranged and the constant turmoil her behavior produced was an attempt to get her parents to form a united front. Indeed, she was partially successful. Her bizarre antics were at times so extreme that her parents barely had time to examine their own problems.

The next time you're in the midst of a family problem, resist your [37] natural urge to think in terms of *right* and *wrong*. Rather, ask yourself, "What is going on here and why?" In our era of no-fault car insurance and no-fault divorce, it makes increasing sense to have no-fault (or all-fault) family problems.

7. Get Rid of Old Emotional Baggage. When people enter into any   38
new relationship, they come to the new with a lot of old fears and
unhealed emotional wounds. Unless you look at your own history
honestly, you're likely to unwittingly re-create the same unhappy mess
that gave you so much pain in the past.

Rachel Dorton grew up in an unhappy household in which her father   39
frequently had affairs. When she married, with fidelity her top priority,
Rachel chose Mal, a hardworking, earnest accountant. For a time, all went
well. After several months of marriage, however, Rachel became
increasingly suspicious when Mal did audits in distant cities. She made
his life miserable with constant suspicion and pleas for reassurance. After
several sessions of counseling, Rachel came to realize that, without
conscious intent, she was re-creating the very experiences she had hated
so much as a child. As she faced her feelings squarely, she was able to
become less provocative, and she came to understand that some men—
particularly Mal—could indeed be trusted.

During periods of severe stress, it's astounding how people may treat   40
others the same way they were treated by their parents. Ed Richardson
had had a rough childhood. His father, a hardworking train conductor,
would often take abuse from passengers and arrive home irritable and
tense. Sometimes he would beat Ed severely. "You're no good," his father
would proclaim. "You're a nothing."

Ed resolved that he would never hit his own children or call them   41
names. For years his resolve held, but then Ed's company went bankrupt
and he was forced to take a job he despised. The family had to retrench
and move to a smaller home. During this crisis, Ed's oldest boy cut school
and was caught shoplifting. Ed brought the boy home and began to beat
him. To his horror he found himself yelling, "You're no good . . . you're
a nothing." Shaken by this experience, Ed got professional help. It took
him a while to put things back together, but it helped when he realized
that, when the chips are down, most people do unto others what has been
done unto them.

At its best, a nourishing family serves as a safe haven enclosed by   42
invisible walls of love and concern. In such a family, individuals can
replenish diminished feelings of self-esteem.

At its worst, a family can become a red-hot crucible in which ancient   43
conflicts brew and boil and are reenacted again and again. Most frequently,
however, families just seem to bumble along with little emotional insight
into how the family itself may be responsible for intensifying or perpetuating
a family member's problem.

Solving family problems has never been easy. As a practicing 44
psychologist, I know that good intentions alone are usually not enough.
Effective action most often follows accurate understanding. With a little
practice, care and use of these seven steps, the chances are good that you'll
be able to lower the tension level in the best family of all—your own.

FIRST IMPRESSIONS

Freewrite for ten minutes on one of the following.

1. Did you enjoy reading this selection? Why or why not?

2. Did any of the stories Dr. Sugarman tells remind you of experiences
   you've had? Which ones? Explain.

3. Do you think "the perfect family" exists? Explain your answer.

VOCABULARY CHECK

A. Circle the letter of the word or phrase that best completes each of the
following four items.

1. In the sentences below, the word *anachronism* means
   a. something undesirable.
   b. something unfair.
   c. something common.
   d. something out of place in the present time.

   "The idea of the typical, happy family is becoming an
   anachronism. . . . I often wonder if the perfect American family
   ever did exist. If it did, I haven't met it often in the past few years."
   (Paragraphs 10–11)

2. In the sentences below, the word *breached* means
   a. strengthened.
   b. broken.
   c. written.
   d. signed.

   "Eventually, he accused her of having a lover and of being 'a
   tramp, like you were when I met you and like you'll always be.'
   With these words their contract was breached, and both sought the
   services of attorneys." (Paragraph 30)

3. In the sentences below, the word *catalyst* means
    a. something which causes change.
    b. tragic accident.
    c. criticism.
    d. penalty.

    > "Many family contracts, like the Butlers', tend to disintegrate when one member of the family begins to grow. And that's really all right, if the family can use the anxiety that inevitably results as a catalyst to foster healthy mutual growth." (Paragraph 31)

4. In the sentences below, the word *retrench* means
    a. remain in one place.
    b. increase in size.
    c. cheer up.
    d. cut back on expenses.

    > "[T]hen Ed's company went bankrupt and he was forced to take a a job he despised. The family had to retrench and move to a smaller home." (Paragraph 41)

B. Circle the letter of the answer that best completes each of the following four items. Each item uses a word (or form of a word) from "Words to Watch."

5. A *chronic* illness is an illness that
    a. affects the lungs.
    b. is quickly cured.
    c. seems as if it will never go away.

6. You should be *wary* of a
    a. dangerous animal.
    b. pet rabbit.
    c. trusted friend.

7. When Jenny's mom told her to clean her room, Jenny *placated* her by
    a. shouting, "Do it yourself."
    b. saying, "I'll do it tonight, I promise."
    c. pretending not to hear her.

8. Michael's many *aptitudes* include
    a. a nice car.
    b. a talent for learning foreign languages.
    c. red hair.

READING CHECK

Central Point and Main Ideas

1. Which sentence best expresses the central point of the entire selection?
    a. Family members need to discuss issues with each other in a straightforward way.
    b. "Contracts" within a family can have both good and bad results.
    c. Family members will get along better if they follow certain steps.
    d. There are seven common ways that people in a family upset one another.

2. The topic sentence of paragraph 7 is its
    a. first sentence.
    b. third sentence.
    c. next-to-last sentence.
    d. last sentence.

3. Which sentence best expresses the main idea of paragraph 18?
    a. Mr. Raymond planned to take his family on a camping trip.
    b. Mrs. Raymond wanted her hard-working husband to enjoy their family vacation.
    c. Mrs. Raymond's failure to be honest with her husband led to a disastrous family vacation.
    d. After the Raymonds arrived at their campsite, Mrs. Raymond began to have physical problems.

Key Supporting Details

4. In order to "get rid of old emotional baggage," family members should
    a. stop comparing themselves with fictional TV families.
    b. negotiate better contracts.
    c. stop classifying their children as Good Guys and Bad Guys.
    d. look honestly at their own history.

5. ___*F*___ TRUE OR FALSE? Communication stops when people stop talking.

6. Parents who "make their blueprints flexible"
    a. want their children to be exactly like them.
    b. want their children to be improved versions of themselves.
    c. have a secret master plan for their children.
    d. consider their children's needs and talents, not just their own dreams.

Inferences

7. The author implies that
    a. it is often a good idea for family members to communicate through a third family member.
    b. parents do not have enough expectations for their children.
    (c.) identifying the real cause of a family problem is the first step in solving that problem.
    d. once a family is in crisis, it can never really recover and become healthy.

8. The author implies that
    a. a family's problems are often the fault of one troublemaking child.
    b. family members should ignore their own desires and give in to what others want.
    (c.) a crisis in a family can actually lead to healthy growth and development.
    d. once a family agrees to an unspoken contract, that contract must never be broken.

The Writer's Craft

9. Which method of introduction does the author use in this selection?
    (a.) Anecdote (Story)
    b. One or more questions
    c. Shifting to the opposite
    d. Broad to narrow

10. Which method of conclusion does the author use in this selection?
    a. Summary
    b. Final thought
    (c.) Final thought and summary
    d. None of the above

DISCUSSION QUESTIONS

1. As you were growing up, did you ever compare your own family to another family (real or imaginary) that you thought was more ideal? What are some ways that family was better or worse than your own family?

2. Who does Sugarman seem to believe is more to blame for family problems—parents or children? What examples from the selection support your answer? Do you agree with him? Why or why not?

3. What are some negative ways that people in this selection got attention from other family members? Why do you think they behaved in the ways they did? How could they have gotten attention in less destructive ways?

4. Sugarman suggests seven strategies for creating peace at home. Can you think of another step that families could take in order to communicate better or reduce family tensions? Give an example of what happens when this step is not taken, and how the same situation would be affected if it *were* taken.

PARAGRAPH ASSIGNMENTS

1. Choose *one* of Sugarman's seven steps that would be especially useful for your own family to practice. Write a paragraph explaining which step you have chosen and why. Your topic sentence could be something like this: "My family would communicate better if we would stop playing Telephone." The rest of your paragraph would include specific examples from your own family's experience to illustrate your point.

2. Write a paragraph in which you propose an eighth step that Daniel Sugarman might include in his next edition of this essay. As Sugarman often does, begin by presenting a story (real or imaginary) in which this step is not taken. Then explain how the family would be better served by following the step you are writing about.

ESSAY ASSIGNMENTS

1. Write an essay in which you explain the three steps suggested by Sugarman that would be most helpful for keeping peace in your own home. Focus your essay with a thesis statement like this one: "There would be peace in my home if my family followed three of Sugarman's steps: _____, _____, and _____."

   For each of the steps, give examples of occasions when the step would be useful. For example, if you choose "Tell it like you feel it" as one of your steps, your paragraph on that step might begin like this:

   • My family would really benefit if we would "tell it like we feel it." For example, my mother pretends it doesn't bother her when my brother ignores her birthday and Mother's Day. But down deep . . .

2. Where is a place, other than the home, where keeping the peace is important to you? Write an essay about several ways to keep the peace in another environment. For instance, you might write about keeping the peace in the classroom, in your school as a whole, in your workplace, in your neighborhood, or on an athletic team. You may use some of the same steps that Sugarman writes about, or you may come up with your own. Include examples, as Sugarman does, that relate specifically to the environment you are writing about.

Unit Four

Educating Ourselves

24

Dare to Think Big
Dr. Ben Carson

Preview

How "uncool" to lug around an armload of books, pay attention in class, and think seriously about the future! But Dr. Ben Carson not only admits that he was massively uncool in his high-school years; he says that non-coolness can have tremendous rewards. After being born into poverty in inner-city Detroit, Dr. Carson, now chief of pediatric neurosurgery at the Johns Hopkins Children's Center, rose to become one of the world's most respected surgeons. This piece is an excerpt from Dr. Carson's book *The Big Picture*.

Words to Watch

deplorable (2): wretchedly bad; miserable
cavernous (4): resembling a cave
spontaneous (5): unplanned; impulsive
graphically (8): vividly
gratification (8): satisfaction
bevy (9): group

I do not speak only to parent groups. I spend a lot of time with students, 1
such as those I encountered not long ago on a memorable visit to Wendell
Phillips High School, an inner-city school on Chicago's south side.

Before I spoke, the people who invited me to the Windy City held a reception in my honor. There I met and talked with school officials and local religious leaders, many of whom informed me about the troubled neighborhood where the school is located. They indicated that gang influence was prevalent, living conditions were deplorable° in the surrounding public housing developments, dropout statistics were high, and SAT scores were low. 2

It sounded like a lot of other high schools I have visited around the country. Yet so dire were these warnings that, on the crosstown drive to the school, I could not help wondering what kind of reception I would receive from the students. 3

I need not have worried. When I walked into Wendell Phillips High School, its long deserted hallways gave the building a cavernous°, empty feel. The entire student body (1,500 to 2,000 strong) had already been excused from class and was assembled quietly in the school's auditorium. A school administrator, who was addressing the audience, noted my entrance through a back door and abruptly interrupted his remarks to announce, "And here's Dr. Carson now!" 4

All eyes turned my way. Immediately students began to applaud. Some stood. Suddenly they were all standing, clapping, and cheering. The applause continued the entire time I walked down the aisle and climbed the steps onto the auditorium stage. I couldn't remember ever receiving a warmer, more enthusiastic, or more spontaneous° reception anywhere in my entire life. 5

I found out later that a local bank had purchased and distributed paperback copies of my autobiography, *Gifted Hands*, to every student at Wendell Phillips. A lot of those teenagers had evidently read the book and felt they already knew me. By the time I reached the microphone, the noise faded away. I felt overwhelmed by their welcome. 6

I did what I often do when facing such a young audience. I wanted them thinking seriously about their lives and futures. So I quickly summarized my earliest years as a child, about my own student days back at Southwestern High School in Detroit. I referred briefly to the incident when my anger nearly caused a tragedy that would have altered my life forever. I recounted my struggles with peer pressure, which sidetracked me for a time. 7

Then I talked about the difference between being viewed as cool and being classified as a lowly nerd. I find that serves as a graphically° relevant illustration for my message on *delayed gratification*°—a theme I hit almost every time I speak to young people. 8

The *cool* guys in every school are the ones who have earned a varsity letter in some sport—maybe several sports. They wear the latest fashions. They know all the hit tunes. They can converse about the latest 9 blockbuster movies. They drive sharp cars and seem to collect a bevy° of beautiful girlfriends.

The *nerds* are the guys always hauling around an armload of books, 10 with more in their backpack. They wear clean clothes—and often big, thick glasses. They even understand the science experiments. They ride the school bus, or worse yet, their parents drive them to school. Most of the popular girls would not be caught dead speaking to them in the hallway between classes.

The years go by, and graduation draws near. Often the cool guy has 11 not done well in school, but his personality wins him a job at the local fast-food franchise, flipping hamburgers and waiting on customers. The nerd, who has won a scholarship, goes off to college.

A few more years go by. The cool guy is still flipping burgers. Maybe 12 he has even moved up to Assistant Shift Manager by now. The girls who come in to eat lunch may notice and smile at him. He is still cool.

The nerd finishes up at college and does very well. Upon graduation 13 he accepts a job offer from a Fortune 500 company. With his first paycheck, he goes to the eye doctor, who replaces those big, old, thick glasses with a pair of contacts. He stops at the tailor and picks out a couple of nice suits to wear. After saving a big chunk of his first few paychecks, he makes a down payment on a new Lexus. When he drives home to visit his parents, all the young women in the old neighborhood say, "Hey, don't I know you?" Suddenly, they do not want to talk to the guy behind the fast-food counter anymore.

The first guy—the cool guy—had everything back in high school. So 14 what did he get for all that?

The other guy was not cool at all—but he was focused. Where did he 15 go in the long run?

"And that," I told my audience, "is how we have to learn to think about 16 life! With a long-term view. A Big-Picture perspective!"

Those students at Chicago's Wendell Phillips High School could not 17 have been more attentive as I recounted the things this former nerd has seen and done. They listened to me explain and illustrate the incredible potential that resides in the average human brain. They even seemed receptive to my challenge that they begin to use those brains to plan and prepare for the future. So, as I wrapped up my talk by daring them to THINK BIG, I did something I had never done before, though I realized it could backfire if I had read this audience wrong. But since they had been such a responsive group, I decided to risk it.

I concluded by asking that auditorium full of high school students for 18 a show of hands. "How many of you are ready, here today, to raise your hands and say to me, to your teachers, and to your peers, 'I want to be a nerd'?"

Although many of them laughed, almost all the students of Wendell   19
Phillips High School raised their hands as they stood and applauded and
cheered even louder than when I had walked in.

FIRST IMPRESSIONS

Freewrite for ten minutes on one of the following.

1. Did you enjoy reading this selection? Why or why not?

2. What's the difference at your school between a "nerd" or a "cool"
   person? Are the standards similar to those that Dr. Carson describes?

3. Do you know popular high schoolers whose lives went downhill after
   graduation? Explain your answers. What might have accounted for
   these changes?

VOCABULARY CHECK

A. Circle the letter of the word or phrase that best completes each of the
   following four items.

1. In the sentences below, the word *prevalent* means
   a. absent.
   (b.) widely present.
   c. desirable.
   d. unimportant.

   > "There I met and talked with school officials and local religious
   > leaders . . . about the troubled neighborhood where the school is
   > located. They indicated that gang influence was prevalent. . . ."
   > (Paragraphs 2–3)

2. In the sentences below, the word *dire* means
   (a.) alarming.
   b. misleading.
   c. reassuring.
   d. amusing.

   > "They indicated that . . . living conditions were deplorable in the
   > surrounding public housing developments, dropout statistics were
   > high, and SAT scores were low. . . . [S]o dire were these warnings that,
   > on the crosstown drive to the school, I could not help wondering what
   > kind of reception I would receive from the students." (Paragraph 3)

3. In the sentence below, the word *abruptly* means
   a. falsely.
   b. quietly.
   c. slowly.
   (d.) suddenly.

   > "A school administrator, who was addressing the audience, noted my entrance through a back door and abruptly interrupted his remarks to announce, 'And here's Dr. Carson now!'" (Paragraph 4)

4. In the sentence below, the word *summarized* means
   (a.) gave a brief account of.
   b. showed pictures of.
   c. wrote a story about.
   d. complained about.

   > "So I quickly summarized my earliest years as a child, about my own student days back at Southwestern High School in Detroit." (Paragraph 7)

B. Circle the letter of the answer that best completes each of the following four items. Each item uses a word (or form of a word) from "Words to Watch."

5. My mother took one look at the *deplorable* apartment I had just rented and asked,
   a. "How in the world can you afford all this luxury?"
   (b.) "Why would you want to live in an awful place like this?"
   c. "Well, it's nice, but isn't it much too big for just one person?"

6. Because the classroom was so *cavernous*, students
   (a.) felt like tiny peas in a huge peapod.
   b. had to crowd together so tightly their desks almost touched.
   c. begged the janitor to turn on the air conditioning.

7. Earl and his brother hugged each other in a *spontaneous* show of affection. In other words, their show of affection was
   a. not genuine.
   b. only temporary.
   (c.) not planned beforehand.

8. Most workers would feel a sense of *gratification* if they
   a. were fired with no explanation.
   (b.) were named "Employee of the Year."
   c. learned that a coworker had stolen credit for their good ideas.

READING CHECK

Central Point and Main Ideas

1. Which sentence best expresses the central point of the entire selection?
    a. In a talk to high-school students, Dr. Ben Carson encouraged them to focus on long-term goals.
    b. The student body of a tough inner-city high school listened politely to Dr. Ben Carson's talk.
    c. Dr. Ben Carson, a famous surgeon, was considered a nerd in high school.
    d. Guys who earn varsity letters, know all the current music, and drive sharp cars seem to collect the most girlfriends in high school.

2. Which sentence best expresses the main idea of paragraph 6?
    a. A local bank had bought and passed out copies of Dr. Carson's autobiography.
    b. Because the students had read and enjoyed Dr. Carson's autobiography, they gave him a warm welcome.
    c. Many of the students at the Wendell Phillips High School had already read Dr. Carson's autobiography, *Gifted Hands.*
    d. Dr. Carson was pleased by his reception at the high school.

3. Which sentence best expresses the main idea of paragraph 13?
    a. The nerd does well in college and even lands a job with a Fortune 500 company.
    b. After a well-paying job lets him afford contacts, nice clothes, and a nice car, the nerd becomes more attractive to women.
    c. When the nerd graduates from college, he can afford a cool wardrobe.
    d. Later in life, the cool guy is sure to envy the nerd's accomplishments.

Key Supporting Details

4. Dr. Carson arrived at Wendell Phillips High School
    a. worried about how the students would respond to him.
    b. confident that his speech would be a big success.
    c. favorably impressed by what he had heard from community leaders.
    d. very late.

5. The students at Wendell Phillips High School
   a. had been excused from class to hear Dr. Carson speak.
   b. skipped school on the day that Dr. Carson spoke.
   c. had unusually high SAT scores.
   d. worked in fast-food restaurants.

6. Peer pressure
   a. sidetracked Dr. Carson for a while during his teenage years.
   b. never affected Dr. Carson during his teenage years.
   c. was less of a problem during Dr. Carson's teen years than it is now.
   d. affected Dr. Carson in positive ways during his teenage years.

7. ___F___ TRUE OR FALSE? Dr. Carson often ends his talks to high school audiences by inviting them to say, "I want to be a nerd."

Inferences

8. From the article, the reader might conclude that
   a. Dr. Carson was considered cool in high school.
   b. planning for the future can mean giving up some pleasure today.
   c. Dr. Carson hardly ever speaks to parent groups.
   d. the visit to Wendell Phillips High School was Dr. Carson's first to Chicago.

9. Dr. Carson implies that
   a. girls in high school aren't impressed by cool guys.
   b. the cool guy in high school wasn't thinking about his future.
   c. the cool guy in school had a "Big Picture" perspective on his life.
   d. when the nerd got his first paycheck, he should have saved it instead of spending it on clothes and contact lenses.

The Writer's Craft

10. What audience did Dr. Carson seem to have in mind when he wrote this essay?
    a. High-school administrators
    b. High-school students
    c. Parents of high-school students
    d. High-school dropouts

DISCUSSION QUESTIONS

1. It doesn't seem likely that Dr. Carson, a highly educated adult, often uses words like "cool" and "nerd" in his own conversation. Why, then, do you think he chose to use such language in his speech at Wendell Phillips High School? What effect do you think it had on the students?

2. Do you tend to think much about your future and work towards future goals? Or are you more inclined to live for the moment, assuming that tomorrow will take care of itself? In your opinion, what are the advantages and disadvantages of each approach?

3. Although Dr. Carson was a focused, committed student, he admits that peer pressure and his own hot temper sometimes got in the way of his success. What are some obstacles—internal and external—that stand in the way of your being the best student you can be? What are some ways you might overcome these obstacles?

4. Dr. Carson speaks frequently to high school students because he has learned something about life that he believes can be of value to them. If you were asked to give a single piece of advice to a group of younger students, what would you say?

PARAGRAPH ASSIGNMENTS

1. Write a paragraph about a person you wish would come and talk to students in your school. In your paragraph, answer these questions: Why would you choose this person? What would you like to hear him or her talk about? What value do you think there would be in hearing this person speak? You could begin with a topic sentence like this: "I would like _____ to speak at my school for several reasons."

2. In this essay, Dr. Carson gives an extended definition of a "cool" person. Write a paragraph in which you give your own definition of "cool." What, in your opinion, makes a person truly cool? Provide specific examples to illustrate your points.

ESSAY ASSIGNMENTS

1. Judging from the reception they gave him, the students at Wendell Phillips admired and respected Ben Carson. Write an essay about three individuals whom you admire. They may be people you know personally, such as friends or family members, or someone well-known whom you have never met—or a combination of the two. A possible thesis statement for this essay would be: "_____, _____, and _____ are the people I admire the most." In your essay, explain exactly what you so admire about each person. In the conclusion of your essay, reflect upon what the choices you have made—the people you have chosen to write about—say about you and your values.

2. In "Dare to Think Big," Dr. Carson contrasts "nerds" and "cool people." Write an essay in which you contrast two other groups that are common in high schools. Besides stating the differences between the two groups, provide vivid examples to illustrate those differences. For example, did the two groups dress differently? Did they deal with classwork differently? Behave in the hallways in contrasting ways? Have different ways of looking at themselves and treating others?

   Here are some contrasting groups you might consider writing about:

   - Athletes / non-athletes
   - Readers / non-readers
   - Fashion followers / fashion foes
   - Scholars / non-studiers
   - Slackers / hard workers
   - Partiers / non-partiers

25

A Change of Attitude
Grant Berry

Preview

No one was more surprised than Grant Berry to find himself in college. His high-school experience did little to prepare him for a life of learning. But somehow, as father of two with a full-time job, he returned to school to pursue a college degree. Berry's transformation from a reluctant student to a passionate one is the subject of this essay.

Words to Watch

striven (3): tried
suavely (4): in a sophisticated manner
immaculately (4): perfectly clean
tedious (6): boring
trudging (6): moving with great effort
nil (6): zero
smugly (8): in a way that demonstrates self-satisfaction
deprivation (16): state of being without possessions
battering (22): pounding

For me to be in college is highly improbable. That I am doing well in 1 school teeters on the illogical. Considering my upbringing, past educational performance, and current responsibilities, one might say, "This guy hasn't got a chance." If I were a racehorse and college was the track, there would be few who would pick me to win, place, or show.

When I told my dad that I was going back to school, the only   2
encouragement he offered was this: "Send me anywhere, but don't send
me back to school." For my father, school was the worst kind of prison,
so I was raised believing that school at its best was a drag. My dad
thought that the purpose of graduating from high school was so you never
had to go back to school again, and I adopted this working stiff's
philosophy.

I followed my dad's example like a man who double-crossed the mob   3
follows a cement block to the bottom of the river. My dad has been a
union factory worker for more than two decades, and he has never
striven° to be anything more than average. Nonetheless, he is a good man;
I love him very much, and I respect him for being a responsible husband
and father. He seldom, if ever, missed a day of work; he never left his
paycheck at a bar, and none of our household appliances were ever carted
off by a repo-man. He took his family to church each week, didn't light
up or lift a glass, and he has celebrated his silver anniversary with his
first, and only, wife. However, if he ever had a dream of being more than
just a shop rat, I never knew about it.

On the other hand, my dreams were big, but my thoughts were small.   4
I was not raised to be a go-getter. I knew I wanted to go to work each day
in a suit and tie; unfortunately, I could not define what it was I wanted to
do. I told a few people that I wanted to have a job where I could dress
suavely° and carry a briefcase, and they laughed in my face. They said,
"You'll never be anything," and I believed them. Even now I am envious
of an immaculately° dressed businessman. It is not the angry type of
jealousy; it is the "wish it were me" variety.

Since I knew I was not going to further my education, and I didn't   5
know what I wanted to do except wear a suit, high school was a disaster.
I do not know how my teachers can respect themselves after passing me.
In every high school there are cliques and classifications. I worked just
hard enough to stay above the bottom, but I did not want to work hard
enough to get into the clique with the honor roll students.

Also, I had always had a problem with reading. When I was a kid,   6
reading for me was slow and tedious°. My eyes walked over words like a
snail trudging° through mud. I couldn't focus on what I was reading,
which allowed my young, active mind to wander far from my reading
material. I would often finish a page and not remember a single word I
had just read. Not only was reading a slow process, but my
comprehension was nil°. I wasn't dumb; in fact, I was at a high English
level. However, reading rated next to scraping dog poop from the tread of
my sneakers. I didn't yet know that reading could be like playing the
guitar: the more you do it, the better you get. As far as reading was
concerned, I thought I was stuck in the same slow waltz forever.

In junior high and high school, I read only when it was absolutely   7
essential. For example, I had to find out who Spiderman was going to
web, or how many children Superman was going to save each month. I
also had to find out which girls were popular on the bathroom walls. I'm
ashamed to say that my mother even did a book report for me, first
reading the book. In high school, when I would choose my own classes,
I took art and electronics rather than English.

Even though I was raised in a good Christian home, the only things I   8
cared about were partying and girls. I spent all of my minimum wage
paycheck on beer, cigarettes, and young ladies. As a senior, I dated a girl
who was twenty. She had no restrictions, and I tried to keep pace with her
lifestyle. I would stay out drinking until 3:00 a.m. on school nights. The
next morning I would sleep through class or just not show up. It became
such a problem that the school sent letters to my parents telling them that
I would not be joining my classmates for commencement if I didn't show
up for class once in a while. This put the fear of the establishment in me
because I knew the importance of graduating from high school.
Nonetheless, I never once remember doing homework my senior year. Yet
in June, they shook my hand and forked over a diploma as I smugly°
marched across the stage in a blue gown and square hat.

Since I felt I didn't deserve the piece of paper with the principal's and   9
superintendent's signatures on it, I passed up not only a graduation party,
but also a class ring and yearbook. If it were not for my diploma and
senior pictures, there would not be enough evidence to convince a jury
that I am guilty of attending high school at all. I did, however, celebrate
with my friends on graduation night. I got loaded, misjudged a turn,
flattened a stop sign, and got my car stuck. When I pushed my car with
my girlfriend behind the steering wheel, mud from the spinning tire
sprayed all over my nice clothes. It was quite a night, and looking back,
it was quite a fitting closure for the end of high school.

After graduation I followed my father's example and went to work,   10
plunging into the lukewarm waters of mediocrity. All I was doing on my
job bagging groceries was trading dollars for hours. I worked just hard
enough to keep from getting fired, and I was paid just enough to keep
from quitting.

Considering the way my father felt about school, college was a subject   11
that seldom came up at our dinner table. I was not discouraged, nor was
I encouraged to go to college; it was my choice. My first attempt at
college came when I was nineteen. I had always dreamed of being a disc
jockey, so I enrolled in a broadcasting class. However, my experience in
college was as forgettable as high school. My habit of not doing
homework carried over, and the class was such a yawner that I often

forgot to attend. Miraculously, I managed to pull a C, but my dream was weak and quickly died. I did not enroll for the next term. My girlfriend, the one who kept me out late in high school, became pregnant with my child. We were married two days after my final class, which gave me another excuse not to continue my education.

My first job, and every job since, has involved working with my hands and not my head. I enjoyed my work, but after the money ran out, the month would keep going. One evening my wife's cousin called and said he had a way that we could increase our income. I asked, "How soon can you get here?" He walked us through a six-step plan of selling and recruiting, and when he was finished, my wife and I wanted in. Fumbling around inside his large briefcase, he told us we needed the proper attitude first. Emerging with a small stack of books, he said, "Read these!" Then he flipped the books into my lap. I groaned at the thought of reading all those volumes. If this guy wanted me to develop a good attitude, giving me books was having the opposite effect. However, I wanted to make some extra cash, so I assured him I would try.

I started reading the books each night. They were self-help, positive-mental-attitude manuals. Reading those books opened up my world; they put me in touch with a me I didn't know existed. The books told me I had potential, possibly even greatness. I took their message in like an old Chevrolet being pumped full of premium no-lead gasoline. It felt so good I started reading more. Not only did I read at night, I read in the morning before I went to work. I read during my breaks and lunch hour, waiting for signal lights to turn green, in between bites of food at supper, and while sitting on the toilet. One of the books I read said that there is no limit to the amount of information our brains will hold, so I began filling mine up.

The process of reading was slow at first, just as it had been when I was a kid, but it was just like playing the guitar. If I struck an unclear chord, I would try it again, and if I read something unclear, I would simply read it again. Something happened: the more I read, the better I got at it. It wasn't long before I could focus in and understand without reading things twice. I began feeling good about my reading skills, and because of the types of books I was reading, I started feeling good about myself at the same time.

The income from my day job blossomed while the selling and recruiting business grew demanding, disappointing, and fruitless. We stopped working that soil and our business died, but I was hooked on reading. I now laid aside the self-help books and began reading whatever I wanted. I got my first library card, subscribed to *Sports Illustrated*. I found a book of short stories, and I dove into poetry, as well as countless newspaper articles, cereal boxes and oatmeal packages. Reading, which had been a problem for me, became a pleasure and then a passion.

Reading moved me. As I continued to read in a crowded lunch room,   16
sometimes I stumbled across an especially moving short story or
magazine article. For example, a young Romanian girl was saved from
starvation and deprivation° by an adoptive couple from the U.S. I quickly
jerked the reading material to my face to conceal tears when she entered
her new home filled with toys and stuffed animals.

Not only did reading tug at my emotions, it inspired me to make a   17
move. All those positive-mental-attitude books kept jabbing me in the
ribs, so last fall, at age twenty-seven, I decided to give college another try.
Now I am back in school, but it's a different road I travel than when I was
a teenager. Mom and Dad paid the amount in the right-hand column of
my tuition bill then, but now I am determined to pay for college myself,
even though I must miss the sound of the pizza delivery man's tires on my
blacktop driveway. I hope to work my way out of my blue collar by
paying for school with blue-collar cash.

As a meat-cutter, I usually spend between 45 and 50 hours a week   18
with a knife in my hand. Some weeks I have spent 72 hours beneath a
butcher's cap. In one two-week period I spent 141 hours with a bloody
apron on, but in that time I managed to show up for all of my classes and
get all of my homework done (except being short a few bibliography
cards for my research paper).

Working full time and raising a family leaves me little free time. If I   19
am not in class, I'm studying linking verbs or trying to figure out the
difference between compound and complex sentences.

There are other obstacles and challenges staring me in the face. The   20
tallest hurdle is a lack of time for meeting all my obligations. For instance,
my wife works two nights a week, leaving me to care for my two daughters.
A twelve-hour day at work can lead to an evening coma at home, so when
Mom's punching little square buttons on a cash register, I hardly have the
energy to pour corn flakes for my kids, let alone outline a research paper.

Going to college means making choices, some of which bring   21
criticism. My neighbors, for example, hate my sickly, brown lawn
sandwiched between their lush, green, spotless plots of earth, which
would be the envy of any football field. Just walking to my mailbox can
be an awful reminder of how pitiful my lawn looks when I receive an
unforgiving scowl from one of the groundskeepers who live on either side
of me. It is embarrassing to have such a colorless lawn, but it will have to
wait because I want more out of life than a half-acre of green turf. Right
now my time and money are tied up in college courses instead of fertilizer
and weed killer.

But the toughest obstacle is having to take away time from those I love   22
most. I am proud of the relationship I have with my wife and kids, so it

tears my guts out when I have to look into my daughter's sad face and explain that I can't go to the Christmas program she's been practicing for weeks because I have a final exam. It's not easy to tell my three-year-old that I can't push her on the swings because I have a cause-and-effect paper to write, or tell my seven-year-old that I can't build a snowman because I have an argument essay to polish. As I tell my family that I can't go sledding with them, my wife lets out a big sigh, and my kids yell, "Puleeze, Daddy, can't you come with us?" At these times I wonder if my dream of a college education can withstand such an emotional battering°, or if it is even worth it. But I keep on keeping on because I must set a good example for the four little eyes that are keeping watch over their daddy's every move. I must succeed and pass on to them the right attitude toward school. This time when I graduate, because of the hurdles I've overcome, there will be a celebration—a proper one.

FIRST IMPRESSIONS

Freewrite for ten minutes on one of the following.

1. Did you enjoy reading this selection? Why or why not?

2. What is the attitude in your family towards higher education? Is it similar to that of Berry's parents, or is it different? Explain.

3. Do you do any reading for pleasure? If not, what keeps you from enjoying reading?

VOCABULARY CHECK

A. Circle the letter of the word or phrase that best completes each of the following four items.

1. In the sentences below, the word *cliques* means
    a. grades.
    b. schools.
    c. groups.
    d. sports.

    > "In every high school there are cliques and classifications. I worked just hard enough to stay above the bottom, but I did not want to work hard enough to get into the clique with the honor roll students." (Paragraph 5)

2. In the sentences below, the word *mediocrity* means
   a. luxury.
   b. heavy drinking.
   c. unemployment.
   (d.) low quality.

   > "After graduation I followed my father's example and went to work, plunging into the lukewarm waters of mediocrity. . . . I worked just hard enough to keep from getting fired, and I was paid just enough to keep from quitting." (Paragraph 10)

3. In the sentences below, the word *fruitless* means
   a. easy.
   b. illegal.
   (c.) unsuccessful.
   d. enjoyable.

   > "[T]he selling and recruiting business grew demanding, disappointing, and fruitless. We stopped working that soil and our business died. . . ." (Paragraph 15)

4. In the sentence below, the word *scowl* means
   a. sincere smile.
   b. favor.
   (c.) angry look.
   d. surprise.

   > "Just walking to my mailbox can be an awful reminder of how pitiful my lawn looks when I receive an unforgiving scowl from one of the groundskeepers who live on either side of me." (Paragraph 21)

B. Circle the letter of the answer that best completes each of the following four items. Each item uses a word (or form of a word) from "Words to Watch."

5. Which of the following characters would you expect to be *suave*?
   a. A homeless panhandler.
   (b.) A European prince.
   c. A circus clown.

6. When she inspected her teenage son's room and found it *immaculate*, Mrs. Kreider
   a. asked, "How do you find anything in all this mess?"
   b. said, "Unlock this door right away!"
   c. clutched her chest, saying, "I think I'm going to have a heart attack. It's so *clean!*"

7. "How was the movie?" Celia asked. "It was great, if you like *tedious* movies," her sister answered. In other words, her sister found the movie very
   a. funny.
   b. frightening.
   c. boring.

8. Many child-raising experts say that instead of spanking a misbehaving child, parents should try *deprivation*. For instance, a parent could
   a. take away the child's bicycle for a day or two.
   b. buy the child a new toy.
   c. shout at the child.

READING CHECK

Central Point and Main Ideas

1. Which sentence best expresses the central point of the entire selection?
   a. Berry was never encouraged to attend college or to challenge himself mentally on the job.
   b. After years of not caring about education, Berry changed his attitude and came to love reading, gain self-esteem, and attend college.
   c. Berry's wife and children often do not understand why he is unable to take part in many family activities.
   d. Berry was given a high-school diploma despite the fact that he did little work and rarely attended class.

2. Which sentence best expresses the main idea of paragraph 13?
   a. Influenced by self-help books, Berry developed a hunger for reading.
   b. People who really care about improving themselves will find the time to do it and to simplify.
   c. Self-help books send the message that everyone is full of potential and even greatness.
   d. There is no limit to the amount of information the brain can hold.

3. Which sentence best expresses the main idea of paragraph 22?
    a. Berry's decision to attend college is hurting his long-term relationships with his wife and daughters.
    b. Berry has two children, one who is three and another who is seven.
    c. Berry enjoys family activities such as attending his children's plays and building snowmen.
    (d.) Although he misses spending time with his family, Berry feels that graduating from college will make him a better role model for his children.

Key Supporting Details

4. The author's reading skills
    a. were strong even when he was a child.
    (b.) improved as he read more.
    c. were strengthened considerably in high school.
    d. were sharpened by jobs he held after high-school graduation.

5. Berry's father
    a. was rarely home while the author was growing up.
    b. often missed work and stayed out late at bars.
    c. was a college graduate.
    (d.) disliked school.

6. The first time the author attempted college, he
    a. quit in order to spend more time with his children.
    b. could not read well enough to understand the material.
    c. did so well he immediately signed up for a second course.
    (d.) often skipped class and rarely did his homework.

7. Today, Berry works as a
    a. college instructor.
    b. stay-at-home dad.
    c. disc jockey.
    (d.) meat cutter.

Inferences

8. In stating that his graduation night "was quite a fitting closure for the end of high school," Berry implies that
    a. he was sorry high school was finally over.
    b. car troubles were a common problem for him in high school.
    (c.) his behavior had ruined that night just as it had ruined his high-school education.
    d. despite the problems, the evening gave him good memories, just as high school had given him good memories.

9. We can infer that from paragraph 21 that the author
   a. does not tend his lawn because he enjoys annoying his neighbors.
   b. receives a lot of mail.
   c. is willing to make sacrifices for his college education.
   d. has neighbors who care little about the appearance of their property.

The Writer's Craft

10. The first sentence of paragraph 4 indicates which kind of relationship to the material that came before it?
    a. Illustration (the author is giving an example of what he has just explained)
    b. Contrast (the author is showing that what follows is different from what has gone before)
    c. Addition (the author is adding a detail to a list of items)
    d. Time order (the author is telling the next part of the story)

DISCUSSION QUESTIONS

1. As Berry read self-help books, his attitude about himself and learning improved. In fact, reading those books eventually led him to go to college. Have you ever read a book that influenced the way you thought, acted, or felt about yourself? What was it you read and how did it affect you?

2. Although Berry's father did not encourage him to go to college, Berry sees many good things about his dad. In what ways was his father a positive role model for him? From Berry's own actions as an adult, what valuable lessons might he have learned from his father's example?

3. Berry discusses some of the difficulties he faces as a result of being in college—struggling to find time to meet his obligations, giving up lawn care, spending less time with his family. If you are in college now, what difficulties do you face as a result of fitting college into your life? If you plan to go to college someday, what do you think will be some of the obstacles you might face?

4. In closing his essay, Berry writes that at his college graduation, "there will be a celebration—a proper one." With what earlier event is he contrasting this graduation? Judging from how Berry describes himself and how he has changed, how do you think the two celebrations will be different?

PARAGRAPH ASSIGNMENTS

1. Children are strongly influenced by their parents and other important adults in their lives. For example, Berry followed his father's example of disliking school and getting a job that did not require him to use his mind.

   Think about your growing-up years and the adults who influenced you, both positively and negatively. Then write a paragraph about one of those persons and his or her influence on you. Provide plenty of specific details to show the reader exactly how the person affected you. Your topic sentence should be something like one of the following:

   - My aunt's example proved to me that I never want to be a teenage mother.

   - From my elementary-school art teacher, I learned that I was a talented and creative person.

   - My father has shown me how to be a loving husband and father.

2. Write a paragraph about one memory of yours that concerns reading. That memory may be a positive or negative one. For example, you may remember the pleasure of having a parent read to you at bedtime. Or you may remember being humiliated when you made a mistake reading in front of the class. Describe in detail exactly what you remember. End your paragraph by explaining why you think that memory has stayed with you so strongly.

ESSAY ASSIGNMENTS

1. Berry writes that he is looking forward to his college graduation and "a proper celebration." Write an essay about a celebration in your life. Such an event might be a graduation, a family reunion, a prom, a school program you participated in, or a wedding. Your introduction should include a thesis statement such as "For several reasons, my mother's wedding to her second husband was an event I will never forget." Then write a scene-by-scene narrative that takes your reader from the planning and anticipation of the event through the celebration itself. Use many sharp, descriptive details to help your readers clearly see events, decorations, clothing, cars, the weather, and so on. Be sure to add meaning to your story by revealing what you were thinking and feeling throughout the event.

2. Berry did not have a realistic idea of what he wanted to do after high school, although he did like to imagine himself in a good-looking suit and carrying a briefcase. What vision do you have of yourself in the future? Write an essay in which you state what you hope to be doing ten years from now. Then describe in your supporting paragraphs three different obstacles or challenges that you will face in pursuing your goal. Explain why those challenges are significant ones for you and just how you plan to overcome them.

26

From Nonreading to Reading
Stacy Kelly Abbott

Preview

A home empty of books, a ready supply of drugs and alcohol, and little support for education—this is the recipe for a nonreader. As the product of such an environment, Stacy Kelly Abbott initially accepted his status as someone who would just never be able to read well. But as time went on, he realized how much his lack of skills was handicapping him. Here is the story of an adult nonreader's courageous struggle to improve his situation.

Words to Watch

marginal (1): limited, minimal
reinforcement (4): support
peers (6): people of the same class, age, etc., such as classmates
jargon (8): the specialized vocabulary of a given field
retain (11): keep in mind, remember
abstractly (11): concerning general ideas (not specific things), theoretically

Reading is the key to success in American society. Everything our   1
society is and does depends on that one word. In addition to the thousands

of illiterates we hear about on television and in magazines, there is an unspoken and silent category of people never mentioned. This is the group of people who can read, but not quite well enough to feel comfortable or successful with it. According to *Time* magazine, "There are over seventy-five million illiterate people in America. Another forty million are termed 'marginal° readers.'" This is the group that I fit into. I am not totally comfortable with reading, but I am able to get by. Slowly and gradually the role of reading in my life is changing from nonexistent to partially existent to existent.

As early as I can remember there were never any recreational books in our home. It just was not something that was thought to be needed—or wanted, for that matter. My wife tells me that the most important thing for a preschooler to have is exposure to reading. They need to have books to look at and "play" read. She has bought our daughter an entire library, and she is only one. Sometimes when I think about it, I think, "It's not fair! Why didn't my parents buy me books and read to me like my wife does to our daughter?" Of course, until my wife told me, I never knew books were supposed to be a part of your early childhood. This was my very first setback in reading. I had absolutely no exposure to any type of stories, poetry, or even picture books before I entered kindergarten. This was my first step on a road to nonreading.

I remember being excited when I entered kindergarten. In my memory, I was not slower or behind the other children. First grade was about the same. I kept up fairly well, and though I do not remember learning the actual mechanics of reading, I still learned to read at the first grade level.

What I learned in school was the end of it. I had absolutely no reinforcement° at home of what I learned at school. It was at this point that drugs and alcohol were entering my life. My father was an alcoholic, and my three brothers and sisters were all teenagers at this time in my life. My two brothers had already dropped out of school, and my sister was well on her way too. Drugs and alcohol were not considered wrong at my house. They were an everyday part of my life. I did not know everyone else's home was not like that. It was inevitable that I try them when they were so readily available. This was my next step on the road to nonreading.

Second grade was where major problems began surfacing. I was held back in second grade, and my second year I was placed into Resource classes. I could no longer fit into regular classes. I could not read past a first grade level. Second grade is where most of my memories of early school are. It was here that my self-esteem plummeted downward. I realized I was slower than the other children. Sometimes children can be really cruel. They teased and told me I was stupid.

School and my self-esteem continued on this downward path for   6
several years. Around junior high it seemed to get worse. This is when
Resource became an embarrassment. It was shameful to be so "stupid." It
was not so bad when I was in the Resource class because most of the
others were about on my level. Reading aloud in front of this group was
sort of calming. It was not bad at all. But I still had to take some regular
classes. This was where the humiliation was horrible. I could read a little,
but reading in front of this group of peers° was impossible. I just stuttered
along. This is how the remainder of my school career went. Resource was
satisfying, but regular classes were awful. Somehow I stuck with school
and did not quit.

All my brothers and sisters dropped out, but they still lived at home.   7
Drugs and alcohol were still readily available. I do not recall exactly
when, but sometime while I was in high school my brother found out that
I could not read. He began teasing and taunting me. It was horrible. I was
one of those millions of marginal readers who graduated from high school
barely able to function in American society. I made sure I maintained a
job where no reading was required. Life was fine for several years, but I
was still continuing down the road to nonreading.

The beginning of the change in my life came when I became active in   8
my church. It is common for young men in my church to serve a mission.
This idea was not so bad, except that all the reading and learning required
to be successful was overwhelming. My desire to get my life in order
finally convinced me to serve a mission. I learned to read much better, but
only on church-related things. It was kind of like learning a jargon° for a
job. I really still did not read very well at all.

About a year after I came home from my mission, I got married. It was   9
then that I realized what bad shape I was really in. I had accumulated
several delinquent bills simply because I could not read the contents of
late notice letters. I even almost lost my home. By this time in my life, my
fear of reading aloud haunted me. When I was in school I really did not
care what other people thought too much. Now I really cared what people
thought of me. I did not want my wife to think any less of me because of
my problem. My wife convinced me that I was okay and she could help
me learn to read better.

With her urging, I began college by taking a summer class. I had been   10
married for a year and had a daughter who was one week old. I read on
an elementary school level, and my fear of reading aloud was a
nightmare. My wife assured me that she had been through four years of
college and had never had to read aloud. I took her word for it. I was
taking a developmental reading class, and the very first day of class the
teacher called on me to read a passage aloud. Somehow I struggled

through it, humiliated and all. When I told my wife what happened, she could not believe it! But she still reassured me that I could do it. I went and spoke with the teacher about my problem, and she was very understanding. All during the summer and fall my wife helped me by reading all my material onto tape and making notes for me. I was quickly seeing all the benefits reading had. Those few years had started me on the path to becoming a reader.

I struggled with school and worked really hard. We discovered that the   11
Texas Rehabilitation Commission could help with fees and tutors for reading. The commission sent me for testing, and it was discovered that I had a visual-spatial learning disability. This explained why it was so hard for me to retain° things and think abstractly,° both of which are required in college. I have received all my textbooks on tape to help me read my books. I have purchased a phonics program to help me with my reading, and it is going slow but steady. I am making my way down the road of active reading.

As I look back over the past four years, I see all the things that have   12
happened to make me see how important reading is. I am not where I want to be yet, but I will be in a year or two. I can say this with confidence now. I see reading now as a key to unlocking my whole future, especially my financial future. No more will there be the fear of having to fill out an application for employment in front of someone. I will be able to fill it out with ease, because I will know how to READ. No more will there be the fear of my daughter asking me to read her a book and me having to say "not right now." No more will there be the fear of delinquency letters because of my inability to read. Reading has truly come from a totally nonexistent part of my life to a very existent and essential part of my life. Reading has simply helped me "to be."

FIRST IMPRESSIONS

Freewrite for ten minutes on one of the following.

1. Did you enjoy reading this selection? Why or why not?

2. Were story books and picture books available in your home when you were very young? What are your earliest memories of books and reading?

3. Do you agree with the statement "Reading is the key to success in American society"? Explain your answer.

VOCABULARY CHECK

A. Circle the letter of the word or phrase that best completes each of the following four items.

1. In the sentence below, the word *inevitable* means
   a. unavoidable.
   b. unlikely.
   c. good.
   d. deadly.

   > "It was inevitable that I try [drugs and alcohol] when they were so readily available." (Paragraph 4)

2. In the sentences below, the word *plummeted* means
   a. increased.
   b. fell quickly.
   c. renewed.
   d. was noticed.

   > "Second grade is where most of my memories of early school are. It was here that my self-esteem plummeted downward. I realized I was slower than the other children." (Paragraph 5)

3. In the sentences below, the word *taunting* means
   a. offering to help.
   b. watching.
   c. insulting.
   d. following.

   > "I do not recall exactly when, but sometime while I was in high school my brother found out that I could not read. He began teasing and taunting me. It was horrible." (Paragraph 7)

4. In the sentence below, the word *delinquent* means
   a. recently paid.
   b. overdue.
   c. overpaid.
   d. badly written.

   > "I had accumulated several delinquent bills simply because I could not read the contents of late notice letters." (Paragraph 9)

B. Circle the letter of the answer that best completes each of the following four items. Each item uses a word (or form of a word) from "Words to Watch."

5. Paul is *marginally* interested in Gail. In other words, he
   a. has a slight interest in her.
   b. is enormously interested in her.
   c. has absolutely no interest in her.

6. When I announced that I was going to win first prize in the five-hundred-yard dash, my brother offered me *reinforcement* by saying,
   a. "In your dreams, turtle boy."
   b. "I know you can do it."
   c. "Well, maybe, but some of those other guys look awfully fast."

7. Teenagers are often warned not to give in to *peer* pressure, which can be defined as pressure from
   a. parents, teachers, and other influential adults.
   b. the media, such as TV shows, advertisements, and movies.
   c. teenage friends and acquaintances.

8. Because Shelly finds it difficult to *retain* information, she took a
   a. spelling course.
   b. math course.
   c. memory course.

READING CHECK

Central Point and Main Ideas

1. Which sentence best expresses the central point of the entire selection?
   a. There were no recreational books in the author's home while he was growing up.
   b. Abbott has improved his reading by getting his textbooks on audio tape and by using a phonics program.
   c. There are forty million marginal readers in the United States.
   d. Despite coming from an unsupportive home and having a learning disability, Abbott is learning to read.

2. Which sentence best expresses the main idea of paragraph 2?
   a. Abbott's wife has purchased an entire library for their daughter.
   b. The first obstacle to Abbott's reading was the lack of books in his home when he was a child.
   c. Abbott is confident his daughter will be a strong reader.
   d. There are numerous story, poetry, and picture books available for preschool children.

3 . Which sentence best expresses the main idea of paragraph 4?
    a. Drugs and alcohol were not considered wrong in Abbott's home.
    b. Two obstacles to Abbott's reading were his family's lack of support for school and their use of drugs and alcohol.
    c. Abbott's brothers dropped out of school, and his sister was on her way to doing the same.
    d. Children often imitate what they see their parents or siblings doing.

Key Supporting Details

4. According to this selection, marginal readers
    a. are completely illiterate.
    b. are rare in the United States.
    c. can read, but not very well.
    d. are very comfortable with reading and often attend college.

5. _F_ TRUE OR FALSE? Abbott's poor reading ability prevented him from serving a mission for his church.

6. The testing that Abbott was given in college revealed that he
    a. had a serious disease.
    b. had a visual/spatial learning disability.
    c. was not intelligent enough to do college work.
    d. could read much better than he previously thought.

Inferences

7. Abbott implies in paragraph 2 that
    a. he thinks his wife is foolish for buying books for their baby daughter.
    b. he respects his wife's judgment about their daughter and reading.
    c. there were not many story, poetry, or picture books published for children when he was little.
    d. his daughter can already read at an advanced level.

8. Abbott implies that a person with a learning disability
    a. is unlikely to ever learn to read.
    b. may deal better with the disability once it is identified.
    c. is probably mentally ill as well.
    d. should not expect to go to college.

9. In the final paragraph of the reading, Abbott implies
   a. that previously, he could not read well enough to fill out a job application.
   b. that he has been reluctant to tell his little daughter about his reading problems.
   c. that he has gotten into financial trouble because of his inability to read.
   (d.) all of the above.

The Writer's Craft

10. Abbott has organized his essay using
    a. listing order, by listing different areas in which his inability to read held him back.
    (b.) time order, discussing the steps in the process of his becoming a nonreader and then a reader.
    c. contrast, by showing the differences between being a nonreader and being able to read.
    d. comparison, by showing the similarities between his learning to read and his young daughter's reading experiences.

DISCUSSION QUESTIONS

1. Abbott's wife bought books for their baby daughter when the child was clearly too young to learn to read. In your opinion, can such a young child benefit from being exposed to books? If so, in what ways?

2. Abbott identifies three factors that contributed to making him a non-reader: a lack of exposure to books as a child, little support for education from his family, and easy access to drugs and alcohol. Which of those three do you think had the greatest negative impact on him? Why? What are some ways parents can contribute to making a child a reader and a successful student?

3. Abbott started first grade with very little preparation for learning. As a result, his excitement about school soon turned to humiliation and disappointment. What do you think schools could do to help children like Abbott?

4. Throughout Abbott's life, people have humiliated him for being a poor reader. Why, then, do you think he has been willing to write this essay, letting countless other people know about his problem?

PARAGRAPH ASSIGNMENTS

1. What is one of your earliest memories concerning books and/or reading? Write a paragraph describing that memory. Your topic sentence could be something like one of the following:

   - My mother's reading aloud to us in the evening was a special time in our house.

   - When our teacher began reading books to us in school, I became convinced that reading could be fun.

   - What I remember is that there were many activities in our house, but reading was never one of them.

   Include as much detail as possible: How old were you? Where were you, and who were you with? What reading material was involved? How did you feel about it? Conclude with a statement about why you think this memory has stayed with you.

2. Abbott was singled out in his school because he was considered "slow." What person do you remember from your school days who seemed slower than average? Write a paragraph describing this person. How was he or she different than other students? How did you and your schoolmates respond to him or her? Looking back, do you wish you had done anything differently?

ESSAY ASSIGNMENTS

1. What can parents do to help their children to be successful students? Write an essay in which you identify three actions you think parents can take to provide a positive environment for learning. A possible thesis statement for this essay is "Parents could help their children succeed in school by _____, _____, and _____." You might want to begin by rereading Abbott's essay and noting what his parents did—or didn't—do, and the negative effects those actions had on his chances of success.

2. Imagine a day in which your ability to read had been taken from you. Write an essay describing, from the moment you wake up until you go to sleep that night, how your life would be affected. Include not only significant effects, such as those on your performance in school, but also smaller ones, such as how you would know the difference between junk mail and important letters.

27

Reading to Survive
Paul Langan

Preview

In an ideal world, the adults in a child's life are kind and gentle. Surrounded by their love and protection, the child has a safe place to learn and to grow. But what happens when the adults in a child's world are terrifying or, at best, helpless? Growing up in such a world, Ryan Klootwyk learned to create his own safe place—one where books became his protectors, his escape, and, finally, his salvation.

Words to Watch

glared (2): stared angrily
vulnerable (4): easily hurt
glimpse (6): quick view or look
took its toll (9): demanded a high price
oozing (11): slowly flowing
intimidation (17): fear caused by threats
cycle (19): series of repeated events
stalk (19): follow in a threatening way
drudgery (27): boring, unpleasant work
lingered (30): were slow to disappear
transition (32): change
resentment (39): anger at having been treated unfairly

"Drink it. It will make a man out of you."   1

Ryan Klootwyk jerked his head away from the cup of beer that his   2
stepfather Larry was shoving in his face. "But I don't like how it smells,"
he pleaded. For a moment, Larry just glared° drunkenly at the eight-year-
old boy, his bloodshot eyes like two cracked windows. Then he raised the
cup high in the air and poured the contents on Ryan's head. As Larry
stormed out of the room, Ryan sat quietly at the table drenched in the
stinking fluid. He was relieved. Larry could have done much worse; he
usually did.

Nearly twenty years later, Ryan remembers that moment as if it were   3
yesterday. He tells the story, sitting at another table—his own—with his
wife and two young sons. Watching his kids play, Ryan thinks how
different their childhood is from his own. "My children will never have to
go through what I went through," he says, shaking his head. "Never."

Ryan's childhood home was shattered by heroin. Both his parents   4
were addicts. When Ryan was six years old, his father died, an apparent
drug-related suicide. Alone and vulnerable,° his mother soon brought a
new man into their home. This was Larry.

When Larry first entered Ryan's life, he seemed friendly. He took   5
Ryan and his brother, Frank, fishing. He bought new furniture for the
house, and Ryan's mother told the kids to call him "Dad." The two lonely
young boys started to accept Larry in his new role. But Larry was keeping
a secret from the family. Underneath his pleasant exterior, Larry was a
monster.

Ryan's first glimpse° into Larry's true nature occurred a few months   6
after he had moved in with the family. Ryan's dog—one that had
belonged to Ryan's father—had an accident on the carpet. High and
drunk, Larry announced he was going to kill the dog. Horrified, Frank
shouted for him to stop. "That's my dad's dog! That's my dad's dog!" he
screamed.

Larry ignored Frank's screams, but when their mother heard the   7
commotion and yelled, "Larry, what are you doing?" he snapped. Seven-
year-old Ryan watched in helpless horror as Larry beat her, hitting her
face with his fists. "My childhood ended that night," Ryan says today. "I
hid behind the table and watched him. I had no idea why he acted that
way. I only knew I was scared that he would kill one of us." Ryan, Frank
and their mother fled into the boys' bedroom. Immediately, Larry
cornered them there and issued a stern warning. "Don't you ever, ever
mention your father to me again," he hissed. Terrified, the little boys
could only stare.

As Larry wandered away, Ryan felt emptiness and terror threaten to   8
overwhelm him. There was nowhere to go; there was no one to turn to.

But a comforting thought broke through his despair. Reaching under his bed, he pulled out a battered copy of his favorite book, *The Five Chinese Brothers*. Crawling into bed, he quickly lost himself in the familiar pages. Thoughts of Larry's brutality, of fear, of pain, of humiliation faded as he read the story of the brave, clever little brother who saved everyone. Ryan was only seven, but he had already found the lifeline that would keep him afloat through the horrifying years ahead. He had discovered books.

Larry supported himself by robbing nearby households and businesses. With the police constantly trailing him, he had to keep moving. The moves would often occur without notice. "I would come home from school, and we'd be out the door," Ryan remembers. Traveling from motels to shelters, from friends' houses to apartments, Ryan lived in six different states and passed through fifteen separate schools, never staying in one place more than a year and a half. The constant moving took its toll.° "I wanted to be a normal kid," he says, "but transferring from school to school made that impossible. The only people who were constant in my life were my mother and my brother. They were the only ones who knew how bad things were. My biggest fear as a child was that I would lose them, that I would be totally alone." 9

When Ryan was eight years old, that fear almost came true. This time, the family was in Texas. Even drunker and angrier than usual, Larry began kicking and stomping on Ryan's mother. Frank, now nine years old, made a desperate effort to protect her. When he stepped between Larry and his mother, shouting "Don't hit her!" Larry turned on the boy. He kicked him in the face with his heavy black boots. Frank crumpled to the floor. 10

For the rest of that evening, little Ryan watched over his brother and tried to comfort him. "I could see that his eye was swollen shut, and pus and fluid were oozing° out of it," he recalls. "Nothing Larry ever did hurt me inside more than when he hurt my brother like that," says Ryan, his voice wavering. Alone in the darkness with his silent, wounded brother, Ryan quietly sobbed through the night. 11

The next day Frank was a little better, and his mother took him to the hospital. Ryan went along. Larry instructed the boys to lie about what had happened. "Tell them you were playing baseball and Frank got hit in the head with the bat," Larry said. The boys and their mother obediently lied, but the injury still made people at the hospital suspicious. A police officer questioned the kids, but they stuck to Larry's story. 12

"I wanted to tell the truth, but we were so afraid of Larry," says Ryan. He still feels the frustration of those days. "We knew what would happen if we told the truth. They would take him away, he would be in jail for a short time, and then he would come out and get us, and he would kill 13

Mom." Without the boys' cooperation, the police could do nothing. And a few weeks later, Larry, aware of the watchful eye of the police, decided to move the family again. In yet another state and another school, the beatings continued.

Amazingly, amidst the constant abuse at home, Ryan did well in school. "School was the one safe place in my life. When I was in school, I was away from Larry. I was free from threats to my family. I could pretend to be a normal kid," recounts Ryan. 14

As a third-grader, Ryan won a school reading contest. The prize was a copy of *Charlotte's Web*. The book quickly became a new favorite. In it, a little runt pig, Wilbur, has his life saved twice: first by a kind little girl, and then by a clever and loving spider, Charlotte. Charlotte's first word to Wilbur is "Salutations!" Like Wilbur, Ryan had no idea what the word meant. He appreciated Charlotte's explanation to Wilbur: "Salutations are greetings," she said. "When I say 'salutations,' it's just my fancy way of saying hello." Ryan loved Charlotte for her friendship and kindness to lonely little Wilbur. 15

Charlotte and Wilbur joined the five Chinese brothers and Ryan's other favorite characters as pieces in a shield between him and the horrors of his home life. "Reading was a way I could forget about everything," he said. "It was the only thing that was completely in my control. I am not sure if I would have survived without it." He looked for things to read the way a hungry child might look for food that others had overlooked. "Once I even found some old history textbooks in the school trash can. To someone, those old books were trash, but to me they were a treasure. I took them home and read them cover to cover." 16

Ryan's success at school had no effect on his troubled home. Each time he transferred to a new school, he concealed the painful truth of his home, of his mother's addiction, of the constant moves, and of Larry. Ryan's strong grades and good adjustment to school were all his teachers saw. Outwardly he seemed to be doing well. Inwardly, he was begging for help. "Sitting in all those classrooms, I remember thinking 'Why doesn't anyone do something about what is happening?'" Ryan remembers. "I desperately wanted someone to ask about us, to investigate, to care. I was incapable of asking for help. I was ashamed about what was happening to us, ashamed at what Mom allowed to go on, ashamed that I couldn't do anything about it. And, on top of all that, I was afraid that if someone found out about our family, they might separate my mother and brother and me. I was so scared, I just kept it all inside," he explains. In silence, Ryan endured years of abuse, violence, and intimidation° at the hands of Larry. "I just hoped that we would run away from Larry one day. That is what kept me going." 17

When Ryan was ten years old, his dream almost came true. His   18
mother took the two boys and fled to Michigan, not letting Larry know
where they were going. For three months, Ryan was free of the constant
threat of violence. But the freedom did not last. Ryan returned from
school one day to find Larry sitting on the couch with a smile on his face.
"Hi," he said smugly.

Ryan could barely speak. "My soul dropped. I just wanted to cry. It was   19
as if something inside me died." Again the cycle° of terror began. This
time, Ryan's mother sought legal help. A judge granted her a restraining
order that barred Larry from being near her home. Larry's response was to
stalk° the family. Lying in bed one night soon after the order had been
issued, Ryan heard a window break. When he went to investigate, he found
Larry punching his mother. She managed to call the police, but Larry ran
away before they arrived. For three more years the family ran from Larry,
moving from town to town and from school to school.

As Ryan grew up, so did his tastes in reading. Instead of make-believe   20
heroes like Charlotte and the clever Chinese brother, Ryan was drawn to
real-life stories of brave men and women. He read biographies of
Abraham Lincoln, once a poor boy who would walk miles to borrow a
book. He read of Frederick Douglass, a former slave who became a fiery
speaker for human rights. Larry's stalking continued until Ryan's mother
became involved with a new boyfriend. The two men got into a fight in
the street outside Larry's house, and Larry was almost killed. At last, he
disappeared from Ryan's life.

At the age of thirteen, Ryan felt that life was starting at last. Ryan's   21
mother overcame her drug addiction and moved into a nicer apartment.
For the first time in his life, Ryan was able to attend the same school for
more than a year. He began to put down roots, make friends, feel at home.
The future looked bright—briefly. Then Ryan's mother announced she
could no longer afford the apartment they were living in. They were going
to move again.

The news that he would have to uproot his life once again shocked   22
Ryan. This time, he rebelled. "I was thirteen, and I had had it," he
remembers. "I did not want to move any more. For the first time in my
life, I had gotten a chance to have a normal healthy life, and now someone
was going to take it away again." Ryan begged and pleaded for his mother
to stay, but she refused. "When we moved, something inside me snapped.
It is sad to say, but in ninth grade I just stopped caring. I figured no one
ever seemed to care about me, so why should I?"

Ryan's grades reflected his changing attitude. In just months he went   23
from a B+ student to a student who got D's and F's. "I started skipping
school, hanging out with the wrong crowd, and then using drugs. I just

gave up. All the anger that had built up inside all those years was coming out, and nobody could do anything to stop me." A low point occurred when a cousin called, asking Ryan if he knew someone who would buy stolen jewelry. Ryan arranged the sale. After he and his cousin spent the eighty dollars they'd made on drugs and whiskey, Ryan asked who owned the jewelry. The cousin had stolen it from his own parents, Ryan's aunt and uncle.

Because of Ryan's poor performance in school, he was sent to a high   24
school for troubled young people. There he was surrounded by students who spent much of their time trying to find a way to smoke marijuana in class. Fights were common. Far more attention was given to discipline than to learning. Once again, overwhelmed by the surrounding violence, Ryan retreated to the one safe place he knew—the world of books.

"I cut school to go to the public library and read," he remembers. "At   25
school, it was clear that the teachers had given up on the students. They were more like babysitters than anything else. But at the library—away from the dangers of school—I could read and learn about anything I wanted." By this time, he was drawn to stories from the pages of military history books. He read about prisoners of war who survived long years of unspeakable torture. One book in particular, *The Forgotten Soldier*, moved him. It told the story of a man fighting his own personal war against himself as World War II rages around him. The author had been a prisoner. Ryan thought of himself as a kind of prisoner, too. But unlike Ryan, the author had pulled himself out of his prison and into a better life. Ryan was still locked inside his own private jail.

Somehow, despite poor grades and a complete lack of direction, Ryan   26
managed to graduate from high school. He went to work as an industrial painter. While working long hours at manual labor, Ryan had time to think about his life since Larry disappeared. "I realized that I had lost control of my life. I asked myself, 'Is this what I want? Is this all there is?'" In order to cope with his own dissatisfaction, Ryan continued reading. "I worked all day and read all night," says Ryan. "I read true stories about people who overcame incredible obstacles, about people who survived wars and concentration camps. I would get depressed because I'd read about people doing amazing things, and I wasn't doing anything except complaining."

Ryan's constant reading and the drudgery° of his work forced him to   27
re-think the choices he had made. "I said to myself, 'How did I get here? What am I doing? Where am I taking my life?'" His self-examination was painful. "I became aware of how I had hurt myself, how I had wasted time and made poor choices. But I could not see anything in my future except more of the same. It all seemed like a big nothing. I grew very depressed."

Then things got worse. On the job one day, Ryan slipped off a pedestal   28
and shattered his wrist. He couldn't work. His wife was pregnant, and
now she had to work more hours to support their household. Feeling
scared and sorry for himself, Ryan went to see his brother Frank.

"I was looking for sympathy when I went over there," Ryan admits. "I   29
told him I had no income, no food, no money to buy food, no way to
support my wife." But Frank didn't want to listen to Ryan's complaints.
Instead, Frank gave Ryan the best advice he could think of. With disgust
in his voice, Frank said, "Why don't you go back to school and get an
education so you can be somebody when you do grow up?"

"I wanted to punch his lights out," Ryan says. "I had come over to find   30
a friendly, supportive brother, and instead I found someone telling me
what to do." Angry and frustrated, Ryan barged out of his brother's home.
Yet Frank's words lingered° with him. "The more I thought about it, the
more I realized that what Frank said was right. I needed to take charge of
my life, and I needed to hear someone say it. Today I thank Frank for
telling me the truth."

One of the next books to make an impression on Ryan was *Embattled*   31
Courage. In that book, soldiers who fought the long-ago American Civil War
spoke of what the war had done to them and their innocent dreams. "Once
again, I realized that people who go through hell can learn to cope with life."

These long-dead soldiers were in Ryan's mind a year later when he   32
enrolled in Muskegon Community College in Michigan. He was the first
one in his family to go to college. The transition° was not easy.

"The first day I set foot on campus, I was terrified," he says. "I looked   33
around and saw that I was ten years older than most of my fellow
students, and I thought, 'What am I doing here?' I was sure that everyone
in the school was looking at me, thinking I was stupid for being so old.
Sometimes I still feel that way," he admits.

"But worse than anything was my fear of failure. I was afraid that I   34
wasn't prepared for the demands of college, since my high school years
had been such a waste. I thought if I failed, then I would be a complete
failure in life, that I wouldn't amount to anything, that everything that
happened years earlier would have beaten me."

But over the course of his first semester, Ryan's fear faded. His   35
constant reading over so many years had done more than help him to
survive: it had helped prepare him for college. Ryan quickly became one
of the strongest students in his classes. His love of learning had been
buried under the years of abuse and poor choices, but it had not died. "I
had given up on school for so long, but when I stepped into college, my
mind woke up again," Ryan says. "It was like being reborn." After two
years in community college, Ryan was a solid A student.

His college work inspired Ryan to decide on a direction for his life. 36
"For years, I survived because I read books about people who kept on
fighting, who kept on struggling in the face of horror. At college, I
realized that I could teach these same stories to others. It became clear to
me that what I wanted to do with my life was to be a history teacher."

Ryan has made his goal a reality. He went on to Grand Valley State 37
University, where he recently earned a degree in secondary education.
Upon completing a job practicum, he will start teaching high-school
history.

"When I read books about extraordinary people, when Larry was 38
hurting us or when I was depressed, I would say to myself, 'If they can
survive, so can I,'" says Ryan. "Today, there are people everywhere—kids
and adults—who are fighting to survive just as I was. Abuse, drugs,
violence—the problems are still out there; they aren't going away. But if
just one person can learn to make it, either by my story or the ones I teach,
then all that I have been through is worthwhile," he says. "You have to
learn from the past to build your future. That is the lesson of history."

"I have another mission too," he says, watching his two sons playing 39
nearby. His older boy, Ryan Richard, is five years old; Reid, his second
son, is three. "It is to be something for them that I never had. . . ." He
pauses for a moment, picks up Ryan Richard, and gives him a warm hug.
"A dad," he says, cradling his son. His eyes are moist when he puts Ryan
Richard down. Reid doesn't notice his father coming over to hug him. He
is engrossed in his favorite book—*Goodnight Moon*—one which has
been read to him so many times that he can recite the words by memory.
Ryan puts his big hand gently on Reid's small shoulder and embraces
him. "They are what I live for most," Ryan says, drying his eyes. "When
I look in their faces, when I see them looking back at me—safe, secure,
and loved—I know why I am here. And despite all my anger and
resentment° for so many years, I feel thankful."

He sits on the floor with Reid. "Can we read, Daddy?" Reid asks 40
hopefully.

"Yeah, but you have to start," Ryan replies. 41

Reid's childish voice carefully recites the book's first line: *In the great* 42
green room there was a telephone and a red balloon . . .

Ryan smiles. He is writing his own kind of book, the book of his life. 43
A painful chapter has ended, and a new one filled with promise and
possibilities has begun.

FIRST IMPRESSIONS

Freewrite for ten minutes on one of the following.

1. Did you enjoy reading this selection? Why or why not?

2. One of Ryan's favorite first books was *The Five Chinese Brothers*. What was the first book you remember liking? What do you remember about it?

3. When you were a child, what activities did you enjoy most? Why did you like these particular activities?

VOCABULARY CHECK

A. Circle the letter of the word or phrase that best completes each of the following four items.

1. In the sentence below, the word *exterior* means
   a. outward appearance.
   b. threats.
   c. secrets.
   d. genuine kindness.

   "Underneath his pleasant exterior, Larry was a monster." (Paragraph 5)

2. In the sentence below, the word *commotion* means
   a. radio.
   b. laughter.
   c. noisy confusion.
   d. sudden silence.

   "Larry ignored Frank's screams, but when their mother heard the commotion and yelled, 'Larry, what are you doing?' he snapped." (Paragraph 7)

3. In the sentences below, the word *despair* means
   a. confidence.
   b. optimism.
   c. lack of interest.
   d. hopelessness.

   "There was nowhere to go; there was no one to turn to. But a comforting thought broke through his despair." (Paragraph 8)

4. In the sentences below, the word *concealed* means
   a. confessed.
   b. laughed about.
   c. bragged about.
   (d.) hid.

   > "Each time he transferred to a new school, he concealed the painful truth of his home, of his mother's addiction, of the constant moves, and of Larry. Ryan's strong grades and good adjustment to school were all his teachers saw." (Paragraph 17)

B. Circle the letter of the answer that best completes each of the following four items. Each item uses a word (or form of a word) from "Words to Watch."

5. Because the dog acted so *intimidated* around its master, we guessed that the master
   a. loved the dog very much.
   (b.) was cruel to the dog.
   c. didn't pay much attention to the dog.

6. Movie stars sometimes have to deal with *stalkers*—people who
   a. send them fan letters.
   b. write nasty reviews about their movies.
   (c.) follow them and seem intent on harming them.

7. Irene's summer plans sound like *drudgery*. She has been hired to
   (a.) spend all day loading crates of recycled newspapers onto trucks.
   b. perform as a "mermaid" at Sea World.
   c. be the social director on a ship cruising the Caribbean.

8. Naturally Robert feels some *resentment* toward his boss. The boss
   (a.) stole Robert's best ideas and took credit for them.
   b. gave Robert the best office in the building, with a gorgeous view of the city.
   c. hired him even though Robert had just been released from prison.

READING CHECK

Central Point and Main Ideas

1. Which sentence best expresses the central point of the entire selection?
    a. Ryan Klootwyk was abused as a child.
    b. Even though he received no support at home, Ryan Klootwyk developed a love of reading and did very well in elementary school.
    c. Ryan Klootwyk, who loves reading, became a straight-A student in college.
    d. Inspired by books, Ryan Klootwyk overcame child abuse and poor choices and has become a success both as a college graduate and as a parent.

2. Which sentence best expresses the main idea of paragraph 17?
    a. Ryan's miserable home life was reflected in his grades at school.
    b. Ryan became used to hiding the truth about his home situation.
    c. Ryan was ashamed that his mother allowed Larry to mistreat them all.
    d. Ryan put up with years of abusive treatment from Larry.

3. Which sentence best expresses the main idea of paragraph 26?
    a. As he read about people he admired and compared himself to them, Ryan became less satisfied with the choices he had made in his own life.
    b. Larry's disappearance brought Ryan contentment with his life.
    c. Although he had made very little effort in high school, Ryan did manage to graduate.
    d. Ryan enjoyed reading about people who had survived difficult situations, including wars and concentration camps.

Key Supporting Details

4. When Ryan was in third grade,
    a. he ran away from home.
    b. he won a copy of *Charlotte's Web*.
    c. he finally told a teacher the truth about Larry.
    d. Larry beat him so badly he had to go the emergency room.

5. Ryan rebelled and began doing poorly in school when
    a. Frank moved away from home.
    b. Ryan's mother announced that they were moving again.
    c. Larry and Ryan's mother got married.
    d. Larry killed the dog that had belonged to Ryan's father.

6. Now that he has completed college, Ryan plans to become a(n)
   a. drug and alcohol counselor.
   b. elementary school teacher.
   c.) history teacher.
   d. police officer.

7. __T__ TRUE OR FALSE? Ryan's mother eventually overcame her drug habit.

Inferences

8. We can conclude that Ryan's brother Frank
   a. lent Ryan money after Ryan hurt his wrist.
   b. liked Larry more than Ryan did.
   c.) wanted Ryan to be more independent and self-reliant.
   d. had graduated from college himself.

9. From paragraphs 39–43, we can conclude that
   a. Ryan Richard has problems with reading.
   b. Ryan gets tired of reading *Goodnight Moon* over and over again to Reid.
   c. Ryan is unwilling to show much emotion.
   d.) Ryan is a much better father to his sons than Larry was to Ryan and his brother.

The Writer's Craft

10. What is the *best* explanation of the title of this essay, "Reading to Survive"?
    a. Ryan's reading gave him an idea of how his family could escape from Larry's abuse.
    b. Many of the people Ryan read about used reading as a way to overcome difficult circumstances.
    c.) Ryan's ability to escape into books helped him survive his life's difficult circumstances.
    d. Ryan read a lot because Larry threatened to kill him if he didn't read.

DISCUSSION QUESTIONS

1. As a child, Ryan used books as a "lifeline" to escape his troubled home life. When you are troubled or stressed, what do you do to make yourself feel better? Does your "lifeline" work as well for you as books worked for Ryan? Explain.

2. Ryan's favorite book when he was little was *The Five Chinese Brothers*. Later, he found a new favorite: *Charlotte's Web*. From what his story tells you, why do you think these two books appealed so much to Ryan? If you also had a favorite book when you were younger, why did you like it so much?

3. Ryan kept silent about the abuse going on in his home because he was so afraid of Larry. Which people could a child in a similar situation go to for help? How could those people help the child without making the situation worse?

4. "You have to learn from the past to build your future," Ryan says. What lessons has Ryan learned from the past? What lessons from your past could help you build your future?

PARAGRAPH ASSIGNMENTS

1. What book has been important to you at some time in your life? If not a book, perhaps there has been a short story, song, article, or even a movie or television show that you have cared about. Write a paragraph in which you describe what the source of inspiration was and why it was so special to you. Start your paragraph with a topic sentence that identifies the item and its special appeal, like either of these:

   • The book *I Know Why the Caged Bird Sings* taught me that the human spirit can rise above even the most difficult circumstances.

   • Anne Frank's *The Diary of a Young Girl* showed me that even people with real human failings can have remarkable qualities.

2. Ryan was angry when his brother, Frank, gave him stern advice instead of the sympathy Ryan was looking for. Later, though, Ryan realized Frank was right. Have you ever been angry at someone for telling you something you didn't want to hear, only to realize later that he or she was right to say it? Write a paragraph describing what happened. Alternatively, write about a time when you told someone a painful truth that he or she didn't want to hear.

ESSAY ASSIGNMENTS

1. Ryan could easily write an essay with a thesis like this: "To me, Larry defined the meaning of the word *cruelty*." He would then proceed to describe several different ways that Larry was cruel, or several different incidents that demonstrated Larry's cruelty. Think of a person who defines a certain quality for you. Such a quality might be (among many others) courage, kindness, messiness, selfishness, hospitality, irritability, generosity, carelessness, or cheerfulness. Write an essay in which you make it clear why this person defines that term for you. Use a thesis statement that identifies the person and names the quality, like either of these:

   - After living with my stepfather for five years, I can truly say that for me, he defines the meaning of the word "kindness."

   - When you look up the word "grouchy" in the dictionary, you ought to find a picture of our landlord, Mr. Stevens.

   Include sharp, specific details and illustrations to help your reader clearly see that person.

2. Ryan has decided to become a history teacher, in part because that career will allow him to help others by sharing with them the kind of stories that inspired him. What is a career that you have considered pursuing or have decided to pursue? Write an essay discussing in detail several reasons why you think that particular career would be worthwhile or enjoyable. If possible, interview at least one person who has chosen this career to get ideas and quotations for your essay.

28

Flour Children
Lexine Alpert

Preview

When is a sack of flour like a baby? The answer is this: when it needs to be dressed, carried, and protected twenty-four hours a day. For students in one San Francisco high school, three weeks of being "parents" to their "flour children" teaches them lessons their teacher hopes they will never forget.

Words to Watch

at random (2): without a plan; haphazardly
acknowledge (4): admit
circumstantial evidence (4): indirect evidence; evidence that allows certain conclusions to be drawn
novelty (5): something interesting primarily because it is unusual or new
intruding (7): getting in the way
swaddled (9): wrapped tightly
consensus (9): opinion held by most or all members of a group

"Hey, Mister V., what are you doing dressed like that?" says a student as he enters the classroom at San Francisco's Mission High School. "I'm getting ready to deliver your baby," replies the sex education teacher, in surgical greens from cap to booties. "Do you have to take this thing so seriously?" asks another, laughing nervously as she watches her teacher bring out rubber gloves. "Yes, babies are a serious matter," he answers. As the students settle into their seats, Robert Valverde, who has been teaching sex education for four years—and "delivering babies" for three—raises his voice to convene the class.

"Welcome to the nursery," he announces. "Please don't breathe on the babies. I just brought them from the hospital." The students' giggles quickly change to moans as Valverde delivers a "baby"—a five-pound sack of flour—to each student. "You must treat your baby as if it were real twenty-four hours a day for the next three weeks," he says. "It must be brought to every class. You cannot put the baby in your locker or your backpack. It must be carried like a baby, lovingly, and carefully in your arms. Students with jobs or other activities must find babysitters." To make sure the baby is being cared for at night and on weekends, Valverde calls his students at random°. "If the baby is lost or broken, you must call a funeral parlor and find out what it would cost to have a funeral," he says. The consequence is a new, heavier baby—a ten-pound flour sack.

Valverde came up with the "flour baby" idea after hearing that some sex education classes assign students the care of an egg; he decided to try something more realistic. "A flour sack is heavier and more cumbersome—more like a real baby," Valverde says. To heighten the realism, he has the students dress their five-pound sacks in babies' clothes, complete with diaper, blanket, and bottle.

"The primary goal is to teach responsibility," says Valverde. "I want those who can't do it to see that they can't, and to acknowledge° that the students who can are doing something that is very difficult and embarrassing." After thirty-six classes and more than a thousand students, Valverde's project seems to be having the effect he wants. "I look at all the circumstantial evidence°—the kids are talking to their parents in ways they never have talked before, and for the first time in their lives, they are forced to respond to an external environment. They have to fill out forms every day saying where they'll be that night and who's taking care of the baby. If their plans change, I make them call me and say who's with the baby. They're forced to confront people's comments about their babies."

Lupe Tiernan, vice-principal of the predominantly Hispanic and Asian inner-city high school, believes Valverde's class has helped to maintain the low number of teenage pregnancies at her school. "His students learn that having a baby is a novelty° that wears off very quickly, and by three weeks, they no longer want any part of it," she says.

At the beginning of the assignment, some students' parental instincts emerge right away. During the first week, sophomore Cylenna Terry took the rules so seriously that she was kicked out of her English class for refusing to take the baby off her lap and place it on the floor as instructed. "I said, 'No way am I putting my baby on the floor.'" Others, especially the boys, learn early that they can't cope with their new role. "I just couldn't carry the baby around," says Enrique Alday, 15. "At my age it was too embarrassing so I just threw it in my locker." He failed the class.

By the second week, much of the novelty has worn off, and the students are beginning to feel that the babies are intruding° on their lives. "Why does it have to be so heavy?" Cylenna Terry grumbles. "It's raining out—how am I supposed to carry this baby and open up my umbrella at the same time?" She has noticed other changes as well. "There's no way a boy is even going to look at me when I have this in my arms. No guys want to be involved with a girl who has a baby—they just stay clear."   7

Rommel Perez misses baseball practice because he can't find a baby-sitter. Duane Broussard, who has helped care for his one-year-old nephew who lives in his household, learns new respect for how hard his mother and sister work at child care. "At least this baby doesn't wake me in the middle of the night," he says. Maria Salinis says, "My boyfriend was always complaining about the sack and was feeling embarrassed about having it around. I told him, 'Imagine if it was a real baby.' It made us ask important questions of one another that we had never before considered."   8

On the last day of the assignment, the temporary parents come to class dragging their feet. Valverde calls the students one by one to the front of the room to turn in their babies. Most, their paper skin now fragile from wear, are returned neatly swaddled° in a clean blanket. But others have ended up broken and lying in the bottom of a trash bin; a half-dozen students° wound up with ten-pound babies. The students' consensus° is that babies have no place in their young lives. "I know that if I had a baby it would mess up my future and hold me down." "After this class, I don't want to have a baby. I couldn't handle it," says fifteen-year-old Erla Garcia. "It was only a sack of flour that didn't cry or scream, didn't need to be fed or put to sleep, and I still couldn't wait to get rid of it."   9

FIRST IMPRESSIONS

Freewrite for ten minutes on one of the following.

1. Did you enjoy reading this selection? Why or why not?

2. Have you ever had to care for a baby for an extended period of time? What about the experience was enjoyable? What was difficult?

3. If your school offered a class like Mr. Valverde's, would you enroll in it? Explain your answer.

VOCABULARY CHECK

A. Circle the letter of the word or phrase that best completes each of the following four items.

1. In the sentence below, the word *convene* means
   a. dismiss.
   b. praise.
   (c.) call together.
   d. sing to.

   > "As the students settle into their seats, Robert Valverde, who has been teaching sex education for four years—and 'delivering babies' for three—raises his voice to convene the class." (Paragraph 1)

2. In the sentences below, the word *consequence* means
   (a.) result.
   b. reward.
   c. reason.
   d. incident.

   > "'If the baby is lost or broken, you must call a funeral parlor and find out what it would cost to have a funeral,' he says. The consequence is a new, heavier baby—a ten-pound flour sack." (Paragraph 2)

3. In the sentence below, the word *cumbersome* means
   a. cold and stiff.
   (b.) clumsy to hold.
   c. fun.
   d. sharply pointed.

   > "'A flour sack is heavier and more cumbersome—more like a real baby,' Valverde says." (Paragraph 3)

4. In the sentences below, the words *cope with* mean
   a. repeat.
   (b.) deal with.
   c. resist.
   d. explain.

   > "At the beginning of the assignment, some students' parental instincts emerge right away. . . . Others, especially the boys, learn early that they can't cope with their new role." (Paragraph 6)

B. Circle the letter of the answer that best completes each of the following four items. Each item uses a word (or form of a word) from "Words to Watch."

5. If you visited the library and picked out a book *at random,* you probably
    a. needed it for a school assignment.
    b. didn't care what you would be reading.
    c. couldn't find it at a bookstore in a paperback edition.

6. After the mayor *acknowledged* that he had faked the election results, the newspaper headline read,
    a. "Mayor Denies He Stole Election."
    b. "Mayor Admits He Stole Election."
    c. "Mayor Refuses to Discuss Election."

7. "Viewers watched the show at first because it was such a *novelty,*" the TV critic wrote. "But now viewers say the show is quite the opposite—that it is
    a. becoming more and more exciting."
    b. sad."
    c. just like everything else on TV."

8. When a young woman says, "He keeps *intruding* on my date!" she is most likely talking about her
    a. boyfriend, who is trying to propose.
    b. little brother, who frequently wanders into the room.
    c. father, who is watching TV in his bedroom upstairs.

READING CHECK

Central Point and Main Ideas

1. Which sentence best expresses the central point of the entire selection?
    a. A San Francisco high school teaches sex education in unusual ways.
    b. Students in Mr. Valverde's sex education class are required to treat sacks of flour like babies, even to the point of finding babysitters for them.
    c. Some students in Mr. Valverde's sex education class take very good care of their flour-sack babies, while others neglect and abuse them.
    d. By caring for flour-sack babies, students in Mr. Valverde's sex education class learn how much hard work and commitment goes into caring for a real child.

2. The main idea of paragraph 2 is that
   a. Mr. Valverde calls students at home to make sure they are taking care of their babies.
   b. if students break or lose their flour sacks, they must find out how much a funeral would cost.
   c. students are not allowed to put their babies in their lockers or backpacks.
   (d.) the students are expected to treat their flour sacks just as if they were real babies.

3. Which sentence best expresses the main idea of paragraph 8?
   (a.) Caring for the flour-sack babies makes students take the idea of having a baby seriously.
   b. One girl realized her boyfriend was embarrassed about having the baby around.
   c. Before caring for his baby, one boy didn't realize how hard his mother and sister worked at child care.
   d. Because he could not find a babysitter, one student missed baseball practice.

Key Supporting Details

4. Students who break or lose their five-pound flour sack
   a. fail the class.
   b. have to admit in front of the class that they would make poor parents.
   c. have to help a fellow student care for his or her baby.
   (d.) are given a ten-pound flour sack.

5. As a result of the flour-sack experiment, Maria Salinis and her boyfriend
   (a.) talked together about important questions.
   b. broke up.
   c. decided they would never have a baby.
   d. got married.

6. __T__ TRUE OR FALSE? The author suggests that in Mr. Valverde's class, boys were more likely than girls to decide that they couldn't cope with being a "parent."

7. Which of the following ideas does *not* appear in the article?
   a. Mr. Valverde makes random calls to students' homes to make sure they're caring for their babies.
   b. One student missed baseball practice because he couldn't find a babysitter.
   c. Students are required to dress their flour-sack babies in clothes.
   d. Students must get up several times each night to check on their babies.

Inferences

8. The article implies that the flour-sack program
   a. is currently in its first year.
   b. is frequently criticized by students' parents.
   c. is supported by the school administration.
   d. has been discontinued.

9. From the selection, we might conclude that
   a. students who have taken the class have fewer teen pregnancies than those who haven't.
   b. Mr. Valverde became a father himself at a very young age and doesn't want others to make the same mistake.
   c. most students consider the flour-sack program silly and quickly forget about it.
   d. having learned a great deal about caring for babies, Mr. Valverde's students are likely to have babies as soon as possible.

The Writer's Craft

10. In general, this reading is organized according to which of the following patterns?
    a. Listing order: a list of the problems in being a teenage parent
    b. Cause-effect: explaining the reasons why teenagers become parents
    c. Comparison-contrast: comparing and contrasting the experience of students who have had the class with that of students who have not had it
    d. Time order: the experience of one group of students over the period of the class

DISCUSSION QUESTIONS

1. In what ways is a "flour baby" like a real baby? What can it teach teenagers about parenthood? What *can't* it teach about parenthood?

2. In your opinion, how big a problem is teen parenthood? Are teenagers, in general, capable of being good parents? Why or why not?

3. If you were asked to help design a high-school program aimed at lowering the rate of teen pregnancy for that school, what would some of your ideas be?

4. Teen pregnancy is only one of the problems that high-school students face. What are some other issues that teenagers confront? What kinds of courses, similar to Mr. Valverde's, might help them deal with these problems?

PARAGRAPH ASSIGNMENTS

1. Write a paragraph that begins with one of the following topic sentences:

   • I think that, in general, teenagers make poor parents.

   • I think that, in general, teenagers make good parents.

   In your paragraph, defend your point of view. Be as specific as possible, providing clear examples rather than making general statements.

2. Imagine that a teenage cousin of yours—male or female—was thinking about becoming a parent. Write that cousin a letter in which you explain at least one important point you think he or she should consider before making his or her decision.

ESSAY ASSIGNMENTS

1. It has often been pointed out that while people need to pass a test in order to get a driver's license, they can become parents without doing any preparation at all. Ideally, what requirements do you think there should be for parenthood? Write an essay about three ways you think people should prepare themselves before they become parents. Those preparations might be emotional, mental, financial, physical, or professional, or they might fall into some other category. In your essay, explain exactly why you think each kind of preparation would make people better parents. Here are possible thesis statements for this essay:

   - Three requirements for parenthood are lots of energy, financial stability, and emotional maturity.

   - To prepare for being parents, people should _____, _____, and _____.

2. How would your life be affected if you had a child to care for? Write an essay in which you describe several ways in which your life would be different if you were responsible for a baby. Reread "Flour Children" to help you think of the effects in very concrete terms—for instance, what would you do with the baby while you attended school, worked, or spent time with your friends? What would you do if it became ill? How would you support the baby? How would your plans for the future be affected? How do you think members of the opposite sex would view you? Conclude your essay with some final thoughts about the overall effect a baby would have on your life.

29

In Praise of the F Word
Mary Sherry

Preview

Many adults with a high-school education find that they lack basic skills needed to function in the working world. As a result, they enroll in "educational-repair shops," such as the adult-literacy program in which essayist Mary Sherry teaches. But, Sherry asks, how did these students manage to graduate from high school in the first place? Her answer to that question, and her suggestions for reform, were first published as a "My Turn" column in *Newsweek* magazine.

Words to Watch

trump card (4): a tactic that gives one an advantage (like a trump suit in card games)
flustered (6): nervously confused
composure (6): calmness and self-control
radical (6): extreme
conspiracy (11): a secret plan

Tens of thousands of eighteen-year-olds will graduate this year and be   1
handed meaningless diplomas. These diplomas won't look any different from those awarded their luckier classmates. Their validity will be questioned only when their employers discover that these graduates are semiliterate.

Eventually a fortunate few will find their way into educational-repair   2
shops—adult-literacy programs, such as the one where I teach basic
grammar and writing. There, high-school graduates and high-school
dropouts pursuing graduate-equivalency certificates will learn the skills
they should have learned in school. They will also discover they have
been cheated by our educational system.

As I teach, I learn a lot about our schools. Early in each session I ask   3
my students to write about an unpleasant experience they had in school.
No writers' block here! "I wish someone would have had made me stop
doing drugs and made me study." "I liked to party and no one seemed to
care." "I was a good kid and didn't cause any trouble, so they just passed
me along even though I didn't read well and couldn't write." And so on.

I am your basic do-gooder, and prior to teaching this class I blamed   4
the poor academic skills our kids have today on drugs, divorce, and other
impediments to the concentration necessary for doing well in school. But,
as I rediscover each time I walk into the classroom, before a teacher can
expect students to concentrate, he has to get their attention, no matter
what distractions may be at hand. There are many ways to do this, and
they have much to do with teaching style. However, if style alone won't
do it, there is another way to show who holds the winning hand in the
classroom. That is to reveal the trump card° of failure.

I will never forget a teacher who played that card to get the attention   5
of one of my children. Our youngest, a world-class charmer, did little to
develop his intellectual talents but always got by. Until Mrs. Stifter.

Our son was a high-school senior when he had her for English. "He sits   6
in the back of the room talking to his friends," she told me. "Why don't you
move him to the front row?" I urged, believing the embarrassment would
get him to settle down. Mrs. Stifter looked at me steely-eyed over her
glasses. "I don't move seniors," she said. "I flunk them." I was flustered.°
Our son's academic life flashed before my eyes. No teacher had ever
threatened him with that before. I regained my composure° and managed to
say that I thought she was right. By the time I got home I was feeling pretty
good about this. It was a radical° approach for these times, but, well, why
not? "She's going to flunk you," I told my son. I did not discuss it any
further. Suddenly English became a priority in his life. He finished out the
semester with an A.

I know one example doesn't make a case, but at night I see a parade   7
of students who are angry and resentful for having been passed along
until they could no longer even pretend to keep up. Of average
intelligence or better, they eventually quit school, concluding they were
too dumb to finish. "I should have been held back," is a comment I hear
frequently. Even sadder are those students who are high-school graduates

who say to me after a few weeks of class, "I don't know how I ever got a high-school diploma."

Passing students who have not mastered the work cheats them and the employers who expect graduates to have basic skills. We excuse this dishonest behavior by saying kids can't learn if they come from terrible environments. No one seems to stop to think that—no matter what environments they come from—most kids don't put school first on their list unless they perceive something is at stake. They'd rather be sailing. ₈

Many students I see at night could give expert testimony on unemployment, chemical dependency, abusive relationships. In spite of these difficulties, they have decided to make education a priority. They are motivated by the desire for a better job or the need to hang on to the one they've got. They have a healthy fear of failure. ₉

People of all ages can rise above their problems, but they need to have a reason to do so. Young people generally don't have the maturity to value education in the same way my adult students value it. But fear of failure, whether economic or academic, can motivate both. ₁₀

Flunking as a regular policy has just as much merit today as it did two generations ago. We must review the threat of flunking and see it as it really is—a positive teaching tool. It is an expression of confidence by both teachers and parents that the students have the ability to learn the material presented to them. However, making it work again would take a dedicated, caring conspiracy° between teachers and parents. It would mean facing the tough reality that passing kids who haven't learned the material—while it might save them grief for the short term—dooms them to long-term illiteracy. It would mean that teachers would have to follow through on their threats, and parents would have to stand behind them, knowing their children's best interests are indeed at stake. This means no more doing Scott's assignments for him because he might fail. No more passing Jodi because she's such a nice kid. ₁₁

This is a policy that worked in the past and can work today. A wise teacher, with the support of his parents, gave our son the opportunity to succeed—or fail. It's time we return this choice to all students. ₁₂

FIRST IMPRESSIONS

Freewrite for ten minutes on one of the following.

1. Did you enjoy reading this selection? Why or why not?

2. Which would you prefer, an easy-going teacher or a demanding one? Why?

3. Were you ever threatened with failure in a school situation? What factors were responsible for your predicament? What finally happened?

VOCABULARY CHECK

A. Circle the letter of the word or phrase that best completes each of the following four items.

1. In the sentence below, the word *validity* means
   a. worth.
   b. signatures.
   c. curiosity.
   d. supply.

   "[The diplomas'] validity will be questioned only when their employers discover that these graduates are semiliterate." (Paragraph 1)

2. In the sentence below, the word *impediments* means
   a. questions.
   b. skills.
   c. obstacles.
   d. paths.

   "I blamed the poor academic skills our kids have today on drugs, divorce, and other impediments to the concentration necessary for doing well in school." (Paragraph 4)

3. In the sentences below, the word *priority* means
   a. failure.
   b. something extremely important.
   c. waste of time.
   d. source of amusement.

   "Suddenly English became a priority in his life. He finished out the semester with an A." (Paragraph 6)

4. In the sentences below, the word *merit* means
   a. value.
   b. cruelty.
   c. hard work.
   d. failure.

   "Flunking as a regular policy has just as much merit today as it did two generations ago. We must review the threat of flunking and see it as it really is—a positive teaching tool." (Paragraph 11)

B. Circle the letter of the answer that best completes each of the following four items. Each item uses a word (or form of a word) from "Words to Watch."

5. The instructor seemed *flustered* when she entered the room; she
   a. glared angrily at all of us.
   b. dropped her papers and couldn't find her grade book.
   c. was humming a tune and smiling to herself.

6. Under pressure, Evan always exhibits *composure*. He
   a. stays cool, calm, and collected.
   b. loses his temper very easily.
   c. begins giggling nervously.

7. My brother made a *radical* change in his appearance when he
   a. lost five pounds.
   b. shaved off his waist-length hair and his beard.
   c. began parting his hair on the left side of his head instead of the right.

8. The movies that almost always involve some sort of *conspiracy* are
   a. romance movies.
   b. comedy movies.
   c. spy movies.

READING CHECK

Central Point and Main Ideas

1. Which sentence best expresses the central point of the entire selection?
   a. Before students will concentrate, the teacher must get their attention.
   b. Many adults cannot read or write well.
   c. English skills can be learned through adult literacy programs.
   d. The threat of a failing grade should be returned to our classrooms.

2. Which sentence best expresses the main idea of paragraph 6?
   a. According to his teacher, Sherry's son sat at the back of the room, talking to his friends.
   b. Mrs. Stifter said that she didn't move seniors; she flunked them.
   c. The fear of failure motivated Sherry's son to do well in English.
   d. Sherry was at first nervous and confused to learn that her son might fail English.

Key Supporting Details

3. After she told her son Mrs. Stifter's plan to flunk him, Sherry
   a. started helping him with his homework.
   b. had a long talk with him about why he was doing poorly.
   c. didn't say anything further.
   d. suggested that he change his seat in her class.

4. Many of the students in Sherry's night course
   a. are single parents.
   b. went to the same high school as her son.
   c. have dealt with substance abuse or unemployment.
   d. want to be teachers themselves.

5. According to the author, students who are "passed along" in school
   a. are lucky.
   b. eventually feel angry and resentful.
   c. don't get into trouble.
   d. will never learn basic writing skills.

6. According to the author, a fear of failure
   a. is healthy.
   b. does not motivate people.
   c. hurts more than it helps.
   d. affects young students, but not her adult students.

Inferences

7. The author implies that our present educational system is
   a. doing the best that it can.
   b. the best in the world.
   c. not demanding enough of students.
   d. very short of teachers.

8. The author implies that Mrs. Stifter
   a. disliked her son.
   b. expected more from seniors than from younger students.
   c. had only recently started teaching at her son's school.
   d. had never actually failed anyone.

9. ___F___ TRUE OR FALSE? Sherry has realized that students cannot be expected to do well in school when they are dealing with unpleasant home environments.

The Writer's Craft

10. The author's primary purpose in this article is to
    a. inform readers that many adults participate in adult literacy programs.
    b. inform readers that teachers like Mrs. Stifter still exist.
    c. entertain readers with stories of students who have been threatened with failing grades.
    (d.) persuade readers that high schools should have stricter requirements for passing courses and graduating.

DISCUSSION QUESTIONS

1. Do you know anyone who has failed or almost failed a course? What effect did the experience have on that person?

2. Most people think of failing a course as a negative experience. Why, then, does Sherry call it a positive teaching tool? In what ways can the threat of flunking be positive for students?

3. Besides the threat of failure, what are some other ways that teachers can motivate students? What have teachers done to make you want to work harder for a class?

4. People often look back on their education and realize that some of the teachers they learned the most from were their strictest teachers. Who do you think you have learned more from, strict teachers or easygoing ones? Give examples to support your point.

PARAGRAPH ASSIGNMENTS

1. Have you (or has someone you know) ever gotten an F for a course? Write a paragraph describing what happened. What led to the poor performance? What effect did the failing grade have? Did the grade act as a motivation to work harder? Start your paragraph with a topic sentence such as "Failing tenth grade English was the best thing that could have happened to me."

2. This essay is about one method of motivating students—the threat of failure. As you look back over your own classroom experiences, what are some other means of motivating students that you've observed? Write a paragraph that describes one other method teachers can use to motivate students. Give specific examples of how that method can work, and perhaps conclude by stating under what circumstances you think the method is effective.

ESSAY ASSIGNMENTS

1. Sherry's son will probably never forget the day his mother told him he was going to fail English if he didn't work harder. Think back to a specific memory, either positive or negative, you have from your school days. Then write an essay about this event. Perhaps you won an award for your academic work, musical ability, art work, or athletic skill. Maybe you were disciplined by a teacher or accused of cheating. Use plenty of vivid details so readers can understand how you felt about the experience. Here are sample thesis statements for this essay:

   - Being named "most improved player" on my basketball team changed my whole attitude about participating in sports.

   - The day I overheard a teacher complaining about me in the teachers' lounge was one of the most humiliating of my life.

2. Sherry mentions students in her night class who have made education a priority despite having serious personal problems. Those students are committed to taking responsibility for their own success, rather than using their problems as an excuse for failure. Who have you seen rise above his or her personal problems in order to reach a goal? You might think of a student who manages to do well in school despite a troubled home situation or a physically disabled person who doesn't let a handicap keep him or her from an active life. Write an essay describing one or more such people. In the essay, be sure to make clear how each person has taken responsibility for his or her own problems and actions.

30

The Professor Is a Dropout
Beth Johnson

Preview

When Lupe Quintanilla was told "You can't learn," she accepted those humiliating words and left formal education behind her. But when her children were told the same thing, a fire was lit in Lupe's soul. Determined to help her children succeed, Lupe discovered abilities within herself she had never dreamed existed.

Words to Watch

authoritarian (4): expecting obedience without question
fluent (10): able to use language smoothly and easily
radical (16): extreme
plant (29): a person put somewhere to spy
renowned (36): famous
destiny (37): fate; one's path in life

Guadalupe Quintanilla is an assistant professor at the University of   1
Houston. She is president of her own communications company. She trains law enforcement officers all over the country. She was nominated to serve as the U.S. Attorney General. She's been a representative to the United Nations.

That's a pretty impressive string of accomplishments. It's all the more   2
impressive when you consider this: "Lupe" Quintanilla is a first-grade
dropout. Her school records state that she is retarded, that her IQ is so low
she can't learn much of anything.

How did Lupe Quintanilla, "retarded" nonlearner, become Dr.   3
Quintanilla, respected educator? Her remarkable journey began in the
town of Nogales, Mexico, just below the Arizona border. That's where
Lupe first lived with her grandparents. (Her parents had divorced.) Then
an uncle who had just finished medical school made her grandparents a
generous offer. If they wanted to live with him, he would support the
family as he began his medical practice.

Lupe, her grandparents, and her uncle all moved hundreds of miles to   4
a town in southern Mexico that didn't even have paved roads, let alone any
schools. There, Lupe grew up helping her grandfather run his little
pharmacy and her grandmother keep house. She remembers the time
happily. "My grandparents were wonderful," she said. "Oh, my
grandfather was stern, authoritarian°, as Mexican culture demanded, but
they were also very kind to me." When the chores were done, her
grandfather taught Lupe to read and write Spanish and do basic arithmetic.

When Lupe was 12, her grandfather became blind. The family left   5
Mexico and went to Brownsville, Texas, with the hope that doctors there
could restore his sight. Once they arrived in Brownsville, Lupe was
enrolled in school. Although she understood no English, she was given an
IQ test in that language. Not surprisingly, she didn't do very well.

Lupe even remembers her score. "I scored a sixty-four, which   6
classified me as seriously retarded, not even teachable," she said. "I was
put into first grade with a class of six-year-olds. My duties were to take
the little kids to the bathroom and to cut out pictures." The classroom
activities were a total mystery to Lupe—they were all conducted in
English. And she was humiliated by the other children, who teased her for
being "so much older and so much dumber" than they were.

After four months in first grade, an incident occurred that Lupe still does   7
not fully understand. As she stood in the doorway of the classroom waiting
to escort a little girl to the bathroom, a man approached her. He asked her,
in Spanish, how to find the principal's office. Lupe was delighted. "Finally
someone in this school had spoken to me with words I could understand, in
the language of my soul, the language of my grandmother," she said.
Eagerly, she answered his question in Spanish. Instantly her teacher
swooped down on her, grabbing her arm and scolding her. She pulled Lupe
along to the principal's office. There, the teacher and the principal both
shouted at her, obviously very angry. Lupe was frightened and embarrassed,
but also bewildered. She didn't understand a word they were saying.

"Why were they so angry? I don't know," said Lupe. "Was it because   8
I spoke Spanish at school? Or that I spoke to the man at all? I really don't
know. All I know is how humiliated I was."

When she got home that day, she cried miserably, begging her   9
grandfather not to make her return to school. Finally he agreed.

From that time on, Lupe stayed at home, serving as her blind grand-   10
father's "eyes." She was a fluent° reader in Spanish, and the older man loved
to have her read newspapers, poetry, and novels aloud to him for hours.

Lupe's own love of reading flourished during these years. Her   11
vocabulary was enriched and her imagination fired by the novels she
read—novels which she learned later were classics of Spanish literature.
She read *Don Quixote*, the famous story of the noble, impractical knight
who fought against windmills. She read thrilling accounts of the Mexican
revolution. She read *La Prensa*, the local Spanish-language paper, and
Selecciones, the Spanish-language version of *Reader's Digest*.

When she was just 16, Lupe married a young Mexican-American   12
dental technician. Within five years, she had given birth to her three
children, Victor, Mario, and Martha. Lupe's grandparents lived with the
young family. Lupe was quite happy with her life. "I cooked, sewed,
cleaned, and cared for everybody," she said. "I listened to my
grandmother when she told me what made a good wife. In the morning I
would actually put on my husband's shoes and tie the laces—anything to
make his life easier. Living with my grandparents for so long, I was one
generation behind in my ideas of what a woman could do and be."

Lupe's contentment ended when her children started school. When   13
they brought home their report cards, she struggled to understand them.
She could read enough English to know that what they said was not good.
Her children had been put into a group called "Yellow Birds." It was a
group for slow learners.

At night in bed, Lupe cried and blamed herself. It was obvious—not   14
only was *she* retarded, but her children had taken after her. Now they, too,
would never be able to learn like other children.

But in time, a thought began to break through Lupe's despair: Her   15
children didn't seem like slow learners to *her*. At home, they learned
everything she taught them, quickly and easily. She read to them
constantly, from the books that she herself had loved as a child. *Aesop's
Fables* and stories from *1,001 Arabian Nights* were family favorites. The
children filled the house with the sounds of the songs, prayers, games, and
rhymes they had learned from their parents and grandparents. They were
smart children, eager to learn. They learned quickly—in Spanish.

A radical° idea began to form in Lupe's mind. Maybe the school was   16
wrong about her children. And if the school system could be wrong about
her children—maybe it had been wrong about her, too.

Lupe visited her children's school, a daring action for her. "Many 17
Hispanic parents would not dream of going to the classroom," she said.
"In Hispanic culture, the teacher is regarded as a third parent, as an
ultimate authority. To question her would seem most disrespectful, as
though you were saying that she didn't know her job." That was one
reason Lupe's grandparents had not interfered when Lupe was classified
as retarded. "Anglo teachers often misunderstand Hispanic parents,
believing that they aren't concerned about their children's education
because they don't come visit the schools," Lupe said. "It's not a lack of
concern at all. It's a mark of respect for the teacher's authority."

At her children's school, Lupe spoke to three different teachers. Two 18
of them told her the same thing: "Your children are just slow. Sorry, but
they can't learn." A third offered a glimmer of hope. He said, "They don't
know how to function in English. It's possible that if you spoke English
at home they would be able to do better."

Lupe pounced on that idea. "Where can I learn English?" she asked. 19
The teacher shrugged. At that time there were no local English-language
programs for adults. Finally he suggested that Lupe visit the local high
school. Maybe she would be permitted to sit in the back of a classroom
and pick up some English that way.

Lupe made an appointment with a counselor at the high school. But 20
when the two women met, the counselor shook her head. "Your test
scores show that you are retarded," she told Lupe. "You'd just be taking
space in the classroom away from someone who could learn."

Lupe's next stop was the hospital where she had served for years as a 21
volunteer. Could she sit in on some of the nursing classes held there? No,
she was told, not without a diploma. Still undeterred, she went on to
Texas Southmost College in Brownsville. Could she sit in on a class? No;
no high-school diploma. Finally she went to the telephone company,
where she knew operators were being trained. Could she listen in on the
classes? No, only high-school graduates were permitted.

That day, leaving the telephone company, Lupe felt she had hit 22
bottom. She had been terrified in the first place to try to find an English
class. Meeting with rejection after rejection nearly destroyed what little
self-confidence she had. She walked home in the rain, crying. "I felt like
a big barrier had fallen across my path," she said. "I couldn't go over it; I
couldn't go under it; I couldn't go around it."

But the next day Lupe woke with fresh determination. "I was 23
motivated by love of my kids," she said. "I was not going to quit." She got
up; made breakfast for her kids, husband, and grandparents; saw her
children and husband off for the day; and started out again. "I remember
walking to the bus stop, past a dog that always scared me to death, and
heading back to the college. The lady I spoke to said, 'I told you, we can't

do anything for you without a high-school degree.' But as I left the building, I went up to the first Spanish-speaking student I saw. His name was Gabito. I said, 'Who really makes the decisions around here?' He said, 'The registrar.'" Since she hadn't had any luck in the office building, Lupe decided to take a more direct approach. She asked Gabito to point out the registrar's car in the parking lot. For the next two hours she waited beside it until its owner showed up.

Impressed by Lupe's persistence, the registrar listened to her story. 24 But instead of giving her permission to sit in on a class and learn more English, he insisted that she sign up for a full college load. Before she knew it, she was enrolled in four classes: Basic Math, Basic English, Psychology, and Typing. The registrar's parting words to her were "Don't come back if you don't make it through."

With that "encouragement," Lupe began a semester that was part 25 nightmare, part dream come true. Every day she got her husband and children off to school, took the bus to campus, came home to make lunch for her husband and grandparents, went back to campus, and was home in time to greet Victor, Mario, and Martha when they got home from school. In the evenings she cooked, cleaned, did laundry, and got the children to bed. Then she would study, often until three in the morning.

"Sometimes in class I would feel sick with the stress of it," she said. 26 "I'd go to the bathroom and talk to myself in the mirror. Sometimes I'd say, 'What are you doing here? Why don't you go home and watch *I Love Lucy?*'"

But she didn't go home. Instead, she studied furiously, using her 27 Spanish-English dictionary, constantly making lists of new words she wanted to understand. "I still do that today," she said. "When I come across a word I don't know, I write it down, look it up, and write sentences using it until I own that word."

Although so much of the language and subject matter was new to Lupe, 28 one part of the college experience was not. That was the key skill of reading, a skill Lupe possessed. As she struggled with English, she found the reading speed, comprehension, and vocabulary that she had developed in Spanish carrying over into her new language. "Reading," she said, "reading was the vehicle. Although I didn't know it at the time, when I was a girl learning to love to read, I was laying the foundation for academic success."

She gives credit, too, to her Hispanic fellow students. "At first, they 29 didn't know what to make of me. They were eighteen years old, and at that time it was very unfashionable for an older person to be in college. But once they decided I wasn't a 'plant'° from the administration, they were my greatest help." The younger students spent hours helping Lupe, explaining unfamiliar words and terms, coaching her, and answering her questions.

That first semester passed in a fog of exhaustion. Many mornings,   30
Lupe doubted she could get out of bed, much less care for her family and
tackle her classes. But when she thought of her children and what was at
stake for them, she forced herself on. She remembers well what those
days were like. "Just a day at a time. That was all I could think about. I
could make myself get up one more day, study one more day, cook and
clean one more day. And those days eventually turned into a semester."

To her own amazement perhaps as much as anyone's, Lupe discovered   31
that she was far from retarded. Although she sweated blood over many
assignments, she completed them. She turned them in on time. And,
remarkably, she made the dean's list her very first semester.

After that, there was no stopping Lupe Quintanilla. She soon realized   32
that the associate's degree offered by Texas Southmost College would not
satisfy her. Continuing her Monday, Wednesday, and Friday schedule at
Southmost, she enrolled for Tuesday and Thursday courses at Pan
American University, a school 140 miles from Brownsville. Within three
years, she had earned both her junior-college degree and a bachelor's
degree in biology. She then won a fellowship that took her to graduate
school at the University of Houston, where she earned a master's degree
in Spanish literature. When she graduated, the university offered her a job
as director of the Mexican-American studies program. While in that
position, she earned a doctoral degree in education.

How did she do it all? Lupe herself isn't sure. "I hardly know. When   33
I think back to those years, it seems like a life that someone else lived." It
was a rich and exciting but also very challenging period for Lupe and her
family. On the one hand, Lupe was motivated by the desire to set an
example for her children, to prove to them that they could succeed in the
English-speaking academic world. On the other hand, she worried about
neglecting her family. She tried hard to attend important activities, such
as parents' meetings at school and her children's sporting events. But
things didn't always work out. Lupe still remembers attending a baseball
game that her older son, Victor, was playing in. When Victor came to bat,
he hit a home run. But as the crowd cheered and Victor glanced proudly
over at his mother in the stands, he saw she was studying a textbook. "I
hadn't seen the home run," Lupe admitted. "That sort of thing was hard
for everyone to take."

Although Lupe worried that her children would resent her busy   34
schedule, she also saw her success reflected in them as they blossomed in
school. She forced herself to speak English at home, and their language
skills improved quickly. She read to them in English instead of Spanish—
gulping down her pride as their pronunciation became better than hers
and they began correcting her. (Once the children were in high school and

fluent in English, Lupe switched back to Spanish at home, so that the children would be fully comfortable in both languages.) "I saw the change in them almost immediately," she said. "After I helped them with their homework, they would see me pulling out my own books and going to work. In the morning, I would show them the papers I had written. As I gained confidence, so did they." By the next year, the children had been promoted out of the Yellow Birds.

Even though Victor, Mario, and Martha all did well academically, Lupe realized she could not assume that they would face no more obstacles in school. When Mario was in high school, for instance, he wanted to sign up for a debate class. Instead, he was assigned to woodworking. She visited the school to ask why. Mario's teacher told her, "He's good with his hands. He'll be a great carpenter, and that's a good thing for a Mexican to be." Controlling her temper, Lupe responded, "I'm glad you think he's good with his hands. He'll be a great physician someday, and he is going to be in the debate class." 35

Today, Lupe Quintanilla teaches at the University of Houston, where she has developed several dozen courses concerning Hispanic literature and culture. Her cross-cultural training for law enforcement officers, which helps bring police and firefighters and local Hispanic communities closer together, is renowned° throughout the country. Former President Ronald Reagan named her to a national board that keeps the White House informed of new programs in law enforcement. She has received numerous awards for teaching excellence, and there is even a scholarship named in her honor. Her name appears in the Hispanic Hall of Fame, and she has been co-chair of the White House Commission on Hispanic Education. 36

The love of reading that her grandfather instilled in Lupe is still alive. She thinks of him every year when she introduces to her students one of his favorite poets, Amado Nervo. She requires them to memorize these lines from one of Nervo's poems: "When I got to the end of my long journey in life, I realized that I was the architect of my own destiny°." Of these lines, Lupe says, "That is something that I deeply believe, and I want my students to learn it before the end of their long journey. We create our own destiny." 37

Her love of reading and learning has helped Lupe create a distinguished destiny. But none of the honors she has received means more to her than the success of her own children, the reason she made that frightening journey to seek classes in English years ago. Today Mario is a physician. Victor and Martha are lawyers, both having earned doctor of law degrees. And so today, Lupe likes to say, "When someone calls the house and asks for 'Dr. Quintanilla,' I have to ask, 'Which one?' There are four of us—one retarded and three slow learners." 38

FIRST IMPRESSIONS

Freewrite for ten minutes on one of the following.

1. Did you enjoy reading this selection? Why or why not?

2. Have you ever come across students for whom English is a second language? Or is English a second language for you? What problems do these students (or you) face? What are they (or you) doing to cope?

3. When you were younger, did your parents ever talk to your teachers about how you were doing in school? What attitude did they have toward your teachers or your school?

VOCABULARY CHECK

A. Circle the letter of the word or phrase that best completes each of the following four items.

1. In the sentences below, the word *flourished* means
   (a.) grew.
   b. stood still.
   c. was lost.
   d. was delayed.

   "Lupe's own love of reading flourished during these years. Her vocabulary was enriched and her imagination fired by the novels she read. . . . " (Paragraph 11)

2. In the sentences below, the word *undeterred* means
   a. hopeless.
   b. highly educated.
   (c.) not discouraged.
   d. delighted.

   "Could she sit in on some of the nursing classes held there? No, she was told, not without a diploma. Still undeterred, she went on to Texas Southmost College in Brownsville." (Paragraph 21)

3. In the sentences below, the word *vehicle* means
   a. transportation.
   b. loss.
   c. method. *(circled)*
   d. difficulty.

   > "'Reading,' she said, 'reading was the vehicle. Although I didn't know it at the time, when I was a girl learning to love to read, I was laying the foundation for academic success.'" (Paragraph 28)

4. In the sentence below, the words *instilled in* mean
   a. frightened in.
   b. forced onto.
   c. passed on to. *(circled)*
   d. forgot about.

   > "The love of reading that her grandfather instilled in Lupe is still alive." (Paragraph 37)

B. Circle the letter of the answer that best completes each of the following four items. Each item uses a word (or form of a word) from "Words to Watch."

5. I knew my new boss was *authoritarian* when I asked, "How shall I do this?" and she answered,
   a. "Gosh, I don't know. How do you think would be best?"
   b. "The only way—my way." *(circled)*
   c. "I'll get back to you on that."

6. A *fluent* liar is one who
   a. almost never lies.
   b. lies, but feels guilty about it almost immediately.
   c. tells lies easily. *(circled)*

7. Kitty Litter, a famous actress, is *renowned* for her height—6 feet 4 inches. In other words, she is
   a. well-known for her height. *(circled)*
   b. envied for her height.
   c. made fun of for her height.

8. Speaking of her latest husband, Rock Bottom, Miss Litter said, "*Destiny* led me to Rock." In other words, she believes that
   a. meeting Rock was the best thing that ever happened to her.
   b. meeting Rock was the worst thing that ever happened to her.
   c. it was her fate to be married to Rock. *(circled)*

READING CHECK

Central Point and Main Ideas

1. Which sentence best expresses the central point of the entire selection?
    a. Lupe Quintanilla enjoys reading.
    b. Lupe Quintanilla's experience vividly shows what is wrong with the American educational system.
    c. Through hard work and persistence combined with a love of reading and learning, Lupe has created a distinguished career and helped her children become professionals.
    d. In school, Spanish-speaking students may experience obstacles to aiming for a professional career.

2. Which of the following sentences expresses the main idea of paragraphs 19–24?
    a. People at school, a hospital, and a telephone company rejected Lupe's requests for an education.
    b. Overcoming rejections and disappointment, Lupe finally found someone who gave her a chance to learn English by enrolling at a college.
    c. Lupe discovered that the college registrar had the authority to decide who could attend college and who could not.
    d. College counselors were eager to enroll Lupe in English classes despite her academic background.

3. Which sentence best expresses the main idea of paragraph 34?
    a. Lupe's children blossomed in school as she continued to speak English to them and was a role model for them.
    b. Lupe was afraid that her children would resent the busy schedule that kept her from spending as much time with them as she would have liked.
    c. Wanting her children to know both English and Spanish, Lupe switched to speaking Spanish at home once her children knew English.
    d. After helping her children with their homework, Lupe would do her own homework.

Key Supporting Details

4. Lupe realized that her children were *not* retarded when
    a. they got good grades at school.
    b. they were put in the group called "Yellow Birds."
    c. she saw how quickly they learned at home.
    d. they read newspapers, poetry, and novels to her.

5. Lupe's training for law enforcement officers
   a. teaches them to speak Spanish.
   (b.) brings police, firefighters, and local Hispanic communities together.
   c. offers a scholarship named in her honor.
   d. teaches Hispanic literature and culture.

Inferences

6. The sentences below suggest that
   a. although Lupe was not very intelligent at first, she became more intelligent once she learned English.
   b. Lupe really did know English.
   c. there are no IQ tests in Spanish.
   (d.) for school IQ tests to be accurate, they must be given in a language the student understands.

   "Once they arrived in Brownsville, Lupe was enrolled in school. Although she understood no English, she was given an IQ test in that language. Not surprisingly, she didn't do very well." (Paragraph 5)

7. We might conclude from the reading that
   a. a school system's judgment about an individual is always accurate.
   b. it is often better for a child to stay home rather than attend school.
   (c.) by paying attention and speaking up, parents may remove obstacles to their children's education.
   d. working parents should accept the fact that they cannot attend important events in their children's lives.

8. The last line of the reading suggests
   a. that retarded people can become successful professionals.
   (b.) that people should not blindly accept other people's opinion of them.
   c. that Lupe's children are smarter than she is.
   d. all of the above.

The Writer's Craft

9. The author's purpose in writing this article is to
   a. inform readers of the difficulties facing Spanish-speaking students in American schools.
   b. entertain readers with the story of Lupe Quintanilla's achievement in learning English.
   c. persuade readers that students should not be considered inferior simply because they do not speak English.
   (d.) do all of the above.

10. In general, the author's attitude towards Lupe Quintanilla is
    a. critical.
    b. amused.
    c. uncertain.
    (d.) admiring.

DISCUSSION QUESTIONS

1. Lupe credits her fellow Hispanic students with being a great help to her in college. Is there anyone in your life—a teacher, family member, or friend—who has helped you through challenging times during your education? Explain what your obstacle was and how this person helped you to overcome it.

2. Lupe found that her school responsibilities conflicted with her duties as wife and mother. What kinds of personal responsibilities have you had to juggle as a student? These may include a job, a difficult home situation, your social life, your extra-curricular activities, or anything else that poses a challenge to your academics. How have you balanced these obligations with your role as student?

3. By the end of Lupe's story we see the serious mistakes made by those who called her "retarded" and her children "slow learners." Was there ever a time when you felt people misjudged you? What did they say about you that was wrong, and how did it make you feel? Explain how you reacted to their judgments—did you accept their remarks or did you fight to disprove them?

4. Lupe is an outstanding example of a person who took charge of her life. Would you say that you have taken charge of your life? Describe how you have done so, or describe what you think you must still do to truly be the "architect of your own destiny."

PARAGRAPH ASSIGNMENTS

1. Lupe remembers very clearly the bewilderment and humiliation she felt when her first-grade teacher scolded her. What is an embarrassing memory you have from your early school years? Write a paragraph telling what happened, beginning with this topic sentence: "Although it happened years ago, I'll never forget the day when _____." In your paragraph, make clear just who was involved, what the circumstances were, and exactly why you felt embarrassed. Conclude your paragraph by telling how, if at all, your view of the event has changed now that you are older.

2. Lupe's early memories of reading include reading out loud to her grandfather. Write a paragraph describing some of your earlier memories of reading. What did you read, and where? Did anyone read out loud to you? Did you read out loud to anyone? To make your paragraph come alive, include titles of favorite books and explain what those particular books meant to you.

ESSAY ASSIGNMENTS

1. When Lupe ran into obstacle after obstacle in her search to learn English, she nearly gave up. Write an essay that begins with a time you felt extremely discouraged. In your essay, explain what brought you to that point. Then describe what happened next. What options did you consider? How did you proceed? Were you able to improve the situation, or did it remain discouraging? Conclude by explaining how the situation was finally resolved. Your thesis statement might be similar to one of the following:

    • When my first boyfriend (*or* girlfriend) broke up with me, I felt as if my life was over.

    • Failing to make the basketball team was extremely discouraging, but I finally got over it.

2. In order to serve the needs of the largest possible group of people, most schools are designed for students who fall into what might be called the "middle of the road" category—average students without special educational needs. As the story of Lupe and her children illustrates, people who fall outside that "middle" category can find school challenging. In your opinion, which types of students are not well served by the average school? You might think of students who are not fluent in English, who have learning differences, who are unusually gifted in some way, who have problems fitting in socially, and so on. In your essay, describe two or three such categories of students. Provide specific examples of people who fall into the categories and of the problems they face in school. As you discuss each category, offer a suggestion or two as to how schools could better serve the needs of those students.

31

Learning Survival Skills
Jean Coleman

Preview

Sometimes the best teacher is a student. That is certainly the case with Jean Coleman, whose experience as a community-college student has given her a wealth of experience to share with others. You won't find the kind of insight Coleman has in any college catalog. She has gained it the hard way—through experience—and offers it as a gift to you.

Words to Watch

vocational (5): work-related
paralegal assistant (7): a person trained to assist a lawyer
persist (10): continue on
endured (13): carried on despite hardship
hostile (14): unfriendly
developmental (17): meant to improve skills in a subject
grim (24): gloomy
projected (25): gave the impression of
destinies (31): fates

For four years I was a student at a community college. I went to night   1
school as a part-time student for three years, and I was able to be a full-
time student for one year. My first course was a basic writing course
because I needed a review of grammar and the basics of writing. I did well
in that course, and that set the tone for everything that followed.

It is now eleven years since I started college, and I have a good job 2
with a Philadelphia accounting firm. When I was invited to write this
article, the questions put to me were, "What would you want to say to
students who are just starting out in college? What advice would you
give? What experiences would it help to share?" I thought a lot about
what it took for me to be a successful student. Here, then, are my secrets
for survival in college and, really, for survival in life as well.

"Be Realistic."

The first advice that I'd give to beginning students is: "Be realistic about 3
how college will help you get a job." Some students believe that once they
have college degrees the world will be waiting on their doorsteps, ready
to give them wonderful jobs. But the chances are that unless they've
planned, there will be *nobody* on their doorsteps.

I remember the way my teacher in a study-skills course dramatized 4
this point in class. He pretended to be a student who had just been handed
a college degree. He opened up an imaginary door, stepped through, and
peered around in both directions outside. There was nobody to be seen. I
understood the point he was making immediately. A college degree in
itself isn't enough. We've got to prepare while we're in college to make
sure our degree is a marketable one.

At that time I began to think seriously about (1) what I wanted to do 5
in life and (2) whether there were jobs out there for what I wanted to do.
I went to the counseling center and said, "I want to learn where the best
job opportunities will be in the next ten years." The counselor referred me
to a copy of the *Occupational Outlook Handbook* published by the United
States government. The *Handbook* has good information on what kinds of
jobs are available now and which career fields will need workers in the
future. In the front of the book is a helpful section on job hunting. The
counselor also gave me a vocational° interest test to see where my skills
and interests lay.

The result of my personal career planning was that I eventually 6
graduated from community college with a degree in accounting. I then got
a job almost immediately, for I had chosen an excellent employment area.
The firm that I work for paid my tuition as I went on to get my bachelor's
degree. It is now paying for my work toward certification as a certified
public accountant, and my salary increases regularly.

By way of contrast, I know a woman named Sheila who earned a 7
bachelor's degree with honors in French. After graduation, she spent
several unsuccessful months trying to find a job using her French degree.
Sheila eventually wound up going to a specialized school where she
trained for six months as a paralegal assistant°. She then got a job on the

strength of that training—but her years of studying French were of no practical value in her career at all.

I'm not saying that college should serve only as a training ground for a job. People should take some courses just for the sake of learning and for expanding their minds in different directions. At the same time, unless they have an unlimited amount of money (and few of us are so lucky), they must be ready at some point to take career-oriented courses so that they can survive in the harsh world outside.   8

In my own case, I started college at the age of twenty-seven. I was divorced, had a six-year-old son to care for, and was working full time as a hotel night clerk. If I had had my preference, I would have taken a straight liberal arts curriculum. As it was, I did take some general-interest courses—in art, for example. But mainly I was getting ready for the solid job I desperately needed. I am saying, then, that students must be realistic. If they will need a job soon after graduation, they should be sure to study in an area where jobs are available.   9

"Persist."°

The older I get, the more I see that life lays on us some hard experiences. There are times for each of us when simple survival becomes a deadly serious matter. We must then learn to persist—to struggle through each day and wait for better times to come—as they always do.   10

I think of one of my closest friends, Neil. After graduating from high school with me, Neil spent two years working as a stock boy at a local department store in order to save money for college tuition. He then went to the guidance office at the small college in our town. Incredibly, the counselor there told him, "Your IQ is not high enough to do college work." Thankfully, Neil decided to go anyway and earned his degree in five years—with a year out to care for his father, who had had a stroke one day at work.   11

Neil then got a job as a manager of a regional beauty-supply firm. He met a woman who owned a salon, got married, and soon had two children. Three years later he found out that his wife was having an affair. I'll never forget the day Neil came over and sat at my kitchen table and told me what he had learned. He always seemed so much in control, but that morning he lowered his head into his hands and cried. "What's the point?" he kept saying in a low voice over and over to himself.   12

But Neil has endured.° He divorced his wife, won custody of his children, and learned how to be a single parent. Recently, Neil and I got letters informing us of the twentieth reunion of our high-school graduating class. Included was a short questionnaire for us to fill out that ended with this item: "What has been your outstanding accomplishment   13 since graduation?" Neil wrote, "My outstanding accomplishment is that I have survived." I have a feeling that many of our high-school classmates, twenty years out in the world, would have no trouble understanding the truth of his statement.

I can think of people who started college with me who had not yet 14
learned, like Neil, the basic skill of endurance. Life hit some of them with unexpected low punches and knocked them to the floor. Stunned and dismayed, they didn't fight back and eventually dropped out of school. I remember Yvonne, still a teenager, whose parents involved her in their ugly divorce battle. Yvonne started missing classes and gave up at midsemester. There was Alan, whose girlfriend broke off their relationship. Alan stopped coming to class, and by the end of the semester he was failing most of his courses. I also recall Nelson, whose old car kept breaking down. After Nelson put his last two hundred dollars into it, the brakes failed and needed to be replaced. Overwhelmed by his continuing car troubles, Nelson dropped out of school. And there was Rita, discouraged by her luck of the draw with teachers and courses. In sociology, she had a teacher who wasn't able to express ideas clearly. She also had a mathematics teacher who talked too fast and seemed not to care at all about whether his students learned. To top it off, Rita's adviser had enrolled her in an economics course that put her to sleep. Rita told me she had expected college to be an exciting place, but instead she was getting busywork assignments and trying to cope with hostile° or boring teachers. Rita decided to drop her mathematics course, and that must have set something in motion in her head, for she soon dropped her other courses as well.

In my experience, younger students seem more likely to drop out than 15
do older students. I think some younger students are still in the process of learning that life slams people around without warning. I'm sure they feel that being knocked about is especially unfair because the work of college is hard enough without having to cope with other hardships.

In some situations, withdrawing from college may be the best response. 16
But there are going to be times in college when students—young or old— must simply determine, "I am going to persist." They should remember that no matter how hard their lives may be, there are many other people out there who are quietly having great difficulties also. I think of Dennis, a boy in my introductory psychology class who lived mostly on peanut butter and discount-store white bread for almost a semester in his freshman year. And I remember Estelle, who came to school because she needed a job to support her sons when her husband, who was dying of leukemia, would no longer be present. These are especially dramatic examples of the faith and hope that are sometimes necessary for us to persist.

"Be Positive."

A lot of people are their own worst enemies. They regard themselves as   17
unlikely to succeed in college and often feel that there have been no
accomplishments in their lives. In my first year of college especially, I
saw people get down on themselves all too quickly. There were two
students in my developmental° mathematics class who failed the first quiz
and seemed to give up immediately. From that day on, they walked into
the classroom carrying defeat on their shoulders the way other students
carried textbooks under their arms. I'd look at them slouching in their
seats, not even taking notes, and think, "What terrible things have gone
on in their lives that they have quit already? They have so little faith in
their ability to learn that they're not even trying." Both students hung on
until about midsemester. When they disappeared for good, no one took
much notice, for they had already disappeared in spirit after that first test.

They are not the only people in whom I have seen the poison of self-   18
doubt do its ugly work. I have seen others with surrender in their eyes and
have wanted to shake them by the shoulders and say, "You are not dead.
Be proud and pleased that you have brought yourself here to college.
Many people would not have gotten so far. Be someone. Breathe. Hope.
Act." Such people should refuse to use self-doubts as an excuse for not
trying. They should roll up their sleeves and get to work. They should
start taking notes in class and trying to learn. They should get a tutor, go
to the learning center, see a counselor. If they honestly and fully try and
still can't handle a course, only then should they drop it. Above all, they
should not lapse into being "zombie students"—ones who have given up
in their heads but persist in hanging on for months, going through hollow
motions of trying.

Nothing but a little time is lost through being positive and giving   19
school your best shot. On the other hand, people who let self-doubts limit
their efforts may lose the opportunity to test their abilities to the fullest.

"Grow."

I don't think that people really have much choice about whether to grow   20
in their lives. To not be open to growth is to die a little each day. Grow or
die—it's as simple as that.

I have a friend, Jackie, who, when she's not working, can almost   21
always be found at home or at her mother's house. Jackie eats too much
and watches TV too much. I sometimes think that when she swings open
her apartment door in response to my knock, I'll be greeted by her
familiar chubby body with an eight-inch-screen television set occupying
the place where her head used to be.

Jackie seems quietly desperate. There is no growth or plan for growth   22
in her life. I've said to her, "Go to school and study for a job you'll be
excited about." She says, "It'll take me forever." Once Jackie said to me,
"The favorite time of my life was when I was a teenager. I would lie on my
bed listening to music and I would dream. I felt I had enormous power, and
there seemed no way that life would stop me from realizing my biggest
dreams. Now that power doesn't seem possible to me anymore."

I feel that Jackie must open some new windows in her life. If she does   23
not, her spirit is going to die. There are many ways to open new windows,
and college is one of them. For this reason, I think people who are already
in school should stay long enough to give it a chance. No one should turn
down lightly such an opportunity for growth.

"Enjoy."

I hope I'm not making the college experience sound too grim.° It's true   24
that there are some hard, cold realities in life, and I think people need to
plan for those realities. But I want to describe also a very important fact—
that college is often a wonderful experience. There were some tough times
when it would have been easy to just give up and quit, like the week when
my son's babysitter broke her arm and my car's radiator blew up. If school
had not been something I really enjoyed, I would not have made it.

To begin with, I realized soon after starting college that almost no one   25
there knew me. That might seem like a depressing thought, but that's not
how it felt. I knew that people at college had not made up their minds about
what kind of person Jean Coleman was. I imagined myself as shy, clumsy,
and average. But in this new environment, I was free to present myself in
any way I chose. I decided from my first week in school that my college
classmates and instructors were going to see the new, improved Jean. I
projected° a confidence I didn't always feel. I sat near the front in every
class. I participated, even took the lead, in discussions. Instead of slipping
away after class, I made a point to chat with my teachers and invite other
students to have coffee with me. Soon I realized that my "act" had worked.
People regarded me as a confident, outgoing woman. I really liked this new
image of myself as a successful college student.

Another of the pleasures of college was the excitement of walking into   26
a class for the first time. At that point, the course was still just a name in
a catalog. The possibilities for it seemed endless. Maybe the course would
be a magic one sweeping me off my feet. Maybe the instructor would be
really gifted in opening students' minds to new thoughts. Maybe through
this course I would discover potential in myself I never knew existed. I
went into a new class ready to do everything I could—through my
listening, participation, and preparation—to make it a success. And while

some courses were more memorable than others, I rarely found one that didn't have some real rewards to offer me.

I even enjoyed the physical preparation for a new class. I loved going 27 to the bookstore and finding the textbooks I'd need. I liked to sit down with them, crack open their binding and smell their new-book scent. It was fun to leaf through a textbook and see what seemed like difficult, unfamiliar material, realizing that in a few weeks I'd have a better grasp of what I was seeing there. I made a habit of buying a new spiral-bound notebook for each of my classes, even if I had others that were only partially used. Writing the new course's name on the notebook cover and seeing those fresh, blank sheets waiting inside helped me feel organized and ready to tackle a new challenge. I was surprised how many other students I saw scribbling their class notes on anything handy. I always wondered how they organized them to review later.

Surely one of the best parts of returning to school was the people I've 28 met. Some of them became friends I hope I'll keep forever; others were passing acquaintances, but all of them have made my life richer. One of the best friends I made is a woman named Charlotte. She was my age, and she, like me, came back to school after her marriage broke up. I first met Charlotte in a basic accounting class, and she was scared to death. She was convinced that she could never keep up with the younger students and was sure she had made a big mistake returning to college. Since I often felt that way myself, Charlotte and I decided to become study partners. I'll never forget one day about three weeks into the term when I found her standing in the hallway after class, staring as if into space. "Charlotte?" I said, and she turned to me and broke into a silly grin. "Jean, I get it!" she exclaimed, giving me a quick hug. "I just realized I was sitting there in class keeping up as well as anyone else. I can do this!" Seeing Charlotte's growing confidence helped me believe in my own ability to succeed.

I found that I was looked to as an "older, wiser woman" by many of 29 my classmates. And while I didn't pretend to have all of the answers, I enjoyed listening to their concerns and helping them think about solutions. My advice to them probably wasn't much different from what other adults might have said—take college seriously, don't throw away the opportunities you have, don't assume finding "the right person" is going to solve all the problems of life, and start planning for a career now. But somehow they seemed to find listening to such advice easier when it came from me, a fellow student.

Getting to know my instructors was a pleasure, as well. I remember 30 how I used to think about my high-school teachers—that they existed only between nine and three o'clock and that their lives involved nothing but teaching us chemistry or social studies. But I got to know many of my college instructors as real people and even as friends. I came to think of my instructors as my partners, working together with me to achieve my goals. They weren't perfect or all-knowing—they were just people, with their own sets of problems and shortcomings. But almost all were people who really cared about helping me get where I wanted to go.

In Conclusion

Maybe I can put all I've said into a larger picture by describing briefly   31 what my life is like now. I have many inner resources that I did not have when I was just divorced. I have a secure future with the accounting firm where I work. My son is doing OK in school. I have friends. I am successful and proud and happy. I have my fears and my loneliness and my problems and my pains, but essentially I know that I have made it. I have survived and done more than survive. I am tough, not fragile, and I can rebound if hard blows land. I feel passionately that all of us can control our own destinies.° I urge every beginning student to use well the chances that college provides. Students should plan for a realistic career, get themselves organized, learn to persist, be positive, and open themselves to growth. In such ways, they can help themselves find happiness and success in this dangerous but wonderful world of ours.

FIRST IMPRESSIONS

Freewrite for ten minutes on one of the following.

1. Did you enjoy reading this selection? Why or why not?

2. What careers most interest you? Which of those careers do you think would offer the best job prospects?

3. Do you know anyone who seems to you like a "zombie student"? Why do you think he or she behaves this way?

VOCABULARY CHECK

A. Circle the letter of the word or phrase that best completes each of the following four items.

1. In the sentences below, the word *peered* means
   a. twirled.
   (b.) looked.
   c. joked.
   d. hid.

   > "He opened up an imaginary door, stepped through, and peered around in both directions outside. There was nobody to be seen." (Paragraph 4)

2. In the sentence below, the word *expanding* means
   a. closing.
   b. shrinking.
   (c.) enlarging.
   d. confusing.

   > "People should take some courses just for the sake of learning and for expanding their minds in different directions." (Paragraph 8)

3. In the sentences below, the word *dismayed* means
   a. satisfied.
   b. rude.
   c. excited.
   (d.) discouraged.

   > "Life hit some of them with unexpected low punches and knocked them to the floor. Stunned and dismayed, they didn't fight back and eventually dropped out of school." (Paragraph 14)

4. In the sentence below, the word *overwhelmed* means
   a. questioned.
   b. strengthened.
   (c.) defeated.
   d. unconcerned.

   > "Overwhelmed by his continuing car troubles, Nelson dropped out of school." (Paragraph 14)

B. Circle the letter of the answer that best completes each of the following four items. Each item uses a word (or form of a word) from "Words to Watch."

5. If the rain *persists* this afternoon,
   (a.) we will have to cancel our picnic.
   b. there will be good weather for the outdoor wedding.
   c. we will have to water the garden ourselves.

6. Cheryl said, "I *endured* my long stay in the hospital because of
   (a.) daily visits from my friends, which cheered me up."
   b. terrible, constant pain."
   c. the awful hospital food and the boredom."

7. The neighbor's dog is so *hostile!* It
   a. rolls over on its back and begs me to scratch its stomach every time it sees me.
   (b.) snarls and shows its teeth every time I come near it.
   c. lies sleeping in the yard all day, not even opening its eyes when I walk by it.

8. The letter from my cousin included the *grim* news that he
   a. is graduating from college with honors.
   (b.) has lung cancer.
   c. and his wife have adopted a beautiful baby.

READING CHECK

Central Point and Main Ideas

1. Which sentence best expresses the central point of the entire selection?
   a. All people experience great problems in the course of their lives, but they should not allow their problems to discourage them.
   (b.) Following certain guidelines will help you succeed in school and in life.
   c. Older adults may have a better attitude toward school than younger students.
   d. A number of common obstacles prevent people from succeeding in college.

2. Which sentence best expresses the main idea of paragraphs 3–8?
   a. Students should make sure that college prepares them for a career that they will enjoy and in which jobs are available.
   b. The author discovered in the *Occupational Outlook Handbook* which kinds of jobs are available now and which will be available in the future.
   c. The author's friend Sheila ended up with a job that had nothing to do with her college degree.
   d. The author is now working as an accountant and also toward becoming a certified public accountant.

3. Which sentence best expresses the main idea of paragraph 30?
   a. The author realized that her college instructors had private lives of their own.
   b. The author enjoyed getting to know and working with her college instructors.
   c. In high school, the author thought her teachers had no private lives.
   d. The author realized that most of her college instructors weren't perfect.

Key Supporting Details

4. The author feels that people who drop out of school
   a. usually have a good reason.
   b. never have a good reason.
   c. often give up too quickly.
   d. always have bigger problems than those who stay in school.

5. The author saw herself as shy, clumsy, and average, but decided to
   a. pretend she was more confident than she actually was.
   b. sit in the middle of the class so no one would notice her.
   c. get involved in school clubs.
   d. drop out of any classes that seemed worthless.

6. The author
   a. took a straight liberal-arts curriculum.
   b. switched from being a French major to an accounting major.
   c. took accounting classes and ended up with a degree in art.
   d. took some general-interest classes but ended up with a degree in accounting.

Inferences

7. The author implies that successful people
   a. don't need to struggle in school.
   b. manage to avoid problems.
   (c.) welcome opportunities to grow.
   d. are unusually lucky.

8. From paragraph 25, we can conclude that in college the author
   a. became depressed.
   b. met many of her fellow students from high school.
   c. had no self-doubts.
   (d.) significantly gained self-confidence.

9. The author suggests that
   a. older college students are very lonely.
   b. older college students always have to work harder at their studies than younger students.
   (c.) younger students often welcome the company of older students.
   d. after a certain age, people should not return to college.

The Writer's Craft

10. The author's main purpose in writing this article is to
    a. entertain readers with stories about things that can go wrong at college.
    b. inform readers about the best careers available to college graduates today.
    (c.) persuade readers to give themselves the best possible chance of success in college.
    d. inform readers about her own success in college.

DISCUSSION QUESTIONS

1. What do you think Coleman means in paragraph 17 when she says, "A lot of people are their own worst enemies"? Have you ever observed anyone seemingly getting in the way of his or her own success? Have you ever done it yourself? Explain.

2. According to Coleman, students should plan for a career that both interests them and offers future job opportunities. What type of career interests you, and why? What degree would help you enter that field? Do you have any idea what the job prospects in that field might be?

3. Coleman ends her introduction (paragraphs 1–2) by stating, "Here, then, are my secrets for survival in college and, really, for survival in life as well." She then makes five points: "Be Realistic," "Persist," "Be Positive," "Grow," and "Enjoy." Which of those points represents the biggest challenge for you right now? Why?

4. Although the author encourages students to make practical career plans, she also writes, "People should take some courses just for the sake of learning and for expanding their minds in different directions." What are some courses you would like to take "just for the sake of learning"? What about them appeals to you?

PARAGRAPH ASSIGNMENTS

1. As you read Coleman's selection, which of her "survival skills" seems of most personal value to you? Do you value that skill because you already possess it and know how helpful it's been to you? Or is it valuable because you *don't* possess it, and know that you need it? Write a paragraph about which one of Coleman's survival skills really stands out for you, explaining in detail exactly why. Your topic sentence can be something like this: "Of all the secrets for survival that Coleman describes, the one that speaks most directly to me is _____."

2. What is something that you have really enjoyed learning? That "something" might be a manual skill, like repairing an engine, or an intellectual pursuit, like learning about the Civil War. Write a paragraph about the experience. Explain what you learned, how you learned it, and what made it so enjoyable for you. Conclude your paragraph by discussing what you discovered about yourself in the process.

ESSAY ASSIGNMENTS

1. Coleman categorizes college students in several ways, including students who give up when they hit an obstacle, students who take a negative attitude toward being in college, and students who have persistent, positive attitudes.

   Write an essay about three categories of students whom you have observed (at any stage of your education). Include plenty of details about just what makes those students fit into the category you are discussing. Those details might have to do with their physical appearance, their classroom behavior, their conversation, or other characteristics. Your thesis statement might be one such as the following: "The students at my school seem to fall into three distinct categories: those who work hard, those who never work, and those who work just enough to get by."

2. Coleman writes, "There are times for each of us when simple survival becomes a deadly serious matter. We must then learn to persist—to struggle through each day." What have been your most challenging struggles so far? Write a paper describing the challenges, what you had to do to deal with them, and how things worked out. You may also wish to comment on how you'd handle the challenges today if faced with them.

   As you work on the drafts for this paper, consider including the following:

   - Exact quotations of what you or other people said at the time (as Coleman does in paragraphs 22 and 28)
   - Descriptions of revealing behavior, actions, and physical characteristics (as Coleman does in paragraphs 21, 27, and 28)
   - Time transitions to clarify relationships between events (as Coleman does in paragraph 6).

Unit Five

Examining Social Issues

32

Tickets to Nowhere
Andy Rooney

Preview

We've all heard or read about lucky people who have won millions of dollars in lotteries. One California man, for example, won over ten million dollars on his very first lottery ticket. Stories like that are enough to keep many people hopefully "investing" in the lottery week after week. But Andy Rooney, in this essay from his syndicated column, has another story to tell.

Words to Watch

determined (4): holding firmly to a purpose
slithered (6): slid from side to side
come over the wires (11): be broadcast
fidgeted (12): moved nervously
clutched (13): held tightly

Things never went very well for Jim Oakland. He dropped out of high school because he was impatient to get rich, but after dropping out he lived at home with his parents for two years and didn't earn a dime.

He finally got a summer job working for the highway department holding up a sign telling oncoming drivers to be careful of the workers ahead. Later that same year, he picked up some extra money putting fliers under the windshield wipers of parked cars.

Things just never went very well for Jim and he was 23 before he left   3
home and went to Florida hoping his ship would come in down there. He
never lost his desire to get rich; but first he needed money for the rent, so
he took a job near Fort Lauderdale for $4.50 an hour servicing the
goldfish aquariums kept near the cashier's counter in a lot of restaurants.

Jim was paid in cash once a week by the owner of the goldfish   4
business, and the first thing he did was go to the little convenience store
near where he lived and buy $20 worth of lottery tickets. He was really
determined° to get rich.

A week ago, the lottery jackpot in Florida reached $54 million. Jim   5
woke up nights thinking what he could do with $54 million. During the
days, he daydreamed about it. One morning he was driving along the main
street in the boss's old pickup truck with six tanks of goldfish in back. As
he drove past a BMW dealer, he looked at the new models in the window.

He saw the car he wanted in the showroom window, but unfortunately   6
he didn't see the light change. The car in front of him stopped short and
Jim slammed on his brakes. The fish tanks slid forward. The tanks broke,
the water gushed out, and the goldfish slithered° and flopped all over the
back of the truck. Some fell off into the road.

It wasn't a good day for the goldfish or for Jim, of course. He knew   7
he'd have to pay for the tanks and 75 cents each for the fish, and if it
weren't for the $54 million lottery, he wouldn't have known which way
to turn. He had that lucky feeling.

For the tanks and the dead goldfish, the boss deducted $114 of Jim's   8
$180 weekly pay. Even though he didn't have enough left for the rent and
food, Jim doubled the amount he was going to spend on lottery tickets.
He never needed $54 million more.

Jim had this system. He took his age and added the last four digits of the   9
telephone number of the last girl he dated. He called it his lucky number . . .
even though the last four digits changed quite often and he'd never won with
his system. Everyone laughed at Jim and said he'd never win the lottery.

Jim put down $40 on the counter that week, and the man punched out
his tickets. Jim stowed them safely away in his wallet with last week's   10
tickets. He never threw away his lottery tickets until at least a month after
the drawing just in case there was some mistake. He'd heard of mistakes.

Jim listened to the radio all afternoon the day of the drawing. The   11
people at the radio station he was listening to waited for news of the
winning numbers to come over the wires° and, even then, the announcers
didn't rush to get them on. The station manager thought the people
running the lottery ought to pay to have the winning numbers broadcast,
just like any other commercial announcement.

Jim fidgeted° while they gave the weather and the traffic and the news.   12
Then they played more music. All he wanted to hear were those numbers.

"Well," the radio announcer said finally, "we have the lottery numbers   13
some of you have been waiting for. You ready?" Jim was ready. He
clutched° his ticket with the number 274802.

"The winning number," the announcer said, "is 860539. I'll repeat   14
that. 860539." Jim was still a loser.

I thought that, with all the human interest stories about lottery   15
winners, we ought to have a story about one of the several million losers.

FIRST IMPRESSIONS

Freewrite for ten minutes on one of the following.

1. Did you enjoy reading this selection? Why or why not?

2. Have you ever played the lottery? If you have, did you win? If you
   have not, is there a reason you have not?

3. What kind of a person would you say Jim is? What role does the
   lottery seem to play in his life?

VOCABULARY CHECK

A. Circle the letter of the word or phrase that best completes each of the
following four items.

1. In the sentences below, the phrase *his ship would come in* means
   a. he could join the navy.
   b. he would enjoy the beach.
   c. he would get lucky.
   d. there would be a challenging job.

   "[H]e was 23 before he left home and went to Florida hoping his ship
   would come in down there. He never lost his desire to get rich. . . ."
   (Paragraph 3)

2. In the sentence below, the word *gushed* means
   a. dripped slowly.
   b. dried.
   c. poured.
   d. held.

   "The tanks broke, the water gushed out, and the goldfish slithered
   and flopped all over the back of the truck." (Paragraph 6)

3. In the sentence below, the word *digits* means
   a. letters.
   b. single numbers.
   c. rings.
   d. area codes.

   "He took his age and added the last four digits of the telephone number of the last girl he dated." (Paragraph 9)

4. In the sentence below, the word *stowed* means
   a. discovered.
   b. bought.
   c. knew.
   d. put.

   "Jim stowed them safely away in his wallet with last week's tickets." (Paragraph 10)

B. Circle the letter of the answer that best completes each of the following four items. Each item uses a word (or form of a word) from "Words to Watch."

5. The police officer was *determined*
   a. to get shot by the thief.
   b. to catch the thief.
   c. by his superiors.

6. An animal that moves by *slithering* along is the
   a. snake.
   b. bear.
   c. goose.

7. "What is bothering Clara?" Amy asked. "She is so *fidgety* today!" Amy thinks that Clara seems
   a. very sad.
   b. relaxed.
   c. anxious.

8. You might *clutch* something that
   a. sticks to your hands.
   b. is too hot to touch.
   c. you don't want to lose.

READING CHECK

Central Point and Main Ideas

1. Which sentence best expresses the central point of the entire selection?
    a. Everyone dreams of winning the lottery.
    b. The more money you invest in lottery tickets, the better your chances of winning.
    (c.) Jim was foolish to plan on getting rich by winning the lottery.
    d. Jim Oakland is a very unlucky man.

2. Which sentence best expresses the main idea of paragraph 6?
    (a.) Jim's daydreaming caused an automobile accident.
    b. Jim was sure he would be driving a BMW soon.
    c. Jim slammed on the brakes to avoid hitting the car in front of him.
    d. Many goldfish died in a car accident.

3. Which sentence best expresses the main idea of paragraph 8?
    a. Jim's boss deducted $114 from Jim's paycheck.
    b. After his boss deducted $114 from his paycheck, Jim could not afford to buy food or pay his rent.
    (c.) Although his reduced paycheck would not cover rent or food, Jim spent twice as much as usual on lottery tickets.
    d. Jim wanted to win the lottery more than ever.

Key Supporting Details

4. According to the reading, Jim dropped out of school because he
    a. was not a very good student.
    b. had to support his family.
    (c.) was in a hurry to get rich.
    d. was offered a well-paying job in Florida.

5. Jim slammed on his brakes because
    a. a BMW pulled into his lane.
    b. he saw his boss coming.
    (c.) he was late in noticing that the car in front of him was stopping for a red traffic light.
    d. it was time to turn on the radio and hear the winning lottery number for that week.

Inferences

6. The author implies that Jim's idea of success for himself was
   a. reaching a goal he had worked hard for.
   b. getting a degree and a career.
   c. being lucky enough to win something.
   d. marrying a wealthy woman.

7. From reading paragraphs 5–8, we can infer that
   a. Jim frequently had auto accidents.
   b. Jim had been drinking.
   c. Jim's daydreaming about becoming rich actually cost him money.
   d. the pickup truck Jim was driving had poor brakes.

8. The author implies that
   a. Jim's parents were wealthy.
   b. Jim's boss was unfair to him.
   c. Jim's next lottery ticket would be a winner.
   d. Jim will probably continue playing the lottery.

The Writer's Craft

9. The author uses direct quotations
   a. frequently throughout the story.
   b. only when Jim speaks.
   c. not at all in the story.
   d. only near the end of the story.

10. What is the *best* explanation of why Rooney titled this selection "Tickets to Nowhere"?
    a. Jim Oakland bought lottery tickets but didn't know what he would do with the money if he won.
    b. Lottery players waste their lives buying "tickets" that take them nowhere.
    c. Because Jim Oakland was so distracted by the lottery, he had a traffic accident and got a ticket.
    d. Lottery tickets don't take people to a physical place, but they can take people to riches.

DISCUSSION QUESTIONS

1. Do you know anyone who, like Jim Oakland, depends more on luck than on hard work or ability? In what ways is this person like or unlike Jim? Do you respect the person? Why or why not?

2. Suppose that five years from now, you could have $500,000. How would you feel about yourself if you had earned that money? Would you feel any differently about yourself if you had won it—say, in a lottery? Explain your answers.

3. The story about Jim Oakland suggests that he never dates the same girl for very long. From what you know about Jim, what do you think are some possible reasons that he has a difficult time maintaining a relationship with a girlfriend? What do his choices concerning the lottery suggest about the kind of boyfriend or husband he would be?

4. As you read the selection, did you think that Jim would win the lottery, or that he would lose? What about the way Rooney wrote the selection made you think that?

PARAGRAPH ASSIGNMENTS

1. Have you ever had a time of really good or bad luck? Perhaps you got new neighbors, and your families became close friends. Maybe you met the person who is now your boyfriend or girlfriend. Perhaps you found a part-time job that suited your schedule and interests perfectly. On the other hand, perhaps a favorite teacher became ill, and you had to spend the rest of the year with a substitute teacher you disliked. Or maybe a parent lost his or her job, and money become scarce for your family. Write a paragraph describing a lucky or unlucky experience you've had. Begin your paragraph with a topic sentence similar to this one: "Recently, I had a period of really good luck (*or* really bad luck)." Provide plenty of details so that the reader will understand just why the time was so lucky or unlucky for you.

2. Clearly, some people are born into situations that are easier to handle than other people's. But aside from that, do you think some people are simply luckier than others? Or do people create their own "good luck" and "bad luck"? Write a paragraph explaining your answer. Use real-life examples you have witnessed to illustrate your point.

ESSAY ASSIGNMENTS

1. By writing about Jim Oakland and his experience with the lottery, Rooney uses just one extended example to illustrate his stand on a controversial issue and to persuade readers to agree with him. Write your own essay in which you take a position on an important issue. Perhaps, for example, you think that high schools should (or should not) require students to wear uniforms, that schools should replace grades with written evaluations, that the sale of tobacco should be made illegal, that junk food should be banned from school cafeterias, that young people should not date until they are 18, or that parents should never spank disobedient children. Focus your essay with a thesis statement similar to one of the following:

   - For several reasons, spanking a disobedient child probably does more harm than good.

   - High schools should require students to wear uniforms for several reasons.

   As Rooney does, defend your position by describing in detail the experiences of one person. Be sure to make it clear how that person's experience illustrates the point you are making. If you prefer, you may use the experiences of two or more people.

2. Jim is a person who is sort of drifting through life, hoping that a stroke of luck will give him everything he wants. As the title of the piece suggests, he is headed nowhere. Do you know someone who is, in your opinion, similarly headed nowhere? Perhaps it is a student who rarely does homework and doesn't seem to think about his or her future. Maybe it's an adult who skips from job to job and is often unemployed. Write an essay about this person and his or her "path to nowhere." Provide plenty of examples of the person's choices and behavior, and make it clear how you think those individual choices or behavior are part of a larger pattern.

33

An Electronic Fog Has Settled Over America
Pete Hamill

Preview

What would you do if your children—once bright and lively and high achievers in school—became dull and passive and began failing their courses? One father's observation of his family's downhill slide is reported here by columnist Pete Hamill. The man's search for a culprit turns up some alarming facts and leads, finally, to his own living room.

Words to Watch

deteriorate (1): worsen in quality
erratic (3): irregular
hustling (3): hurrying
staggered (7): shocked
accumulated (12): gathered
compromise (13): to settle differences by giving something up
projected (14): given an impression of
dominated (14): controlled
voluntary (16): done willingly, without being forced
disconsolate (18): unhappy

The year his son turned fourteen, Maguire noticed that the boy was   1
getting dumber. This was a kid who had learned to talk at fourteen
months, could read when he was four, was an A student for his first six

years in school. The boy was bright, active, and imaginative. And then, slowly, the boy's brain began to deteriorate°.

"He started to slur words," Maguire told me. "He couldn't finish   2
sentences. He usually didn't hear me when I talked to him and couldn't answer me clearly when he did. In school, the A's became B's, and the B's became C's. I thought maybe it was something physical, and I had a doctor check him out. He was perfectly normal. Then the C's started to become D's. Finally, he started failing everything. Worse, the two younger kids were repeating the pattern. From bright to dumb in a few short years."

Maguire was then an account executive in a major advertising agency;   3
his hours were erratic°, and the pace of his business life was often frantic. But when he would get home at night and talk to his wife about the kids, she would shake her head in a baffled way and explain that she was doing her best. Hustling° from the office of one account to another, Maguire pondered the creeping stupidity of his children. Then he took an afternoon off from work and visited his oldest boy's school.

"They told me he just wasn't doing much work," Maguire said. "He   4
owed them four book reports. He never said a word in social studies. His mind wandered, he was distracted, he asked to leave the room a lot. But the teacher told me he wasn't much different from all the other kids. In some ways, he was better. He at least did some work. Most of them, she told me, didn't do any work at all."

Maguire asked the teacher if she had any theories about why the kids   5
behaved this way.

"Of course," she said. "Television."   6

Television? Maguire was staggered°. He made his living off   7
television. Often, he would sit with the kids in the TV room and point out the commercials he had helped to create. Television had paid for his house in the suburbs, for his two cars, his clothes, his food, the pictures on the walls. It even paid for the kids' schools.

"What do you mean, television?" he said.   8

"Television rots minds," the teacher said flatly. "But most of us figure   9
there's nothing to be done about it anymore."

At work the next day, Maguire told his secretary to do some special   10
research for him. Within a week, he had some scary numbers on his desk. The Scholastic Aptitude Tests (SATs) showed that the reading scores of all American high-school students had fallen in every year since 1950, the year of television's great national triumph. The mathematics scores were even worse. The average American kid spent four to six hours a day watching television and by age sixteen had witnessed eleven thousand homicides on the tube.

"I came home that night, and the kids were watching television with   11
my wife," he said. "I looked at them, glued to the set. They nodded hello

to me. And suddenly I got scared. I imagined these four people, their brains rotted out, suddenly adding me to the evening's homicide count because I wanted them to talk to me. I went to the bedroom, and for the first time since college, I took down *Moby-Dick* and started to read."

In the following week, Maguire accumulated° more and more ideas 12 about the impact of television on the lives of Americans. All classes and colors had been affected intellectually; reading requires the decoding of symbols, the transforming of a word like *cat* into a cat that lives in the imagination. Television shows the cat. No active thought is required. Television even supplies a laugh track and music to trigger the emotions the imagination will not create or release.

"I read somewhere that the worst danger to kids who become TV 13 addicts is that while they are watching TV, they're not doing anything else," Maguire said. "They're not down in the schoolyard playing ball, or falling in love, or getting into fights, or learning to compromise°. They're alone, with a box that doesn't hear them if they want to talk back. They don't have to think, because everything is done for them. They don't have to question, because what's the point if you can't challenge the guy on the set?"

Television had also changed politics; Maguire's kids had political 14 opinions based on the way candidates looked and how they projected° themselves theatrically. Politics, which should be based on the structure of analysis and thought, had become dominated° by the structures of drama, that is to say, by conflict.

"I knew Reagan would win in a landslide," Maguire said. "As an actor, 15 he fit right into the mass culture formed by thirty years of television."

Maguire tried to do something. He called a family conference after 16 dinner one night, explained his discoveries, and suggested a voluntary° limiting of television watching or its complete elimination for three months.

"I said we could start a reading program together," he told me. "All 17 read the same book and discuss it at night. I told them we'd come closer together, that I'd even change my job so I could be home more and not work on television commercials anymore."

After ten minutes, the kids began to squirm and yawn, as if expecting a 18 commercial. Maguire's wife dazed out, her disconsolate° face an unblinking mask. He gave up. Now, when he goes home, Maguire says hello, eats dinner, and retreats to his bedroom. He is reading his way through Balzac*.

Beyond the bedroom door, bathed in the cold light of the television 19 set, are the real people of his life. Their dumbness grows, filling up the room, moving out into the quiet suburban town, joining the great gray fog that has enveloped America.

---

*A nineteenth-century French author who wrote nearly one hundred novels.

FIRST IMPRESSIONS

Freewrite for ten minutes on one of the following.

1. Did you enjoy reading this selection? Why or why not?

2. How much television did you watch as you were growing up? How much television do you watch now? Do you think watching TV has affected you in any way? Explain.

3. Would you put any restrictions on your children's TV watching? Explain.

VOCABULARY CHECK

A. Circle the letter of the word or phrase that best completes each of the following four items.

1. In the sentence below, the word *pondered* means
    a. ignored.
    b. thought carefully about.
    c. slowed.
    d. tried to remember.

    "Hustling from the office of one account to another, Maguire pondered the creeping stupidity of his children." (Paragraph 3)

2. In the sentences below, the word *distracted* means
    a. hard-working.
    b. staying in one place.
    c. not paying attention.
    d. talkative.

    "He never said a word in social studies. His mind wandered, he was distracted, he asked to leave the room a lot." (Paragraph 4)

3. In the sentence below, the word *trigger* means
    a. shoot.
    b. set off.
    c. hold back.
    d. prevent.

    "Television even supplies a laugh track and music to trigger the emotions the imagination will not create or release." (Paragraph 12)

4. In the sentence below, the word *enveloped* means
   a. mailed.
   b. left.
   c. wrapped around.
   d. escaped from.

> "Their dumbness grows . . . moving out into the quiet suburban town, joining the great gray fog that has enveloped America." (Paragraph 19)

B. Circle the letter of the answer that best completes each of the following four items. Each item uses a word (or form of a word) from "Words to Watch."

5. Because their marriage seemed to be *deteriorating*, the couple
   a. started seeing a marriage counselor.
   b. celebrated with a second honeymoon.
   c. felt relieved that it was getting better.

6. When the doctor realized that Dad had an *erratic* heartbeat, the doctor
   a. congratulated Dad on his good health.
   b. ordered Dad to the hospital for some tests.
   c. was not concerned.

7. Naturally, I was *staggered* when
   a. the postman put a letter intended for my neighbor in my mailbox.
   b. I saw that the cost of gasoline had gone up five cents a gallon.
   c. I met my identical twin, who I never knew existed, in the dentist's office.

8. In *Gone with the Wind,* Scarlett O'Hara *accumulated* boyfriends. She obviously
   a. made fun of men.
   b. was shocked by men.
   c. was attractive to men.

READING CHECK

Central Point and Main Ideas

1. Which sentence best expresses the central point of the entire selection?
   a. Maguire's son became stupid because he watched so much TV.
   b. Declining SAT scores seem to be linked to increased TV watching.
   c. Ironically, the industry that Maguire made his living from was harming his family.
   (d.) The influence of television has produced a generation of people who cannot think for themselves.

2. Which sentence best expresses the main idea of paragraph 2?
   a. Like their older brother, Maguire's youngest children began doing poorly in school.
   (b.) Maguire's children were becoming less bright, and there was no obvious explanation why.
   c. Maguire suspected that his son had a physical problem that was affecting his intelligence.
   d. Maguire's son couldn't speak clearly, hear well, or keep up with his studies.

3. Which sentence best expresses the main idea of paragraph 10?
   a. Maguire asked his secretary to research the effects of television on children.
   b. The reading and math SAT scores of American kids have fallen every year since 1950.
   (c.) The research done by Maguire's secretary revealed some surprising and frightening facts about television's effects on children.
   d. The average American kid watches four to six hours of TV a day and witnesses thousands of TV homicides.

Key Supporting Details

4. Maguire was certain that Reagan would be elected president of the United States because Reagan
   a. had pledged to raise America's SAT scores.
   b. had once worked as a television advertising executive.
   (c.) had been an actor who still appealed to mass-media tastes.
   d. ran a campaign based on the structure of analysis and thought.

5. When Maguire came home and found his family watching TV, ignoring him except to nod hello, he suddenly felt
   a. terribly sad.
   b. furious.
   c. frightened.
   d. loving.

6. ___F___ TRUE OR FALSE? According to the article, the average American child spends two to four hours a day watching television.

Inferences

7. The article implies that
   a. Maguire was very pleased that President Reagan was elected.
   b. Maguire's two younger children had never done well in school.
   c. Maguire's children would have been better students if Maguire had been home more.
   d. Maguire's children would have been better students if there were no TV set in the house.

8. From the way the article ends, we can reasonably conclude that
   a. Maguire's wife and children will eventually join him in his reading program.
   b. Maguire's children will soon be doing better in school.
   c. Maguire will quit his job in the advertising agency.
   d. the Maguires' problem exists in many households in the United States.

9. We can conclude the author would agree that the worst effect of TV is that it
   a. makes kids violent.
   b. lowers kids' SAT scores, thus making them less able to attend good colleges.
   c. makes people passive observers in life, rather than active participants.
   d. discourages people from reading.

The Writer's Craft

10. The phrase "electronic fog" in Hamill's title refers to
    a. the spread of television programming across the country.
    b. the television-caused stupidity that has crept across America.
    c. the violent content of many television programs.
    d. students' SAT scores, which have fallen every year since 1950.

DISCUSSION QUESTIONS

1. Do you agree with the argument that television makes people less intelligent and more passive? Why or why not?

2. Are there other reasons you can think of for the steady fall in SAT scores since 1950? What are they?

3. As you were growing up, how much television did you and your family watch? Was the TV on most of the time, or did you and your family watch TV only when a special program was on? What, if any, restrictions were put on your TV watching?

4. Based on your answers to the previous question, explain how you will deal with television in your home if you become a parent (or, if you already are a parent, how you do deal with it). How will your attitude toward TV be similar to or different from that of your parents? What, if any, restrictions will you (or do you) put on your children's TV watching? Explain.

PARAGRAPH ASSIGNMENTS

1. This essay reflects the huge role that television has come to play in our society. Most Americans literally could not imagine living without TV—over 99 percent of American households own at least one set. What is one other invention or product that has become a near-necessity for most Americans? Write a paragraph explaining what that product is, what role it plays in Americans' lives, and how you think people would react if they were forced to do without it. Your paragraph might begin like this: "These days, Americans would find it almost impossible to do without _____."

2. Overall, do you think television has been a positive influence in your life—or a negative influence? Write a paragraph explaining your answer. Explain specifically how you think TV has helped or hurt you.

ESSAY ASSIGNMENTS

1. Write an essay about your life as a TV watcher. Choose two to three periods of your life—maybe your preschool years, your adolescent years, and the present—and describe your viewing habits during each of those periods. Provide plenty of details. For instance, where did you do most of your viewing? Who was with you? What were your favorite shows? What was usually going on around you as you watched? What time of day did you do most of your watching, and how long did you watch? A possible thesis statement for this essay is "My life as a TV watcher falls into two (*or* three) distinct periods." In your conclusion, comment on how your viewing habits have changed or stayed the same over the years.

2. Maguire made an effort to get his family to reduce its TV watching and to read more, but the essay suggests that his attempt came too late. If you have children some day (or if you already have them), what are several qualities or habits that you strongly hope that they will possess? How will you try to instill these qualities or habits in your children? Write an essay that explains both what these hoped-for characteristics are, and, as specifically as possible, how you will encourage your children to develop these characteristics.

34

The Quiet Hour
Robert Mayer

Preview

Families who do not own a TV set are considered an oddity in modern-day America. "But what do you do for entertainment?" or "How do you keep up with what's happening?" they are asked by puzzled friends who cannot imagine life without their electronic companion. According to Robert Mayer, however, getting rid of TV—at least for a brief period each day—would expand, rather than limit, a family's options.

Words to Watch

slack (2): loose
scenario (3): imagined scene
byword (5): often-stated principle
byproduct (7): side effect
bugaboo (12): steady source of concern
invalid (12): not effective
saturation (13): state of being full
radical (14): extreme
pompous (14): having an exaggerated importance
drivel (14): nonsense

What would you consider an ideal family evening? Call me a romantic,   1
but that question calls up in my mind pictures of parents and children

lingering around the dinner table to cozily discuss the day's events; munching popcorn from a common bowl as they engage in the friendly competition of a board game; or perhaps strolling through their neighborhood on an early summer evening, stopping to chat with friends in their yards.

Let me tell you what "an ideal family evening" does not conjure up for   2
me: the image of a silent group of people—the intimate word "family" seems hardly to apply—bathed in the faint blue light of a television screen that barely illuminates their glazed eyes and slack° jaws.

Yet we all know that such a scenario° is the typical one. I would like   3
to suggest a different scenario. I propose that for sixty minutes each evening, right after the early-evening news, all television broadcasting in the United States be prohibited by law. Let us pause for a moment while the howls of protest subside.

Now let us take a serious, reasonable look at what the results might be   4
if such a proposal were adopted.

New Explorations

Without the distraction of the tube, families might sit around together   5
after dinner and actually talk to one another. It is a byword° in current psychology that many of our emotional problems—everything, in fact, from the generation gap to the soaring divorce rate to some forms of mental illness—are caused, at least in part, by failure to communicate. We do not tell each other what is bothering us. Resentments build. The result is an emotional explosion of one kind or another. By using the quiet family hour to discuss our problems, we might get to know each other better, and to like each other better.

On evenings when such talk is unnecessary, families could rediscover   6
more active pastimes. Freed from the chain of the tube, forced to find their own diversions, they might take a ride together to watch the sunset. Or they might take a walk together (remember feet?) and explore the neighborhood with fresh, innocent eyes.

Pros and Cons

With time to kill and no TV to slay it for them, children and adults alike   7
might rediscover reading. There is more entertainment and intellectual nourishment in a decent book than in a month of typical TV programming. Educators report that the generation growing up under television can barely write an English sentence, even at the college level. Writing is often learned from reading. A more literate new generation could be a major byproduct° of the quiet hour.

A different form of reading might also be dug up from the past: 8
reading aloud. Few pastimes bring a family closer together than gathering
around and listening to Mother or Father read a good story.

It has been forty years since my mother read to me, a chapter a night, 9
from *Tom Sawyer*. After four decades, the whitewashing of the fence,
Tom and Becky in the cave, Tom at his own funeral remain more vivid in
my mind than any show I have ever seen on TV.

When the quiet hour ends, the networks might even be forced to come 10
up with better shows in order to lure us back from our newly discovered
diversions.

Now let us look at the other side of the proposal. What are the negatives? 11

At a time when "big government" is becoming a major political 12
bugaboo°, a television-free hour created by law would be attacked as
further intrusion by the government on people's lives. But that would not
be the case. Television stations already must be federally licensed. A
simple regulation making TV licenses invalid° for sixty minutes each
evening would hardly be a major violation of individual freedom.

It will be argued that every television set ever made has an "off" knob; 13
that any family that wants to sit down and talk, or go for a drive, or listen
to music, or read a book need only switch off the set, without interfering
with the freedom of others to watch. That is a strong, valid argument—in
theory. But in practice, it doesn't hold up. Decades of television saturation°
have shown us the hypnotic lure of the tube. Television viewing tends to
expand to fill the available time. In practice, the quiet hour would not limit
our freedom; it would expand it. It would revitalize a whole range of
activities that have wasted away in the consuming glare of the tube.

A Radical° Notion?

Economically, the quiet hour would produce screams of outrage from the 14
networks, which would lose an hour or so of prime-time advertising
revenues; and from the sponsors, who would have that much less
opportunity to peddle us deodorants and hemorrhoid preparations while
we are trying to digest our dinners. But given the vast sums the networks
waste on such pompous° drivel° as almost any of the TV "mini-series,"
I'm sure they could make do. The real question is, how long are we going
to keep passively selling our own and our children's souls to keep
Madison Avenue on Easy Street?

At first glance, the notion of a TV-less hour seems radical. What will 15
parents do without the electronic babysitter? How will we spend the quiet?
But it is not radical at all. It has been only about forty-five years since
television came to dominate American free time. Those of us 55 and older

can remember television-free childhoods, spent partly with radio—which at least involved the listener's imagination—but also with reading, learning, talking, playing games, inventing new diversions, creating fantasylands.

It wasn't that difficult. Honest.   16

The truth is, we had a ball.   17

FIRST IMPRESSIONS

Freewrite for ten minutes on one of the following.

1. Did you enjoy reading this selection? Why or why not?

2. How would you feel if TV programming were prohibited for an hour every evening? Why would you feel that way?

3. What is your favorite way of spending time with your loved ones? What do you enjoy about it?

VOCABULARY CHECK

A. Circle the letter of the word or phrase that best completes each of the following four items.

1. In the sentence below, the word *lingering* means
   a. rushing.
   b. leaving.
   c. staying.
   d. arguing.

   > "[A]n ideal family evening . . . calls up in my mind pictures of parents and children lingering around the dinner table to cozily discuss the day's events." (Paragraph 1)

2. In the sentences below, the word *subside* means
   a. investigate.
   b. persuade.
   c. inform.
   d. quiet down.

   > "I propose that for sixty minutes each evening . . . all television broadcasting in the United States be prohibited by law. Let us pause for a moment while the howls of protest subside." (Paragraph 3)

3. In the sentences below, the word *diversions* means
   a. facts.
   b. stories.
   c. amusements.
   d. friends.

   > "[F]orced to find their own diversions, they might take a ride together to watch the sunset. Or they might take a walk together (remember feet?) and explore the neighborhood. . . ." (Paragraph 6)

4. In the sentences below, the word *revitalize* means
   a. permanently discontinue.
   b. limit.
   c. bring back to life.
   d. betray.

   > "In practice, the quiet hour would not limit our freedom; it would expand it. It would revitalize a whole range of activities that have wasted away in the consuming glare of the tube." (Paragraph 13)

B. Circle the letter of the answer that best completes each of the following four items. Each item uses a word (or form of a word) from "Words to Watch."

5. The grieving young widow marched into the lawyer's office and said, "My darling old husband left me everything in his will. Give me my $600 million immediately." The lawyer smiled gently and said, "My dear, your husband's will is *invalid*—
   a. so here is your money. Have a great time."
   b. you see, he never signed it. It's worthless."
   c. but it must be around here somewhere. I'm sure we'll find it."

6. When the second-grade teacher mentioned that little Johnny's stories were *saturated* with blood, guns, and knives, Johnny's parents
   a. were concerned that their son was so interested in violence.
   b. were pleased that their son's stories were so free of violence.
   c. wondered if they should buy Johnny a computer so he could write more neatly.

7. When asked, "Won't you introduce yourself to the group?" the *pompous* man answered,
   a. "Oh, would you mind doing it for me? Speaking in public makes me so nervous."
   b. "I'd prefer not to. I like to just blend into the crowd."
   c. "I don't need to introduce myself! Everyone here knows who I am."

8. "Every paragraph of this research paper is pure *drivel*," the teacher wrote. She apparently felt the research paper was
   a. brilliant and original.
   b. well organized.
   c. truly bad.

READING CHECK

Central Point and Main Ideas

1. Which sentence best expresses the central point of the entire selection?
   a. Television shows need to improve in order to compete with other family activities.
   b. Many people will argue that a "quiet hour" interferes with their basic freedoms.
   c. Before TV, people entertained themselves in a variety of ways.
   d. Banning TV for an hour each day would enrich our lives.

2. Which sentence best expresses the main idea of paragraph 5?
   a. After dinner, many families watch television instead of talking about their problems.
   b. Three problems of modern society are an increasing generation gap, a soaring divorce rate, and mental illness.
   c. Many of our emotional problems are caused by lack of communication.
   d. A "quiet hour" would improve family life by giving us time to communicate with one another.

3. Which sentence best expresses the main idea of paragraph 14?
   a. The benefits of a "quiet hour" are more important than its disadvantages to networks and sponsors.
   b. Networks and sponsors should stop advertising deodorants and hemorrhoid preparations during dinner.
   c. The networks waste the huge sums of money gained from ads on terrible programs.
   d. The networks will not support a "quiet hour."

Key Supporting Details

4. ___T___ TRUE OR FALSE? The author states that reading often improves our writing skills.

5. The author feels that an enforced "quiet hour"
   a. would bankrupt TV networks since fewer commercials could be aired.
   (b.) is not an extreme idea because TV didn't dominate Americans' free time until just a few decades ago.
   c. could improve people's overall health since they would not be on the couch eating junk food while they were watching TV.
   d. would interfere with our freedom to spend an evening as we please.

6. According to the article, television stations currently
   (a.) must be federally licensed.
   b. make little profit from commercials.
   c. are not regulated by the government.
   d. voluntarily provide a "quiet hour" in many states.

Inferences

7. We can conclude that the author believes reading
   (a.) involves the imagination more actively than watching TV does.
   b. is better when it is done aloud.
   c. is less interesting than watching TV.
   d. can easily be done while watching TV.

8. The author implies that our freedom to shut off the TV is limited by
   a. the increasing number of TV's in every household resulting from the decreasing price of TV sets.
   (b.) the hypnotic effect of television.
   c. not enough time being available for TV watching.
   d. the high quality of certain TV shows.

The Writer's Craft

9. The author organizes paragraphs 5–10 according to
   a. listing order: listing the ways that TV networks would fight against the idea of a TV-free hour.
   (b.) listing order: listing the ways that a TV-free hour would benefit families.
   c. time order: from the time TV was introduced to the present.
   d. time order: from the time the average family gets up in the morning until bedtime.

10. What is the author's primary purpose in writing "The Quiet Hour"?
    a. To entertain readers with stories about what people did in the days before TV.
    b. To inform readers about the problems caused by people's failure to communicate.
    c. To persuade people that turning off the TV would benefit individuals and families.
    d. To persuade television networks to give up some of their profits.

DISCUSSION QUESTIONS

1. What were family evenings like in your home as you grew up? Which did they resemble more: those described in paragraph 1 of the reading or those described in paragraph 2?

2. How many hours a day do you watch TV now? If you cut down your viewing time by an hour or so a day, how do you think you would use that time? What activities might you do—or do more of?

3. In order to make their argument stronger, authors often raise possible objections against it and then point out the weaknesses in those objections. What objections does Mayer raise to his own thesis, and how does he show the weaknesses of these objections? (See paragraphs 12–15.) Do you agree with him? Why or why not?

4. Mayer writes, "With time to kill and no TV to slay it for them, children and adults alike might discover reading." He suggests one way to help children learn to enjoy books: by having parents read aloud to them. What are some other ways that parents could help their children enjoy reading?

PARAGRAPH ASSIGNMENTS

1. Mayer claims that television has a largely negative effect on children and families. Do you agree? Write a paragraph in which you defend one of the following statements: "I believe TV is generally a harmful influence on children and families" or "I believe TV is not all that bad for children and families." Use specific examples to support your argument.

2. What is one television show that you really enjoy? Write a paragraph that describes that show and why you like it. In your paragraph, quickly summarize what the show is about (remember, your reader may never have seen it). Then list two or three good features of the program. Illustrate each of these good features with a specific example from the show.

ESSAY ASSIGNMENTS

1. Mayer's purpose in "The Quiet Hour" is to persuade readers that a daily hour with no television at all would be a good idea. Write an essay in which you try to persuade your readers of the benefits of several other changes in their personal lives. For example, you might try to convince them to eat a low-carbohydrate diet, to begin a daily exercise program, and to spend at least one hour a day reading. Your thesis statement might be one like this: "Here is my plan for a three-part improvement program that can change people's lives."

   Or you might try a humorous, opposite approach: "Here is my plan for a three-part destruction program that might be fun at first but that would in no way benefit a person's life."

2. Mayer believes that getting rid of TV for an hour each evening would benefit society. What is another widely accepted aspect of modern life that you would like to see less of? Write an essay proposing the elimination of something you think is a negative influence on society. Don't worry if your proposal is impractical—let your imagination run wild as you describe how life would be improved without, for example, money, beauty pageants, shopping malls, alcohol, advertisements, telephones, computers, automobiles, or professional sports. In your supporting paragraphs, explain the drawbacks of the particular aspect of modern life you've chosen. You might conclude by imagining what a world without that annoyance would be like.

35

Rudeness at the Movies
Bill Wine

Preview

Have you been the victim of other moviegoers' thoughtless talking and noisy eating? Do you slump in your seat, despairing, when a fellow viewer discloses what is going to happen next—right before it happens? If so, you will sympathize with film critic and columnist Bill Wine, who contends that an "epidemic of rudeness" is sweeping through movie theaters today.

Words to Watch

spritzes (4): sprays
engulfed (9): swallowed up
galling (14): irritating
invariably (16): always
superfluous (16): unnecessary
prescient (20): knowing what will happen beforehand
waxing (21): becoming
provocation (23): urging
gregarious (25): sociable
Fascist-like (27): like dictators

Is this actually happening or am I dreaming?   1
  I am at the movies, settling into my seat, eager with anticipation at the   2
prospect of seeing a long-awaited film of obvious quality. The theater is

absolutely full for the late show on this weekend evening, as the reviews have been ecstatic for this cinema masterpiece.

Directly in front of me sits a man an inch or two taller than the Jolly   3
Green Giant. His wife, sitting on his left, sports the very latest in fashionable hairdos, a gathering of her locks into a shape that resembles a drawbridge when it's open.

On his right, a woman spritzes° herself liberally with perfume that her   4
popcorn-munching husband got her for Valentine's Day, a scent that should be renamed "Essence of Elk."

The row in which I am sitting quickly fills up with members of Cub   5
Scout Troop 432, on an outing to the movies because rain has canceled their overnight hike. One of the boys, demonstrating the competitive spirit for which Scouts are renowned worldwide, announces to the rest of the troop the rules in the Best Sound Made from an Empty Good-n-Plenty's Box contest, about to begin.

Directly behind me, a man and his wife are ushering three other   6
couples into their seats. I hear the woman say to the couple next to her: "You'll love it. You'll just love it. This is our fourth time and we enjoy it more and more each time. Don't we, Harry? Tell them about the pie-fight scene, Harry. Wait'll you see it. It comes just before you find out that the daughter killed her boyfriend. It's great."

The woman has more to say—much more—but she is drowned out at   7
the moment by the wailing of a six-month-old infant in the row behind her. The baby is crying because his mother, who has brought her twins to the theater to save on exorbitant babysitting costs, can change only one diaper at a time.

Suddenly, the lights dim. The music starts. The credits roll. And I   8
panic.

I plead with everyone around me to let me enjoy the movie. All I ask, I   9
wail, is to be able to see the images and hear the dialogue and not find out in advance what is about to happen. Is that so much to expect for six bucks, I ask, now engulfed° by a cloud of self-pity. I begin weeping unashamedly.

Then, as if on cue, the Jolly Green Giant slumps down in his seat, his   10
wife removes her wig, the Elk lady changes her seat, the Scouts drop their candy boxes on the floor, the play-by-play commentator takes out her teeth, and the young mother takes her two bawling babies home.

Of course I am dreaming, I realize, as I gain a certain but shaky   11
consciousness. I notice that I am in a cold sweat. Not because the dream is scary, but from the shock of people being that cooperative.

I realize that I have awakened to protect my system from having to   12
handle a jolt like that. For never—NEVER—would that happen in real life. Not on this planet.

I used to wonder whether I was the only one who feared bad audience   13
behavior more than bad moviemaking. But I know now that I am not. Not
by a long shot. The most frequent complaint I have heard in the last few
months about the moviegoing experience has had nothing to do with the
films themselves.

No. What folks have been complaining about is the audience. Indeed,   14
there seems to be an epidemic of galling° inconsiderateness and outrageous
rudeness.

It is not that difficult to forgive a person's excessive height, or   15
malodorous perfume, or perhaps even an inadvisable but understandable
need to bring very young children to adult movies.

But the talking: that is not easy to forgive. It is inexcusable. Talking—   16
loud, constant, and invariably° superfluous°—seems to be standard
operating procedure on the part of many movie patrons these days.

It is true, I admit, that after a movie critic has seen several hundred   17
movies in the ideal setting of an almost-empty screening room with no
one but other politely silent movie critics around him, it does tend to spoil
him for the packed-theater experience.

And something is lost viewing a movie in almost total isolation—a   18
fact that movie distributors acknowledge with their reluctance to screen
certain audience-pleasing movies for small groups of critics. Especially
with comedies, the infectiousness of laughter is an important ingredient
of movie-watching pleasure.

But it is a decidedly uphill battle to enjoy a movie—no matter how   19
suspenseful or hilarious or moving—with non-stop gabbers sitting within
earshot. And they come in sizes, ages, sexes, colors and motivations of
every kind.

Some chat as if there is no movie playing. Some greet friends as if at   20
a picnic. Some alert those around them to what is going to happen, either
because they have seen the film before, or because they are self-
proclaimed experts on the predictability of plotting and want to be seen
as prescient° geniuses.

Some describe in graphic terms exactly what is happening as if they   21
were doing the commentary for a sporting event on radio. ("Ooh, look,
he's sitting down. Now he's looking at that green car. A banana—she's
eating a banana.") Some audition for film critic Gene Shalit's job by
waxing° witty as they critique the movie right before your very ears.

And all act as if it is their Constitutional or God-given right. As if their   22
admission price allows them to ruin the experience for anyone and
everyone else in the building. But why?

Good question. I wish I knew. Maybe rock concerts and ball games—   23
both environments which condone or even encourage hootin' and

hollerin'—have conditioned us to voice our approval and disapproval and just about anything else we can spit out of our mouths at the slightest provocation° when we are part of an audience.

But my guess lies elsewhere. The villain, I'm afraid, is the tube. We have seen the enemy and it is television.   24

We have gotten conditioned over the last few decades to spending most of our screen-viewing time in front of a little box in our living rooms and bedrooms. And when we watch that piece of furniture, regardless of what is on it—be it commercial, Super Bowl, soap opera, funeral procession, prime-time sitcom, Shakespeare play—we chat. Boy, do we chat. Because TV viewing tends to be an informal, gregarious°, friendly, casually interruptible experience, we talk whenever the spirit moves us. Which is often.   25

All of this is fine. But we have carried behavior that is perfectly acceptable in the living room right to our neighborhood movie theater. And that *isn't* fine. In fact, it is turning lots of people off to what used to be a truly pleasurable experience: sitting in a jammed movie theater and watching a crowd-pleasing movie. And that's a first-class shame.   26

Nobody wants Fascist-like° ushers, yet that may be where we're headed of necessity. Let's hope not. But something's got to give.   27

Movies during this Age of Television may or may not be better than ever. About audiences, however, there is no question.   28

They are worse.   29

FIRST IMPRESSIONS

Freewrite for ten minutes on one of the following.

1. Did you enjoy reading this selection? Why or why not?

2. Do you think the author is right about today's moviegoers, or is he unfair to them? Why?

3. How do you feel when a stranger is rude to you? What, if anything, do you do about it?

VOCABULARY CHECK

A. Circle the letter of the word or phrase that best completes each of the following four items.

1. In the sentence below, the word *ecstatic* means
   a. very enthusiastic.
   b. cautious.
   c. missing.
   d. disappointing.

   > "The theater is absolutely full for the late show on this weekend evening, as the reviews have been ecstatic for this cinema masterpiece." (Paragraph 2)

2. In the sentence below, the word *exorbitant* means
   a. too loud.
   b. too high.
   c. boring.
   d. interesting.

   > "The baby is crying because his mother, who has brought her twins to the theater to save on exorbitant babysitting costs, can change only one diaper at a time." (Paragraph 7)

3. In the sentence below, the word *malodorous* means
   a. pleasant.
   b. expensive.
   c. bad-smelling.
   d. flowery.

   > "It is not that difficult to forgive a person's excessive height, or malodorous perfume, or perhaps even an inadvisable but understandable need to bring very young children to adult movies." (Paragraph 15)

4. In the sentence below, the word *condone* means
   a. punish.
   b. forbid.
   c. fear.
   d. overlook.

   > "Maybe rock concerts and ball games—both environments which condone or even encourage hootin' and hollerin'—have conditioned us to voice our approval and disapproval . . . when we are part of an audience." (Paragraph 23)

B. Circle the letter of the answer that best completes each of the following four items. Each item uses a word (or form of a word) from "Words to Watch."

5. "It really *galls* me to hear you answer the telephone like that," Mr. Roberts said to his son. Apparently his son
   a. answers the phone very politely.
   b. never answers the phone.
   c. answers the phone in an inappropriate way.

6. Someone who is *invariably* bad-tempered
   a. very rarely gets angry.
   b. seems angry, but really isn't.
   c. seems always angry.

7. If your paper contains *superfluous* details, your instructor is likely to tell you to
   a. get rid of them.
   b. add more of them.
   c. explain them more fully.

8. Which of these quotations would a *gregarious* person agree with?
   a. "The more I see of people, the better I like my dog."
   b. "People who need people are the luckiest people in the world."
   c. "There's no such thing as a free lunch."

READING CHECK

Central Point and Main Ideas

1. Which sentence best expresses the central point of the entire selection?
   a. Going to the movies used to be more fun than it is today.
   b. The rude behavior of today's audiences is ruining the movie-going experience.
   c. People like to talk while watching television.
   d. Ushers must control the behavior of movie audiences.

2. Which sentence best expresses the main idea of paragraph 16?
   a. Most people talk too much.
   b. Some loud talking during movies is acceptable.
   c. Talking during a movie is inexcusable.
   d. Screaming "Fire!" in a theater is wrong.

3. Which sentence best expresses the main idea of paragraph 25?
   a. Most of our screen-viewing time is spent watching TV, not watching movies in theaters.
   b. Television offers a wide variety of programs, from Shakespeare plays to soap operas.
   c. We have become accustomed to talking while watching TV.
   d. Many homes have television sets in their living rooms and bedrooms.

Key Supporting Details

4. _F_ TRUE OR FALSE? The Cub Scouts in Wine's dream are throwing popcorn at each other.

5. The author feels that movie comedies
   a. are best viewed alone in a silent screening room.
   b. cause people to talk even more than other movies.
   c. lose something if they are not seen in the company of others.
   d. are not as good as they were when he began his career as a movie critic.

Inferences

6. We might conclude that
   a. when the author was younger, he was just as rude as the people he describes.
   b. the author has occasionally asked other movie-goers to be quieter, but gotten little cooperation.
   c. the author is going to quit his job as a movie critic because of the rude audiences.
   d. the author now watches movies only in a screening room with other critics.

7. _F_ TRUE OR FALSE? The author implies that teenagers are the rudest members of movie audiences.

8. At the end of the article, the author implies that unless audiences become quieter,
   a. movie theaters will be closed.
   b. everyone will watch less television.
   c. children will no longer be allowed to go to movie theaters.
   d. ushers will have to force talkers to be quiet or leave.

The Writer's Craft

9. In paragraphs 1 through 10, the author
   a. states the central point of the selection.
   b. states the thesis of the selection and then presents examples and statistics to back it up.
   c. gives a realistic example of how movie audiences behave.
   (d.) gives an exaggerated example of how movie audiences behave.

10. In paragraphs 23 through 26, the author
   (a.) discusses the causes of rudeness at the movies.
   b. discusses the effects of rudeness at the movies.
   c. illustrates rudeness at the movies.
   d. illustrates other types of rudeness.

DISCUSSION QUESTIONS

1. Do you agree with the author's theory about why some people are rude at the movies? What might be some other causes for this behavior?

2. Certain movies seem to bring out the worst in people. Which ones? Why?

3. Wine uses humorous exaggeration to make many of his points. For example, he claims that the man in front of him is "an inch or two taller than the Jolly Green Giant." Find other examples. Do you think this technique is effective, given the subject matter of Wine's essay?

4. In what activities besides moviegoing do you frequently observe rude behavior? What is the effect of such behavior on other people?

PARAGRAPH ASSIGNMENTS

1. Assume that you are the manager of a movie theater, and you have been receiving complaints from patrons about excessive talking and other inconsiderate behavior that has spoiled their movie watching. Write a paragraph—possibly to be put on a sign in the theater lobby—trying to convince patrons to be more considerate of those sitting near them. Your paragraph might begin something like this: "Movies are wonderful entertainment, and the management of Movie Magic Cinemas wants every patron to enjoy our films. For the sake of everyone in the audience, we ask our patrons to follow a few guidelines for courteous viewing."

2. Many people would agree with Wine that going to the movies can be an annoying experience. In addition, the ability to rent videos or DVD's allows viewers to watch movies comfortably at home. In spite of all that, people still go to the movies. Why? Write a paragraph explaining why people still pay to see movies in theaters. Include several reasons, pointing out the benefits of each.

ESSAY ASSIGNMENTS

1. Write an essay about a time someone was especially rude to you. Explain what happened, how you reacted, and how you felt about it. Conclude by explaining why your response was a good one, or by telling what you wish you had done instead. Your thesis statement could be similar to one of the following:

   - It was very rude of my uncle to loudly comment at a family gathering that I had gained weight.

   - When I went to the police station to report the theft of my bicycle, the officer there treated me rudely.

2. Write an essay about several situations or places besides a movie theater where people are apt to be rude and inconsiderate. Like Wine, use specific examples of how people behave. Try to persuade your reader that the behavior you are describing is a real problem and should be stopped. You can write about some of the following situations or any others you can think of:

   - waiting in line at the supermarket
   - waiting in line for tickets to a concert
   - shopping at a department store during a sale
   - riding in a crowded bus
   - driving during rush hour

36

My Daughter Smokes
Alice Walker

Preview

Alice Walker is a famous novelist. She is also a mother. Like mothers everywhere, she would do nearly anything to protect her child from harm. How bitter, then, to see her daughter choose a habit that could end her life. From the starting point of her daughter's smoking, Walker branches into a broader discussion of tobacco, its role in society, and the way it has been corrupted by an ever larger and wealthier industry.

Words to Watch

consort (2): spouse
pungent (3): having a sharp, bitter taste
dapper (4): stylishly dressed
perennially (6): continually
ritual (12): activity done regularly
futility (16): uselessness
empathy (17): understanding
denatured (17): changed from its natural state
mono-cropping (17): growing of single crops apart from other crops
suppressed (18): kept down
cajole (20): gently urge

My daughter smokes. While she is doing her homework, her feet on the bench in front of her and her calculator clicking out answers to her algebra problems, I am looking at the half-empty package of Camels tossed carelessly close at hand. Camels. I pick them up, take them into the kitchen, where the light is better, and study them—they're filtered, for which I am grateful. My heart feels terrible. I want to weep. In fact, I do weep a little, standing there by the stove holding one of the instruments, so white, so precisely rolled, that could cause my daughter's death. When she smoked Marlboros and Players I hardened myself against feeling so bad; nobody I knew ever smoked these brands.

She doesn't know this, but it was Camels that my father, her grandfather, smoked. But before he smoked "ready-mades"—when he was very young and very poor, with eyes like lanterns—he smoked Prince Albert tobacco in cigarettes he rolled himself. I remember the bright-red tobacco tin, with a picture of Queen Victoria's consort°, Prince Albert, dressed in a black frock coat and carrying a cane.

The tobacco was dark brown, pungent°, slightly bitter. I tasted it more than once as a child, and the discarded tins could be used for a number of things: to keep buttons and shoelaces in, to store seeds, and best of all, to hold worms for the rare times my father took us fishing.

By the late forties and early fifties no one rolled his own anymore (and few women smoked) in my hometown, Eatonton, Georgia. The tobacco industry, coupled with Hollywood movies in which both hero and heroine smoked like chimneys, won over completely people like my father, who were hopelessly addicted to cigarettes. He never looked as dapper° as Prince Albert, though; he continued to look like a poor, overweight, overworked colored man with too large a family; black, with a very white cigarette stuck in his mouth.

I do not remember when he started to cough. Perhaps it was unnoticeable at first. A little hacking in the morning as he lit his first cigarette upon getting out of bed. By the time I was my daughter's age, his breath was a wheeze, embarrassing to hear; he could not climb stairs without resting every third or fourth step. It was not unusual for him to cough for an hour.

It is hard to believe there was a time when people did not understand that cigarette smoking is an addiction. I wondered aloud once to my sister—who is perennially° trying to quit—whether our father realized this. I wondered how she, a smoker since high school, viewed her own habit.

It was our father who gave her her first cigarette, one day when she had taken water to him in the fields.

"I always wondered why he did that," she said, puzzled, and with some bitterness.

"What did he say?" I asked.   9

"That he didn't want me to go to anyone else for them," she said,   10
"which never really crossed my mind."

So he was aware it was addictive, I thought, though as annoyed as she   11
that he assumed she would be interested.

I began smoking in eleventh grade, also the year I drank numerous   12
bottles of terrible sweet, very cheap wine. My friends and I, all boys for
this venture, bought our supplies from a man who ran a segregated bar
and liquor store on the outskirts of town. Over the entrance there was a
large sign that said COLORED. We were not permitted to drink there,
only to buy. I smoked Kools, because my sister did. By then I thought her
toxic darkened lips and gums glamorous. However, my body simply
would not tolerate smoke. After six months I had a chronic sore throat. I
gave up smoking, gladly. Because it was a ritual° with my buddies—
Murl, Leon, and "Dog" Farley—I continued to drink wine.

My father died from "the poor man's friend," pneumonia, one hard   13
winter when his bronchitis and emphysema had left him low. I doubt he
had much lung left at all, after coughing for so many years. He had so little
breath that, during his last years, he was always leaning on something. I
remembered once, at a family reunion, when my daughter was two, that
my father picked her up for a minute—long enough for me to photograph
them—but the effort was obvious. Near the very end of his life, and largely
because he had no more lungs, he quit smoking. He gained a couple of
pounds, but by then he was so emaciated no one noticed.

When I travel to Third World countries I see many people like my   14
father and daughter. There are large billboards directed at them both: the
tough, "take-charge," or dapper older man, the glamorous, "worldly"
young woman, both puffing away. In these poor countries, as in American
ghettos and on reservations, money that should be spent for food goes
instead to the tobacco companies; over time, people starve themselves of
both food and air, effectively weakening and addicting their children,
eventually eradicating themselves. I read in the newspaper and in my
gardening magazine that cigarette butts are so toxic that if a baby
swallows one, it is likely to die, and that the boiled water from a bunch of
them makes an effective insecticide.

My daughter would like to quit, she says. We both know the statistics   15
are against her; most people who try to quit smoking do not succeed.*

There is a deep hurt that I feel as a mother. Some days it is a feeling   16
of futility°. I remember how carefully I ate when I was pregnant, how

---

*Three months after reading this essay, my daughter stopped smoking.

patiently I taught my daughter how to cross a street safely. For what, I sometimes wonder; so that she can wheeze through most of her life feeling half her strength, and then die of self-poisoning, as her grandfather did?

But, finally, one must feel empathy° for the tobacco plant itself. For 17 thousands of years, it has been venerated by Native Americans as a sacred medicine. They have used it extensively—its juice, its leaves, its roots, its (holy) smoke—to heal wounds and cure diseases, and in ceremonies of prayer and peace. And though the plant as most of us know it has been poisoned by chemicals and denatured° by intensive mono-cropping° and is therefore hardly the plant it was, still, to some modern Indians it remains a plant of positive power. I learned this when my Native American friends, Bill Wahpepah and his family, visited with me for a few days and the first thing he did was sow a few tobacco seeds in my garden.

Perhaps we can liberate tobacco from those who have captured and 18 abused it, enslaving the plant on large plantations, keeping it from freedom and its kin, and forcing it to enslave the world. Its true nature suppressed°, no wonder it has become deadly. Maybe by sowing a few seeds of tobacco in our gardens and treating the plant with the reverence it deserves, we can redeem tobacco's soul and restore its self-respect.

Besides, how grim, if one is a smoker, to realize one is smoking a 19 slave.

There is a slogan from a battered women's shelter that I especially 20 like: "Peace on earth begins at home." I believe everything does. I think of a slogan for people trying to stop smoking: "Every home a smoke-free zone." Smoking is a form of self-battering that also batters those who must sit by, occasionally cajole° or complain, and helplessly watch. I realize now that as a child I sat by, through the years, and literally watched my father kill himself; surely one such victory in my family, for the rich white men who own the tobacco companies, is enough.

FIRST IMPRESSIONS

Freewrite for ten minutes on one of the following.

1. Did you enjoy reading this selection? Why or why not?

2. Have you ever been (or are you now) a smoker? Why did you begin smoking? If you still smoke, what are your reasons for continuing?

3. Do you know anyone whose health has obviously been harmed by smoking? What symptoms does he or she have? Does he or she still smoke? If so, why?

VOCABULARY CHECK

A. Circle the letter of the word or phrase that best completes each of the following four items.

1. In the sentences below, the word *emaciated* means
   a. thin.
   b. muscular.
   c. healthy.
   d. gray-haired.

   > "Near the very end of his life, and largely because he had no more lungs, he quit smoking. He gained a couple of pounds, but by then he was so emaciated no one noticed." (Paragraph 13)

2. In the sentence below, the word *eradicating* means
   a. curing.
   b. feeding.
   c. destroying.
   d. controlling.

   > "[O]ver time, people starve themselves of both food and air, effectively weakening and addicting their children, eventually eradicating themselves." (Paragraph 14)

3. In the sentences below, the word *venerated* means
   a. honored.
   b. ignored.
   c. ridiculed.
   d. forgotten.

   > "For thousands of years, it has been venerated by Native Americans as a sacred medicine. They have used it extensively. . . ." (Paragraph 17)

4. In the sentence below, the word *redeem* means
   a. destroy.
   b. save from evil.
   c. treat with contempt.
   d. loosen.

   > "Maybe by sowing a few seeds of tobacco in our gardens and treating the plant with the reverence it deserves, we can redeem tobacco's soul and restore its self-respect." (Paragraph 18)

B. Circle the letter of the answer that best completes each of the following four items. Each item uses a word (or form of a word) from "Words to Watch."

5. Noticing that her son looked especially *dapper*, Mrs. Robinson remarked,
    a. "Are you going to play basketball?"
    b. "I wish you wouldn't go around looking like such a slob."
    c. "You're looking very sharp today. Are you meeting someone special?"

6. A man who is *perenially* interested in other people's business would get the reputation of being
    a. really nosy—a busybody.
    b. the quiet loner type, who rarely interacts with anybody.
    c. very sarcastic, always making fun of other people.

7. If mowing the lawn on Saturdays is a family *ritual*, it is apparent that
    a. the family never does it on Saturday.
    b. the family does it every Saturday.
    c. everyone in the family hates doing it.

8. Rick expressed *empathy* for his sister, who had just broken up with her boyfriend, by saying,
    a. "Oh, grow up. Don't make such a fuss about it."
    b. "You must really feel sad right now. Can I do anything to help?"
    c. "I knew he'd dump you eventually."

READING CHECK

Central Point and Main Ideas

1. Which sentence best expresses the central point of the entire selection?
    a. Most people who try to quit smoking are not successful.
    b. The pain Walker feels over her daughter's smoking leads her to think about all the harm done by the tobacco industry.
    c. Native Americans have used the tobacco plant for thousands of years as a sacred medicine and in ceremonies of prayer and peace.
    d. Tobacco ads that show healthy, attractive people are misleading.

2. Which sentence best expresses the main idea of paragraph 4?
    a. For Walker's father and others, the reality of smoking was very different from the images shown in ads and movies.
    b. Walker's father smoked because he wanted to look like Prince Albert.
    c. No one rolled his or her own cigarettes by the 1950s.
    d. Walker's father was poor, overweight, and overworked.

3. Which sentence best expresses the main idea of paragraph 5?
   a. Walker does not know when her father began to cough.
   b. When Walker was her daughter's age, she was embarrassed to hear her father wheezing.
   c. Walker's father's cough began quietly, but it grew to become a major problem.
   d. Walker's father had great difficulty climbing stairs.

Key Supporting Details

4. Walker is especially upset that her daughter smokes Camel cigarettes because
   a. she believes Camels to be especially bad for people's health.
   b. Camels are the brand that Walker herself smoked as a teenager.
   c. Walker's father, who died as a result of smoking, smoked Camels.
   d. they are filtered.

5. When Walker's father picked up his granddaughter at a family reunion, he
   a. burned the child with his cigarette.
   b. put her down quickly so he could have another cigarette.
   c. warned her against smoking.
   d. was too weak to hold her for long.

6. ___F___ TRUE OR FALSE? Walker's daughter has stated that she has no intention of quitting smoking.

Inferences

7. We can infer that Walker
   a. believes people who are poor, uneducated, and nonwhite have been especially victimized by the tobacco industry.
   b. believes that the tobacco plant should be made illegal.
   c. remains furious with her father about her daughter's decision to smoke.
   d. believes Native Americans were wrong to honor the tobacco plant.

8. We can assume that, for Walker, smoking as a teenager was
   a. strictly forbidden by her parents.
   b. an exciting experiment.
   c. quickly habit-forming.
   d. the end of her friendship with Murl, Leon, and "Dog" Farley.

9. We can conclude that Walker's daughter
    a. did not care that her mother was concerned about her smoking.
    (b.) may have been helped to quit smoking by her mother's essay.
    c. has no clear memories of her grandfather.
    d. blamed her aunt for encouraging her to smoke.

The Writer's Craft

10. What audience did Walker seem to have in mind when she wrote this essay?
    a. Executives of the tobacco industry
    b. Citizens of the Third World who are being targeted by tobacco advertising campaigns
    c. Only her daughter, who Walker hoped would stop smoking after she read the essay
    (d.) Her daughter plus anyone else who smokes

DISCUSSION QUESTIONS

1. What would you do if you had a friend who was involved in self-destructive behavior, such as smoking, excessive drinking, or drug use? Would you ignore the behavior? Would you try to persuade the friend to stop the behavior? What would be the risks of either choice?

2. It's clear that smoking is a health hazard. Study after study shows that smoking leads to a variety of diseases, including cancer, emphysema, and heart disease. It has also become clear that second-hand smoke—smoke that non-smokers breathe when they are around smokers—is dangerous as well. If you had the power to do so, would you make smoking illegal or put any legal restrictions on smoking? Or do you believe that smoking should continue to be an individual's right? Explain.

3. What is a bad habit of yours that you have tried to break? How successful were you? What made breaking that habit difficult?

4. Suppose that you had a sixteen-year-old son or daughter. What rules would you expect him or her to obey while living in your home? Would you, for example, have a curfew for your child? Would you allow him or her to smoke in your home? How would you respond if you learned that he or she was drinking, using drugs, or becoming sexually active?

PARAGRAPH ASSIGNMENTS

1. In her essay, Walker is critical of the glamorous, healthy image presented by cigarette advertisements. Write a paragraph in which you describe what you think an honest cigarette advertisement would look like. Who would appear in the ad? What would they be doing? What would they be saying?

    In preparation for this assignment, you might study two or three cigarette ads, using them as inspiration. Your topic sentence might be something like this: "A truly honest cigarette advertisement would not tempt anyone to smoke."

2. Write a paragraph in which you try to persuade a friend to quit smoking. In it, explain in detail three reasons you think he or she should quit. Use transitions such as *first of all, secondly, another*, and *finally* as you list the three reasons.

ESSAY ASSIGNMENTS

1. Think of three bad habits that you have. Perhaps you spend money impulsively, put things off until the last minute, eat too much junk food, speak before you think, or bite your nails. Write an essay explaining how you believe you acquired the habits, how you think they harm you, and how you could get rid of them. Here is a possible thesis statement for this essay: "There are several bad habits that I would love to break."

2. According to Walker, a viewer of movies from the 1940s and 1950s would get the idea that people could "smoke like chimneys" with no bad effects. What are some unrealistic images that today's movies and TV shows present? To answer that question, write an essay from the point of view of an alien from another planet. In order to learn more about the human race, you, the alien, are watching today's movies and TV shows. Write about at least three unrealistic—or just plain wrong—ideas that today's films and television teach you about human beings and society. Use specific examples from movies and TV shows to illustrate your points. Here are a few sample topic sentences for supporting paragraphs in this essay:

    - "Humans sustain themselves with bubbly drinks and messy food combinations."
    - "Humans play a wide variety of puzzling games."
    - "Young and mature humans speak somewhat different languages."

37

Here's to Your Health
Joan Dunayer

Preview

"It doesn't get any better than this." "Here's to good friends." "Good times never felt so good." According to its advertising slogans, alcohol makes life better. But does it? In this piece, Joan Dunayer looks behind the attractive advertisements to find an ugly reality.

Words to Watch

tequila (1): a strong liquor made from a Mexican plant
segment (2): part
defy (2): to challenge
voluntary (2): not required; done by choice
myth (3): a false belief
illusion (8): false impression
irony (12): a meaning that is the opposite of what is actually said

As the only freshman on his high school's varsity wrestling team, Tod 1
was anxious to fit in with his older teammates. One night after a match, he was offered a tequila° bottle on the ride home. Tod felt he had to accept, or he would seem like a sissy. He took a swallow, and every time the bottle was passed back to him, he took another swallow. After seven swallows, he passed out. His terrified teammates carried him into his

home, and his mother then rushed him to the hospital. After his stomach was pumped, Tod learned that his blood alcohol level had been so high that he was lucky not to be in a coma or dead.

Unfortunately, drinking is not unusual among high-school students or, for that matter, in any other segment° of our society. And that's no accident. There are numerous influences in our society urging people to drink, not the least of which is advertising. Who can recall a televised baseball or basketball game without a beer commercial? Furthermore, alcohol ads appear with pounding frequency in magazines, on billboards, and in college newspapers. According to industry estimates, brewers spend more than $600 million a year on radio and TV commercials and another $90 million on print ads. In addition, the liquor industry spends about $230 million a year on print advertising. And recently, Joseph E. Seagram & Sons, Inc. decided to defy° the liquor industry's voluntary° ban on radio and TV ads for hard liquor. The company began running commercials for its Crown Royal Canadian Whiskey on a Texas TV station.

To top it all off, this aggressive advertising of alcohol promotes a harmful myth° about drinking.

Part of the myth is that liquor signals professional success. In a slick men's magazine, one full-page ad for Scotch whiskey shows two men seated in an elegant restaurant. Both are in their thirties, perfectly groomed, and wearing expensive-looking gray suits. The windows are draped with velvet, the table with spotless white linen. Each place-setting consists of a long-stemmed water goblet, silver utensils, and thick silver plates. On each plate is a half-empty cocktail glass. The two men are grinning and shaking hands, as if they've just concluded a business deal. The caption reads, "The taste of success."

Contrary to what the liquor company would have us believe, drinking is more closely related to lack of success than to achievement. Among students, the heaviest drinkers have the lowest grades. In the work force, alcoholics are frequently late or absent, tend to perform poorly, and often get fired. Although alcohol abuse occurs in all economic classes, it remains most prevalent among the poor.

Another part of the alcohol myth is that drinking makes you more attractive to the opposite sex. "Hot, hot, hot," one commercial's soundtrack begins, as the camera scans a crowd of college-age beachgoers. Next it follows the curve of a woman's leg up to her bare hip and lingers there. She is young, beautiful, wearing a bikini. A young guy, carrying an ice chest, positions himself near to where she sits. He is tan, muscular. She doesn't show much interest—until he opens the chest and takes out a beer. Now she smiles over at him. He raises his eyebrows and, invitingly, holds up another can. She joins him. This beer, the song concludes, "attracts like no other."

Beer doesn't make anyone sexier. Like all alcohol, it lowers the levels   7
of male hormones in men and of female hormones in women—even when
taken in small amounts. In substantial amounts, alcohol can cause
infertility in women and impotence in men. Some alcoholic men even
develop enlarged breasts, from their increased female hormones.

The alcohol myth also creates the illusion° that beer and athletics are   8
a perfect combination. One billboard features three high-action images: a
basketball player running at top speed, a surfer riding a wave, and a
basketball player leaping to make a dunk shot. A particular light beer, the
billboard promises, "won't slow you down."

"Slow you down" is exactly what alcohol does. Drinking plays a role   9
in over six million injuries each year—not counting automobile
accidents. Even in small amounts, alcohol dulls the brain, reducing
muscle coordination and slowing reaction time. It also interferes with the
ability to focus the eyes and adjust to a sudden change in brightness —
such as the flash of a car's headlights. Drinking and driving, responsible
for over half of all automobile deaths, is the leading cause of death among
teenagers. Continued alcohol abuse can physically change the brain,
permanently impairing learning and memory. Long-term drinking is
related to malnutrition, weakening of the bones, and ulcers. It increases
the risk of liver failure, heart disease, and stomach cancer.

Finally, according to the myth, alcohol generates a warm glow of   10
happiness that unifies the family. In one popular film, the only food
visible at a wedding reception is an untouched wedding cake, but beer,
whiskey, and vodka flow freely. Most of the guests are drunk. After
shouting into the microphone to get everyone's attention, the band leader
asks the bride and groom to come forward. They are presented with two
wine-filled silver drinking cups branching out from a single stem. "If you
can drink your cups without spilling any wine," the band leader tells
them, "you will have good luck for the rest of your lives." The couple
drain their cups without taking a breath, and the crowd cheers.

A marriage, however, is unlikely to be "lucky" if alcohol plays a major   11
role in it. Nearly two-thirds of domestic violence involves drinking. Alcohol
abuse by parents is strongly tied to child neglect and juvenile delinquency.
Drinking during pregnancy can lead to miscarriage and is a major cause of
such birth defects as deformed limbs and mental retardation. Those who
depend on alcohol are far from happy: over a fourth of the patients in state
and county mental institutions have alcohol problems; more than half of all
violent crimes are alcohol-related; the rate of suicide among alcoholics is
fifteen times higher than among the general population.

Advertisers would have us believe the myth that alcohol is part of   12
being successful, sexy, healthy, and happy; but those who have suffered

from it—directly or indirectly—know otherwise. For alcohol's victims, "Here's to your health" rings with a terrible irony° when it is accompanied by the clink of liquor glasses.

FIRST IMPRESSIONS

Freewrite for ten minutes on one of the following.

1. Did you enjoy reading this selection? Why or why not?

2. Do you agree that movies, TV shows, and advertising present alcohol in a deceptively positive light? Can you think of any that show the harm alcohol can do?

3. Do you know anyone who has had a negative experience because of alcohol use? What happened to that person? Did he or she continue to use alcohol following the incident? How did that person's experience affect your thinking about alcohol?

VOCABULARY CHECK

A. Circle the letter of the word or phrase that best completes each of the following four items.

1. In the sentence below, the word *prevalent* means
   a. weak.
   b. colorful.
   c. widespread.
   d. inexpensive.

   "Although alcohol abuse occurs in all economic classes, it remains most prevalent among the poor." (Paragraph 5)

2. In the sentences below, the word *substantial* means
   a. large.
   b. reasonable.
   c. weak.
   d. pleasing.

   "Beer . . . lowers the levels of male hormones in men and of female hormones in women—even when taken in small amounts. In substantial amounts, alcohol can cause infertility in women and impotence in men." (Paragraph 7)

3. In the sentence below, the word *impairing* means
   a. damaging.
   b. doubling.
   c. postponing.
   d. teaching.

   "Continued alcohol abuse can physically change the brain, permanently impairing learning and memory." (Paragraph 9)

4. In the sentence below, the word *generates* means
   a. removes.
   b. hides.
   c. produces.
   d. follows.

   "Finally, according to the myth, alcohol generates a warm glow of happiness that unifies the family." (Paragraph 10)

B. Circle the letter of the answer that best completes each of the following four items. Each item uses a word (or form of a word) from "Words to Watch."

5. An example of a *segment* of the population is
   a. a survey of the population.
   b. African American males between the ages of 17–25.
   c. the population as a whole.

6. The beautiful princess *defied* the terrifying dragon by
   a. crying out, "Ooh, I am so frightened! Where is a handsome prince to save me?"
   b. offering him the king and queen to eat if he would spare her life.
   c. shouting, "I'm not afraid of you, garbage breath! Get out here and fight!"

7. It is *voluntary* to pay
   a. taxes.
   b. for a friend's dinner.
   c. a parking ticket.

8. Lucinda's belief that Victor really loved her was an *illusion*; Victor
   a. soon married her, was a wonderful husband, and they lived happily ever after.
   b. soon revealed that he was a con man interested only in her money.
   c. loved her dearly, although circumstances made it impossible for them to be together.

READING CHECK

Central Point and Main Ideas

1. Which sentence best expresses the central point of the entire selection?
    a. Advertising promotes the idea that alcohol makes people sexy, successful, and happy.
    b. Advertisers spend a lot of money to promote false ideas about alcohol.
    c. Advertisers should be more careful to tell the truth, as young people are easily influenced by ads.
    d. Like the freshman on the wrestling team, teenagers often engage in foolish behavior to win the acceptance of their friends.

2. The topic sentence of paragraph 2 is its
    a. first sentence.
    b. second sentence.
    c. third sentence.
    d. last sentence.

3. Which sentence best expresses the idea of paragraph 5?
    a. Students who drink heavily tend to make low grades.
    b. Drinking and lack of success often go hand in hand.
    c. A large percentage of heavy drinkers are poor.
    d. Employees who drink heavily are often fired from their jobs.

Key Supporting Details

4. What is the total amount that brewers spend per year on TV, radio, and print ads?
    a. $60 million
    b. $90 million
    c. $690 million
    d. $900 million

5. Which of the following is *not* listed in paragraph 9 as a physical risk of long-term drinking?
    a. Heart disease
    b. Lung cancer
    c. Malnutrition
    d. Liver failure

6. According to paragraph 11, what percentage of violent crimes are alcohol-related?
   a. 25 percent
   b. Nearly 50 percent
   (c.) Over 50 percent
   d. 75 percent

7. Which of the following problems that affect children is linked to alcohol abuse by their parents?
   a. Juvenile delinquency
   b. Child neglect
   c. Birth defects
   (d.) All of the above

Inferences

8. We can logically infer that Tod
   a. had been an alcohol abuser for some time prior to the incident mentioned in this story.
   (b.) did not realize how powerful tequila was.
   c. suffered permanent brain damage as a result of his tequila overdose.
   d. was suspended from the wrestling team.

9. ___F___ TRUE OR FALSE? We can conclude that the author believes light beer is not harmful.

The Writer's Craft

10. The beginning of the article is best described by which of the following statements?
    a. It is a personal anecdote—or brief story—about how the author herself has been affected by alcohol advertising.
    b. It is a series of questions about alcohol advertising and its effects.
    (c.) It is an anecdote that illustrates how a teenager accepted the myth about alcohol use.
    d. It is a scenario about happy, successful alcohol users—in other words, an idea that is the opposite of the one the essay will develop.

DISCUSSION QUESTIONS

1. Dunayer presents and then refutes four false ideas about alcohol. What are these four ideas? According to Dunayer, what is the reality behind each? To what extent do you agree or disagree with Dunayer?

2. If it's true that "beer doesn't make anyone sexier," why do you think so many young people drink so much beer in social situations? What are they hoping to achieve?

3. Think about a wine, liquor, or beer ad you have seen in a magazine, in a newspaper, or on television. What part of the alcohol myth described in "Here's to Your Health" does that ad promote? What details of the ad contribute to that element of the myth?

4. Cigarette advertising is no longer allowed on television. Do you think beer ads should also be outlawed on TV? Should cigarettes and/or beer ads be banned from newspaper and magazines, too? Why or why not?

PARAGRAPH ASSIGNMENTS

1. Few people go through life without being exposed to the negative effects of alcohol. In a paragraph, describe an unpleasant or dangerous incident you have been aware of, or experienced yourself, in which alcohol played a part. Who was involved? What happened? In what way did alcohol contribute to the situation? How did the incident end? How did you feel about what happened? You might begin with a topic sentence similar to the following: "An unpleasant incident last year taught me how dangerous alcohol can be."

2. The advertising and sale of cigarettes are topics of much debate. Some legal restrictions already exist: cigarettes are not advertised on television, they are not to be sold to minors, and warning labels on cigarettes inform consumers of health risks associated with smoking. In addition, cigarette smoking is banned in an increasing number of public places, such as restaurants and office buildings. In your opinion, are these restrictions necessary? Should even more restrictions be imposed on the tobacco industry? Or should cigarettes be advertised and sold like any other product and smoked wherever people wish? Decide which of these questions you would answer with a "yes," and then write a paragraph that explains your opinion.

ESSAY ASSIGNMENTS

1. As this article shows, alcohol advertisements are often based on the claims that alcohol makes people more successful, sexier, healthier, and happier. Find several alcohol advertisements (TV or print ads) that you believe promote one or more of those claims. Write an essay in which you explain how each of your ads illustrates one particular claim. As Dunayer does in paragraphs 4 and 6, describe the ads carefully, pointing out exactly how each one supports a particular part of the myth. Your thesis statement could be something like this:

   - Two whiskey ads and a beer commercial demonstrate several aspects of the myth described by Joan Dunayer in "Here's to Your Health."

2. According to advertisements, alcohol makes people successful, happy, and sexy. The abuse of alcohol, however, often has quite the opposite effect. Write an essay in which you describe what more truthful alcohol advertisements would look like—ones that showed the negative side of drinking. What images would you include in such advertisements? You might organize your essay by addressing several of the positive views about alcohol mentioned in the article and describing an ad that would contradict each of these false ideas.

38

A Drunken Ride, a Tragic Aftermath
Theresa Conroy and Christine M. Johnson

Preview

It is a sequence of events that occurs all too often—high-school kids gather for a party that quickly turns drunken and raucous. The party spills out into the roadways, and an evening of alcohol-fueled celebration turns into a nightmare of twisted metal, mangled bodies, and anguished survivors. As this article makes clear, the horror of such a night does not end with the funerals of those who died.

Words to Watch

vehicular homicide (6): killing with a vehicle
carnage (19): massive slaughter
catharsis (62): refreshing release of emotional tension
fathom (64): understand
tamperproof (65): unable to be changed improperly
curtail (68): cut back on
impair (76): weaken
faculties (76): abilities
incarcerate (79): put in prison
vicariously (94): by imagining someone else's experience
adherence (95): sticking

subsidized (97): financed
peer-group (97): made up of people of a similar age, grade, etc.
welling (104): rising and ready to flow

When Tyson Baxter awoke after that drunken, tragic night—with a   1
bloodied head, broken arm, and battered face—he knew that he had killed
his friends.

"I knew everyone had died," Baxter, 18, recalled. "I knew it before   2
anybody told me. Somehow, I knew."

Baxter was talking about the night of Friday, September 13, the night   3
he and seven friends piled into his Chevrolet Blazer after a beer-drinking
party. On Street Road in Upper Southampton, he lost control, rear-ended
a car, and smashed into two telephone poles. The Blazer's cab top
shattered, and the truck spun several times, ejecting all but one passenger.

Four young men were killed.   4

Tests would show that Baxter and the four youths who died were   5
legally intoxicated.

Baxter says he thinks about his dead friends on many sleepless nights   6
at the Abraxas Drug and Alcohol Rehabilitation Center near Pittsburgh,
where, on December 20, he was sentenced to be held after being found
delinquent on charges of vehicular homicide°.

"I drove them where they wanted to go, and I was responsible for their   7
lives," Baxter said recently from the center, where he is undergoing
psychological treatment. "I had the keys in my hand, and I blew it."

The story of September 13 is a story about the kind of horrors that   8
drinking and driving is spawning among high-school students almost
everywhere, . . . about parents who lost their children in a flash and have
filled the emptiness with hatred, . . . about a youth whose life is burdened
with grief and guilt because he happened to be behind the wheel.

It is a story that the Baxter family and the dead boys' parents agreed   9
to tell in the hope that it would inspire high-school students to remain
sober during this week of graduation festivities—a week that customarily
includes a ritual night of drunkenness.

It is a story of the times.   10

The evening of September 13 began in high spirits as Baxter, behind the   11
wheel of his gold Blazer, picked up seven high-school chums for a
drinking party for William Tennent High School students and graduates
at the home of a classmate. Using false identification, according to police,
the boys purchased one six-pack of beer each from a Warminster
Township bar.

The unchaperoned party, attended by about fifty teenagers, ended 12
about 10:30 p.m. when someone knocked over and broke a glass china
cabinet. Baxter and his friends decided to head for a fast-food restaurant.
As Baxter turned onto Street Road, he was trailed by a line of cars
carrying other partygoers.

Baxter recalled that several passengers were swaying and rocking the 13
high-suspension vehicle. Police were unable to determine the vehicle's
exact speed, but, on the basis of the accounts of witnesses, they estimated
it at fifty-five miles per hour—ten miles per hour over the limit.

"I thought I was in control," Baxter said. "I wasn't driving like a nut; 14
I was just . . . driving. There was a bunch of noise, just a bunch of noise.
The truck was really bouncing.

"I remember passing two [cars]. That's the last I remember. I 15
remember a big flash, and that's it."

Killed in that flash were: Morris "Marty" Freedenberg, 16, who landed 16
near a telephone pole about thirty feet from the truck, his face ripped from
his skull; Robert Schweiss, 18, a Bucks County Community College
student, whose internal organs were crushed when he hit the pavement
about thirty feet from the truck; Brian Ball, 17, who landed near Schweiss,
his six-foot-seven-inch frame stretched three inches when his spine was
severed; and Christopher Avram, 17, a premedical student at Temple
University, who landed near the curb about ten feet from the truck.

Michael Serratore, 18, was thrown fifteen feet from the truck and 17
landed on the lawn of the CHI Institute with his right leg shattered.
Baxter, who sailed about ten feet after crashing through the windshield of
the Blazer, lost consciousness after hitting the street near the center lane.
About five yards away, Paul Gee, Jr., 18, lapsed into a coma from severe
head injuries.

John Gahan, 17, the only passenger left in the Blazer, suffered a 18
broken ankle.

Brett Walker, 17, one of several Tennent students who saw the 19
carnage° after the accident, would recall later in a speech to fellow
students: "I ran over [to the scene]. These were the kids I would go out
with every weekend.

"My one friend [Freedenberg], I couldn't even tell it was him except 20
for his eyes. He had real big, blue eyes. He was torn apart so bad. . . ."

Francis Schweiss was waiting up for his son, Robert, when he received a 21
telephone call from his daughter, Lisa. She was already at Warminster
General Hospital.

"She said Robbie and his friends were in a bad accident and Robbie 22
was not here" at the hospital, Schweiss said. "I got in my car with my
wife; we went to the scene of the accident."

There, police officers told Francis and Frances Schweiss that several 23
boys had been killed and that the bodies, as well as survivors, had been
taken to Warminster General Hospital.

"My head was frying by then," Francis Schweiss said. "I can't even 24
describe it. I almost knew the worst was to be. I felt as though I were
living a nightmare. I thought, 'I'll wake up. This just can't be.'"

In the emergency room, Francis Schweiss recalled, nurses and doctors 25
were scrambling to aid the injured and identify the dead—a difficult task
because some bodies were disfigured and because all the boys had been
carrying fake driver's licenses.

A police officer from Upper Southampton was trying to question 26
friends of the dead and injured—many of whom were sobbing and
screaming—in an attempt to match clothing with identities.

When the phone rang in the Freedenberg home, Robert S. and his wife, 27
Bobbi, had just gone upstairs to bed; their son Robert Jr. was downstairs
watching a movie on television.

Bobbi Freedenberg and her son picked up the receiver at the same 28
time. It was from Warminster General. . . . There had been a bad accident.
. . . The family should get to the hospital quickly.

Outside the morgue about twenty minutes later, a deputy county 29
coroner told Rob Jr., 22, that his brother was dead and severely
disfigured; Rob decided to spare his parents additional grief by
identifying the body himself.

Freedenberg was led into a cinderblock room containing large drawers 30
resembling filing cabinets. In one of the drawers was his brother, Marty,
identifiable only by his new high-top sneakers.

"It was kind of like being taken through a nightmare," Rob Jr. said. 31
"That's something I think about every night before I go to sleep. That's
hell. . . . That whole night is what hell is all about for me."

As was his custom, Morris Ball started calling the parents of his son's 32
friends after Brian missed his 11:00 p.m. curfew.

The first call was to the Baxters' house, where the Baxters' sixteen- 33
year-old daughter, Amber, told him about the accident.

At the hospital, Morris Ball demanded that doctors and nurses take 34
him to his son. The hospital staff had been unable to identify Brian—until
Ball told them that his son wore size 14 shoes.

Brian Ball was in the morgue. Lower left drawer.   35

"He was six foot seven, but after the accident he measured six foot ten, 36
because of what happened to him," Ball said. "He had a severed spinal
cord at the neck. His buttocks were practically ripped off, but he was
lying down and we couldn't see that. He was peaceful and asleep.

"He was my son and my baby. I just can't believe it sometimes. I still   37
can't believe it. I still wait for him to come home."

Lynne Pancoast had just finished watching the 11:00 p.m. news and was   38
curled up in her bed dozing with a book in her lap when the doorbell rang.
She assumed that one of her sons had forgotten his key, and she went
downstairs to let him in.

A police light was flashing through the window and reflecting against   39
her living-room wall; Pancoast thought that there must be a fire in the
neighborhood and that the police were evacuating homes.

Instead, police officers told her there had been a serious accident   40
involving her son, Christopher Avram, and that she should go to the
emergency room at Warminster General.

At the hospital she was taken to an empty room and told that her son   41
was dead.

Patricia Baxter was asleep when a Warminster police officer came to the   42
house and informed her that her son had been in an accident.

At the hospital, she could not immediately recognize her own son   43
lying on a bed in the emergency room. His brown eyes were swollen shut,
and his straight brown hair was matted with blood that had poured from
a deep gash in his forehead.

While she was staring at his battered face, a police officer rushed into   44
the room and pushed her onto the floor—protection against the hysterical
father of a dead youth who was racing through the halls, proclaiming that
he had a gun and shouting, "Where is she? I'm going to kill her. I'm going
to kill him. I'm going to kill his mother."

The man, who did not have a gun, was subdued by a Warminster   45
police officer and was not charged.

Amid the commotion, Robert Baxter, a Lower Southampton highway   46
patrol officer, arrived at the hospital and found his wife and son.

"When he came into the room, he kept going like this," Patricia Baxter   47
said, holding up four fingers. At first, she said, she did not understand that
her husband was signaling that four boys had been killed in the accident.

After Tyson regained consciousness, his father told him about the   48
deaths.

"All I can remember is just tensing up and just saying something,"   49
Tyson Baxter said. "I can remember saying, 'I know.'

"I can remember going nuts."   50

In the days after the accident, as the dead were buried in services that   51
Tyson Baxter was barred by the parents of the victims from attending,
Baxter's parents waited for him to react to the tragedy and release his grief.

"In the hospital he was nonresponsive," Patricia Baxter said. "He was 52
home for a month, and he was nonresponsive.

"We never used to do this, but we would be upstairs and listen to see 53
if Ty responded when his friends came to visit," she said. "But the boy
would be silent. That's the grief that I felt. The other kids showed a
reaction. My son didn't."

Baxter said, however, that he felt grief from the first, that he would cry 54
in the quiet darkness of his hospital room and, later, alone in the darkness
of his bedroom. During the day, he said, he blocked his emotions.

"It was *just* at night. I thought about it all the time. It's still like that." 55

At his parents' urging, Baxter returned to school on September 30. 56

"I don't remember a thing," he said of his return. "I just remember 57
walking around. I didn't say anything to anybody. It didn't really sink in."

Lynne Pancoast, the mother of Chris Avram, thought it was wrong for 58
Baxter to be in school, and wrong that her other son, Joel, a junior at
William Tennent, had to walk through the school halls and pass the boy
who "killed his brother."

Morris Ball said he was appalled that Baxter "went to a football game 59
while my son lay buried in a grave."

Some William Tennent students said they were uncertain about how 60
they should treat Baxter. Several said they went out of their way to treat
him normally, others said they tried to avoid him, and others declined to
be interviewed on the subject.

The tragedy unified the senior class, according to the school principal, 61
Kenneth Kastle. He said that after the accident, many students who were
friends of the victims joined the school's Students Against Driving Drunk
chapter.

Matthew Weintraub, 17, a basketball player who witnessed the bloody 62
accident scene, wrote to President Reagan and detailed the grief among
the student body. He said, however, that he experienced a catharsis° after
reading the letter at a student assembly and, as a result, did not mail it.

"And after we got over the initial shock of the news, we felt as though
we owed somebody something," Weintraub wrote. "It could have been us 63
and maybe we could have stopped it, and now it's too late. . . .

"We took these impressions with us as we then visited our friends who 64
had been lucky enough to live. One of them was responsible for the
accident; he was the driver. He would forever hold the deaths of four
young men on his conscience. Compared with our own feelings of guilt,
[we] could not begin to fathom° this boy's emotions. He looked as if he
had a heavy weight upon his head and it would remain there forever."

About three weeks after the accident, Senator H. Craig Lewis (D., 65
Bucks) launched a series of public forums to formulate bills targeting
underage drinking. Proposals developed through the meetings include

outlawing alcohol ads on radio and television, requiring police to notify parents of underage drinkers, and creating a tamperproof° driver's license.

The parents of players on William Tennent's 1985–1986 boys' basketball team, which lost Ball and Baxter because of the accident, formed the Caring Parents of William Tennent High School Students to help dissuade students from drinking. 66

Several William Tennent students, interviewed on the condition that their names not be published, said that, because of the accident, they would not drive after drinking during senior week, which will be held in Wildwood, New Jersey, after graduation June 13. 67

But they scoffed at the suggestion that they curtail° their drinking during the celebrations. 68

"We just walk [after driving to Wildwood]," said one youth. "Stagger is more like it." 69

"What else are we going to do, go out roller skating?" an eighteen-year-old student asked. 70

"You telling us we're not going to drink?" one boy asked. "We're going to drink very heavily. I want to come home retarded. That's senior week. I'm going to drink every day. Everybody's going to drink every day." 71

Tyson Baxter sat at the front table of the Bucks County courtroom on December 20, his arm in a sling, his head lowered and his eyes dry. He faced twenty counts of vehicular homicide, four counts of involuntary manslaughter, and two counts of driving under the influence of alcohol. 72

Patricia Ball said she told the closed hearing that "it was Tyson Baxter who killed our son. He used the car as a weapon. We know he killed our children as if it were a gun. He killed our son." 73

"I really could have felt justice [was served] if Tyson Baxter was the only one who died in that car," she said in an interview, "because he didn't take care of our boys." 74

Police officers testified before Bucks County President Judge Isaac S. Garb that tests revealed that the blood-alcohol levels of Baxter and the four dead boys were above the 0.10 percent limit used in Pennsylvania to establish intoxication. 75

Baxter's blood-alcohol level was 0.14 percent, Ball's 0.19 percent, Schweiss's 0.11 percent, Avram's 0.12 percent, and Freedenberg's 0.38 percent. Baxter's level indicated that he had had eight or nine drinks—enough to cause abnormal bodily functions such as exaggerated gestures and to impair° his mental faculties°, according to the police report. 76

After the case was presented, Garb invited family members of the dead teens to speak. 77

In a nine-page statement, Bobbi Freedenberg urged Garb to render 78
a decision that would "punish, rehabilitate, and deter others from this
act."

The parents asked Garb to give Baxter the maximum sentence, to 79
prohibit him from graduating, and to incarcerate° him before Christmas
day. (Although he will not attend formal ceremonies, Baxter will receive
a diploma from William Tennent this week.)

After hearing from the parents, Garb called Baxter to the stand. 80

"I just said that all I could say was, 'I'm sorry; I know I'm totally 81
responsible for what happened,'" Baxter recalled. "It wasn't long, but it
was to the point."

Garb found Baxter delinquent and sentenced him to a stay at Abraxas 82
Rehabilitation Center—for an unspecified period beginning December
23—and community service upon his return. Baxter's driver's license was
suspended by the judge for an unspecified period, and he was placed
under Garb's jurisdiction until age 21.

Baxter is one of fifty-two Pennsylvania youths found responsible for 83
fatal drunken-driving accidents in the state in 1985.

Reflecting on the hearing, Morris Ball said there was no legal 84
punishment that would have satisfied his longings.

"They can't bring my son back," he said, "and they can't kill Tyson 85
Baxter."

Grief has forged friendships among the dead boys' parents, each of whom 86
blames Tyson Baxter for their son's death. Every month they meet at each
other's homes, but they seldom talk about the accident.

Several have joined support groups to help them deal with their losses. 87
Some said they feel comfortable only with other parents whose children
are dead.

Bobbi Freedenberg said her attitude had worsened with the passage of 88
time. "It seems as if it just gets harder," she said. "It seems to get worse."

Freedenberg, Schweiss, and Pancoast said they talk publicly about 89
their sons' deaths in hopes that the experience will help deter other
teenagers from drunken driving.

Schweiss speaks each month to the Warminster Youth Aid Panel—a 90
group of teenagers who, through drug use, alcohol abuse, or minor
offenses, have run afoul of the law.

"When I talk to the teens, I bring a picture of Robbie and pass it along 91
to everyone," Schweiss said, wiping the tears from his cheeks. "I say, 'He
was with us last year.' I get emotional and I cry. . . .

"But I know that my son helps me. I firmly believe that every time I 92
speak, he's right on my shoulder."

When Pancoast speaks to a group of area high-school students, she 93 drapes her son's football jersey over the podium and displays his graduation picture.

"Every time I speak to a group, I make them go through the whole 94 thing vicariously°," Pancoast said. "It's helpful to get out and talk to kids. It sort of helps keep Chris alive. . . . When you talk, you don't think."

At Abraxas, Baxter attended high-school classes until Friday. He is one of 95 three youths there who supervise fellow residents, who keep track of residents' whereabouts, attendance at programs, and adherence° to the center's rules and regulations.

Established in Pittsburgh in 1973, the Abraxas Foundation provides an 96 alternative to imprisonment for offenders between sixteen and twenty-five years old whose drug and alcohol use has led them to commit crimes.

Licensed and partially subsidized° by the Pennsylvania Department of 97 Health, the program includes work experience, high-school education, and prevocational training. Counselors conduct individual therapy sessions, and the residents engage in peer-group° confrontational therapy sessions.

Baxter said his personality had changed from an "egotistical, 98 arrogant" teenager to someone who is "mellow" and mature.

"I don't have quite the chip on my shoulder. I don't really have a right 99 to be cocky anymore," he said.

Baxter said not a day went by that he didn't remember his dead friends. 100

"I don't get sad. I just get thinking about them," he said. "Pictures pop 101 into my mind. A tree or something reminds me of the time. . . . Sometimes I laugh. . . . Then I go to my room and reevaluate it like a nut," he said.

Baxter said his deepest longing was to stand beside the graves of his 102 four friends.

More than anything, Baxter said, he wants to say good-bye. 103

"I just feel it's something I *have* to do, . . . just to talk," Baxter said, 104 averting his eyes to hide welling° tears. "Deep down I think I'll be hit with it when I see the graves. I know they're gone, but they're not gone."

FIRST IMPRESSIONS

Freewrite for ten minutes on one of the following.

1. Did you enjoy reading this selection? Why or why not?

2. If you were the parent of one of the boys who were killed, would you have responded to Tyson Baxter in the same way the parents in the story did? Or would you feel differently? Explain.

3. Do you know of alcohol-related accidents involving students? Did the accidents seem to have any effect on other students' attitudes toward drinking?

VOCABULARY CHECK

A. Circle the letter of the word or phrase that best completes each of the following four items.

1. In the sentence below, the word *spawning* means
   (a.) producing.
   b. preventing.
   c. protecting.
   d. predicting.

   > "The story of September 13 is a story about the kind of horrors that drinking and driving is spawning among high-school students almost everywhere . . . ." (Paragraph 8)

2. In the sentence below, the word *appalled* means
   a. relieved.
   (b.) horrified.
   c. pleased.
   d. aware.

   > "Morris Ball said he was appalled that Baxter 'went to a football game while my son lay buried in a grave.'" (Paragraph 59)

3. In the sentence below, the word *deter* means
   a. punish.
   b. pay.
   (c.) prevent.
   d. hide.

   > "Freedenberg, Schweiss, and Pancoast said they talk publicly about their sons' deaths in hopes that the experience will help deter other teenagers from drunken driving." (Paragraph 89)

4. In the sentence below, the word *averting* means
   a. opening.
   (b.) turning away.
   c. asking.
   d. thinking of.

   > "'I just feel it's something I *have* to do, . . . just to talk,' Baxter said, averting his eyes to hide welling tears." (Paragraph 104)

B. Circle the letter of the answer that best completes each of the following four items. Each item uses a word (or form of a word) from "Words to Watch."

5. "No one can really *fathom* eternity," said the preacher. He meant that no one can
   a. live for all eternity.
   b. believe in eternity.
   c. grasp the meaning of eternity.

6. Trina has really *curtailed* her cigarette smoking. She
   a. has cut back from a pack a day to just two cigarettes.
   b. never has smoked and swears she never will.
   c. has developed from an occasional smoker into a constant chain smoker.

7. Natalie *impaired* her chances of winning the class presidency by
   a. blanketing the hallways with her posters, photographs, and campaign promises.
   b. not campaigning at all, so few people even knew she was running.
   c. being an honest, good-natured candidate whom most people liked.

8. Richie likes to get his thrills *vicariously*, so he
   a. sky-dives, bungee-jumps, and mountain-climbs.
   b. sits comfortably in his living room watching people do dangerous stunts on TV.
   c. plays lots of contact sports, such as football.

READING CHECK

Central Point and Main Ideas

1. Which sentence best expresses the central point of the entire selection?
   a. The experience of Tyson Baxter and his friends should serve as an example to teens of the dangers of drinking and driving.
   b. The parents of the boys killed in the accident have never forgiven the driver, Tyson Baxter.
   c. Drinking has become a routine part of life for many teenagers.
   d. Because of a high-school student's drunk-driving accident, a state senator began work on a bill targeting underage drinking.

2. Which sentence best expresses the main idea of paragraph 8?
   a. Many people are affected by the consequences of high-school students' drinking and driving.
   b. Parents who lose their children may be consumed with hatred.
   c. The driver of the automobile feels a great deal of grief and guilt.
   d. High-school students across the country are drinking and driving more.

3. Which sentence best expresses the main idea of paragraphs 56–61?
   a. Tyson Baxter went to a football game.
   b. Following the accident, many students at William Tennent High joined the school's Students Against Driving Drunk chapter.
   c. There were various reactions when Tyson Baxter returned to school.
   d. Many students avoided Tyson Baxter when he returned to school.

Key Supporting Details

4. Which of the following was *not* a consequence of the accident?
   a. Students pledged not to drink during senior week at Wildwood, New Jersey.
   b. A senator held a series of public forums to think up ways to fight underage drinking.
   c. Many William Tennent students joined a Students Against Driving Drunk chapter.
   d. The parents of the boys who died began to meet every month.

5. ___F___ TRUE OR FALSE? Of all the teens in the car, Baxter had the highest blood-alcohol level.

6. The task of identifying the bodies was made more difficult because
   a. the boys' friends were sobbing and screaming.
   b. the bodies were badly disfigured.
   c. the boys were carrying fake identification.
   d. of all of the above.

Inferences

7. From the comments made at court by the parents of the victims, we can infer that the parents
   a. did not blame their own sons for their underage drinking.
   b. believed Baxter had gotten false identification for their sons.
   c. felt all of the victims that survived should be punished.
   d. felt all of the above.

8. We can infer from the statements made by seniors in paragraphs 67–71 that
   a. many students at Baxter's high school had not heard of his accident.
   b. graduation parties will be strictly chaperoned.
   c. some students do not take seriously the dangers of alcohol abuse.
   d. the drinking age is lower in Wildwood than in other places.

9. We can assume that after being released from Abraxas, Tyson Baxter will
   a. never drive a car again.
   b. visit the graves of the four boys killed in the accident.
   c. become a role model in the fight against drunk driving.
   d. pretend that the accident never happened.

The Writer's Craft

10. The authors begin and end their article with
    a. remarks by the author about the dangers of drunken driving.
    b. quotations from Tyson Baxter.
    c. quotations from the police who were first on the scene of the accident.
    d. quotations from parents of the boys who died.

DISCUSSION QUESTIONS

1. The authors write in paragraph 14: "'I thought I was in control,' Baxter said. 'I wasn't driving like a nut; I was just . . . driving.'" What does this tell us about the effects of alcohol on drivers?

2. To what extent do you think Tyson Baxter was responsible for the accident? Do you feel his passengers also were at fault in any way? If so, to what extent were they also responsible? Is there anyone else that you think is partly to blame for the accident?

3. What do you think would be an appropriate punishment for Tyson Baxter? If you were the judge in his case, what sentence would you give him? Why?

4. Why do you think that, even after knowing what had happened to Tyson Baxter and his friends, some of his classmates would brag about their plans to "drink very heavily" during senior week? What, if anything, do you think could change those students' attitudes about drinking?

PARAGRAPH ASSIGNMENTS

1. While drunk drivers can be any age, a large percentage of them are young. Write a paragraph explaining what you think would be a truly effective way of making young people understand the horrors of drunk driving. Keep in mind that the young are being cautioned all the time and that some of the warnings are so familiar that they probably have little impact. What approach would be so unusual, dramatic, or unexpected that it might really get young people's attention? Start your paragraph with a topic sentence such as the following: "Here is a way to truly convince the young of the horrors of drunk driving." Then, in the rest of your paragraph, develop your suggestion in great detail.

2. Tyson Baxter's friends might still be alive if he had not been drunk when he drove. But there is another way their deaths could have been avoided—they could have refused to get into his car. Such a refusal would not have been easy; after all, nobody likes to embarrass, anger, or offend a person who has offered him or her a ride. To help your readers prepare for such an occasion, write a paragraph in which you suggest one or more ways to turn down a ride with a driver who may be drunk.

ESSAY ASSIGNMENTS

1. People have different views about how severely Tyson Baxter should be punished. Some believe that the drunk boys in his car share the blame for what happened. Others say that by offering to drive, Baxter assumed total responsibility for the accident. Write an essay about what you think would be an appropriate punishment for Tyson Baxter, and why. Your thesis statement should state the chosen punishment—for example:

   • The most appropriate punishment for Tyson Baxter would be life imprisonment.

   • For several reasons, Tyson Baxter should have received a one-year sentence to a minimum-security prison.

   Your supporting paragraphs should develop the various reasons why that punishment is appropriate.

2. Drinking and driving is one of the more tragic, unwise activities that young people get involved in. What are some other dangerous, unwise, or silly activities or behaviors that teenagers (and/or adults) often get caught up in? Write an essay describing three of these activities and people's involvement in them. Your essay may be serious or light-hearted. In either case, provide lots of specific examples of each behavior and how the people involved are affected by it.

39

Living the Madison Avenue Lie

Joyce Garity

Preview

Unplanned pregnancies, lost futures, AIDS and other sexually-transmitted diseases, and a shattered sense of self—these are only a few of the results when teens buy into the sexual lie made popular by the media. But when young people grow up bombarded by seductive images, what are the chances that they will resist? Social worker Joyce Garity tells the story of one teenager and her attempts to live out the lie that sex is as problem-free as a cover girl's complexion.

Words to Watch

suffice it (1): it is enough
leering (3): looking in a manner suggesting sexual desire
waif-thin (3): thin as a neglected child
abandon (6): complete surrender; giving up any controls on behavior
pedestrian (6): ordinary
irony (7): inconsistency between what is expected and what actually happens
Shangri-la (7): an imaginary paradise
cynical (8): full of contempt
double talk (8): purposely unclear language
snickers (8): says smugly
innuendo (8): suggestion

simulated (9): pretended
copulation (9): intercourse

A few years ago, a young girl lived with me, my husband, and our 1
children for several months. The circumstances of Elaine's coming to us
don't matter here; suffice it° to say that she was troubled and nearly alone
in the world. She was also pregnant—hugely, clumsily pregnant with her
second child. Elaine was 17. Her pregnancy, she said, was an accident;
she also said she wasn't sure who had fathered her child. There had been
several sex partners and no contraception. Yet, she repeated blandly,
gazing at me with clear blue eyes, the pregnancy was an accident, and one
she would certainly never repeat.

Eventually I asked Elaine, after we had grown to know each other well 2
enough for such conversations, why neither she nor her lovers had used
birth control. She blushed—this porcelain-skinned girl with one child in
foster care and another swelling the bib of her fashionably faded overalls—
stammered, and blushed some more. Birth control, she finally got out, was
"embarrassing." It wasn't "romantic." You couldn't be really passionate, she
explained, and worry about birth control at the same time.

I haven't seen Elaine for quite a long time. I think about her often, 3
though. I think of her as I page through teen fashion magazines in the
salon where I have my hair cut. Although mainstream and relatively
wholesome, these magazines trumpet sexuality page after leering° page.
On the inside front cover, an advertisement for Guess jeans features junior
fashion models in snug denim dresses, their legs bared to just below the
crotch. An advertisement for Liz Claiborne fragrances shows a barely
clad young couple sprawled on a bed, him painting her toenails. An
advertisement for Obsession cologne displays a waif-thin° girl draped
stomach-down across a couch, naked, her startled expression suggesting
helplessness in the face of an unseen yet approaching threat.

I think of Elaine because I know she would love these ads. "They're 4
so beautiful," she would croon, and of course they are. The faces and
bodies they show are lovely. The lighting is superb. The hair and makeup
are faultless. In the Claiborne ad, the laughing girl whose toenails are
being painted by her handsome lover is obviously having the time of her
life. She stretches luxuriously on a bed heaped with clean white linen and
fluffy pillows. Beyond the sheer blowing curtains of her room, we can
glimpse a graceful wrought-iron balcony. Looking at the ad, Elaine could
only want to be her. Any girl would want to be her. Heck, *I* want to be her.

But my momentary desire to move into the Claiborne picture, to trade 5
lives with the exquisite young creature pictured there, is just that—
momentary. I've lived long enough to know that what I see is a marketing

invention. A moment after the photo session was over, the beautiful room was dismantled, and the models moved on to their next job. Later, the technicians took over the task of doctoring the photograph until it reached full-blown fantasy proportions.

Not so Elaine. After months of living together and countless hours of watching her yearn after magazine images, soap-opera heroines, and rock goddesses, I have a pretty good idea of why she looks at ads like Claiborne's. She sees the way life—her life—is supposed to be. She sees a world characterized by sexual spontaneity, playfulness, and abandon°. She sees people who don't worry about such unsexy details as birth control. Nor, apparently, do they spend much time thinking about such pedestrian° topics as commitment or whether they should act on their sexual impulses. Their clean sunlit rooms are never invaded by the fear of AIDS, of unwanted pregnancy, of shattered lives. For all her apparent lack of defense, the girl on the couch in the Obsession ad will surely never experience the brutality of rape.

Years of exposure to this media-invented, sex-saturated universe have done their work on Elaine. She is, I'm sure, completely unaware of the irony° in her situation: She melts over images from a sexual Shangri-la°, never realizing that her attempts to mirror those images left her pregnant, abandoned, living in the spare bedroom of a stranger's house, relying on charity for rides to the welfare office and supervised visits with her toddler daughter.

Of course, Elaine is not the first to be suckered by the cynical° practice of using sex to sell underwear, rock groups, or sneakers. Using sex as a sales tool is hardly new. At the beginning of this century, British actress Lily Langtry shocked her contemporaries by posing, clothed somewhat scantily, with a bar of Pear's soap. The advertisers have always known that the masses are susceptible to the notion that a particular product will make them more sexually attractive. In the past, however, ads used euphemisms, claiming that certain products would make people "more lovable" or "more popular." What is a recent development is the abandonment of any such polite double talk°. Advertising today leaves no question about what is being sold along with the roasted peanuts or artificial sweetener. "Actually, size does matter," snickers° an innuendo°-filled ad for Tequiza beer. Pop sensation Christina Aguilera introduces a fragrance titled "Fetish." An ad for a Ralph Lauren cologne shows a fully-clothed man embracing an apparently naked woman. A billboard for Levi's shows two jeans-clad young men on the beach, hoisting a girl in the air. The boys' perfect, tan bodies are matched by hers, although we see a lot more of hers: bare midriff, short shorts, cleavage. She caresses their hair; they stroke her legs. A jolly fantasy where sex exists without consequences.

But this fantasy is a lie—one which preys on young people. Studies   9
show that by the age of 20, 75 percent of Americans have lost their
virginity. In many high schools—and an increasing number of junior
highs—virginity is regarded as an embarrassing vestige of childhood, to
be disposed of as quickly as possible. Young people are immersed from
their earliest days in a culture that parades sexuality at every turn and
makes heroes of the advocates of sexual excess. Girls, from toddlerhood
on up, shop in stores packed with clothing once thought suitable only for
streetwalkers—lace leggings, crop tops, and wedge-heeled boots.
Supermarket checkout lanes are lined with magazines whose covers
feature topics like "Ten Things Your Man Really Wants In Bed" and
"Your Must-Have Fashion and Sex Horoscope." Parents drop their
children off at concerts featuring simulated° on-stage masturbation or
pretended acts of copulation°. Young boys idolize sports stars like the late
Wilt Chamberlain, who claims to have bedded 20,000 women. And when
the "Spur Posse," eight California high-school athletes, were charged
with systematically raping girls as young as 10 as part of a "scoring"
ritual, the beefy young jocks were rewarded with a publicity tour of talk
shows, while one father boasted to reporters about his son's "manhood."

In a late, lame attempt to counterbalance this sexual overload, most   10
schools offer sex education as part of their curriculums. In 2000, 35 states
required schools to provide information about HIV/AIDS and other
sexually-transmitted diseases, and 19 states required more general sex-ed
courses. But sex-ed classes are heavy on the mechanics of fertilization and
birth control—sperm, eggs, and condoms—and light on any discussion of
sexuality as only one part of a well-balanced life. There is passing reference
to abstinence as a method of contraception, but little discussion of
abstinence as an emotionally or spiritually satisfying option. Promiscuity is
discussed for its role in spreading sexually transmitted diseases. But the
concept of rejecting casual sex in favor of reserving sex for an emotionally
intimate, exclusive, trusting relationship—much less any mention of
waiting until marriage—is foreign to most public-school settings. "Love
and stuff like that really wasn't discussed" is the way one Spur Posse
member remembers his high-school sex-education class.

Surely teenagers need the factual information provided by sex-   11
education courses. But where is "love and stuff like that" talked about?
Where can they turn for a more balanced view of sexuality? Who is telling
young people like Elaine, my former houseguest, that sex is not an adequate
basis for a healthy, respectful relationship? Along with warnings to keep
condoms on hand, is anyone teaching kids that they have a right to be
valued for something other than their sexuality? Madison Avenue,
Hollywood, and the TV, music, and fashion industries won't tell them that.
Who will?

No one has told Elaine—at least, not in a way she comprehends. I 12
haven't seen her for a long time, but I hear of her occasionally. The baby
boy she bore while living in my house is in a foster home, a few miles
from his older half-sister, who is also in foster care. Elaine herself is
working in a local convenience store—and she is pregnant again. This
time, I understand, she is carrying twins.

FIRST IMPRESSIONS

Freewrite for ten minutes on one of the following.

1. Did you enjoy reading this selection? Why or why not?

2. Do you agree that today's media overemphasize sex? If so, what
   effects do you think this emphasis has on young people?

3. Have you ever taken a sex-education course? What did the course
   teach you? Do you think it taught what young people really need to
   know? Explain.

VOCABULARY CHECK

A. Circle the letter of the word or phrase that best completes each of the
following four items.

1. In the sentences below, the word *scantily* means
   a. warmly.
   b. shabbily.
   c. fashionably.
   (d.) inadequately.

   > "Using sex as a sales tool is hardly new. At the beginning of this
   > century, British actress Lily Langtry shocked her contemporaries
   > by posing, clothed somewhat scantily, with a bar of Pear's soap."
   > (Paragraph 8)

2. In the sentences below, the word *euphemisms* means
    a. harshly critical terms.
    (b.) indirect, vague terms.
    c. vulgar, crude terms.
    d. direct, honest terms.

    > "The advertisers have always known that the masses are susceptible
    > to the notion that a particular product will make them more sexually
    > attractive. In the past, however, ads used euphemisms, claiming that
    > certain products would make people 'more lovable' or 'more
    > popular.'" (Paragraph 8)

3. In the sentence below, the word *vestige* means
    a. mistake.
    b. acceptance.
    c. prize.
    (d.) leftover.

    > "In many high schools—and an increasing number of junior highs—
    > virginity is regarded as an embarrassing vestige of childhood, to be
    > disposed of as quickly as possible." (Paragraph 9)

4. In the sentences below, the word *promiscuity* means
    a. having only one sexual partner.
    (b.) lacking standards in selection of sexual partners.
    c. refraining from sexual activity.
    d. using contraception.

    > "Promiscuity is discussed for its role in spreading sexually
    > transmitted diseases. But the concept of rejecting casual sex in
    > favor of reserving sex for an emotionally intimate, exclusive,
    > trusting relationship . . . is foreign to most public-school settings."
    > (Paragraph 10)

B. Circle the letter of the answer that best completes each of the following
    four items. Each item uses a word (or form of a word) from "Words to
    Watch."

    5. "Jeff is always *leering* at me," Janine remarked. "He looks at me as if
        he
        a. was scared to death of me."
        b. really can't stand me."
        (c.) was hungry and I was the last pork chop on the plate."

6. Donna *abandoned* herself to the double-fudge chocolate layer cake, saying
    a. "I'll diet tomorrow—give me a fork and a really big plate."
    b. "I don't care for chocolate."
    c. "Give me just the tiniest slice possible, please."

7. The movie star was surprisingly *pedestrian* in real life; he
    a. never went anywhere without a bodyguard, personal secretary, and stylist.
    b. did his own laundry and was listed in the phone book.
    c. lived in an enormous house modeled after an 18th-century Italian castle.

8. Uncle Marco looks like a big, jolly Santa Claus. The *irony* is that
    a. he is nasty, selfish, and bad-tempered.
    b. he is exactly that: jolly, laughing, and good-natured.
    c. his beard has been white since he was a young man.

READING CHECK

Central Point and Main Ideas

1. Which sentence best expresses the central point of the entire selection?
    a. School sex-education classes fail to teach teens what they need to know about sex.
    b. Elaine, the author's houseguest, was irresponsible to have so many unplanned pregnancies.
    c. Today, magazine advertising messages are more direct than they used to be.
    d. The media are harmfully convincing young people that life and happiness are all about sex.

2. Which sentence best expresses the main idea of paragraph 5?
    a. The people in the Claiborne pictures were just models.
    b. A minute after the photograph was taken, the beautiful room was taken apart.
    c. The author realizes that the photograph was fantasy, not reality.
    d. The author envies the beautiful woman in the photograph.

3. Which sentence best expresses the main idea of paragraph 8?
    a. When sex was used to sell products in the past, it was done in a fairly subtle way.
    (b.) Although sex has long been used to sell products, today's advertising is more obviously sexual than ever before.
    c. Using sex in advertisements works better for some products than others.
    d. Advertisements for everything from soap to cologne to jeans somehow use sex as a selling tool.

Key Supporting Details

4. When she was asked about her unborn baby's father, Elaine said that she
    a. did not want to talk about him.
    (b.) was not sure who he was.
    c. was convinced he was going to marry her.
    d. thought he looked like a movie star.

5. Elaine had not used birth control because
    a. it was too expensive.
    b. her parents forbade her to get it.
    c. she wanted to become pregnant.
    (d.) she thought it was embarrassing.

6. According to Garity, what percentage of Americans have lost their virginity by the age of 20?
    a. 15 percent
    b. 30 percent
    (c.) 75 percent
    d. 90 percent

7. __*F*__ TRUE OR FALSE? The father of one of the members of the California "Spur Posse" was deeply embarrassed by his son's behavior.

Inferences

8. The author implies that
    a. Elaine was a relative of hers.
    b. she often opens her home to unwed teenage mothers like Elaine.
    (c.) trying to copy a glamorous sexual lifestyle has left Elaine in a very unglamorous position.
    d. she believes Elaine's experience is highly unusual.

9. The author implies that sex-education courses
   a. are totally ineffective.
   b. actually make young people more likely to become sexually active.
   c. should be required in every American school.
   d. do not address the most important aspects of human sexuality.

The Writer's Craft

10. In order to prove her case that the media is filled with sexual images, the author relies primarily upon
    a. examples from advertisements.
    b. testimony from experts.
    c. statistics.
    d. quoted comments from advertising executives.

DISCUSSION QUESTIONS

1. Do you feel that your attitudes towards sex and intimacy have been influenced by television, the movies, ads, and commercials? Explain.

2. Did you ever attend a sex-education class? What did it teach? What *didn't* it teach? What changes would you have made to improve the course? If you didn't attend such a class, do you think you missed something important? Explain.

3. In arguing against the emphasis on sexuality in our culture, Garity focuses on potential dangers to young women. How do you think our highly sexualized culture affects young men? Are they also at risk? Explain.

4. As Garity shows, the media and other influential parts of our culture often glamorize casual sex and sexual excess. Is there anything that parents can do to counteract that influence on their children? What could other authority figures or organizations do to help young people develop a healthier, more balanced view of sexuality?

PARAGRAPH ASSIGNMENTS

1. Assume that your community is debating whether to offer a sex-education program to middle-school children. Along with several other residents, you have been asked to explain why you think such a program should or should not be offered. Write a paragraph stating your position and several reasons for it. Use a topic sentence such as "A sex-education program should (*or* should not) be offered at our middle school for several reasons." Where possible, illustrate each reason with concrete, persuasive examples from your own and other people's experiences.

2. As Garity shows, children today are bombarded with images that affect their views of their own sexuality. What is another troubling message that you think young people often receive from advertising, movies, TV, or other forms of mass media? Write a paragraph explaining what that message is and what its negative effects can be. Provide several examples of how that message is delivered.

ESSAY ASSIGNMENTS

1. Write an essay developing Garity's point that advertisements contribute to careless, irresponsible sex. Begin by finding two or three magazine ads that you feel contain subtle—or not so subtle—messages about sex. In your essay, describe the ads and interpret their sexual messages. Keep the ads nearby as you write so that you can describe them with the same sort of vivid detail as Garity does. Your thesis statement might be similar to one of the following:

   - Ads such as the attached, with their strong sexual content, should not be printed in magazines read by today's young people.

   - Both the pictures and the text of the attached ads present harmful sexual images.

2. In order to put an individual, human face on the problem she is discussing, Garity focuses much of her essay on Elaine. Choose a specific person—someone you are actually acquainted with—whose experience illustrates a problem that concerns you. You might select, for example, a classmate who is failing in school, a friend who is involved in a gang, an abused woman, a man with an alcohol problem, or a drug-abusing teenager. Write an essay about this person and how his or her experience illustrates a larger social problem. As Garity does, provide plenty of specific details about the person, making clear how this problem has influenced his or her life.

40

Staying Power
Jennifer Lin

Preview

A gunshot rings out; sirens wail and a crowd gathers. Neighbors watch sadly as a woman from a faraway country cradles her dying husband. It's another playing out of an all-too-familiar tragedy in the city. The story could have ended there, with nothing but anger and sorrow to show for it. Instead, a community has come together, determined that this time, caring and common humanity will triumph over emptiness and despair.

Words to Watch

twinge (6): sudden, sharp pain
redemption (22): salvation
relentless (28): showing no sign of stopping
numbed (28): made unable to feel anything
closed ranks (28): came together as a tightly unified group
loitering (30): remaining in an area for no obvious reason
barricaded (30): protected with a barrier
revel (30): take pleasure in
bemoaned (31): express grief over (something)
prim (32): neat and tidy
bustled (32): was busily alive
prospered (42): succeeded financially
chockablock (47): very full
oscillating (47): moving back and forth

paraphernalia (54): accessories
feisty (72): energetic and determined
gauge (75): measure
resolve (75): determination
compost (77): fertilizer
oasis (78): a pleasant, green place in the middle of a desert-like area
pergola (80): a decorative shelter
salvaged (80): saved from destruction and put to use
extravaganza (87): a lavish, spectacular project
saturated (87): soaked
mementos (91): things intended as reminders

To her neighbors, she's Miss Moon, the Korean lady who runs the little   1
grocery store on 52nd Street near Fairmount Park. Her real name is Yoon
Suk Lee. The Moons were the couple who ran the store three years ago.

Mrs. Lee doesn't mind the wrong name. The fact is, she only knows   2
her friends from the neighborhood by one name. In a black marbled
notebook by the cash register, she has jotted some of their numbers in
pen. There's Stanley, Wanda, Monica, Graham, Coffee.

Stanley—James Stanley, 53, who has an auto-body shop a block   3
away—ducks into her West Parkside store every day without fail.

"Everything OK, Miss Moon?" he asks. He's a big man from   4
Georgia—6 feet, 4 inches big—and when he fixes his gaze on the tiny
woman behind the bulletproof glass, he expects an honest answer.

And on bad days, sad days, when a customer may notice tears, word   5
will get out. Stanley will tell Wanda, who will hurry to the store and use
the wordless language of women—a pat, a look, a hug—to tell her,
"We're here."

Her neighbors have helped her get through the last few months. They   6
understand her sorrow, struggle with their own rage, and feel a twinge° of
shame about what happened.

For it was someone from the neighborhood, police say, who killed her   7
husband.

The tip of the pistol, cold and hard, was pressed to the middle of her   8
forehead. She cannot forget how it felt that November evening.

Moon, where's the money bag?   9

Yoon Suk Lee was flat on her back, on the floor by the register. The   10
robber, one of two, gripped her neck in his gloved hand. She couldn't see
his face. A black-and-red bandana covered it. But that voice . . .

Moon, where's the money bag?   11

She knew that voice. She heard it every day.   12

Moon, where's the money bag?   13

By the grill and deli case in back, the second robber aimed his gun at 14
her husband and another worker. But her husband darted around the
counter, picked up a big can of ketchup, and threw it.

The robber with his hand on her throat spun around. Mrs. Lee heard a 15
pop. Five steps away, her husband, the father of her two children, fell to
the floor.

Wanda Lytle, a neighbor and friend, heard the gunshot, then sirens. 16
She ran outside. In front of the store, a crowd vibrated with the news of
the shooting.

Inside, she found the grocer's wife kneeling beside her husband. 17

"I'm looking at her and she's holding him, telling him over and over 18
to get up," Lytle remembers.

Three days later, police arrested two 17-year-olds. Donald Brown and 19
Christopher Walker were charged with murder as adults and held without
bail. Both have pleaded not guilty and are expected to be tried in the fall.

Brown grew up three blocks from the store. Walker lived with his 20
mother three doors away.

Neighbors thought they had seen the last of Mrs. Lee on that night of 21
November 4. The robbers stole $500 and left her husband, Duk Sang Lee,
50, bleeding to death in the aisle of his store. "I would've closed and not
come back," said Monica Jordan, a neighbor and friend.

But persuading the 48-year-old widow to stay has become a cause for 22
some of her neighbors. They see it somehow as part of West Parkside's
redemption°.

After the shooting, Lytle, who lives in the next block and visits the 23
store daily, told Mrs. Lee, "You're not leaving us. We need you."

And James Stanley made it his business to keep an eye on her. "That's 24
my daily mission—to console her," he said.

Their efforts are working. 25

"A lot of people worry about me," Mrs. Lee said. "That's why I stay 26
here."

In West Parkside, the murder has stoked anger about guns and drugs, 27
the twin horsemen ravaging the neighborhood. Talk to anyone there and
he or she can rattle off names of victims of revenge killings, drive-by
shootings, drug overdoses. None of the dead lived to see 30.

The relentless° violence has numbed° people. But when the Korean 28
grocer was gunned down in his store during the dinnertime rush,
neighbors closed ranks°.

"We need to grab back this neighborhood and grab back our children," 29
declared Lytle, who has lived within walking distance of the store for 37
of her 46 years. "His death was a turning point. It shook this place up."

West Parkside does not leave a good first impression. Too many 30
homes are rotting and empty. Porches sag from neglect. Knots of truants

spend suspicious time loitering° around pay phones. Old-timers who live in tidy rowhouses barricaded° with metal gates and deadbolts revel° in what West Parkside was—and lament what it has become.

"It's just falling apart," Geneva Murray bemoaned°. "And no matter 31 how much Crazy Glue you put on it, it's not sticking together."

Murray, 54, has lived in the same prim° rowhouse on Columbia 32 Avenue near 52nd since she was nine years old. Her parents were one of the first black couples to move into what was then a Jewish neighborhood. The Baptist church on the corner used to house a synagogue, and from Parkside to Lancaster Avenues, 52nd Street bustled°.

"Two hoagie shops, two cleaners, a meat market, a fruit market, a 33 hobby shop, a restaurant and a hardware store," Murray recalled. "All you had to do was walk out of the house to go to the store."

Today, all that's left is a bar—and Mrs. Lee's grocery. 34

Murray recited the store's history: Opened decades ago by black 35 merchants, who sold it to a Greek man, who turned it over to a Korean couple—the Moons—who sold it to the Lee family three years ago.

Without the store, neighbors would have to walk under the looming 36 Amtrak train trestle to Lancaster Avenue just to buy milk or a loaf of bread.

"There are no more black stores and white people, they've been long 37 gone," said an African American friend of Mrs. Lee's. "If she would go, you could go for blocks and blocks and not find a store here."

Yoon Suk Lee has worked in some kind of mom-and-pop store since 38 the day she arrived in Philadelphia as a newlywed from South Korea in 1980.

Her husband came from a grocery family. Of eight siblings, three had 39 stores in the city. An older brother introduced Mrs. Lee to her future husband in Seoul.

The couple became merchants for the reason so many new immigrants 40 run corner stores: It's a way to make a living without speaking much English. Their first business was a dry cleaners near Temple University. Next came a take-out seafood business in North Philadelphia, then a grocery store in Southwest Philadelphia.

"I like the grocery business," Mrs. Lee said in halting English. "At the 41 seafood restaurant, the hours were too long. We were open to midnight."

Asian merchants have prospered° in this mom-and-pop trade, but it is 42 a risky business. Almost every day in the city, the owner of a grocery store or deli is robbed, according to police statistics.

From 1988 to 1999, 100 Asians were murdered in Philadelphia—a 43 third of them during holdups in businesses such as grocery stores, chain stores, delis or take-out restaurants. Last year, three Asian merchants were slain: a Korean grocer in North Philadelphia, killed during a robbery; a

Chinese teenager, shot execution-style at his father's take-out restaurant in Tioga; and Duk Sang Lee.

Feeling vulnerable to crime, many Korean grocers are getting out of   44
the business; some are selling to newly arrived Dominican immigrants.

A few years ago, Yoon Suk Lee and her husband tried to get out. They   45
sold their store in Southwest Philadelphia to a Chinese merchant and
looked for a business like a dry cleaners in the suburbs, where they live.
When nothing turned up, Duk Sang Lee bought the West Parkside grocery
from his older sister, the original Miss Moon.

"We decided to go back to what we were used to," his widow said.   46

The store is just a sliver of floor space with chockablock° shelves.   47
Mrs. Lee sells necessities: diapers and cereal, shampoo and macaroni,
cake mixes and milk, dog food, cat food, baby food. She carries one of
just about everything: a deadbolt, a pair of jumper cables, an oscillating°
fan. It's all there, from hair extensions to sweatsocks.

Two Korean relatives and an African American neighbor work with   48
her, mostly handling take-out orders from the grill in back of the store.

From the start, the Lees got along with most customers. Neighbors   49
liked their polite way. Mr. Lee used common sense. If a kid stole
something, he told a parent instead of calling the cops every time.

Both of them were churchgoers, and on Monday morning, Mrs. Lee   50
would chat with some of the ladies about her church service, and they, in
return, would tell her about theirs.

Monica Jordan liked the way Mr. Lee teased her when her two-year-   51
old daughter whined for candy.

"She's hungry," he implored on the girl's behalf.   52

"No, she's greedy," Jordan joked in reply.   53

Not everything was sweetness and nice. Some customers complained   54
about prices. A few didn't like the fact that the store sold single cigars and
cigarettes and rolling papers—paraphernalia° for smoking dope. Mrs. Lee
told a neighbor that she was afraid to stop selling the items for fear of
harassment.

Kids could be rude. Adults could be rude. And some patrons were   55
rankled that outsiders who looked different, spoke differently, and didn't
even live in the neighborhood were making money off them.

Across Philadelphia, grocery stores are flash points for racial hostility.   56
Like Jewish merchants before them, Asian store owners are symbols of
the monied class in neighborhoods where there often is little money.

"You just got bad folks out there who feel you owe them something   57
just because you're rich," James Stanley said.

Jordan has given her own teenage son a lecture about the Korean   58
grocers. "I told him, 'Even if they're not your race, you don't be
disrespectful,' " she said. "They're humans like you."

The day after the murder, Stanley placed a bouquet on the doorstep of 59 the grocery store. Monica Jordan left a teddy bear holding a heart.

When Korean relatives came to clean the store, Wanda Lytle started to 60 pray on the sidewalk. Out front, someone placed a poster that read "Rest in Peace Moon," for neighbors to sign.

On the door, the grocer's family posted directions to the viewing at a 61 Korean church.

The church was miles away, in Northeast Philadelphia. Jordan 62 borrowed a neighbor's car. Stanley gave some of the women a lift. Others took the bus up Roosevelt Boulevard to Cottman Avenue. And on the evening of November 7, more than 40 neighbors showed up at the Sei Han Baptist Church.

They arrived early. Wanda Lytle remembered how Duk Sang Lee had 63 invited her so many times to come to church with him some Sunday, but she'd never taken him up on his offer. She thought of that as she bent into the casket to kiss his cheek.

Yoon Suk Lee stood in a receiving line of relatives, including the 64 couple's 11-year-old son and 19-year-old daughter. None of the neighbors knew the children. They rarely came to the store.

When Jordan approached the receiving line, Mrs. Lee saw her and 65 broke away. The Korean woman went straight towards the younger black woman and threw her arms around her neighbor.

"Why?" the widow sobbed. "Why?" 66

Mrs. Lee's neighbors believe they know why. 67

"There's nothing in this community for young people," Lytle said. 68 "There are no jobs here. Right now, the streets have our children."

And from Robert Kinnard, 47, a respiratory therapist who lives around 69 the corner from the store: "Young kids are told to do things to prove themselves. And this [holdup] is one of the things. It didn't make sense."

And Ella Francis, a 75-year-old retired art teacher: "This is one of our 70 lowest points. If you talk to kids on the streets, you don't hear anyone who says, 'I can make it. I can do it.'"

The old woman despairs. "They've resigned themselves almost to the 71 point of suicide. They don't care about life."

Francis is a feisty° activist who doesn't just live in West Parkside; she 72 loves it. She founded the Parkside Neighborhood Association in 1977 to save Fairmount Park green space from a parking lot for the Mann Music Center.

She traveled to Minneapolis to persuade a giant computer company to 73 invest in a technology center for Parkside. She helped to start a day-care center. She encouraged neighbors to enroll in computer training programs. She prodded City Hall to spend millions clearing sixty-five acres for industrial development.

But none of it has stopped the neighborhood's slide. People continue 74
to move out, according to the 2000 census. In the last ten years, the
population has dropped by 25 percent in the area bounded by Parkside
Avenue to the north, Lancaster Avenue to the south, Belmont Avenue to
the east, and Bryn Mawr Avenue to the west. One out of three residents
lives below the poverty line.

Although bleak, the statistics don't gauge° resolve°. "This community 75
doesn't have to be in the trouble that it's in," Kinnard said.

He wants to make his block a drug-free zone. At night, he patrols the 76
streets as part of a Town Watch. His wife is working with some of the
neighborhood women to keep children active this summer. They want to
organize arts and crafts camp, bus trips, block parties.

And Stanley is doing his best to keep everyone up to his elbows in 77
compost°. The auto repairman believes the soil can restore the soul. He
sees ugly and thinks impatiens, camellias, wisteria, sunflowers, daylilies
and black-eyed Susans.

He tore up an alleyway of packed dirt next to his house and auto body 78
shop on 52nd. He planted big, leafy plants with a tropical look—hostas,
ferns and umbrella-size "elephant ears." He laid stones for a winding path
in his narrow oasis°.

Then he looked across the street. He hired out-of-work neighbors and 79
bored children to turn an eyesore lot into a vest-pocket park, with
manmade hillocks and tufts of flowering shrubs.

Then he looked around the corner. He had his neighborhood crew 80
clear another lot fronting busy Parkside Avenue. He planted a vegetable
patch. He erected a makeshift pergola° of white pillars salvaged° from
abandoned homes. He took the side rails from an old crib and built an
archway. He recycled empty cans of paint thinner from his garage, glued
them end to end, painted them white, and added more columns.

"When I came out here, I was dealing with druggies and poor people," 81
Stanley explained. "I used them for gardening. They've grown to know
me and I respect them. This area has changed."

His motto: "Your home is what you make it." 82

Which goes a long way to explain why he doesn't want the grocer's 83
widow to flee Parkside.

It upsets many neighbors to know that two of their own have been 84
accused of murdering the Korean grocer. Many of the friends of the
Korean couple also know the families of the two teenage suspects.
Stanley is godfather to the younger brother of Donald Brown.

"Everyone knows everyone here, we're just that tight," Kinnard said. 85
"It's like someone in the family has violated you."

On a dreary spring day, a rainstorm howled through the city, forcing 86 the hooded kids in front of the grocery store to huddle closer.

Across the street, a truckload of soil that was delivered for Stanley's   87
latest extravaganza°—"I want an all-white flower garden"—looked like a
mound of black velvet, rich and saturated° with rain.

Mrs. Lee waited on customers from behind an inch-thick bulletproof   88
window. Her neighbors finally persuaded her to install the protective
glass. Wanda Lytle said Mr. Lee had resisted the idea, telling her, "If I
have to put up a glass shield, then I don't need to be here." But friends and
family told her to install protection for her own sake.

Mrs. Lee has thought about selling the store, but only because the work   89
is so hard, the hours so long. But she doesn't expect to be going anywhere
soon. She has college tuition to pay and a younger child to raise. Her
daughter is studying graphic arts in New York City, while her son goes to
a public school in Montgomery County, where the family lives.

She said if she ever did leave, the neighborhood wouldn't be the   90
reason. "I actually don't have fear anymore," Mrs. Lee said.

In the basement of the store, she has three big trash bags filled with   91
dried flowers and stuffed animals—mementos° that neighbors left on her
doorstep after the murder.

"My husband all the time joking," she said in her fractured way. "He   92
happy man."

In back, her cook grilled a hamburger patty and onions. With each   93
press of his spatula, grease hissed and sizzled, filling the store with warm,
oily wafts. The phone rang, and Monica Jordan called in her lunch order.
The front door opened, and Stanley stepped out of the rain.

Mrs. Lee had just learned that the gardens were his creations.   94

"Stanley, I didn't know that," she teased him. "Why didn't you tell me?"   95

"Oh," he said with a smile, "there's a lot of hidden beauty down here."   96

FIRST IMPRESSIONS

Freewrite for ten minutes on one of the following.

1. Did you enjoy reading this selection? Why or why not?

2. Why do you think the neighbors want Mrs. Lee to stay in the
   neighborhood? If you were Mrs. Lee, would you stay? Explain.

3. Are there people of various races and ethnic backgrounds living in your
   neighborhood? In general, how do the people from these different groups
   get along? If your neighborhood has mostly people of one racial or ethnic
   group, how welcome do you think people of other groups would be if
   they moved in?

VOCABULARY CHECK

A. Circle the letter of the word or phrase that best completes each of the following four items.

1. In the sentence below, the word *stoked* means
    a. taken away.
    b. risked.
    c. stirred up.
    d. lessened.

    "In West Parkside, the murder has stoked anger about guns and drugs. . . ." (Paragraph 27)

2. In the sentence below, the words *vulnerable to* mean
    a. comfortable with.
    b. unaffected by.
    c. likely to experience.
    d. understanding of.

    "Feeling vulnerable to crime, many Korean grocers are getting out of the business; some are selling to newly arrived Dominican immigrants." (Paragraph 44)

3. In the sentences below, the word *implored* means
    a. begged.
    b. shouted.
    c. criticized.
    d. remembered.

    "Monica Jordan liked the way Mr. Lee teased her when her two-year-old daughter whined for candy.
    'She's hungry,' he implored on the girl's behalf." (Paragraphs 51–52)

4. In the sentence below, the word *rankled* means
    a. pleased.
    b. surprised.
    c. annoyed.
    d. placed in order.

    "And some patrons were rankled that outsiders who looked different, spoke differently, and didn't even live in the neighborhood were making money off them." (Paragraph 55)

B. Circle the letter of the answer that best completes each of the following four items. Each item uses a word (or form of a word) from "Words to Watch."

5. Because the fire downtown was *relentless*, the firefighters
   (a.) called in additional fire companies to help them fight it.
   b. knew they would have the fire put out soon.
   c. notified police that the fire seemed to have been set on purpose.

6. My aunt *revels* in her memories of
   a. being extremely poor and hungry as a child.
   b. her unhappy first marriage.
   (c.) being voted "Teacher of the Year" by her students.

7. For the last half-hour, I've been listening to my brother *bemoan* the fact that
   a. the prettiest girl in his algebra class invited him to a dance.
   b. he'll be a starting player in this weekend's basketball game.
   (c.) his car has broken down and he can't afford to repair it.

8. Their housecleaning business has *prospered*, so Kevin and Terry have
   a. given the business up and are looking for other, better jobs.
   (b.) hired more help and given themselves raises.
   c. had to declare bankruptcy.

READING CHECK

Central Point and Main Ideas

1. Which sentence best expresses the central point of the entire selection?
   a. No matter what residents and authorities do, they cannot stop the rapid decline of many inner-city neighborhoods.
   (b.) The murder of a shopkeeper has brought residents of a troubled area together in an effort to rescue and renew their neighborhood.
   c. Although violence in West Parkside was nothing new, neighbors were shocked by the murder of a shopkeeper in their neighborhood.
   d. Conflict between members of different racial groups was inevitable in Philadelphia's West Parkside neighborhood.

2. Which sentence best expresses the main idea of paragraphs 30–34?
   a. West Parkside, with its neglected houses, does not make a good first impression.
   b. Old-timers in West Parkside live in tidy rowhouses.
   c. West Parkside is in poor condition now, but it was once pleasant and tidy.
   d. West Parkside was once a Jewish neighborhood.

3. Which sentence best expresses the main idea of paragraphs 75–81?
   a. There is hope for urban neighborhoods.
   b. Two of Mrs. Lee's neighbors are working to improve their West Parkside neighborhood.
   c. Robert Kinnard, a member of Town Watch, wants to make his block of West Parkside a drug-free zone.
   d. James Stanley has involved other members of the community in creating flower and vegetable gardens.

Key Supporting Details

4. The young men arrested for Duk Sang Lee's killing
   a. were strangers from out of state.
   b. had never been in the Lees' store before the killing.
   c. were James Stanley's sons.
   d. lived near the Lees' store.

5. If Mrs. Lee's store closed, neighbors would
   a. shop at the supermarket down the street.
   b. shop at one of the black-owned grocery stores nearby.
   c. have to walk for blocks to find a grocery store.
   d. shop at one of the other Korean-owned groceries in the neighborhood.

6. The bulletproof window in Mrs. Lee's store
   a. shattered when the gunmen shot her husband.
   b. was ordered by her husband, but arrived after his murder.
   c. is usually open, because Mrs. Lee doesn't like to use it.
   d. is something Mrs. Lee's friends convinced her to get after the murder.

Inferences

7. We can infer from the article that
   a. Mrs. Lee will never leave West Parkside.
   b. Mr. and Mrs. Lee planned to return to Korea some day.
   (c.) Mrs. Lee would have left West Parkside by now if not for her neighbors.
   d. Mrs. Lee's children will eventually run the West Parkside store.

8. We can conclude from the article that
   a. most people in West Parkside are prejudiced against Koreans.
   (b.) Mrs. Lee is better off financially than many people in West Parkside.
   c. Mr. and Mrs. Lee sometimes cheated their customers.
   d. the young men arrested for Mr. Lee's murder had worked in the store.

9. Which of the following statements can we infer that James Stanley, Wanda Lytle, and the rest of the neighbors might agree with?
   a. The people who killed Mr. Lee should be punished as severely as possible.
   b. The boys who are accused of killing Mr. Lee could not have done it.
   c. You can't really blame the people who killed Mr. Lee for what they did because they grew up under poor conditions.
   (d.) There is no excuse for murder, but we understand why kids growing up here feel hopeless about life.

The Writer's Craft

10. The author supports her statement that "Asian merchants have prospered in this mom-and-pop trade, but it is a risky business" (paragraph 42) with
    a. quotations from Asian merchants.
    b. an anecdote about Mr. Lee.
    (c.) police statistics.
    d. an excerpt from a newspaper story.

DISCUSSION QUESTIONS

1. Would you call this story primarily a sad one or a happy one? What is sad about it? What parts of it could be called happy?

2. This article mentions that many corner groceries are being run by Korean immigrants. Where you live, are certain businesses run mainly by people from one country? What are those businesses, and who runs them? What reasons can you think of that certain businesses might attract specific ethnic groups?

3. The murder of Mrs. Lee's husband was a crisis that pulled the surrounding community together. Have you seen a problem or crisis pull together people in your family or community who were not previously closely connected? What was the problem? Who responded to it, and how?

4. Unfortunately, severely depressed neighborhoods like West Parkside are common within American cities. What factors do you think go into destroying a once-healthy community? Who is to blame? What, if anything, can be done to undo the damage?

PARAGRAPH ASSIGNMENTS

1. What, to you, is a place of beauty near where you live? Is it a garden? A tree? A park? A particular building? A tub of flowers on an apartment balcony? Write a descriptive paragraph about that place, providing such rich details that your reader experiences the beauty of it as you do. It does not need to be a big, dramatic kind of beauty— sometimes the beauty that means most to us is small, unexpected, and hardly noticeable. Your topic sentence will alert your reader to what you are going to describe, as in the following examples:

   • Beside my grandmother's apartment steps is a beautiful patch of pinks and petunias.

   • A stained-glass window in my church is a beautiful sight.

2. James Stanley is a person who, when he sees a problem, does something about it. We can see this in both his relationship with Mrs. Lee and his efforts to beautify his community. Write a paragraph about a person you know who, like Stanley, has stepped forward to take responsibility for a problem. For example, perhaps a local merchant saw that young people needed recreational opportunities, so he or she sponsored a basketball team. Or perhaps a resident, concerned about making the community safe, organized a Town Watch program.

   In your paragraph, make clear just what the problem was, who it was that took action, and just what he or she did. Conclude by stating the results of this person's efforts.

ESSAY ASSIGNMENTS

1. Several residents of West Parkside suggest that young people in the neighborhood are growing up without hope of a better life and without belief in themselves. What factors do young people need in order to grow up feeling optimistic about life and their own abilities? Write an essay in which you name two or three such factors and explain why they are important to young people. Use a thesis statement similar to this one: "To grow up with a positive attitude, young people need _____, _____, and _____."

   Here are some factors you might consider including: good role models, a stable home, educational opportunities, and consistent discipline. In your essay, give specific examples of how each factor works in a young person's life, and explain what is lost when that factor is absent.

2. What are some problems that exist in your neighborhood? They could be like the severe ones that exist in West Parkside—drugs, crime, unemployment, poverty—or less alarming ones, such as the lack of certain facilities (for example, a library, shopping center, or places of recreation). Write an essay in which you explain two to three problems in detail and propose possible solutions to each of the problems. Conclude with what you think ordinary residents of your community could do to bring those solutions about.

Additional Writing Assignments

Note: Each of the following twenty assignments asks students to read two essays and then to write a paper based on both. The assignments are listed in the order in which the primary essay in each pair appears in the book.

1   The Scholarship Jacket

A *narrative* is simply a story told in the order in which the events occurred. A first-person narrative like "The Scholarship Jacket" (page 44) has special power, because the writer can tell not only what happened, but also how he or she felt about it. Write a first-person narrative about a memorable event in your life. As Marta Salinas does, use rich sensory details (how things looked, sounded, smelled, tasted, felt) as well as your own emotional responses to make the reader experience the event as you did. Before beginning your paper, read "Shame" (page 232), another example of a vividly detailed first-person narrative.

2   A Small Victory

As shown by the response to Steve Lopez's original column, "A Small Victory" (page 63) evoked strong emotions from the people who read it. Lopez had carefully chosen details to make his readers see Mrs. Knight as he did: a small, frail woman, elderly and dignified, being victimized by a large, faceless bureaucracy.

Write a description of a person who evokes a similarly strong emotional response from you. Your first task will be to state your central point, using a sentence that puts into sharp, tight focus just what the rest of your paper will explain. Your central point might be like one of these:

- My grandmother, although softspoken, is the strongest and most determined person I've ever known.

- The man who runs the convenience store in our neighborhood seems as if he carries a grudge against the whole world.

In your paper, provide plentiful details to show your reader just what you mean. As Lopez does, include bits of dialogue, so that your reader can hear your subject in his or her own words.

Before you write, be sure to read "All the Good Things" (page 203), paying special attention to the brief, but sharply drawn, description of Mark Eklund. Notice how the carefully chosen details make clear why Mark was so special to his teacher.

3 From Horror to Hope

Cultural expectations are the expectations others have of us because of our ethnic group, gender, religion, or socio-economic status. Cultural expectations often affect what we can or can't (or think we should or shouldn't) do. For example, in "From Horror to Hope" (page 85), Phany Sarann was discouraged from pursuing an education because, in her native culture, schooling was not considered important for a woman. How do you think cultural expectations have affected your life (positively or negatively)? Write a paper in which you explain one or more ways cultural expectations have affected you. For inspiration, read "The Professor Is a Dropout" (page 340), and look for ways that cultural expectations affected the author and her children.

4 Migrant Child to College Woman

In "Migrant Child to College Woman" (page 96), the reader learns of the process Maria Cardenas went through in her transformation from a frightened, barely literate girl to a courageous, successful adult. The essay "Rowing the Bus" (page 242) describes the steps involved in another person's transformation: in this case, from a victim of bullying to a defender of the bullied. Write a paper in which you describe a significant, gradual change that you have (or someone you know has) gone through. Use transitional words like "first," "next," "after that," and "finally" to emphasize that this change was a process, rather than something that happened in one single step.

5   He Was First

As "He Was First" (page 110) demonstrates, many baseball fans were shocked at first to see black and white athletes playing on the same field. But just a few years later, the children of those fans thought nothing of seeing African American athletes participating in professional sports. This is just one example of how parents' and children's attitudes towards racial issues can differ. How do your racial attitudes differ from the attitudes held by your parents? Are you, for example, more likely to have friends of different races than they are? Do you feel differently about interracial dating and marriage than they do? Write a paper that states how you and your parents differ in your attitudes about race, and give examples illustrating those differences.

(Alternatively, you could write about how you and your parents differ on another important social issue, such as capital punishment, gun control, abortion, women's rights, or gay rights.)

Read the essay "Staying Power" (page 447) for some insight into how people of different races can learn to value one another's common humanity.

6   Responsibility

In his essay (page 151), author Scott Peck provides what is in a sense a lengthy definition of the word "responsibility." He describes what responsibility is, gives vivid examples of irresponsible behavior, and suggests the negative consequences of living without a sense of personal responsibility. Write a paper in which you define another desirable human trait, such as courage, kindness, maturity, wisdom, patience, compassion, perseverance, or tolerance. As Peck does, give your reader clear examples of how people behave when they possess that trait, as well as how they behave when they do not. Before writing, read "Anxiety: Challenge by Another Name" (page 159) to see how another writer defines a trait we all sometimes possess.

7   The Bystander Effect

In "The Bystander Effect" (page 169), the author relates several well-publicized incidents to make her point that bystanders are reluctant to get involved, even when someone's life seems to be in danger.

Look through recent editions of your local newspaper to find two or three stories in which people act in surprising ways. (Those surprising actions may be either positive or negative.) Write a paper in which you explain what happened in each incident and why you found the people's actions surprising. Then provide your best theory about why the people involved acted as they did. Your theories will be based not only on the facts in the newspaper story, but also on your own observations of human nature.

In his essay "Responsibility" (page 151), psychiatrist Scott Peck illustrates his belief that rather than take responsibility for their own lives, people often act in self-destructive ways. His story may give you some evidence for your theories.

8   All the Good Things

Write a paper in which you expand on what Sister Helen's students did in "All the Good Things" (page 203). Choose a person whom you like and admire, and select three "good things" about that person. In your paper, state what those "good things" are, and describe in detail how you have seen those things demonstrated in the person's life. Whenever possible, give examples of those "good things" in action. Before writing, read Alex Haley's essay, "Thank You" (page 133) to see how one writer made his readers understand why he valued certain people highly.

9   The Yellow Ribbon

In "The Yellow Ribbon" (page 212), Vingo has taken responsibility for what he has done wrong, then asked his wife for forgiveness and acceptance. As the story touchingly shows, she gladly gives that forgiveness.

When have you needed forgiveness? Or when have you been asked for forgiveness by someone who has hurt you? Write a paper describing what happened. Begin by explaining whatever you (or the other person) did that was wrong. Then describe how you thought and felt as you considered what had happened. As Hamill does, keep the reader in suspense as to whether you were forgiven (or gave your forgiveness) until the end.

For another story about someone who was working to regain the trust of people he had hurt, read "Joe Davis: A Cool Man" (page 74).

10 What Do Children Owe Their Parents?

After reading "What Do Children Owe Their Parents?" (page 221), write a paper in which you suggest at least three guidelines, based on your own experience and observations, for healthy parent-child relationships. Include specific examples of common parent-child conflict, and show how your guidelines would help in such circumstances. Reading "Seven Ways to Keep the Peace at Home" (page 263), before you begin to write will get your ideas flowing.

11 Shame

In "Shame" (page 232), Dick Gregory relates an incident in which an insensitive teacher humiliated him. Almost everyone has a teacher who stands out in his or her memory, because the teacher was either exceptionally good or remarkably bad. Drawing upon your own experience as a student, write a paper based on one of the following two central points:

- "Everyone should be lucky enough to have a teacher like _____."
- "No one should be forced to learn from a teacher like _____."

In your paper, provide at least three reasons why this teacher was the best or worst you ever had. Support each of those reasons with examples that vividly illustrate the points you are making.

For an example of an experienced, effective teacher, read "In Praise of the F Word" (page 332), paying special attention to the character of Mrs. Stifter.

12 Flour Children

"Flour Children" (page 323) describes one school's unusual program designed to encourage high school students to postpone parenthood. Pretend that you have been asked to come up with several additional ideas aimed at reducing teen pregnancy in local schools. Those ideas could include classroom programs, guest speakers, field trips, special projects, or anything else you think might be effective. Write a paper in which you fully describe two or three of those suggestions. Reading "Living the Madison Avenue Lie" (page 437), which gives you a glimpse into the reality of one teenage mother's experience, may give you some ideas.

13 In Praise of the F Word

In her essay "In Praise of the F Word" (page 332), Mary Sherry writes of people who have a "a healthy fear of failure." Write a paper in which you explore the idea of "a healthy fear of failure." Consider such questions as these: In what way is that fear healthy? How do people acquire it? How does it affect their actions? What happens if someone does not acquire such a fear? Before writing, read Andy Rooney's essay, "Tickets to Nowhere" (page 369), to see an example of someone who apparently lacks a "healthy fear of failure."

14 The Professor Is a Dropout

A *catalyst* is defined as "an agent that provokes or speeds significant change or action." Although Lupe, in "The Professor Is a Dropout" (page 340), was terrified of going back to school, her concern for her children acted as the catalyst that pushed her into action. Write a paper about a catalyst that has pushed you into making some positive change in your life. That catalyst might have been a flash of insight, a remark you heard, something you read, an incident in which you participated or which you learned about second-hand, or any other force that provoked you to action. Explain in detail what the catalyst was and exactly what change you made because of it. You will find an example of a catalyst in "From Nonreading to Reading" (page 300), in which the author discusses an experience that motivated him to make a change in his life.

15 Learning Survival Skills

"Learning Survival Skills" (page 353), shares a number of secrets which are valuable for succeeding in school. Write a paper in which you provide secrets of success in another field. You might consider offering tips on how to succeed in the workplace (in general, or within a specific occupation), on an athletic team, in a romantic relationship, in a friendship, or as a neighbor. To see another example of an essay based on a series of suggestions, read "Seven Ways to Keep the Peace at Home" (page 263).

16 An Electronic Fog Has Settled Over America

"Electronic Fog" (page 377) argues that television is producing a generation of people who have forgotten how to think. What is another negative effect you think TV has on young people? (Or instead of TV, you may choose another powerful influence on today's young people, such as advertising, the Internet, video games, movies, music videos, or popular music.) Write a paper in which you state your concern. Your central point might be something like this: "I am concerned that the Internet influences young people to be isolated and self-centered." The rest of your paper will state your reasons and present arguments in support of those reasons. For another essay that presents a writer's arguments against an aspect of popular culture, read "Living the Madison Avenue Lie" (page 437).

17 The Quiet Hour

Robert Mayer suggests in "The Quiet Hour" (page 386) that an "ideal family evening" can be many things, but that watching TV isn't one of them. Write a paper in which you defend one of the following statements:

- I agree with Robert Mayer. An ideal family evening involves turning off the TV.
- I think that Robert Mayer is wrong. Watching TV together is an ideal family evening.

In your paper, state your reasons for agreeing or disagreeing with Mayer, and provide details to back up your reasons. Before writing, read "An Electronic Fog Has Settled Over America" (page 377) to learn about one family's differing opinions about the role of TV in their lives.

18 Rudeness at the Movies

In "Rudeness at the Movies" (page 395), Bill Wine protests the "epidemic of rudeness" he says is sweeping movie audiences. What is another "epidemic" you would like to put a stop to? Perhaps it involves clothing that's in bad taste, or TV "comedies" that aren't funny, or entertainers that lack talent. Write a paper in which you, like Wine, humorously critique your epidemic of choice. Feel free to use exaggerated examples, as Wine does, to drive your point home.

Pete Hamill's "An Electronic Fog Has Settled Over America" (page 377) will provide you with a serious critique of what the author could have called "an epidemic of stupidity."

19 My Daughter Smokes

In "My Daughter Smokes" (page 404), Alice Walker describes influences that may cause people to adopt one unhealthy habit: smoking. Write a paper about an unhealthy habit that you find hard to resist. It might, for example, be smoking or drinking, overeating, choosing the wrong foods, or not exercising. In your paper, state what the tempting habit is, several influences that make you want to indulge in that habit, and what you think the consequences of that habit have been for you. The essay "Here's to Your Health" (page 413), which discusses media messages that encourage people to begin the unhealthy habit of drinking, may provide some useful insights.

20 A Drunken Ride, a Tragic Aftermath

As "A Drunken Ride, A Tragic Aftermath" (page 422) shows, a single event can have widespread consequences. In this case, an accident has had far-reaching effects on individuals, families, a school, and a town. Write a paper in which you show the connection between a single event—a cause—and its effects. That cause and its effects may have affected just you or a larger community. Before writing, read "A Change of Attitude" (page 288), which describes a specific incident in the author's life and its life-altering effects, to see another example of a cause-effect essay.

Reading Performance Chart

Note: To obtain your score, give yourself 5 points for each correct Vocabulary Check item and 6 points for each correct Reading Check item.

Title of Selection	Vocabulary Check (40%)	Reading Check (60%)	TOTAL SCORE
1. Bird Girl	_____	_____	_____
2. The Scholarship Jacket	_____	_____	_____
3. Life Over Death	_____	_____	_____
4. A Small Victory	_____	_____	_____
5. Joe Davis	_____	_____	_____
6. From Horror to Hope	_____	_____	_____
7. Migrant Child	_____	_____	_____
8. He Was First	_____	_____	_____
9. Night Watch	_____	_____	_____
10. Thank You	_____	_____	_____
11. Winners, Losers	_____	_____	_____
12. Responsibility	_____	_____	_____

Title of Selection	Vocabulary Check (40%)	Reading Check (60%)	TOTAL SCORE
13. Anxiety	_____	_____	_____
14. The Bystander Effect	_____	_____	_____
15. Don't Let Stereotypes	_____	_____	_____
16. Dealing with Feelings	_____	_____	_____
17. All the Good Things	_____	_____	_____
18. The Yellow Ribbon	_____	_____	_____
19. What Do Children Owe	_____	_____	_____
20. Shame	_____	_____	_____
21. Rowing the Bus	_____	_____	_____
22. Bullies in School	_____	_____	_____
23. Seven Ways	_____	_____	_____
24. Dare to Think Big	_____	_____	_____
25. A Change of Attitude	_____	_____	_____
26. Nonreading to Reading	_____	_____	_____
27. Reading to Survive	_____	_____	_____
28. Flour Children	_____	_____	_____
29. In Praise of the F Word	_____	_____	_____
30. Professor Is a Dropout	_____	_____	_____
31. Learning Survival Skills	_____	_____	_____
32. Tickets to Nowhere	_____	_____	_____
33. An Electronic Fog	_____	_____	_____
34. The Quiet Hour	_____	_____	_____
35. Rudeness at the Movies	_____	_____	_____
36. My Daughter Smokes	_____	_____	_____
37. Here's to Your Health	_____	_____	_____
38. A Drunken Ride	_____	_____	_____
39. Living the Mad Ave Lie	_____	_____	_____
40. Staying Power	_____	_____	_____

Acknowledgments

Abbott, Stacy Kelly. "From Nonreading to Reading." Reprinted by permission.

Alpert, Lexine. "Flour Children." Reprinted by permission.

Barkin, Dorothy. "The Bystander Effect." Reprinted by permission.

Berger, Kathleen. "Bullies in School." From *The Developing Person: Through the Life Span,* 4th ed. Copyright © 1998 by Worth Publishers, Inc. Reprinted by permission.

Berry, Grant. "A Change of Attitude." Reprinted by permission.

Broderick, Bill. "Life Over Death." Reprinted by permission.

Cardenas, Maria. "Migrant Child to College Woman." Reprinted by permission.

Carson, Dr. Ben. "Dare to Think Big," from *The Big Picture* by Dr. Benjamin Carson with Gregg A. Lewis. Copyright © 1999 by Benjamin Carson. Used by permission of Zondervan Publishing House.

Coleman, Jean. "Learning Survival Skills." Reprinted by permission.

Collier, James Lincoln. "Anxiety: Challenge by Another Name." Originally published in *Reader's Digest,* December 1986. Reprinted by permission of the author.

Conroy, Theresa, and Christine M. Johnson. "A Drunken Ride, A Tragic Aftermath," from The *Philadelphia Inquirer.* Copyright © 1986, *The Philadelphia Inquirer.* Reprinted by permission.

DeLeon, Clark. "Bird Girl." *The Philadelphia Inquirer*, 1987. Reprinted by permission.

Dunayer, Joan. "Here's to Your Health." Reprinted by permission.

Garity, Joyce. "Living the Madison Avenue Lie." Reprinted by permission.

Gregory, Dick. "Shame." From *Nigger: An Autobiography*, copyright © 1964 by Dick Gregory Enterprises, Inc. Used by permission of Dutton Signet, a division of Penguin Putnam Inc.

Haley, Alex. "Thank You." Published in *Parade* Magazine, 1982. Copyright © 1982 by Alex Haley. Reprinted by permission of John Hawkins & Associates, Inc.

Hamill, Pete. "An Electronic Fog Has Settled Over America." Originally published in *Los Angeles Magazine*, January 16, 1982. Reprinted by permission of International Creative Management, Inc.

Hamill, Pete. "The Yellow Ribbon." Reprinted by permission of International Creative Management, Inc.

Heilbroner, Robert L. "Don't Let Stereotypes Warp Your Judgments." Reprinted by permission.

Johnson, Beth. "Joe Davis: A Cool Man." Reprinted by permission.

Johnson, Beth. "The Professor Is a Dropout." Reprinted by permission.

Kellmayer, John. "He Was First." Reprinted by permission.

Landers, Ann. "What Do Children Owe Their Parents?" Originally published in *Family Circle,* September 1, 1978. Permission granted by Ann Landers and Creators Syndicate.

Langan, Paul. "Reading to Survive." Reprinted by permission.

Lin, Jennifer. "Staying Power," from *The Philadelphia Inquirer Magazine*, May 20, 2001. Reprinted by permission.

Logan, Paul. "Rowing the Bus." Reprinted by permission.

Lopez, Steve. "A Small Victory," from *The Philadelphia Inquirer.* Copyright © 1990, *The Philadelphia Inquirer.* Reprinted by permission.

Mayer, Robert. "The Quiet Hour." Originally appeared as a "My Turn" in *Newsweek*. Adapted and used with permission of the author.

Mrosla, Sister Helen P. "All the Good Things." Originally published in *Proteus*, Spring 1991. Reprinted by permission as edited and published by *Reader's Digest* in October, 1991.

Peck, M. Scott. "Responsibility," from *The Road Less Traveled.* Copyright © 1978 by M. Scott Peck, M. D. Reprinted by permission of Simon & Schuster.

Popkin, Roy. "Night Watch," Originally appeared in *The National Observer*, December 1, 1964. Subsequently published in *Reader's Digest*, September 1965. Reprinted by permission of Dow Jones & Company, Inc., and *Reader's Digest*.

Rooney, Andy. "Tickets to Nowhere." © Tribune Media Services, Inc. All Rights Reserved. Reprinted with permission.

Salinas, Marta. "The Scholarship Jacket," from *Nosotras: Latina Literature Today*, edited by María del Carmen Boza, Beverly Silva, and Carmen Valle. Copyright © 1986 by Bilingual Press/Editorial Bilingüe, Arizona State University, Tempe, AZ. Reprinted by permission.

Sarann, Phany. "From Horror to Hope." Reprinted by permission.

Schulz, Charles. PEANUTS cartoon on page 11. Reprinted by permission of United Feature Syndicate, Inc.

Sherry, Mary. "In Praise of the F Word." Reprinted by permission.

Sugarman, Daniel. "Seven Ways to Keep the Peace at Home." Reprinted by permission.

Verderber, Rudolph F. "Dealing with Feelings," from *Communicate!* 6th ed., copyright © 1990. Reprinted with permission of Wadsworth, an imprint of the Wadsworth Group, a division of Thomson Learning.

Walker, Alice. "My Daughter Smokes," from *Living by the Word: Selected Writrings 1973–1987.* Copyright © 1987 by Alice Walker. Reprinted by permission of Harcourt, Inc.

Wightman, Dan. "Winners, Losers, or Just Kids?" *Los Angeles Times*, July 25, 1979.

Wine, Bill. "Rudeness at the Movies." Reprinted by permission.

Index